THE INVENTION OF ANGELA CARTER

THE INVENTION OF ANGELA CARTER

A Biography

Edmund Gordon

OXFORD
UNIVERSITY PRESS

OXFORD
UNIVERSITY PRESS

Oxford University Press is a department of the University of Oxford.
It furthers the University's objective of excellence in research, scholarship,
and education by publishing worldwide. Oxford is a registered trade mark of
Oxford University Press in the UK and certain other countries.

Published in the United States of America by Oxford University Press
198 Madison Avenue, New York, NY 10016, United States of America.

Originally published in the United Kingdom as The Invention of Angela Carter by
Chatto & Windus, an imprint of Vintage, 2016.

Library of Congress Cataloging-in-Publication Data
Names: Gordon, Edmund, author.
Title: The invention of Angela Carter : a biography / Edmund Gordon.
Description: New York : Oxford University Press, 2017. | Includes
bibliographical references and index.
Identifiers: LCCN 2016042329| ISBN 9780190626846 (hardback) |
ISBN 9780190626860 (epub)
Subjects: LCSH: Carter, Angela, 1940–1992. | Authors, English—20th
century—Biography. | BISAC: BIOGRAPHY & AUTOBIOGRAPHY / General. |
BIOGRAPHY & AUTOBIOGRAPHY / Literary.
Classification: LCC PR6053.A73 Z682 2017 | DDC 823/.914 [B] —dc23 LC record
available at https://lccn.loc.gov/2016042329

1 3 5 7 9 10 8 6 4 2

Printed by Sheridan Books, Inc.,
United States of America

For Sophie

'Self-possession. To be in possession of oneself. That's the only thing really.'
Angela Carter, journal, 1972

Contents

Contents

Introduction

At the end of November 1991 – when she had stopped receiving treatment for the tumours that had advanced like 'tiny Rottweilers' across her lungs and onto her lymph nodes – Angela Carter was approached to be the subject of a film for *Omnibus*, the BBC's flagship arts series. 'I should stress', wrote the producer, Kim Evans, 'that collaboration could take one of several forms – the most important thing is for you to choose the one you feel happiest with . . . The extent of the collaboration is really up to you.'

Angela no longer had the strength of a healthy fifty-one-year-old. She was often short of breath, and was becoming increasingly housebound as the cancer progressed. But here was a chance to take stock of her life and work, to represent herself to posterity, and specifically (as she told her nurse) to record something that her eight-year-old son, Alexander, might view in later years. She agreed to be interviewed for the programme, but explained that due to the severity of her illness, Evans's suggestion of filming 'either in spring or summer' wasn't going to be possible: there was no time to lose.

The production team arrived at her south London home on the morning of 16 January 1992, and stayed for most of the day. They had to keep breaking so that Angela could rest. In the days that followed, though, she continued to channel her diminished energies into the project. She wrote Evans a flurry of notes, making requests and offering suggestions about almost every aspect of the production, from the music (she proposed the Goldberg Variations) to the visual effects ('might we be able to matte "C[ompany] of W[olves]" [for which she had co-written the script] onto the Granada screen?'). At around the same time, she was planning her funeral in meticulous detail, selecting readings (from her own and others' work) and pieces of music that she felt reflected aspects of her character. 'A funeral', she had written almost a decade earlier, 'is no longer an invitation to share a common distress at the ubiquitousness of mortality': both the service and the film were opportunities to affirm her individuality. The need to do this had been with her since childhood. 'I always thought that she knew who she was,' said her friend and fellow novelist Salman Rushdie. 'She knew that she was Angela Carter. But she wouldn't have minded a few other people knowing.'

She died exactly a month after recording the interview. By the time the film was broadcast, in September, Angela Carter was a household name. Her obituaries in the British press received more space than any others published that year except those of Francis Bacon, Willy Brandt and Marlene Dietrich. Their tone was rhapsodic. 'Angela Carter . . . was one of the most important writers at work in the English language.' 'She interpreted the times for us with unrivalled penetration.' 'Her imagination was one of the most dazzling of this century.' Three days after she died, Virago (the publishing house with which her name was most closely associated) sold out of her books. Over the course of the next academic year, the British Academy received forty proposals for doctoral research into her work – compared to three on the whole of the eighteenth century.

Her long-term admirers regarded this sudden outpouring of acclaim – which was on a different scale to anything she had previously received – with a touch of exasperation. For more than twenty-five years, Angela Carter had been producing novels, short stories and journalism that stood defiantly apart from the work of her contemporaries. At a time when English literature was dominated by sober social realists, she played with disreputable genres – Gothic horror, science fiction, fairy tale – and gave free rein to the fantastic and the surreal. Her work is by turns funny, sexy, frightening and brutal, but it's always shaped by a keen, subversive intelligence and a style of luxuriant beauty. She was concerned with unpicking the mythic roles and structures that underwrite our existences – in particular the various myths of gender identity – and during the last decade of her life she was beginning to emerge as a feminist icon. But it was only now, when her voice had been silenced, that her genius became widely acknowledged.

The *Omnibus* documentary was a first glimpse of the newly canonised author, and it made a powerful impression. Images of Anton Furst's lavishly surreal set designs for *The Company of Wolves* are interspersed with shots of Angela herself in the comparably wonderful environment of her home: over her shoulder there are saffron-coloured walls, crimson shutters, and a beautifully painted fairground horse. Her long white hair is tied up with a pink and purple scarf. The effects of her medication – steroids and morphine – can be discerned in her face, which is very flushed, very full. Her voice rings with obscure emotion when she says:

> I never believe that I'm writing about the search for self. I've never believed that the self is like a mythical beast which has to be trapped and returned, so that you can become whole again. I'm talking about the negotiations we have to make to discover any kind of reality. I tend to think it's the world that we're looking for in the forest.

'Why should anyone be interested in my boring, alienated, marginal, messy life?' she had wondered ten years earlier, when a small but ardent group of admirers had first expressed such an interest. But even as she framed the question, she was gesturing towards one of the strongest links between her life and her work, which was about 'the nature of alienation'. It was an unusual subject for a middle-class Englishwoman, raised in the capital city of the British Empire, educated at a private school and a good civic university. She refused identification with any of these things, feeling that although alienation could be painful, 'integration means giving up one's freedom of being, in that one becomes mastered by one's role'.

This belief – that our selves are neither false nor true, but merely roles we either master or are mastered by – is one of the central themes of Angela Carter's fiction. Her characters wear their personalities like so many fancy-dress costumes. She was explicit about viewing femininity as a 'social fiction', part of a culturally choreographed performance of selfhood. She wasn't the first person to make this observation – but she may have been the first to greet it so warmly, as a licence for boundless self-invention.

The story of her life is the story of how she invented herself, of how she progressed from a shy, introverted childhood, through a nervy, aggressively unconventional youth, to a happy, self-confident middle age. 'By the end, her life fitted her more or less like a glove,' wrote the critic Lorna Sage, who from the mid-1970s was one of her closest friends and staunchest champions. 'But that was because she had put it together, by trial and error, *bricolage*, all in the (conventionally) wrong order.'

Her own personality displayed splashes of fancy dress. She enjoyed making people laugh, and had a knack for the startling, side-splitting phrase. She swerved between registers, from foul-mouthed demotic to jargon-strewn highbrow, so abruptly that neither seemed to be quite her natural voice. At other moments she spoke with such exquisite courtesy, accompanied by such pantomime gestures of deference (tilted head, gathered palms), that people tended to suspect her of irony ('It was almost as if she was presenting a satirical version of herself,' said the novelist Kazuo Ishiguro, who met her when he was a student, and she a tutor, on the creative writing MA at the University of East Anglia). Her warmth and generosity felt more authentic – she wrote sympathetically to fellow authors who'd been subjected to unkind treatment in the press, went out of her way to help those younger than herself, and would drop everything to comfort friends who'd suffered break-ups or bereavements, on more than one occasion baking a cake for them and travelling across London to deliver it – but even these qualities could strike people as containing an element of masquerade. 'She had a sort of granny persona that she did with me,' recalled Lorna Sage's daughter Sharon. 'We both knew that it was performance, but it was still nice.'

Her face was unusually mobile, her expression modulating swiftly from uncertainty to amusement ('watching her was sometimes like looking at someone under water, sometimes like seeing a diver break cover at the surface', wrote her friend and editor Susannah Clapp). She had a girlish, delicate voice, high-pitched and quite posh, with a few flat south London vowels sprinkled about like ballast. Her conversation tended to circle back on itself as she refined a point or improved a phrase: hearing her speak, you get a strong sense of how her mind worked, how she wrote. She would leave long pauses while she collected her thoughts, often waving a hand in the air, as if to net the *mot juste*. She had a mild stutter – perhaps the silences were partly to disguise it – and she put emphasis in strange places in a sentence. Her talk ebbed and flowed, her pauses ending in a rush of speech, as if the pressure of thought had been building up. Her laughter came just as suddenly, but in two distinct varieties. The most frequent was a barely audible wheezing chuckle, accompanied by a mischievous, conspiratorial glint in her grey-blue eyes. But when she laughed properly, her mouth fell open, her whole face creased up, and she turned a startling shade of red. It's a very infectious laugh. Even watching it on film, it's hard not to join in.

The way people look, how they speak, the quality and frequency of their laughter – all these things help shape our understanding of them, for if we invent ourselves, we also invent one another. Angela knew this. In 1969, she wrote: 'I feel like Archimedes and have just made what seems to me a profound insight – that one's personality is not a personal thing at all but an imaginative construct in the eye of the beholder.' Even so, she loathed it when people constructed her in ways that weren't compatible with how she saw herself. Several witnesses recall the party at which an editor at a national newspaper – a woman who had idealised her as 'a New Age role model, an earth mother' – asked her to write something on the summer solstice at Stonehenge. Angela looked 'pityingly' at the woman and said: 'You just haven't got me, have you dear?'

But writers continue to be invented and reinvented by their readers, long after their own last words on the matter. As Auden wrote of Yeats's death: 'he became his admirers'. Angela Carter has become hers in ways that have often ignored her wish not to be defined by her roles. Her obituaries demonstrated an impulse towards myth-making and sanctification. They emphasised her gentleness, her wisdom and her 'magical' imagination, at the expense of her intellectual sharpness, her taste for violent and disturbing imagery, and her exuberant sensuality. 'She had something of the Faerie Queene about her,' wrote the novelist and cultural critic Marina Warner in the *Independent*, 'except that she was never wispy or fey.' That nod towards complexity was rare. In the *New York Times*, Salman Rushdie identified her straightforwardly with 'the Fairy Queen', adding that 'English literature has lost its high sorceress, its benevolent white witch.' In the *Sunday Times*, her editor and confidante Carmen Callil described her as 'the oracle we all consulted', and her friends as 'an enchanted circle'. The novelist Margaret Atwood, writing in the *Observer*, went even further in flattening this complicated modern writer into the shape of an age-old female archetype: 'The amazing thing about her, for me, was that someone who looked so much like the Fairy Godmother . . . should actually *be* so much like the Fairy Godmother. She seemed always on the verge of bestowing something – some talisman, some magic token you'd need to get through the dark forest, some verbal formula useful for the opening of charmed doors.'

Sometimes this mythic version of Angela Carter has taken on a life of its own. Two days after she died, an 'appreciation' appeared in the *Guardian*. Its author, Veronica Horwell, who lived near Angela in the south London district of Clapham, described their first encounter in a local supermarket: 'She caught me smiling sentimentally at her boy. Wordlessly, she opened my hand and dropped a ripe pomegranate into the palm.' Horwell's last sighting of this 'exotic' figure was 'one morning of fast-moving skies after she must have known about her cancer', when she found her smoking cigarettes 'in a bad-prefect-behind-the-bike-sheds way' on the bench by the Underground where the local drunks tended to gather:

> She caught my eye, stretched out her arms along the bench back and spread out the strong hands to take in the 1911 municipal clock, Telecom booth, bus shelter with its proposals of South Downs days out, conjunctions of glamorous transpontine traffic. 'Much wilder than Tokyo,' she said, and lit another wicked ciggie from the butt of the last.

This depiction of Angela struck her friends and family as an outrageous farrago. Edward Horesh, an economist who had been close to her since the mid-1960s, fired off an indignant letter to the paper, complaining that Horwell's recollections did 'not seem in character – not even the silent gift of a ripe pomegranate', and that the suggestion that his friend was a secret smoker was particularly far-fetched: 'Angela gave up smoking about 10 years ago. After she heard that she had contracted cancer she told me how much she hated the sight of anyone smoking . . . She was much too honest a person to pretend.' His hurt and bewilderment surged forth as the letter continued: 'Did Angela live in a world of Horwell's fantasies rather than the streets of Clapham?' he demanded.

One answer is that she lived in both places. During the five years I've spent researching Angela Carter's life, her closest friends (including Horesh) have told me things that can't be true. Fantasy has a habit of corrupting memory. This is something that biographers – who invent their subjects out of various kinds of evidence, including testimony – need to bear in mind. A further consideration in this case has been that Angela lived to an unusual extent (even by the standards of her profession) in her own fantasies. She wasn't always a reliable witness to her own life. 'I do exaggerate, you know . . . I exaggerate terribly,' she once admonished a friend who she feared had taken her too seriously. 'I'm a born fabulist.' But she believed that even the most imaginatively sculpted confession could reveal truths about the confessor's experience:

> Autobiography is closer to fiction than biography. This is true both in method – the processes of memory are very like those of the imagination and the one sometimes gets inextricably mixed up with the other – and also in intention. 'Life of' is, or ought to be, history: that is, 'the life and times of'. But 'my life' ought to be (though rarely is)

a clarification of personal experience, in which it is less important (though only tactful) to get the dates right. You read so-and-so's life of somebody to find out what actually happened to him or her. But so-and-so's 'my life' tells you what so-and-so thought about it all.

Actually, 'what happened to him or her?' is only one of the questions we usually expect a 'Life of' to answer. Others include: 'what was it like to meet him or her?' and: 'what was it like to be him or her?' This book tells a story about Angela Carter that draws on the stories others have told about her, as well as on many of the stories she told about herself. I've tended to rely on her account when I haven't encountered anything that obviously undermines it. My guiding principle has been one of the last things she ever wrote: 'the *really* important thing is narrative . . . We travel along the thread of narrative like high-wire artistes. That is our life.'

PART I

CHAPTER ONE

A matriarchal clan

'Once upon a time, deep in the heart of the country, there lived a pretty little girl whose mother adored her, and her grandmother adored her even more.' Angela first heard the story of Red Riding Hood from her own grandmother. This was deep in the heart of Yorkshire, where the old woman had lived when she was a girl. As she spoke, candlelight enlarged the shadows on her rough and rumpled face. What big eyes, what a big mouth she had . . . 'All the better to eat you up!' she said, and pounced, roaring like a hungry wolf, while Angela squirmed and giggled and squeaked in delight.

The sluggish, brownish river Dearne extends for some thirty miles along the upper periphery of the South Yorkshire coalfield, worming its way through land dazed and disfigured by centuries of heavy industry. Since the closure of the mines in the 1980s, the towns along its banks have fallen on hard times – their high streets are now sad successions of takeaways, betting shops and cheerless pubs, many of them boarded up – but they were once the thriving beneficiaries of Britain's industrial expansion.

Coal was mined in the settlement of Wath-upon-Dearne as early as the seventeenth century, and when the gargantuan Manvers Main colliery opened its gates in 1870, mining replaced agriculture as the region's major industry. Workers were soon pouring into the town from the surrounding countryside: in 1871, Wath's population stood at just over 2,000; by 1901 it had swollen to 8,500. There were several churches, an athletics ground with a large pavilion, musical and dramatic societies, and two railway stations, one reserved for transporting coal, the other enticing holidaymakers to the coast or into the great cities of the north. Angela Carter's maternal great-grandfather, Henry Stones, worked laying plates on the railways, but he later became – like most local boys and men – a labourer at the coal pits.

Her grandmother, Jane Stones, was born in Wath on 13 July 1876. The house she grew up in (next door to the one where – some seventy years later – she told Angela fairy tales) was a two-up, two-down terraced miner's cottage right on the edge of the town. There was no running water – the weekly wash was taken at the slipper bath in the town centre – and the outdoor lavatory was reached by means of a communal access lane, which meant a long walk with a candle-lantern if she needed to go before bed. The two-bedroom cottage must have been uncomfortably cramped: Jane was one of six children, though only four of them survived beyond infancy.

Jane worked as a chambermaid during her teenage years, a job Angela thought she must have been 'bloody awful' at. She was a brusque, headstrong, pragmatic girl who spoke with a thick Yorkshire accent, and had no time for frivolity or weakness. 'Every word and gesture of hers displayed a natural dominance, a native savagery,' Angela wrote. Godfearing and superstitious, she was full of old sayings, and would opine over the cradles of newborn babies: 'It's a wise child that knows its own father' – a phrase that her granddaughter made use of in the title of her final novel. Wise Children is a madcap jaunt (led by septuagenarian twin sisters Nora and Dora Chance) around the 'illegitimate' side of British culture, and it gains much of its piquant flavour from Angela's pride in her family history.

She tended to emphasise the picturesque, folksy aspects of her grandmother's personality: she frequently described her as 'a witch', and told one interviewer that Jane had 'second sight', before adding: 'of course, it was all guess-work'. This was a characteristic move: the impulse towards romanticism briefly indulged, then undermined by a no-nonsense punchline. If the whimsy was inherited from her father, then the bluntness came very definitely from her mother's side of the family. She also claimed that her grandmother was 'functionally illiterate', which crosses the border of romanticisation into the realm of outright falsity. Jane was a lot more sophisticated than Angela liked to admit. Her education was basic, but it wasn't non-existent – she was part of the first generation to benefit from the Elementary Education Act of 1870, which guaranteed schooling until the age of thirteen – and in spite of her superstitions, she had a good deal of worldly acumen and drive. She respected literature and the arts, and was evidently ambitious enough to imagine a life for herself beyond the horizons of Wath-upon-Dearne.

By the time she left school, escaping the town was becoming a matter of some urgency. In 1893 the price of coal fell, and the miners' wages were slashed. They tended to be bound by contracts that offered no protection from the vagaries of the market. At the same time, their working conditions were punishing: the mines were poorly ventilated, and accidents were commonplace. Most colliers, even boys as young as thirteen, laboured for between ten and fourteen hours a day, and those who worked deep underground saw daylight only on Sundays; their health was usually ruined by the time they were forty, and their life expectancy was well below sixty. Now even these modest standards were under threat.

By the beginning of August, colliers in most mining districts in England and Wales had voted to strike. It was the worst industrial dispute the country had ever known: the mine owners were inflexible, the export of coal ground more or less to a halt, and within two months starvation menaced large parts of Wales, the Midlands and the north. An editorial in *The Times* called it 'a national calamity'. On 7 September, an argument broke out between striking miners and the colliery manager at Featherstone Main in West Yorkshire and quickly escalated into rioting: the troops were called in, and sixteen miners and bystanders were shot. Two of them died. The next day, in anticipation of further violence, soldiers from the Suffolk Regiment were sent north to Garforth, Nottingham, Barnsley and Pontefract: the Pontefract detachment was broken up into small parties, one of which was quartered in the Manvers Main colliery in Wath.

Jane Stones was seventeen years old. Her father and her brother both worked in the pits, and it's likely that they took a dim view of her fraternising with the soldiers; but Jane wasn't an easy person to control. Walter Farthing was a twenty-four-year-old private, well travelled and sexually experienced (one of the few things that can be ascertained about his early life is that within eight months of joining the army he had twice been hospitalised with gonorrhoea). Their courtship must have been intense: it lasted only a few weeks. By 21 October, all parties had returned to headquarters, and in March 1894, Walter was despatched to India. For seven years he wrote each week to Jane; with a characteristic lack of sentimentality, she destroyed his letters, but kept the stamps.

*   *   *

5

Walter's first posting was in Malabar, a remote, hilly and (even by late Victorian standards) underdeveloped region of what is now Kerala. In October 1895 he was sent briefly to Rangoon, and from there to Port Blair in the Andaman Islands, a large penal settlement containing more than 12,000 (mostly political) prisoners. It was a notorious place: on a visit in 1872, Lord Mayo, the Viceroy of India, had been stabbed to death by a convict. The shock of the assassination, which has been described as 'one of the first acts of modern jihad', penetrated to the furthest corners of the empire. Since then the British had maintained an uneasy presence on the islands, assailed by disease (malaria was rife), and regarded with suspicion by the locals, who refused to take money, so that all commerce had to be undertaken using rum or top hats for currency.

To the soldiers, Port Blair seemed like the edge of the world. A subaltern who served there at the same time as Walter described a sense of isolation so intense that after a few weeks 'we [began] to think seriously of discarding our clothes' – an idea which would have seemed pretty desperate to the average Victorian reader. Perhaps resentment at their own exile goes some way towards explaining the brutality with which they treated their prisoners. Floggings were routine, as were summary executions. There were also sinister medical experiments: in the 1880s, prison doctors had force-fed high doses of cinchona alkaloid (the bark of a tree known for its antimalarial properties) to a sample group of 1,000 prisoners, most of whom died. The suicide rate among the convicts was appallingly high. There were also frequent escape attempts, the most successful ones by raft to Burma: venturing inland meant going into the jungle, at the risk of being killed by tribesmen armed with bamboo spears or bows and arrows.

Angela doesn't seem to have looked very closely into her grandfather's military service, but she did show signs of discomfort about being descended from an imperialist. She indulged in some fairly wishful thinking about him. Walter died five years before she was born, and there is simply no evidence to support the claims she liked to make: that he 'became radicalised' after witnessing 'the contradictions inherent in the Raj', or that in later life he 'chaired a meeting at which Lenin spoke'. These details belong to the biography of the grandfather she would have designed for herself, not the one she had. Her older brother, who did know Walter in the last years of his life, remembered him as 'very much an ex-military, upright, senior NCO type'. If he was radicalised, it didn't prevent him from doing his job to the very best of his ability: he impressed his superiors in Port

6

Blair – who described his service as 'exemplary' – and in October 1898 he was promoted to sergeant.

Nor was his departure from the army a matter of having had enough. He might easily have progressed further through the ranks. But one day in 1899, while off duty, he sat idly loosening a belt buckle with his bayonet. He must have pressed too hard: the blade flew upwards, gashing his right eye. The cornea was ruptured and he was left half-blind, a cloudy white mass obscuring most of his pupil. It was impossible for him to carry out his duties any more. His doctor wrote: 'He is <u>much depressed</u>, his <u>general health has suffered considerably</u>, and he <u>urgently</u> requires change to England.'

Before he sailed, Walter assembled a few mementos of his years abroad: 'an ebony elephant, spears, a carved coconut shell representing the Hindu cosmogeny, beautiful shells from tropical seas, some with pierced messages: A Present from the Andaman Islands.' These exotic trinkets, scattered amongst the Anglican icons and souvenir china of her grandmother's home, fed into Angela's mental image of Walter. No wonder she felt that 'of all the dead in my family, this unknown grandfather is the one I would most like to have talked to'. As a teenage girl oppressed by the limitations of her home environment, she turned him into a beacon of romance and worldly knowledge: an avatar for all the things she wanted her family to be.

Walter Farthing and Jane Stones were married in Wath on 4 June 1900, almost seven years after they had met. The next morning they left for London, where Walter had been given work as a clerk, keeping the ledgers at the Royal Army Clothing Store (his injury having been sustained off duty, he wasn't entitled to a full civil livelihood). According to family legend, Jane took one look at the dark house he had found for them on Millgrove Street, in the slum district of Battersea, south of the river Thames, and returned to Yorkshire on the next available train. Her horrified father sent her back again.

It's telling that someone as tough and determined as Jane should have faltered at the warren of gloomy streets that was to be her new home. South London was practically a separate city from the great imperial capital north of the Thames. Since the eighteenth century it had been used to house the 'stink industries' – tanneries, with their overpowering stench of bad meat and ammonia; vinegar-makers; breweries; manufacturers of soap and tallow – and other such undesirable trades. People whose lifestyles offended polite sensibilities were likewise driven south of the river: by the mid-nineteenth century, the list of refugees from good taste who had made their homes there included prostitutes, transvestites, and music-hall artistes like the Chance sisters in *Wise Children*, or Fevvers, the winged acrobat in Angela Carter's eighth novel, *Nights at the Circus*.

Angela, in contrast to her grandmother, took enormous pride in coming from 'the *bastard* side of Old Father Thames'. She was conscious of 'the tendency of English fiction, of the English novel, to be about . . . a kind of lifestyle which I associate more with NW3 than with SE25', and set out to celebrate, in her own writing, the more marginalised type of Englishness that she encountered as a child. Her depictions of the locality are often pitched halfway between parodying the north Londoner's impression of it and confirming that impression with defiant glee: south London was a place where 'old men in flat caps complain, at bus stops, about their feet'; where 'a typical . . . headline from the local press was: BABY IN PRAM BITTEN BY RAT'; where 'sounds of marital violence, breaking glass and drunken song echoed around and it was cold and dark and smelled of fish and chips'. None of these sketches looks very much like middle-class Balham, where Angela spent most of her childhood; they're much closer to the atmosphere of her grandparents' shabby and neglected part of Battersea.

The Farthings' first child, Eric, was born on 24 April 1901. Three others followed: Cynthia (known as Kitty) on 6 March 1903; Olive on 7 March 1905; and Cecil on 9 August 1909. The children all had thick black hair and slightly sallow complexions, and they shared a quarrelsome, highly strung, artistic temperament. Jane – who didn't intend the flow of social mobility to dry up in the slums of Battersea – pushed them to work hard. 'My maternal grandparents . . . did believe in work as salvation, in a quite profound moral sense,' Angela said, and she inherited an atheist's version of their protestant work ethic. Respect for the arts was also something that Jane drummed into her children from an early age: although the house on Millgrove Street wasn't much bigger than the one she had grown up in, she installed a piano for the children to play in the front room (by the time Angela was born it was 'so out of tune it sounded like a harpsichord'), and they were encouraged to read books and participate in amateur dramatics. At the weekends, she took them to the cheap seats at Sadler's Wells and the Old Vic, where they saw plays by Ibsen and Shakespeare; a great treat was to see one show in the afternoon, then another one in the evening. In *Wise Children*, her lovingly sustained tribute to her mother's family,

Angela Carter evokes this unabashed working-class passion for 'serious' theatre-going – a pursuit that had become much more exclusive by the time the novel was published in 1991. The memory of its democratic history, passed down from her mother, informed her deeply held sense that Shakespeare was a popular entertainer.

Both of the Farthing boys did well. Jane must have felt gratified at the distance her family had travelled in just two generations: her oldest child, Eric, won a scholarship to Oxford and became a headmaster; her younger son, Cecil, was an even greater credit to her. When he was only seven years old, he spent whole days by himself at the Victoria and Albert Museum, and when he was offered a book for his eighth birthday he chose one on Botticelli. As a scholar in English at King's College London, he ran the Literary Society. Then, after a short period teaching, he took a second degree in history of art at the Courtauld Institute, and was subsequently appointed the Conway Librarian there under Anthony Blunt. In 1941, when the National Buildings Record was established to document architectural treasures destroyed in the Blitz, he was one of the first people appointed to its staff, and after the war he became director of the newly established National Monuments Record. He was a fellow of the Society for Antiquities, secretary of both the British Archaeological Association and the London Topographical Society, and received an OBE in 1967.

'Love is not too strong a term for his feeling for the arts,' Cecil's obituary in *The Times* suggested in 2001. 'His expression and timbre would change markedly when he spoke of a favourite poem or picture, and these feelings and the sense of intimacy with the people and the traditions of the past were the driving force of his life.' It would be difficult to overstate his influence on his niece, who visited him frequently in her teens and early twenties, and sought his advice on some of the major decisions of her life.

Kitty and Olive were not given the same freedoms or opportunities as their brothers. Although Angela was justified in describing the family as 'a matriarchal clan', they were by no means feminists (her claim that her grandmother used to turn up at school sports days wearing a Votes for Women badge on her lapel is about as plausible as the idea that her grandfather was a Leninist). The Farthing women ruled absolutely in the home, where men were regarded as oafish and incompetent interlopers, to be snapped at and bossed around. But there was always a tacit understanding that this female-governed domestic space was less important, somehow, than the male world of moneymaking and career progression, and that there was a natural divide between the two.

Jane played the role of domestic matriarch instinctively: she expected her daughters, and to a lesser extent her sons, to do as she said. Like many parents whose own upbringings took place under very different cultural circumstances to their children's, she never seems to have really understood her daughters, with their grand ambitions and metropolitan manners – and perhaps feeling that she lacked the means to provide the lifestyles that they wanted, she instead mocked their desires and needled their weaknesses. Both of the girls were kept firmly in their place, and neither of them fully emerged from her shadow. When Olive was in her forties, her mother would still look over her shoulder, issuing instructions and criticising her technique, as she cooked Christmas dinner for her family.

Kitty fared much worse. Inspired by her childhood visits to the Old Vic, she wanted to go on the stage; but her ambitions were swiftly crushed, and until her mother's death in 1966 she lived at home with her as a companion and effective factotum. By the time she was in her late thirties, her mind was starting to wander. During the war, she took to roaming the blacked-out streets, enthralled by the flying bombs. As she grew older, her eccentricities became more and more pronounced. She was forever saying goodbye to people on trains and forgetting to get off. She once wrote a formal letter to her bank manager, then added as a PS: 'How are things in Glocca Morra?' She may have suffered from some form of dementia, though it was never diagnosed. When they were children, Angela and her brother adored her. Dora Chance, the all-singing, all-dancing narrator of *Wise Children*, is based on Kitty: the novel is Angela's way of giving her dotty aunt a posthumous taste of the freedom she had never been allowed in life.

Wise Children is also a portrait of the glamorous London that enthralled Olive as a young woman. Working in the 1920s as a cashier in Selfridges, she would gaze in awe at the Dolly Sisters, the beautiful Hungarian dancers and mistresses of Gordon Selfridge, who spent lavishly in the store: their photograph appeared on the first edition of the novel. A delicate child (she had a weak heart following an attack of rheumatic fever in infancy) and a great reader from an early age, Olive was awarded a scholarship to the local girls' grammar school, but she left at fourteen without qualifications. In later years, Angela thought of her clever, stylish, well-read mother as a classic example of frustrated female potential. Olive passed her interest in fashion on to her daughter, but Angela combined it with an interest in semiotics, and came to believe that 'clothes are the visible woman – the detachable skin which expresses inner aspirations, dreams and fantasies' – and that Olive's fondness for snappy headgear and beautiful dresses suggested desires that couldn't be realised by the life of a suburban housewife.

She was a warm, loving, funny woman, who doted on her children and thought it only natural that they should be musically and linguistically gifted. She was also nervous and introspective, 'sometimes sorry for herself', and possessing a 'talent for histrionics'. Her superstitions were legion, and ranged from the commonplace (she thought green was an unlucky colour) to the idiosyncratic (in a thunderstorm, she would cover up the cutlery to prevent it reflecting lightning). Her neuroses were just as various. She was suspicious of tinned food, which, much of it being foreign-made, might easily have been poisoned, and she worried about handling money because it had been touched by God knew who else. She believed that submerging the body in water removed essential oils and that brushing one's teeth damaged the enamel (her daughter blamed the latter conviction for her own recurrent dental problems).

Although she was on the left politically – a Labour supporter her whole life – Olive was extremely conservative on most social issues. She would switch off the television if an actor or presenter had been divorced. She couldn't abide swearing or vulgarity. She liked things to be nice. The only comment her children remembered her making about sex was: 'I wish God had thought of a better way of making babies.' But with her slender figure, her broad, almost Slavic-looking features, and her fashionably bobbed black hair, she turned heads wherever she went. One afternoon around her twentieth year she was approached on the tennis courts by a dapper, handsome Scot.

Well over six feet tall, Hugh Stalker had a hawk-like face, dominated by a toothy, mischievous grin, hooded eyes and a long aquiline nose. He stood very straight and dressed in tweed jackets, colourful bow ties, and glamorous 'Edgar Wallace' hats, which he would doff to ladies he passed in the street. He was traditional in his tastes and conservative in his politics (after he died, Angela discovered his membership of the Scottish Conservative Party – an allegiance he wouldn't have dared admit to when Olive was around), but he had a lyrical bent and a slightly ribald sense of humour. He smoked a pipe and took the occasional dram. He carried a walking stick, though there was nothing wrong with his legs. 'If he had pretensions, they would have been to style as such,' Angela wrote.

A recording of Hugh (speaking in the 1980s, towards the end of his life) has survived. In a slightly high-pitched, fluting voice, his east of Scotland accent hardly dulled by the forty-seven years he spent in London, he talks about his childhood memories. He was born in Macduff – a town that stares bleakly out from the Aberdeenshire coast towards the arctic north – on 24 June 1895, the third child of William Stalker, a master cobbler, and his wife Christina (née McLean). The family lived in narrow rooms above the shop, which was situated in a row of thriving small businesses, among them an inordinate number of fishmongers and ship chandlers. Macduff was a prosperous town at the turn of the century: a lively port with ships delivering wood from Norway and wines from France, and setting out again loaded with grain and herring. Hugh remembered watching the local fifies (traditional fishing boats with two masts and long straight keels) departing: 'it was a marvellous spectacle . . . hundreds of them would sail out together, and people would assemble on the shore to see them off'.

Not all of them came back again. In the graveyard at Macduff, countless tombstones bear the lament: 'Lost at sea'. The funerals of the drowned were magnificent affairs. There was a horse-drawn hearse, driven by the town's dustbin man (who wore an apron, gaiters and a top hat for the occasion), and followed by a procession of freshly scrubbed fishermen in frock coats – a sight that made a big impression on Hugh. Indeed, mourning was something of a local speciality – he also remembered how the town was decked out in flags and black clothing when Queen Victoria died – and the tendency rubbed off on him. Along with his loquacity and his romanticism, the quality Angela most admired in her father was his ability to cry.

His family, on the other hand, she found 'weird beyond belief'. They were strict Calvinists, strait-jacketed with disapproval and guilt, obsessed by puritan ideas of wickedness. Hugh's mother wouldn't light the fire on a Sunday, and piled all the day's washing-up in a bucket for dealing with on Monday morning. His brother William, who inherited the shop, was by all accounts a mean and sanctimonious man. His sister Katie was much warmer, but she drank too much: 'If you opened a drawer anywhere in the house there'd be the chink of bottles,' Angela's brother remembered. There was also a pervasive reek of fish, since Katie was given to feeding all the cats in the area; it would have pleased her to know that the Stalker shop is now owned by the charity Cat's Protection.

By the time he left school at fourteen, Hugh had developed a high standard of literacy and a love of books (he had already read *Don Quixote*, presumably in translation, and it remained his favourite novel). He was apprenticed to the *Banffshire Journal*, and after a couple of years he became a reporter for the *Aberdeen Free Press*, for which he would go round the villages on his bicycle to cover parish meetings. The outbreak of war interrupted his career. He enlisted with the Scots Guards in December 1915, shortly before the Military Service Act came into force, and was sent to France on 5 October 1916, when he was twenty-one. In later life he rarely spoke about his wartime experience, and it's impossible, now, to check exactly where he was deployed, but Angela formed the impression that he was at the Somme. If he was, he probably didn't see the worst of it. When his commanding officers discovered that he had a background in journalism – he had been writing the other men's letters home for them – he was given a staff job writing up reports.

He was lucky to be kept away from the front. When he returned to Macduff, he found that 117 men from the town had died in the trenches. In 1921 a memorial was erected to commemorate them. During his retirement, Hugh would ask his doctor to drive him to the memorial every Remembrance Day, to lay a wreath for his fallen friends and neighbours.

On the morning of 15 August 1922, a fishing party of nine set out from the Loch Maree Hotel near Gairloch in the Scottish Highlands. The hotel had provided them with potted meat sandwiches (turkey and tongue, and chicken and tongue), which all but two of them ate. That evening, the ones who had eaten the sandwiches began to experience difficulty breathing; their speech became clotted and slow; they started seeing double. Nobody recognised the symptoms of botulism, which had never before been recorded in Britain. Five of the seven were dead by the following morning; the other two clung on for a few more days. If there was ever any doubt about the cause, it was laid to rest later that week, when a sandwich that had been discarded was found surrounded by dead seagulls.

Hugh Stalker, who since returning from France had been working for the *Dundee Courier*, was sent to cover the incident. His account gives a strong flavour of his journalistic voice, a wistful tone embroidered with lyrical flourishes. He describes the dead as 'happy tourists, whose whole thought was of the catch that might fall to their skill with the rod and line', before lamenting that 'their day's fishing was to be one tragically remembered by their friends and acquaintances'.

The case attracted national attention, and Hugh's report was read with admiration on Fleet Street. He was offered a job working as a reporter for the Press Association, and he moved to London to take it up. After he had been there three years, the agency was shaken up following the appointment of a new editor-in-chief, and Hugh was given the job of night editor. The role suited his temperament – allowing him a slow start to the day, with lunch at home and every other weekend off – and he remained in it until he retired.

He was the kind of journalist who not only writes stories, but becomes the subject of them. According to one (related in all his obituaries), he once called a correspondent in Lichfield, a man named Bishop who was hours late filing a report on a train crash. Hugh began raging down the phone at him. It must have been a nasty shock to realise that he'd actually been put through to the Bishop of Lichfield. But such was Hugh's charm, he not only mollified the prelate, but also managed to extract an exclusive comment about the train crash for the Press Association. His success in maintaining the affections of colleagues and readers over several thousand nights of stories earned him the nickname 'the Scheherazade of Fleet Street'.

Hugh and Olive were married on Saturday 20 August 1927 at St Saviour's Church, Battersea, and soon settled into their first home at 161 Bedford Hill, Balham. The ostensible reason for selecting this area was that it was on the Northern Line and so convenient for Fleet Street – but it was also a short bus journey from Jane Farthing's home, and Olive seems to have been incapable of putting too much distance between herself and her mother.

Nevertheless, in spite of its geographical connection, Balham was in a different socio-economic world to Battersea. When the Stalkers first moved there, it was a drowsy middle-class enclave of somewhat dishevelled respectability, self-consciously superior to the adjoining neighbourhood of Tooting, but unfashionable for its proximity. In Balham, bank managers and civil servants lived tidy lives behind privet hedges, sent their daughters to private dance classes (classical and tap), attended church sales and went to meetings of the local Rotary Club. The Balham Hippodrome put on music hall and variety shows for audiences of over a thousand, and there were several local cinemas. The area did have its seedier elements – the flashers on Wandsworth Common, the prostitutes at the other end of Bedford Hill – but these were easily ignored, and although Olive sometimes talked about moving to a posher part of London, Hugh never saw the need.

Their first child, William Hugh Stalker (known as Hugh, and within the family as Hughie) was born on 23 December 1928. When he was two years old, the Stalkers moved across Balham to Ravenslea Road, a mile-long Edwardian terrace, overlooking Wandsworth Common at one end and a few minutes' walk from Balham High Road at the other. Behind the houses on the south side of the terrace, up a shallow bank, runs the Victoria to Brighton railway line. A train passed their house at number 121 every few minutes – Olive worried that the vibrations would bring the roof tumbling down – but when there was a gap between them it was possible to hear the birds chirruping on Wandsworth Common. These were happy years for the Stalkers, with frequent trips to the countryside and to the coast in an open-topped sports car. They had a spaniel called Jock. Hughie took piano lessons from a neighbour, and went cycling with his friends. His childhood – at least partly because he was a boy – was much freer than his sister's would be.

This contented period was ended by another war. In September 1939, when Hughie was ten, he was evacuated to Eastbourne. 'Evacuation was really rather like abduction,' he remembered. 'You weren't told where you were going, and your parents weren't told.' Other evacuees have recalled the trauma of being separated from their families, but Hughie had no need to worry on that account. As soon as Olive heard from him, she instructed her husband to rent a flat in Eastbourne, at 15 St Leonard's Road, a long, quiet, tree-lined street a few minutes' walk from the sea. Olive must have discovered that she was pregnant again at around the same time, so perhaps the move was as much in the spirit of evacuating her second child as being reunited with her first.

Angela Olive Stalker was born on 7 May 1940 in the maternity home at 12 Hyde Gardens, Eastbourne. It had been an agitated pregnancy, rounded off by a long and difficult labour: Angela came to worry that it had exacerbated the heart condition from which her mother eventually died. What followed can't have helped. Two weeks after Angela's birth, the decision was made to evacuate British forces from Dunkirk. The south coast of England was now the front line: it had been an idiotic refuge for London children in the first place. The authorities ordered their immediate return home.

But London was hardly a safer place for them to be. On 7 September the Luftwaffe began its assault on the capital, dropping almost 30,000 bombs over the next three weeks. A few days into the barrage, the Stalkers' neighbours at 4 Ravenslea Road were hit. In his eighties, Hughie still remembered 'the feeling of panic' when he arrived home from his emergency school on Clapham Common and saw the mountain of rubble where that morning a house had been. A few weeks later, in the evening of 14 October, fires from incendiary bombs were reported in twenty-five streets in Balham; once again, Ravenslea Road was among them. Another bomb fell into Balham High Road, directly above the northbound platform of the Underground station, where hundreds of people were sheltering; the tunnel collapsed, and effluent from the fractured sewers cascaded in. Sixty-six people died – one of the worst tolls for a single incident in the Blitz. Before there was time to create a diversion, an 88 bus, travelling under the blackout, drove straight into the crater formed by the bomb. Pictures of the half-submerged bus appeared in newspapers all over the world: a surreal illustration of the violent wasteland London had become.

Jane Farthing realised that the city was no place for her grandchildren to be living. But she did know of one place that would be safe from German bombs. The house next door to the one she had grown up in (where her brother and sister still lived) was standing empty. Hugh's work meant that he had to stay in London, but he agreed that his family should get away as quickly as possible. Towards the end of 1940, Jane took Olive, Hughie and Angela with her to Wath-upon-Dearne.

'She was our air-raid shelter,' Dora Chance says of Grandma Chance in *Wise Children*. 'When the bombardments began, she'd go outside and shake her fist at the old men in the sky.' This might be Angela talking (in typically extravagant fashion) about Jane, whose role as saviour and protector made an indelible impression on her. German planes passed over Wath with nerve-jangling frequency during the war, though the closest bombs fell in Sheffield, fifteen miles away. The town itself had hardly changed in forty years: with mining a reserved occupation – necessary to keep the home fires burning and the factories churning out supplies – the pits were still at the centre of its life. Angela remembered watching the colliers 'swaggering' home at the end of the day, then listening to her great-uncle Sidney coughing through the wall for half the night. The first five years of her life were spent in this 'mucky pastoral' environment: she attended the local nursery school and played with the miners' children in the fields behind the cottage. Her grandmother told her stories and sang to her, taught her to whistle and to 'snawk' (that is, to steal) coal for the fire, and generally set about moulding her into the kind of self-sufficient girl her own London-bred daughters were not. 'I think I became the child she had been, in a sense,' Angela reflected. 'She reared me as a tough, arrogant and pragmatic Yorkshire child and my mother was powerless to prevent it.'

Grandmother figures abound in Angela Carter's work, and they tend to share Jane's qualities of toughness, earthiness, and folksy wisdom. They also tend to be sympathetically drawn, even if (as in the two takes on Red Riding Hood in *The Bloody Chamber*, her strange and sumptuous collection of reimagined fairy tales) they come to a sticky end. Mothers, by contrast, are rarely depicted, and are never anything like Olive. This apparent favouritism sometimes leaked into Angela's way of speaking about her family. Her attachment to Jane – who 'seemed to my infant self a woman of such physical and spiritual heaviness she might have been born with a greater degree of gravity than most people' – was so intense that in later years she often talked as if it had just been the two of them living in Yorkshire. If she ever had a daughter of her own, she said, she would name her 'Lulu [after the Louise Brooks character in G. W. Pabst's 1929 film *Pandora's Box*] – and Jane, for her grandmother' – a schema which lightly airbrushes out a generation.

It must have been painful for Olive to watch her daughter being taken over by the parent who still treated her like a child herself. But she lacked the strength to stand up to Jane. Angela took a long time even to notice that there was tension between them. 'With the insight of hindsight,' she wrote in 1976, 'I'd have liked to have been able to protect my mother from the domineering old harridan, with her rough tongue and primitive sense of justice, but I did not see it like that, then.'

CHAPTER TWO

States of grace are always evil

When the Stalkers returned to Ravenslea Road in 1945, it was almost unrecognisable. Many of their neighbours' houses had been bombed into the ground; light seeped through the gaps in the terrace. Many more had been blown wide open, exposing their smoke-blackened interiors. While her parents and her brother tried to resume their former lives, Angela took to exploring the bombsites, collecting shards of broken china and other debris among the ruins. On one occasion she recalled finding something black and bloody in a paper bag, which she realised only years later must have been an aborted foetus. The image haunted her nightmares for months.

Their own house had narrowly escaped damage: it still stands today, looking from the outside much the same as it ever did. It has an austere red-brick facade with a prominent bay window, which throughout Angela's childhood was veiled by net curtains. On the left as you came in was the 'front room', arranged around the bay window onto the street, and dominated by an upright piano (which Hughie played most frequently, although Olive would sometimes bring out her show tune, 'The Stepney Gavotte') and a large radiogram (still a state-of-the-art item in the mid-1940s). Handsome, dark furniture – leather sofas, a mahogany sideboard – occupied much of the remaining space.

At the end of the hall, down a couple of stairs, past a small dining room on the left (which was reserved for Christmas dinner and other times when the Stalkers had guests) was the kitchen. A smallish room, it could accommodate a fireplace and a table, but without much space between them. This was where the family ate, relaxed, and tended to gather. The fireplace meant it was the only room that was reliably warm. The rest of the house would fill with fog on winter days: coming upstairs from the kitchen, they would find themselves engulfed by it.

The kitchen led onto both a scullery and a small back garden, the latter planted with roses, which (against all odds, since nobody paid them much attention) bloomed every summer. Behind the garden was the railway line. Angela's bedroom, directly above the kitchen, looked onto it: the clackety-clack of passing trains was one of the familiar sounds of her childhood, and when she was on the train herself she would glance up at the house, hoping (or so she whimsically said) to catch sight of herself at her bedroom window. Her brother's bedroom was beside hers, and across the landing, facing the street, was their parents' room. At the very top of the house was a loft: Hugh Stalker's office. He always put on his hat to travel between there and the kitchen.

There were a great many books in the house, and newspapers everywhere, since Hugh brought the early editions home from work. To a large extent, his job determined the shape of their lives: the hours he worked meant that their routine was at odds with the rest of the neighbourhood, and he and Olive couldn't enjoy much of a social life. They spent an unusual amount of time together as a family, and the sense of inseparability that developed between them was as reassuring as it could be claustrophobic. On the weekends Hugh had off, they would all go to church on Sunday morning, then take a walk on Wandsworth Common; when he was working, Olive and the children would go by Tube to the Strand and meet him for Sunday lunch at the Lyons Corner House. Most weekdays he would come home in the middle of the night, make Olive tea and bring her biscuits in bed; Angela would hear them talking into the early hours.

She was an intensely loved and thoroughly spoiled child, heaped with gifts and goodies: not just chocolate and ice cream and books, but a doll's house, a toy sewing machine, pretty dresses and expensive shoes. There was a succession of cats for her to play with (her favourite was Charlie, who used to pee in her mother's shoes). When she looked back on her childhood from the vantage point of middle age, she couldn't remember ever being punished. Olive, in particular – finally having her daughter to herself after years of sharing her with Jane – lavished affection on her. She was never put to bed until after midnight, when Hugh came home from work: until then, her mother wanted her for company. The mollycoddling only increased when, in September 1947, Hughie went to Brasenose College,

Oxford on an organ scholarship (his uncle Cecil having encouraged him to apply). After that, Angela had her mother's undivided attention.

Even before Hughie left home, Angela lacked playmates of her own age, and was often left to her own devices. That didn't always mean she had much fun. Like many solitary, imaginative children, she developed a range of hang-ups and private fears. 'She was always terribly serious about everything,' her cousin Nicola Farthing (Cecil's daughter) remembered. She worried fervently about illness and – not unreasonably in the context of the Cold War – nuclear catastrophe. 'My childhood had . . . terrifying self-created monsters,' she wrote in her journal in the 1960s, before hazarding a diagnosis: 'I suppose I was guilty at being so happy & so loved & had to create my own horrors to compensate.' It's an uncharacteristically woolly explanation, absolving herself, and more pointedly her parents, of any real blame – as if guilt were an innate quality in children.

She found some respite from her neuroses in stories of magic and adventure. The Stalkers didn't have a television set until the late 1950s, but the radio was always on, and an early influence was *The Box of Delights*, a *Children's Hour* serial based on John Masefield's 1935 novel. Angela came to regard the serial (which was broadcast three times when she was a girl: in 1943, 1948 and 1955) as 'one of the most potent memories of [her] childhood'. 'In an unselfconscious way', she reflected, '*The Box of Delights*, with its cast of piratical rats and time-travelling Renaissance philosophers, its ineffable atmosphere of snow and mystery . . . used all the resources of radio to create what we now call "magic realism".'

The first books she loved were also works of fantasy: she read her brother's copies of the Grimms' fairy tales and Lewis Carroll's *Alice* books, as well as *The Three Royal Monkeys* by Walter de la Mare and *The Princess and the Goblin* by George MacDonald. These tales found a place in her heart; they were still among her possessions when she died. Another childhood favourite was *The Secret Garden* by Frances Hodgson Burnett, which follows the adventures of a spoiled and wilful girl who, when her parents die overseas, is sent to live in the magical house of her maternal uncle, whom she has never met – plot points which would, reshaped into the stuff of her own allusive art, all feature in Angela Carter's second novel, *The Magic Toyshop*.

She enjoyed writing as much as she enjoyed reading, and couldn't imagine doing one without the other. Her father would bring home long rolls of white paper from work, and she would be set up with a box of crayons, composing stories while her parents chatted to one another. The idea of being published didn't occur to her until much later. Writing was just something she did, 'to amuse myself, to pass the time'.

She always claimed to have written her first novel at the age of six. The manuscript of *Bill and Tom Go to Pussy Market* (or *Tom Cat Goes to Market* – she gave both titles at different times) was lost or thrown away at some point by her mother, but she assured an interviewer that, far from being a work of fantasy, it was 'full of social realism: cats going about their daily business'. Elsewhere, she described it as 'an ill-spelt epic'. Ill spelt it may have been, but in writing it she had discovered one of her favourite motifs. As well as the raunchy version of 'Puss-in-Boots' that appeared in *The Bloody Chamber*, she wrote two feline-themed books for children – *Comic and Curious Cats* and *Sea-Cat and Dragon King* – and cats feature (in minor roles) in most of her novels for adults, too. She always associated the species with domestic happiness. 'I get on well with cats because some of my ancestors were witches,' she wrote in 1974. 'Whenever we feel at home, we secure some cats.'

Although Olive was the one who spent the most time with Angela, and who spoiled her the most extravagantly, Hugh was also an indulgent parent. Already in his mid-forties when she was born – 'just the age to be knocked sideways by the arrival of a baby daughter' – he often returned home laden with treats for her, and only ever told her off when it came to taking sides between her and Olive. 'I would say my father did not prepare me well for patriarchy,' she reflected in 1983. 'He was putty in my hands throughout my childhood.'

In spite of the unsociable hours he worked, Hugh's job had a few redeeming perks, including season tickets to the Proms and a free pass to the Granada chain of cinemas. Sometimes, on his weekends off, he took Angela with him to the Granada, Tooting. The largest and grandest of the 'picture palaces' built throughout Britain in the 1930s, this voluptuous concoction of diverse architectural styles – Angela described it as both a 'dream cathedral' and an 'apotheosis of the fake' – was the model for all subsequent Granada theatres, and is the only former cinema in Britain to be a Grade I listed building.

Entering via the Italianate portico on Mitcham Road, the cinemagoers were ushered by elaborately uniformed staff into a foyer festooned with many-tiered chandeliers, huge gilded columns, Puginian arches and carvings of rampant dragons. From there they went up a wide marble staircase into a long corridor done up in tones of cream, gold and nicotine brown. This corridor was lined on both sides with mirrors: Angela held her breath as she passed between them, since 'anything might materialise in those velvety depths'. Finally, having shown their passes, they were directed up another staircase, at the top of which the vast auditorium – capable of seating more than 3,000 people – opened up above them: a dramatic, thrilling moment. As they found their seats, Angela gazed entranced at the exquisitely intricate panelling of the walls, at the huge gaudy murals of medieval and Shakespearean figures above the orchestra pit, and (especially) at the cyclorama of the night sky that was projected onto the ceiling of the upper gallery.

Exposed to such stylistic excess 'at an age when there is no reason for anything to be real', she treated this fantasy interior as being of a piece with the films she saw there, and came to value artifice and extravagance as artistic virtues. The Granada was the first public building she took any notice of, and it remained the one that meant the most to her. Talking about it in the last weeks of her life, she cast a sidelong light on her own aesthetic: 'it was like the unconscious itself – like cinema itself – public and private at the same time'.

From 1945 until 1951, Angela attended Hearnville Road School, a sprawling yet somehow homely building on the junction of Ravenslea Road, only a couple of minutes' walk from her house. On winter evenings the school was lit by greenish gas lamps and heated by coke stoves; the outdoor toilets regularly froze over, but that didn't stop Angela locking herself in there for the duration of a Scripture lesson about Father Damian and the lepers (leprosy being one of the many diseases she was afraid of contracting).

The headmistress, Miss Edith Cox – a physically imposing woman who wore pastel Queen Mary dresses and arrived at school each day in a chauffeur-driven Rolls-Royce – is still spoken of fondly by many of her former pupils. She achieved impressive results with poor resources, and was proud that every year around five of her pupils gained London County Council scholarships to Christ's Hospital, an independent boarding school in Sussex. The curriculum at Hearnville Road included English, arithmetic, Scripture and geography, and (for the girls) needlework. But the highlight of the school calendar – and Miss Cox's pride and joy – was Empire Day.

A weird mixture of quaintness and triumphalism, this holiday was celebrated nationally on 24 May each year. The playground at Hearnville Road was strung with bunting and Union flags. The children would process up and down, bearing symbols of all the British colonies; at the end of the line came four children dressed up to represent the four nations of Great Britain herself (Angela once played Ulster in a green dress) and carrying their national emblems: a rose, a thistle, a daffodil and a shamrock. Those who weren't directly involved in the pageant stood around singing patriotic songs – 'There'll Always Be An England', 'Rose of England', 'Rule Britannia', 'Land of Hope and Glory' – to the accompaniment of a piano played by Mr Bridgeman, the deputy headmaster. Then there was dancing round the maypole, followed by speeches, and finally cakes and jelly. 'For us kids, there was a tremendous amount of pride on the day,' remembered one former pupil. 'We had a feeling of belonging to a great country and of course a great Empire.'

This was actually something of an illusion: in 1947, India detached herself from Britain, and the children in Miss Cox's playground were still in their teens when the country's shameful behaviour over Suez taught them where they stood in the new world order. But a more immediate challenge to the complacency of Empire Day was posed by the arrival of immigrants from Africa and the Caribbean, many of whom were putting down roots in south London. Around a quarter of the 492 West Indians who disembarked from the *Empire Windrush* at Tilbury Docks on 22 June 1948 – an event widely seen as the beginning of large-scale Afro-Carribean immigration to the UK – were entertained the next day at the Church of the Ascension in Balham, where they introduced the congregation to calypso music. Sizeable West Indian communities were soon established in the south London districts of Stockwell, Croydon, Clapham and Brixton, the latter being referred to as 'Little Harlem' as early as 1952. By the end of the decade the Stalkers had neighbours on Ravenslea Road called Mgbojibwe and Onyekwelu, while at nearby Hildreth Street Market you could buy (to Angela's delight) such exotic foods as yam, goat and black-eyed peas.

She was born just in time to witness the full extent of London's transformation from the class-encrusted heart of a bloated empire to a vibrant and relatively egalitarian multicultural metropolis; she greeted the latter incarnation as a distinct improvement. Part of what drew her to the study of folklore – as with many others who were involved with the folk revival of the 1950s and 60s – was a feeling that Britain had to discover a national identity that wasn't based on ruling the waves. When, as an adult, she returned to live in Balham for a brief period, she was delighted to see that the Hearnville Road playground was 'full of extrovert brown children, now'.

For all the pomp and bluster of Empire Day, the school catered mainly to the children of working-class families. Angela's best friend was a girl called Pamela, who (according to Angela's enthralled account) had a nephew only a year younger than herself, a married sister who had been bitten by a rat, and an uncle who trained greyhounds. They ate penny buns together on Wandsworth Common and joined in playground games called 'In and Out of Windows' and 'Chain He', the latter of which involved rows of children linking arms and chasing each other around.

Angela only felt she could join in these games when she was with Pamela. Making friends was complicated by the fact that she was becoming extremely overweight. She seems to have weighed around six or seven stone when she was only eight years old. Her mother had to buy adult clothes for her. At school, she was known as Fatty and Tubs. She became clumsy, and grew exceedingly self-conscious; she cultivated (and never lost) an artificial delicacy and thriftiness of movement, in which one interviewer discerned a 'desire to make herself invisible'. She stammered – an affliction that forced her to choose her words with care, and which may ultimately have contributed to her magniloquent prose. Once, during a game of 'Chain He', she toppled over – 'like many fat girls, my feet were too small to carry me conveniently' – and was dragged along the asphalt on her face.

Throughout the 1940s, meat, sugar, chocolate, cooking fats, milk, butter and cheese were strictly rationed: it wasn't easy to become obese. Olive must have siphoned off some of her own rations to bulk up Angela's. She may also have been generous with such sugary items as canned fruit and condensed milk, which had been removed from the ration list at the end of the war. 'Canned fruit was a very big deal in my social class when I was a kid,' says the narrator of Angela Carter's story 'The Quilt Maker', which is drawn directly from first-hand experience:

Sunday teatime . . . a glass bowl of canned peach slices on the table. Everybody gossiping and milling about and, by the time my mother put the teapot on the table, I had surreptitiously contrived to put away a good third of those peaches, thieving them out of the glass bowl with my crooked forepaw the way a cat catches goldfish . . .

My mother caught me licking my sticky fingers and laughed and said I'd already had my share and wouldn't get any more, but when she filled the dishes up, I got just as much as anybody else.

Olive babied Angela to a ridiculous degree – putting handkerchiefs behind her head as a prophylactic against nits whenever she sat down in a public place; rubbing so much Zam-Buk ointment on her chest that her top was permanently stained green – and was happy to give her whatever she wanted, so long as it kept them close to one another. It meant that her severely under-confident, introverted, near-friendless daughter was almost wholly dependent on her for reassurance and affection.

In 1948, during his second year at Oxford, Hughie met Joan Smalley: the daughter of missionaries, she had grown up in China, and was studying for a degree in history. Joan was a practical, plain-speaking woman, whose personality complemented Hughie's gentleness and dreaminess. She remembers Angela being 'enormous' when they met, and was very clear about where to lay the blame: 'I thought her mother was crazy. Her mother clung to Angela. She didn't want Angie to grow up.'

In her school report for 1949, Angela was placed sixth in a class of forty-five, receiving judgements of 'good' or 'fairly good' in all subjects except English, at which she was judged 'very good'. In 1951 she came first in the London Essay Competition – an annual event for schoolchildren, sponsored by the RSPCA – for a paper on 'Man's Duty to Animals'; her prize was a copy of *Wild Animals of Britain* by Kenneth Richmond. (Her winning essay hasn't survived.) That summer, she did well enough in her eleven-plus exams to receive a funded place at Streatham Hill & Clapham High School, a 'direct grant' independent school for girls.

The 1944 Education Act (or Butler Act, after the Conservative minister for education who introduced it) had radically shaken up the school system in England and Wales. Among its many innovations, it guaranteed a number of grants to install children from modest backgrounds at private schools such as Streatham Hill & Clapham High. It was one of Angela's pet theories that the Act inadvertently created, for the first time in history, a genuine British intelligentsia – that is, a class of people who didn't believe they were born to rule, who had no stake in maintaining the class-bound structure of British society, but who made their livings through dealing with ideas. According to this theory, the first generation of highly educated, liberally disposed men and women created by the Butler Act, who came of age in the 1960s, were largely responsible for the bracing flavour of that decade. Many of them went on to become academics (John Carey, Philip Dodd), newspaper journalists (Michael White, Janet Street-Porter), playwrights (Michael Frayn, Alan Bennett), poets (Tony Harrison, Geoffrey Hill) and novelists (David Lodge, Malcolm Bradbury), and in many cases they juggled any number of those professions at once. Angela saw herself as a model beneficiary of the system. The Butler Act has been widely credited with providing new educational opportunities for women, and she might also have thanked it for broadening her horizons beyond those of her mother.

The 500-odd girls at Streatham Hill & Clapham High were expected to be studious and self-motivated, and to set their sights on further education; the school had (in its original incarnation as Brixton High School) been sending girls to university since 1894, a record of which it was justifiably proud. According to one of Angela's contemporaries, anyone who took needlework and domestic science instead of Latin and Greek was looked on as 'a bit of a failure'. This academic, aspirational ethos left the girls, as another former student put it, 'unencumbered of the need to fulfil a stereotypical female role'. The headmistress, Miss Margaret Macaulay (a terrifying figure to her charges: tall, gaunt and severely dressed, she taught Latin and Scripture with crisp authoritarianism) was the sister of Mary Ogilvie, who from 1953 was the principal of St Anne's College, Oxford; a handful of girls went there from Streatham Hill & Clapham High every year; many more went on to the red-brick universities or took professional training courses. A report written in 1972 boasts that 'in the last twenty years girls [from the school] have become doctors, artists, musicians, nurses, lawyers, journalists, novelists, teachers, secretaries, accountants, social workers, pharmacists and physiotherapists, to mention only a few'.

Angela arrived at the school just as it was moving back, following the repair of Blitz damage, into its massive, flat, wholly unlovable premises – resembling nothing so much as a glum municipal hospital – at the top of Streatham Hill. The location did, at least, afford fantastic views: from the third floor, it was possible to see as far as Hampstead Heath in one direction and Epsom Downs in the other, with the dome of St Paul's Cathedral (still the tallest building in London in the 1950s) rising like the first bud of spring over the thicket of spires and rooftops in between. The school building was set in private grounds fretted with tennis and netball courts; hockey was played on nearby Clapham Common. The girls were divided into four academic houses, which competed against one another at sports as well as in an annual dramatic competition. There was an extensive programme of extracurricular activities, including an orchestra and a choir, debating and literary societies, and class trips to museums and galleries.

On 22 March 1952, towards the end of her first year at the school, Angela decided that she wanted to become an Egyptologist when she grew up – an ambition prompted by a class trip to the British Museum. Statues of the lion-headed goddess Sekmet, carvings of the gods Osiris, Anubis and Amen-Ra, and intricately decorated mummy cases had sparked off her imagination. She channelled some of her enthusiasm into a poem, 'The Valley of the Kings', which was published that summer in the school magazine:

> Thebes, ancient capital of Egypt,
> Deep in slumber lay,
> Sleeping against the sorrows
> Of another day.
>
> The priests in the temples,
> Chanted psalms and praises,
> 'Amen-Ra!' the voices cried.
> 'Amen-Ra, we thank thee greatly –
> Another night has died!'
>
> In the tombs so far away,
> Ancient kings long vigil keep,
> Till the last bright day is ended
> And the earth shall ever sleep.
>
> Thebes is dead, its temples dead
> No more do beggars crave
> A little food, or money, maybe,
> All is silent as the grave.

In the tombs so far away,
Ancient kings long vigil keep,
Till the last bright day is ended,
And all the earth shall sleep.

The poem is pretty astonishing for an eleven-year-old – not so much for its literary accomplishments (although the way the perspective drifts out from the chanting priests to the end of the world is smartly done) as for its throbbing bass-notes of melancholy. 'The sorrows of another day' indeed. Angela's sense of grief at the remnants of a vanished culture was profound, and the same commemorative instinct was brought to bear on her later study of folklore. She published two more poems in the school magazine, both of which also explored myths of the ancient world. In 1953 there was a poem about the Nativity (it ends on a doubtful, ironic cadence which suggests that aged thirteen she was already questioning her faith), and in 1954 an evocation of the Minotaur.

These poems are the work of a child who was increasingly isolating herself in a mental world constructed from reading and her own imagination. Her former classmates remember her as an eccentric, self-contained girl who made no effort to join in with group activities, and who inspired a vague sense of awe in the rest of them. Although nobody thought of her as unpopular, neither do they remember her being friends with anyone in particular (she once described herself as having been 'lots of people's second-best friend', but this seems to have been an exaggeration). They were all aware that she was clever: her accomplishments in English were well known. By the time she took her O levels, she knew *Great Expectations* 'off by heart', and she later acknowledged Miss Havisham as a source for the many images of wedding dresses in her own fiction. But her results in most other subjects were unremarkable (she was, in her own phrase, 'a one-person "mixed ability" class'). She came near the bottom of the year in mathematics, and she failed Latin O level more than once. Her teachers, viewing such inconsistency as the product of laziness, were tough on her. In all likelihood, they were being unfair – Angela had an acutely developed work ethic, and she liked to succeed wherever she could. One area that certainly caused her difficulty (only partly on account of her weight) was physical education; she was hopeless at hockey, and never did learn how to swim. But still she was criticised and pushed to do better: she felt persecuted and misunderstood.

'I hated school,' she wrote. 'Though perhaps hate is the wrong word, too positive, too passionate, to describe the glum, sullen loathing that overcame me as I daily slouched and dawdled towards the great, grey place.' She felt that having to go to school was 'the punishment for being a child'. That's not an unusual attitude, but in Angela's case it seems to have encroached on her basic sense of herself: 'I felt I had no right to *be* in the world.'

The reach of that phrase – 'in the world' – is telling. Her unhappiness at school was largely an extension of the lack of control she felt at home. As Angela approached adolescence, Olive's obsessive cosseting didn't let up. She continued to dress her – just as if, Hughie thought, his sister was 'a sort of doll'. Even when she was ten or eleven, she wasn't allowed to go to the lavatory on her own. She was made to wash with the bathroom door open well into her teens. Olive was terrified that some catastrophe would befall her if she let her out of her sight: she would slip and injure herself, or drown in the tub. This deluge of parental attention not only robbed Angela of all sense of agency; it also led her to place a high value on solitude, and her isolation at school during these years was doubtless a form of self-protection.

Psychotherapists – especially those influenced by Melanie Klein, whose work Angela read with enthusiasm in the 1970s – often speak about the twin fears of 'abandonment' and 'engulfment'. The former is usually dominant among people who've felt neglected or insufficiently loved during childhood; it manifests itself in a frantic insecurity about adult relationships, a desperate fear of losing the loved one. The latter tends to prevail in people who, like Angela, feel overwhelmed by their parents' demands; it manifests itself in a fear of the 'loss of self', a bristling terror of annihilation, and can inculcate a ferocious individualism as the only means of defence. As an adult, Angela was vigorous in her efforts to assert and protect her individuality. She dressed, spoke and wrote in such a way as to distinguish herself from the crowd, and would end friendships and sexual relationships abruptly (and often, from the other person's perspective, bewilderingly and hurtfully) if she felt she was being 'taken over'. But during her early adolescence – before she had developed any coherent strategy for dealing with it – her sense of engulfment, the drowning sensation of her autonomy being crushed, was utterly debilitating.

She began to feel 'blindingly unhappy'. She lacked control over even the smallest corners of her life, and felt oppressed by the prospect of the 'bleak, blank stretch' of years ahead of her. She slept badly, and would often read for half the night. In thrall to her neurotic instincts, she became increasingly drawn to the literature of disaster. In 1951, *The Day of the Triffids* was being serialised in the *Daily Sketch*, one of the many papers her father brought home from work. The idea of a blind world 'obsessed and indeed terrified' her. She also read the science-fiction magazine *Amazing Stories*, with its tales of shape-shifting aliens and malevolent robots. But these imagined cataclysms couldn't distract her from the upheavals that were beginning to take place within her own body.

Claustrophobic intimacy jostled with a penchant for strict respectability at Ravenslea Road: a combination that was bound to cause turbulence during a young girl's passage to womanhood. Sex was never spoken about. As late as her thirteenth or fourteenth year, Angela thought that the navel had something to do with intercourse. Nor was she in any way prepared for the onset of puberty. In a journal entry from 1977 she recalled her surprise at the arrival of her first pubic hairs:

> I can remember . . . the mild agitation I felt when I first found them growing; I fingered my slit & it felt, not hairy, but as if the flesh were crimped. How old would I have been then? Eleven? As I was probing around meditatively, in bed, one morning, probably late one Saturday morning, my father came in with a cup of tea for me & said: 'Don't let me catch you doing that again.' It was years before I found out what he thought I'd been doing.

In *The Sadeian Woman* (her 1979 non-fiction book about the Marquis de Sade and the construction of gender roles), Angela Carter described sexual activity as the 'most elementary assertion of the self' – perhaps that association can be traced back to her being made to feel, as a young girl who saw her identity being infringed on all sides, that she should be ashamed of her body's sexual development. At the same time, she wasn't allowed to keep the changes she was going through private. She once told a friend that when she was growing up, Olive regularly sniffed her discarded knickers. Even if this is an embellishment or exaggeration, it's true to Angela's sense of the terrible invasiveness to which she was subjected.

Throughout her writing life, female sexuality was a taboo she was at pains to overturn. *The Magic Toyshop* – her second novel, written in the winter of 1965–6, when she was plotting her escape from another oppressive domestic situation – recreates the stifling atmosphere of her teenage years. The story takes place mainly in south London during the 1950s ('around the time I was 13 or 14'), and follows its heroine Melanie after she is sent to live with her uncle, a daemonic puppeteer. It is full of lucidly remembered period detail: Sweet Afton cigarettes with the picture of Robert Burns on the packet; Guinness hoardings trumpeting 'A Man's Drink!'; and countless varieties of sweet and stodgy food – tinned peaches, bread and butter pudding, ice-cream cornets, apple pie with custard – which Melanie won't eat because she thinks that, if she gets fat, 'nobody would ever love her and she would die a virgin'. Her virginity is much on her mind. The novel begins with her first apprehension of herself as a sensual being:

> The summer she was fifteen, Melanie discovered she was made of flesh and blood. O, my America, my new found land. She embarked on a tranced voyage, exploring the whole of herself, clambering her own mountain ranges, penetrating the moist richness of her secret valleys, a physiological Cortez, da Gama or Mungo Park.

But constrained, controlled and spied on in her uncle's home, Melanie is unable to satisfy her erotic instincts. She feels that she is 'in limbo and would be for the rest of her life'; she resents being 'so young and inexperienced and dependent'. Sex is both a wonderful and a hideous idea, valued largely as the end of innocence – as manifested in her attraction to her cousin by marriage, Finn, whose 'terrifying maleness' and 'ferocious, unwashed, animal reek' don't dampen her desire. When she reread the novel in the mid-1980s, Angela was struck 'with the intense sense of adolescent longing in it, an extraordinary sexual yearning. What it reminded me of was endless afternoons alone in a room smelling of sun-warmed carpet, stuck in the Sargasso Sea of adolescence when it seems that you are never going to grow up.'

It's also a novel about self-invention: Melanie is searching for an identity for herself. She is trying to decide what kind of woman she wants to be, but the available female role models – her mute aunt Margaret, her stolid nurse Mrs Rundle – are woefully uninspiring. The family is the frame for all this, and rejection of the family is the only solution. Melanie's eventual affirmation of self – and of sexual autonomy – brings the dramatic change she has been praying for, and the novel ends with her and Finn standing in the garden while behind them the family home, containing all of their childhood possessions and memories, burns down.

The Magic Toyshop is Angela Carter's first version of the Fall, a fairy tale of 'the fortunate expulsion from an evil Eden'. In an interview in the 1970s she said: 'Eden is always evil . . . states of grace always are.' These are the words of someone who had suffered the intense discomfort of artificially prolonged innocence – someone whose childhood had been a state of grace from which she had longed to fall. It was a theme she would visit again and again.

On 2 January 1954, a day mired in fog and drizzle, Hughie married Joan Smalley in the south London neighbourhood of Purley. Angela was a bridesmaid: the wedding pictures show her with her hands clasped in front of her, wearing a slightly lost expression: in spite of her stately build, she appears much younger than her almost fourteen years. Hugh is standing beside her, laughing vigorously at some joke that only he appears to have heard. Olive is between him and the newly-wed couple, her face turned slightly away from the camera, apparently so as to keep one eye on her daughter.

The following year, Olive suffered a heart attack. From that time on she was never entirely well: she lacked the strength to do many of the things she had before. Hugh eventually set up a bed for her in the dining room so that she wouldn't have to climb the stairs, and brought her meals in on a tray. 'A good deal of the joy evaporated from their lives,' Angela wrote. But whatever else she had to abandon, Olive doesn't seem to have relaxed her hold over her daughter, or calmed her neurotic attitude to her.

That summer, Angela took to arriving early at school – it must have been purely for the sake of escaping home. She would get there at the same time as a girl from the year below called Jacqueline Anthony. While they waited for the day to begin, they wandered round the grounds together – Anthony remembers Angela's 'curious way of walking, with her hands behind her back like the Duke of Edinburgh'. They mainly talked about sex. Angela explained about lesbianism (which she had presumably learned about from a book), and pointed out the members of staff she thought were that way inclined. The older girl's eloquence and intellectual confidence made a powerful impression on the younger one: 'I longed to be like her,' Anthony confessed. 'She spoke so fluently and so colourfully, and had such strong opinions.' She was growing into herself, and beginning to enjoy her power to shock.

In Olive's relationship with her own mother, Angela could see that an infantilising parent–child dynamic could persist for decades if the umbilical cord wasn't properly severed. When she was seventeen, she decided that the time had come to put some emotional distance between herself and Olive. The first thing she did was to seek a doctor's advice about losing weight. She was put on a rigorous diet: at the start of 1958, she weighed something between thirteen and fifteen stone; by that summer, she had shrunk to around ten stone. She looked much healthier for it, and whether because she knew she did, or because she had finally resisted her mother's will, or both, she became more assertive in other areas of her life. She began choosing her own clothes, opting for the close-fitting black garments that were 'a positive sign of depravity' in the late 1950s (a typical outfit consisted of 'black-mesh stockings, spike-heeled shoes, bum-hugging skirt, jacket with a black fox collar'). Hughie was astonished by the transformation: 'I remember going back to Balham and the door opened and this sylph appeared.' Nicola Farthing was just as struck: 'I went back to my parents' flat one day, and Angela had arrived . . . And there was this beatnik, this slinky thing that was Angela, pencil-thin with black winklepickers on, striking a pose, leaning against the wall. She'd come to show off her new shape.'

Olive was vehemently against the diet (she wanted her daughter 'to stay fat and dependent on her', Joan says). But Angela was determined to forge her own identity. She started smoking – Olive was horrified, and told her it would turn the inside of her belly black. She took to swearing, openly and elaborately. Olive could only take so much, and began pushing back furiously against Angela's new-found self-assertiveness.

The breakdown of Angela's and Olive's relationship was as ugly as it was rapid. In spite of their closeness through most of her childhood, Angela's memories of her mother were forever stained with 'our later discords, our acrimonious squabblings'. Her determination to go through with the break is testament to her bravery. Although Olive's protectiveness was by almost any standards excessive, teenage girls in the 1950s were expected to abide by their parents' wishes. Nothing in Angela's background had set her up as a rebel, and (at least to begin with) she had to force herself to upset her mother. It can't have been easy for Olive, either: after a lifetime of acquiescing to her own mother, she must have felt utterly betrayed. She enlisted Hugh's support, and threatened Angela with his rage. But it was her own rage that stuck most painfully in Angela's memory:

> My mother . . . always selected the susceptible point, plunged in her scalpel & then mercilessly twisted it. Tears she regarded merely as first blood; but she could not qualitatively differentiate between her grievances. Her fears that I wore my skirts too short corroded her heart just as much – & were as real – as her fears I was surreptitiously injecting myself with heroin. Skipping through [*Portnoy's Complaint* by Philip Roth, the narrator of which is emotionally crippled by his intrusive, guilt-inflicting mother] I recognised her immediately.

That makes it sound as if the unpleasantness flowed in only one direction, but Angela was very often the aggressor. She came to enjoy provoking Olive, and took to saying whatever she thought would go down worst, usually something iconoclastic, blasphemous or obscene. There was doubtless an element of malice in this: she went on to write sympathetically of matricide in her unproduced film script *The Christchurch Murder*, and in *The Sadeian Woman* of a transgression much more disturbing than matricide: Eugénie de Mistival's rape of her mother ('a form of punishment uniquely fitted for her crime against pleasure') in Sade's *Philosophy in the Boudoir*. But above and beyond any conscious vindictiveness, there was a kind of joy, not only in laying claim to her own personality, but in discovering the anarchic fun, the ebullient comedy, of lobbing a well-timed phrase like a hand grenade at her audience, and watching it detonate.

Cecil Farthing and his wife Ann were sympathetic to Angela's predicament. She enlisted them as undercover agents in her war against her parents. Olive wouldn't allow her to go out with boys, so she took to asking her uncle and aunt to say she was spending the evening with them. Nicola Farthing remembers her ringing them up frequently for this reason. They were always happy to cover for her. After Ann died in 1989, Angela wrote a letter to Cecil in which she belatedly expressed her gratitude ('I never properly thanked you at the time, and I'd hate it if my "thank you" was one of those things that ended up never being said'). She recalled 'the endless kindness & hospitality &, indeed, understanding you & she both showed me, hospitality to a number of strange friends of mine, too, without flinching!'

It's unclear who these 'strange friends' were – they don't seem to have been girls from her school. She probably met them, and whichever boys she was seeing, through the sixth-form society that Streatham Hill & Clapham High ran with five other schools (two girls' and three boys'), which met five times a year 'for lectures, music, social functions and so on'. It seems unlikely, though, that she became very close to any of them. 'My adolescent rebellion was considerably hampered by the fact that I could find nobody to rebel with,' she wrote in 1983. 'I now recall this period with intense embarrassment, because my parents' concern to protect me from predatory boys was only equalled by the enthusiasm with which the boys I did indeed occasionally meet protected themselves against me.'

Perhaps another thing that drove Angela to unfasten herself from her parents at this time was that – her formal education having now outstripped theirs – she was developing a rich inner life that she was unable to share with them. Intellectually, these were crucial years. As well as whatever concerts and lectures she was attending through the sixth-form society, she was going regularly, by herself, to the National Film Theatre, where she gained a detailed knowledge of cinematic history. She was entranced by the iconic actresses of German cinema – Louise Brooks in *Pandora's Box*, Marlene Dietrich in *The Blue Angel* – who were, to a body-conscious teenager actively trying to craft her own self-image, fascinating studies in constructed femininity:

> I loved these faces, I loved them as faces. I loved them as objects . . . What's interesting about [*The Blue Angel*], it's before her face becomes Dietrich's face really, it's before it's really lacquered. And I was able to watch the progression of her lacquering as she becomes more unreal. More and more an object, more and more an object of desire. This is the fascination of it. How that face is created from, you know, from raw material, how it's invented, like a piece of cookery really, a piece of haute cuisine. And this was, you know, for me, this was the fascination, how it's done.

It was only later that she could start to ask herself *why* it was done. This question came to fascinate her: *The Passion of New Eve*, which was written against the background of the 1970s women's movement, explores the cultural hang-ups that lie behind the fantasy creation of a Dietrich-like

35

actress. For now, though, it was enough simply to notice the fact of the makeover, and to examine its process.

At school, she was relishing her study of English and French literature. Her earliest surviving notebook shows that she was plunging deep into the canon (*Othello* and *Hamlet* might be encountered by an ordinarily diligent student, but *Cymbeline* and *Troilus and Cressida* aren't on many sixth-form reading lists). She was discovering many of the writers who would continue to mean the most to her: Chaucer, Marvell, Blake. An even more important discovery came when her 'very unusual' French teacher, Miss Syvret, lent her a record of a Comédie-Française actor reading poems by Baudelaire and Rimbaud. This was a critical moment in Angela's life. She 'wore that record out' before returning it, smitten by the 'dark, sinuous voice' of the actor, and by the renegade, dandyish flavour of the writing. It was after listening to it a few times that she decided she wanted to become a writer: 'That record was my trigger. It was like having my skull opened with a tin opener and all its contents transformed.' She would later put the exuberance, the linguistic razzmatazz of her prose, down to the influence of French poetry. And it's worth noting that many of the writers who had the greatest impact on her throughout her life – Baudelaire and Firbank, certainly, but also Nabokov, Melville and Joyce – were to some extent dandies, fastidiously ornamenting and personalising their style, perfecting writing as a display of self.

Her teachers were impressed by her enthusiasm, and she was encouraged to apply to Oxford. She was keen on the idea, until Olive announced that she and Hugh would rent themselves a flat in the city so that they could remain close to her, just as they had rented a flat in Eastbourne when Hughie was evacuated there. Angela knew that her mother was quite serious about this. She dropped all talk of going to university. In the summer of 1958 she received A levels in English literature (with distinction) and French, but she didn't pass any other subjects. She had begun to think of marriage as the only way of escaping her parents' home.

CHAPTER THREE

Flight from a closed room

If Angela imagined that her parents would make fewer demands on her once she'd given up on university – that they'd allow her to loiter glumly round the house until a husband came along – then she had badly underestimated them. Hugh insisted that she got a job: he wasn't going to let her throw away her education by marrying 'some nitwit'. Within weeks of receiving her A level results, he found her work as a reporter on the Croydon *Advertiser* – the largest of the *Advertiser* group's nine local papers in Kent, Surrey and Greater London – at a salary of £2.50 a week, rising to £3 after six months' probation. Angela took the job 'kicking and screaming . . . saying no, no, no'.

'I never thanked him,' she reflected, more than twenty years later. 'It never even occurred to me that he was doing something rather progressive.' In the depths of her self-pity, she wasn't paying attention to how the world she lived in functioned. By the end of the 1950s, women comprised thirty-three per cent of the total workforce, but the majority were in traditionally female roles – they were secretaries, nurses, teachers – and those who worked with men didn't tend to advance far. Journalism (like politics, finance, medicine and the law) was an overwhelmingly male profession. When Angela joined the *Advertiser*, she was 'the token woman' on a staff of twenty writers, and she had to adapt herself quickly to a self-consciously masculine environment.

The paper was run out of an imposing four-storey building – its facade striped with pilasters, its roof elaborately gabled – on Croydon High Street. It was entered through a revolving door, and backed onto the noisy vegetable market at Surrey Street. The newsroom was smoke-filled and cacophonous:

the persistent din of clacking typewriters and ringing phones meant that all conversations had to be shouted. It made a change from the genteel atmosphere of Streatham Hill & Clapham High School, and Angela soon warmed to the role of reporter. ('It was obviously a better bet than a lot of the things I could do,' she later admitted. 'Even I could see that.') The sense of shabby romance she discovered in it remained an important component of her self-image, and as late as 1983 – with seven novels, two collections of stories, and an ongoing academic position to her name – she gave her occupation as 'journalist' when being admitted to hospital for the birth of her son.

Her colleagues soon began thinking of her as 'one of the lads'. This was a matter of her swearing ('I'd never heard a woman use the F-word in my life, but Angie did it all the time'), her smoking ('she was one of the most devout smokers on the staff, rarely without a fag drooping from the corner of her mouth'), and her willingness to join the men for a drink after work ('back in those days, if you said to a girl "Come to the pub with a group of us," most of them would say "No, I don't think so," but Angela would say "Yeah, okay." And that was the difference'). In later years, Angela often expressed the view that masculinity and femininity were simply 'behavioural modes', only loosely connected to the facts of sexual differentiation. Her success in inhabiting the conventionally masculine role of reporter may have laid the foundations of this belief, which was at the heart of her feminist consciousness.

But just because she had rejected her mother's dainty brand of femininity didn't mean she wanted to be regarded as 'one of the lads'. Several of her fellow reporters fancied themselves as ladies' men. She couldn't help noticing that their flirtatious gestures and lewd remarks – noisily pitched at the secretaries and female subeditors – were never directed at her. Though she maintained a show of jaunty self-assurance, it made her feel wretched.

At least until she reached her mid-thirties, Angela's intellectual composure co-existed with intense physical self-consciousness. She was fairly tall – almost five feet nine by the time she was eighteen – and naturally wide-boned. She once described herself as 'a great, lumpy, butch cow, physically extremely clumsy, titless and broadbeamed, a kind of hockey captain'. On other occasions she said she looked like 'Britannia on the old penny coins' and like 'a Russian female all-in wrestler'. This intensely critical perspective on her looks wasn't helped by the apparent indifference of the first men she got to know outside her family.

One evening, returning by train from Croydon to Balham, she found herself alone in the carriage with a French sailor. They started talking and he offered her a Gauloises. As she bent towards the match, he shoved his hand up her skirt. 'And I was <u>pleased</u>. Pleased because it was the first attention a man had shown me in six months, and I was working in an office full of men.' That attitude depressed her when she recalled it a decade or so later, but in 1958 – 'adolescent, clever, neurotic to a twinkling pitch' – her lack of confidence prevailed over her feminist instincts.

By the end of the year, her physical insecurities were swelling into full-blown obsessions. Her weight had now dropped below nine stone, but she wanted to become even thinner. She thought that achieving a waif-like frame was the only way she could make herself attractive to men. 'Attempted suicide by narcissism,' she called it, remembering this period some fifteen years later. 'Clearly, more was going on in my psyche than that, but sexual vanity was my justification.' By the end of January she had dwindled to 'between five and a half and six stone'. She started to exhibit the ghoulish symptoms of the morbidly underweight. Her periods stopped. She lacked energy and felt morose. 'At this point,' she wrote, 'I became an anorexic.'

Psychologically, the diagnosis fits Angela very well. 'Some analysts interpret the food the young woman rejects as the mother she is distancing herself from,' writes Lisa Appignanesi in *Mad, Bad and Sad*, her history of women and mental illness since 1800. 'Whatever theorization of anorexia clinicians prefer, one note persists in all accounts. The anorectic's fear and rejection of food are also a rejection of any kind of intrusion.' The Italian psychotherapist Mara Selvini Palazzolli (whose book *Self-Starvation* Angela reviewed in 1974) identifies two common features of anorexics: they have a heightened awareness of the cultural baggage attached to femininity; and they lack a sense of personal autonomy, usually due to having an overprotective mother. That sounds a lot like Angela. Even so, we should be cautious about accepting her testimony too readily: her GP's records haven't been preserved, nor have any photos from the first half of 1959 survived, so all we have to go on are her 'confessions of an ex-anorexic', and the memories of others. And while her own statements on the matter are definite enough, very few people who knew her at the time are willing to accept them as true. Her *Advertiser* colleagues don't remember her eating much apart from yoghurt, which she would snack on at her desk;

but neither do they remember her looking cadaverous, as she said she did, and as a woman who was five feet eight and weighed only five and a half stone would. Hughie thought that 'the talk of anorexia was slightly overdramatising it'. Joan is a bit more corroborative, saying that 'it was certainly on the edge of anorexia'. It may well have been. But Angela *was* an incorrigible self-dramatiser: 'between five and a half and six stone' was the measurement she gave in public, but writing to a friend in 1969, she estimated her lowest ever weight at seven and a half stone.

Two things are certain: that for the rest of her life, whenever she was unhappy, Angela had an 'automatic . . . not-eating reaction'; and that Olive was frantically concerned for her health. Their arguments took on a new, hysterical tone: 'Her mum kept trying to get her to eat cream buns and so on because she was terrified she would die,' remembers Joan. Nevertheless, when Olive discovered that Angela had stopped menstruating, her first, furious thought was that her daughter was pregnant – clearly, she still wasn't allowing her much privacy.

Even if Angela didn't become quite as emaciated as she later claimed, her weight loss had obviously reached a point at which it was damaging her health as much as her obesity ever had; and it was evidently connected to her uncertain self-image and her miserable sense that she lacked any other means of self-determination. She was desperately confused, and still felt tyrannised by her parents' demands: 'I didn't know what they wanted of me, nor did I know what I wanted for myself.' Compared to the volatile atmosphere at Ravenslea Road, the *Advertiser* 'functioned as a kind of benign day-clinic, where my patent insanity was taken in good part'. Within a year, the condition had ameliorated – but by that time, she had taken dramatic steps to wrest control of her life from Hugh and Olive.

Angela's *Advertiser* colleagues never thought of her as under-confident. The ultramasculine, ultraconservative mood of the office soon became the object of her anarchic instincts. Ignoring the paper's strict dress code, she began wearing wide-brimmed hats, bright 'ethnic' dresses and black fishnet stockings. Joe Steeples – who joined the *Advertiser* shortly after she did, and became one of her closest friends on the staff – thought she looked 'like a cross between Quentin Crisp and the Wicked Witch of the West'. Some of his colleagues were a lot less kind. Her eccentricity baffled and infuriated the more chauvinistic among them, which was almost certainly part of the point. Writing in 1967 about the 'gaudy rags' of the flower-power generation, Angela argued that dressing outrageously is really a way of disguising yourself: 'One passes oneself off as another, who may or may not exist . . . Though the disguise is worn as play and not intended to deceive, it does nevertheless give a relaxation from one's own personality and the discovery of maybe unsuspected new selves. One feels free to behave more freely.' By dressing unconventionally, she immunised herself against conventional opinion. Her colleagues remember the day she came in wearing green lipstick. The chief reporter, Noel Wain (brother of the novelist John Wain), rounded on her: 'What the fucking hell is that?' Angela asked what the fucking hell it had to do with him.

She might not have escaped censure for this behaviour if her father hadn't been such a prominent figure on Fleet Street. Hugh Stalker had given a talk to the *Advertiser* staff shortly before Angela joined, and he was friendly with the editor, Bob Taylor. Whether because of this connection or not, it does seem that Taylor went easy on her. By her own admission, she had 'a demonic inaccuracy' when it came to matters of fact. She was good at capturing the atmosphere of a court case, but would leave crucial details (such as verdicts) out of her reports. She irritated the subeditors by trying to sneak puns and literary allusions into her copy. On more than one occasion she was asked to leave the magistrate's court because of her 'avant-garde' get-up. When she was sent to cover the annual general meeting of the Croydon Deaf Children's Society, she came back saying that she hadn't been able to, because 'they hadn't heard her knocking'. But rather than reproaching or getting rid of her, Taylor made her a features writer.

It was an inspired move. Angela was never interested in court cases or council meetings, but now she could pursue the subjects she cared about, and develop her prose style while doing so. She reviewed books, plays and records; wrote essays on 'The Pin-Up of Yesteryear' and 'The Railway Station as an Art Form'; and riffed on south London history. On the whole, these pieces lack the intellectual resourcefulness and coruscating style of her later essays: they often have the relentless jollity typical of women's magazine writing in the 1950s ('There was nothing stuffy and formal about this fashion parade!' – not an obvious Angela Carter sentence). But in the best of them, and increasingly as she grew more confident, a personal voice begins to emerge.

This was partly a matter of calculation: most pieces in the *Advertiser* were anonymous, but Angela realised that if she used the first person frequently enough, the subs would be forced into giving her a byline. So the everyday sights of Croydon became springboards for philosophical reflection. The cards in a newsagent's window provided an opportunity for 'a free course in the sociology of the suburbs', and provoked a blunt ethical question: 'am I being oversensitive in seeing a menace . . . in the increasing number of flats to let that specify "no coloureds" or "adult Europeans only"?' She had a good laugh at a collection of smutty post-cards from 1917, featuring an almost fully clothed model in a variety of seductive poses, but then allowed her imagination to drift out into the future:

> so, indeed, in another 40 years' time, the rangy model girls with their 'expressive' faces, so often seen in the magazines of today, will end up in the 2001 equivalent of a junk shop. And someone in those days will laugh kindly at the dream girls of the 1960s and compare them unfavourably with a contemporary blonde Venus (who, maybe, will really come from Venus) or a moon faced Moon maiden.

There are also flashes of feminism. Reviewing an album by Marlene Dietrich in 1959, she speaks on behalf of her gender:

> I think women admire Marlene Dietrich so much because she looks as if she ate men whole, for breakfast, possibly on toast. And – 'Cor, serve 'em right,' one thinks. She is a sort of devastating, feminine revenge on the entire male sex.

This is amazingly close to Angela Carter's mature voice (the disarming frankness of 'Cor, serve 'em right', the wild comic flourish of 'possibly on toast'). It's also amazingly outspoken. The 1950s and early 1960s were by and large a fallow period for British feminism, with a huge cultural emphasis placed on the nuclear family and housewifely duty; Betty Friedan's *The Feminine Mystique* wouldn't appear for another four years. Angela's later avowal that 'I can date to . . . the summer of 1968, my own questioning of the nature of my reality as a *woman*' has often been taken to describe the beginnings of her interest in sexual politics. That might be when she became intellectually engaged with questions of gender identity, but the seeds of her feminist consciousness – no doubt cultivated by the chauvinistic atmosphere of the *Advertiser* offices – were already there.

*   *   *

The piece about Marlene Dietrich is one of a large number of record reviews Angela wrote during this period. She liked 'the high, wild uplands of modern jazz' – Count Basie and Duke Ellington were among her favourites – as well as George Gershwin, Ella Fitzgerald and Cole Porter. She was dismissive of 'commercial cha-cha', and reserved her greatest scorn for slickly varnished chart-toppers such as Cliff Richard, Tommy Steele and Billy Fury ('the fancy-name brigade', she called them, apparently forgetting her enthusiasm for Jelly Roll Morton). She felt that all the artistically interesting stuff was happening on the sidelines, and began to position herself squarely against the mainstream: 'Prolonged study of best-selling-record charts forces me to acknowledge that "pop" music has reached the crest of a wave of pure idiocy. Music for morons is taking over.'

Access to avant-garde music was made easier in the 1950s by the still fairly new phenomenon of independent record labels. One of the first independents in the UK was Tempo, established in 1946 by Colin Pomroy, Ron Davies and Jack Clough. In 1949, Pomroy split from the others and founded an even smaller label called Jazz Collector, reissuing rare 78s from defunct American labels such as Paramount. Print runs were minuscule, and most copies were sold in Pomroy's shop, a tiny record store 'like a taxi office' in West Kensington. Angela reviewed a number of his records: 'Jazz fans and folk-music fanciers should not be without these discs,' she wrote. 'Though the top ten customers would find them strong meat indeed.'

Pomroy's second in command was a twenty-seven-year-old industrial chemist (he spent most of his working hours in the laboratory at Dunlop) called Paul Carter. Angela probably met him at the shop in Kensington. Her first impression was of 'a simple, artsy Soho fifties beatnik'. He was softly spoken and reserved: 'humble' is a word his friends often use to describe him, but Angela soon realised that he was excruciatingly shy, much shyer even than she was. He wore dark polo-neck jumpers and shabby duffel coats. His face was square and somewhat pudgy – a friend of Angela thought he looked like 'an amiable teddy bear' – but she herself discerned a simian quality to his features, with his soulful brown eyes, prominent ears, and the thick flush of hair descending from his Adam's apple. Later, when she saw him eating bananas in bed, she said she feared for their children.

It seems likely that Paul was the first man to take a genuine romantic interest in Angela; no doubt she found his calm, undemonstrative manner appealing after the ferocious torrent of Olive's love. Though she later dismissed their relationship as a matter of sheer expedience – 'I finally bumped into somebody who would . . . have sexual intercourse with me' was how she put it in 1983 – there were several things that attracted her to Paul in those early days. His 'gentleness' and semblance of 'moral virtue' were especially appealing – both were qualities she felt lacking in herself. It's clear from the journals she started keeping a year or so later that she was very much in love.

Paul took music extremely seriously. He played several instruments (including the trumpet, the recorder and the English concertina), had a good singing voice, and derived a lot more pleasure from helping out at Pomroy's shop than from his day job in the laboratory at Dunlop. His great passion was for the traditional music of the British Isles. In 1958, the folk revival was just taking off. Impressed by the work of such pioneering collectors as Peter Kennedy and Alan Lomax (who had been broadcasting traditional songs on the BBC since the early 1950s), Paul persuaded Pomroy to set up an offshoot label, simply named Collector, issuing live record-ings of English, Irish and Scottish folk music. He began travelling to rural areas at the weekends, scouring the pubs for unknown fiddlers, pipe play-ers, whistle players and singers, and he also cornered American performers when they were passing through London. First for Collector, and later for Topic, he made field recordings of gypsy musicians such as Phoebe Smith, Harry Lee and the Willets family, and also worked with leading artists of the folk revival, including Louis Killen, Sandy Paton and Peggy Seeger.

The London folk scene in the 1950s was amateurish and sociable: there were regular singarounds in the upper floors of pubs; nobody was booked to perform, and nobody was paid. Angela wrote for the *Advertiser* about a meeting of the Croydon Folk Club, which welcomed all comers at the Swan and Sugar Loaf every Friday night: 'If you know some good songs, the door is open, just come in and sing.' Paul took her to a few of the better-known central London clubs (such as the Troubadour in Earls Court, where Bob Dylan played on his first visit to London in 1962), and introduced her to friends such as the musician and music historian Reg Hall, who found her 'nice, witty, a little abrasive, a little way out in the way she dressed'.

Paul, she said, taught her everything she knew about traditional music. It was perhaps his most important gift to her. 'The study of the traditional song of these islands is something of a liberal education in itself,' she averred, and it wasn't a great stretch to apply some of the things she was beginning to appreciate about folk music – that it was a democratic art form which was anybody's to do with as they pleased, a great tradition overlooked if not actively dismissed by the arbiters of culture, an outlet for the 'creative urge of the anonymous masses' – to the folk tales she had first encountered, almost twenty years ago, in a secluded Yorkshire mining community. She went on to write sleeve notes to at least three of the records Paul produced or recorded for Topic – *Troubled Love* and *Early in the Spring* by Peggy Seeger, and *Ballads and Broadsides* by Louis Killen – in which she displayed much the same empathy and insightfulness with which she would later write about such tales as 'Red Riding Hood' and 'Beauty and the Beast'.

There were strong links between the folk scene and the newly formed Campaign for Nuclear Disarmament (CND). The movement had been started by a group of left-wing intellectuals in January 1958, in response to J. B. Priestley's call for Britain to 'defy this nuclear madness into which the spirit of Hitler seems to have passed': its inaugural meeting in February was attended by more than 5,000 people. That Easter, a three-day march from Trafalgar Square to the nuclear research facility near Aldermaston in Berkshire gained intense media attention, and cemented CND in the public consciousness as a major political force.

Angela and Paul became enthusiastic members. They were fairly typical activists: young, leftish, middle-class folk fans. 'From 1958 the Aldermaston march was a sort of national meeting for practically all the folk clubs,' remembered the singer John Foreman. 'It was a singing march.' One of the records Paul produced at this time was of the London Youth Choir performing *Songs from Aldermaston*. (Sample lyric: 'some people say the world's a horrible place / but it's just as good or bad as the human race'.) According to one observer, CND was 'a tremendous stimulation of . . . love affairs', and the sense that they were working together against the massed forces of conservatism, the slavering cheerleaders of annihilation, doubtless strengthened Angela's attraction to Paul. 'We were always being picked up and going limp and being carried into vans by policemen,' she reminisced – but she liked to romanticise things, and that 'we' may not have included her.

At one point she thought about writing 'a CND novel'. It would be called *And Tomorrow's Doomsday* – a nod to the Romantic author Thomas Lovell Beddoes, who used the phrase in a late poem – and would be 'a black joke ending with the 4 minute warning in [Trafalgar] Square one

Easter Day'. She never got round to writing it, and she drifted away from the movement, disillusioned, in the aftermath of the Cuban missile crisis. But she retained 'moving and beautiful memories' of the early marches: 'It seemed, then, that in the face of those immense shows of serene public indignation – exhibitions of mass sanity, as they were . . . protest might change things.'

All of this stood in thrilling contrast to the conventionality of Ravenslea Road. There's no doubt that a large part of what drew Angela to Paul was what he seemed to represent: not only an escape route from her childhood home, but another way of living altogether. She brought him home to meet her parents, and he made them a present of a record he'd produced: *The Songs of Robert Burns* performed by a young Glaswegian vocalist called Robin Hall. Some of the lyrics were a bit bawdy – 'My love, she's but a lassie yet / We'll let her stand a year or twa / She'll no be half so saucy yet!' – which upset Olive, and delighted Angela. Hugh thought that Paul was 'wet behind the ears'.

The summer of 1959 was the warmest in living memory: writing a couple of years later, Angela recalled 'the smell of omelette & fried potatoes along the Charing Cross Road, eating salad in Mario's, going to the pictures with the sun shining, walking through lovely Sunday afternoon city streets, kissing for hours in the shop with the sun creeping through the venetian blinds'. Their embraces had 'a desperate quality, as if taking place at midnight, on a cliff, with thunder & lightning & the end of the world at hand'. Perhaps that was because they hadn't yet had sex: Paul insisted they should be engaged first. Just over a year after she had left school, Angela accepted his proposal of marriage.

In the early 1960s, more people were getting married than at any other time in British history. Even so, at nineteen, Angela was a little on the young side. To her parents, who had been so ambitious for her, it seemed a particularly cruel act of rebellion. Her father was unable to hide his disappointment – he had her whole career mapped out, all the way to Fleet Street, and he was devastated at the thought of her throwing it away. At first he refused to give his consent, but Angela told him that she was happy enough to live with Paul without getting married, if that was her only option. Hugh relented, but the rows didn't end there. Olive was distraught at the prospect of losing her daughter so soon, and her nagging and prying gathered urgency. The night before the wedding, she became incensed when she discovered that Angela hadn't bought herself new underwear for the occasion.

The service was held at St Mary's Church, Balham, on 10 September 1960. Paul wore a red tie (which made Angela's grandmother, Jane Farthing, suspect he was a communist), while his best man wore scuffed, tawny-coloured shoes with a black suit (which met with disapproval from the stylishly turned out father of the bride). Angela, for once, was beyond her mother's reproach: she looked beautiful in a white dress with her dark hair piled up on top of her head; at around nine and a half stone, she seems to have made a complete recovery from her anorexia. Afterwards there was lunch at a pub off Wandsworth Common, at which Jane ladled sugar into her champagne and over her smoked salmon, and was heard commenting that she 'wouldn't go to the lavatory' in the hat her older son Eric's wife, Lina, was wearing. Angela and Paul left the reception and went for dinner at the Palace Chinese restaurant in Croydon, where (to everybody's embarrassment) they bumped into a party of Angela's colleagues from the *Advertiser*. That was the extent of their honeymoon: on 12 September, Angela was back at work.

In Angela Carter's fiction – as in fairy tales – the heroine often makes a dramatic gesture, forsaking everything, giving up her oppressive past for an uncertain future. *The Magic Toyshop* – the novel that most powerfully evokes her childhood – ends with Melanie and Finn looking at each other 'in a wild surmise' as the family home is destroyed by fire. In her fourth novel, the hard-edged apocalyptic fable *Heroes and Villains*, the heroine leaves the stifling comfort of the community she has grown up in with a barbarian: 'she loved nobody in this place but beyond it lay the end of all known things'. When the gesture is getting married, the tone is even more doubtful. 'The Bridegroom' – a short story which appeared in *Bananas* in 1979 – ends with its heroine replacing one husband with another: 'she had lived for only as long as the silence in which she chose whose victim she would be. Freedom had betrayed her. Yet what else could she have done? The only liberty she possessed was choosing her master.' This was how Angela came to feel about her decision to marry Paul. 'I admit it,' she wrote in her journal only a couple of years later. 'Marriage was one of my typical burn-all-bridges-but-one acts; flight from a closed room into another one.'

By comparison to her existence in her parents' home, though, the freedom that marriage afforded her was immense. She clearly enjoyed the element of nest-making it involved. She moved with Paul into a furnished flat – they had nothing of their own – in Birdhurst Rise, a somewhat forlorn South Croydon crescent studded with fat semi-detached villas and connecting at both ends to an almost equally quiet, if slightly longer and more accessible, suburban street. Going by the accounts of people who visited her there, and the fragments of her own writing that have survived from this period, she seems to have liked taking charge of running a home. Although she never became very diligent about doing those parts of the housework that didn't interest her (ironing, cleaning, washing up), she immediately warmed to the more creative aspects of domestic life (cooking, decorating, entertaining), and writing less than a year after she married she described the 'sense of perfect order . . . that I get when I open my kitchen cupboard & see the tins & jars & packages & smell the faint rich coffee smell'.

Of her earliest sexual experiences, Angela wrote only that they were 'embarrassing', because of her almost total lack of knowledge. Her experiments in cooking were much more successful. The first cookbook she bought was *Plats du Jours, or Foreign Food* by Patience Gray and Primrose Boyd. Elizabeth David was another early influence. Angela became very good at cooking hearty, unfussy Continental dishes such as ratatouille and coq au vin. But she always had (as several of her friends observed) a former fat girl's attitude to food. She loved preparing it, and loved others eating it, but didn't over-indulge herself. Nor did she drink much: guests often felt frustrated by her habit of pouring them a single glass of wine, then corking the bottle and putting it back in the fridge, never to emerge again.

A few of her colleagues – Joe Steeples, Peter Carver and John Henty – used to visit Birdhurst Rise to listen to Paul's records and eat the stews Angela had prepared. On Friday nights they would often go to the Classic Cinema in South Croydon, 'to watch something *nouvelle vague*, avante-garde, and ever so boring that only [Angela] had ever heard of'. One of these boring avant-garde films was *Breathless* (*À bout de souffle*), which Angela found 'a revelation' when it was released in 1960. For her, Jean-Luc Godard was the artist who most powerfully defined the times: 'My whole experience of the next decade can be logged in relation to Godard's movies as if he were some sort of touchstone.'

Around this time, she began working on a novel. Her experience of writing for the *Advertiser* had empowered her to do this: 'It must have given me a certain degree of self-confidence, because, I mean, the glamour and magic of seeing one's name in print was nothing to me, I'd seen my name in print every single week.' Her colleagues remember that when they visited Birdhurst Rise, Angela's portable typewriter usually had pages of the novel she was working on sticking out of it, and that sometimes she would let them read bits.

No fiction from this period has survived, but we do know what the major literary influences were on this lost early novel, and what cultural currents it was battling against. British fiction in the late 1950s and early 1960s tended to be formally stiff and verbally gaunt, in conscious retreat from the lush complexities of modernism. The landscape was dominated by such traditionalist figures as Angus Wilson (a former librarian at the British Museum) and C. P. Snow (a senior civil servant), who encouraged comparisons with the grand nineteenth-century authors looming behind them (Dickens for Wilson, Trollope for Snow). The forces of iconoclasm were represented by 'Angry Young Men' like Kingsley Amis and Alan Sillitoe, who daringly put lower-middle- and working-class characters centre stage, but who remained as committed to social realism as the literary establishment they sought to displace. There were a few outliers – Anthony Burgess being perhaps the most prominent – who valued linguistic and imaginative energy over social and psychological detail, but Angela doesn't appear to have encountered their work until the mid-1960s.

She was bored by the contemporary novels that came her way, and turned for inspiration to the previous generation ('the period . . . 1903–23 now looks as though it was England's last artistically vital one', she wrote almost twenty years later in an essay about Katherine Mansfield). Her favourite writer at this time was D. H. Lawrence, and *Sons and Lovers* was 'very much the first novel we all wanted to write':

> Those themes – that naked confrontation with the self, most passionate of all encounters for a bourgeois individualist; with the family; with sex; with the challenge of the world; the novel that justifies your own existence, the justification, above all, for that murder of the parent, which is to say, the murder of the self as a child, which is the beginning of adult life.

What appealed to her was Lawrence's ability to 'quicken the pulse,' something few living authors seemed remotely interested in doing. She believed that she 'would have given up reading altogether at an early age' had it not been for the whiff of sexiness and scandal surrounding *Lady Chatterley's Lover*, which was cleared of obscenity (but only in a court of law) when she was twenty. A colleague slipped a copy on to her desk – 'even the cover seemed to blush'. All the same, her admiration for the phallus-worshipping Lawrence does suggest that her feminism was, at this stage, embryonic. She went cool on him soon enough ('D. H. Lawrence embarrasses me,' she wrote in her journal in 1965 – 'am I growing up?'), but there was always something a bit Oedipal about the way she denounced her former hero (even going so far as to out him, in a remarkable essay of 1975, as a latent transvestite), and in 1982 she wrote that 'the uncomfortable fact remains that he is, simply, the greatest English novelist of this century'.

Towards the end of 1960, Paul left his unrewarding job at Dunlop. Presumably this was a matter of choice, although the company no longer holds a record of his employment, so it's impossible to say for sure. What's certain is that for a while Angela became the sole breadwinner (though Paul still brought in a few pounds here and there from record sales), and in all likelihood (given the prevailing customs of the day) she was still doing most of the housework, too. This can't have been an ideal arrangement from her perspective, but it seems to have had an even worse effect on Paul. He began to exhibit what Angela came to know as his 'indrawn moods'. These were periods when he would retreat into complete silence – he wouldn't look up from his book when she came into the room, and made only a 'simple, minimal, stranger's response' to anything she said – which could last for days at a time. Her colleagues were left in no doubt as to how this was affecting her. On 21 March 1961, with Paul still out of work, John Henty noted in his diary: 'Angela depressed.' On 23 March: 'Angela still despondent.' On 11 April: 'Angela was more than just quiet – she was not even there – mentally, that is.'

Hughie – who had become a music teacher after leaving Oxford – was concerned. He stepped in to help when he saw an advert in the *Times Educational Supplement* for a lectureship in chemistry at the newly founded Bristol Technical College (absorbed into Bristol Polytechnic in 1970, and now part of the City of Bristol College). Paul applied for the job and was accepted.

'I suppose you'll have to go with him,' Angela later recalled her mother saying. She didn't think twice: the move was an opportunity to 'end [her] status as their child' once and for all. She left the *Advertiser* at the end of July, a month before they were due to leave London, and began searching for a place to live. She wrote application letters to the BBC and the *Bristol Evening Post*. The sense of making a new start was intoxicating. On 4 August she announced to her former colleagues that she was pregnant. 'She was happy,' says John Henty, who was among those she told. 'No doubt she was happy about it.'

CHAPTER FOUR

Just a wife

The Bristol suburb of Clifton – a rambling network of sloping alleys and raised Georgian crescents, set into the cliffs above the Avon gorge – is the city's last breath before the Downs, the river, and beyond, the open countryside. In spite of its grand eighteenth-century architecture, the area has a relaxed, villagey atmosphere. The buildings are painted in soft pastel colours. Gulls circle overhead. But during the 1960s this picturesque neighbourhood – formerly and subsequently one of Bristol's most expensive – was in a state of semi-dilapidation. Its ramshackle mood is captured in Angela Carter's third novel, *Several Perceptions*: 'Many of the shops were boarded up, to let, or sold second-hand clothes, or had become betting shops . . . tufts of weeds and grass sprouted from every cranny and broken windows were roughly patched with cardboard, if at all.'

For most of their time there, the Carters lived on Royal York Crescent, an enormous, sweeping terrace, uphill from everywhere. Their ground-floor flat at number 38 had two expansive rooms with high ceilings and vast sun-welcoming windows. The front room doubled as a bedroom: they filled it with books, musical instruments and dark Victorian furniture, and hung a silk kimono on the wall as a decoration. The kitchen had dramatic views of the Clifton Suspension Bridge, a feat of engineering which Angela thought 'possibly the greatest work of art produced in the nineteenth century'. A connecting double door between these two rooms could be kept open to create a single lavish space. Off to the side of the kitchen was a small back room, which Angela used as a study. There was no bathroom – they shared with the couple who lived upstairs – and no hot water. They had to stoke the coal fire each morning, and during the winter months they often kept their coats and jumpers on indoors.

Beyond Clifton, the city was booming at the beginning of the 1960s, eagerly propelling itself into the late twentieth century. Old terraces were being pulled down to make way for new housing estates. There were ballrooms and discos, and several twenty-four-hour bingo parlours. The Mecca Leisure Group was investing £2.5 million to build the New Bristol Centre, the largest pleasuredome in Europe, towering over its Georgian surroundings on Frogmore Street. By the end of the decade it contained an ice rink, a cinema, a casino, several bowling alleys and a dozen licensed bars. Its centrepiece was the 2,000-capacity Locarno Ballroom, where bands such as The Who and The Jimi Hendrix Experience performed; the ceiling was illuminated with a twinkling firmament of little lamps, and at midnight hundreds of balloons were released for the dancers to pop with their cigarettes.

'Everyone was terribly conscious that Bristol was happening,' remembered one of Angela's neighbours on Royal York Crescent. Artists and writers were showing up from all over the country. By 1964 there were more than 300 local pop groups (*Western Scene*, Bristol's very own beat paper, listed them: 'Johnny Slade and the Vikings; Dean Prince and the Dukes; Mike Tobin and the Magnettes; Johnny Carr and the Cadillacs . . .'). Throughout the decade the city was particularly renowned for its dramatic output, and during the years Angela lived there it was home to several well-known playwrights, including Peter Nichols, who in 1967 had a major success with *A Day in the Death of Joe Egg*; Peter Terson, whose *Zigger Zagger* (also 1967) caused a stir as one of the first fictional treatments of football hooliganism; and Charles Wood, who in 1965 wrote *Help!*, the second Beatles film. The BBC's documentary unit was based in Bristol, and from 1962 it was headed by the director John Boorman, while the members of the Bristol Old Vic repertory company included Peter O'Toole, and the theatre critic of the *Bristol Evening World* was Tom Stoppard, whom Angela saw, once, 'across a crowded room'. She later said that her early years in the city were like living in a museum: there were wonderful things everywhere she looked, but for all she had to do with them, they might as well have been sealed behind glass.

Her life there wasn't the one she had been dreaming of when she left London. She knew nobody in the city, and with Paul at work all day she was spending most of her time locked into the solitary routines of a housewife. She was often lonely and bored, but her opportunities for going out were pathetically scarce. Wrapped up in Paul's overcoat, she took 'sick, mindless wanders' around the old town, and signed on at the Labour Exchange for one pound and nineteen shillings a week. She haunted the auction rooms at the end of Royal York Crescent, where she bought such decorative Victorian bric-a-brac as an enormous collection of sardine tins (she later described this as 'wilfully eccentric and whimsical' behaviour). Her applications to the BBC and the *Bristol Evening Post* had been unsuccessful; she asked for work at George's bookshop – at that time the only bookshop in the centre of the city – but was turned down there as well. It meant, she noted, that she had no excuse for not following her dreams: 'I must strive to be an artist, after all.'

We know a fair amount about what Angela was thinking and feeling during this period because on 29 October 1961, she began keeping a journal; she would continue to do so, on and off, until she was diagnosed with cancer almost thirty years later. These lined A4 exercise books – their covers plastered with cigarette cards and pictures cut from magazines – are highly idiosyncratic documents. They are not (like the diaries of Virginia Woolf, for example) daily records of her activities and thoughts. They're a lot less structured or comprehensive than that. Working notes – sentences copied from books she was reading; ideas for stories; draft paragraphs; poems in progress – occupy the evenly numbered pages. Occasional jottings from life – descriptions of scenes and events; brief studies of friends and acquaintances; reflections on her moods, hopes and fears – are on the odd ones. Often, during especially busy or turbulent periods, she wrote nothing at all. Even when she did, she sometimes tore out the pages afterwards, or scored through them with dark felt tip. Yet there is a wealth of personal detail in what remains.

Her earliest journal reveals not just how lonely she was during her first year in Bristol, but how thoroughly she sought to occupy herself in literary work. She wrote poems and prose fiction, struggling to forge a distinctive voice. The fiction employs an eclectic range of styles and genres, from terse social realism to implausible comic yarns with sub-Roald Dahlish twists. None of it has the distinctive dazzle of her mature work. She found the weakness of what she was producing, in spite of her best efforts, frustrating and frightening. Behind every failed story lurked the horrible thought that she didn't have what it took to be a writer: 'I'm intelligent, I know, but untrained & without discipline, so that simply living is gradually blunting my mind, tarnishing it like silver.'

Among the best of her early fiction to have survived is a short, naturalistic story called 'The Baby'. It concerns a young married couple, not unlike Angela and Paul. The man is 'some years older' than the woman and has a 'playful way of speaking to her, as though she were a child'; he is prone to worrying and brooding, and has 'an unreasoning anger when something thwarted him . . . when a cinema was so full they could not get in; when they got on the wrong train; once, when he had lost a glove'. She thinks of herself as 'the girl who would never be free again, secured with not one but a million chains of love'. There is a listlessness to the story: the woman gets pregnant, and begins to feel increasingly distant from her husband. They have a row – a minor squabble, about nothing really – and it ends with him sulking in bed, and her crying beside him in the darkness: 'She thought that when the baby came, she would have something she could call her own and love on her own conditions . . . And as she wept, her allegiance to her husband was crumbling; she owed more allegiance to the still fish-shaped embryo that swam in her womb.'

'The Baby' is built on solid autobiographical foundations. Paul's gloomy spells and touchy, drawn-out silences had followed them to their new home. Angela's journals are full of references to him being 'depressed', 'indrawn', 'contracting almost to a pin-point', and going into 'one of his massive infantile sulks'. These moods were extremely difficult for her, not least because she felt (or was made to feel) that she was responsible for them. One thing that reliably upset Paul was her devil-may-care attitude to doing the housework. Increasingly, she found it an exhausting and utterly unrewarding constraint on her freedom:

> It never ends, the buggering about with dirty dishes, coal pails, ash bins, shitbins, hot water, detergent . . . There is no stop for me; never no rest, never ever again, on & on & on . . . I have just scrubbed the sink. It must be scrubbed tomorrow, too. I'm so tired I can't think, or write, or read. I tumble, glazed & bladderful, from bed & swing into the fire-kettle-porridge-bread routine.

It has been estimated that in 1961 the average British housewife spent seven and a half hours each day on her chores. That wouldn't leave much time for writing, and Angela wasn't willing to sacrifice her literary ambitions to thankless domestic tasks. Before long the dust lay so thick on the kitchen surfaces at Royal York Crescent that visitors often wrote things in it. There tended to be dozens of empty milk bottles in the shared hallway, which Angela said were nothing to do with her, 'they simply bred in the corridor.'

She felt that Paul was ashamed of her 'vile, dirty habits'. Coming home to find that the housework had once again been neglected in favour of writing, he upset her by saying: 'another day wasted'. She describes him becoming 'angry & . . . indrawn . . . because the kitchen floor was dirty (I forgot to wash it); because the dresser shelves were dirty (I forgot to wash them); because I've sawn great jags in the dresser through cutting the bread (I forgot to use the chopping board)'. Another sulk was brought on when the Hodges – the upstairs neighbours with whom the Carters shared their bathroom – complained that Angela was leaving drips of piss on the lavatory seat. 'My God', she wrote in her journal, 'women are physiologically fashioned so they drip; it's God's way. Mrs H. ain't got no bladder.'

Paul was evidently a restrictive and at times an enervating person to live with, but it would be wrong to view him as an ogre; a few years later, Angela described him as someone who '[muddled] along, basically unenlightened, wanting to believe the best of people, trying to be nice, but constantly tripped up by his own psyche . . . an erratic person, [who] has a kiddie's windmill for a heart'. His assumption that his wife would dote on him – that she would more or less subordinate her own ambitions to the task of looking after him – wouldn't have seemed egregious by the standards of his generation. The chauvinistic attitudes of the 1950s were still in rude health during the early 1960s. It was widely assumed – so widely, indeed, that it was enshrined in various bureaucratic rules and procedures – that the man of the house was, if not the sole earner, then certainly the executive source of all higher decisions and responsibilities within the home. In financial matters, British women were treated more or less as children: they often received an allowance from their husbands for household expenses, but they had no legal right to any savings they made from it; they needed the signature of a male guarantor to take out a mortgage, the justification being that few women worked for long enough periods to pay one off; those who were self-employed tended to find that the Inland Revenue sent their tax rebates directly to their husbands. In return for all this financial security, women were expected to keep themselves presentable, to be responsive to their husbands' sexual, emotional and conversational requirements, and (above all) to keep a tidy and smooth-running home.

But Angela had married precisely to get away from being somebody's marionette; she didn't want that role again. She consciously strove to assert her own interests within the relationship. Although she later told friends and interviewers that she was 'just a wife' during this period, it wasn't how she liked to think of herself at the time. She wanted to be respected and indulged as a creative artist; she wanted Paul to recognise the dignity of her ambitions, and to make as few demands on her as possible.

Though she doesn't seem to have been aware of it, her attitude to Paul resembled, to an astonishing extent, Olive's attitude to her as a child: 'I don't really want him to have a personality at all,' Angela confessed to her journal. 'I just want him to be warm & responsive & loving & entirely subordinated to me.' But Paul was none of these things, and her earliest journal reveals a desperate battle of wills between them. Where chilly indifference was his weapon of choice, she went in for tearful scenes ('I go all to pieces & cry & cry'); but this only made him withdraw further into himself, and she quickly became sick of 'bruising [herself] against his stolid, brutal silence'.

There was always a tension between Angela's fear of engulfment and her romantic sensibility. She wanted warmth and passion, even as she wanted to be free from emotional demands (a contradiction that she explored in her novels *Love* and *The Infernal Desire Machines of Dr Hoffman*). The latter need was partly what drew her to Paul in the first place, but he was constitutionally unable to provide the affection she sought from him, or even to 'accept expressions of love gracefully'. She found herself harbouring an excess of emotion that she didn't know what to do with. 'I want to cry with love, I feel heavy & aching with love,' she wrote. 'I want to touch him all the time, with my hands & my mouth (poor luv, it annoys him).' He once told her that this was precisely why their relationship worked: because he was so introverted, and she was so warm. 'There's a flaw to this logic, somewhere,' she commented.

Nevertheless, when Paul was in good spirits, she could believe that the relationship did work. It was easy to see things that way on 4 November, when they went to a fireworks display on the Downs. The weather had been mild since they'd moved to Bristol, but that evening the temperature plummeted; people wore big jumpers and huddled close together, and Angela noted the expressions of joy on faces lit by the flashing carousel of colours. She was moved and stimulated by the display ('Too bad that so many writers have mucked around with fireworks,' she wrote in her journal, a sign of how little confidence she had in her powers of description at this stage; her first collection of stories, published in 1974, was titled *Fireworks*). Back at the flat, she and Paul turned out the lights and lit sparklers in the sitting room. Then they made love on the sofa – 'a new experience'.

She woke the next morning with a terrible cold. She wasn't good with colds – 'they dehumanise me so' – and spent the next few days lying around in bed, smoking menthol cigarettes, and (it's clear from her journal) being extremely needy. Paul became 'very indrawn'. Though it would take Angela a long time to acknowledge the fact, they were a remarkably ill-matched couple: neither of them was willing to relinquish much independence, yet both of them required selflessness and solicitude from the other. Years later, she told a friend that she'd had 'more meaningful relationships with people I've sat next to on aeroplanes'.

She missed her parents terribly. To travel, in the space of a year, from the obsessiveness and overfamiliarity of their home in London to the anonymity and isolation of her life in Bristol was a lot more than she had bargained for. She was twenty-one, but in her journals she often sounds like a very young girl: 'I'm unhappy enough to die. I want to go home. I want to go home. I want to go home.'

When she did go home, for Christmas, she was overcome with affection for her parents and her brother. 'My family is unique & stupendous & quite adorable,' she wrote. 'I love them so much it hurts.' Even so, she couldn't resist winding up Olive, who had selected a large frozen turkey for Christmas lunch. At 11.30 that morning it was still frozen, 'wallowing pinkly in a bowl of hot water in the sink like a fat old man in a hip bath'. It took a while to reach their plates, but everybody was in high spirits and getting on well, until Olive eventually brought the roasted bird into the dining room. Angela looked up and said: 'Oh good, here comes the fucking turkey.' And out it went again. Hughie regarded the incident as typical: 'Angela would do things to upset my mother, to upset the apple cart at home. If things were going normally, she'd go, Oh God, this isn't good enough, we'll have to do something to make it more interesting.'

Returning to Bristol after the holiday, her situation seemed much worse. With Paul 'mooning silently about' and her writing still failing to catch light, she felt hopeless. 'Oh dear, why did I marry?' she asked herself. 'The first freedom is gone, now. I want to move on. Not from Paul; with him, but he is not footloose like me.'

Just as it had been when she was a child, Angela's unhappiness was chaperoned by hulking neuroses. In January 1962, an outbreak of smallpox at St Luke's hospital in Bradford was receiving shrill front-page coverage in the national press. Angela – living 200 miles away – became obsessively anxious about contracting the disease. She decided she could only quell her nerves by going to the doctor's to get inoculated. The waiting room was 'full of fat, happy, giggling babies'; she was the only adult who had come on her own behalf. She felt she was 'taking the vaccine out of the arms of babes & sucklings'. But she went through with it, even so.

The difficulties that Angela faced, both in her writing and in her marriage, became marginally less oppressive as she started developing a life outside the home. Among the earliest friends she made in Bristol were Peter and Janet Swan, a relaxed and sociable couple who lived on Cornwallis Crescent, the street nestled one tier below Royal York Crescent on the hill of Georgian terraces that cascades down to the river. Peter was an artist, specialising in abstract 'landscape forms' and monochrome portraits with a naïve folk-art affect; Janet was mainly occupied with looking after their children.

The Swans remember Angela as 'wacky', an eccentric and somewhat gauche young woman, of whom they were very fond, owing to her warmth, her intellectual curiosity and her mischievous sense of humour. Like most people who knew her at this time, they had no inkling of the unhappiness and self-pity that are so sharply apparent in the pages of her journals: she didn't expose her innermost feelings, and tried only to show her lively, quick-witted side to the world. She dressed for effect – 'there was a dramatic style about her, not like anybody else's' – but more oddly than elegantly, in tattered fur coats and floppy wide-brimmed hats. This ancient-looking wardrobe, coupled with her passion for Victoriana and her hesitant way of speaking, contributed to a sense that she was somehow much older than her years. Peter describes her as 'twenty-one going on sixty-one', while Janet says she seemed like 'an old maid'.

Janet's memories also cast light on the pregnancy that Angela had announced to her *Advertiser* colleagues, and which must have informed the composition of 'The Baby':

> She played the sort of elderly aunt to little children like ours. She had this big sweetie jar, and she would say: 'Have a sweetie.' She was curious about children. The very first time I met her – we knew Paul already, and he brought her to the flat to introduce her to us, and I remember she'd been to the loo and she was walking back through the flat to where the baby was lying in its cot, and she looked rather objectively at this baby and said: 'I thought I was going to have one of those.' She said it was a phantom pregnancy. She didn't seem emotional about it.

Phantom or 'hysterical' pregnancies can involve all the major symptoms of actual pregnancy – swollen belly, tender breasts, missed periods – except for the crucial one. There is no consensus about their causes, but they have been viewed as arising from fears of barrenness – an interpretation that might be taken to cast light on Angela's attitude to her literary endeavours as much as to her relationship with Paul. She was given to psychosomatic conditions. A few years later, when she'd started taking more of an interest in Freud, she began referring to herself half-jokingly as a hysteric: 'I always have to interpret my physical symptoms as if they were the bloody Tarot pack.' And although she didn't usually describe them as phantom pregnancies, she was on several subsequent occasions convinced – on the basis of such slender evidence as a marginally delayed period – that she was carrying a baby. In 1972, following another false alarm, she consulted a friend's gynaecologist, 'a nice, old-fashioned feminist, who diagnosed me thus: that I'm enamoured of the idea of having children, but like to keep it strictly as a fantasy'. Angela thought this analysis 'perfectly just'. But it was a fantasy that she seems to have indulged only during markedly uncertain or frustrating times in her life.

Through the Swans, she met John and Jenny Orsborn, who lived on Saville Place, a grandly proportioned spur road, divided from Royal York Crescent by the shabby thoroughfare of Regent Street. John styled himself as a painter, but he never sold enough canvasses to make a living from it, and supplemented his meagre income by riffling through abandoned buildings for any goodies – ornamental toilet flushes, well-made door handles – that could be sold on to one of the local junk dealers. Jenny did whatever work – such as serving in cafés and bars – she could fit around looking after their young son.

The Orsborns took to visiting Angela at Royal York Crescent for coffee on weekday mornings, when Paul had left for work. Jenny remembers her fondly – 'She had a nice sense of humour and a laugh that could empty the room, a belly laugh if something was funny, despite having quite a gentle voice' – but it was John to whom Angela was most powerfully drawn. He was unlike any man she had previously met: tall, handsome in a vulpine sort of way, fair-haired and neatly bearded, he had an air of danger about him, a sort of Heathcliffian wildness. He could be cruel (he once told the Swans that he couldn't imagine sleeping with Angela because of her 'awful teeth' and 'puce-coloured' face) and he was quite capable of using people to get what he wanted. But he was also witty and charismatic, full of energy and ideas. He considered himself an intellectual, talked in a dazzling stream of insights and ideas, and had lots of affairs. In her journal Angela goes from calling him a 'shitbag' in one entry, to writing in the next: 'Orsborn is <u>all right</u>, a good guy.'

The heart of the Clifton scene – and a favourite haunt of John Orsborn – was the Greyhound pub on Princess Avenue. Angela began going there quite frequently, and she used it as the model for the pubs in both *Shadow Dance* and *Several Perceptions*. Although the landlord was Polish, it served Spanish food, and had an imported Spanish bartender and posters of bullfighting on the walls ('nights in a garden of never-never Spain', Angela wrote in *Shadow Dance*). Invariably overcrowded, dense with smoke and talk, it had, in 1961, the kind of nonconformist spirit that would become so widespread later in the decade. Its clientele was largely made up of aspiring writers, out-of-work actors, penniless painters and musicians. They were promiscuous (Angela joked about making a film about Clifton society: the camera would pan slowly around the Greyhound, showing all the regulars, and at the end a voiceover would say: 'Everybody in this pub has been to bed with everybody else') and they were dissolute (every so often, the police would raid the premises for drugs).

Angela was fascinated by this slice of 'provincial bohemia'. Clifton struck her as 'very innocent and pastoral and semi-criminal . . . very seedy and picturesque'. It was a more or less uncharted landscape, as roundly neglected by English literature as the south London of her childhood, and just as vibrant and odd. She decided to make it the focus of her own writing, hoping to capture 'the genius loci of this strange area . . . The curious away-from-London, away-from-everything feel of it all.'

Just as important to Angela's life in Clifton (though not involved in the world of the Greyhound) were Nick and Corinna Gray. They both came from artistic, bohemian London families – Nick's mother was the food writer Patience Gray, whom Angela revered – and according to Corinna, they were consciously trying to escape this background. They wanted to live 'as conventionally as possible', to which end they had married young, moved to a provincial suburb and had two children in quick succession. But to someone from Angela's middle-class background, they must have seemed anything but conventional. Nick had a variety of jobs, ranging from a fishmonger's van driver to an antique dealer's assistant, during the time she knew him; he rarely stuck at anything for very long. Corinna had studied at the Central School of Art and Design, and shortly after Angela met her she began a second degree in animated film at the University of Bristol. She had long hair, a quirky style of dressing, and a somewhat ethereal manner. She and Nick ran Punch and Judy shows together during the school holidays, and later organised tours of Bristol in their narrowboat *Redshank* (it was being a passenger on this vessel that inspired Angela to buy a barge of her own in the 1980s). Angela felt that they were 'not of this world', and that they brought 'a breath of Hampstead wherever they go'.

She and Paul began meeting them every Thursday evening to go to the pub, where the men would drink and talk, and the women would sit there 'being rather bored by them', according to Corinna. Angela liked Corinna's off-centre poise, her fearlessness about embracing her idiosyncrasies, and they developed an extremely close friendship, which endured until the end of Angela's life. At its heart was a rare creative affinity: they hatched an abortive plan to do a children's book together (Angela writing, Corinna illustrating), and Corinna (having reverted to her maiden name of Sargood) did the artwork for *The Virago Book of Fairy Tales* in 1990 and its successor volume in 1992, her macabre, carnivalesque woodcuts perfectly complimenting Angela's selection of material. '[Angela] was a very visual person,' she recalled, 'which is one of the reasons we got on; we liked the same sorts of things. And perhaps we liked one another because we were both sort of outcasts from proper society.'

*   *   *

These friendships rendered Angela's life in Bristol considerably less claustrophobic; but writing remained her priority. 'What I want is a voice,' she wrote in March 1962, 'something personal and unmistakable, that people will instantly recognise & say, "That's Angie". At the moment, I don't care particularly whether I'm good or bad.'

Between January and May, she redoubled her efforts to find a style of writing that would proclaim her individuality in this way. She composed her first drafts longhand, using an old-fashioned pen: 'I like using a proper pen better than fountain pens or biros & things because the continual pauses to dip in the ink afford a breathing space, in which to consider & brood & plan what one is writing.' Then she typed up a second draft, before going over it again in pen. During this period, she worked on a novel titled *The Star Gazers* (it hasn't survived, but her notes suggest that it was a Gothic murder story set in Bristol and informed by themes from astrology), and completed about five short stories and a dozen poems. She began sending them out for publication, and on 10 February received the 'great psychological blow of having first rejection slip from a "little magazine"'.

The stories she was working on were increasingly set in the world of bohemian squalor and loose sexual mores that she had encountered through John Orsborn and the Greyhound. They are a curious mixture of virtuosity and clumsiness, veering from beautifully vivid details ('her dry bush of hair susurrated like old newspapers in a small wind') to hasty globs of histrionic action ('"You're just too bloody much, aren't you," said David. Beads of sweat appeared on his forehead and he darted from the room'). But their style is much richer than that of 'The Baby', and the distinctive tone of Angela Carter's early novels is beginning to emerge: that blend of social commentary and psychodrama, in which the characters have ordinary enough (if thoroughly bohemian) existences, but extraordinary fantasy lives. These stories aren't fully formed, but they do reveal the spark of authentic creativity: they're unlike anything written by anyone else.

Typical of this period is 'The Events of a Night', in which Leonie and David, a destitute brother and sister, both having abandoned their parents, go for a late-night walk in a city that strongly resembles Bristol, and end up sleeping together. The next day David locks Leonie into his flat: 'She wandered around his room in a fury because only her brother would think he had the right to lock her up, the inalienable right of family and that of love, for this was the kind of irrational thing people did when they were in love.' The story ends in theatrical style, with David killing himself by jumping out of the window, and his sister gamely contributing to the performance: 'Mechanically, as if she knew this were expected of her, Leonie began to scream.' Several of Angela Carter's characteristic tropes – incest, theatricality, mirrors, folklore – feature in this early work, although the mixture is awkwardly stirred.

Another story, 'The Man Who Loved a Double Bass', is also set in the world Angela was living in at the time, but its focus is tighter, its touch considerably surer. Set during the trad-jazz boom of the early 1960s, it follows a group of musicians called the West End Syncopaters whose 'souped-up version of "West End Blues" (plus new vocal) had penetrated to the lower reaches of the top twenty'. Its hero is the group's bass player, Johnny Jameson, an artist of such integrity he doesn't even notice that trad has become fashionable. The story is pitched between a skit on contemporary manners and a fantasia on artistic 'madness' and authenticity. In July 1962 it won first place in the *Storyteller* magazine short-story competition, and became Angela Carter's first published work of fiction.

Some of the distance between 'The Baby' and such stories as 'The Events of a Night' and 'The Man Who Loved a Double Bass' can be attributed to Angela's exposure to new influences in the period between writing them. In January she had read *Ulysses* for the first time, describing it in her journal as 'quite magnificent'. Joyce's impact on English fiction in the early 1960s was minimal (hardly any greater than Rimbaud's or Baudelaire's were), and the delight that Angela took in *Ulysses* speaks to her continuing dissatisfaction with her immediate literary environment. The novel revealed to her a way of writing in English without succumbing to the fustiness that she felt scented the pages of most English novels. Twenty years later, she wrote that without its example she 'would not even have had the possibility of a language':

> [Joyce] carved out a once-and-future language, restoring both the simplicity it had lost and imparting a complexity. The language of the heart and the imagination and the daily round and the dream had been systematically deformed by a couple of centuries of use as the rhetorical top-dressing of crude power. Joyce Irished, he Europeanised, he decolonialised English: he tailored it to fit this century, he drove a giant wedge between English literature and literature in the English language and, in doing so, he made me (forgive this personal note) free.

She was also feeling her way back into journalism during this period, taking whatever freelance commissions she could find. At the beginning of 1962, she contributed two articles on folk music to the *Western Daily Press*, which was something of a crucible for literary talent in the early 1960s: Tom Stoppard, Zulfikar Ghose and B. S. Johnson – all of whom, later in the decade, wrote works of fiction that pointedly departed from the conventions of realism – also contributed to the paper's arts pages during these years. Angela's pieces display enormous confidence in her material, and represent an advance on the witty, slangy, personal voice she had started to develop during her time at the *Advertiser*. They are also deeply revealing about her interest in the English folk revival:

> Few nations have spent quite as long as England in creating an official mask . . . What are we like? Oh, you know. Reserved. Imperturbable. Anti-romantic. Practical. A bit fumbly and embarrassed when it comes to sex . . . But study our folk heritage, our great and still living heritage of rough and ready poetry, and there is the authentic face. The man who emerges from English folk song is as merry as a cricket, as lecherous as a goat, a Gargantua in appetites and mirth, with a pulsing vein of lyric poetry in his body.

The 'authentic' Englishman she found in folk music had all the qualities she prized most in herself. Rude, warm, romantic, funny: this was the type of person she was trying to be. But to see these qualities as essential to the national character required a spectacular act of faith. In the Englishman she saw the most of in her personal life, the 'reserved', 'anti-romantic', 'imperturbable' mask looked uncomfortably like the true face.

One of the poems Angela wrote at this time is called 'Love's Impossibility'. It begins: 'To speak of love is to betray / My independent yesterday'. The idea that love is self-deceit is a recurring theme in her journals during the first half of 1962. She felt stung by Paul's coldness towards her, which seemed to travesty their closeness in the summer of 1959. She began to feel that her desire for that first happiness to endure had been a childish fancy that she'd done well to outgrow:

> Through marriage & love one learns the painful lesson of the temporary nature of contact. Love is a shortened form of so many things; respect,

reverence, sexual compatibility & understanding. And basically it means knowing when to leave well alone, when to keep silent, when to respect someone else's personal isolation.

Lonely is only a sad word when we don't understand what it means. 'Lonely from the beginning of time until now' is the mountainous landscape within us, our own dignity, self-respect, self-containment.

'Self-containment' wasn't quite what she had wanted when she described herself as 'heavy & aching with love' a few months earlier; Paul's silences had proved a lot more effective than her tears, but rather than admit this, Angela convinced herself that she'd wanted the same as him all along. That meant conceiving of herself as a much tougher and more radically alienated person than she had done, and viewing her flight from Olive's intrusive style of parenting as a more basic flight from human intimacy: 'I married for privacy,' she wrote on 5 May, '& in our love we respect each others' privacies.'

It's likely that Paul didn't notice the extent to which Angela was withdrawing from him. On the surface, their relationship in the summer of 1962 was much what it had been in the summer of 1959. They went to the cinema, they attended CND demonstrations together, and they even set up a 'Folksong and Ballad' night at the Lansdown pub in Clifton. According to the country blues guitarist Ian Anderson, it had a reputation for being 'very hard line [and] traditional . . . you weren't allowed in with guitars and stuff like that'. Corinna Gray went once, but was put off by the sight of 'all these middle-class people singing Durham miners' songs'. That may be parodying it a little: Paul's connection to Topic Records meant that they could attract some well-known performers. Musicians would come to stay with them at Royal York Crescent, and Angela would cook for them ('it was all very odd and all intimately connected with the folk music phenomenon and also with how well I do the earth mother bit', she wrote a few years later). In the summer of 1962, she made an awestruck note in her journal: 'Peggy Seeger sleeping on my floor.' The occasion was evidently a bit less significant from Seeger's perspective: she has no memory of meeting Angela at all.

On her twenty-second birthday, 7 May 1962, Angela felt 'empty and forlorn', with 'nothing to show for it but one grey hair'. Her uncle

Cecil Farthing came to visit her, and took her out to lunch at an Italian restaurant. Realising how unhappy she was, he suggested that she apply to study English at the University of Bristol. 'If you've got a degree, you can always get a job,' she remembered him telling her. 'You can leave your husband any time you want.' Her lack of a third A level could now be overlooked since, he pointed out, she would be applying as a mature student.

Britain's universities were, at that moment in history, beginning to assume new significance in the national consciousness. Before the war, they had been the sanctums of a privileged and bookish few; the majority of lawyers, doctors and even prime ministers had done without degrees. But as a result of the 1944 Education Act, there had been a massive upsurge in the number of people taking A levels, and with the introduction of universal student grants at the beginning of the year, anyone who had the inclination and the requisite ability was, at least in theory, able to attend university. In practice, there weren't enough places to accommodate the new demand, and a strenuous programme of expansion was underway. Angela knew that if she became a student it would mark her out as unusually clever, lucky and ambitious: fewer than ten per cent of eighteen- to twenty-one-year-olds were in higher education, and only a quarter of those were women.

Angela almost certainly regretted the adolescent truculence that had led her to sabotage her chances of getting into Oxford. At any rate, the idea of doing something that would get her out of the house and which would potentially be good for her writing – while providing a safety net if it failed to come to anything – appealed to her. She applied, was interviewed, and received an offer to begin studying for the Special Degree of BA in English ('Special' meaning simply that English wasn't taken in conjunction with any other subject) that October. Fees were £67 per annum, but due to the introduction of student grants, valued at £380 per annum, she would have more money of her own than she had ever had before. It would be – much more than her work as a reporter or her subsequent role as a housewife, both of which had left her beholden to men – her first real taste of independence.

CHAPTER FIVE

A *slapstick nightmare*

The University of Bristol occupies a series of lofty, architecturally diverse buildings on the wide, busy, light-ensnaring streets where Clifton meets the city proper, and a smattering of eighteenth-century town houses in the surrounding area. During the 1960s the English department was at Berkeley Square, an attractive Georgian terrace built around leafy central gardens, just across Queen's Road from the magnificent, cathedral-like structure of the Wills Memorial Building, in which the library was housed; it would have taken Angela no more than fifteen minutes to walk there each morning from Royal York Crescent.

Her timetable was not especially demanding, but it kept her at the university for most of each weekday. It comprised lectures ('not too many of them and not all compulsory'), seminars and tutorials, and she was expected to spend several hours each day in the library. The course was divided into three main periods – the fourteenth century; the sixteenth and seventeenth centuries; and the 'modern' period from 1800 to 1925 – all of which were given more or less equal attention until students began to specialise towards the end of their degree. Chaucer and Shakespeare were compulsory authors, but beyond that, students had a good deal of freedom about which texts they concentrated on for their final exams. In her first year, Angela would mainly have been occupied with the literature of the sixteenth and seventeenth centuries, and with practical criticism, although she also took short introductory courses on the growth of the English language, on Old English, and on Saxon art and civilisation.

The department was headed by the distinguished Shakespearian critic L. C. Knights (a founding editor of *Scrutiny*, and author of the seminal study *How Many Children Had Lady Macbeth?*), whose compulsory seminars on practical criticism were described by one of Angela's contemporaries as 'astonishingly brilliant'. Angela's first impressions were rather less flattering:

> Professor Knights is a delicate, thin idiot, with dark-rimmed glasses that seem an integral part of his face. His nose is so thin one expects light to shine through it. He has a somewhat hesitant delivery, con-tinually ducking his head forward, for all the world like a fragile, long-legged bird – crane or stork – tugging absent-mindedly at an invisible, intransigent worm.

It isn't surprising that she took against him: she had an instinctive aversion to the critical tradition he espoused. *Scrutiny* was, as the Marxist critic Terry Eagleton has put it, 'not just a journal, but the focus of a moral and cultural crusade'. Its editors, led by the redoubtable Cambridge don F. R. Leavis, abhorred popular culture, and had rigid ideas about the proper function of criticism, which included the development of 'mature', 'complex', 'serious' responses to literature, and the maintenance of aesthetic 'standards'. They divided texts into the good, the bad and the frivolous according to set rules – coming down hard on the so-called pathetic and intentional fallacies, sentimental adjectives and showy alliteration – and they disdained historical and philological analysis, believing that the task of the critic was to read books in a discerning manner, not to research them. The journal had ceased publication in 1953, but its influence on British universities persisted until the end of the 1960s, and although Knights sometimes departed from the *Scrutiny* line (and had in fact been renounced by Leavis for his disloyalty by the time Angela met him – 'as a head of department . . . I had to work with men and women whose tastes and aptitudes differed widely from my own,' he rather sheepishly explained), he went on believing until the end of his career in what he called the 'educational project associated with *Scrutiny*'.

His seminars would have set out to equip students with the attitudes necessary to confront the maelstrom of modern culture and make the appropriate aesthetic judgements: that Shakespeare was a good writer, and John Galsworthy a bad one, for example. Actually, Angela would have agreed with this assessment – she had some pretty rigorous standards of her own – but she wouldn't have liked being told what to like, nor would she have approved of the idea that 'seriousness' was the ultimate literary virtue (or even a perceptible one in Shakespeare's case). She later parodied the Leavisites as the 'eat up your broccoli' school of literary criticism, and opined that the 'arrogant provincialism' of the *Scrutiny* movement had produced a baleful effect on British novelists, most of whom had studied English at top universities.

The only part of the syllabus that remained untouched by the influence of Leavis was Middle English literature (partly because philology was an essential component of its study); Angela said that was why she inclined towards it, but the bawdy, romantic, folklorish tradition of Chaucer, Langland and the Gawain poet would probably have aroused her sympathies under any circumstances. It was taught by the popular medievalist and grammarian A. B. (Basil) Cottle, whose teaching methods were as eccentric as they were effective: he delighted in puns and quips, and demonstrated the rigours of medieval transcription by getting his students to copy out passages from languages they couldn't speak. A non-smoking teetotaller, modest, generous-spirited and witty, Dr Cottle was a man of eclectic interests, ranging from etymology, archaeology and church history to the composition of limericks, literary spoofs and comic pantomimes (the latter being 'remarkable for their lack of plot or incident', according to one obituarist). He had been part of the Enigma code-breaking team at Bletchley Park during the war, and later became a fellow of the Society of Antiquaries, but he retained a sceptical, humorous attitude towards the establishment, which perhaps explains why, in spite of his accomplishments both as a scholar and as a teacher, he still (at the age of fifty-five) hadn't made it past the rank of senior lecturer. 'Tales are best divided into pious and impious,' he told his students; 'the latter are far less common and far more interesting.' This mischievous, iconoclastic attitude appealed to Angela, especially when contrasted with what she saw as the tweedy elitism of L. C. Knights. She wrote that Cottle 'made the study of Middle English literature a constant source of delight', and that 'there were times . . . when the lecture room actually disappeared and we were chasing griffins or riding through the woods with Gawain'.

All students at Bristol took an additional (subsidiary) subject in their first year; Angela opted for philosophy. She attended lectures and read such seminal works as Descartes' *Discourse on Method* (which she didn't get along with – 'how can anyone take him seriously after this?') and Hume's *Treatise on Human Nature* (which she did – 'I am shattered by Hume; he is tremendous'). She also read Freud's *Interpretation of Dreams* around this time. The language of psychoanalysis thrilled her, unlocking as it did a dark tapestry of symbolism – not unlike the violent and suggestive imagery of medieval literature – in everyday discourse. It had a profound influence on her way of looking at the world, one that intensified over the course of the next decade, and which is most dramatically expressed in her two career-defining books of 1979, *The Bloody Chamber* (in which well-known fairy tales are ransacked for their psycho-sexual content, such that Red Riding Hood seduces the wolf and Beauty morphs into a beast) and *The Sadeian Woman* (which views the marquis' furious imaginings as anticipating Freud's thinking on femininity).

Married, four years older than the recent school-leavers she found herself sitting alongside in seminars and lectures, and with almost three years of paid employment behind her, Angela felt out of place during her first term at the university. Inevitably, her sense of estrangement enhanced the aura of self-containment that had affected her school peers. It's hardly surprising that this apparent detachment – coupled with her determination to assert her individuality through the clothes she wore and the way she spoke – communicated itself to some of the other students as arrogance. They were struck by the self-consciously bohemian figure she cut, arriving at lectures wearing jeans and her trademark wide-brimmed hat, or sometimes a beret, and smoking perpetual cigarettes. She stood out in the conservative atmos-phere of a university where, as one (male) contemporary remembers, 'most of the female students were nice young ladies from the Home Counties, wearing Alice bands and so on'. They left her well alone, but her ostenta-tion was at least partly a strategy for overcoming her natural shyness. 'I wish they'd at least <u>speak</u> to me at the University,' she wrote in her journal: 'say "hello," & "how are you?" & "who are you?" I had the feeling the other day that if I fell dead on the floor of the philosophy lecture, nobody would come & pick me up.'

She began to gravitate towards the other mature students on her course. One of these was Neil Curry, who at twenty-eight was even more ancient than she was. He had already had plays produced in his native Newcastle and at the Edinburgh Festival by the time he went to Bristol, and his poems had appeared in the *Times Literary Supplement*. Angela wasn't particularly impressed by his work, but she did find him interesting and engaging, and his achievements aroused her competitive instincts. She began to sit with him in lectures and to go to the auction house with him. They joked about the recent school-leavers – whom they referred to as 'the children' – and talked about literature. 'It was obvious that Angela was writing,' he says. 'She talked of herself as a writer. She had such self-confidence that she never appeared ridiculous; you thought of her as a writer.'

One of the 'children' she did get on with was Rebecca Neep – Rebecca Howard, as she later became – a glamorous eighteen-year-old student from a wealthy suburban-Liverpool background, who was involved in university dramatics. Rebecca, who remained close to Angela until the end of her life, remembers the impressions she formed of her during their time at Bristol:

> She always struck me as someone who was far too big for that place [because of] the amazing energy and vitality and brainpower that she had. We were always aware that she was going to fly. But there was a kind of naïvety about her. I think she was such an individual person, so there were certain aspects of life she probably wasn't quite so clued up about. Sort of practicalities, I mean. When I first met her I got the impression that she'd had quite an insular sort of existence. She was on a very sharp learning curve . . . She always had these odd mannerisms, quirks, which I think perhaps came from being shy . . . I think being outspoken was something that she'd tried, and it had worked, so she pushed it – she was keen on pushing boundaries – and I think because people responded to that, she became more flamboyant.

People who knew Angela later in life rarely thought of her as shy, or self-conscious, or naïve – nor did everyone who knew her in the 1960s think these things about her – but Rebecca's observations suggest that her strong opinions and outrageous jokes were still part of a conscious performance: that public recitation of selfhood through which she believed the identity was padded out.

The extramural hub of student life was the Berkeley Café on Queens Road, a short walk from the English department: Angela and her friends would go there after lectures. A spacious but somehow claustrophobic building, with an intrinsic air of dinginess (it is now a Wetherspoons pub), the Berkeley was fogged with cigarette smoke right up to its high-domed ceiling, and had a dark stain on the floor which some people said was Peter O'Toole's vomit, and others claimed was his blood, spilled in a fight.

With its traditional menu (toasted teacakes and pots of Earl Grey were staples) and its steady constituency of old ladies, the Berkeley was an unlikely repository for the youthful, iconoclastic spirit of the times. But towards the end of her life, Angela spoke of having met situationists and anarchists there, and said that they had influenced her politics more than anyone else. It's a somewhat doubtful claim – she doesn't seem to have been at all involved in student radicalism, and she cast a conventional Labour vote in the 1966 general election ('to vindicate Mrs Pankhurst's gallant fight to let me have the opportunity') – but it's also clear that she sympathised with the dynamic, subversive spirit of these fringe ideologies. Her socialism was broadly speaking an inheritance from her mother, but it always had a sharply individualist flavour. Though she had a sentimental affection for the working classes, her objection to high capitalism was its entrenchment of class divisions, and thus its unequal distribution of freedoms. Asked in a late interview which was more important to her, socialism or feminism, she replied without hesitation: the latter was really a branch of the former.

Rebecca Howard described the Berkeley as having a relaxed intellectual atmosphere: 'you would talk about feminism or politics or whatever, and we'd also gossip a lot, because Angie loved gossip, about who was sleeping with who. That kind of thing.' Martin Hoyle – a mature student at the Old Vic Theatre School, who lived a few doors down from the Carters on Royal York Crescent and became friends with Angela around this time – knew her by sight from the Berkeley: 'She'd sit there staring at people,' he says. Others remember her 'holding court', and the noisy cackling ignition of her laughter sounding across the room (a consequence of the strange acoustics produced by the domed ceiling).

After years of being cooped up, of not living the kind of life she wanted, Angela felt that the horizon had suddenly opened up. 'It is only recently that I've been with people I really, truly like at all,' she admitted. The world was alive with possibilities: intellectual, artistic, political, sexual. But she was too conscious of forging her own identity to take full advantage of them. 'I talk about myself too much,' she wrote in her journal: 'instead of watching & listening to other people, I try & exhibit my own original & exciting personality – whereas I am, in fact, merely a stupid young bitch & will only learn more by watching, watching, listening, listening. And forcing other people to talk.'

The original and exciting personality was best exhibited when making people laugh, and Angela's jokes weren't always kind. Martin Hoyle was hurt when, after a dinner party at which Rebecca's partner had come in tired from work and gone straight to bed, it reached him that Angela had

gone around telling people that 'Martin bored him to sleep.' Neil Curry
agrees that 'she could be cruel . . . She was quite brilliant at taking the
piss out of people. She went between warmth and coldness. She could be
difficult to be friends with.' But Rebecca, who became closer to Angela
than either Neil Curry or Martin Hoyle ever did, saw a side of her that
was more consistently likeable: 'if you said something silly you could get
told off, but I don't remember her ever being malicious . . . She was always
a very warm and very caring friend, and at one or two really low points
in my life she was a real help. I mean, she really was incredibly caring.'

One thing that everybody who knew her at this time agrees on is that
she didn't socialise much in the evenings – 'Presumably that was because
Paul was at home,' Rebecca says. 'I met him a few times, when I went to
her flat at Royal York Crescent. He just seemed pleasant, quiet, into cats.'
Neil Curry formed a similarly vague impression of Angela's married life: 'I
don't remember her ever saying anything against Paul. But then, I hardly
remember her mentioning him.'

In September 1963, at the beginning of her second year at the university,
Angela made a brief, plaintive note in her journal: 'Paul is sad.' Looking
back at that entry in May 1965, she recognised it as the beginning of
'eighteen months of purgatory'. Paul had fallen into a deep depression. His
'inward moods' expanded to envelop his entire character: he and Angela
became like strangers inhabiting the same house, going for days on end
without exchanging more than a few words. She tried her hardest to look
after him, but it wasn't easy, and in spite of the excitement of her life at the
university, she felt increasingly unhappy. Then, on 16 December, she made
another short entry in her journal: 'Perhaps it's Paul I'm tired of? Oh no.'

It's conspicuous that Paul's first major depression coincided with her
developing a life outside the home. Later, the publication of her books would
drive him into himself in a less pronounced but nonetheless comparable
manner. But that isn't to deny the reality of his illness. In 1968, following
another episode, Angela wrote: 'It's clear that his depression is a biochemical
and environmental freak, unconnected with existential anguish, but fairly
closely connected, alas, with "mauvaise honte".' She later told several of
her friends that he underwent a long course of electroconvulsive therapy
around this time. That may well be true: the treatment was common in
Britain throughout the 1960s, with approximately 50,000 patients each

year, many of them suffering from depression. But we only have Angela's word to go on that Paul was one of them, and she doesn't appear to have mentioned the treatment to anyone until a few years later. Then again, nor does she appear to have mentioned Paul's illness at the time.

They spent that Christmas with her family in Balham. Joan was passing their room one day when she heard Angela crying inside. She went downstairs and told Paul: 'I thought maybe he would go up and comfort her.' But he didn't stir. It was Joan's first intimation of any difficulties in her sister-in-law's marriage.

It says a lot about Angela's fundamental toughness, as well as her capacity for self-containment, that she dealt with this lonely and exhausting business on her own. She was also studying hard and looking after the house single-handedly, and they were putting up a near-constant stream of visiting musicians for the folk club. In a letter of 1968 she wrote about

> the utterly crazy way we lived during the worst periods of Paul's illness, when we had people lying about the flat virtually all the bloody time waiting placidly to be fed, watered and entertained and they'd never even make their beds or do the washing-up and they'd get all stroppy if we had friends of our own in or wanted to go out by ourselves. (I think it was cos he couldn't bear to be alone with me.)

In spite of getting 'tired of' Paul, she doesn't seem to have seriously considered leaving him during this period. Partly, that was because she feared that he would kill himself if she ever did. The idea of suicide by gas recurs throughout her novels of the 1960s, the images becoming starker and more macabre as the decade progresses: Morris in *Shadow Dance* contemplates it; Joseph in *Several Perceptions* attempts it; Annabel in *Love* carries it off. Behind that anxiety it is possible to glimpse Angela's uncertainty about her own place in the world. She always had an instinct for looking after people, and it was flattering to feel that she was essential to Paul. A few months later, she gave the following thought to Morris in *Shadow Dance*: 'you can't waste love. Only the most reckless housewife throws it away.'

The coldness and silence of her home life meant that Angela immersed herself all the more intensively in literature. Reading was always a visceral activity for her – she devoured novels, cracking their spines, tearing through them – and from the notes she kept in her journal it appears that between

September 1963 and July 1965 she finished at least 200 books: an average of two and a half a week. Most of these had some bearing on her degree, but although she studied no books published after 1925, and none in translation, she also read several contemporary novels during this period, including *Cat's Cradle* by Kurt Vonnegut and *An Unofficial Rose* by Iris Murdoch, as well as major European works such as Kafka's *The Castle* and Dostoevsky's *The Idiot*.

She formed an intense dislike for Jane Austen after reading *Mansfield Park* ('an obnoxious book'), *Emma* ('Ugh!') and *Pride and Prejudice* ('Just can't take her'), and also took against Henry James ('he does go on') and W. B. Yeats ('he seems to be an utter, drivelling fool'). But she was overwhelmed by *Molloy* and *Watt* ('Beckett is great, great, great; why can't I write like bloody Beckett'); by Anthony Burgess's *Inside Mr Enderby* ('a splendid novel'); and by Northrop Frye's *Fearful Symmetry* ('brilliant, superb, wonderful'). *Lolita* had a profound effect on her. She felt that Nabokov was wrong to have so stubbornly denied the insights of psychoanalysis – that in doing so he reduced the novel to 'a brilliantly executed bit of *commedia dell'arte noir*' – but she was exhilarated by the grand luxuriance of his prose, and by his darkly comic vision.

During their second year at the university, Angela and Neil Curry took over the literary society. They invited writers to give talks, though they found it hard to attract anyone well known: among their most notable speakers were the poet Vernon Watkins, and David Thompson, the art critic of *The Times*. They wrote to the poet R. S. Thomas, but he never replied. When Charles Tomlinson (himself a poet who would probably have been a bigger draw than either Watkins or Thompson, and who was also a lecturer at the university) said he could put them in touch with Basil Bunting, Angela said she couldn't countenance inviting someone with such a silly name.

They also put out a magazine of student writing – a few typed-up and stapled-together A4 sheets, titled *Vision*. In terms of content it was a fairly typical undergraduate review, a diverse mixture of short fiction and poetry, most of it tiresomely derivative and overwrought. Easily the best things in it are the poems of her own that Angela published under the pseudonym Rankin Crowe – a misspelling (perhaps deliberate, perhaps not) of the name of an early twentieth-century cowboy whose ghosted memoir, *Rankin Crow in the Oregon Country*, she must have known. She found cowboys desperately romantic, and at around this time went to see *A Fistful of Dollars* more than once at the cinema. But why did she adopt a pseudonym at all? It may have been partly a matter of embarrassment (she described *Vision* as 'obnoxious' even while she was editing it), or tactical modesty (it never inspires confidence when an editor is her own star contributor), but the explanation she offered at the time was that she did it 'for the reasons most women who write sooner or later find themselves using masculine names, unless they are those quivering-sentimentality-type females who trade on being women . . . I do not really write like a woman & some men may get upset.'

This is obviously a bit of a joke, but the equation of 'quivering-sentimentality' and writing 'like a woman' can't be dismissed as mere facetiousness. Although she later acknowledged that there were other ways of writing like a woman (and would surely have been embarrassed that she'd once tried to pass her work off as a man's), Angela retained a profound distaste for a certain kind of feminine writing – as examples of its perpetrators she cited Edna O'Brien, Joan Didion and Jean Rhys – in which she felt that being a woman was presented as a condition of victimhood. It was an attitude she loathed. Her own feminism derived from the premise that men and women were fundamentally alike, and however much she resented the patriarchal assumptions of British society, she felt that women bore some responsibility for their perpetuation if they simply blamed male aggression: in doing so they conspired in maintaining their status as the weaker sex. The only way to combat having one's selfhood subsumed by one's gender was to be self-assertive, and to reject the implied enormity of gender difference. As she put it in *The Sadeian Woman*: 'My anatomy is only part of an infinitely complex organisation, my self.'

A couple of years after leaving university she wrote to her friend Carole Roffe:

Men are different to women, as far as I can see, only in their bio-logical organisation. Somebody asked me who my favourite women writers were the other day, meaning, I guess, some kind of writers who expressed a specifically feminine sensibility – I said Emily Brontë, who's pure butch, and cursed myself afterwards because the greatest feminine writer who's ever lived is Dostoevsky, followed closely by Herman Melville, who has just the kind of relish of beautiful boys that emancipated ladies such as yourself express. And D. H. Lawrence is infinitely more feminine than Jane Austen, if one is talking about these qualities of sensitivity, vulnerability and perception tradition-ally ascribed by male critics to female novelists . . . D. H. Lawrence's tragedy was he thought he was a man.

According to this schema, the poems Angela published as Rankin Crowe do tend towards the masculine – 'sensitivity' and 'vulnerability' are not among their most prominent qualities. The most interesting of them is a long poem titled 'Unicorn', a very arty, slightly undercooked, but wholly unusual piece of work, which mixes free verse, prose, and ballad stanzas, and prefigures Angela Carter's mature work in its sardonic attitude to myth. The central conceit comes from Sir Thomas Browne's instruction that the only way to catch a unicorn is to send a virgin into the woods: the creature 'soon leaps into her lap when he sees her and hence gets caught'. This eye-poppingly sexual image evidently amused Angela. Her virgin is not only naked, but blatantly carnal, 'raw and huge', with breasts 'like carrier bags' and 'curious plantations of pubic hair'. The unicorn is 'drawn by the fragrance of her moist / garden plot'. But she rejects the role of passive sex object:

> I have sharp teeth inside my mouth,
> Inside my dark red lips,
> And lacquer slickly hides the claws
> In my red fingertips.
>
> So I conceal my armoury.
> Yours is all on view.
> You think you are possessing me –
> But I've got my teeth in you.

Poetry was, more or less exclusively at this point, the form in which she explored ideas and indulged her penchant for the fantastical. 'This sounds very pretentious,' she wrote in the letter accompanying an unsuccessful submission to *Stand* magazine, 'but I'm trying to work out a sort of blend of entertaining visual imagery and meaningful, even didactic content.' To show what she meant, she provided a commentary on her 'Poem for Robinson Crusoe' – in which the castaway teaches the island parrots 'to remind him of his identity ("Robinson Crusoe!") / and thus he alienated his self-pity / after the manner of Brecht' – which she said was 'about the necessity of constructive creative activity'.

Twelve years later, she told Neil Astley of Bloodaxe Books that the poetry she had written in the 1960s was 'of its period, kind of hippy quaint'. That may be true in some respects, but it was flying in the face of literary fashion – this was a time when spare, straightforward, semi-confessional volumes such as Ian Hamilton's *Pretending Not to Sleep* and Philip Larkin's

The Whitsun Weddings were garnering acclaim – and the first poems Angela had accepted for publication were uncharacteristically quiet, naturalistic, and altogether lacking in ideas. In September 1963, she and Paul had acquired a cat (she was white, with 'lavender ears' and 'bracken-coloured eyes'; Angela described her compulsively, over and over again, in her journals, but they don't appear to have bothered naming her – she is always referred to as 'my cat' or 'Pussy'). Angela composed two studies of her in free verse: 'My Cat in Her First Spring', and 'Life-Affirming Poem About a Small Pregnant White Cat', both of them wholly unaffected attempts to evoke the creature's physicality in simple language. Peter Redgrove accepted them for the seventh edition of *Universities Poetry*, a prestigious annual that, for the 1964–5 edition, had attracted 1,030 submissions from 256 authors.

This was the greatest recognition that Angela had so far received for her writing, and she must have been pleased. But she was conscious that she hadn't published – or even written – anything really significant yet. The early 1960s were a time when very young writers were being fetishised: Shena Mackay (whom Angela admired) and Françoise Sagan (whom she didn't) being two of the most prominent. Angela was already several years older than either of them had been when their first novels appeared. On 13 May 1964, a week after her birthday, she suffered her by now traditional pangs of distress at her advancing age: 'I am twenty-four years old and hate it – am terrified by it.' She felt she had nothing much to show for all those years upon the earth. But that was about to change.

In the summer of 1964 – the vacation between her second and third years at the university – Angela began writing a novel set in 'the semi-criminal, semi-beatnik fringe of a provincial city'. The idea of a character named Honeydripper – a promiscuous, attractive, somewhat unhinged young man – had first come to her at the beginning of 1963. In that original incarnation, he was a rather sorry figure:

> Honeydripper crouched defensively in his dark blue duffel coat. He had a loose, dark-red lipped modish face & rather a lot of dark brown hair & long hands on which the veins stuck out. He said he was working on a thesis but nobody except the committee from which he obtained four pounds ten shillings a week for books & maintenance believed him. He spent his days desultorily reading newspapers & talking

to people & chatting up girls & his evenings in drinking bitter & finding out where the parties were & his nights were not infrequently passed in sex, which Julie said derisively was his sole creative talent.

She had tried using this character in a variety of abortive projects – including 'a very hip short story' titled 'Fucking' – but his basic lassitude had drained them of vitality. Her need to give artistic shape to the Clifton demi-monde would have to find another outlet. She was still seeing a lot of John Orsborn, a fairly typical inhabitant of the world she wanted to write about: she decided to model Honeydripper on him. The character's dark brown hair became blond; he lost the academic income and went into the junk trade; his creative talents multiplied; he became charismatic and manipulative; he gained 'an inexpressibly carnivorous mouth' and large, pale eyes. The resulting figure was, as Jenny Orsborn saw it, a 'very thinly disguised' version of her husband.

But Honeybuzzard (as Honeydripper eventually became) is much nastier and more frightening than John Orsborn ever was: he is a sadist, a sexual predator, and ultimately a killer. Angela once claimed that he was 'based on an acquaintance of mine who carved his name into somebody', but there's no trace of who this alternative model might have been, and it's likely that she invented him on the spur of the moment: she didn't feel compelled to inform her publishers of his existence. At any rate, whether he was a composite figure or just a loonier-than-life version of John Orsborn, the demonic Honeybuzzard now filled her imagination, and her plans for him swelled to the dimensions of a novel. Its major themes would be mutability, madness and masquerade. It would be called *Shadow Dance*.

By the end of July she was two-thirds of the way through a first draft. The original manuscript hasn't survived, but the synopsis she sent out to publishers has, and it's clear that the outline of the story didn't change. It concerns a girl called Ghislaine whom Honeybuzzard has knifed – scarring her atrociously, 'from eyebrow to navel' – and quite possibly raped. She returns, after being released from hospital, to confront him in the pub. There she bumps into his partner in the junk trade, Morris Grey, a depressive, unhappily married 'bad painter' with a face 'like an El Greco Christ' (the critic Marc O'Day has suggested that Morris and Honeybuzzard are two sides of the same personality, and indeed John Orsborn's biography is distributed fairly evenly between them). But Honeybuzzard is away in London, and for almost a third of the novel he remains an ominous off-stage presence, while Morris suffers paroxysms of vicarious guilt, having himself taken advantage of Ghislaine in the past. Now all she wants is 'to weep and glitter with public tears and fatten her undernourished little self on them', but she's denied even that meagre satisfaction. At the end of the novel, Honeybuzzard strangles her in the 'disordered attics' of an abandoned house, leaving her naked body surrounded by candles for Morris to find, her hands crossed over her breasts, her eyes shut down with pennies, her mouth gaping open.

Shadow Dance is palpably not the creation of a happy person. It's a dark, spiky, misanthropic piece of work. It does contain jokes, but they tend to be sour send-ups of romantic language in a heartless world. When Morris asks Honeybuzzard's girlfriend, Emily, whether she's happy with him, she says: 'I love him, I love him. When he touched me up on Mitcham Common . . .' Its metaphors are routinely succulent, but they sometimes leave a nasty taste in the mouth: a smashed beer bottle produces 'dregs of brown liquor [that] spilled and gleamed like the shiny backs of a nest of disturbed beetles running over the stones'; the flowers in the churchyard where Ghislaine was attacked 'browned at the edges and reeked of halitosis and finally dropped down dead'; children playing in the park look 'as if butter wouldn't melt in their eyes'.

This was the first time Angela had put everything she had into a piece of writing: her dislikes and anxieties, her interest in clothes, music, Victorian bric-a-brac and provincial bohemia, and above all her reading. The prose often bears the impress of other writers:

> Morris felt like his own shadow, moving silently past windows where television sets glowed whitely, bluely; where roses spread in a red, yellow and pink plastic fan in lustre vases; where plaster Alsatian dogs romped between red plush curtains. They saw hardly another walker. A girl in shorts whirled by on a beautiful, young bicycle. A car slid by with cushions on its wheels. That was all.

The 'whitely, bluely' glowing televisions have a Nabokovian hue, and the girl on the 'beautiful, young bicycle' has travelled directly from the pages of *Lolita*, where the phrase crops up more than once. Elsewhere in *Shadow Dance*, 'a panting, wet-lipped nymphet with jutting nubile breasts' makes an appearance, and there are also gusts of Poe, Dostoevsky and Swift, of *Alice in Wonderland*, of fairy tales, folk songs and pop songs.

But perhaps the novel's most striking achievement is its densely textured portrait of the relations between men and women, and its utterly unsentimental attitude to its female characters. Ghislaine, we're told, 'used to look like the sort of young girl one cannot imagine sitting on the lavatory or shaving her armpits or picking her nose'; but when Morris sees her after she's been attacked, he is seized with the conviction that his beer tastes of her: 'of her metallic deodorant sweat and the foundation cream she smeared over her lips to make them pale and a chemical smell of contraceptives and her own sexual sweat'.

Ghislaine's disfigurement is in part a metaphor for what Angela Carter is doing to the literary female form – the myth of the perfect, sanctified woman that still inhabited most novels and poems in the 1960s. She starts off as a figure from male fantasy ('sweet, white, innocent and childish, like ice-cream'), but with a strong sexual pulse (that line about her innocence is from a passage in which she's posing for dirty photos). She becomes – like several of Angela Carter's later heroines, including Fevvers in *Nights at the Circus* and the Chance sisters in *Wise Children* – a woman of lurid physicality. The scar on her face looks like a 'chasm', and implies blood: men are embarrassed by it. In being made more human, her sexuality has become disturbing – an unsettling irony.

But if the novel exhibits a feminist sensibility, it isn't a very programmatic or clubbable one. Morris's wife, Edna, is just the kind of self-ordained victim Angela despised. When not in the mood for sex, 'she would sigh and put on her martyred smile . . . and weakly clasp her long hands and say that if he wanted her, very badly . . .' Morris's infidelities upset her, but only because they're so infrequent: 'she would have found some satisfaction in having a persistently unfaithful husband, just as she would have found satisfaction in physical ill-treatment'. This view of women (or at least of some women) as being complicit in their own subjugation drew strong words from Angela's fellow feminists in the 1980s.

Another character completes the novel's trio of female leads. This is Emily, whom Honeybuzzard brings with him when he finally returns from London. A practical, unimaginative girl, sensual, self-sufficient and serene, she is the only character whom the novel treats with a hint of affection. She dotes on Honeybuzzard, but drops him abruptly when she learns what he did to Ghislaine. It is she who calls the police in the final scene (Morris tries to stop her). But when it comes to offences short of murder and rape, she adopts a much more tolerant attitude ('she was a charitable girl'), as she makes clear in this conversation with Morris:

> 'What is the name of your cat?' Morris asked her courteously.
> 'Tom', she said.
> 'Why is that?'
> 'Because he's all male.'
> 'But doesn't it ejaculate around the house? Isn't that inconvenient?'
> 'It can do what it likes. You don't castrate somebody just because it makes it more convenient for yourself, do you?'

One would hope not. Yet this belief that everybody, men and women (and even cats), should be free to do more or less what they please, and to be more or less who they want – a belief that was of great and growing importance to Angela – is at the crux of the utterly distinctive voice that erupts into life in *Shadow Dance*.

Angela's final examinations were made up of nine three-hour papers; instead of a tenth paper, she opted to write a dissertation, for which her supervisor would be Dr Cottle. Titled 'Some Speculations on Possible Relationships between the Medieval Period and 20th Century Folk Song Poetry', this very long (120 typewritten pages) essay is extraordinarily discursive, personal and opinionated. It is much too eccentric to succeed fully as an academic paper, while being too jargon-ridden to appeal hugely to a general audience. But it is interesting for the way it conveys the thickening of her interests at this time – combining her most significant recent enthusiasms (folk music, medieval literature) with preoccupations that derive largely from her family background (European folklore, music hall) – and it demonstrates a remarkable level of erudition for a twenty-four-year-old undergraduate.

She wrote it up between September and December 1964, finding the process stressful, her work interrupted by the constant trilling of folk singers in her flat. 'For relaxation', she was translating (from the Middle Scots) William Dunbar's long poem *The Tua Mariit Wemen and the Wedo* which she described as 'one of the most obscene poems in the language . . . all knobby and warty with these great alliterative clusters'. In fact, what she was doing was more of a cover version than a translation. She changed a reference to 'hideous Mohammed' to 'some nigger bastard', since, she reasoned, the former phrase had lost much of its emotive power over the centuries, but her 'fascist and illiberal' alternative would ruffle readers' feathers in just the right way. It appeared in the *London Magazine* in March 1966.

On 13 January 1965, Angela sent the manuscript of *Shadow Dance* to William Heinemann Ltd., the British publishers of Dostoevsky and D. H. Lawrence, as well as of contemporary authors including Anthony Powell, Patricia Highsmith and Anthony Burgess (she said that she decided on the firm because Carter would be listed immediately after Burgess in the catalogue). In her covering letter she described the novel as a black comedy: 'I think it is very funny; certainly it makes me laugh . . . When I wrote it, I was trying to be funny and at the same time horrific, to create something of the atmosphere of a slapstick nightmare, because life is like that, isn't it.'

Angela didn't have an agent, and hadn't addressed her letter to a specific editor, so the manuscript found its way on to what is these days known as the slush pile, along with hundreds of other novels from obscure hopefuls. It was spotted there by a young editor called Janice Robertson, who was trying to develop her own list. She knew immediately that she had found what she was looking for: 'I thought, "Here's a writer of exceptional talent." Every sentence was remarkable. You didn't see that sort of thing more than once every five years or so.' For a second opinion she sent it to the young novelist Margaret Forster, who was working for Heinemann as an external reader, and also showed it to her colleague Roland Gant, the editorial director in charge of fiction. Both of them were enthusiastic, but Gant felt that the book needed to be cut, and that the ending needed to be rewritten.

On 7 April, almost three months after Angela had sent her the manuscript, Janice wrote back saying that *Shadow Dance* had received 'several readings' in the office, and that they were all excited about the idea of publishing it, but that she wanted to discuss the possibility of 'a certain amount of revision work for it'. Angela went to London later that month, and they had lunch in a 'very nice, incredibly cheap' Italian restaurant near the Heinemann offices off Curzon Street in Mayfair (Angela 'hardly ate anything', Janice remembered). They got on well: they were about the same age, had compatible tastes in literature, and shared a love of cats. Angela 'was eccentric and delightful and a little bit bewildering. She had very definite opinions.' Nevertheless, she was open to doing the revisions that Heinemann wanted. Janice asked whether she had any other projects in mind, and Angela outlined her plans for a non-fiction book based on the life of Merlin, and a modern prose version of *Sir Gawain and the Green Knight*.

Janice was concerned that John Orsborn might sue over his resemblance to Honeybuzzard. Angela persuaded him to sign a letter promising that he wouldn't: 'my mate says, having read "S.D.", that he can't see what I am fussing about as he can't see anything at all in it which could remotely reflect on himself . . . he is perfectly happy about it'. But Jenny Orsborn remembered her husband being 'very upset' and 'angry' about his depiction in the novel: quite aside from how unflattering it was, he worried that he might get into trouble over the scenes in which Morris and Honeybuzzard break into abandoned buildings, at least one of which was taken directly from his life.

Angela revised *Shadow Dance* for 'three weeks or so' – juggling it with revising for her final exams – and sent a second draft to Janice on 27 June. 'I haven't changed the main structure,' she explained, 'but have tried to get the main relationship (which, I think now, after brooding on it, is probably that between the two men – if you recall the story after all this time!) more into the foreground'. She had also made various cuts, which rendered 'the whole thing . . . more poetic and oblique'. Janice was much happier this time, but still had some qualms about the ending; Angela went to London again in early August to discuss it. She redid the ending and sent what she made clear was the final version – 'I don't think I can do any more to it, & am as satisfied as may be' – on 16 August. The following week she and Paul (who had started to emerge from the worst of his depression in May) went to Ireland.

The purpose of the trip was evidently something to do with folk music: perhaps Paul was recording an Irish singer for Topic, or perhaps they were scouting for musicians to play at their club. They started out in Dublin, where they went to a fiddler's club in a corrugated-iron hut behind a bookmaker's. Angela thought the city looked 'just like Joyce says it looks', and although she recognised that 'it was poverty [that] kept it so bitterly beautiful', she didn't like it any less for that.

From there they went to Sligo, then to Connemara, and finally to Galway city, where gypsies with 'hair the colour of bitter beer' slept in their carts and begged during the day. This was the first time Angela had been abroad, and she was overwhelmed by the experience. She made expressionistic, somewhat sentimental notes in her journal: 'the eyes round here are blue with looking to America'; 'the landscape is primeval, you expect to see pterodactyls'. She decided to learn what she called 'Irish Gaelic', and said that she wanted to live in Connemara, 'if ever I have enough money'. She never did live there, but she and Paul returned several times over the next few years.

When they got back to Royal York Crescent on 1 September, Angela learned that she had been awarded an upper-second-class degree – she had been hoping for a first. But the bad news was amply cushioned by a letter from Janice Robertson, offering an advance of £150 for hardback publication of *Shadow Dance*. Angela wrote back the same day: 'I am extremely pleased . . . Great, great, great! as they say.' Speaking to an interviewer in 1977, though, she claimed she hadn't been overly excited by the offer: 'I know it's awful, but all I really felt was: *about fucking time.*'

CHAPTER SIX

Giving the flash more substance

'My first husband wouldn't let me get a job after I graduated from university,' Angela told a friend in 1980. 'So I stayed at home and wrote books instead, which served the bugger right.' It's a characteristic exaggeration. Paul was never very supportive of her writing, but (perhaps for that very reason) he seems to have put pressure on her to find some other sort of employment. Before she went to the university, they had a 'mild row' about it: 'I just don't want to work,' she had written then. 'I want to stay snugly by the fire & scribble, scribble, scribble, because, when I'm in the mood, this is my deepest pleasure.' Studying had become another pleasure, and she wasn't about to risk either of them for the sake of a job.

As summer faded into autumn, she put together an application to write an MA thesis, provisionally titled 'Legends of Merlin in Middle English' – a topic that would feed into the book she had proposed to Heinemann – and began studying for the degree, with Dr Cottle as her supervisor, in November. It was standard practice at the university for students to enrol on the MA before expanding their theses into PhDs, and it's likely that this was what Angela intended. She was put forward as a candidate for a Major State Studentship (a prestigious bursary administered by the British Academy), but it appears her application was rejected, presumably because she had achieved only a second-class BA.

She wasn't under any immediate financial pressure – American rights to *Shadow Dance* were bought by Simon & Schuster for $2,000 (about £700), and UK paperback rights went to Pan for £750. But she had no reason to suppose that her luck would continue. The novel aside, her output during this period consisted entirely of arty poems and experimental short stories, and she was becoming used to the impecunious world of small presses and student magazines. Her *Universities Poetry* contributions had been noticed by Barry Tebb, a Leeds-based poet, who included some of her work in an anthology titled *Five Quiet Shouters*; this in turn was seen by Cavan McCarthy, a student at the University of Leeds and editor of *Tlaloc*, a magazine dealing mainly in concrete poetry. He published a few of Angela's poems there, and offered to bring out 'Unicorn' as a free-standing pamphlet. She published a couple more poems in the University of Leeds magazine *Poetry and Audience*, and two short stories, as well as a clutch of articles and book reviews, in the University of Bristol magazine, *Nonesuch*. She had also begun contributing to the *Aylesford Review*, a Carmelite literary journal whose contributors were mainly Roman Catholic poets. These publications provided some mild exposure, but they weren't bringing in any money, and her attempts to break into the better-known and better-paid reviews were getting nowhere: between January and April 1966 she received rejection slips from the *Paris Review*, the *London Magazine*, the *Transatlantic Review*, *Poetry Review* and *Agenda*. She wasn't going to survive as a writer unless she started another novel.

The earliest stirrings of *The Magic Toyshop* came via a line from André Breton's *First Surrealist Manifesto*. Over and over again, throughout the winter of 1965–6, Angela repeated it in her journal: 'the marvellous alone is beautiful'. She admired the surrealists' efforts to recapture the child's sense of wonder, the value they placed on the imagination and desire, their romanticism – how for them 'the beautiful is put at the service of liberty'. Over the next few years, their influence on her writing grew increasingly pronounced – reaching its apogee in her sixth novel, *The Infernal Desire Machines of Dr Hoffman* – before declining in the mid-1970s, when she began to find the movement's idealised, fondly patronising view of women (sources of mystery and beauty, but not creative spirits in their own right) impossible to square with her developing feminist consciousness. But as late as 1978, she wrote that 'the old juices can still run . . . when I hear that most important of all surrealist principles: "The marvellous alone is beautiful."'

She must have read the line in translation (the original French, *il n'y a même que le merveilleux qui soit beau*, is unambiguous), for she was soon putting her own spin on it. On 3 October she wrote:

does 'the marvellous alone is beautiful' mean:
a) 'the MARVELLOUS alone is beautiful',
or
b) 'the marvellous ALONE is beautiful'?
In future, I shall read ALONE as a noun

These diverse ideas – the beauty of marvels and the beauty of being alone – were becoming strangely tangled in her mind, in a way that recalled her childhood and adolescence. Once again, she felt trapped in a claustrophobic domestic situation, beyond which lay the frightening unknown. She had reread *The Box of Delights* in 1964. She made her first notes for *The Magic Toyshop* in November 1965:

> clockwork cat catching clockwork mouse
> a dumb woman with red eyebrows
> a toy theatre in which you take part

The meaning of these images was unclear to her at first. 'I think writing – or my kind of writing – is a process of self-analysis, of interpreting one's imagery and constantly mining inside oneself,' she wrote in 1968. That sounds like a statement of belief in the surrealist project, with its Freudian faith in the expressiveness of dreams, and its vision of writing as self-discovery. In later years, she was fond of citing Balzac's view that all fiction is 'symbolic autobiography', and elsewhere she wrote: 'our external symbols must always express the life within us with absolute precision; how could they do otherwise, since that life has created them?'

Melanie in *The Magic Toyshop* is the first incarnation of a character who appears in several of Angela Carter's early short stories, and in her fourth novel, *Heroes and Villains*: a neurotic teenage girl, clever, bored and self-absorbed. 'The bourgeois virgin', Angela called her in 1982: 'At the time [of writing those books] I would have hotly denied that she was me, but I can see now that she must have been.' Perhaps the most conspicuous feature of Angela's 'symbolic autobiography' – if that phrase can be taken to describe her entire *oeuvre*, as well as specific works within it – is the way this crabbed, introspective figure is replaced by fleshier, happier women in her later work.

The Magic Toyshop is structured as a malevolent fairy tale, and written with an eerie lucidity. It opens with Melanie in the comfortably bourgeois surroundings of her parents' home in rural England; they're abroad, and meanwhile she indulges her every whim. One night, unable to sleep, she puts on her mother's wedding dress, and climbs the apple tree in the garden. The following morning she learns that her parents have been killed in a plane crash, and she superstitiously blames the disaster on her nocturnal transgression: 'She went into her bedroom. She met herself in the mirror, white face, black hair. The girl who killed her mother.'

Along with her younger brother Jonathan and baby sister Victoria, the orphaned Melanie is sent to live with her mother's estranged brother, the toymaker Uncle Philip, in his south London shop; his wife, Aunt Margaret (a mute Irishwoman, 'frail as a pressed flower'), and her brothers, Finn and Francie (a pair of roguish musicians), also live on the premises. Uncle Philip turns out to be a sadistic and manipulative patriarch, much more interested in puppets than in people. At one point – in one of the novel's most hypnotic and disturbing set-piece scenes – he forces Melanie to play Leda in a puppet show, and has her mock-raped by a mechanical swan. His watchful, scheming presence casts a pall over every aspect of life in the shop. Even Melanie's and Finn's growing attraction to one another is soured by it: 'he wanted me to fuck you', Finn explains at one point. 'I'm not going to do what he wants even if I do fancy you.' Eventually, after he discovers that Francie and Aunt Margaret are incestuously involved with one another, Uncle Philip sets fire to the toyshop. Melanie and Finn escape into the garden: 'Nothing is left but us,' she says to him.

As the novel took shape, past and present collided in Angela's imagination. Uncle Philip was a grotesquely exaggerated version of Paul Carter ('but he was a depressed chemist rather than a mad scientist', she explained to a presumably baffled interviewer). Finn and Francie were based on the Irish folk musicians who were 'in & out of the house' in Bristol while she was writing the book. The 1950s detail, the carefully textured south London backdrop, the atmosphere of sexual longing and compromised privacy were all taken from her childhood. One obvious reading of this assemblage presents itself: her current domestic situation made her feel infantilised. She hazarded a slightly more straightforward interpretation of her own: 'I thought, tentatively, that maybe it was, very loosely, about growing up & having the comfortable things peeled off one, but I could be wrong.'

Once she had settled on this theme, the novel became an increasingly conscious engagement with *Paradise Lost* (Milton, she said, taught her 'a great deal about the methodology of fantasy'.) The poem's genetic legacy is easily discerned in the novel's features: the fateful transgression involving an apple tree; the autocratic God-figure of Uncle Philip; the toyshop as a sort of secularised Eden. Finn and Francie were given the surname Jowle because of its proximity to *jowl*, the Cornish for devil. The novel's ending – a man and woman alone in the garden – was 'quite consciously borrowed from the end of *Paradise Lost*'. Angela found the last lines of the poem captivating, 'not because of any religious thing but for its qualities of pure myth – as a paradigm of human relations, I suppose'. Adam and Eve are banished from Eden:

> The world was all before them, where to choose
> Their place of rest, and Providence their guide.
> They, hand in hand, with wandering steps and slow,
> Through Eden took their solitary way.

By the end of January 1966, Angela had written the first 30,000 words of what was to become a 50,000-word book. She described it in a letter to Janice Robertson as 'a Gothic melodrama about a sort of South Suburban bluebeard toymaker & his household . . . It should be finished before the leaves come out, with luck, Merlin permitting.' True to her word, she delivered the manuscript at the beginning of April. Janice was enthusiastic, but received a reader's report from Barbara Comyns (the author of eleven sharply idiosyncratic novels of her own, fleetingly popular in the late 1950s, now best remembered as 'a precursor to Angela Carter'), who thought it 'a queer little book'. Angela didn't argue with this assessment:

> she's put her finger on my weakest spot, which is a tendency to a batty
> kind of whimsicality. This is okay under control but embarrassing when
> it gets out of hand . . . The thing is, it is <u>meant</u> to be off-balance &
> episodic & nightmarish &, if it has this quality, I don't want to revise
> it right out! But I'm sure we'll work something satisfactory out.

She signed a contract for £150 with Heinemann on 19 May. In June Simon & Schuster offered an advance of $2,500 as 'a measure of confidence' in her future career, although Peter Schwed, her American editor, made it clear that he had preferred *Shadow Dance* to the new book.

Angela later described the speed with which she composed her early novels – one every year between 1965 and 1969 – as the product of 'neurotic compulsion', and writing *The Magic Toyshop* does seem to have kept her doubts and anxieties about her marriage at bay: as soon as she had finished work on it, she became uneasy. On 3 April she began to suspect that she was pregnant: 'I feel nauseated & have vague pains. My reactions are so ambivalent I cannot sort them out. It would/will certainly be a lesson to me.' In spite of the difficulties in her relationship with Paul, they were still having sex (as late as February 1969, a few months before she left him, she wrote: 'it is only very rarely and then not for long that I have disliked touching him. Touching Paul, in fact, remains one of my simplest, most radiant pleasures.') But he was reluctant to become a father, and Angela knew that her desire to become a mother wasn't very sensible given her frustration with the maternal role she already played in the marriage. 'I most wanted Paul's children when I most wanted to protect him,' she told a friend a couple of years later. 'Presumably I've created a very bad mother/child thing partly for lack of a real child, partly because this is one of the many ways that people fit together, I suppose.' Even so, she found it hard to repress her maternal instincts. In the pages of her journal she sometimes wrote as if parenthood would be a solution to all their problems: 'if only he would let me have babies. If only.'

This time, the imagined pregnancy didn't last long, but it was replaced by a more startling psychosomatic condition: a creeping 'paralysis' of her writing arm. She felt 'almost desperate'. Her doctor recognised that anxiety was the likely cause, and prescribed Librium. On 24 May she wrote in her journal: 'the drug seems to be working & my arm feels almost its old self. But I felt so bad.' That sounds encouraging enough, but she follows it with a strange remark which suggests that she wasn't entirely free from anxiety: 'I don't really know the difference between feeling bad & dramatising feeling bad to make myself seem more interesting to myself.' Shortly afterwards, she wrote:

> I am all confused & don't know what to do. I am a writer. Am I a writer? What is it all about. I know I shall go on, improving, getting less flashy or, rather, giving the flash more substance. If I was a man, it would be so much simpler, although I don't want to be a man, I love myself too much, I think I am sexy & beautiful & I think, I feel, that although this may not be so & I am really a scruffy wreck, I am not bugged by being a woman because I am sure of my femininity, sure enough to wonder what it would be like to make love with a

woman. Shit, I am writing this for the reader over my shoulder. I am the most self-conscious thing that ever breathed.

She may have been writing for the reader over her shoulder, but the passage says more about her overwrought state of mind than anything else. That long sentence about 'being a woman' is a semantic vacuum, swirling with contradictions and non-sequiturs. But at least one thing was clear: 'I want – I know I want – to chuck my MA.' She wrote to Dr Cottle:

> You will know by now that I am unable to continue as a full-time research student due to very pressing personal reasons. I am distressed because I feel I've let you down, disappointed you. But I hope to continue as a research student on a part-time basis, when things are less rough.
>
> I want to thank you for all sorts of kindnesses you may never even have noticed and for the privilege of working with you. I hope to do so again.

Probably, like the 'very pressing personal reasons' she cited as grounds for abandoning her thesis, her desire to pick it up again later was a sort of half truth. Academia was too narrow a stage for the role she hoped to inhabit. Among the highly charged journal entries she wrote during the spring of 1966, there is one line that has the ring of authentic self-knowledge: 'I need to be extraordinary.'

Ditching the academic work appears to have galvanised her, and she began to concentrate on her literary career with a renewed sense of purpose. She had started making notes for the novel that became *Several Perceptions* while she was working on *The Magic Toyshop*, but her ideas for it were still in flux, and she wouldn't begin the writing for another few months. In the meantime, she sought out new opportunities for journalism.

On 11 May she travelled to Cardiff to see Bob Dylan perform at the Capitol Theatre. This was the third date of his UK tour (the first had been at the ABC Theatre in Belfast on 6 May, and the second was at the Colston Hall in Bristol on the 10th), but he had already aired his new electric sound in other parts of the world, and the concerts were causing a stir. He began by playing a solo set, accompanying himself on an acoustic guitar and harmonica, in the style that had made him the darling of the folk scene.

Then, after a short break, he re-emerged with a five-piece electric band. This transformation was greeted with boos and heckles from large sections of the audience, and the press were scarcely any more sympathetic, suggesting that he was trying to ape Mick Jagger. It's testament to Angela's openness to new forms that she was so enthusiastic. Though she was still writing sleeve notes to the records Paul produced for Topic during this period, she felt she was outgrowing the 'innocent liberal' world of singarounds and CND marches. She admired such songs as 'Like a Rolling Stone' and 'Ballad of a Thin Man' for their 'mature savagery', and felt that Dylan was 'approaching an artistic maturity of a most unexpected kind'.

Shortly afterwards, she went to see The Who in the Locarno Ballroom. She was less keen on their music than she had been on Dylan's, but she was intrigued by it nonetheless, describing it variously as a 'shock of noise', 'aural crazy paving being bulldozed away', 'a process of abstraction', and 'sci-fi sound'. She interviewed the band backstage, as they were packing away such instruments as had survived the ritual smashing-up with which they ended their shows ('this orgy of destruction should come as catharsis, a tremendous release of wound-up tension', Angela wrote; 'it didn't come off tonight'). She scribbled down her impressions of the green room: 'couple of birds sit around, blonde, just sitting . . . gaggle of fans, boys & girls, at the door. Is it sex or knowing these kids have made it while young & they want to touch them to get their magic?' Pete Townshend struck her as slightly younger than he had on stage – 'early twenties rather than mid-twenties' – but she was impressed by his intelligence and his lack of pretension. John Entwistle, the bassist, lay slumped in a chair, eyes closed, spent from the manic exertion of the performance. Keith Moon, the now legendary drummer, towelled his 'slightly spotted' back. Angela sold her articles on both Dylan and The Who to the *London Magazine*, and was paid £7 for the former, £12 for the latter.

In June she took a job washing dishes in the café at Bristol Zoo. It's clear that she planned from the outset to use this experience as the basis for another piece of writing, rather than doing it exclusively for the three shillings and sixpence an hour she was paid: she made detailed notes about it in her journal and later worked them up into an article, which appeared in the *Guardian* on 17 September.

The café sold ham or pork pie, with a side of chips or salad, or chips and salad: a notice informed customers that 'the management regrets it is unable to serve chips alone'. There was also cake, ice cream, and scones with blackcurrant jam, which made the washing-up water turn 'the most awful, purplish colour, a kind of death colour' in the sink. By the end of the day, Angela found that her hands were 'tacky' from rinsing heaps of sugar from unfinished cups of tea.

There were eight other women working in the kitchen: 'They are all old and most are fat,' Angela wrote. 'Their feet are swollen but they move with the rhythmic precision of dancers.' Flo (renamed Ruby in the article) was in charge of the washing up. She was 'huge as fate, but selectively huge', her fat having 'settled on top, like a fall of snow'. She was 'very rude and very coarse', and laughed a lot. The only man there was Fred (Alf in the article), who worked the chipping machine. The women made him the butt of various saucy jokes – 'he's been with every woman here', Flo told Angela, with a wink – 'but, all the same,' Angela wrote, 'he always gets his cup of tea sugared for him and first choice of the plate of cakes for, after all, he is a man'. He also got paid four shillings an hour: sixpence more than any of the women were getting.

It was the women who held Angela's attention. She observed them carefully, noting down their conversations, their habits, their physical peculiarities. 'I am beginning to understand about femininity,' she wrote in her journal. 'These women . . . are like rocks, or rock, the basic, living fabric of the world. The work is something they do, they accept it, don't question it. It makes me almost cry.' In spite of the indulgences given to Fred, the café was a female-governed zone, not altogether dissimilar from the domestic world of her mother's family, but poorer, ruder, and with a greater spirit of sisterhood. It was a type of environment that would become much less common during Angela's adulthood, as the sexes became less polarised, and men and women began increasingly to occupy one another's traditional spaces. Perhaps that was why it made such an impression on her. Recalling it in June 1991, when she was facing cancer and casting her mind back over the social changes she had witnessed in half a century, she was once again overcome with emotion: Flo and her colleagues 'wouldn't have recognised Simone de Beauvoir if she'd dropped in for a coffee, but all of them had a deep, ingrained conviction of the moral superiority of women and the tyrannical economic power of men'. It was a sort of instinctive feminism, and she recognised its spirit in the women's movement of the 1970s.

* * *

On 22 August 1966 – a month after she turned ninety – Angela's grandmother, Jane Farthing, suffered a fatal heart attack. Angela had last seen her in April, and had been moved by how frail she was, 'all faded away from herself', her hands 'fat & twisted with arthritis', her eyes 'quite sunk in her head'. Now the towering figure of her early childhood was gone. It was the first time Angela had lost anyone she had been close to, and memories of those long-ago days in Yorkshire, being told stories by the light of a guttering candle, filled her mind. The following year she embarked on a series of fairy tales for young children.

The funeral was held in the south London suburb of Morden, a short journey from Jane's home in Battersea. The Stalkers went by car, and joined a long procession of slow-moving vehicles following a hearse. At the last minute they realised that this dignified cortège was leading them to the wrong funeral: they had to make a breakneck U-turn to reach the church on time. Angela described the service itself as a 'plastic' affair, featuring 'piped organ music'. Afterwards, the mourners gathered round while Jane's coffin was lowered into the ground. Olive worried that her uncle Sidney would tumble in after it: 'People are always falling into graves at funerals,' she said. Two 'beatnik' gravediggers, 'straight Hamlet', lolled around in jeans, waiting for the mourners to disperse. Angela felt that the occasion lacked the solemnity her mood required: 'I was surprised how nothing it all was.'

Shadow Dance was published later that month. The jacket featured a blurb from Anthony Burgess, who professed 'envy' at Angela Carter's 'remarkable descriptive gifts', and predicted that she would develop into a major author. Burgess was never exactly sparing with his praise, but his admiration for Angela's work appears to have been genuine. The feeling was very much reciprocated: she was 'knocked out that Anthony Burgess of all people likes *Shadow Dance*'. She wrote to him ('a few stuttering lines') courtesy of Heinemann, and received an invitation to his house in Chiswick, where they finally met two years later. They only saw each other a couple of times after that – once in Bristol in 1973, once in Dublin in 1982 – but they maintained a correspondence for many years. It was Angela's first literary alliance, and she was 'enormously pleased and flattered' by it.

In 1966, the English literary landscape was still dominated by linguistically modest, structurally solid works of social realism, many of them concerned with recent national history. The year's most talked-about novels included *The Jewel in the Crown* by Paul Scott (the first instalment of his 'Raj Quartet', a sequence chronicling the last days of British rule in the subcontinent, in the tradition of E. M. Forster's *A Passage to India*) and *The Soldier's Art* by Anthony Powell (the eighth instalment of *A Dance to the Music of Time*, which had opened in 1920s Eton and had duly reached the officers' mess halls of the Second World War, where it took on a flavour of Evelyn Waugh's *Sword of Honour* trilogy). Rumblings of a more innovative and irreverent literary trend – as could be felt at the Edinburgh Festival, where Tom Stoppard's play *Rosencrantz and Guildenstern Are Dead* had its first performance – received considerably less attention.

Shadow Dance was reviewed widely enough, though often fleetingly, in the midst of first-novel round-ups. Most commentators regarded it, for better or worse, as a voguish affair, addressing the interests and anxieties of the emerging counterculture. The *Sunday Times* reviewer, Margaret Haltrecht, wrote that 'for all its strangeness', it was 'strongly contemporary in feeling', while Marigold Johnson, writing anonymously in the *Times Literary Supplement*, praised the 'poetic vision of Heaven and Hell' folded into the 'contemporary world of bearded young junk shop dealers'. The Scottish poet Edwin Morgan, writing in the *New Statesman*, felt that the novel's subject matter – which he summarised as 'Victoriana, Pop Art, Beardsleyesque rooms, dark glasses, casual lust and violence' – was 'a little too fashionable', but he declared himself impressed by Angela Carter's 'decided talent for the grotesque scene, the nightmarish atmosphere, the alarming uncertainties of human relationships'. Reviewing the novel on the BBC Home Service, Vernon Scannell found it 'very promising indeed . . . brave and beautiful', and pointed out that 'we are too close to the Moors trial to dismiss as implausible the nature or the consequences of [Honeybuzzard's] obsessions'. He concluded that '*Shadow Dance* takes chances on every page, comes a cropper now and then, but manages to end, slightly absurd, yet radiant and splendid as youth should be and sometimes, in fact, is.'

The worst notice was in the *Manchester Evening News*, whose anonymous reviewer was the only one who seemed to realise that *Shadow Dance* was meant to be funny. Noting Angela's hobby of collecting Victorian junk (mentioned in her capsule biography on the inside cover), he suggested that 'she can add this book to her collection'. That must have hurt: in spite of her apparent confidence in her abilities, Angela had a thin skin for criticism. Writing to console Pat Barker for a negative review in 1982, she confessed to fixating on them herself:

> in my experience, a few cheap, cutting remarks by some tin-pot reviewer whose name I don't even recognise can hurt more, & fester longer, than anything, & somehow seem to cancel out praise from people whose opinion is worth something . . . God knows why that is; it is to do with all kinds of insecurities & fears & kind of like 'The Emperor's New Clothes' – as if the one person with the contrary opinion is bound, by some Protestant logic, to be right.

But in spite of that slap down from the *Manchester Evening News*, *Shadow Dance's* reception was exciting for a twenty-six-year-old debut novelist, and Angela enjoyed her first taste of public recognition. She became something of a celebrity in Clifton. People began pretending much closer friendships with her than in fact they had, a phenomenon that pleased and annoyed her in equal measure. Several of her acquaintances claimed to have spotted themselves in the novel, but Angela denied that she'd based any of the characters on real people (John Orsborn must have kept quiet about the letter she'd made him sign). The attention went to her head a bit: 'I'm not giving autographs until I get my Nobel Prize,' she wrote to Cavan McCarthy – a joke, but one that betrays a measure of egotism all the same. (The last English novelist to receive the prize had been John Galsworthy, thirty-four years earlier.)

Her friends felt that with her sense of accomplishment came a further loosening of her attachment to Paul. 'Everything was kind of opening up for Angela,' Rebecca Howard remembered. 'You could sense that she was moving on . . . I think he was left sort of floundering in her wake.' Hughie and Joan Stalker formed a similar impression: 'Paul began to resent the fact that she was having such a good time . . . he wouldn't open letters from the BBC or the printers or the publishers or whatever, he'd go into a silence.' Angela later told a friend that he didn't speak to her for three weeks after *Shadow Dance* was published.

If Paul regretted that she had ever written the novel, he wasn't the only one. Her mother thought it a 'lewd and outrageous' book, and asked: 'What do you want to write about all that copulation for? We get enough of it on television.' This criticism was still on Angela's mind when she received proofs of *The Magic Toyshop* in January. The cover showed a puppet, his face contorted in ecstasy, with a fat, phallic tongue emerging from his trousers – Angela was appalled. 'Is indecent exposure the trendy thing this season?' she asked Janice. 'What can I say to my mother?'

Towards the end of 1966, Angela wrote a piece about the English folk singer Fred Jordan, and sent it to *New Society*, a left-of-centre (though scrupulously non-partisan) weekly magazine which published social and cultural criticism from a non-academic standpoint. Founded in 1962, the magazine sought to be 'self-questioning, anti-metropolitan, anti-Westminster gossip, anti-literary . . . Humane, rational, unsnobbish.' It specialised in essays that deconstructed the minutiae of everyday life (the configuration of adolescent value systems, the politics of pornography, the aesthetics of ice-cream vans), from a line-up of contributors that included John Berger, E. P. Thompson and Michael Wood. As Angela put it in 1982:

> It pioneered, and maintains, a kind of social reportage, a documentary writing, that treats the background as the foreground. As a result, it is rarely surprised by events . . . It has a good record for asking awkward questions – about child benefits, about high-rise flats, about the care of the old, the mad, the forgotten.

The 1960s were a fertile period for British journalism, but of all the magazines that sprang to print in that nonconformist decade (including *Oz*, *Time Out*, the *New Left Review* and *Private Eye*), *New Society* was the one whose editorial stance chimed the most closely with Angela's sensibility, and whose backing was the most important for her career. Her piece about Fred Jordan was accepted, and the magazine's editor, Paul Barker, sensing that he had found a star contributor, suggested that she come to see him in London. He recalled the meeting as somewhat disconcerting:

> She was dressed all in black, topped with a large black floppy hat . . . We had an office tucked away at the back of a building, flanked by fruit and veg wholesalers, in the old Covent Garden. She walked in, very erect, and spoke with an odd mixture of hesitancy and point-blank self-assurance . . . She looked like someone off the Left Bank.

He told her that some of her pieces were 'a bit too Hogarthian' – which was, he later explained, his shorthand for 'sentimental working-class history' – and encouraged her to write more critically: 'her aggressive outsiderishness and her wit gave her a position from which to attack'.

Over the next two decades her pieces for the magazine (often numbering thirteen or fourteen a year) ranged from analyses of make-up and high-street fashion, through dispatches about Japanese culture, to reflections on pornographic magazines and television advertising. From the publication of her first piece in February 1967 until the early 1980s, the magazine was her natural home as a non-fiction writer (a position later usurped by the *London Review of Books*), and she continued to write for *New Society* until, its readership having declined during the Thatcher years, it was absorbed into the *New Statesman* in 1988. As Barker recalled: 'She became central to what the magazine was about.'

That winter, Angela had the idea of writing a non-fiction book about provincial nightlife. Originally titled *Good Times*, but soon renamed *A Bunch of Joys: Scenes from City Nights*, it would be a work of social reportage, capturing the moment at which the new forms of entertainment flourished side by side with the old, in a Britain where the provinces were full of life. Janice liked the sound of it, and offered an advance of £200, half to be paid up front, the rest on publication.

As part of her research, Angela found work as a hostess in the Locarno Ballroom, bringing drinks to the tables and collecting the empties while the house band played songs from the hit parade and young men 'of the fifties, smooth rocker type' danced with 'mod and pretty' young women who favoured 'black-rimmed eyes, cropped hair and diminutive smocks which bared their arms'. She was paid seventeen shillings and sixpence for four and a quarter hours' work on weeknights; five shillings more on Fridays, when the ballroom was open until 1 a.m.; and one pound and five shillings on Saturdays, when the ballroom was at its busiest and she worked from 7.15 p.m. until 1 a.m. That wasn't nearly enough money to survive on, and many of the hostesses had other jobs during the day, though most of them hadn't yet reached their twentieth birthdays (Angela kept her own age a secret). There were two men behind the bar: a 'boy . . . filling in time before he went to university', and 'a big, raw-boned young man in a white jacket'. The latter tried to grope the hostesses as they passed, but they wriggled away from him, casting aspersions on his masculinity over their shoulders.

The casual misogyny of the ballroom grated on Angela. The hostesses were made to wear body-hugging yellow-and-white striped cheongsams with white tights: it was an outfit in which she felt ridiculous. The dress was slit up the left side to the thigh, so that

> an unwise freedom of movement caused the skirt to fall away, revealing the entire leg to the curious. When this happened as one was clearing a table, there would be a ritual roar of simulated lust and one would either be asked, 'Did you know you've torn your skirt?' or 'Aren't you cold, with that big hole in your skirt?' There was little variation on these two remarks. We girls returned small, grim smiles.

'When young men are rude, I spill drink on them,' she reported to Janice. But when they weren't rude – and as often as not they just sat there looking terrified, especially the really young ones – they aroused her sympathy. She thought of them at the start of the evening, putting on their nice clean shirts and combing back their hair, 'with perhaps high hopes of magic and romance in the ballroom'; only to remain stiffly seated in their all-male groups, watching the girls dance – 'an infinitely tormenting display of inno-cent provocation' – or even just passing out drunk in their finery. Some of them, she reflected, had come all the way from Wales.

She worked on *A Bunch of Joys* throughout the winter of 1966 and into January 1967, finding it 'more difficult and maybe less true than fiction'. Her experiences in the Locarno formed the first chapter of the book. Much of the writing is witty and vivid, and there are some sharp observations on 1960s nightlife: 'dancing is ceasing altogether to be a social thing and is evolving into a pure form of abstract self-expression. Girls dance alone or in clumps and, even when they are dancing opposite a boy, one can only tell they are together by the direction in which they are pointing.' All the same, it's possible that it has more to offer us now, as a historical document, than it could ever have offered a contemporary audience. The voice Angela created for it is essentially journalistic: she proves herself a clear-eyed witness to events, but rarely troubles to decipher them. A greater problem is the book's essential scrappiness: its chapters range over subjects as miscellaneous as wrestling, rock music, and the New Year's Eve celebra-tions in a couple of Clifton pubs, and its approach is just as uneven, with Angela putting herself at the centre of the action in some places (as in the ballroom), while in others she makes do with interviewing the participants, or simply watching from the fringes.

She sent the manuscript to Janice at the end of January, and on 17 March 1967 received the disheartening news that Heinemann had decided not to publish (though as a gesture of faith in her career, they decided not to seek repayment of the £100 they had already given her). She managed to sell a few of the chapters as free-standing pieces – to the *Guardian*, the *Daily Telegraph* and *New Society* – and some of the material she'd accumulated found its way into her fiction. The ballroom features in *Love*, and the retired busker who was the subject of another chapter – and whom she had already used in a poem for the *Aylesford Review* – appears in *Several Perceptions* as Sunny Bannister. Altogether, it wasn't a disastrous outcome, and Angela doesn't seem to have regretted the book's loss for long: 'this one died about the fifth month, it was a natural miscarriage', she wrote across her notes for it at a later date.

Bristol Technical College was housed in a clump of vast, grey Victorian buildings that had originally served as the dormitories of an orphanage: the corridors and stairwells were oppressively narrow, and most of the windows too high to look out of. In 1965, the college had begun sharing these gloomy premises with the newly established University of Bath, whose permanent campus was under construction. The two institutions lived together 'in a somewhat incestuous relationship', according to a study of the arrangement made shortly afterwards: 'it was confusing and difficult to dissociate the two'.

One evening, during the period Angela was researching her graduate thesis, Paul had invited one of his University of Bath colleagues home to Royal York Crescent. Edward Horesh was a left-wing economist with a strong interest in literature and the arts. Gangly, bespectacled and highly cerebral, he loved to argue, often purely for the sake of it, taking up whatever position his companions were most likely to disagree with. Angela was fascinated and somewhat awed by him. 'His ability for abstract thought both chills & impresses me,' she wrote. 'Chills more than impresses. To talk coolly about corporal punishment is to forget the lash of the whip on the shoulders.' Nevertheless, he was her intellectual match in a way that very few of her university or Clifton friends were, and she enjoyed talking to him. Over the course of the year they became increasingly friendly, and by the beginning of 1967 they were doing the weekly shop together at Sainsbury's on Wednesday evenings.

This quaint domestic ritual is somehow hard to square with the outlandish figure Angela cut at this time. Her hair was styled in what she described as 'a reasonably suave Jimi Hendrix cut', and she had taken to hennaing it to disguise the grey, so that its colour was now coppery rather than its natural dark chestnut – but she tended to hide it, anyway, beneath one of her enormous wide-brimmed hats. She had lost one of her front teeth (it had probably been extracted, rather than knocked out: she made numerous trips to the dentist during this period, and in 1968 she wrote that 'the only time I have genuinely wished an end to this sad charade was one time when I had inexpressible toothache'), but for several months she didn't have a denture fitted, and simply smiled with a gap. She identified in this respect with Lee in her fifth novel, *Love*, who has also lost a front tooth, and feels that it 'took away the suspicion he might be simple-minded for it gave his gapped but dazzling smile a certain ambiguity'. That wasn't how Angela's own gap tended to strike people: 'I think she went out of her way to be and look eccentric,' Edward Horesh recalled. Her local newsagent, meanwhile, referred to this black-clad, floppy hatted, gap-toothed figure as 'the witch'.

Through Edward – though Paul evidently didn't stand in her way – she began teaching 'liberal studies', on a freelance basis, to economists at the University of Bath. She seems to have enjoyed the work: she played the students folk and pop records, encouraged them to smoke pot (though she was never much of a pot smoker herself), and generally assumed the role of emissary from the exotic world of the arts. The exact terms of her employment are hard to reconstruct – the university hasn't kept any record of her working there, and the payments detailed in her journal vary wildly both in size and frequency – but she appears to have made around £60 in 1967 from occasional teaching at both the University of Bath and Bristol Technical College. On one of her visits, she introduced herself to Edward's friend Carole Roffe, who was doing graduate work in psychology at the former institution.

Carole was younger than Angela, but had graduated from the University of Bristol a couple of years earlier, and had already been through a marriage and a divorce. She was given to 'severe depressions', but maintained an air of ironic detachment and intellectual self-confidence. She was passionate about women's liberation, as it was beginning to be called. After her marriage, she had embraced the permissive society – she had, by her own account, had over a hundred lovers by the time she met Angela – and had travelled extensively in Europe, hitch-hiking around the continent several times. Slim and smallish, she cut a striking figure with her long blonde hair, tinted glasses, and prodigious cigarette habit. She became the model for the psychiatrist in *Love*: 'a young woman . . . dressed entirely in black and lavishly hung about with hair of metallic yellow. Her eyes were concealed behind tinted glasses and her voice was as if smoked also, dark-toned and husky.'

Even before they met, Carole knew Angela by reputation, had read and admired her stories in *Nonesuch*, and was aware that she had published a novel. But her first impression was not flattering: she recalled 'an ugly, gawky girl with a mottled face and a mass of wire wool hair who seemed ill at ease in her body' approaching her desk at the technical college. She had heard Angela and Paul being referred to as 'the Folk Singing Carters', which she described as 'a fact hardly likely to endear her to me': Carole was in tune with the zeitgeist, and by 1966 the folk music scene was becoming passé: 'it smelt heavily of the late fifties'. Angela's initial assessment of Carole was hardly less critical than Carole's was of her. In her journal she described her as

> a nice bird but so smug, it's funny. I wonder how deep this apparent sense of being a member of an intellectual elite goes; to me, being as I am such a mass of puritan virtue, she & her friends seem shallow. Though I suppose I am jealous because she has so many friends.

In spite of these mutually disdainful first impressions, they were evidently intrigued by one another, and started to pursue a friendship. Carole liked Angela's 'odd mixture of diffidence and boldness', while Angela respected Carole's greater experience of the world, admired her 'strength & peculiar integrity', and thought that she was 'in many ways much more, as they say, artistic than I'. They had both read and admired Salvador Dalí's novel *Hidden Faces* (Angela drew on its imagery in *The Infernal Desire Machines of Dr Hoffman*), and the discovery that they had such an esoteric reference point in common was an early milestone in their relationship.

They began to see each other most days of the week: they would sit in Angela's front room, on either side of the fireplace, each in a Victorian button-back chair (Angela in the blue one, Carole in the orange), smoking and talking all afternoon, until Paul returned from work. They talked about, in Carole's words, 'our lives, our loves, our families . . . every book we had read, film we had seen, experience that had stayed with us'. It became one of the closest and most important friendships of Angela's life. 'They would talk to each other in virtual shorthand,' according to a boyfriend of Carole who often saw them together. Carole was more emphatic: 'It was like a love affair.'

Their correspondence – more than 1,000 pages of it on Angela's side alone, the overwhelming bulk of which was written when she was in Japan – bears out this impression of their relationship. Angela had at last found someone to whom she could speak about Paul's depression and her own feelings of uncertainty and frustration. She responded to Carole's instinctive self-assurance, set store in her advice, and in 1972 thanked her for 'prodding & pushing & propagandising me so that I took my life into my own hands'. It was no easy task: 'her background was such', Carole wrote a few years later, 'that she could only come to the idea of freedom slowly'.

CHAPTER SEVEN

Happiness is ego-shaped

By 1967, hippies were becoming a familiar sight in Clifton: men in kaftans, women with flowers in their hair; Angela called them the *papillons dorées* – the gilded butterflies. If there was a pinch of irony in her attitude towards them, she also identified with their ostentatious refusal to conform: 'There was a yeastiness in the air . . . due to a great deal of unrestrained and irreverent frivolity,' she later recalled. 'Everyday life, even where I was living, in Bristol, took on the air of a continuous improvisation.' Towards the end of the year she wrote her 'Notes for a Theory of Sixties Style', an admiring analysis of 'the startling dandyism of the newly emancipated young'. She argued that the sartorial eclecticism of the hippy generation – their appropriation of everything from military jackets to Mexican wedding dresses – meant that clothes were being 'robbed of their symbolic content' and turned into nothing more nor less than a 'dramatisation of the individual . . . the presentation of the self as a three-dimensional art object, to be wondered at and handled'.

The improvised, performative nature of selfhood is a major theme of the novel she began writing in March 1967, and the emergence of flower power ('a haze of colour') is its intricately painted backdrop. *Several Perceptions* is a return to the territory of *Shadow Dance* – the promiscuous demi-monde of Clifton bohemia – but the atmosphere has changed beyond all recognition. Gone are the bearded junk dealers and long-suffering housewives: the men now wear earrings and denim jackets, have long hair, and go to the newsagent's barefoot, while the women wear ponchos or T-shirts with their names stencilled across the breast, take drugs, and are just as likely to walk out on their boyfriends as vice versa. Frequent references to the war in Vietnam enhance the novel's contemporary flavour. In a retrospective essay about the 1960s, Angela wrote:

> Wars are great catalysts for social change and even though it was not specifically *our* war, the Vietnam war was a conflict between the First World and the Third World, between Whites and Non-Whites and, increasingly, between the American people, or a statistically significant percentage thereof, and Yankee imperialism . . . But why should Britain have been so caught up in the consequences of US foreign involvement? The more I think of it, the odder it seems . . . that so much seemed at stake in Vietnam, the very nature of our futures, perhaps.

She told a friend that Joseph Harker, the novel's shambolic hero, was based on a neighbour at Royal York Crescent, but he also resembles the original version of Honeybuzzard/Honeydripper – he retains 'a certain illegitimate intellectual status' in spite of having dropped out of university, and spends his time 'contemplating new bizarre and ingenious methods of sexual intercourse', a pursuit described as 'his only creative activity'. Profoundly alienated ('sad, hopeless and full of baffled murderous thoughts as some animal in a very small cage'), he is given to random, trivial acts of both kindness and cruelty, and is plagued by freaky dreams he has trouble distinguishing from reality.

After his girlfriend leaves him, he tries to kill himself by turning on the gas and striking a match; but the explosion only burns his hands and blasts out the windows, letting in 'the sweet evening air' and saving him from asphyxiation. His survival undoes his faith in external reality ('Somehow, he thought, he had contravened the laws of cause and effect') and he decides that he might as well live according to impulse from now on. He releases a badger from the zoo, sleeps with his best friend's mother, and airmails a turd to Lyndon B. Johnson. All of this is described with unmistakable glee: the novel has the effervescent mood of a Shakespeare comedy. It ends with a Saturnalia, a raucous house party on 24 December (it was intended to be blasphemous, and Angela was disappointed that none of the reviewers seemed to notice), at which Joseph spontaneously decides to make 'friends with time again', and to engage with society on society's terms: to haul himself back from the brink of insanity. But this unexpectedly happy ending may be the novel's final, blackest joke: it's possible that the final scene is a dream, and that Joseph has sunk into a bottomless psychosis.

The Scottish psychiatrist R. D. Laing – one of the intellectual pin-ups of the 1960s counterculture – was a major influence on *Several Perceptions*. Laing approached mental illness as a product of the sufferer's relation to society: psychotics and schizophrenics were people who couldn't make sense of their dysfunctional circumstances, and their illnesses were expressions of the radical alienation that ensued. This account was seized on by Angela's generation: madness could be viewed as a beautifully authentic response to an inauthentic world. Angela was fairly explicit about the influence of these ideas on the novel: 'Speaking very loosely, *Several Perceptions* is about madness as a failure to adjust to a mad society'.

Laing's most famous book, *The Divided Self* – published in 1960 and a slow-burning success over the next decade – brought together his ideas on psychiatry and psychoanalysis, philosophy and religion, society and the family, via case studies of the patients he'd encountered over the years in Glasgow's psychiatric hospitals. It had a profound effect on Angela: 'it made madness, alienation, hating your parents . . . glamorous'. Perhaps what most powerfully captured her attention was Laing's concept of 'ontological insecurity'. While an ontologically secure person has a 'centrally firm sense of his own and other people's reality and identity', an ontologically insecure person lacks any fixed understanding of who he or she is, and as a result is locked in a continuous struggle to maintain any sense of personal identity. They fear 'engulfment' by others and the 'implosion' of external reality. In extreme cases, a radical division occurs between their 'inner self' and a 'false self' that they present to the world.

Angela was riveted by these ideas. But she was suspicious of Laing's concept of an essential 'inner self', of which the schizophrenic's 'false self' was a betrayal. In *Several Perceptions* she mixes Laing's idea of 'ontological insecurity' with a concept of selfhood derived from empiricist philosophy. The novel's title and epigraph come from Hume: 'The mind is a kind of theatre, where several perceptions successively make their appearance, pass, re-pass, glide away and mingle in an infinite variety of postures and situations.' This was how Angela claimed to experience things herself. She wrote about 'my own very strongly held self-image as a random blur of reactions', a conception of selfhood which she felt 'gives one a certain freedom. If personality is in a state of flux, always a random, indeterminate collection of responses, reflexes, intimations and false reflections in the minds of other people, well, this is freedom.'

In the final chapter of *The Divided Self*, Laing illustrates some of his ideas through a case study of 'Julie', a schizophrenic. Her illness appears to stem from her relationship with her mother, who it transpires was a demanding and repressive parent, unintentionally stifling Julie's individuality by trying to shape her in her own image. 'I wasn't mothered I was smothered,' Julie tells Laing, who concludes that faced with such an overbearing mother, a child must develop a firm sense of her own identity, or else go mad.

Perhaps this was a bit close to home. Joseph's parents do make a brief appearance in *Several Perceptions*, but they're hardly the domineering gargoyles Laing would have posited:

His father was a newsagent and tobacconist who worked hard all his life. His mother was just an ordinary housewife who worked hard all her life . . . His bewildered father surveyed a son who was hardly there at all and said from time to time: 'But we've always done the best for you, I can't understand it,' while his mother, with the odour of roasting turkey caught in the springes of her hair, remonstrated: 'Don't go on at the boy, Father, after all, it's Christmas.'

But Joseph has a sort of surrogate parent in the form of the enormous, alcoholic, heavily made-up mother of his best friend Viv. Mrs Boulder is a prostitute – 'love is her business' – whose 'terrifying naked eyes' are 'full of solicitude and pure motherly care' when we first encounter her, and whose 'expressionless voice . . . nevertheless carried deep blue hints of poignant symbolic overtones'. Her cloyingly maternal, disturbingly sexual presence pervades the novel. It's against her pillows ('retaining a ghostly female perfume') that Joseph recuperates after the gas explosion; the snowfall that covers the city in the final scene is compared to her naked body. Joseph is able to draw this analogy because a couple of nights earlier he has visited her at home and had sex with her: 'he wanted to reach the uncreated country of fountain and forest deep inside her'. He dreams of being 'gone for good, dead and buried all at once in the polar night of Mrs Boulder's belly'. The relationship was based on the alchemical story (recounted in Jung's *Mysterium Coniunctionis*) of Beya and his sister Gabricus; she absorbs him entirely into her body when they have sex – an 'engulfment image' which Angela found 'quite offensive'.

By the time she started writing the novel in March 1967, she had been making notes on it for almost a year. Its working title was *A Dream Book*. She began writing it in the first person, but abandoned the attempt fairly promptly. Even after that, she found it much more difficult than either of her previous novels had been. With its precarious central perspective and its jump-cuts 'borrowed from Godard', it involved technical challenges of a kind she hadn't previously encountered, and when she wrote the final chapter she found she had to go back and revise almost everything that had gone before. She finally completed it in early December, and felt 'both bemused and excited . . . Some of it I genuinely didn't know I had in me.' She wrote to Carole: 'I am less shuffling and furtive about this novel than about the others because it seems to me the first promising first novel [sic] I've written, not mad freaks like the other two.' On 16 December she sent the manuscript to Janice with an accompanying letter:

> It is very short (about 45,000 words) but, really, exceedingly com-
> plex . . . technically, it's a failure; the hero is only intermittently
> alive . . . On the other hand, it's very beautifully written. I think,
> really, it is an interesting failure but it is tremendously important to
> me because writing it helped to show me the limitations of what I can
> do and what I can't do, helped me work out some personal obsessions
> and gave me some indications of where I am going to go from here.
> In its warped, fragile way, it is a novel of ideas and the questions it
> raises are no less real because they're quite insoluble. In a way, it's
> about moral responsibility.

Janice was enthusiastic: 'I think it is the best thing you have done so far.' She offered an advance of £250, a significant increase on what Heinemann had paid for the first two novels. Simon & Schuster offered $2,500, the same as they had paid for *The Magic Toyshop*.

Between delivery and publication, Angela found herself a literary agent. Irene Josephy had a fairly distinguished list of clients, including the journalists Nicholas Tomalin and Paul Foot, the humourist and TV personality Patrick Campbell, and the poet Adrian Mitchell. An eccentric, gin-soaked Jewish lady, who believed in astrology and claimed never to wash her long grey hair, she divided her time between agenting and translating Russian novels. Another of her clients, the humourist Gyles Brandreth, described her offices on London's Craven Street: 'a tiny desk in the corner of [a] vast, empty room. Bare floor-boards, bare walls, manuscripts in piles on the floor around her. All day long she sits there, sipping at a glass of gin and water, taking calls, making calls, doing deals.' When Janice met her, she thought she was 'a bit like Angela, really'.

* * *

When she looked back on the 1960s from the relative contentment of subsequent decades, Angela was able to write as sharply about the sexual revolution as she ever had about the flamboyant new fashions or the defiant swagger of pop music. In an essay on the porn star Linda Lovelace – written in 1974, after Angela had gained some first-hand experience of the permissive society – she paused to deliver a coruscating Marxist analysis of permissiveness, pointing out that the very notion implies a fundamental authoritarianism:

> Now I am permitted as much libidinal gratification as I want. Yippee!
> But who is it who permits me? Why, the self-same institutions that
> hitherto forbade me! So, I am still in the same boat, though it has
> been painted a different colour. I am still denied authentic sexual
> autonomy, perhaps even more cruelly than before . . . I have acquired
> an illusory sense of freedom that blinds me more than ever to the
> true nature of freedom itself.

For most of the 1960s – as a young woman who had only ever slept with her husband and who felt increasingly restless and resentful of her situation – the nature of freedom looked a little different. Carole slept with whomever she wanted, and claimed not to give a hoot about romantic love. Angela was impressed by her relaxed attitude: 'I have nothing but praise and admiration for your modus vivendi,' she told her – 'and of course envy.'

It isn't easy to nail down the exact chronology – all we have to go on are a couple of undated letters and the frequently contradictory accounts of participants and onlookers – but around the time she left the university, it seems that Angela had begun looking for opportunities to be unfaithful to Paul. Her Clifton friend Janet Swan noticed a change in her around this time: 'She started going out more, to parties where drugs were taken, she was definitely presenting herself.' But until the winter of 1966–7, all the men she propositioned appear to have been uninterested: 'Not because of Paul particularly, but because she was gauche.' One man – a neighbour on Royal York Crescent who took her back to his room, where they sat side by side on the bed – remembered being put off by the sight of her unshaven legs disappearing into her baseball boots. Another, when she tried to touch him, 'reacted like when Glumdalclitch scoops up Gulliver . . . terror and dismay'. Angela tended to think that these eleventh-hour rejections were a product of the men's discomposure when faced with a sexually assertive woman:

Women tend to be raised with a monolithic notion of 'maleness', just as men are raised with the idea of a single and undifferentiated femininity. Stereotyping. *Real* men, especially when approached by women acting in ways they're not supposed to act, can behave like fifteen-year-old girls in the photostory magazines. This can come as a shock.

The first man with whom she appears to have had any luck was her friend John Orsborn (who had once told the Swans that he couldn't imagine sleeping with her; using him as the villain in *Shadow Dance* had evidently been a first-class seduction technique, even if that wasn't the intention). For a brief period in the winter of 1966–7 they had a sexual relationship. Angela described it as an 'aborted' and 'one-sided' affair, while John gave friends to understand that he was 'screwing' her. Jenny Orsborn says that her own friendship with Angela didn't suffer during this period – 'it didn't affect how I felt about her at all' – but it's clear from Angela's journals that, at least from her perspective, things were tense between them:

> this is the first thing that has happened to me for years & I am loth to have it stop. Also, it is good for my ego (happiness is ego-shaped) to see myself as [John] sees me, a sweet, cool, flower in the sun; &, especially as [Jenny] sees me, an exotic, treacherous femme fatale.

In according herself the role of femme fatale, she cast Jenny as the tragic wronged wife. Early in 1967 she wrote in her journal: 'the classic climax of this, the beautiful logic of the situation resolving itself, Jenny should kill or try to kill herself . . . I wish Jenny would try to kill herself.'

This eruption of Angela's ugliest nature – an indication of her intense emotional investment in the affair – is worth noting. It wasn't how she liked to see herself (she stuck a picture from a magazine over the page on which she'd written that line, though it subsequently came loose), and it wasn't a side that she often allowed others to see. But it was murkily, fitfully there.

In many ways, John was much more Angela's type than Paul ever was – more artistic, more virile, more proletarian – and she found the contrast intoxicating. When he ended the relationship, she was distraught. She told Carole that she felt bewitched by him, and resorted to magic to cure herself ('Granny wasn't a witch for nothing'). In her journal she wrote:

Since I do not fully understand what the phrase 'in love' means, I shall say that I used to think about him so much that his image webbed in fantasy & grew princefully bejewelled with thoughts. This image of him/not him, which possessed me, displaced almost completely my usual preoccupations, such as, for example, the weather & watching my cat put back its ears like spoons to listen behind her. Now I am happy to say there is room for these things again. I wrote his name on a piece of paper and fired it with a match. When I looked at him again, he had vanished entirely, as if smoke, or all the time, a mirage, anyway.

Even if she got over her infatuation as easily as this suggests, the way the relationship ended had a discouraging effect on her. The affair had (perhaps unconsciously) been a dry run for leaving Paul, and the unhappiness it caused her made her less inclined to take the plunge for real. To further dampen her wanderlust, Paul was going through a period of relative good humour. In her journal, around the time that her relationship with John was coming to an end, she wrote: 'we are so happy together, Paul and me, I see that now'. To Carole, shortly afterwards, she wrote:

Paul is all new and shiny, there is this absurd but marvellous sense of newness. I've always known, deep down, I was somehow obliterating him, which is easily enough converted to resentment that he is obliterating me; this is the way one lives with the grislier aspects of one's own personality, I suppose. But, now that the time he needed me for a mother is over (which he did and which it is) we can at least begin to try being separate but equal, in the basis of an emotional structure that, whatever crazy things it's been built out of over the years, <u>does</u> contain a good deal of mutual respect . . . There is now, for me, at least the possibility of a dynamic relationship in the sense of leaving room for the maximum amount of change in both of us whilst continuing to love, as in the best-regulated families. Which mine was not; I learned to love, to protect and to cherish but not to leave well alone.

*   *   *

The Magic Toyshop was published on 12 June 1967, with an initial print run of 1,600 copies. Its reception was almost entirely positive. Elizabeth Berridge, writing in the *Daily Telegraph*, thought that 'Angela Carter has done that unusual thing: she has written a second novel which is strides ahead of her first, for which she was highly praised . . . Formidable is surely the word to describe her kind of talent.' Sarah Curtis, writing anonymously in the *Times Literary Supplement*, agreed: 'Angela Carter has a bizarre but unquestionable talent.' In the *Guardian*, Christopher Wordsworth described the book as 'a cruel and lyrical little fantasy' that 'genuinely gripped me'. Virtually the only dissenting voice was Ian Hamilton, the influential poet and critic, who once said that he viewed 'suffering' and 'control' as the great literary virtues, and who through his editorship of the *Review* championed the work of poets who wrote in spare, unfussy English and were in proper control of their suffering: Al Alvarez, John Fuller, Jon Silkin, Clive James. (Not a single female poet was featured in the *Review* until its ninth issue, which was devoted to the work of the recently deceased Sylvia Plath; over the ten years of its existence it featured just two living female poets – Denise Levertov in 1964, and Molly Holden in 1970.) Hamilton was never likely to be a great admirer of Angela Carter. Writing in the *Listener*, he found *The Magic Toyshop* 'indulgent' and 'unremittingly inventive', concluding that 'what ought to be rather terrifying (so the heroine's ever-widening eyes insist) too often turns out to seem just cosily peculiar and easily grown out of'.

Several reviewers emphasised the novel's fairy-tale qualities. In the *Observer*, Claire Tomalin remarked that 'Angela Carter writes like a very up-to-date Hans Andersen', while Kay Dick in the *Sunday Times* described the novel as 'Hans Andersen mixed with the Brothers Grimm'. Angela must have been pleased with these comparisons. That summer, between novels, she wrote a trio of fairy tales – titled 'Jack and His Faithful Friends', 'The Magicked Rose', and 'Rosemary and Elizabeth' – each about 2,500 words long. None of them has survived, but the references to them in Angela's letters suggest that they were traditional bedtime stories, 'more like Grimm than Hans Andersen, not at all like Oscar Wilde, very simply written'. She enjoyed the work – what she called the 'lucidity' of writing for children – and planned to do enough tales to fill a book.

Janice put her in touch with Mary Whitehead, the children's editor at Heinemann, who liked the stories but had some doubts about whether a collection of fairy tales would sell. Angela responded by proposing 'a simple narrative framework' to tie them together: they would be told by monkeys, and the book would be called *The Monkey's Magic Reader*. Whitehead liked this idea even less, but she did like the additional stories Angela sent, especially 'Miss Z, the Dark Young Lady' and 'The Donkey Prince'.

The first of these demonstrates a sure understanding of how the form works, the principle that it should mix mundane and marvellous elements, or that 'a fairy tale is a story where one king goes to another king to borrow a cup of sugar', as Angela later expressed it. After her father kills King Parrot, Miss Z sets out to the land of the green lions, equipped with 'her magic dress and a paper bag full of cheese sandwiches', to persuade the other parrots to come back to the Parrot Jungle. Some feminist critics – such as Andrea Dworkin, in her 1974 book *Woman Hating* – have denounced the fairy tale as a patriarchal form, but in Angela Carter's hands it is anything but: Miss Z is always dealing with the hot-headed idiocy of the men she encounters. Her father kills King Parrot with his catapult. 'I fear you acted rashly,' she tells him. A unicorn tells her that he'll destroy the green lions for her. She reflects that she doesn't want to destroy them, 'only to speak to them sensibly'. When the unicorn does battle with the ruler of the lions, she grows bored and throws her dress over them to make them fall asleep.

'The Donkey Prince' also features women calmly countering male aggression: when Bruno is adopted by a queen, he doesn't realise that it was her father who turned his people into donkeys, and that this is her way of making amends. Her magic apple goes missing, so he sets out in search of it. With the help of a little girl called Daisy, he climbs the Savage Mountain, home of the Wild Men. It is Daisy who comes up with all the ideas and ruses that see them through. ('A working girl knows how to use her wits,' she says.)

Mary Whitehead forwarded the stories to Simon & Schuster, feeling that if an American publisher could be persuaded to share the cost of commissioning illustrations, then 'a book of 25,000 to 30,000 words containing 10 to 12 stories' might be a worthwhile endeavour. Word came back after a few weeks that the Americans liked the stories, but felt they were too reminiscent of the Brothers Grimm. Angela was asked if she could do something a bit different, perhaps with more 'gore'. She responded: 'I fear my particular forte is gentler and more poetic.' Simon & Schuster eventually decided to publish 'Miss Z' and 'The Donkey Prince' as free-standing books – they paid $1,500 for each of them, and Heinemann offered an additional £250 to publish both in the UK. It was almost as much as Angela was receiving for her adult novels. She was thrilled with the intricate, willowy illustrations commissioned from the American artist Eros Keith, finding them 'exactly – even uncannily – right' for the stories. *Miss Z* was published in Britain and the US in October 1970; Heinemann intended to publish *The Donkey Prince* the following year, but when Angela moved her adult books elsewhere, they felt there was no point continuing with her children's books, and cancelled the contract; it has only ever appeared in the USA.

That summer, Angela enrolled in evening classes at the West of England College of Art, an institution she cheerfully described as 'the worst art school in the country'. She had always loved to draw. She found it relaxing, involving as it did a process of concentrated and receptive looking, without any of the fraught mental exertion of writing novels. Over the course of her life, she produced an enormous number of still lifes and portraits (many of them featuring cats) in pencil and crayon. Her style was naïve, a surge of strong lines, bulbous shapes and primary colours; her flowers have a resemblance to Georgia O'Keeffe's, and her watermelons might have been plucked from one of Frida Kahlo's fruit paintings.

Most of the students in the evening class were older women 'doing therapy, splashing about in oil paints', while the tutor moved between them lavishing praise on their efforts: '"Only Mrs Gifford would paint like that" – "That's a beaut, a real beaut" – "What an interesting beginning."' Even so, Angela can't have found it an altogether worthless experience. The following year she applied to the college as a full-time student, but was turned down on the basis (or so she said) that students were expected to commit fully to the degree, and her habit of writing and publishing novels suggested a dilettantish attitude towards the visual arts. She wore this verdict as a badge of pride, often inscribing the books she gave to friends with a doodle, beneath which she would scrawl some variation on the words: 'And they wouldn't let me into art school, the bastards! They said I was a dilettante.'

As the summer drew to a close, Paul succumbed to another depressive episode, and Angela's recent lease of enthusiasm for her marriage began to falter. A new, bitter tone creeps into many of her journal entries around this time: 'as I try & grow, as I submit myself to change to help him, as I make allowances & act tenderly & do all the things a good wife should, my fucking understanding, my kind heart, so I am building a better & stronger cage for myself every day & in every way'. 'Nobody is responsible for anybody else,' she told herself. She felt that she had spent much too long passively accepting a situation that made her miserable:

> It seems to me I have only recently become a person and begun to apprehend the nature of the labyrinth & maybe see ways out. It is September 1967, already, how fantastic. Autumn again, full of leaf. The years are getting shorter.

Around Christmas, Paul entered a 'spontaneous remission period'; but Angela was unable to recapture her mood of a few months earlier: 'when I can't find excuses for certain aspects of his behaviour because he's depressed, they just send me quietly wild'. In her letters to Carole she went back and forth over her reasons for staying with him, her reasons for wanting to leave, as if by totting up the pros and cons she would eventually come to know her mind. 'I'd rather like you to tell me what your trained, observer's eye has made of my marriage,' she demanded at one point, before immediately overruling herself: 'I suppose I want confirmation that my position is, in fact, intolerable, and this is rather a lot to ask, actually.' Actually, it was asking no more than Carole had already provided, but Angela didn't want to hear it all again: 'I don't think I could stand the emotional tempest of splitting up & there's this terrible narcissus thing of not being able to bear the thought of P. unhappy without me. So I'll just have to peg on, I suppose.' In another letter, she struck an even more cynical note: 'I am dependent on the idea of somebody being dependent on me; some people call this syndrome "love".'

CHAPTER EIGHT

The edge of the unimaginable

Angela was idly browsing in George's Bookshop one afternoon when she came across a copy of *New Worlds* magazine. Visibly avant-gardish – its covers featured M. C. Escher drawings and collages by Eduardo Paolozzi – the quarterly publication had become, under Michael Moorcock's editorship, a showcase for the 'New Wave' of science fiction, a movement with an affinity to surrealism, which sought to reclaim the genre from nerdy teenage boys and use it as an instrument for probing the social and psychological conditions of the near future. A character in a *New Worlds* story was less likely to go boldly into outer space than to go slowly mad in the terrible aftermath of an all too credible catastrophe. J. G. Ballard, one of the magazine's regular contributors and editorialists, formulated its credo in arresting terms: 'the only truly alien planet is Earth'.

This was Angela's first exposure to the genre since reading John Wyndham and *Amazing* magazine as a child, and she was intoxicated by the 'immaculately glazed savagery' of work by Moorcock and Ballard in particular. 'When I read those mid-sixties issues of *New Worlds* I realised it was possible to scrap almost everything I found oppressive about [the mainstream] apparatuses of fiction,' she wrote:

> It seemed to me that that was how the late sixties felt, that that was how it was like . . . And it was only, it seemed to me, the group of writers who were loosely connected with *New Worlds* that were actually dealing with the new circumstances in which we found ourselves, as British people in a society that had changed quite radically since we'd been grown up. And also as beings in

the world, because we were the generation that grew up with the reality of nuclear weapons.

The novel she worked on between January 1968 and January 1969 – shutting herself in the back room for 'twelve hours a day more or less' – seizes on these new techniques as a way of exploring alienation. *Heroes and Villains* is a post-apocalyptic fairy tale, a headlong departure from the domestic settings of her first three novels. It started out with the idea of writing 'a love story set in a period when the word "love" was not part of the vocabulary'. But as it developed, the setting shifted from the distant past to the dystopian future: a few decades after a nuclear disaster has obliterated Western civilisation, life has become nasty, brutish and short, and the concept of love has been more or less forgotten. In this atrophied society, people are divided into three hereditary classes: Professors (guardians of knowledge, who live in walled settlements and preserve many of the routines and traditions of the former civilisation), Workers (both agricultural and domestic) and Soldiers (who are meant to protect and police the others, but who are rapidly developing 'an autonomous power of their own'). Outside society are the Barbarians (bandit tribes, who live in the forests and mount regular bloody raids on the settlements) and the Out People (radioactive mutants, who haunt the streets of ruined cities, and are regarded as verminous by Professors and Barbarians alike). 'What I was envisaging was a world divided between the people who'd been in the shelters and the ones who hadn't,' Angela told an interviewer in 1985. She conceived of the novel as another version of the Fall (for a while, she flirted with calling it *Adam and Eve at the End of the World*) as well as 'an attempt to cross-fertilise Jean-Jacques Rousseau & Henri Rousseau' (she cut one of the latter's lush other-wordly pictures out of a magazine, and pinned it over her desk while she worked).

Marianne – a Professor's daughter and the novel's impetuous teenage heroine – is warned of how dangerous the Barbarians are, but she hopes they will visit her settlement anyway, because at least it 'would make some kind of change'. She is (after Melanie in *The Magic Toyshop*) another incarnation of the 'bourgeois virgin', a bored, cosseted middle-class girl praying for someone or something to come along and shake things up. She lives in a white tower – 'made out of steel and concrete' rather than ivory, but still – and has never left the staid sanctuary of her settlement. When the Barbarians do attack, she watches the 'tremendous confusion' of the battle from a high window, and when she sees one of the marauders run injured into a shed, she's more excited than afraid.

She waits until after dark, then brings him food; he tells her that his name is Jewel and asks if she'll leave the settlement with him. But he doesn't set much store by her consent, and immediately declares that she's his hostage. After he takes her back to his tribe, she is swiftly disabused of her romantic notions; he rapes her, and she is forced to marry him. So she goes from her stultifying childhood home to a distant community, trapped in a nightmare marriage to a man who has 'a chronic gift for unhappiness'. It isn't hard to unpick the strands of symbolic autobiography in this.

Angela researched the novel carefully, anchoring the fantasy to solid facts: she worked out which animals could survive in the English countryside after escaping from a zoo, and read books about tribal societies, snakebites, midwifery and witchcraft. To begin with, she imagined the Barbarians as a biker gang, and read *Hell's Angels* by Hunter S. Thompson for any details she could purloin. But when she was halfway through a first draft, the strikes and protests of May 1968 erupted in Paris, consuming her attention, and knocking the novel off course. 'It started to feel like living on a demolition site,' she later wrote about this period. 'One felt one was living on the edge of the unimaginable.' She noted down the movement's slogans – 'I treat my desires as reality because I believe in the reality of my desires'; 'Be realistic, ask the impossible'; 'It is forbidden to forbid' – and familiarised herself with some of its intellectual touchstones.

Several books that were venerated by the sixty-eighters had a profound influence on *Heroes and Villains*, and on much of Angela's subsequent intellectual development. In *The Savage Mind*, Claude Lévi-Strauss argues that 'savage' and 'civilised' intellects are fundamentally alike, that all known societies have common mechanisms including classificatory systems and myths, and that myths are the opposite of works of art. Angela copied several long passages into her journal. She also read *Minima Moralia* by Theodore Adorno, who argued that 'the feminine character, and the ideal of femininity on which it is modelled, are products of masculine society'. After encountering his ideas, Angela felt a 'heightened awareness of the society around me', and began wondering about 'the social fictions that regulate our lives', and in particular about how 'that social fiction of my "femininity" was created, by means outside my control'. Her feminism, which until now had been largely instinctive, was beginning to acquire an intellectual edge.

'I suppose I started getting interested in things when I was twenty-eight,' she told an interviewer: 'I started getting interested in ideas, and *Heroes and Villains* is the result of that.' It approaches the status of women in society much more self-consciously than any of its predecessors had. Even so, it isn't a perfectly refined production. Angela was rare among novelists in her partiality to theory, but she wasn't a philosopher or a demagogue, and she tended to jumble up bits of Marxist, feminist, structuralist, post-colonial and psychoanalytic theory in her books, using them because they interested her, rather than seeking to reconcile them and fashion a sleek intellectual product. 'I have a jackdaw kind of a mind that picks up bright shiny things and takes [them] back to its nest,' she told an audience at the Adelaide Festival in 1984.

The biggest stumbling block for a feminist reading of *Heroes and Villains* is the scene in which Jewel rapes Marianne: it has been interpreted as a consequence of her desire (though Angela tended to be much more interested in desire itself than its consequences), and was roundly condemned by radical commentators in the 1970s and 80s. Writing to an academic who had inquired about 'attacks on her work by some feminists', Angela said that she put in 'that distinctly ideologically dodgy rape scene . . . for reasons of pure sensationalism', and that she couldn't 'defend [it] on any other grounds except that "H and V" is *supposed* to share a vocabulary with the fiction of repression . . . Note, however, that it doesn't make Marianne feel degraded – it makes her absolutely *furious*.'

All the same, it's clear from Angela's correspondence at the time of writing the novel that she didn't regard Jewel as its villain. In June she wrote: 'I'm not too sure myself what the novel is about except that love is a dysfunctional (new word) apparition & Jewel is supposed to be a bit like the hero of "L'Age D'Or", or perhaps the ultimate Magic Other.' Six months later, her ideas were still a bit tangled: 'it looks like pretentious gibberish at about 4 o'clock in the morning', she confessed to Janice.

It says something about Angela's priorities at this point in her life that her uncertainty regarding the novel's intellectual quality didn't really bring it down in her estimation. As she approached the end, she wrote to Carole: 'I am really quite pleased with it, it is a juicy, overblown, exploding Gothic lollipop.' Her publishers agreed that it was 'very good'. She signed a contract with Heinemann for an advance of £400 on 20 March 1969; Simon & Schuster offered $2,500 for American rights in August, and paperback rights were bought by Pan for £625 in October. It was also published in Holland, becoming the first of her novels to be translated, and earning her an additional £80. She was 'terribly pleased . . . partly because I rather want to live in Amsterdam for a while, one day'.

Work on the novel was made easier by an unprecedented lack of distractions that year. By the summer of 1968, Angela's Bristol circles were much smaller than they had been, and looked set to shrink further. Edward Horesh was getting ready to move to Bath; Rebecca Howard had left for London soon after graduation, and now Carole Roffe, having been offered a job as a psychologist for the Civil Service, began renting her spare room. She returned to visit Angela for occasions such as American Independence Day (in celebration of which Angela cooked a Boston black-bean stew, and Edward read the Gettysburg Address), sometimes bringing her new boyfriend John Lockwood, a philosophy graduate of the University of Hull, who worked with her at the Civil Service. He was very handsome, with long and luxurious hair, a bulletproof jawline and a muscular physique; Angela thought he had 'a look of [Jean-Paul] Belmondo', her favourite actor at this time due to his appearance in several Godard films. In 1969, John and Carole moved to Bradford, Carole having taken a job at the nearby University of Leeds, and they saw even less of one another, though they kept in close touch by mail.

Martin Hoyle was still around, working for the BBC in Bristol, but that summer he was spending most of his time in London, recording a programme called *Free for All in the Arts*. The format involved pitching invited critics, artists and writers against 'ordinary' members of the public: 'the idea was that the ordinary people would put the poncey critics to shame with their sturdy common sense', he explained. 'It just doesn't work. You'd get Edward Lucie-Smith standing up and spouting about art and sitting down. The housewife from Stevenage is just cowering.' He invited Angela to hear Stevie Smith reading from her *Novel on Yellow Paper*. The audience stood around Smith in a large circle while she read, then fired questions at her from all sides – 'a bizarre circus', Angela thought. For A. S. Byatt, who was also there, it was 'like a bullring':

On the way out this very disagreeable woman stomped up to me, and she said, 'My name's Angela Carter. I recognised you and I wanted to stop and tell you that the sort of thing you're doing is no good at all, no good at all. There's nothing in it — that's not where literature is going.' That sort of thing. And off she stomped.

The sort of thing Byatt was doing was writing novels that sought to balance nineteenth-century solidity with twentieth-century ingenuity, mixing George Eliot with Iris Murdoch and a dash of metafictional complexity, aiming for what she has described as 'self-conscious realism'. Angela would have viewed this project as rather airless. She may also have associated Byatt with her sister, Margaret Drabble, a practitioner of what later became known as the Hampstead novel, and like Byatt an admirer of F. R. Leavis (in another version of the story, Byatt has Angela saying: 'the sort of thing you and your sister are doing just won't work'). The incident clearly reveals Angela's competitiveness with two female novelists of her own generation, both of whom were much better known than she was at this point – but it also shows exactly what she was defining herself against.

Byatt sensed a degree of nervousness in her accuser: 'I knew she was shy when she said that . . . I thought, this is just gauche, and I didn't hold it against her at all . . . it was something she believed and she just thought she should make it clear.' Angela's own account of the incident supports this interpretation, while adding another layer of psychological detail: 'Byatt is a very intelligent literary lady who appears to have read everything in fiction and takes it all pretty seriously,' she wrote to Carole. 'She terrified me and made me feel effete and flippant.'

But if feelings of inferiority played any part in her confrontation with Byatt, they were a bit misplaced at a moment when her career was starting to take off. On 2 May, she heard that *The Magic Toyshop* had received the John Llewellyn Rhys Prize, worth £100, beating novels by Nigel Patten, Jeremy Seabrook and Angus Wolfe Murray. Pan, who were bringing out the paperback, tried to capitalise on this success by arranging an interview with Kenneth Pearson in the *Sunday Times*. 'They fail to realise it could well be a traumatic experience for everyone concerned,' Angela told Carole. 'I feel it my duty to make [the book] as hard to sell as possible.' This was a bit of a pose (her rationale was that 'Harold Macfuckingmillan' was on Pan's board of directors, though she had been happy enough for Pan to buy the paperback rights in the first place), but she was true to her word: 'Things are happening to Miss [*sic*] Carter, but communicating them is not exactly her primary concern,' Pearson complained in his remarkably short profile. Angela was presented with her cheque by Mrs John Llewellyn Rhys at a party on 17 July at the Heinemann offices, to which she took Carole as her guest. She wore a big dress with a floppy collar and glasses. Her hair was cut very short. In the photographs taken that night, she looks happy.

The prize may have softened the blow of the poor reception her next novel got in the press a few weeks later. John Higgins in the *Sunday Telegraph* was typical in viewing *Several Perceptions* as a disappointment, 'muted and blurred' in comparison to Angela Carter's first two novels. Most of the praise it did receive was very faint indeed. John Hemmings in the *Listener* opined that 'what is so intriguing about Miss [sic] Carter's writing is that so little in it betrays the hand of the woman novelist'. The *Evening News* described it as 'compelling in its own obscure way'; an anonymous reviewer in the *Observer* allowed that 'Miss [sic] Carter presents us with some briefly beguiling scenes'; Christopher Wordsworth in the *Guardian* applauded the 'many small sunbursts' of good writing; and Michael Wood in *New Society* compared it to 'a pop record you liked, but probably won't remember'. Unexpectedly enough, one of the few reviewers who was enthusiastic about the novel was Richard Church, the elderly poet, memoirist, and book critic of *Country Life*: he praised its 'astonishingly brilliant technique', 'the beauty of its prose', 'its poetic imagery', and its 'fundamentally moral outcry' against 'our crumbling manners and taboos', recommending it as 'a work of art . . . sophisticated, not crude'. It was a lovely review, but *Country Life*'s readership wasn't the constituency Angela hoped to appeal to. She came to the conclusion that the novel was 'a complete failure because all the wrong people like it'.

Worse even than the tepid critical response was the discovery that her friends weren't wild about *Several Perceptions*. Edward accused her of being 'a monster of sentimentality' when he read it. Carole suggested that using the Vietnam War as an expressionist backdrop was 'more or less a confession of spiritual poverty'. This criticism really deflated Angela, who responded:

> I am becoming reconciled to the fact that you don't like my books; it saddens me but there it is . . . I guess the book's main fault is that it isn't clearly defined enough; it doesn't live up to its own intellectual pretensions, partly because the quasi-realist mode is not my scene. I've tried to do a conjuring trick which doesn't come off; I've put various emblematic figures in the back bar of the 'Greyhound' and,

to my chagrin, watch them pass unnoticed in the throng . . . One paragraph is both good and interesting and, as I say, some of the jokes are pretty funny (at least, to me); and, honestly, this is more than I've managed so far.

This was a considerable devaluation of her opinion on finishing the book, and she would continue to revise it downwards in her estimation. Years later, shortly before *The Passion of New Eve* was published in 1977, she suggested that *Several Perceptions* was the only one of her novels that she really couldn't stand: 'It does embarrass me. Because I think I was too young to do it. Suffering appears as a form of decoration in it, which I think is awful.'

For all that her career was gathering velocity, Angela felt that her life had stalled at the beginning of 1969. She was still fretting over whether or not to leave Paul, but she hadn't spoken to him about her feelings – it doesn't seem to have occurred to her that she might have done – and as a result he was entirely oblivious to the desperate condition of their relationship. In February she wrote:

I've been haunted by 'Strawberry Fields Forever' for days; 'living is easy with eyes closed'. How trite. How true. It's easy if you can do it; Paul can. I can't. He's so content in this illusory structure of a happy marriage that I am beginning to feel all thin and two dimensional, like a figment of his imagination.

These feelings persisted into the spring. By then the peaceable mood of the 'Summer of Love' had been displaced in her imagination by the violence and fury of May 1968. In March, she began making notes for another Clifton novel, one whose tone was a far cry from the optimism of *Several Perceptions*. It was inspired by Benjamin Constant's 1816 novel *Adolphe*, which had 'knocked [her] out' when she read it at the beginning of the year. Perhaps the strength of her reaction was down to finding echoes in the novel of her situation with Paul: *Adolphe* tells the story of its narrator's attempts to extricate himself from a turbulent, emotionally ambivalent, mutually destructive romance. Angela read it in French, 'sacrificing innumerable nuances of meaning and the benefits of an introduction for the sheer joy of the language, which is like a string quartet', and admired it for its 'absolute sense of honesty' about 'the rhetoric of the heart'.

The novel that would become *Love* – its working title was *The Gates of Paradise* – inherits several of its features from *Adolphe*. Both are exquisitely stylised short novels about 'the rhetoric of the heart'; both view romantic attachments as intolerable constraints on personal freedom; and both end in sensational style, with a woman's death. But where Constant's novel is reflective, composed, urbane, Carter's is savage, primary coloured, expressionistic. It follows a love triangle comprising Annabel, a 'sick' and 'disturbed' young art student; her husband Lee, a secondary-school teacher with a 'very tender heart', whose 'grand passion' is for 'freedom'; and his half-brother Buzz, a 'malign' and perverted petty criminal.

Love is soaked in the painfully claustrophobic atmosphere of an unworkable marriage. Lee finds Annabel 'quite incomprehensible'. She has painted their room, filled it with her belongings – 'the palpable evidence of her own secrets' – and made her husband a stranger there. She has fantasies of 'totally engulfing' him. From the start of their relationship, he is unfaithful to her. When he has sex with a woman called Carolyn in the course of a party at their flat, Annabel slashes her wrists: 'she could not incorporate this manifestation of his absolute otherness anywhere into her mythology, which was an entirely egocentric universe'. A psychiatrist at the hospital where she's treated tells Lee that, for the sake of his wife's health, he has to get her away from Buzz, who shares their flat. 'There is a condition of shared or, rather, mutually stimulated psychotic disorder known as *"folie à deux"*. Your brother and your wife would appear excellent candidates for it.'

Buzz has been insinuating himself deeper and deeper into his sister-in-law's affections, seemingly out of rivalrous antipathy for Lee. After Lee evicts him, Buzz finally sleeps with Annabel. When she returns to the flat, she gasses herself.

Lee was initially drawn to Annabel on account of her vulnerability, but over the course of the novel he realises there is nothing much he can do for her. He feels crushed by his responsibilities ('think of it this way', her psychiatrist tells him; 'There is a sick girl who needs care and can only turn to you'). After he marries her, he is troubled 'by the conviction that he had done something irreparable'. But when she kills herself, he realises that 'nothing but death is irreparable'.

Angela thought of *Love* as an 'anti-Laing novel', in contrast to the 'pro-Laing' standpoint of *Several Perceptions*. By 1969, in light of her experience with Paul, she had come to feel that, far from being a courageous stand against the world's hypocrisies, mental illness was a piteous retreat from human contact. She told an interviewer that Lee was 'in my terms a perfectly moral person, who wants to do good, who wants to help, and he can't. And that's ultimately what destroys him, that he's incapable of fulfilling his own moral expectations of himself.' This was how she was beginning to feel about her own responsibilities towards Paul. '"LOVE" is autobiographical,' she wrote to Carole after the book was published. 'I might well be Lee; I even put in clues like knocking out his front tooth, dammit, and nobody guessed!' In another letter she wrote: 'if some biographer of the far-distant future got hold of the reference to Paul . . . in which I compared him to Annabel in LOVE – oh, there'd be meat there!'

It is tempting, after reading those lines, to treat the novel as a straightforward portrait of her marriage, the husband-and-wife dynamic disguised by a crafty gender switch. A lot of it rewards this construal. Annabel resents Lee's privacy, 'since she felt that privacy was her exclusive property and nobody else had much right to it'. She wants 'to reduce him to not-being'. He tries to be tender with her, but it's rejected. His infidelities are 'only to be expected' under the circumstances. Eventually, he becomes detached – a detachment he sees as necessary to maintaining his 'precarious autonomy'. So far, the association between Angela/Lee and Annabel/Paul seems fairly solid. But *Love* remains a work of the imagination, and not everything in it yields to such a simple-minded reading. Lee ties Annabel up and beats her; it's safe to assume that Angela never did this to Paul.

If Lee and Annabel are dream-versions of Angela and Paul, then Buzz comes from an altogether more shadowy part of Angela's psyche. When she reread the novel almost twenty years later, she wrote: 'he's come out of the pages to haunt me, whoever he was, the creation of my discontent . . . he is something to do with my libido, I think, the perpetually renewed fountain of desire who is the female myth or fantasy or dream of the male, the woman's imaginary idea of male sexuality'.

She approached writing the novel in a practical manner, concerning herself less with ideas than with questions of narrative technique. 'A lot of [*Love*] is an exercise in style,' she told an interviewer in 1976:

I might be bothered about, like, the nature of alienation and so on, but these aren't really the problems that my work presents to me – they are, how to get A out of a room so that B can come into it without them meeting. They're constructional problems, grammatical problems, problems connected with imagery (where you can overload something so

much that it becomes meaningless), problems of tautness, of tension . . .
I still find the first half of *Love* very exciting narratively . . . It's flawed,
it falls into two halves, the first half is I think very nicely balanced and
structured and has a really very nice flow, and then there's the problem
of how to finish it, and the narrative does change gear.

In order to solve some of these problems she looked to the examples of other
writers. She immersed herself in French literature, reading, in addition to
Benjamin Constant, such authors as Balzac, Rousseau and Rétif de la Bretonne.
In April she made a list of other things she meant to read or reread while
working on the novel, including Nabokov ('for precision') and *Wuthering
Heights* ('for passion'). The result is perhaps Angela Carter's most classically
stylish work. It mixes long, plush sentences with short, austere ones, to create a beautifully textured prose. Lee's pupil Joanne falls in love with him:

An unhappy adolescent will clutch at any straw. Joanne, who was
dissatisfied, incorporated her schoolteacher in her own illusory web
where, quite unknown to himself and entirely without his consent,
he led a busy, active life of high adventure and almost continuous
sexual intercourse. She had never received much real affection. Her
mother was dead and her father an alcoholic. When she was a small
child, she found a wounded pigeon beside the railway line. Its breast
and leg were hurt. She nursed it until it grew better and exercised it
by allowing it to fly round and round her room. At first, as it learned
once more how to fly, it blundered about from mantelpiece to chest
of drawers like a raw beginner, bungling every movement, but soon
it gained confidence and swooped around beneath the ceiling with
the heavy grace of pigeons. It slept in the bottom of her wardrobe.
One night it escaped from her room and fluttered downstairs into the
kitchen where it sat on the plate rack of the gas stove, cooing, until
the sound irritated her father, who kicked it to death.

The way the paragraph moves from Joanne's imaginative freedom to the
pigeon's actual freedom, and its abrupt curtailment, suggests there won't
be much luck for any of them. On 19 May, Angela wrote to Carole: 'This
novel, as promised, remains in the French style but technically is turning
into a film de Alain Resnais . . . It's turning Gothic, of course.'

Revisiting *Love* in 1986 from 'the plump cheerfulness of middle-age',
Angela tried to force herself 'painfully back inside the skin of that thin,

unhappy young woman who wrote such a violent, anguished book about the savage landscape of the human heart'. She was a bit bewildered by it, and felt the need to set the record straight: 'I have nothing against love as such. Only against the kind of relationship it forces on people. Perhaps I should have called the novel "Marriage".'

It's a measure of how narrowly Angela Carter's writing has been pigeonholed – by her admirers and her detractors alike – that *Love* has generally been read as a fable of patriarchal oppression and feminist self-determination, with Annabel as the brothers' defiantly wayward victim. It's an interpretation that involves contorting the text into some painfully unnatural shapes, but that hasn't stopped a number of usually sensible critics embracing it. 'The heroine's refusal to grow up is clearly for Carter the most honest and telling thing about her,' writes Lorna Sage, who views the novel as a 'fairy tale of the perfect, suffering woman'. John Bayley complains that 'although [Carter] feels sorry for Buzz, she sticks . . . to the party line: instructing us that female bodies must not be treated as objects'. Katie Garner applauds the novel's efforts 'to provide Annabel with an empowering femininity', while Sue Roe argues the complete opposite – 'she has no femininity . . . she is Jung's emptied woman' – and declares that she kills herself 'because this ultimate embodiment of the primitive woman has no precedent in the male imagination; she dies, in artistic terms, partly because Carter's project for *Love* was to rewrite Benjamin Constant's *Adolphe* from the point of view of the female'. If that had been her project, then the novel would have been a bizarre and worrying failure, since it actually inhabits Lee's perspective much more often than it does Annabel's. But these readers seem to find it inconceivable that Angela Carter's sympathies could have resided with the male protagonist. They have invented a wholly synthetic author, unnaturally clear in her intentions and consistent in her outlook, and perfectly receptive to the praise or censure they want to aim at her.

She had imagined how it would be. In 1969, while she was work-ing on *Love*, Boston University (presumably roused by her receiving the John Llewellyn Rhys Prize) wrote offering to acquire her manuscripts. She 'dreamed a gaggle of Eng Lit students were dancing on my grave', an idea she found 'exquisitely satisfying and profoundly irritating'. Satisfying because she believed in what she was doing as a writer, enjoyed flattery, and would have liked to see her reputation grow. But irritating because she recognised the academy's tendency to suck the life out of books, to co-opt them into making points and taking stands. Years later, towards the end of her life, she wrote crabbily to an academic who had asked her to explain the imagery in one of her novels:

> I had no intention, when I first started being published, of writing illustrative textbooks of late feminist theory to be used in institutions of education and the thought that I'm taught in universities makes me feel rather miserable. I stopped enjoying museums when I realised they were places where beautiful things go when they die; I feel somewhat the same about literature departments.

It's a dismal irony that since her death her reputation has been so firmly interred within these scholarly sarcophagi. As late as 1982, there had been next to no academic interest in her books ('I once met someone who wanted to write a thesis on me, but they didn't after they talked to me,' she told the audience at a science-fiction conference). But every year since her death, dozens of papers have appeared with titles such as '"His Peremptory Prick": The Failure of the Phallic in Angela Carter's *The Passion of New Eve*' or 'The Violence of Gendering: castration images in Angela Carter's *The Magic Toyshop*'. She has been reduced to the status of a pamphleteer, a writer who created not art but argument.

She didn't always help herself: in a widely quoted interview, she told John Haffenden that her novels were often 'straightforwardly intellectual arguments'; in the *Omnibus* documentary she said that her characters have 'always got a tendency to be telling you something'. But she also said things like: 'I never know what a novel is about until I've finished it', and 'I write to ask questions, to argue with myself, not to provide answers'. These remarks have been more or less ignored by academic commentators, who tend to treat her as though she always wrote in the grip of an agenda.

To a reasonably impartial reader, the personality that emerges from her work bears no resemblance at all to the po-faced polemicist of her academic afterlife. As Jan Dalley wrote in a review of her posthumously published *Collected Stories*: 'it does Angela Carter no favours to credit her with this add-water-and-stir political correctness – she is a much spikier, more oblique and cussed, and indeed more flawed writer, as well as more truly original'. She was exorbitantly various, resistant to being absorbed into any movement or genre, perpetually trying on new roles and identities, both in her life and her work. 'I would regard myself as a feminist writer, because I'm a feminist in everything else and one can't compartmentalise these things,' she wrote, and several of her novels and stories do take the experience of women as a standout theme. But just as every action she performed wasn't a mimed commentary on gender inequality (she didn't cook feminist food or take feminist baths, though she was still a feminist while cooking and bathing), so her fiction can't be boiled down to a set of neat intellectual perspectives. Neat is the last thing she ever was or wanted to be.

In February 1969, Janice contacted Angela with an enticing proposal: an American producer called Leonard Field wanted to turn *The Magic Toyshop* into a 'low-budget film to be produced in England'. Angela stood to receive a figure 'in the neighbourhood of $25,000' for the option, plus ten per cent of the film's total budget if she agreed to write the script. This was potentially life-changing money, and she jumped at the opportunity.

Janice had been told that Field's 'background is in motion pictures and he has produced on Broadway', but that might have been putting it a bit grandly. His background in motion pictures appears to have been limited to inheriting a chain of cinemas in Iowa. He had produced a few Broadway plays, but most of them had closed after very short runs. During the war he had been in the Signal Corps with John Cheever, whose biographer, Blake Bailey, describes him as 'a not-very-successful theatre producer', and makes no mention of a film career. Nevertheless, he had the money to indulge his enthusiasms, and he put it where his mouth was; in addition to paying lavishly for the option (there is no record of what the amount finally agreed on was, but it was sufficiently generous for Angela to celebrate when she received it in September), he offered her $3,500 to write a 140-page script, with the guarantee of a further $1,500 in the event of the film being released.

Angela had never seen a film script before, let alone written one, so she asked him to send her some examples. In May she went to London to run over a few ideas with him and told Janice that they were 'getting along splendidly'. Back in Bristol, though, her enthusiasm waned. Writing a screenplay, she told Carole, was 'One Big Drag . . . I think it's partly the element of going backwards that distresses me, for *Magic Toyshop* was written three or four years ago and is full of such hideous infelicities I tremble to open it. It's just work, in fact, and terribly difficult to get down to.'

By mid-August she had managed to hammer out a first draft, but at eighty-six pages, it was much shorter than the script she had been contracted to write. She was informed that Field wasn't willing to pay her for it, since it didn't meet the terms they had agreed on: 'This does not mean that he is not pleased with what he has received (indeed, he feels that you have made an excellent beginning) but, rather, he would like you to do more work.' She diligently fleshed out a new draft, although she lacked any interest in the project by this stage. Not long afterwards she wrote that 'the film thing appears to be falling apart', and on 5 December she received word from Field that, although he still wanted to make the picture, it was too difficult working long-distance, and he hoped to find somebody in the United States to write the script instead. Angela was sanguine: 'I have been very handsomely paid for wasting my time . . . I'm really very pleased he doesn't want me to write any more scripts cos I've got other things to do, anyway.' The whole project soon fizzled out, and Angela seems to have more or less forgotten that it had ever happened. When she was approached by Granada Television to write a script for David Wheatley's film of The Magic Toyshop in 1985, she never mentioned that she had attempted to write one before.

Later that spring, on 26 March, she received the surprising (but very welcome) news that Several Perceptions was to be given the prestigious Somerset Maugham Award, worth £500. The rules, laid down by Maugham himself, stipulated that the money should be spent on foreign travel. Angela, who had never been further abroad than Ireland, wanted to visit Japan. Many of her acquaintances thought this idea was crazy. As Paul Barker wrote: 'it is hard now to appreciate how strange a decision [it] was. Japan was then simply a place that made cheap toys, imitation Western branded goods, and had done many horrible things in the war. No one knew anything about it.' In later life, Angela gave a variety of explanations for her decision, ranging from a desire to go somewhere that was untouched by Judaeo-Christian morality (but had decent food and drinkable water), through a love of Japanese cinema, to having been dared to go by a friend. Perhaps a combination of these things was responsible. She had always thought of it as a beautiful culture – her novels of the 1960s are studded with references to it – and she had recently read The Makioka Sisters by Junichiro Tanizaki, who she thought was 'one of the world's great novelists'.

Paul was keener on going to America, for the music. They agreed to spend a month or so travelling around the USA together; then, at the end of the summer, Paul would return home for the new academic term, and Angela would carry on alone to Tokyo, where she would spend six weeks, before going via Hong Kong to Bangkok (which she optimistically thought of as 'the Venice of the Orient'), rejoining him in Bristol when the prize money ran out. This plan raised a few eyebrows among their friends. Corinna's husband, Nick Gray, told Paul that if Angela went to Asia by herself, she wouldn't come back; but Paul crossly dismissed the warning.

He had some reason to feel secure: outwardly, Angela gave every impression of being committed to a future with him. On 15 July, only a fortnight before they were due to leave for America, they moved house, from the ground floor of number 38 to the fifth floor of number 27 Royal York Crescent. It was 'a typical Clifton move': their friends found it all a bit comic (the more so because the Carters employed a removals firm to help them shift their things a few doors down the road), but the new flat was bigger and lighter than the old one, with its own bathroom and a kitchen raised one floor above.

The 15th was a hot day – the temperature well into the thirties – midway through the sunniest spell the South-West had seen in a decade. The removal men soon became irritated with lugging musical instruments and crates of books up five flights of stairs. 'I think they particularly objected to carrying about on their heads things like 67 back numbers of "Rave" magazine and a dozen empty Keiller marmalade jars and pictures of pigeons, cats with kittens, etc.,' Angela wrote. 'We gave them beer and extra money and they kept suggesting perhaps we were planning on opening a library . . . Never in my life have I felt so alienated from the proletariat and I became grovelling and apologetic.' Martin Hoyle, who had the ground-floor flat at number 27, remembered coming home to find the hallway blocked by 'all these wretched men carrying furniture', and Angela among them, seeming to be agitated:

Angela had, I think, one of her slightly assumed naïve/neurotic moments: she seemed to be upset, and I said, 'What's the matter?' . . . she said: 'One of the removal men asked, "Where does this go?" and I said, "Put it in the junk room" and he said, "Which one is that?"' She professed she was upset by this, but I think it was just a joke.

She was probably more genuinely distressed than he realised. The move was bringing home to her both the stultifying nature of her life with Paul, and her own timidity in allowing it to continue. Packing up her things at 38 Royal York Crescent, she 'kept finding little bits of discarded selves . . . the flat was like a kind of sewer, a repository for these [nine] wasted years'.

The Carters flew to New York on 29 July. They arrived in the aftermath of the Stonewall riots, when the city was fractious and twitchy in the midsummer heat. A few weeks earlier, the first American troops had withdrawn from Vietnam (an outcome which Angela thought was 'in human terms . . . the single most glorious event since the abolition of slavery'), but in August the headlines were dominated by gun battles between Black Panthers and police, the bombing of the Marine Midland building on Broadway by a radical left-wing activist, and the gruesome murders perpetrated by the Manson family in Los Angeles and the Zodiac killer in San Francisco. Angela felt that the status quo 'couldn't hold on much longer. The war had been brought home.' She found Manhattan 'a very, very strange and disturbing and unpleasant and violent and ter-rifying place . . . The number of people who offered to do me violence was extraordinary.' The trip was the basis for the expressionist portrait of New York in *The Passion of New Eve* – it's depicted as a society in the last stages of moral and economic collapse – which she described as 'only a very slightly exaggerated picture, not of how it was in New York but of how it felt that summer'. She met one of the models for Tristessa – the novel's transvestite leading lady – in Max's Kansas City, the legendary nightclub in the East Village, where the house band was the Velvet Underground, and the clientele was composed largely of artists, writers and musicians, including such luminaries as Andy Warhol, William Burroughs and Patti Smith.

Angela and Paul spent three days in the city before travelling by Greyhound bus through Connecticut, Maryland, Virginia, Tennessee, Mississippi, Louisiana, Texas, New Mexico, Arizona and California. Angela wrote to Carole:

Riding the buses is weird, since one sees only the Other America – the poor people, spades, Mexies, mountain men & European tourists.

Everyone else is in a car or plane. Eating at bus station cafés in strange dawns, each station identifiable only by the differing postcards in the stand & the sugar lollipops labelled A Present from Knoxville . . . Or Phoenix or Memphis depending on the town. Black girls twisting their hair into spikes & applying the de-kinking fluid as the bus roars at 70mph through a Mississippi night, a fanfare of electrographics heralds another city.

The rush of the prose suggests something of the disorientation produced by visiting eleven states in just over a month. She hardly had time to process her impressions of one before moving on to the next. In New England they spent a few nights sleeping in a log cabin in a redwood forest. In Virginia they stayed with a Scottish weaver who 'brewed Typhoo tea while nibbling imported shortbread & sighing for black pudding as though it were the fruits of a lost Eden'. In Arizona ('the most beautiful, barren, wild place') they passed a Comanche village, and through the bus window Angela watched a young boy throwing stones at a wasted Chevrolet – 'the only glimpse I caught in all my travels in America of the vanishing American himself'. On the Berkeley campus of the University of California, 'saffron-robed figures sang and danced "Hare Krishna", to my exquisite embarrassment, and everywhere they advertised burgers – hamburgers, bullburgers, broil-erburgers, every kind of burger including Murphy's Irish Shamrockburger'. She thought that America was 'like a Godard movie, like all the Godard movies playing at once', but also 'a nation entirely without voluptuous-ness'. It was an ambivalence that stayed with her, though she returned to the country several times. At the very end of her life – having lived for periods in Texas, Iowa, Rhode Island and New York State – she wrote: 'I think of the United States with awe and sadness, that the country has never, ever quite reneged on the beautiful promise inscribed on the Statue of Liberty . . . and yet has fucked so much up.'

The only constant was her travelling companion. But Paul isn't men-tioned in either of the short pieces of journalism she wrote about the trip (for BBC Radio 3 and the *Author*), or in the journal entries she made while they were there, or even in her letters to Carole. It's an eloquent omission, as her later descriptions of the journey make clear. The narrator of 'The Quilt Maker' recalls travelling by bus around the USA, 'somewhere along my thirtieth year', in the company of 'a man who was then my husband'. At the bus station in Houston, Texas, she asks him for money ('he used to

carry about all our money for us because he did not trust me with it')
to buy a peach from a vending machine. There are two peaches available
in separate compartments of the machine, and she selects the smaller one;
he teases her about this instinctive self-denial. 'If the man who was then
my husband had not told me I was a fool to take the little peach,' she
says, 'then I would never have left him, for in truth, he was, in a manner
of speaking, always the little peach to me.'

Even so, she hadn't finally decided on leaving Paul when, on 3 September,
they boarded separate flights at San Francisco airport. It's clear from subsequent letters that they parted on good terms: there had been no dramatic
bust-up, and the plan was still for her to return to Bristol in late October.
Neither of them imagined that it would be their last moment together as
a married couple.

CHAPTER NINE

Vertigo

In an unpublished autobiographical fragment, written during the summer of 1971, Angela described her first glimpse of the city in which her life was transformed:

> I arrived by air, in the dark. When night descended over the ocean, many unfamiliar stars sprang out in the sky; as we approached land, there began to blossom below me such an irregular confusion of small lights it was difficult to be certain if the starry sky lay above or below me. So the aeroplane ascended or descended into an electric city where nothing was what it seemed at first and I was absolutely confused. I was seized with vertigo.

It's an expressionistic passage, but 'vertigo' sounds about right. This was the first time Angela had travelled alone, and the seething, neon-corrupted spectacle of Tokyo would have given even the most seasoned adventurer pause. It was the largest city on the planet, with a population hurtling towards 12 million: its bewildering traffic junctions and labyrinthine alleyways were choked with 'hordes of purposeful human beings', all of whom appeared to be occupied – buying things, selling things, building things – in 'a ceaseless controlled frenzy of industry'. But Angela was delighted to note that these perpetually bustling people tended to 'laugh and/or smile all the time, a strange thing among city dwellers'. And although she found Tokyo 'architecturally vile', she also thought it was a city of ubiquitous beauty: 'cups, saucers and plates are beautiful. Any paper parcel is beautiful. The faces around one are often beautiful.'

She described it as both a 'garish, bedizened, breathtakingly vulgar megalopolis', and 'one of the most truly civilised cities in the world'.

She had arrived at a liquid moment in its history: it was no longer the despoiled and traumatised capital of a defeated nation, nor yet the economic titan it was on its way to becoming. It jangled with the gaudy accessories of hypermodernity – vending machines on street corners; chewing-gum dispensers in the backs of taxis; neon signs at eye level and throbbing, dazzling electro-graphics overhead – but its infrastructure was only marginally ahead of the developing world. The sewers reeked, the air was thick with pollution, and rats darted incessantly from shadow to shadow. There were numerous tramlines, but only six subway lines, and one small airport. It was still essentially a low-rise town, just beginning to stir and stretch itself towards the heavens: the 500-foot Kasumigaseki building gave new shape to the horizon, and several more skyscrapers were under construction. Angela – coming from a declining economic power whose buildings were old and whose pride was suffering – was excited to be somewhere that had 'its history . . . before it rather than behind it or within it'.

'This is probably the most absolutely non-boring city in the world,' she wrote to Carole. As she came to understand its scrambled topography, she gravitated towards Shinjuku, and the pleasure district of Kabukicho, a lurid stretch of bars, dance halls, coffee houses and hostess clubs, haunted by artists and students, and anyone else who valued cheap entertainment and easy encounters with strangers ('kind of Greenwich Village' was how Angela explained it to friends in England). She began 'spending most of [her] time in coffee houses listening to modern jazz on the stereo'. They were good places to take refuge from the tumult of the city: 'if you order a cup of coffee, you can spend hours there chatting with someone, reading a book, writing a letter, or doing whatever you like'.

Her favourite coffee house was the Fugetsudo, a traditional wooden building spread across two floors and entered via a lanterned doorway off a narrow alley, with an atmosphere of 'hashish-dream somnolence'. It was a magnet for Western backpackers – many arrived there directly from the airport – and the preponderance of white women made it, in turn, a magnet for local men. 'Japanese men pursue European women,' Angela told an interviewer in 1972. 'One is the object of a quite incredible erotic curiosity, bordering on the hysterical. It is our size, our bigness, our fairness which drives them wild.' She enjoyed receiving their attentions, especially the younger ones: 'When they grow their hair long they look like the best kind of Red Indian, and nature often blesses them with very impressive cheekbones and passionately sensitive mouths,' she enthused. 'And they move very beautifully. Yes, indeed.' The experience of travelling alone – of successfully striking out by herself – had awakened her libido. She felt a 'nascent sense of independence . . . And I am, for the first time in my life, conscious of sexual frustration.'

To begin with, she seems to have been cautious about satisfying it. Early on in her stay, she reported meeting a Russian wrestler and going back to his hotel room, where he flung her on the bed. She made her excuses and left. 'I didn't want to sleep with him or I would have, right?' she asked Carole. 'Or was it my mother rising up in my heart to thwart my desires once again?' If it was, she soon subdued her. Shortly afterwards she met 'a middle-aged Brooklyn Jew', and spent a week with him at the Tokyo Station Hotel, an experience she described as 'my first adult sexual relationship'. The man in question was almost certainly Hal Burnell, a Brooklyn-based illustrator, who was forty-six in 1969 (not Jewish, though). More than thirty years later, he recalled meeting Angela 'in the Tokyo railroad station': 'this beautiful, red-haired woman was standing with her back against a wall. A face as red as her hair, totally lost. I'd been in Japan for quite some time, and recognising the situation, rescued her. We spent the week or so together before I continued on my way West.' The relationship wasn't significant enough to undo her attachment to Paul, but it did allow for a more insouciant attitude towards him. She decided to spend a year in Japan, regardless of his movements: 'if he wants to come with me, he can do so, & if he doesn't, not'.

One evening, towards the end of September, a twenty-four-year-old Japanese man approached Angela's table at the Fugetsudo. He was a couple of inches shorter than she was and neatly made, well dressed and graceful in his movements. He had a slight stammer, an easy smile, and a charming, not-quite-fluent style of speaking English. His skin, which was 'the colour of a brown paper parcel', was lightly scabbed with acne – the only real flaw in his photogenic good looks. An unpublished story describes the scene: '"Where are you from?" he asked her . . . "England," she said. "That must be terribly boring," he said & gave her the great international seducer's smile.'

His name was Sozo Araki. He had recently dropped out of a degree course in political science at Waseda University, with the intention of becoming a novelist; while he worked on his first book, he was scraping a living as a private tutor. They talked about Dostoevsky, Faulkner and Alan Sillitoe, and about the student protests that were convulsing the city that summer. But whatever intellectual pleasure they found in one another, the attraction between them was overwhelmingly physical. 'I thought she was like a Hollywood actress,' Sozo remembered. 'Like Katharine Hepburn.' Angela, for her part, found him 'incredibly beautiful'.

He took her to one of the many 'love hotels' – establishments whose hospitality is offered by the hour – that are scattered around even the most respectable districts of Tokyo. They range in style from the crudely functional to the weirdly luxurious; Angela, who was fascinated by them, described several in her journals, poetry and fiction during this period, including one with 'a mirror on the ceiling and lascivious black lace draped round a palpably illicit bed', and another with 'an authentic red light' and a 'passion machine, which relayed to us, in return for a 100 yen piece, the rising crescendo of a panting girl against a very tinny & quite unsuitable musical background – "the Blue Danube", I think, played at very high speed'. But the place Sozo took her to that evening is probably the one that features in 'A Souvenir of Japan', a story that makes use of her experience in an unusually direct way:

> We were shown into a room like a paper box. It contained nothing but a mattress spread on the floor. We lay down immediately and began to kiss one another. Then a maid soundlessly opened the sliding door and, stepping out of her slippers, crept in on stockinged feet, breathing apologies. She put a tray down on the matted floor beside us and backed, bowing and apologising, from the room whilst our uninterrupted kiss continued. He started to unfasten my shirt and then she came back again. This time, she carried an armful of towels. I was stripped stark naked when she returned for a third time to bring the receipt for his money. She was clearly a most respectable woman and, if she was embarrassed, she did not show it by a single word or gesture.

The next morning, while Sozo played *pachinko* (a Japanese version of pinball, to which he was more or less addicted), Angela went back to her hotel to shower and change. She remembered this moment in feverish detail: 'The maid . . . indicating to me so clearly in sign language: "Where were *you* last night?" that I blushed; at which she shrieked with laughter'.

She had arranged to meet Sozo at 11 a.m. in front of the Kinokuniya bookstore in Shinjuku. They went to a coffee house and had a breakfast of toast and boiled eggs, then walked to the Waseda University campus. After a while, they went to another love hotel near Takadanobaba station. The previous night, Angela had found the sex disappointing; this time it was revelatory, for both of them. Sozo retained a memory of Angela sitting up in bed afterwards, brushing her hair.

For the rest of her life, Angela looked back on this period as 'my First Real Affair'. Over the next few days she devoured all she could learn about Sozo. She described him as 'a romantic of the most extreme kind . . . [he] possesses extreme charm, an intellect all the more remarkable because it is absolutely analytic & incapable of any kind of synthesis, and a relentless conviction of the utter futility of everything'. His main enthusiasms were Elvis Presley and *pachinko*; he also shared Angela's love of Dostoevsky. She nicknamed him Alyosha (after the cheerful youngest sibling in *The Brothers Karamazov*), while he called her Myshkin (after the love-torn hero of *The Idiot*). She was, for the first time in years, utterly absorbed in the present. Paul was 'like a figure through the wrong end of a telescope'. It dawned on her that this sense of immediacy and agency was exactly what she had been looking for, a realisation that made her feel 'like a character in a cheap novel'.

The speed with which she fell in love with Sozo does have a somewhat novelettish quality. From the day they met, they had little more than a fortnight together before she was due to leave Japan: during that time she visited both Nara and Kyoto (she thought that the latter city was 'very like Bristol' and even located 'the Kyoto version of the Berkeley'), so they can't have spent more than twelve full days in one another's company. They slept with each other only nine or ten times, she told Carole. It was a remarkably short acquaintance on which to base important decisions about the future. But her attraction to Sozo had become tangled with her new sense of freedom. Looking back on the early days of their relationship a couple of years later, she accepted this point of view:

> His face did not, when I first met him, seem to me the face of a stranger; it seemed a face long known & well remembered, a face that had always been somehow imminent in my consciousness as an idea that now found a perfect visual expression . . . plainly, he was an object created in the mode of fantasy; his image was already present somewhere in my head, & I was seeking to discover him in reality, searching every face for the right face – that is, the face that corresponded to my notions of the imagined face of the one I should love.

As her departure drew near she made up her mind to leave Paul. She accepted a job in Tokyo 'with a drunken Irishman in a school teaching businessmen English'. This sounded 'a bit like death', but she thought it was preferable to teaching in a girls' school, and she needed a working visa if she was to be allowed back into Japan. 'I do feel a bit scared,' she wrote: 'I feel like I was 19 again, only grown-up, this time.' Her flight to Hong Kong was booked for 15 October. At the airport she cried, and promised Sozo that she would return; then, in a final, private gesture of extravagant symbolism, she took off her wedding ring and left it in an ashtray in the departure lounge.

She spent five days in Hong Kong, where she was mainly occupied with consolidating the decisions she had made in Tokyo. She wrote to Carole, explaining what had happened: 'I fell in love & realised that Paul is a selfish pig, lousy in bed & shockingly insensitive. It took me a while to get over feeling sorry for him but, in some respects, he's a monster, & I don't want to see him again, ever. And I expect I shall be quite shockingly cruel when it comes to it.' That last sentence was sheer bravado: she also wrote to Edward Horesh and Corinna Gray, asking them to keep an eye on him. Then she wrote to Paul himself: it must have been a horrible letter to compose, and though it hasn't survived, it's safe to assume that she wasn't gratuitously cruel. Next she wrote to Janice, saying that all her mail should be forwarded to her agent, Irene Josephy, from now on. She also wrote – either in a spirit of dismissing her last great infatuation, or because he was one of the few people who understood what she had gone through with Paul – to John Orsborn:

> I plan to go back to Japan to live & I do not intend to live in Bristol, or with Paul, any more. I'm telling you this, partly because I think you'll be interested, partly because the letter I wrote him instructing him of my intentions will be plopping through his post box about now & he might need some help in accepting it. I can't live with him any more or I'll kill myself & that's that & I don't much care what happens to him, though I feel I ought to; nevertheless, if you could keep an eye on him . . . well, it might help.

Finally, she wrote to Sozo, reaffirming the promises she had made him, and enclosing a copy of The Magic Toyshop, which she had found in a Hong Kong bookshop (she had searched in vain for one of her books to give him in Tokyo).

What she saw of Hong Kong itself, with its jumble of Chinese and British influences, produced in her an 'unwilling respect' for her compatriots:

> the British talent for seedy compromise is really a splendid thing – this filthy, squalid, messy city is not a relic of colonialism any more but a huge, corrupt & really rather hopeful indication that our race will be able to survive, in however shabby a way. This cheers me up as I've become very conscious here of being a European, being white & coming from a part of the world whose history is almost over. In Japan, to say I came from England was like saying I came from Atlantis, or that I was a unicorn.

From Hong Kong she travelled to Bangkok, where she spent the last four days of her journey. Perhaps her response to the city was the product of exhaustion, but she found it a squalid and degraded place: 'truly,' she wrote to Carole, 'everything the Americans touch they turn into a gigantic brothel, & this spoiled paradise is rather distressing. It isn't really safe for a white woman to walk alone.' Even so, she must have gone out a bit while she was there, since she later reported having gone to bed with a French soldier who had served in the Algerian War. But she appears to have spent most of her time reading Borges, and was 'bowled over by the extraordinary possibilities those new methods of organization opened up'. Her excitement at his work, combined with the experience of having seen more than ten cities in the past three months, reinvigorated her, and she made a plan for a new novel, which would take the form of 'an inventory of imaginary cities'. This idea would eventually – through a series of gradual refinements – become *The Infernal Desire Machines of Dr Hoffman*.

Angela's plane touched down at Heathrow early in the morning of 25 October. In Tokyo and Hong Kong, far from the judgements of family and friends, it had been relatively easy to place her future in the care of her emotions; now she had to face the consequences. She knew that Bristol would be 'too hot to hold me'. But she was even more anxious of facing her parents. Olive viewed divorce as a shameful moral failing, a dreadful stain on a man's or (especially) a woman's character. Perhaps this was one of the reasons why Angela had stayed with Paul for so long: she knew that leaving him would provoke a fresh crisis in her relationship with her mother. She wrote to Carole asking if she could come and live with her in Bradford for 'three months or so'; in the meantime she stayed with Rebecca Howard at her house on Child Street, in the down-at-heel, essentially transient west London district of Earls Court.

In this prosaic setting, she became uncomfortably aware of 'how much, not so much of self-deceit but of sleight of hand, went into the effortful creation of the idea of myself in love'. The things she had felt in Japan seemed fanciful now, and the tangible evidence of the affair was not the stuff of fairy-tale romance: she had picked up a sexually transmitted infection, perhaps from Sozo, perhaps from the Frenchman she had slept with in Bangkok; either way, it was 'a bad introduction to the permissive society'. She also suspected that she was pregnant, although she recognised that this notion was 'irrational and . . . really, I suppose, a last-ditch stand of my unconscious in my hopeless attempt to crash the culture barrier'.

Crashing the culture barrier was important if she was to hold her nerve. Believing herself in love had given her the courage to take charge of her life, but now that she doubted the emotion, she couldn't allow her sense of liberation to falter. Shortly after she arrived in London she wrote Sozo a letter, in which she made 'an interesting Freudian slip':

> In the way one does in the first treacherous flush, I wrote: 'I feel I belong to you.' When I read it back, however, I realised I had, in fact, written: 'I feel I belong to me.' So I tore the letter up, because I felt I had suddenly defined my existential position and though I shall be very hurt if he forgets me, that is really his problem & nothing to do with me.

* * *

Angela's sense of independence was soon coming under sustained pressure. Paul bombarded her with letters and phone calls at Child Street: 'he alternately blusters and cajoles, & informs me I am not to use his name in future if I don't return to him', she told Carole. His tactics ranged from telling her that the trip was 'an adventure' from which she would soon come down, through embarking on a new relationship of his own and feeding her the details in a clumsy attempt at making her jealous, to changing the locks on their flat – a move which Angela thought was 'the contemporary equivalent of putting a notice in the "The Times" saying one will not be responsible for one's wife's/husband's debts'. Responding to her assessment of the problems in their marriage, he wrote: 'it's no good saying I never heard you talking about your unhappiness, I get the feeling you didn't really want to talk about it', and: 'The communication barrier is easy enough to break through, with a little understanding.' These remarks made her furious, and she developed an 'icy cruelty' in her dealings with him: 'he's plainly in a bad way but I find I don't care', she told Carole (to whom she also forwarded his letters): 'I never want to see the pig again.' She told him she was returning to Japan immediately, but in fact she was having trouble with her visa application, the job teaching English to businessmen having fallen through, and she planned to lie low in Bradford until it was resolved.

It's striking how vigorously she stoked her contempt for Paul during these weeks, and how ruthless she became. Perhaps the effort was psychologically necessary ('a free woman in an unfree society will be a monster', she wrote ten years later in *The Sadeian Woman*). If she'd allowed herself to feel sorry for him, even for a moment, her courage might easily have faltered. Martin Hoyle saw him shortly after he'd received her letter from Hong Kong:

> I met him that morning, and I've always remembered this, because his eyes were red. I was walking back towards the Crescent and he was emerging from it, and he said: 'Angela's left me. She's sent me a letter saying "Thank you for nine years of marriage, I'm not coming back."' He took it very, very, very badly. I had to go and talk to him for a long time because he couldn't sleep at night. He'd occasionally come down and chat to me or just sit there . . . He was shattered.

His feelings don't seem to have healed entirely with the passage of time. When, more than forty years later, I wrote to him asking if he'd be willing to talk about his life with Angela, I received a polite but very firm refusal: 'I have no wish at all to trawl through that part of my past . . . Please do not bother to contact me again.'

Against this turbulent personal background, *Heroes and Villains* was published in November. The novel had risked alienating Angela's admirers, but almost all of the reviews approved of the new direction her work was taking. In *The Times*, Judith Frankel praised it as 'a remarkable step into the darkness', observing that the sinister mood of *Shadow Dance* and *The Magic Toyshop* had become 'out-and-out, no-bones-about-it Gothic' in the new book. 'Angela Carter's is an altogether original talent,' she declared. Even those reviewers who weren't quite so enthusiastic found plenty to admire in *Heroes and Villains*. Jane Miller, writing anonymously in the *Times Literary Supplement*, agreed that it was 'richly imagined, never whimsical and extraordinarily believable', but felt that it was let down by 'occasional pretentiousness' in the later chapters, after Marianne joins the Barbarian tribe. This cavil didn't stop her from describing it as 'in many ways a remarkably effective novel.'

It was a strong reception, but Angela hardly noticed: 'I find I am not particularly interested in my reviews this time though that vague feeling of anti-climax when one of my books comes out & nobody takes a blind bit of notice hasn't done my sense of being much good'. By 'nobody', she meant her publishers. They didn't throw her a launch party, and she wasn't required to give any interviews this time round. Janice asked her out for a drink, which was 'as far as Heinemann would go in the feting stakes'.

Manningham is an attractive Victorian suburb about a mile north of Bradford city centre, its gently sloping terraces, stately civic buildings and colossal spiring mills tending to be wrought from a soft, honey-coloured stone (though when Angela arrived there, long before the clean-ups of the 1990s, they were mostly black with soot). To a modern visitor, the elegant period architecture can come as a surprise: in recent decades the area has shouldered a reputation as a tinderbox of racial division and economic decline. It's probably best known for the riots that flared briefly but devastatingly in 1995 and again in 2001, as sections of the overwhelmingly Muslim population faced off against far-right agitators and the police. But in 1969 it was home to a flourishing and genuinely multicultural community: large numbers of immigrants had lived there since the late nineteenth century – German Jews, Hungarians, Italians and Poles, as well as the more recent arrivals from India and Pakistan – all drawn by the promise of comfortable housing and plentiful jobs in the textile industry. Angela delighted in the strange juxtapositions afforded by the ethnic mix: 'vodka in the windows of the off-licences, next to the British sherry, brown ale and dandelion and burdock', and 'signs everywhere in Urdu' in a landscape dominated by weeping gas lamps, belching chimneys, and statues of stern Victorian industrialists.

Carole and John lived on Athol Road, a long row of two-up, two-down houses huddled under the massive shadow of Lister's Mill, the largest silk factory in the world. Angela moved all her possessions into the spare room, having moved them out of Royal York Crescent while Paul was at work. On

28 November she wrote to Janice that she was 'installed happily . . . with books, typewriter, big coal fire & part shares in the family cat, which is nice'. During the day she worked on *Love*, which she had barely touched since she left for America four months earlier. John – who was doing a master's degree at the University of Leeds, and therefore spent more time in the house than Carole did – had a chance to observe Angela's working habits: 'She did not find writing novels easy,' was the opinion he formed. 'I mean, the number of cigarette packets she got through . . . She settled down straightaway in the morning to try and get a full day in, and it was horrendous, you'd be treading on eggshells.' She was also very reluctant to go out: 'She had this mad idea that she might bump into someone and it would get back to Paul that she hadn't yet gone to Japan. I think probably, like many people would be in that situation, she was a bit worried that if she saw him too soon he would persuade her to come back and she would agree.'

When Carole and John did coax her out of the house it was usually to see something at the Bradford Playhouse or the Leeds Film Theatre, or to visit an art gallery. Occasionally they went to either of two local pubs, the Upper Globe or the Lower Globe, but Angela 'wasn't that big on going out to pubs'. Partly, John felt, because social situations stoked her insecurities:

> We'd be going to do something, like go to a gallery or something, we wouldn't stay long, we might call for a drink on the way back. So Angela would appear in jeans and sweater, a typical folk-music look – and then suddenly she'd vanish again, and she'd re-emerge in this tiny little short skirt and fishnet stockings, and a flower in her hair . . . I think Angela had various devices to deal with her self-consciousness, and of course they mostly didn't work. They mostly drew attention to her weirdnesses.

She was, however, a generous and solicitous housemate. Often, if John had been out, she would have found a passage in a book to interest him when he returned. After a while, left by themselves for most of each day, they began sleeping together. Carole was aware of this development from the start, and both she and John insisted that it wasn't a problem: theirs was an open relationship, and both of them saw other people. Nevertheless, Angela evidently felt guilty about it, and a few months later she wrote to Carole apologising for 'my maladroit handling of the pre-Christmas thing I briefly had with him'. From John's perspective, there was a different problem: 'As soon as we started to have sex, Angela . . . disappeared.' He meant that she retreated into herself. 'It was very disturbing,' he recalled:

> I think if you feel a great affection for someone, and it's accompanied by sexual desire . . . I think we all tend to expect that if it's going to work sexually, its going to lead to even greater closeness, because you're sharing something quite special. It doesn't have to be monogamous, but just because it's not monogamous doesn't mean it's not special. But as soon as we started, it was like, 'Where are you?'

When he ended the sexual side of their relationship, saying that he thought they were incompatible in that respect, Angela responded angrily, claiming that Carole had turned him against her. It was, John thought, an 'absolutely outrageous' allegation: Carole had been nothing but supportive, both through the long saga of Angela's unhappy marriage, and the tawdry melodrama of its dissolution. But Angela was once again casting herself in the role of femme fatale. In her journal she wrote: 'I suppose I feel that everything I have is up for sale; my most secret & perverse desires, the things I love & I am not responsible for the fact that I might betray anybody at any time.' This was her new conception of herself: no longer a passive and frustrated wife, but fickle, greedy, unrepressed, the kind of woman who abandoned her husband with as little grief as she might crush out a cigarette. Almost ten years later, in a piece for *New Society*, she argued that 'the significance of the femme fatale lies not in her gender but in her freedom'.

The narrative Angela was constructing for herself was about to take an unpleasant twist. She had avoided seeing her parents since she'd been back in England, but shortly before Christmas she received distressing news: Olive had collapsed and been rushed to hospital, where she was found to have suffered a massive pulmonary embolism, a direct result of the vascular heart disease that had blighted her health for years. Angela went with her brother Hughie and his wife Joan to St James's Hospital in Balham, but Olive took one look at her and turned to face the wall. If she had struggled to accept Angela's marriage in the first place, she would never forgive her for walking out on it. She died on 20 December, having cut her daughter out of her will.

The distance that Angela had fought so hard to establish between them was now infinite, impossible to bridge. The timing of Olive's death can only have exacerbated this feeling. It was a horribly literal manifestation of the thing Angela had always feared: that striking out for herself would leave her with nobody to fall back on; that her only choice was between engulfment and abandonment. It's clear from the distortions and omissions that perforate the accounts she gave to friends how badly she wished that things had happened differently. A few months later she wrote to Carole about a 'sideboard my mother practically begged me to recover [from Paul] with her dying breath'. She doesn't seem to have ever spoken about the way things really ended between them.

It was a 'memorably ghastly' winter. She moved back into Ravenslea Road to keep her father company, and sat in the kitchen trying to write while he – who had 'suddenly got old & rather frail' – came in and made cups of instant coffee and constantly readjusted the table lamp. The house seemed strange: she hadn't lived there in a decade, and now it was eerily depleted. But she was horrified, nonetheless, when Hugh announced that he was going to sell it and move back to Scotland. For the rest of her life, Angela associated the loss of her childhood home with the loss of her mother (asked in a late interview about the lack of mothers in her work, she explained that in her imaginative topography, houses stood for mothers).

She was utterly disorientated. In a letter to Carole she related a strange incident: walking home one afternoon, absorbed in her thoughts, she stepped out in front of a lorry; it squealed to a halt only a few inches from her. She started laughing. The driver, presumably in a state of shock, remonstrated with her. 'Afterwards, I really thought, "How can I tell I haven't been killed?"'

The only thing was to focus on her return to Tokyo. She took Japanese lessons with 'a nice young girl' whose father had been a professor of medicine at Tokyo University, and immersed herself in the bureaucracy of obtaining a visa, booking flights, and putting her affairs in order. She went to endless meetings with her publishers, her accountant, and the Japanese Embassy. By 19 March she had obtained permission to stay for a year in Japan engaged in 'cultural activities', and she booked a flight for 19 April. She spent a good deal of time at the dentist: her teeth were in 'a deplorable state', and she looked forward to being able to smile without showing them. All this activity distracted her, but as the date of her departure neared she recalled the vertiginous mood of her first glimpse of Tokyo. She opened a Japanese bank account; when she was given the address, she went home and was sick from nerves. Her hand was unsteady when, at the start of 1970, she wrote in her journal:

> I feel so strange. No home. Nothing familiar, any more. I feel quite empty, like a husk with the kernel gone, quite lacking in energy & prey to vague fears. My stomach feels all twisted up with nerves; I'm not precisely unhappy, only a little scared & apprehensive, I suppose, like the newborn wanting to retreat back to the womb, knowing it is impossible & knowing there is no womb-surrogate anywhere, now.

Angela Carter's paternal grandfather, William Stalker, outside the Stalker shop in Macduff

Angela's parents, Hugh Stalker and Olive
Farthing, on their wedding day, 20 August 1927

Hugh and Olive with baby Hughie, 1929

A matriarchal clan: Jane Farthing (centre) with her daughters Kitty (left) and Olive (right) standing behind her. Angela Carter's final novel, *Wise Children*, is in part a tribute to these three women

Angela in 1946, outside the Knowles Hotel, Macduff

'A dream cathedral': the Granada cinema, Tooting, where Angela spent many enchanted evenings with her father

Hughie Stalker and Joan Smalley on their wedding day, 2 January 1954. Angela is second from the left, beside her parents, looking much younger than her almost fourteen years

'Tubs' at school: Angela (centre) in 1956

Angela in the early 1960s; she thought she looked 'like a Russian female all-in wrestler'

Top: Royal York Crescent, Clifton, Bristol, where Angela lived from 1961 until 1969

Left: Angela and Paul Carter on their wedding day, 10 September 1960

Below: Angela and Paul, early 1960s. In later years she spoke dismissively about their relationship, but it's clear from her journals that in the beginning they were very much in love

Shadow Dance
by Angela Carter

I've read this book
with admiration, horror, and
other relevant emotions, including
gratitude that we seem to have here
a very distinctive talent that's going to be a major one.
Angela Carter has remarkable descriptive gifts,
a powerful imagination and
—what I admire and envy more than anything—a
capacity for looking at the mess of contemporary
life totally without flinching.

Anthony Burgess

new worlds
Speculative Fiction   July 1967   3s.6d.

Thomas M. Disch: Camp Concentration
Ballard · Aldiss · MacBeth · Zelazny

Top left: First edition of
Shadow Dance (1966)

Top right: *New Worlds*
magazine, which Angela
read with excitement in
the mid-1960s, and which
sent shockwaves through
her own fiction

Right: Anthony Burgess,
Angela Carter's first great
champion, and one of the
contemporary authors
she most admired

Inventing a look: (clockwise from top left) author photos for *The Magic Toyshop* (1967) in folk music mode; *Several Perceptions* (1968), with trademark black floppy hat; and *Heroes and Villains* (1969), with 'reasonably suave Jimi Hendrix cut'

Angela Carter, John Lockwood and Carole Roffe, 1969. 'Our friendship is one of the great central relationships of my life,' Angela told Carole, and their correspondence sustained her through some difficult times in Japan

'The most absolutely non-boring city in the world': Tokyo, late 1960s

Fishermen on Kujukuri beach, where Angela wrote *The Infernal Desire Machines of Dr Hoffman* in the winter of 1970–1

Angela in 1972, shortly after she returned from Japan

PART II

CHAPTER TEN

The dressing-up box of the heart

On 19 April 1970 – an unseasonably cold and gloomy day – Sozo Araki stood in the arrivals hall of Haneda airport, his legs shaking uncontrollably. He had never expected Angela to honour her promise to return to him. As he scanned the tired faces coming down the escalator from passport control, he felt he had drifted scarily out of his depth. When Angela finally appeared, she looked (as he later recalled) every bit as apprehensive as he was, and much older than he remembered. Catching sight of him, she mustered 'an awkward, forced smile'.

The awkwardness persisted during the taxi ride to their hotel. Even in the six months that Angela had been away, Tokyo had changed dramatically – skyscrapers sprouting all along the horizon, familiar landmarks bulldozed and replaced – and as she looked out of the car window she found it hard to get her bearings. The city, she came to feel, was 'a living image of impermanence', its weirdly mutable landscape provoking 'an uneasy suspicion that nothing is real'. But perhaps the strangest thing of all was her presence there. To travel more than halfway round the world for the sake of a man she had known for less than a fortnight (and that six months ago) was an act of audacity that teetered on the edge of lunacy. They were, she realised, strangers. Making it work was going to require all her reserves of romanticism, imagination and will.

Almost as soon as they reached their hotel room, they undressed and went to bed: Angela told Carole that they didn't emerge until 4.30 p.m. the following day. Shortly afterwards, she wrote in her journal: 'sustained by passion only, we walk the tightrope of desire and acrobatically perform the double somersault of love without a safety net'. It's the first appearance of a phrase that evidently meant a lot to her, variations of it occurring in 'A Souvenir of Japan', in her poem 'Only Lovers', and in an early draft of her story 'Flesh and the Mirror' (all three of which are based directly on her relationship with Sozo), as well as in *The Infernal Desire Machines of Dr Hoffman* (which is drawn from the relationship in a rather less direct way), and in *Nights at the Circus*. The line, with its explicit association between love and performance, seems to suggest the mechanism of what she had previously called 'the effortful creation of the idea of myself in love'. At the end of the two years she spent living in Tokyo she wrote that she had 'taken certain ideas (like living for love) as far as they will go'. Again, it's a striking way of putting it – as if her grand act of passion was primarily an intellectual exercise.

It hadn't occurred to Sozo that he and Angela would move in together when she returned to Tokyo, but she had assumed that they would, and he was swept along on the current of her fantasy. On the morning of Wednesday 22nd they began looking for a place to rent. Neither of them anticipated it being a difficult process, but they hadn't counted on the thoroughgoing bigotry of Japanese culture at the beginning of the 1970s. They went to a lettings agency near their hotel: the old man behind the desk took one look at Angela and brusquely told Sozo that he didn't accept foreigners as tenants. By the end of the day it had become a familiar refrain. They traipsed from one agency to the next – they posed as fiancées, cousins, business associates – but the result was always the same. That evening, Angela wrote, 'Sozo began to cry, quietly, and said he'd never realised what cunts his fellow-countrymen were.'

The obvious solution was for Angela to let Sozo handle the arrangements on his own, without revealing to the agents that he'd be living with a European woman. But she was adamant that she wasn't going to cede her independence to him in any respect: 'I <u>didn't</u> want to move into a flat with him in entire control of the situation,' she told Carole. 'I suppose I feel that if I lived in someone else's house again, the prison doors would clank to behind me.' So the following day she contacted the British Council, and was put in touch with an agency that specialised in finding accommodation for foreigners. On the Friday morning they were shown a flat in Meguro, a respectable residential area, where the views were of row upon row of shingle rooftops, patches of well-tended foliage, and lines of clean washing rippling in the wind. They were a ¥60 train ride in one direction from the

Marunouchi business district, with its morning crowds of harried commuters, and a ¥60 train ride in the other direction from Shinjuku, with its evening crowds of festive drinkers; but in Meguro itself, Angela wrote, 'it always seems to be Sunday afternoon . . . It is difficult to find a boring part of Tokyo but, by God, I have done it.'

The flat was on the ground floor of a two-storey house about halfway down a sloping alley; the main room had a floor made up of six tatami mats (a single mat being roughly the size of an adult Japanese lying down). Once they had installed a mattress measuring 'about two foot six by five foot ten', and a low table that they bought in an antiques shop, there wasn't much room for anything else. The bathroom and kitchen were each about half the size of the bedroom. But in spite of how cramped it was, the rent was steep by British standards – ¥38,000 (the equivalent of about £40) per month – and since Sozo earned considerably less than her, Angela anticipated having to cover the bulk of it. 'I'm going to have to support him,' she wrote to Carole. 'It will be a great test of his character to see how he responds.'

They moved in on 29 April. Because it was the emperor's birthday, the local children were all home from school. Angela described the scene in an essay for *New Society*:

> They were playing 'catch' around the back of the house and a little boy came to hide in the embrasure of the window. He glanced round and caught sight of me. He did not register shock but he vanished immediately. Then there was a silence and, shortly afterwards, a soft thunder of tiny footsteps. They groped round the windows, invisible, peering, and a rustle rose up, like the dry murmur of dead leaves in the wind, the rustle of innumerable small voices murmuring the word: 'Gaijin, gaijin, gaijin' (foreigner), in pure, repressed surprise.

It occurred to her that she was 'the first coloured family in this street'. The phrase carries a heavy consignment of irony, but that doesn't mean she found the situation comfortable. It was 'a painful and enlightening experience to be regarded as a coloured person . . . to be defined as Caucasian before I was defined as a woman'. Over the weeks that followed the children tormented her, booby-trapping the front door with cans of Fanta so that they spilled all over her when she opened it, and stuffing mounds of earth into the letter box. 'When they put shit in it,' she resolved, 'I shall move.'

*   *   *

They settled into a mildly dissolute routine, rising around midday to boil eggs in the kettle, sitting on the floor to eat them using chopsticks, then getting back into bed to read and make love and doze a while longer. Tokyo soon began to feel like Earls Court. They divided the shopping, cooking and cleaning between them. Twice a week, Sozo visited his bedridden sister-in-law on the other side of Meguro to cook and clean for her, and to take her children (his nephews) to the park; he tutored most afternoons. While he was gone, Angela went to the Fugetsudo coffee house, where she wrote letters to her friends in England and chatted to other foreigners; on her way home she often stopped at the supermarket, where she would scour the shelves for cans with English words, or pictures, on the labels. Her life at Royal York Crescent seemed a long time ago.

During those first few months of the relationship, she thought of Sozo as the living opposite of Paul. He was, for a start, 'very happy & very funny', given to cracking puerile jokes and playing the fool. And though he wasn't free from neuroses, he didn't appear to regard them as her responsibility. 'He shows no signs of dependence on me at all,' she wrote, with palpable relief. She felt that he was (again in contrast to Paul) her intellectual equal, and psychologically very similar to her: an intense romantic, given to bouts of extreme melancholy, but not real depression. He was also given to grand demonstrations of passion, and often (jokingly, Angela tended to think) suggested that they should contrive a love suicide. 'The most interesting and the most disturbing thing about this relationship is, he is exactly like me,' she wrote. They spent hours on end talking to one another, and she found a 'peculiar anguish' in knowing that, while Paul had understood every word she said, 'but had no grasp of the ideas underneath the words', Sozo could have grasped every idea, if only he'd had a better command of the language.

She could see that some of this was wishful thinking: that by concentrating on the ways in which Sozo was similar to her and different from Paul, she wasn't looking directly at him. 'I knew him as intimately as I knew my own image in a mirror,' she wrote of the character based on him in 'A Souvenir of Japan'. 'In other words, I knew him only in relation to myself . . . At times, I thought I was inventing him as I went along.'

Nor was she altogether blind to his defects, even in those early days: 'I am both absolutely in love with him, so that he seems the only real thing in the world, and irritated beyond measure by his unpunctuality, his vagueness, his (yes) absent-mindedness and a curious capacity for seeming to be lying when he is, in fact, telling the truth.' She found him unconscionably lazy (he spent far too much time, she thought, adopting 'Gauginesque poses' on the mattress and playing *pachinko*) as well as 'radiantly unreliable' (though only in some respects: 'I can rely on [him] absolutely for sex, tenderness, consideration and a constant attempt at – interpretation, perhaps, rather than understanding'). He was also very proud, a quality which struck her as almost comically Japanese. He attached a great deal of pride to his writing, and she felt that he wouldn't stay with her for long unless he published something, and could regard himself as her equal in that respect. Then again, she worried that *she* wouldn't cope very well if he turned out to be a genius: 'because he's not published anything, I tend not to take the pile [of manuscripts] in the cupboard seriously', she confessed. 'But, of course, I hadn't published anything when I was 24 and he does manifest most of the symptoms of an actual writer – in particular, a serene dissociation from the consequences of his fantasies . . . and a tendency towards self-dramatisation.'

Sozo was determined to prove his usefulness to Angela, and early on in their relationship, he attempted to teach her Japanese when he returned from tutoring in the early evening. It wasn't a success: there were only 'five or six lessons max' before she gave up. When she had been living in Tokyo for three months, she still knew no Japanese, except for 'Welcome, Mr Cat', with which she greeted the two-tailed Siamese that lived next door. She was pretty ashamed, Sozo thought, of her failure in this respect; but she told Carole that she liked the fact that Sozo didn't put any pressure on her to learn the language, and elsewhere she wrote that not speaking Japanese, and so having to interpret the culture entirely through its visual aspect, was an invaluable 'apprenticeship in the language of signs'.

In the evenings, Sozo took the train to Shinjuku to go drinking with his friends, and at first Angela went with him. But his friends were all men – 'I am a bit like a phoenix or a unicorn,' Angela wrote – and none of them spoke much English. Sozo felt that 'English was necessary for her to enjoy life':

> Her problem with talking to foreigners was that she refused to talk to them like a kindergarten nurse. She talked to everybody like she talked to her friends in England. She never changed her pronunciation, or spoke in simpler sentences. She always tried to express herself as fully as possible.

She was also entirely honest about her responses to people, which meant that 'she had a lot of small arguments with everybody': 'when she couldn't agree with somebody she wouldn't hide her feelings, she would say: "That is the stupidest thing I've ever heard."' Sozo says that his friends liked her, but found her intimidating ('Angela doesn't like stupid boys like us,' one of them told him). When, after only a few weeks, he started going out by himself in the evenings, Angela put it down to a cultural difference. 'On the other hand,' she mused, 'if a Clifton bloke shacked up with a Japanese girl who couldn't speak a word of English, she wouldn't half cast a blight on the interaction in the Greyhound.'

She spent the night of her thirtieth birthday as she spent many others during this period, sitting up alone in the apartment, waiting for and worrying about Sozo. She felt certain that he was seeing other women, but claimed that this wasn't what bothered her: 'I just wish I knew when he was coming home, that's all.' It often wasn't until 5 a.m., when the trains started up again. She was sometimes angry with him when he returned, but she disliked herself for adopting this possessive role – 'tinkering with another person's autonomy is rather a dreadful thing' – and the truth was that she had begun to love having the night-time to herself, using it to work in, watching the sky getting gradually lighter and listening to the dawn chorus. The routine she established during these months – writing all night, then sleeping for half the day – was one she returned to, when circumstances allowed, for the rest of her life.

Sozo doesn't remember Angela writing anything during the period they were living together in Tokyo. He says that she spent her time 'reading and chatting . . . she loved to talk all the time'. His perspective is inevitably blinkered – she tended to work at night, when he was out – but his impression that she wasn't writing suggests how much more relaxed about it she had become. Shortly after she returned to England in 1972, she told an interviewer that her psychological compulsion to write had faded when she left her marriage, and the evidence bears this out: she wrote seven novels (including two lost early ones) during less than a decade married to Paul Carter; in the remaining twenty-two years of her life, she wrote only four. The comparison isn't entirely scientific: she increased her production of short stories, journalism and drama during the latter period, as well as writing a book-length essay. But after 1970 she wrote very little poetry, and overall there was a definite dip in her productivity.

At first, she blamed the downturn on her immediate surroundings: 'I can't work in this fucking flat because there is no other room to get up & walk to.' She did, however, complete three short stories while living there – 'The Executioner's Beautiful Daughter', written between May and July, 'A Souvenir of Japan', written between August and September, and 'The Loves of Lady Purple', written between September and December – all of which ended up in *Fireworks*. 'I started to write short pieces when I was living in a room too small to write a novel in,' she claimed in the book's afterword – a bit disingenuously, since she had in fact been writing stories since her early twenties. But the ones she wrote in Japan were light years ahead of her earlier efforts in the form. Exhibiting the influence of Borges, they dispense almost entirely with such conventional trappings as character and plot, focussing their energies instead on the swift creation of an atmospheric world – a glacial mountain kingdom, an expressionistic version of Tokyo, a darkly enchanted fairground – and compelling attention via the play of language and ideas. She told an interviewer that 'The Excecutioner's Beautiful Daughter' had its roots in 'a conversation I had with a bloke I met in a café about static and kinetic fiction . . . "The Executioner's Beautiful Daughter" is absolutely static . . . It's a very verbal structure, it's all about words.' It may not have been, as she claimed, 'the first short piece I ever attempted to write', but it was her first mature achievement in a form that she rapidly made her own.

She also worked on a television script during this period, a process that she found an 'ongoing trauma', recalling the torment of her aborted adaptation of *The Magic Toyshop* the previous year. The project (a commission from ITV) was to write an episode of *The Adventures of Don Quick*, a comic sci-fi series loosely based on *Don Quixote*, in which the bumbling hero (played by Ian Hendry) and his sidekick, Sam Czopanzer (Ronald Lacey), land in a different planet each week and set about fixing what they see as its problems, usually to the severe annoyance of the inhabitants.

Angela's episode was titled 'It Was Such a Nice Little Planet'. Don and Sam arrive in Megalopolis One, a planet-sized super-city (pop: 1,000,000,000) that bears more than a passing resemblance to Tokyo (neon signs light up the night, overcrowding is endemic, and showing the teeth in public is considered 'a highly indecorous act'). But unlike Tokyo it's a totalitarian state, where the Happiness Enforcement Brigade ensures that everyone is happy, all the time. So unhappiness flourishes in secret, taken like a drug. Don links up with a melancholy soul called Mendacious and together they overthrow the regime. But the citizens are furious. They don't want free will: 'they want tranquillity, order, joy; and perhaps the cheap thrill of an illicit tear or two, an insult, a ticket to a peepshow of grief where they do not have to stay for long.' Don and Sam are chased off the planet, which, as they leave it, plunges into the sun.

Angela finished the script in late June, and told Carole that it was 'extraordinarily camp and probably won't be televised because most of the sets out-Barbarella "Barbarella"'. She was right – it wasn't ever televised – but it does have lots of witty touches, and a few memorable lines. Angela was especially proud of the following exchange: Q: 'What's a nice girl like you doing in a place like this?' A: 'Degrading myself.'

For all that Angela was keeping herself busy with minor projects, 1970 was the first year in a decade that passed without her doing much work on a novel. She had finished a first draft of *Love* (still titled *The Gates of Paradise* at this stage) while she was in Bradford in November 1969, but Janice had expressed reservations, especially about the explicit descriptions of sex in the original draft. Angela had revised it while she was staying with her father at Ravenslea Road:

> I cut out the cunnilingus and modified the post-Buzz sex between Lee and Annabel, removing the reference to the residual traces of fraternal semen. I also spent an entire day and night trying to do an instant Flaubert on the ending; thus, probably, fucking it up entirely. When I handed it to Janice and pointed out I had excised the cunnilingus, she was no end of pleased, and I realised, through a blur of weariness, that was all I need have done.

But her sense of closure was premature. Though Janice was now staunchly in favour of the novel, the sales department at Heinemann remained cautious, feeling that it was much too short and wouldn't sell – a position that was bolstered by a glance at the sales figures of Angela's previous novels. Months passed while the company debated it. Eventually, in June, they offered an advance of £250 (£150 less than they had paid for *Heroes and Villains*). Angela thought that the offer was 'fucking derisory'. She sent a telegram to Irene Josephy, instructing her to tell Heinemann to 'take its fivers and insert them up their commodious collective asshole'. She felt oddly disengaged from the consequences of this move. 'Freud would no doubt say this was not unconnected to my getting fucked into a screaming wreck every night but I think it's more to do with getting my head straight.' On another occasion she put her insouciance down to her geographical estrangement from the British literary world: 'I am far too many miles away to keep my finger on the pulse of my career.'

Even so, she was supporting herself for the first time in her life, and would need to make up the lost income. 'What the fuck am I going to do for a living?' she asked Carole. As it turned out, the question didn't warrant that note of panic: there were ample opportunities for English-speakers in Tokyo during the 1970s. She soon found a 'minimal' job – five hours a day, three days a week – at the NHK broadcasting company, turning the erratic English of Japanese translators 'into some semblance of our mother tongue'. She was very funny about this employment in her letters to Carole, presenting it as utterly Kafkaesque: she claimed that they kept producing contracts that she was sure she had never signed, and which showed she had to work more hours, for less pay. Then, after a couple of months, the man who had hired her left the company, and since he was the only one who spoke any English, she realised she wouldn't be able to hand in her notice even if she wanted to. Not that she was in any rush to do that. The work was both interesting and decently paid – she seems to have received ¥100,000 (about £120) a month – and a lot of the time she was free to spend all day reading in the corporation's large English-language library.

Though he doesn't seem to have been entirely conscious of it at this stage, Sozo's all-night absences were his only real weapons in an underlying struggle for dominance of the relationship. He was six years younger than Angela, much less experienced, and (though he denies her claim that she was actively supporting him) in a far weaker financial position. In Britain, during the 1970s, this would have been a difficult situation for many men to accept; to most Japanese men, it would have been unimaginable. Sozo was almost indecently laid-back by the standards of his culture, but he did suffer pangs of abraded male pride: 'Because I was young and stupid, it annoyed me that she was older than me,' he admits. 'I felt that women should be younger than men and smaller than men . . . That was a big thing for me.'

Angela was much more keenly aware of how the power dynamic operated: 'I suspect I <u>am</u> dominating him horribly and edging him further and further from his Japaneseness.' It wasn't something she regretted much. Having spent most of her life being tyrannised by someone else's requirements – first Olive's and then, in spite of her best efforts, Paul's – she was determined not to let it happen again. She was able to impose her desires on Sozo much more easily than she ever had before. But he still had at his disposal this crude, culturally bestowed form of power: to assert his role as a man (who could come and go as he pleased) against hers as a woman (who stayed at home). In 'A Souvenir of Japan', Angela wrote: 'the word for wife, *okusan*, means the person who occupies the inner room and rarely, if ever, comes out of it. Since I often appeared to be his wife, I was frequently subjected to this treatment, though I fought against it bitterly.'

In early June, Angela described in letters to several friends an extraordinarily revealing domestic scene. One evening, as they were undressing, she spotted traces of lipstick on Sozo's underpants. She didn't wear lipstick, herself. Sozo confessed that he had picked up a girl on the subway, taken her to a public park, and after some brief conversation, engaged her in oral sex. In her letters home, Angela said that she found this hilarious. 'If he fancies being sucked off by perfect strangers in Japanese formal gardens, I can only say that I myself have passed through the female equivalent of that phase and feel a complete indifference to the whole thing':

> I think he wanted me to be angry with him but I was laughing too much. Lipstick on his underpants. Dear God, I never had that trouble with Paul . . . I wait with baited breath for what surprises next week may bring. I shall probably discover residual traces of a Mars bar in his anus.

The story seems too cartoonishly vivid and expressive to be true, but Sozo confirms its basic details (in fact, he says, he met the girl in a bar and took her to a hotel – for obscure reasons, he made up the details of the subway and the park). Angela's suspicions about what he was up to when he didn't come home until 5 a.m. were well founded ('I was young,' he says now, with a half-embarrassed, half-proud shrug. 'I tried to keep it a secret'). Her amused tone seems indicative of a basic detachment from the relationship at this stage, for all her extravagant talk of love – an inference that seems to be confirmed by her dismayed reaction to Sozo's later infidelities – but it also lays bare the skill with which she engaged in power games. She maintained that she had no interest in limiting Sozo's freedom of action, but that's not to say she didn't want to overshadow him: 'to be utterly self-revealing', she wrote to Carole a few months later, 'I think I am less interested in making people do what I want, that form of dominance, than of [*sic*] making myself utterly memorable . . . Written down, in cold blood, this looks like megalomaniac fantasy. Anyway, my little dream is to be startling & extraordinary, really.'

Tokyo, like any big city, was full of the sorts of drifter and misfit that Angela naturally warmed to. At the Fugetsudo she was getting to know a ragged crowd of Europeans, Americans and Australians, who – in contrast to the mainstream expat community of diplomats, businessmen and journalists – had come to Japan for no reason beyond an interest in the culture. Even so, they tended to stick together. Most of them taught English, or worked as translators and rewriters. They gathered in coffee houses and Western-style bars (one regular haunt was Lefty's, 'a perfect imitation of a glossy New York bar in a forties film', where the matchboxes were emblazoned with the motto: *Lefty's, the place where everything is All Right*). 'It is rather like the Hemingway expatriate world,' Angela wrote of her new milieu. 'We refer to the Japanese as "them" & discuss them constantly.'

She thought of these new friends as her 'elective family'. The person among them she became closest to was John Yoxall, a gregarious, impulsive, enormously entertaining twenty-seven-year-old Englishman from Staffordshire. He had hitch-hiked from England to India, then continued his journey via Australia to Japan. He had a rich supply of traveller's tales, which he would unfold in rambling, frequently hilarious monologues. People tended either to love him for his warmth and humour, or loathe him for his recklessness and self-absorption. He had a boyish grin, chiselled features, and long, thick, curly hair: Angela thought he was 'extremely beautiful', if 'kind of raw-boned'. It was a purely academic observation, since she was fairly confident that he preferred men. But 'he really likes, admires & respects women', she assured Carole, and even described him as 'an ardent feminist'. 'He is, actually, someone I want to keep all my life,' she declared on another occasion. 'He's good.'

It was Yoxall, she wrote in 1972, 'who made a radical feminist of me'. That claim should probably be taken with a large pinch of salt, although her conversations with him were clearly among the influences on her thinking about gender politics at this time. She had begun describing herself as a feminist before she moved to Tokyo, but living in the city greatly increased her allegiance to the cause. Japanese society seemed to parody the assumptions about sexual difference that she had perceived in Britain, and as such it laid bare their spuriousness ('at least [in Japan] they do not disguise the situation', she later wrote). She was appalled by the 'intense polarity between the sexes', but at the same time it was enlightening to see gender identity being so ludicrously exaggerated, since it seemed to substantiate her belief that it was always a fabrication. The young women she encountered in Tokyo cultivated 'absolute femininity and charm', giggling behind their hands, dressing and making themselves up for maximum cuteness, quite as if they had 'become their own dolls'. By objectifying themselves in this way, they were allowing their identities to be determined by the prescriptions of a masculine society. One of Angela's new European friends, who spoke the language, would frequently hear other men asking her Japanese boyfriend: 'Is she a good lay? How big is her clitoris? etc. etc. etc.' Angela found it all immensely dispiriting. 'This is a heartbreaking country for a feminist,' she wrote to the novelist Andrea Newman, whom she had met in London at a Pan Books party at the beginning of the year.

'Mrs Pankhurst is right,' she wrote to Carole around the same time. 'The men in a society which systematically degrades women also become degraded. And, dear god, this society degrades women.' This observation clearly wasn't meant to exclude the Japanese man she knew best, and his readiness to leave her at home while he was off all night behaving like 'an ambulant penis'. But nor did her awareness of Sozo's chauvinistic traits make her want to leave him. The intensity of the relationship – and in particular of its sexual component – was enough to sustain her interest. 'One has always wondered why oriental women put up with all those centuries of male domination,' she wrote. 'The answer may, in fact, be surprisingly simple.'

If that seems like an unusual thing for a 'radical feminist' to say, then it's probably indicative of a deeper ambivalence to the role. Angela was fiercely resistant to being defined by her gender, but nor did she want to be defined by her membership of any movement, and she enjoyed saying things that upset the ideologically pure. 'My position in any revolution, sexual or otherwise, is always bound to be equivocal because I, basically, don't want to get involved,' she wrote to Carole. One of the expats she knew during this period was:

an American woman's lib. lady . . . who is like a parody of every man's secret notion of a woman's lib. lady. She is inclined to grab the balls of passing Japanese, tweak them and yelp: '<u>That's</u> what it feels like to be a sexual object!' She complains loudly because she always wanted to be an Arctic explorer but her mother made her play with dolls . . . She also – pathetically – positively <u>glows</u> when a bloke so much as approaches her.

By contrast, the woman Angela became closest to in Tokyo was 'not yet fully radicalised'. This was Naine Woodrow, who came from Brisbane, and had recently moved to Japan with her English boyfriend, Ted Holst (a descendant of the composer). Angela wrote that Naine's attitude to being a woman had 'curious elements of Uncle Tomism. I can put it best by saying she would be a completely different person if she were a man.' Nevertheless, she was soon describing her in a letter to Carole as 'the woman I love best after you'. As was often the case, Angela had been drawn to a person because of the contrasts between their personalities: '[Naine] is all perception, with only a little of the solid ballast of intellect. However, she is staggeringly aware of things & is able to articulate states of emotional ambivalence most people do not even dream exist.' She claimed that she was far more interested in what Naine had eaten for breakfast that morning than she was in 'some pseudo-intellectual's theory of revolution', because Naine's experience was always 'real'.

The apparent straightforwardness and authenticity of Naine's experience fascinated Angela. She herself tended to oscillate 'between practising romanticism and hard-headed realism', such that every emotion had to be clinically dissected, and every expression of enthusiasm inoculated with a shot of irony. To a woman whose day-to-day existence was meant to be 'sustained by passion only', such relentless self-consciousness was deeply problematic; it meant that she could only live in the moment for a few moments at a time. By the middle of the summer, she was becoming profoundly disengaged. She wrote to Carole:

> My own persistent discontent makes it impossible for me to regard anything I do as in the least memorable or important. 'Big fucking deal', I say to myself. Okay, I'm living in Tokyo. But this quarter is nothing like [the 1963 film] 'An Actor's Revenge'. I didn't hitch across India

to get here, so that was a drag. I have a nice and interesting little job, and my rewriting activities are bringing in bewildering amounts of yen, but I would rather be working as a bar hostess. I have a desire for sleaziness which I can never be bothered to put into practice. And leading an adequate sex life doesn't seem to have altered either my detachment or my socialising difficulties much.

The fiction that she wrote in Japan reflects this process of disenchantment. Desiderio, the narrator of *The Infernal Desire Machines of Dr Hoffman*, is impervious to the lyrical illusions that assail his native city. 'So much complexity – a complexity so rich it can hardly be expressed in language . . . it bored me,' he says. 'I could not abnegate my reality and lose myself forever as others did, blasted to non-being by the ferocious artillery of unreason. I was too sardonic. I was too disaffected.' In 'Flesh and the Mirror' – a more strictly autobiographical treatment of Angela's life in Tokyo – the narrator describes herself as 'rummaging in the dressing-up box of the heart for suitable appearances to adopt in the city', since 'the definitive world of the everyday with its hard edges and harsh light did not have enough resonance to echo the demands I made upon experience':

> It was as if there were glass between me and the world. But I could see myself perfectly well on the other side of the glass. There I was, walking up and down, eating meals, having conversations, in love, indifferent, and so on. But all the time I was pulling the strings of my own puppet; it was this puppet who was moving about on the other side of the glass. And I eyed the most marvellous adventures with the bored eye of the agent with the cigar watching another audition. I tapped out the ash and asked of events: 'What else can you do?'

Perhaps because Sozo had a similar tendency to see-saw between idealism and ennui (though his fluctuations were a lot less jolting than hers), Angela was soon placing most of the blame for her dissatisfaction on the relationship: 'the real trouble, of course, is that I've gone and got married again, haven't I'. She felt that Sozo was overshadowing her experience of Japan, and preventing her from engaging more fully with the culture: 'I am knocked out by aspects of this country he, as a native, finds boring or else distressing.'

On 30 July, Angela and Sozo took the train from Shinjuku station to see a fireworks display in the suburbs. They joined a huge crowd walking slowly out into fields towards the source of the fireworks, which were released over the river, so that the bursts of tinselled light in the dark sky above were multiplied in the dark water below. They passed stalls selling balloons, goldfish in plastic bags, and various kinds of food: they bought themselves grilled cuttlefish skewers, which they ate as they walked. The policemen lining the way carried paper lanterns. As the night lengthened, the long grass started to rustle with lovers. Angela found the whole experience magical: 'what with working & S's alienation from his culture & resultant internationalised lifestyle, the petty-bourgeois poetry of this country – which is so harmonious & so moving – was beginning to seem as though I had imagined it'.

But Sozo had seen similar displays countless times during his childhood, and soon became restless. 'He was bored by the fireworks, Carole,' Angela wrote a few months later, still dismayed by the unbridgeable distance between their responses. 'I mean, there <u>clearly</u> isn't a common life we can lead.' This episode, which came to seem emblematic of their relationship, provided the narrative meat of 'A Souvenir of Japan':

> 'Are you happy?' he asked. 'Are you sure you're happy?' I was watching the fireworks and did not reply at first although I knew how bored he was and, if he was himself enjoying anything, it was only the idea of my pleasure – or, rather, the idea that he enjoyed my pleasure, since this would be a proof of love. I became guilty and suggested we return to the heart of the city. We fought a silent battle of self-abnegation and I won it, for I had the stronger character.

Writing to Carole in 1971, Angela said that the story was 'not strictly true. To concentrate on a single aspect of a many-faceted situation, which one <u>has</u> to do, nevertheless falsifies the whole thing.' But that's only to state the limitations of all writing, and you couldn't fit a pin between the description of the evening that appears in *Fireworks* and the account she gave Carole the next day. When Sozo read 'A Souvenir of Japan' a few years later, he felt that it was 'accurate'. The story is one of the most plangently beautiful things Angela Carter ever wrote. It ends like this:

> we were surrounded by the most moving images of evanescence, fireworks, morning glories, the old, children. But the most moving of these images were the intangible reflections of ourselves we saw in one another's eyes, reflections of nothing but appearances, in a city

dedicated to seeming, and, try as we might to possess the essence of each other's otherness, we would inevitably fail.

*   *   *

The saga of *Love/The Gates of Paradise* continued to occupy her. On 7 August she received a letter from Peter Schwed, her American editor, who not only rejected the novel on behalf of Simon & Schuster, but advised her that if she published it anywhere she would be labelled a 'Johnny-One-Note':

> THE GATES OF PARADISE is a book that isn't going either to increase your reputation or make you any money. Any Angela Carter devotee would know that she had written this book – the beautiful handling of the language and the imagery is there. But the novel is so very downbeat, and has no real theme or resolution that's apparent, nor do any of the characters enlist the reader's empathy . . . My honest advice would be to put this one on the shelf, at least for the time being.

Angela was outraged by this assessment. She wrote to Carole:

> it seems to me that Lee is a deeply sympathetic character because he is a perfectly normal, exceedingly moral (in the way that you & I use the word), not particularly intelligent but rather responsible person caught in a dilemma which he cannot possibly resolve. This seemed – and seems – to me a genuinely tragic situation, made more tragic by the fact that Lee does understand what is going on . . . Anyway, running through the list of my favourite writers I find they are all Johnny One Notes to a man. I bet people always kept saying 'Fyodor, Fyodor, open up your heart and let the sun shine in.'

Her fifth novel was now without a publisher in either Britain or the US, but the situation doesn't seem to have dented her confidence much. Perhaps this was partly because, in a strange way, her reputation was blossoming in Japan. 'I am constantly meeting people who make wild offers about translating me into Japanese,' she told Janice, with whom she was still in touch despite her irritation with Heinemann. The most serious of these offers came from Kodansha, the largest publishing house in the country, which bought rights to both *Shadow Dance* and *Love* (a translation of the latter appeared in 1974).

Meanwhile, a freelance translator called Masako Ikezuki was approaching various Japanese publishers with a rough version of Angela's children's story *Miss Z, the Dark Young Lady*, to which she had, with Angela's permission, made various small changes ('e.g. Miss Z ought to be blonde in Japan, 'cos nobody finds brunettes particularly exotic when there are 100 million of them milling about', Angela explained to Janice).

Being a novelist also gave Angela a certain status among the expat community, and she had started receiving regular invitations to functions at the British Council and the British Embassy. On 29 August she attended a reception to mark the opening night of the first International Science Fiction Symposium. She spent much of the evening talking to Arthur C. Clarke, who she thought was 'probably the most boring man in the entire universe . . . As I grow older and, from time to time, meet a celebrity, I realise how spurious a thing is fame, how it lights on the most undeserving heads like the random droppings of a giant pigeon.'

In September, Irene managed to secure an offer of £2,000 for *Love* from Rupert Hart-Davis Ltd, a hardback imprint of the Granada group of publishers (paperback rights were included in the deal, and went to Panther, another Granada imprint), whose recent output included Leon Edel's five-volume biography of Henry James, bibliographies of Ronald Firbank, D. H. Lawrence and Ezra Pound, and works of fiction by Robert Coover and Michael Moorcock. 'I am uneasy about [signing a contract with them],' Angela wrote, 'as I cannot remember ever having heard of them.' Nevertheless, it was more money than she was likely to be offered elsewhere; the contract was duly signed, and publication was scheduled for the following May. On 25 September she wrote to Janice at her home address, thanking her for all her support over the previous five years, and urging her not to take the move personally.

Meanwhile, payments were arriving with unforeseen frequency from a variety of other quarters. She had been commissioned to translate an anthology of science fiction (she intended to split the money with Sozo, who would do the actual translation, after which she would touch up his English), and was still writing regular articles for *New Society* at an average rate of £30 per piece. In October, Warner Brothers took an option on *Heroes and Villains*, for which she was paid £600, along with 'a vague promise of several thou if the film is made'. She wasn't paying tax on her earnings from NHK, which made her anxious, but meant that her finances were all the more robust. By the end of the summer, she felt she had too much money. 'I simply do not need to earn as much as this and I've got enough sense to pass up e.g. teaching jobs which would add another lump sum per month but take away too much time and energy. I have this peasant conviction that money in the hand is more real than money in the pipeline – and I'll have to stop that, or I'll never be a great writer.'

In spite of her worries, Angela was well on the way to becoming a great writer. By the beginning of autumn, she had been thinking about her sixth novel for almost a year – a much longer gestation period than she had allowed for any of her previous books – and since returning to Tokyo in April she had been filling up notebooks with the conversations, speeches and scenes that would provide its texture. On 6 October she described it in a letter to Carole:

> It's interesting for me because it will be in the first person – male; the heroine will look exactly like S. on one of his good days, i.e. when I love him. It is to be called: 'Dr Hoffman's Desire Machine', or, possibly, 'Dr Hoffman's Infamous Desire Machine' or 'Dr Hoffman's Infernal Desire Machine' . . . I am pussy-footing about starting the thing because it demands a great deal of research and because I don't really want to get sucked into it and because . . . because I'm scared I'll spend a year on the thing and it will be shit when it's finished and . . . <u>won't make me any money</u>. Neuroses, neuroses!

Presumably another reason for her procrastination was that her living space in Tokyo was 'too small to write a novel'. Towards the end of October, she decided to quit her job at NHK, rent a cottage by the sea for the winter, take Sozo with her, and begin 'No. 6' while they were there (Sozo remembers this as being Angela's decision, and it seems likely that it was, although in a letter to Carole she claimed that it was his). Then, in March or April, she would go to England for the publication of *Love*. It wasn't clear to her whether she would return to Japan afterwards – the winter would tell. She felt that the experience of being alone in the countryside with Sozo for all that time would 'either make the relationship absolute or shatter it' – and she suspected it would be the latter. If she did stay in England, she thought she might try to do graduate research of some kind, perhaps in sociology. 'I really do both want & need more formal education,' she wrote to Carole. 'I find I can't regard (how shall I put it) this Japanese experience as an end in itself.'

By end of the month she had found a house – possibly through Edward Seidensticker, a distinguished American scholar, who spent summers in a neighbouring house – just outside the town of Kujukuri in Chiba Prefecture, about seventy miles east of Tokyo. The landlord was a rich, gay American, who had returned to the US for the winter. Angela gave notice on the apartment in Meguro on 1 November.

On 25 November, four days before she was due to leave, she was sitting in a bar when the television screen filled with the face of Yukio Mishima, Japan's most famous contemporary novelist: he had tried to launch a *coup d'état*, and when it failed, had committed ritual suicide, disembowelling himself before having his head removed by one of his co-conspirators. The standard Japanese reaction – including Sozo's – was one of agonised respect in the face of such courage. The standard European reaction was one of utter incomprehension. Angela's reaction was to call Mishima 'a buffoon'. She wrote an essay about the debacle for *New Society*, in which she made several authoritative insights into Japanese society, observing that Mishima's act 'was an orchestration of certain elements: sadomasochism; the homoeroticism inevitable in a society which has, for the past 800 or 900 years, systematically degraded women; a peculiarly nutty brand of fidelity; narcissism; and authoritarianism . . . these elements unhappily do not fall into those areas of the human psyche that the Japanese repress'. In spite of her failure to learn the language, she had, after a year of living in Tokyo, become a keen and discriminating student of the culture.

CHAPTER ELEVEN

Blueprints for new lifestyles

Kujukuri beach extends for almost forty miles along the coast of the Bōsō Peninsula, the bulging outcrop that dangles off the mainland to Tokyo's east. It faces out over the turquoise immensity of the Pacific towards California, whose white sandy shores, buffered here and there by grassy cliffs, it resembles. When the sun rose – as if emerging whole from the ocean – on the morning of 3 December, Angela felt she had arrived at the edge of the world:

> we have travelled further than the 8,000 miles I originally came to Tokyo from London, for then, in real terms, all I did was move from one suburb to another of the global village. This time, we crossed a mountain, went down the other side and found ourselves in perfectly strange, low lying country flooded with that hallucinatory light, issuing from an excess of sky, which provokes either visions or else a subdued melancholy.

It reminded her in some ways of Macduff, her father's birthplace, where she had spent holidays as a child: men weren't much in evidence in either community (most of them were out at sea), and the women in each had 'similar weather-lacquered, inexpressive faces, squat, durable bodies and hands as hard as those of old-style prizefighters'. All along the beach, the day's catch was laid out to dry in the pale winter sun (the weather was 'like an English April'), amid tropical shells, bits of driftwood, and other odds and ends retrieved by the tide (polythene wrappers, broken beer bottles and, on one occasion while Angela lived there, a dead dog). Since they were some distance from the nearest road, the beach was also used as a highway: women cycled past the house all day, the occasional truck rumbled by loaded with crates of fish, and in the evenings teenagers careered up and down on their motorcycles. At night the temperature plummeted, and all the dogs in the neighbourhood joined in a chorus of howls at the moon. It is the landscape of 'The Smile of Winter', the fourth story in *Fireworks*, which Angela wrote while she was there.

The house, which was separated from the beach by a small pine grove, was fairly large (enormous by the standards they had become used to in Tokyo), and elegantly furnished. A veranda ran all along the side facing the beach, and any of the three main rooms could be entered from the outside. The bedroom was beautiful, with eight tatami mats underfoot, and sliding doors of latticed paper that glowed in the sunlight, so that, Angela thought, it was 'like being inside a shell'. The next room along was also furnished in 'a most refined Japanese style', decked out in tatami, and filled with the landlord's collection of harpsichords. The third room was ('thank god') a modern Western lounge, with wooden floors, a leather sofa and a 'Scandinavian style fireplace'. The only things that Angela didn't like about living there were the toilet (a ceramic hole in the ground over which they had to squat) and the temperature at night (the house had been designed to let air circulate during the summer; it was poorly insulated, and the only source of heat was the fireplace).

Kujukuri town was a twenty-minute walk down the beach. Angela always referred to it as a village, but its amenities were much more generous than that implies. On the dusty main road there were several shops, including a barber's, a post office, a general store, more than one liquor store, and even a small cinema, which changed its bill every fortnight. But the atmosphere was sleepy: the holidaymakers on whom the town depended for its trade stayed away during the winter months. The buildings were 'reminiscent of the Old West' – wooden cabins with unpainted shutters for the most part – and though there were always people on the streets, it was, Angela wrote, 'a curiously silent place'.

The first couple of weeks were difficult. Sozo, in particular, found it hard to settle into their new home. 'It was so boring,' he remembers, 'no girls to see, no bars to go to.' They returned to Tokyo a couple of times, and went out drinking with their separate groups of friends in Shinjuku, or together to the cinema (they saw *That's The Way It Is*, Denis Sanders' documentary about Elvis Presley – 'I was so happy,' Sozo recalls, 'but in a way Angela was happy too, because she said Elvis was so sexy'). They invited friends – including John Yoxall and Sozo's younger sister Koniko – to come and stay with them. On 16 December, Angela typed up her notes for 'No. 6' (a summary of the plot, a list of phrases she wanted to include, a couple of crucial scenes and bits of dialogue that she had already fleshed out) and pinned them to the wall of the room with the harpsichords. But 'God knows if I will write it.'

In fact, she started work the next day, and found herself immediately plunged back into the familiar 'anxiety-ridden, frenetic, exhilarated yet terribly agitated state' of composing a novel. She wrote the first draft long-hand, over 167 lined A3 sheets, sitting on the tatami floor, working from late afternoon until the sun began to bleach the sky the next morning.

In terms of technique, *The Infernal Desire Machines of Dr Hoffman* shares an approach with *Heroes and Villains*, though it is much more confident – both in its method of constructing an imaginary world (actually, several imaginary worlds) and in its ideas – than the earlier novel. Its principal quality is an extraordinary richness – of language, of thought, of imagery – and its principal debt is to surrealism. The eponymous doctor (his name alludes to both the German romantic author E. T. A. Hoffmann, and Dr Albert Hofmann, the man who first synthesised and ingested LSD) is a surrealist extraordinaire, having learned how to make desire manifest. He wages a guerrilla war on the 'solid, drab . . . thickly, obtusely masculine' capital of his unnamed South American country, drenching its streets in the pure products of the unconscious, so that it becomes a kaleidoscopic dreamscape. Street lamps turn into giant flowers; peacocks cluster in concert halls, drowning out the music with their squawks; the bricks in public buildings become mouths that speak. The only person capable of combating this bombardment of the absurd is the Minister of Determination, a man of powerful intelligence but 'limited imagination', who is therefore immune to the doctor's machinations. What ensues is 'a battle between an encyclopaedist and a poet', or to put it another way, between rationality and romance. This tension reverberates throughout Angela Carter's sixth novel, its fantastical imagery jostling for space with ideas derived from Wittgenstein, Lévi-Strauss and Freud.

The story is told by Desiderio – his name means 'the desired one' – who looks back on the war between the doctor and the minister from his cosseted old age. A junior clerk in the minister's office at the beginning of the action, he is subsequently charged (because of his sardonic immunity from the plague of images) with finding and assassinating Dr Hoffman 'as inconspicuously as possible'. By the time he recounts the story he has come to be regarded as a national hero, feted by the young and valorised in the history books: 'posterity's prostitute', as he puts it. He describes his physical pursuit of the doctor over a constantly shifting, vigorously surreal landscape, and his simultaneous emotional pursuit of the doctor's daughter, Albertina, with whom he has fallen in love.

Perhaps more clearly than any of Angela Carter's other novels, *The Infernal Desire Machines of Dr Hoffman* reveals the processes by which she transmuted her day-to-day experience into strange, hallucinatory art. The city in which the narrative opens, with its ephemeral and baffling topography ('the Doctor has liberated the streets from the tyranny of directions and now they can go anywhere they please') and its thrilling strangeness ('nothing in the city was what it seemed – nothing at all!'), is a dream-version of Tokyo. The period of the doctor's campaign, 'the time of actualised desire', represents the period in Angela's life after she left Paul. Albertina not only looks like Sozo (she first appears in the guise of a man: 'his eyelids were vestigial and his cheekbones unusually high . . . he was the most beautiful human being I have ever seen'), she also possesses many of his characteristics ('Don't you think it would be very beautiful to die for love?' she asks Desiderio at one point). The twin poles of romanticism and reason, as represented by the doctor and the minister, are reflections of the warring parts of Angela's psyche.

There isn't much trace, even in the first draft of the novel, of Angela's initial plan to write an 'inventory of imaginary cities', although every chapter does create a new world. All the societies Desiderio passes through have their own religion, political structure and language, and these are meticulously described, as in Borges's story 'Tlön, Uqbar, Orbis Tertius', in which the structures and atmosphere of an existentially ambiguous country are inferred from an encyclopaedia. Desiderio lives for a while among river Indians:

> The speech of the river people posed philosophical as well as linguistic problems. For example, since they had no regular system of plurals but only an elaborate system of altered numerals for denoting specific numbers of given objects, the problem of the particular versus the universal did not exist and the word 'man' stood for 'all man'. This had a profound effect on their societization.

The novel's overarching South American setting was also a nod to Borges. Angela described it as coming from him and from Gabriel García Márquez's strange and voluptuous family saga *One Hundred Years of Solitude*, which had recently appeared in English translation. García Márquez is widely seen as the father, and Borges as the grandfather, of 'magical realism' – a mode that incorporates fantastical elements into fastidiously detailed realist settings, and accords them exactly the same kind of attention as one another. The term has often been used to describe Angela Carter's work, and *The Infernal Desire Machines of Dr Hoffman* is perhaps the book of hers that it most comfortably fits. It was a striking import at the time: although they became familiar commodities during the 1980s and 90s (conspicuous in the work of Salman Rushdie, Ben Okri and Louis de Bernières, among others), Latin American influences were almost entirely alien to the British fiction of the early 1970s.

The other crucial literary influences on *The Infernal Desire Machines of Dr Hoffman* were Wittgenstein, whom Angela read while she was in Chiba ('Jesus, he could have written great science fiction,' she told Carole) and Sade, who provided the template for the picaresque structure (the marquis himself – or someone very like him – makes an appearance at one point). Angela planned to write a loose trilogy of picaresque novels: the second was to be called either *The Great Hermaphrodite* or *Confessions of the Great Eunuch* – 'an allegorical novel, based on the myth of Tiresias, set in early Christian Rome' (this evolved into *The Passion of New Eve*); and the third was to be called *The Manifesto for Year One* – a 'Dostoevskian novel' set in 'a Russian city . . . peopled by students of philosophy', which would feature characters based on John Yoxall and Sozo. She explained to an interviewer a few years later that her decision to utilise the form was partly political:

> *The Infernal Desire Machines of Dr Hoffman*, that was when I began to use these ragged, picaresque, rambling kinds of discourses, because I was trying to short-circuit the question of whom I am addressing. Do they have villas, do they have willies, and so on and so on.

It isn't obvious why she felt that the picaresque was gender-and-class-neutral compared to other modes of writing, but it was probably to do with what she saw as the form's structural affinity with the language of dream. At any rate, *The Infernal Desire Machines of Dr Hoffman* is also a political novel in its content, giving full reign to its author's socialist and feminist principles. It pays close attention to the role of women in all of the places Desiderio visits, from the 'theoretically matrilinear' society of the river people, in which women undergo a bizarre form of genital mutilation whereby their clitorises are elongated so that they enjoy sex more, to the still crueller (but at least less hypocritical) society of the Centaurs, who tattoo their women's faces since they 'believed women were born only to suffer', and for whom 'an unfaithful wife was flayed alive and her hide given to her husband to cover his next marriage bed, a mute deterrent to his new bride to keep from straying'.

For all the attention it pays to abuses of sexual power, though, the novel delights in eroticism. Angela wanted to write about sex without either *Carry On* sauciness or Lawrentian gravity ('the English . . . either don't take sex seriously; or approach it as if it were Canterbury Cathedral on low Saturday'). Instead, she forged a prose of joyful sensuality, alive to the comedy of sexual desire, but never treating sex as comic in itself. When he's living with the river people, Desiderio seduces the grandmother of the nine-year-old girl he has been betrothed to:

> I experienced an almost instantaneous regret as soon as the act was over for I could hardly imagine there was any society in the world which would not think that gaining carnal knowledge of one's hostess and foster grandmother was a gross abuse of hospitality but Mama, smiling (as far as I could tell), sighing and fluttering butterfly kisses all over my remorseful face, told me she had not enjoyed sex since the last circumcision festival in the town of T., the previous April, and that was a very long time ago; that my performance, although improvised, had been spirited enough to give her a great deal of pleasure; and that she was always available in the galley every morning after breakfast and before lunch. Then she wiped us both dry with a handtowel, put on her trousers again and turned her attention back to the shrimp, which had scorched a little.

'I knew myself to be a man without much passion, even if I was a romantic,' says Desiderio, but that doesn't stop him from having sex in every chapter except for the first and the last. Even so, when he reaches the doctor's castle and is shown a room containing hundreds of couples performing 'the death-defying double somersault of love', he is 'awed and . . . revolted'. We soon realise that his love for Albertina is so self-conscious as to be effectively false. She tells him that the Sade character's 'fatal error was to mistake his will for desire':

> I interrupted her with a certain irritation.
> 'But how is one to distinguish between the will and a desire?'
> 'Desire can never be coerced,' said Albertina.

In the end, Desiderio gives up trying to coerce his own desire, chooses reason over passion, and kills not only the doctor, but Albertina too. 'I think I killed her to stop her killing me,' he says. But looking back from his old age, he tells us that he has regretted his decision every day since. This was the choice that Angela felt she would soon have to make regarding her relationship with Sozo, and the consequence that she feared was inevitable.

The novel came quickly, more and more so as she worked: by the beginning of March 1971 she had written just over 40,000 words, and by the end of the month, almost 75,000. She found it a much easier and more enjoyable process than writing any of her previous books. 'I was peaking a bit, stylistically, when I was doing *Hoffman* and the short stories [in *Fireworks*],' she told an interviewer a few years later. 'I'd developed this highly decorative, very tightly structured prose that could almost fit anything, and I was quite consciously utilising it. I mean it was lovely, it was beautiful, because I was in control of it.' In spite of its thematic insistence on the mutually destructive forces of reason and passion, the novel exhibits absolute creative freedom. It was, in part, a product of leaving England and her marriage, and then sequestering herself away from even Tokyo's demands. 'Doing Dr H. just isolated me completely from the passage of time,' she wrote a few weeks after finishing it.

She knew she had made a major breakthrough, and didn't see it only in terms of her own artistic development. That August, she wrote to Carole: 'HOFFMAN is probably, if not a masterpiece, as good as any novel in the English language for 30 years.' Alan Brooke, her editor at Hart-Davis, might not have gone quite that far – he recalls finding it 'very strange' ('I wasn't very familiar with magical realism') – but he had enough confidence in Angela, and enough admiration for her style, not to hesitate over acquiring it. He offered £2,000 for hardback and paperback rights, and Angela signed a contract when she returned to London that summer.

The novel was in a sense an elegy to her relationship with Sozo, but over the period that she was writing it, the relationship matured. 'We seem to get on very well, having worked out a rough schedule for chores and so on,' she wrote when they had been living in Chiba for a fortnight. 'It is the isolation from stress situations that has done it, of course . . . I keep expecting him to behave like Paul, but he never does, not around the house.' After another fortnight, she was more emphatic: 'when there is nobody else around, we get on fantastically well'.

They had swiftly established a pleasant domestic routine. Angela rose earlier than Sozo did, and sat reading under the pine trees until she heard him singing inside the house. Then she would make breakfast, after which they often walked into town together, collecting driftwood for the fire on their way back. Sozo tended to cook dinner – tempura, soup, rice with vegetables – and they alternated the washing-up on a day-by-day basis. While Angela worked on *Hoffman*, Sozo worked on a novel of his own in the next room. The passion that had sustained the relationship in Tokyo dwindled slightly, but Angela found that she could enjoy it with a greater sense of immediacy. She put on weight, but for the first time since childhood didn't mind. Her self-confidence soared. 'He gave me a new me,' she later wrote about this period. Sozo felt that he, too, changed while they were in Chiba: 'I didn't get bored of just talking to Angela in the cottage and cooking and doing laundry. That was enough. I told her I didn't know this kind of life was possible, and I just wanted to live like this. "Yes, everybody does," she said. "But where does the money come from?"'

For four months, they hardly spoke to another living soul. In late January they had 'a weird 2 days in Tokyo, constantly suggesting we went to see our separate friends, but never actually doing so 'cos we didn't want to leave one another'. Almost a year later, after her relationship with Sozo had ended, Angela wrote that Chiba would always be her reference point for happiness. Sozo felt very much the same. 'That was one of the happiest times of my life,' he said, more than forty years later. 'Very few people can have that kind of time in their lives.'

They returned to Tokyo on 29 March, and stayed with Violet – the bedridden sister-in-law for whom Sozo had been shopping and cooking twice a week before they went to Chiba – in her apartment on the other side of Meguro. Her husband (Sozo's older brother Hanio) worked in the Middle East as an engineer, but Violet had fallen ill shortly after moving there with him (Angela described her as having 't.b. of the skin at an advanced stage'), and so she had returned to Tokyo with the two children, Kenichi, aged four, and Akio, aged three.

Angela thought that Violet should really have been in hospital, but 'she can't bear to leave the kids, silly cow'. Cooped up in a small flat with a potentially infectious invalid, Angela's childhood phobias quickly reasserted themselves: she worried that what her hostess *really* had was leprosy, and began experiencing symptoms of her own: 'headaches, stiff arm, crawling skin . . .' But her good nature gained the upper hand over her hypochondria, and she threw herself into helping with the housework and childcare. Violet was half-English, and the children were bilingual, so Angela read to them, and spent hours each day helping them to draw. She seems to have enjoyed the role – Sozo remembers her pleasure at being called 'Aunty Angela' – but at the same time, she had never before had such prolonged exposure to children, and it had a cooling effect on her maternal fantasies:

> I think I'd be rather a good but very authoritarian mother. I'd chain them to their finger paintings in those cages they call kiddiepens & clump them over the head with the shorter Oxford English dictionary at the least squeak . . . [But] 4 hours in their company puts any such sentimental whims out of my head.

Otherwise, she was mainly occupied with planning her visit to England for the publication of *Love* during these weeks. She wrote to Rebecca Howard to find out if she was still living in the house in Earls Court, and on learning that she was, asked to stay there for a while. She set about obtaining a Japanese re-entry permit, and booked a one-way flight to London at the last minute. She told Sozo that she would return in June.

Angela landed at 'Heath Row' – as she called it in mocking tribute to the new prime minister – on 22 April 1971, a year and three days after she had left. She felt like a returning hero, and played up the various ways in which she had changed. She wrote to Carole that she found the Western habit of keeping shoes on inside the house 'disgusting', and that she felt unnerved by all the 'very big, very clumsy, very pink, very menacing people' around her. Before long, she was conscious of becoming 'a Japan bore'. But the ways she had changed since moving to Tokyo were apparent even without her drawing attention to them. 'She was much more sociable,' recalled Edward Horesh. 'Much more self-confident.' Rebecca Howard agreed: 'it was a huge thing, it really was. [She had] a lot more ideas fizzing around and . . . a lot more confidence.'

She stayed with Rebecca in the house on Child Street, but made regular trips around the country to visit other friends and family: to the Cotswolds to see Hughie and Joan (who remembered her asking how they'd feel about having a Japanese brother-in-law), to Bristol to see Nick and Corinna ('a weekend with them is a storybook experience, delicious food full of fresh herbs served on unlikely plates decorated with zebras & giraffes, always some new enthusiasm . . . always some giant catastrophe freshly avoided'), to Bath to see Edward, and to Bradford to see Carole. She was having a fantastic time, and even managed an 'untraumatic' conversation with Paul Carter about getting a divorce.

The only flaw in her mood was that she missed Sozo ('what I really feel about being away from the boy is that the pole of the world is gone'), and he wasn't writing to her frequently enough, or at sufficient length, to elide the distance between them. On a day trip to Brighton, she decided that she wanted to move there with him, or else to 'that respectable working-class area around Victoria [station], so convenient for Brighton & the continent'. She pictured him reading Faulkner on the beach, and was quite confident that he would move to England if she asked him to. She also thought about doing a PhD, the title of which would be 'De Sade: Culmination of the Enlightenment'. When she was between novels, she often made 'blueprints for new lifestyles' in this way.

In London, she attended to business matters. Panther Books – the paperback wing of Granada – was planning to bring out its own edition of *Love* the following year. William Miller, who ran the imprint with his friend John Boothe, became a close friend and ally of Angela over the course of the 1970s. A heavyset man with humorous, intelligent dark eyes, who defined himself as 'a Scot, a homosexual and a socialist' (though he had in fact been born in Kent and educated in Sussex), he was also a heavy drinker, a famous talker and an incorrigible *bon vivant*. But his extravagance only half-disguised a genuine radical streak: in 1958, as co-editor of the Oxford student newspaper *Isis*, he had been imprisoned for breaching the Official Secrets Act when he ran an exposé of Britain's woefully inadequate plans in the event of a nuclear attack; he later risked prosecution under obscenity laws when he and Boothe published the British edition of Alex Comfort's *The Joy of Sex* (it had been turned down by several other UK publishers, and had to be printed abroad).

It was probably during that visit to England in the summer of 1971 that Angela met Miller for a drink at the John Snow pub in Soho, where he introduced her to John Hayes, a young lecturer in philosophy at the University of Essex, who by coincidence was halfway through reading *Heroes and Villains*: he declared himself a fan, and thereby sparked off a friendship that endured until the end of Angela's life. They discussed the Continental theorists who Angela had been reading since the student protests of May 1968 – Adorno, Lévi-Strauss, etc. 'She was into it,' Hayes remembered, 'but I must stress, she had a bit of irony about it. She would never play the part of an intellectual theorist.' 'She always seemed to me to be a reluctant everything,' agreed Hayes' partner John Cox, the opera director who worked with Angela on her adaptation of Virginia Woolf's *Orlando* in 1980. 'There seemed to be a kind of reticence about her when she offered an opinion or entered into a kind of discourse on anything . . . It was dry, it was ironical, but there was also a slight shyness, hesitancy, almost an embarrassment.'

Love was published by Hart-Davis on 17 May, to reviews that were generally cool and sometimes damning. Almost all of them saw the novel as a step backwards into an earlier phase of Angela Carter's career. The poet Robert Nye, writing in the *Guardian*, called it 'a disappointing effort after her brilliant *Heroes and Villains*', adding that the writing was characterised by a certain 'numbness', as though 'the author, having invented people off the top of her head, was determined to keep plugging away with them until the bitter and absolutely predictable end'. In the *Observer*, John Coleman was equally harsh, finding the French style 'a trifle above the matter to which she applies it'. Perhaps the souring of the hippy dream seemed a staler and more dated subject in 1972 than it did in subsequent years: *Love* was reissued by Chatto & Windus in 1987, and went on to become one of Angela Carter's most popular novels.

Just as when she was last in Britain – in an echo that brought the memories of that period surging back – the publication of a novel was closely followed by a death in the family. Angela's paternal uncle, William Stalker, suffered a massive brain haemorrhage, and died shortly afterwards in hospital on 27 May. She delayed booking her return passage to Tokyo, and travelled to Macduff to be with her father, who had moved into a cottage three miles outside the town (achieving 'what every Sicilian in New York, what every Cypriot in Camden Town wants to do, to complete the immigrant's journey, to accomplish the perfect symmetry, from A to B and back again'). Her aunt Katie was still living in the flat above the Stalker shop. They put Angela in William's bed: 'they haven't changed the sheets', she told Carole, evidently repulsed by the thought.

Her distaste extended to her living relatives. Though she hadn't exactly been looking forward to the visit, nor had she allowed 'for the violence of my reactions or the strain it would cause me to keep cool'. Katie allowed the cat to eat from the kitchen table, addressing him as 'Mammy's beautiful pet' and 'my sweet beloved lover'. With her 'destroyed' alcoholic's face, her 'puffed & immense' body, and her 'very slender and shapely' legs, she gave Angela 'the physical horrors'. Her father upset her even more profoundly. He hadn't informed Katie that Angela had left her husband, so she had to break the news herself. She was appalled by the 'total atmosphere of hypocrisy, greasy miserliness, mystification and deceit . . . Katie is a palpable obscenity & my father, in his home environment, is obscene.' Oddly, these feelings gave her a sense of unity with Olive:

> My posthumous rapprochement with my mother has speeded up considerably; presumably [my] passion & hysteria &, I suppose, intelligence come from her . . . I even realise why she was so damnably possessive with her children. Anything that prevented her being alone with my father must have made her life a little less insupportable. I suspect some of the rage she expressed when I left Paul was due to an incoherent jealousy of my ability to escape. This is the first time I've had a real experience of my father unmodified by her presence or in a place where he wasn't in control & really, he is just so fucking <u>stupid</u>.

Nowhere else – neither in Angela's published essays about her family, nor in any of the other references to them in her private letters and journals – does this tone come close to being replicated. She usually expressed absolute devotion to her father, but during those few weeks in the summer of 1971, her feelings became unpleasantly soured. Perhaps it was partly the shock of seeing him so smoothly returned to the world of his childhood, and thus removed from the world of hers: as if his almost fifty years in England had been 'an enormous parenthesis', as she later wrote. She became 'fantastically depressed' by it all, and equipped herself with 'a month's supply of Librium' shortly after returning to London.

Back in the capital she went to the dentist, who did 'horrible things' to her, and to her accountant's office, where she discovered that her taxes were in an even more tangled state than she had thought. She hemmed and hawed about how to return to Tokyo. Would she fly via Malaysia, or perhaps stop off for a night in Bangkok? Or would she use the inheritance she expected from her uncle William to buy a house in London, and then send Sozo the money for a one-way plane ticket? Eventually, she decided to return via Russia, flying to Moscow and then making her way east by plane and train and boat. She was 'both very excited & very trepidatious' about this idea. 'Though the most ghastly things will probably happen, it is something like an adventure.' Her main reservation was that it would keep her away from Sozo 'for another wistful week'.

He still wasn't writing to her as much as she would have liked. She was beginning to feel 'like the girl in "Song of Solomon", sick of love'. She spent hours daydreaming about him. 'I have suddenly realised, with hideous clarity, that if I don't get back to Sozo soon, I shall fall into my first, authentic, clinical depression,' she wrote to Carole. 'It is him I miss, dammit. I miss his funny little ways & his cleverness, his complexity, his guile. All that & perfect sexual compatibility, too. It is well worth coming back all this way to realise I cannot live happily without him.'

On the morning of Monday 12 July she flew to Moscow, which she found 'a pretty place' ('even the tenements boast a lot of gingerbread round the tops') and 'startlingly human', though the Soviet bureaucracy, she said, reduced her to tears. She spent a couple of days there before taking an uncomfortable overnight flight ('there were not enough blankets to go round & no pillows') to Khabarovsk, a city of half a million people, which is smeared clumsily along the gaping mouth of the river Amur, off which a bitter wind blows all year round. Even today, long after the statue of Lenin was pulled down from the main square, Khabarovsk retains an ingrained atmosphere of Soviet drabness and isolation. Angela described it in her journal as 'a desolate town, like a poor white town in Tennessee, wooden houses under a leaden, weeping sky'. From there she took the train to Nakhodka, a twenty-hour journey (Vladivostok, from where the Russia–Japan ferry sails today, was closed to foreigners throughout the Soviet period due to its position as a naval base).

The Trans-Siberian Railway is not a mode of transport for the fainthearted: there are no showers on board, so the stench of sweat soon becomes overwhelming, and the toilets don't accept paper, which means a malodorous, overflowing bin in every cubicle. But perhaps it was a marginally more pleasant experience in 1971 than it is today. The USSR was going through a period of economic expansion, and the trains still retained something of their old imperial elegance. Lace curtains allowed a bit of privacy into cabins that had only two berths each (Angela shared hers with 'a French woman and her awful child'). In the dining car the waiters wore black tie, and served Georgian champagne. The atmosphere of faded grandeur was kind to Angela's imagination. 'It is possible,' she wrote, 'as one sips one's Chekhovian glass of tea and lights a cigarette of the suavest Turkish tobacco, to believe that [the Trans-Siberian Railway] offers an elegiac remembrancer of the kind of luxury that departed our lifestyle when the lights went out over Europe.' In 1974 she made the same journey in the opposite direction, and she drew on her memories of both trips when writing the Siberia section of *Nights at the Circus*.

The crossing from Nakhodka to Yokohama was unpleasant – '2 days of unremitting agony' – thanks to an attack of seasickness. 'I realised I am probably the worst sailor in the world.' She couldn't tolerate even the sight of the heavy Russian food that was served on board. She had sent Sozo a cable from Nakhodka, telling him what time to meet her on the other side. Now she lay queasily in her berth and fixed her thoughts on him. Describing the journey in 'Flesh and the Mirror', she wrote: 'as we rounded the coast in bright weather, I dreamed of the reunion before me, a lovers' meeting refreshed by the three months I'd been gone'.

The boat docked at 7 p.m. on Saturday 17 July. Angela was in such a hurry to disembark that she left her raincoat on board. Coming through customs, she searched the crowds for the face she had been dreaming of since April. But she saw only the faces of indifferent strangers. Sozo wasn't there.

CHAPTER TWELVE

Constructing a personality

Angela's spirits crashed when she found herself abandoned at Yokohama. She hadn't eaten for two days, but she was too upset to think about food, and booked herself onto the next train to Tokyo. She arrived in the city at half-past nine, and went straight to the Fugetsudo, where she learned from acquaintances that Sozo was nearby – 'making, I suppose, the most of his last night of freedom'. Lacking other ideas, she went out to search for him, 'from bar to bar, café to café', hauling her anxiety and her growing anger through the bright Shinjuku streets.

What happened next is played out again and again in Angela's published and unpublished writing from this period, most exhaustively in 'Flesh and the Mirror', several drafts of which survive. It was Saturday night, so the area was full of revellers. She pushed her way through the crowds, past the love hotels and hostess clubs, under the artificial cherry blossom. By 11 p.m., 'the poignancy of my own situation [had overcome] me,' and she gave in to tears. It started to rain. A young man with 'sequin eyes' fell into step beside her. He asked her where she was going, and didn't seem to believe her when she said she was looking for her lover. 'If you can't find him,' he asked, 'will you go to bed with me?'

Angela had already given up hope of finding Sozo, so she went with the young man to a love hotel, where they were given a room with a mirror above the bed. Describing the encounter in a letter to Carole the next morning, she struck a triumphant note:

> It was an absolutely delirious night . . . a grand tour of Japanese eroticism – from bath to bed, innumerable sequences of positions. Ever had

186

your armpits licked? (He'd washed me very carefully first.) He only had 222 yen (a nice round sum) in the world (conceivably people with a great deal of erotic energy are always penniless due to fucking too much to make an honest living by sublimating) so, inevitably, I paid the hotel. Worth every yen . . . It transpired he's an actor with a left-wing group that takes Gogol & Gorki & stuff like that to the workers. His English was minimal but he said one luminous thing: 'I feel your holy body' (presumably meant 'whole' . . .)

But the narrator of 'Flesh and the Mirror' is appalled by the ease with which she has betrayed her lover, and dismayed by the sight of her body twined with a stranger's in the mirror above the bed:

I saw the flesh and the mirror but I could not come to terms with the sight. My immediate response to it was, to feel I'd acted out of character. The fancy-dress disguise I'd put on to suit the city had betrayed me to a room and a bed and a modification of myself that had no business at all in my life, not in the life I had watched myself performing.

Angela told Carole that she and 'the Summer Child' (as she took to calling him in subsequent letters) said 'a choked goodbye', but in the story she implied that their parting was flavoured by awkwardness and shame:

I scrambled out of [his] arms and sat on the edge of the bed and lit a fresh cigarette from the butt of the old one. The rain beat down. My demonstration of perturbation was perfect in every detail, just like the movies. I applauded it. I was gratified the mirror had not seduced me into behaving in a way I would have felt inappropriate – that is, shrugging and sleeping, as though my infidelity was not of the least importance. I now shook with the disturbing presentiment that he with his sequin eyes who'd been kind to me was an ironic substitute for the other one, the one I loved . . .

Therefore I dressed rapidly and ran away as soon as it was light outside.

It's not enough to say that one of these accounts is fiction and the other isn't, and simply to leave it at that: the events they describe are nearly identical, and Angela was just as likely to spruce up the facts in her letters as she was in her stories. The two versions are of equivalent biographical value, in other words, and the best conclusion we can draw is that their differing moods were both present in her encounter with the Summer Child.

Angela had a powerful sex drive, and after three months of celibacy, she must have enjoyed the evening on a purely physical level; at the same time, Sozo's failure to appear at Yokohama may have unsettled her more profoundly than she was willing to reveal to Carole. The roles she was alternating between – that of the perfectly liberated woman (for whom the 'infidelity was not of the least importance'), and that of the woman who was living for love (for whom it was of the utmost importance) – were incompatible. At least one thing was clear: the night was a parody of the 'lovers' meeting' she had been imagining.

When she tracked Sozo down at the Fugetsudo the next morning, it was immediately obvious that something was very wrong. He says that he didn't bother going to the port because he was 'busy', and he assumed that they would run into one another in Shinjuku eventually. As Angela must have feared, his feelings towards her had hardened considerably during her three-month absence. 'He is undergoing some sort of personality crisis which I don't quite understand,' she wrote. 'I think he himself has just realised he's not a student but a dropout & this has come as something of a shock.'

She tried to talk to him about her trip to Macduff and how ill it had made her, but he laughed – a reaction that she thought of as 'Paul Carter activity'. She didn't tell him about the Summer Child, but in a sign of just how detached from her he had become, he volunteered that he had slept with three women while she was gone. She was extremely distressed by this information. 'His passion for sex without contacts – the locking of 2 anonymous sexual objects – sickens me,' she wrote (even though the reunion had been preceded by an anonymous encounter of her own).

The next few days were painful and difficult for them both. They made some effort to resuscitate the relationship, but deep reservoirs of resentment had been exposed on both sides, and most of their conversations descended into squabbling. 'S. has perceived we are engaged in a profound battle for dominance,' Angela wrote to Carole. 'He says I have dominated him completely . . . He has, in Kleinian terms, converted his image of me from Good Breast to Bad Breast & I do not know if it is worth my while going through the whole process of readjusting him to me again.' In another letter, written a few weeks later, she suggested that 'a simpler & less competitive person [than Sozo] might be moved by the fact that I couldn't have written HOFFMAN without him . . . This is how a good wife should feel.

Well, he reacted violently against the wife role.' It was a fairly accurate diagnosis of Sozo's state of mind. 'Frankly,' he explained forty years later, 'I didn't want to be a gigolo any more.'

With Angela away in England, he had found that he could support himself in a modest way without her. He had rented a tiny room – a '2 mat cupboard' – which Angela felt was 'big enough to screw a Japanese girl in & possibly to screw me but hardly to conduct any kind of relationship in'. As it was, she didn't much feel like screwing anyway. 'The thrill has definitely gone, I feel a singular lack of passion,' she told Andrea Newman. Even so, she was scared of breaking up with Sozo, not least because of 'the loss of face involved': she had told everyone in England that she intended to bring him back there with her. But there was no use pretending that fate held anything else in store. 'Splittsville is definitely imminent,' she wrote to Carole.

On 25 July – exactly a week after she had caught up with Sozo at the Fugetsudo – Angela moved her things out of his 'horrible', 'Raskolnikovian' flat, and went to stay with John Yoxall. She told her friends that it was she who had ended the relationship, although 'I am sure he thinks <u>he</u> has left me.' She told Sozo (who was in no doubt that he had left her) much the same thing ('the truth is that I left you'). In the context of the letters she had written to her friends immediately before the split, as well as those she wrote later that summer, it seems fairly clear that Angela was in fact the jilted partner. But it was evidently important to her that she maintained (perhaps to herself as much as to anyone else) that the destructive factor wasn't her domination of Sozo, but his dependence on her. Among her papers is a fragment of a letter that she must have written to him around this time (whether she actually sent a version of it isn't clear). She told him:

> I do not believe it is moral to love somebody unless both partners are entirely free. I mean, that the love can survive partings, can survive changes & – most important of all – does not prevent the lovers from changing themselves, & does not prevent their freedom of action. I say this from experience. It is very easy for people to destroy one another in the name of love. Briefly, however much I love you, I cannot – and <u>will not</u> – take responsibility for you . . . I have struggled to become an independent person & I think you, also, wish to be an independent person.

As the weeks passed, however, it became harder and harder for her to maintain this perspective. Throughout her life, her appetite for independence had been whetted by constrictive personal relationships. Now, for the first time, she was entirely on her own. In a sense, she had achieved what she had always wanted, but she found that her sense of abandonment was as hard to bear as her sense of engulfment had ever been. She wrote that 'my freedom appals me – there is no need to worry about the future, even . . . I feel my self like this grotesque burden.' She no longer had any reason to be in Japan, but faced with an effectively infinite range of choices – she thought about returning to England, or going to America, or to Nepal – she found it impossible to reach a decision, so simply stayed put. All she knew for certain was that she was 'terrified of being alone'.

She and Sozo had parted on reasonably civil terms, and for a few months they continued to see one another socially, but she found it increasingly hard to stay calm around him. On one occasion, he failed to call her when he said he would, so she went round to his apartment (she had hung on to the key), tore up his condoms, and left a note saying that her heart was breaking. On another occasion, she hit him in the face on the street, and on yet another she threw water over him in the Fugetsudo. It was the first intimate relationship of her life that had ended on someone else's terms, and she was overwhelmed by her sense of powerlessness. Yet even as her behaviour grew more violently erratic, she was conscious of performing a role: 'to the extent that I am a romantic, I delight in having a broken heart', she told Carole.

If being broken-hearted was another role, it was one that appears to have consumed her. By the middle of August, her health was suffering. 'I can't eat (except for nectarines, which, mercifully, are plentiful) & when I am on my own I will start crying,' she wrote. 'Because I oscillate violently between reason & desire I can keep my cool – <u>as long as I am not alone</u>.' Still discussing this period almost ten years later, she wrote to her friend and editor Carmen Callil that she 'used to keel over in the street for no reason . . . the world becomes a meaningless void and one forgets things, one is intermittently incoherent'. In her letters to Carole she talked frequently about suicide, and said that she was only able to function with a semblance of normality by medicating herself. She later wrote that 'just a leetle, leetle Valium, not much, one a day for no more than a week or, at most, ten days, took the edge off [the] states of extreme anxiety . . . the attacks of wild, irrational panic, the shaking hands, the loss of appetite'.

She also seems to have used Librium fairly heavily in the months following the break-up. The other things that sustained her during this period were her friendship with John Yoxall and, even more so, her correspondence with Carole. 'You & I are far closer than most human beings ever allow themselves to be with one another,' she told Carole in a letter of 1 September. 'I think that our friendship is one of the great central relationships of my life . . . and I am constantly thankful for it.'

All the happiness and self-assurance that Angela had accumulated since leaving Paul had vanished in a few appalling weeks. She returned to worrying that she was unattractive and unlovable, and that her work wasn't any good. All the same, she had enough self-awareness to realise that she hadn't objectively changed when Sozo left her, and she rebuked herself for allowing the relationship to determine her self-image. She began to see this period of being alone as an opportunity to define herself without reference to anybody else's perception of her.

She moved into a place of her own in early September. It was a 'wee house' in Shinjuku ('yes, Shinjuku at last'), constructed from wood and paper in the traditional Japanese style, with magnolia and bullfrogs that croaked under stones in a small garden at the back. There was no bathroom, so she went each afternoon to the public baths, where she took off her clothes 'in a coolish, mirrored room full of other women taking off or putting on their clothes'. These women gossiped as they washed, but since she spoke no Japanese, Angela couldn't join in, or even eavesdrop. It was a daily dash of salt in the open wound of her loneliness. She acquired a black, white and orange cat – 'more of a patchwork quilt than a cat, really' – to save her from being totally alone in the house. But only in the evenings, when she went out drinking with her European 'family', could she forget about Sozo for a few hours.

Since she felt compelled to go out with friends as often as she could, she wasn't doing much writing. For a while, she found it difficult even to read. But by mid-October, she had begun planning a new book. The working title was *Fictions Written in a Certain City*. It was to contain three stories of around 15,000 words each, linked by their Tokyo setting and by their themes (the 'fugue of love and death'; the city as invention; the experience of never knowing what's real), which would be 'harmonised according to the laws of counterpoint and introduced from time to time with various contrapuntal devices'. The individual stories were 'The Entire City', an elegy to Tokyo, written in the brisk, impressionistic style of travel journalism, but with the odd startling, surreal flourish ('I think I saw death, once, on Akasaka Mitsuke subway station'); 'The Grammar of Existence', which deconstructs Tokyo in the manner of the Continental theorists she had been reading ('If a philosophical problem has the form, "I don't know my way about", the city itself is a philosophical problem'); and 'Victims of Circumstance', which focuses mainly on her relationship with Sozo ('his memory ~~remains~~ remained as a constant irritation in my heart for a long time . . . he revealed to me aspects of my self I never knew existed – desire; cruelty; despair; delight; hypocrisy; bad faith') as well as her encounter with the Summer Child.

She worked on this project, on and off, for the rest of 1971 and into the first few months of 1972. It came excruciatingly slowly – 'HOFFMAN rattled along at such a jolly speed it is v. difficult to readjust to the pains-taking, Flaubertian chiselling away at a phrase' – and her enthusiasm for it repeatedly faltered. On 27 October she wrote: 'this is a very, very hard patch of maturing for me & I'm not sure if I'll come through; I feel the need of a <u>basic</u> change of direction, as though HOFFMAN really were the end of a period in my life, & the pull towards visual expression is becoming v. strong, almost as if I didn't trust words any more'. She ploughed on with the project, even so, but was perpetually looking for different ways of doing it. After she had completed a draft of 'The Entire City', she decided that 'I must perfect a new form if I want to get it right.' She wrote to Carole:

> it actually involves me in creating, oh, Jesus, a theory of knowledge. I am trying to describe this city, Tokyo, as an emanation of myself, as a reflection of my feeling, so that the real world is in a dialectic with the private experience that made me perceive the city in this way . . . I find that I want to write an abstract novel and I am cast-ing about blindly for the form. I think I may have an idea of how to proceed – there are Japanese fictional forms, aptly enough, that are rambling and discursive mood pieces and I'm going to have a bash at working on that.

She wrote at least six drafts of 'Victims of Circumstance', each one shorter than the last. 'I shall end up with about 3,000 beautiful words & a ten-volume notebook,' she joked. She wasn't far wrong. The material was eventually boiled down to the 3,000 words of 'Flesh and the Mirror', which appeared in *Fireworks*. The other two stories never saw the light of day. But the process of working on them does appear to have helped her regain control of herself. By the end of October she was lucid enough to recognise that she had been 'fairly mad' for a while. She still thought about Sozo constantly ('Oh, Jesus, when will this torture <u>end</u>,' she wondered on 27 October), but she no longer felt that her happiness was dependent on him. She wrote to Carole: 'though I want desperately to come home, I don't think I should right now – do you agree? I feel primarily a need to establish myself existentially . . . the way I should have done when I was 19; & crashing back seems a bit of a cop-out, somehow.'

In truth she was looking for much the same thing as ever: a romantic relationship in which her identity was sacrosanct – except that she could see, now, that her own attempts at 'making myself utterly memorable' were as much of a threat to her identity (certainly if that project failed) as someone else attempting to dominate her. What she wanted was 'a sufficiently well-established sense of self [that I] can function adequately, possibly function best, without the help of another', and a relationship in which neither partner saw the other as an extension (or mirror) of themselves.

On 16 November, she went to a party full of expats, and left with about the only Asian male among them, a Korean teenager who had grown up in Osaka (immigrant status was effectively hereditary, and he and his siblings had been denied Japanese citizenship). Angela described him in a letter to Carole:

> Kō. Yes, Kō. Who is, or, rather, was, a virgin; who is 19; who looks like a kind of oriental pierrot, a face of perfect comic gravity & a gravely comic presence, once he feels sure of himself. He makes me laugh. He is a minor Fellini character, in a purple Indian shirt & trodden down baseball boots. He has also all the Holden Caulfield characteristics – a suddenly luminous turn of phrase; a history of running away from home; a confession of mental instability (as if I hadn't <u>known</u>). And he brought me a can of pineapple as a present, because I seduced him.

She discovered soon afterwards that Kō was actually his family name (his given name was Mansu), but she went on calling him Kō nonetheless. As that decision might suggest, the locus of power in the relationship was never in question. He moved in with her almost immediately, and did all the cooking, cleaning and washing up. He was a sort of natural feminist, Angela thought, totally lacking in macho pretensions. It made a soothing change from the demonstrativeness (not to mention the regular infidelities) that had characterised her previous relationship: 'I remember S. saying: "Tell me to kill myself for you & I'll do it." Kō's great gesture of love is cleaning out the lavatory.'

She loved his apparent lack of complication, his self-sufficiency ('he is already a complete person'), his gentleness, and his capacity for delight, all of which stood in sharp contrast to both Sozo and Paul. His English was poor, so their verbal communication had to be done in broad strokes. 'God knows what's in his head, but . . . all of it seems coded messages of a language of joy,' she told Carole. He was extremely inexperienced, but she enjoyed teaching him. He was two inches shorter than her (only slightly taller than Sozo) and poignantly thin. He looked young even for nineteen – 'more a mature 14 . . . Every time I pull down his underpants I feel more & more like Humbert Humbert.' He had, she wrote,

> already contrived to reveal to me further aspects of my self . . . obviously, the maternal impulse. I never realised it was so strong. And, equally obviously, a need to be in control. One doesn't choose 19-year-old virgins (& I did, quite consciously, choose him, if only to seduce him) or feel, afterwards, a compulsion to know them better if one doesn't feel the need to be the dominant partner, though I had to be given an extreme example before I saw this aspect of myself clearly.

She was very aware of 'the stresses the external world will impose on our relationship', and she felt a bit sore about it: 'if I were a man & I had the incredible good fortune to seduce a girl 12 years younger than I who was as bright & freaky & pretty as Kō, everyone would applaud & say: "How splendid." As it is, only Naine & Yoxall would understand . . . the rest of the expatriate circles would raise their eyebrows & say: "But, clearly, she can't get anyone else."' It's true that many of her friends in Japan thought her affair with Kō was 'very strange'. But their bafflement seems to have had as much to do with his lack of English as his age.

It's certainly the case that she was never as emotionally invested in Kō as she had been in Sozo. Nor was the physical side of the relationship as overwhelming. And for all that she appreciated his lack of ego, 'the relationship is so simple', she wrote, 'that, inevitably, I miss the complexities'.

She still thought about Sozo a great deal, though by the end of the year her anguish had faded into a 'wistful sorrow'. In a cruel mood she wrote: 'I suppose [Kō] is really a piece of sexual bric-a-brac . . . Apart from the sheer delight, he <u>does</u> bore me. He has no conversation – not only because of the language barrier.' She knew that their affair could never be a long-term one. But this may well have been what she valued most about it: she saw that she would continue to exist independently of him, and that it was therefore more important for her to establish herself in her own mind than it was to establish herself in his.

At the start of December, she found work at a hostess bar in the Ginza district, an upmarket commercial quarter, crowded with department stores and the flagship outlets of major fashion labels. The bar was called Butterfly; it was 'about the size of a largish studio apartment in Hampstead and somewhat tastefully panelled in beige pseudo-wood, with two chandeliers in a tiered, wedding-cake style'. Because Christmas was only a few weeks away, there was an artificial white tree, and tinsel everywhere. To go with this European look, the *mama-san* was looking for European girls: Angela roped in Naine (who left after only a couple of days, finding it 'creepy') and an American girl called Keith (renamed Suzy in the article Angela wrote about the experience for *New Society*), who had worked in a hostess bar before, so knew what to expect; Angela probably took her along for security as much as anything else. Their job was to indulge and fawn over the male customers, who over the course of the evening would 'regress to behaviour of a masculine crassness sufficient to make a Germaine Greer out of a Barbara Cartland':

> For example, the girls even go so far as to feed their large infants food. 'Open up!' they pipe, and in goes a heaped forkful of raw shellfish or smoked meat. Unaware how grossly he has been babified, the customer masticates with satisfaction. Meanwhile the *mama-san* herself takes ice from the crystal ice-bucket with a pair of silver tongs and pops it into her customers' drinks with gestures of (in the circumstances) ludicrous refinement. And a hostess can hardly call her breasts her own for the duration of the hostilities.

In her *New Society* article Angela talked about placing herself on 'the front line of the battle [between the sexes]'. But it was her 'desire for sleaziness' that had drawn her to the job in the first place, and it was this element that she tended to emphasise in later life. Though she worked in the bar for just one week – barely enough time to gather material for the article – she later spoke as if it had been a major component of her Japanese experience, to the extent that Paul Barker could write, in 1995, that she 'was never sure how close she got to prostitution in Tokyo'. The answer will disappoint scandal-seekers: she didn't get very close at all.

She spent New Year in Osaka, 'in the warm & enormous bosom of the Kō family'. She got on extremely well with them. The parents were from Cheju Do (now Jeju), a volcanic island situated about fifty miles off the southernmost tip of the Korean mainland. Father Kō considered himself a bit of a scholar – 'an old-fashioned Confucian type', according to one of his sons-in-law – and would idle his days away contemplating things. Angela thought he had a 'faintly bewildered air'. He was by all accounts a useless businessman: the mother was the one who kept the family going. She had sold black-market shoes during the Korean War, and subsequently became a bookkeeper. The latter trade had made them fairly rich. They had purchased a string of run-down properties in Osaka and now lived as slum landlords. Angela wrote: 'I have squared [their profession] with my conscience thus: considering how nasty the Japs have been to the Koreans, the Korean minority seems to have every right to exploit the Japs.' It's a sign of how much she liked them that she was ready to go through the small print of her principles on their behalf.

But however much affection she felt for Kō, and however happy she was to meet his family, she still had no intention of committing herself to a future with him. After they returned to Tokyo the next day, she apologised to Carole for rhapsodising over him: 'Kō _is_ lovely; the limitations of the relationship are obvious, so . . .' She began to wonder if she shouldn't leave him sooner rather than later. 'I realise I _still_ have the task of constructing my personality to cope with & it's conceivable that the days of the 3rd Mr Carter are numbered.'

Not for the first (nor for the last) time, uncertainty over her future was accompanied by symptoms of pregnancy. On 9 January she wrote: 'I went off the pill & onto a diaphragm, & have had no period this month & feel v. ill. Either my system is finding the hormonal adjustment agonising; or I really am pregnant.' On 11 January she recorded the following symptoms: 'cessation of menstruation; vaginal discharge; sore breasts; & curious heaviness in the abdomen. Oh, yes. And a conspicuous decline in libido. A total cessation of libido, in fact, but a constant urge to snuggle.' A week later she was 'more or less convinced – with more justification than usual – that I'm pregnant'. Meanwhile, she was vacillating wildly over whether or not to leave Kō: 'I know I will miss him horribly & I am, of course, absolutely terrified of loneliness & of fending for myself; & Jesus God! I will be <u>32</u> in 3 months' time! . . . But is it worth staying on here, even for a month or so, when I feel nothing but boredom & exhaustion, just because I've got a satisfactory but obviously limited relationship?' Her visa expired in April, so she felt she had to make a decision before then. By 2 February she had ascertained that 'a good, English-speaking abortion will cost about £40'. Her readiness to abort Kō's child was in a sense symbolically destructive of their relationship, and four days later, she made up her mind that she would leave him and return to England. Almost as soon as she had reached that decision, she told Carole that she wasn't pregnant after all: 'I was just doing my thing, with a good deal more conviction even than usual; I had a test . . . to the stunned surprise of those in my confidence (Kō and Naine) it was negative.'

Kō was devastated by the thought of Angela leaving. His initial response was to announce that if she had to return to England, then he would come with her. She tried gently to dissuade him, saying that she was nervous of 'swamping' him, and that having herself got married at the age he was now, she knew how easily such an attachment could breed resentment. That line of argument clearly failed to convince him, and on 14 March he returned to Osaka, presumably so as to gain some distance from the relationship and come to terms with its imminent conclusion. Angela told Carole that the prospect of her departure was 'doing all kinds of things to his head, let alone his heart. He is, after all, in love for the first time and he is very, very young.' It was an admission of what she must, on some level, have known early on – that beneath his apparent self-sufficiency, Kō wasn't yet the 'complete person' she had wanted to believe.

She went to Osaka 'to comfort Kō', and was struck by his gestures – 'the childlike delicacy & precision with which he stirs sugar into his coffee; his small sigh of content, that small sigh which . . . rouses in my heart a melting tenderness I can hardly bear; the way he carries his head, like a bird' – all of which 'seemed remembered from far longer ago than a week, because I had grown used to his oddness'. She brought him back to Tokyo with her, and over the next month her affection for him didn't dim. Shortly after she returned to England, she wrote in her journal:

> It <u>was</u> – though blurred by my sickness, psychosomatic pregnancies & whatever, an unusually beautiful affair . . . I can't think what will come next or who will come next; Kō is in my heart, for ever, and maybe I do not want time to blur his perfection at nineteen, his warm, clean, golden flesh, his eyes like the hearts of anemones, his Charlie Chaplin run, his dearness. I think this is maybe the nub of it – you can't possess people; you only borrow them for a time & then give them back to themselves.

*   *   *

In early April, Angela received another discouraging letter from Peter Schwed, effectively terminating her relationship with Simon & Schuster:

> I'm afraid I have nothing but bad news to report about our reaction to THE INFERNAL DESIRE MACHINES OF DR HOFFMAN . . . I very much regret to tell you that all of us thought it much too excessive (to use your own word) and a book that we couldn't possibly do even as well with as the (to me) disappointing sales that we have experienced with some of your novels which we thought so good . . . HOFFMAN is just too much of an odd item to have any chance in our opinion.

'The letter from Simon & Schuster has affected me rather deeply,' Angela wrote. 'I suppose it means that, from now on, I really am going it alone and the chance of becoming rich and famous is no longer an open option . . . The really sickening fear which sometimes affects me is that I am, basically, talentless.' She wrote to Anthony Burgess (still her closest literary ally), telling him that she felt despondent about being a novelist, that the reviews of *Love* had depressed her, and that she worried her career wasn't going anywhere. He replied with a characteristically forthright note, advising her to 'for God's sake get out of Japan . . . The thing to do is to get on with the writing, easier said than done. But what else is there? You <u>must</u> get on with the writing, because you're a good writer. I mean that.' His hectoring tone seems to have done the trick, and during her last few weeks in Tokyo, Angela started work on a new story, 'Penetrating to the Heart of the Forest', another version of the Fall, in which a brother and sister begin to notice one another's developing bodies after they eat the fruit of a forbidden tree.

As her departure neared, Angela spent a lot of time thinking about how her time in Japan had changed her: 'it really has been the most extraordinary experience. I've packed so much into it.' After the manufactured intensity and then the fleeting period of genuine romantic happiness with Sozo, the emotional trauma of the relationship's collapse, the painful but constructive experience of living alone, and the calmness and contentment of her time with Kō, she had a much clearer idea of what she wanted from life: 'what I do feel, really, is that I am a lot more ordinary than I thought. This probably only means I've come to terms with being peculiar; possibly, also, the time for existential leaps is over and I <u>am</u> myself, now.'

PART III

CHAPTER THIRTEEN

Yet another foreign country

Angela returned to London on 24 April 1972, and began renting an attic room on Arundel Place, a somewhat gloomy Georgian terrace in the shabbily handsome, gradually gentrifying borough of Islington, north of the river Thames. The house – number 8 – was owned by a gay couple who gave lavish dinner parties and favoured art nouveau furnishings ('which, senses peeled by the ascetic rigour of Japanese interior decoration, I find altogether TOO MUCH', Angela wrote). There were two other tenants: a German doctor, and a 'beautiful, queer' Irishman in his late twenties, who was studying for his A levels.

Angela's room – like her childhood bedroom – looked down onto the railway tracks behind the house. It was sparsely furnished, with a single bed and a desk, but no armchair or rug. By way of decorating it she handwrote short stories in an exercise book, then tore out the pages and pinned them to the walls. Soon the whole room was covered in these scraps of manuscript.

Islington was still a predominantly working-class neighbourhood in the early 1970s, but its low rents, central location, and atmosphere of neglected grandeur made it an attractive habitat for the less well-to-do sort of literary type. Joe Orton lived there until his murder in 1967; so did B. S. Johnson, until his suicide in 1973. In spite of her bias towards south London, Angela soon warmed to the area. 'The atavistic appeal of these Georgian squares is v. strong,' she wrote, '& it is so English it feels, in a curious way, as though one were abroad.'

All the same, it was a dilapidated inner-city neighbourhood, and unsavoury elements were never far away. Coming back to the house one evening,

Angela heard a man walking behind her. 'I knew it was a man because he was muttering to himself,' she wrote in her journal. 'But I thought he was talking to a friend until his footsteps became menacing & he said: "I'd like to stick my cock between your legs."' She was almost at 8 Arundel Place, so she quickened her pace and hurried up the steps, but then fumbled for the key in her bag, and as the man loomed behind her she became afraid – 'I think he was exposing himself' – until her Irish housemate opened the door and he ran off.

It was an isolated incident, but not quite anomalous, given the national mood of derangement and decay. Angela was 'dreadfully shocked by the state of GB'. Since Edward Heath's surprise election victory in June 1970, inflation and unemployment had risen sharply: wages lost value almost by the month, and a relentless series of strikes and boycotts was jamming some of the essential mechanisms of society. The phones often failed to work, power cuts were commonplace, and the trains dawdled and lurched along without much loyalty to the timetable. A few days after she returned, Angela was travelling down Fleet Street when a group picketing the *Evening Standard* started rocking her taxi – 'it was like that F. Scott Fitzgerald story, "May Day"', she told Carole. In the newspapers she read of bombing campaigns by a rash of terrorist organisations – the Provisional IRA, the anarchist Angry Brigade, the Palestinian group Black September – which had all surfaced while she was in Japan. She began to feel that the death of capitalism might be at hand: 'This feverish, hysterical feeling of being In At The End is very exhilarating,' she wrote to Carole. 'I really do feel excited, this is history and one is living right in it.' She entertained 'the most apocalyptic fantasies', some of which were channelled into 'Elegy for a Freelance', a story set in a crumbling, convulsive London ('it hardly seemed possible that the city could survive the summer'), where terrorists make petrol bombs in mouldy basements, snipers lurk in upper windows, and owning property has been made illegal. The narrator lives 'high up in an attic, in a house in a square'.

High up in her own attic, across the road from Arundel Square, Angela weathered the storm. She saw a lot of Andrea Newman and Rebecca Howard, and had a brief affair with a publisher called Bill, whose English public-school accent 'got on my tits like anything'. It wasn't a very deep relationship. He made no secret of seeing other women, even calling one of them to arrange an assignation while he was in bed with Angela

('I was terribly impressed,' she wrote in her journal). Her romantic attention was still occupied by thoughts of Kō. She felt 'the ache of loss, the amputated feeling . . . mixing in with the memory of what I felt when I split with S. so it is all the more subtly, devastatingly poignant'. She hadn't heard from him since getting back, which she thought was probably a good sign, an indication that he was getting over her. Then, in May, she had a letter from his sister Mina. It revealed that, devastated by Angela's departure, Kō had run away from home and hadn't been heard of since. 'I feel very bad about this,' Angela told Carole. 'I mean, I didn't know he cared.'

A few weeks after getting back, Angela visited Carole in Bradford. From the moment she arrived, the atmosphere was strained. She had a 'sensation of walking on thin ice', and detected 'a positive shutting off – almost an audible click – of interest in my lover, which hurt me very much . . . in my lover & also in the big affair, which was with Japan'. After an uncomfortable few days, she made her excuses and returned to London. On the train back she wrote Carole a furious letter:

> Carole, oh, Carole, you are <u>so</u> demanding! I feel, in some ways, you have idealised me into a version of yourself while I've been away, maybe inevitably, and there is necessarily a jarring of gears when you meet me, than whom few people are more intransigently themselves, once again. But I <u>can't</u> be you, and to demand I should be only brings out the worst in me.

She had been planning to live in Athol Road for part of the summer, but now she began making excuses for staying in London, citing the pressures of work ('far too much') and money ('running out'). Her next letter, dated 16 May, was also full of excuses, this time for not having written sooner. It's a revealing lapse. She often complained, during these months, of how her years in Japan had alienated her from British society – in July she told Anthony Burgess that 'the trouble with travelling is . . . eventually one returns, to find one has merely arrived at yet another foreign country' – but it's conspicuous that, far from drawing tight the threads of belonging, she unpicked the stitches of one of her oldest and closest friendships. Her correspondence with Carole limped on for a while, but it never again had the warmth and intimacy that had characterised it previously, and sometimes their letters descended into outright recrimination. On 16 June, presumably in response to nagging from Carole, Angela wrote:

> I can't stand friction. It's no longer the stuff of life to me. Please don't think badly of me or dramatise the situation. I find the whole thing fairly scrutable & it grieves me, a bit, 'cos I can't really be a support to anyone in any way, except by just standing around being my kooky little self. When people stop enjoying me, I cease to have a function for them, really; & maybe that's what happened. We both used the correspondence somewhat as an end-in-itself, you know; a working out of theories of modus vivendi that, it turns out, are probably incompatible.

Rebecca Howard was given to understand that the decline of Angela's friendship with Carole had to do with Angela's fear of engulfment: 'all I know is that [Angela] used to, if people tried to, in her words, "take her over" . . . she'd just back off, and not want to know any more'. But Carole's role in her life had always been somewhat pushy and intrusive. The change was in Angela – who two years earlier might not have described herself as someone 'than whom few people are more intransigently themselves' – and until the end of her life, Carole felt hurt by her friend's sudden change of heart.

The Infernal Desire Machines of Dr Hoffman was published by Hart-Davis in June. A few months earlier, Angela had included a dedication: 'For Sozo Araki, my more than Albertina.' At the last moment, she asked her publishers to change it to something that reflected her current loyalties: 'For the family, wherever they are, reluctantly including Ivan [the bitter, isolated middle sibling in *The Brothers Karamazov*] who thought he was Alyosha.'

The novel had been a tremendous risk, but in spite of Angela's later avowal that it 'marked the beginning of my obscurity', it was reviewed widely, and with unanimous approval. John Howkins, the *Time Out* reviewer, admiringly described it as 'a real freak . . . an erotic, sexy, energetic, picaresque, escapist dream. The prose is luscious.' Perhaps such accolades from the underground press were only to be expected, but the mainstream press was – if anything – even more flattering. In the *Financial Times*, Isabel Quigley wrote that 'Angela Carter has the kind of electric talent that tingles through whatever she writes. It reminds me a little of Nabokov's . . . She must be far and away the most gifted of our younger novelists.' Elizabeth Berridge, writing in the *Daily Telegraph*, agreed that Angela Carter was 'unique among her contemporaries in her ability to sustain such imaginings and leaven them with humour and poetry', while in the *Sunday Times* John Whitley applauded her 'peacock brilliance' and called *The Infernal Desire Machines of Dr Hoffman* 'her most impressive novel so far'. Even Auberon Waugh, the habitually stodgy and backward-looking critic of the *Spectator*, offered up an ovation: 'I can only testify that I read it enthralled, fascinated and bewitched.' Angela was interviewed for the *Guardian* by Catherine Stott (who reported that 'being a somewhat fey, whimsical person, she had elected not to meet for lunch in any of London's trendy literati trats, but preferred to seek out a Turkish restaurant in most ethnic Stoke Newington'): she was described as being 'somewhat bewildered [by] the acclaim'.

Most pleasingly of all, the book earned Angela the attention of her peers. That year, B. S. Johnson included her in a list of authors 'who [were] writing as though it mattered, as though they meant it, as though they meant it to matter'. Among the handful of others he thought worthy of this praise were Samuel Beckett, John Berger and Anthony Burgess (the three contemporary authors Angela most admired, excepting such distant stars as Nabokov and Borges), as well as Alan Burns, Eva Figes, Rayner Heppenstall, Ann Quinn and Stefan Themerson. The last few formed a loose circle of 'experimental' writers, bound together by Johnson himself, who since the mid-1960s had been trying to sprinkle a bit of Continental spice – metafictional gestures such as intrusive third-person narrators, physical novelties such as holes cut strategically through the pages of a book – over the social-realist soup of British fiction. There's no evidence that Angela had read any of them, and she might not have felt an overwhelming affinity even if she had (she took only a sporadic interest in formal experiment, and tended to prefer juicy prose – writing with 'blood and brains everywhere' – to Johnson's brand of mordant minimalism), but she would certainly have liked being claimed for that side of the struggle.

Commercially, it was a rather different story. By the beginning of August, *The Infernal Desire Machines of Dr Hoffman* had been turned down by 'eight or nine' American publishers. 'I haven't yet actually dared face up to what this <u>means</u>,' Angela wrote. 'It really means I can no longer hope to make a living from writing. This is back at square one with a vengeance – & to think I shared all the fat years with Paul!'

Angela didn't need a great deal of money to enjoy life – 'I always find it easier to tailor my lifestyle to my income than the other way around' – but with only a dribble of royalties from previous novels and the odd £30 cheque from *New Society* coming in, her financial situation was starting to look bleak. Joe Scott-Clark (her editor at *Queen* magazine, to which she had contributed a few paperback reviews in 1967, and a short story, 'The Empress of Cockaigne', in 1968) suggested some of the reasons for her difficulties in a letter supporting her application for an Arts Council grant:

> her first publishers saw her as the author of high-flown literary novels (which indeed she is) and chose to cocoon her rather than subject her to the brashness of the publicity machine. Her subsequent publishers . . . have undergone dramatic structural changes in the last year or two and it may be that energies which could have been well spent on publicizing Miss Carter's works, were instead diverted to other affairs . . .
>
> It may help the Arts Council to come to a decision in Miss Carter's favour to know that [she] is obliged to live very modestly in an Islington attic bed-sitter and genuinely has difficulty making ends meet.

This image of garret life evidently affected the judges, and Angela was awarded £1,000, tax-free, which she received on 10 January 1973. In the meantime, she would have to muddle through. She wrote as much journalism as she could (most of it for *New Society*), tried to sell a few of the short stories she had been writing ('Penetrating to the Heart of the Forest' was bought by the upmarket women's magazine *Nova*), and accepted an invitation to judge the John Llewellyn Rhys Prize (the books she had to read were 'so God awful I feel the writing of fiction should be banned instantly for three years, except for me, of course'). She even – providing a measure of her desperation – persuaded the American producer Leonard Field to let her have another go at *The Magic Toyshop* script. She also applied for two academic jobs, one at the University of East Anglia and the other at University College London. Her referees were John Berger (whom she had met once, probably at a literary party, and with whom she had formed a rapport – 'I admire him very much as a man . . . it really was like meeting Shelley') and Anthony Burgess (who told her: 'if called on, I'll say that you're one of the three best living women novelists, which is probably true'). In spite of these illustrious backers, she wasn't so much as interviewed by either institution. 'When I really want to humiliate myself, I apply for a job at a British University,' she wrote a couple of years later.

Just as it was starting to look as if things might fall apart before she received the Arts Council grant, she was approached by Marion Boyars, joint managing director of Calder & Boyars – an avant-garde independent publishing house whose authors included Samuel Beckett, Alain Robbe-Grillet and William Burroughs – to translate Xavière Gauthier's *Surréalisme et sexualité*, one of the first feminist critiques of the surrealist movement. Published in 1971 and based on her doctoral thesis, Gauthier's book traces the various incarnations of womanhood – 'ranging from the innocent child-woman to the devouring praying mantis' – found in surrealist art and literature, and exposes them all as male fantasies. Angela thought it was 'a very good book indeed, very erudite and extremely pertinent'. Many of its ideas – not to mention its basic approach – influenced *The Sadeian Woman*.

After spending a few days with Gauthier's book, Angela wrote to Boyars that she'd 'like to translate it very, very much indeed – because I'm a woman and, in a slap-dash kind of way, an anarcho-Marxist as well as heavily into . . . the surrealist movement'. She drew up a five-page sample translation, doing it 'very freely, as [Gauthier's] prose style often isn't up to her argument'. On 18 October, Boyars offered a flat fee of £200, 'plus half of whatever we would get from an American publisher', with a deadline of 30 March 1973. Basic Books signed up to publish the translation in the States, but there's no record of what – if anything – they contributed to Angela's finances.

Perhaps the clearest indication of Angela's deteriorating friendship with Carole was her commencement of a relationship with Andrew Travers, a former boyfriend of Rebecca, who had also been at the University of Bristol. Back then he had been heavily into drugs (amphetamines and hallucinogens) and petty crime (vandalism and theft), with noisily held anarchist leanings. Carole hated him, believing him to have burgled her flat when they were undergraduates. Other contemporaries thought he was unhinged. Angela had always seemed to agree, describing him in a letter of 1970 (when they had both been dinner guests at Rebecca's house on Child Street, and Andrew had ruined the evening by shouting at everyone) as 'not only insane but actively unpleasant'.

Her opinion started to change when she ran into him again in the autumn of 1972, at the central London flat of a mutual friend from Bristol. He offered her a lift home in his Morris Oxford saloon, and outside 8 Arundel Place she invited him in for coffee. 'We sat downstairs at a huge table loaded with the detritus of a generous dinner party, the remains of a large leg of roast lamb, fruit, cheese, and so on,' he recalled. 'After wolfing down some of the lamb . . . Angela suddenly sat on my lap.' She had always found him physically attractive, with his slim, lofty build, gaunt features, and hooded blue eyes behind big, rimless glasses; now she felt that he had mellowed, and she was touched by what she saw as his vulnerability. 'Time & ill fortune have wrought certain changes in Andrew,' she wrote later that year, paying tribute to his 'good conduct & amenable demeanour'.

Not everyone could perceive the changes that Angela described. But even his staunchest detractors conceded that Andrew was witty, free-spirited, and intellectually dynamic. It's clear that Angela valued his mind as much as his physical qualities, and her letters to him (most of which were written during the summer of 1973, when she was staying with Edward Horesh in Bath) frequently deviate into discussions of Freud, Baudelaire, Rimbaud, Firbank, Brecht and Tarkovsky, among other artists and thinkers. She later described him as 'one of the few people I ever met who took fiction seriously, as a mode of truth', and also wrote that she saw him 'not [as] an emanation of myself, but an Other with an utterly different mode of being, a rich & extraordinary one that astonishes me'.

The ill fortune Andrew had suffered included a period in the psychiatric unit of Queen Elizabeth Hospital in Welwyn Garden City, where he had been treated for depression, panic attacks, and what he describes as 'post-traumatic stress disorder brought on by ill-advised ingestion of hallucinogenics'. By 1972 he was writing short stories (Angela thought that several of them revealed talent), making collages, and spray-painting political slogans on walls. Shortly afterwards, he began working as an assistant gardener at St Pancras Cemetery, a job that involved driving round the offices of the London Borough of Camden in a van to deliver and maintain flowers grown at the cemetery (Angela enjoyed claiming that he was a gravedigger; when the relationship ended, she told Hughie and Joan it was because 'he brought his work home with him').

On Sunday 5 November, Angela had a row with her landlord at Arundel Place ('I am not entirely innocent,' she admitted, 'my manner has been provocative in the extreme'), and was given two weeks' notice to quit her room. A few nights later, she met the New Zealand-born poet Fleur Adcock at a literary party, and explained her situation. By luck, some of Fleur's friends had just moved out of her house in East Finchley, and she invited Angela to take their room. 'In the interval before she actually moved in,' Fleur recalled, 'I read her extraordinary novels and wondered what sort of a sinister character I had invited to live in my house. As it turned out, there was nothing sinister about Angela, but she came with a boyfriend to whom that adjective could be applied.'

That Angela took Andrew with her to East Finchley suggests that the relationship was already fairly serious. But she still hadn't told Carole about it. Even at this stage – when she needed him to drive her to Bradford to collect the belongings that had been stored there since 1969 – she wrote only that 'my path has crossed with that of Andrew Travers, & he being fortuitously unemployed, offered to drive me, an offer I accepted with a double-take shortly after . . . like, I remembered you weren't speaking to him'. Carole was extremely distressed, not only by Andrew's presence in her home, but by what she suspected were Angela's motives in bringing him there. John Lockwood – who was no longer living with Carole, but remained a close friend – was given her impressions: 'she said Angela's entire manner while she was there, packing Andy's van, was this kind of almost gleeful provocative manner'.

It was the last time that Carole and Angela ever saw one another. Shortly afterwards, Angela wrapped up the correspondence that had sustained her through so many difficult times with one final letter. It reads like a coda to their friendship, an attempt to acknowledge its importance in her life, and to protect its memory from the spread of hard feelings:

> I am perceptive but not sensitive & that can be a dreadful com-
> bination, especially for somebody as sensitive as you. I want to
> apologise for all the various inconveniences I've caused, a lot of
> them quite unwittingly. There is something I want to say everso
> much & that is, that without you I doubt I'd have left Paul. The
> notion of self-determination has carried me a long way on from
> what I was 3 years ago & I can look at my new landlady's lifestyle –
> which is virtually minimal living, days pass, she speaks to no-one,
> she is the Emily Dickinson of East Finchley – without, now, any
> shudder of dread at all & I am and always will be more grateful
> than I can say to you.

*　*　*

East Finchley is a quiet, unassuming neighbourhood, situated in the leafy north-western heights of the metropolis – Angela considered it a 'godforsaken hole accessible only to Highgate village, a part of London I rather dislike'. Fleur's house was on Lincoln Road, a long mid-Victorian terrace with an eclectic mix of residents (ranging from Tony Gould, the literary editor of *New Society*, to a group of Antipodean squatters who played loud music into the early hours). Angela and Andrew had a large bedroom and a kitchen to themselves on the ground floor; Fleur lived upstairs with her teenage son, and worked during the day at the Foreign Office Library.

Though Fleur and Angela later became close, they kept their distance while they were living together. 'I was always slightly in awe of her,' Fleur remembered. 'She was so brilliant and so strange and incredible. I didn't like to sort of encroach on her life.' Very occasionally, they went out together to the Five Bells pub, and Angela would sometimes venture upstairs to the sitting room when Fleur had friends over. But on the whole, she stayed downstairs and focussed on her work.

Andrew remembers her routine: 'she didn't start particularly early in the morning but once she got going it was office hours more or less, broken by phone calls and reading the post and cups of tea and cups of coffee and, if I wasn't driving the van, frantic sex'. She sometimes went out in the evenings to literary parties, but he formed the impression that she didn't enjoy them much: 'I think she found most social interactions quite thwarting, frustrating. "Contactless sociability" was one of her favourite phrases in those days.' He remembers her reading Erving Goffman's essay 'Embarrassment and Social Organisation', which proposes that social discomfiture is a product of slippage between the subject's projected and protected selves: 'she found that incredibly exciting, that idea that people were so painfully trying to live two roles at once, and each role invalidates the other in the embarrassing situation – she found that very exciting, because it chimed with her own experience of making a mess, even of ordering a cup of coffee in a bar or whatever'.

Andrew describes his relationship with Angela as 'intensely sexual' and 'not always dreadfully sentimental'. From almost the very beginning they argued frequently. Looking back, he thinks that their fights were only 'mildly tempestuous' ('there were no knives'), but admits that he was 'a quite difficult person to be around, quite dogmatic, very easily offended, and feeling violent against anybody who offended me'. Angela would have agreed with this assessment. She accused him of 'possessiveness' and 'super-sensitivity'. Believing him to be reading her journal, she left him notes in it: 'Dear Andrew . . . You are lonely when you are with me because you do not apprehend me as a different person, as an other.' She felt oppressed by what she thought was his restricted view of her:

> He does not see me as a subject but as an object on which he projects fantasies of lust & domination & aggression & despair; otherwise, how could he submit me to this atrocious suffering. It is a kind of higher selfishness; an obsession that blots out all the areas of my personality that don't fit with his picture of me. Worse, not only does he see me as his object; he sees himself as his own object, & can take himself so seriously because, at the very deepest level, <u>he does not take himself seriously at all</u>.

Rather than air these grievances, she tended to resort to implacable silence – a tactic reminiscent of Paul Carter. 'You knew you'd done something that annoyed her or angered her,' Andrew remembered, 'but all you would hear would be the pounding of typewriter keys.' Perhaps she felt that passive aggression was her only recourse, that any more open expression of her frustrations would mean an escalation of hostilities on Andrew's side. 'He provokes violence as an excuse to commit violence,' she wrote in her journal. 'His method is to procure hysteria in me – always an easy task – & then keep me on the edge of tears . . . in my fakely calm mood.'

Even so, it's clear that the tensions between them sometimes erupted into ugly scenes. On 17 February 1973, Angela wrote to Anthony Burgess about:

> a spiritual/psychological crise in my cohabitor, whom I call the Roderick Usher of East Finchley, which produced a mild version of the same in me as a girl can't be skipping out of the way of flung missiles all the time and retain her sangfroid, or her togetherness. Half the time I was packing to shift and the other half unpacking. Then he packed in his job (he was working as a gardener's labourer in St Pancras Cemetery, where Belle Crippen is buried) and perked up no end immediately. Because work is bad for one, I suppose. But it was a tumultuous time. However, since I always go for nutters (and they always go for me), I suppose, in some subterranean fashion, I like it.

Whether she actually 'liked it' or (as seems more likely) not, Angela did get a fair amount of conversational mileage out of the 'flung missiles'.

She told several people around this time that her boyfriend had thrown a typewriter at her. Andrew doesn't deny the incident, only that Angela was the missile's target: 'I think I threw a typewriter at something, not at her . . . I never threw anything *at* her.'

Angela would, in 1973, have been newly sensitive to the stench of domestic violence. Among the most conspicuous of the changes to have affected British society while she was away was the rise of the women's movement. When she had left, there had only been four feminist groups in the whole of London; by the end of 1971 there were almost sixty. The intensification of the campaign, stoked by the writing of Sheila Rowbotham and Germaine Greer, reflected long-simmering dissatisfaction among many British women. Their lives had supposedly become much freer during the 1960s, with the contraceptive pill reducing the risk of unwanted pregnancies and washing machines easing the burden of unwanted housework. But these scientific advances had done nothing to alter the underlying structures of a male-dominated society, and even in the utopian climate of the 1968 student movement, the role of women had usually been limited to typing up leaflets and making tea for the male activists. Now the private frustration felt by millions of women – the frustration of being treated as sexual objects and domestic instruments; of suffering lower pay and scarcer opportunities than their male counterparts; of having their identities defined by their anatomy – cohered into a wide-ranging political movement.

Members of the Women's Liberation Workshop (a sort of federal administration for the country's various feminist groups) ran a guerrilla campaign on the London Underground, covering adverts featuring naked women with stickers proclaiming *You earn more as a real whore* and *This advertisement is insulting to women*. In November 1970, protestors stormed the Miss World competition at the Royal Albert Hall, hurling bags of flour over the contestants and chasing the host – a terrified Bob Hope – off the stage. On 6 March 1971, thousands of women marched on Trafalgar Square, bearing aloft a shop mannequin nailed to a cross and a washing line from which hung bras, bodices and corsets, while chanting: 'I'm not just a delectable screwing machine' and 'Biology isn't destiny'. The mood was revolutionary, and by the time Angela returned from Japan, the movement had chalked up some significant victories: in January 1970, Barbara Castle (the Secretary of State for Employment, and by some distance the most prominent female politician in the country) had introduced an Equal Pay Bill; the first refuge for victims of domestic violence had been established in 1971; and at the end of that year the Wimpy chain of burger bars had scrapped its policy of barring admittance to unaccompanied women after midnight.

Asked about her relationship to the movement in 1984, Angela explained that she wasn't 'actively involved in anything. I snipe from the sidelines and I get attacked a lot.' It was always the place where she felt most comfortable. Though she described herself for a while as a 'radical feminist', her politics always had as much in common with the libertarian and socialist tendencies. She never saw the oppression of women as categorically different from other forms of oppression, and believed that if femininity was a cultural construction, forcing the individual into a cramped and demeaning role, then so was masculinity. 'Imagine having to be macho. I can't think of anything more terrible,' she told an interviewer in 1979. 'I suspect that when my sisters think of me – and I don't for a moment imagine that they do that very often – they see me as a bit of an Uncle Tom. I think it's *all* terrible. I think it's terrible for everyone, not just women.'

The depictions of feminists in the mainstream press didn't really allow for such nuanced perspectives. They tended to tar the entire movement with the coarse brush of Valerie Solanas – the American founder of SCUM (the Society for Cutting Up Men) and would-be-assassin of Andy Warhol – and to dismiss it as an absurd sideshow. An *Observer* journalist, sent to cover the first National Women's Conference at Ruskin College, Oxford in April 1970, began her report by noting that the commissioning editor had told her: 'It's easily the most amusing thing that's happening this weekend.' Almost exactly a year later, a *Daily Telegraph* columnist pronounced that the 'overriding impression' of Women's Lib was 'of a deep sexual unhappiness among its members'. The tabloid press, meanwhile, adopted a frankly leering attitude towards women: in November 1970, the *Sun* introduced topless female models on page three of every edition, and both the *Daily Mirror* and the *Daily Star* followed suit shortly afterwards.

The underground press made some efforts to counteract this trend. In autumn 1971, *Frendz* magazine produced a women's issue, co-ordinated by the twenty-year-old journalist Rosie Boycott. At around the same time, Marsha Rowe of *Ink* magazine was organising meetings of women from the underground press, at which they discussed their frustration at being forced to work as glorified secretaries, and shared their experiences of sexual dissatisfaction and illegal abortions.

In 1972 Boycott and Rowe joined forces to set up *Spare Rib*, a magazine that sought to address their colleagues' sense that 'there was a huge gap between what their lives were about and what they read, between the cushioned world of the women's weeklies and the reality of inequality and feminine conditioning'. Working by candlelight due to the ongoing power cuts of that year, using typewriters borrowed from friends, and desks, chairs and filing cabinets from the offices of *Ink*, they produced their first issue in July. It had a rough-and-ready feel – spelling errors were common, the print often broke free from its setting and sloped down the page – but its content was electrifying. There were features on the suffragette movement, on the situation of women in the fourteenth and fifteenth centuries, and on women's attitudes to their breasts, alongside news items on the first female admiral in the US navy, and on the decision of Femfresh, the vaginal-deodorant makers, to target twelve- to- fifteen-year-olds – a move the manufacturers justified by noting that 'with the onset of Women's Lib, their market had been disastrously decreased'. There was a damning review of the first issue of *Cosmopolitan*, which also claimed to be a new kind of magazine for a new kind of woman, but which *Spare Rib*'s reviewer described as 'a promise swathed in fantasy built upon a lie . . . *Cosmopolitan* is to Women's Liberation what Little Black Sambo is to the Black Panthers.'

Angela saw the magazine and liked what it was doing. She rang the editors and they invited her to lunch. She arrived 'tall, slim, and scantily dressed', recalled Rowe: 'she seemed all air and ideas. She was completely focussed on what she wanted to talk about, and these were rather brave things to be saying for the time. She spoke slowly, but she wasn't hesitant, not in terms of intention.' She proposed an interview with the artist Evelyn Williams, who was making large, somewhat grotesque wax figures like vast misshapen dolls, which Angela admired for their sense of 'the loneliness of the child, the loneliness of the mother, the loneliness of mother-and-child as a self-enclosed unit'. The article appeared in March 1973. She followed it, in May, with a piece about sexual politics in Japan, illustrated with her own drawings. She focussed on the misogyny implicit in the exaggerated Japanese versions of femininity: 'the first thing you feel is that they must hate women very much if they subject them to such a rigorous deperson-alisation process'.

Two months later she wrote another piece about sexual relations in Japan, in a somewhat different vein (it was full of prurient detail, such as the information that 'the Turkish baths supply the needy with a brisk masturbatory service at about £7.50'), for a very different publication. *Men Only* had been relaunched in 1971 by Paul Raymond, the proprietor of the UK's first strip club (the Raymond Revuebar in Soho). Along with its stablemate *Club International* – which Angela also wrote several articles for during this period – it mixed smutty articles (D. M. Thomas on dirty words, Howard Nelson on sex in history) with full-colour spreads of naked women. The most interesting of Angela's contributions was 'a custom-tailored short story' for *Club International*. Billed by the editors as 'bizarre and sexy', 'The Upland Road' is in fact a characteristic Angela Carter production, with nods to Kafka and Poe (the plot concerns a man travelling to a castle, where a woman called Madeleine is waiting for him), and though its erotic elements are often comically gratuitous ('"You will get better lodging here," said the woman simply and unbuttoned her green bodice so that there spilled out her fair-skinned breasts with rich, crimson nipples that hardened at the cool touch of the air and quivered as they would have done under my fingers'), they're no more explicit than those in *The Infernal Desire Machines of Dr Hoffman* or *The Bloody Chamber*. And for all its emphasis on the female body, the story is recognisably feminist in intention: the hapless narrator is batted between a series of ferociously liberated women, who hold all the psychological and sexual power.

Pornography split the women's movement – with increasing acrimoniousness as the 1970s progressed, and almost irreconcilably in the early 1980s – and was the subject of several heated articles in *Spare Rib*. Broadly speaking, feminist commentators were divided between those who considered porn to be less an expression of sexuality than a consolidation of male power, a form of violence against women in that it silenced and objectified them in its basic structures (a position put most pithily by the American feminist Robin Morgan, who wrote in 1974 that 'pornography is the theory, and rape is the practice'); and those who argued that there was a hard line between fantasy and action, and that women could (indeed, should) enjoy porn every bit as much as men did.

Angela found the first view especially tiresome. 'I think some of the Sisters make too much of a fuss about porn,' she said in 1984. 'They imply also that women who don't make a fuss are in some way in complicity. I think that's bananas. Violence against women is husbands beating their wives to a pulp.' But she wasn't much more tolerant of the idea that there was no causal relationship between pornography and the wider world. Her own view was that it stood in the same relationship to the world as any other sort of cultural production:

> We've almost forgotten that it was Lady C[hatterley] who opened the floodgates to reasonably priced, readily available porn . . . The real irony of the decision of the good men and true who lifted the ban on Lawrence's peculiar sexual fantasies was the notion that prevailed that, if a book was both a dirty book and a work of literature – a *good* dirty book – then the art would disinfect the filth . . . Behind this theory lies the typically British notion that art is utterly useless and has no effect whatsoever on the man in the street. Art is so irrelevant it doesn't need censorship . . .
>
> Porn degrades the image of women; but so does much of the advertising industry and so, dammit, does 'Lady C' herself, and a whole lot of world-class art-literature that isn't even dirty at all.

Angela's socialist consciousness meant she believed that pornography *was* an expression of power relations, but only in so far as everything else was, and that like everything else, it was capable of expressing those relations differently. This insight dovetailed with her thinking on the Marquis de Sade, who she believed had – by treating his female characters as 'beings of power' and acknowledging the full extent of their sexuality – 'put pornography in the service of women, or, perhaps, allowed it to be invaded by an ideology not inimical to women'. His work demonstrated the possibility of 'the moral pornographer', which is what she aimed to be when writing for *Men Only* and *Club International*.

The chance to explore some of these ideas in more depth came when Rosie Boycott threw a lunch party in honour of the Polish–American novelist Jerzy Kosiński. Angela sat next to Carmen Callil, a thirty-five-year-old Australian publicist who was now running her own agency, having previously worked alongside William Miller and John Boothe at Panther. Fiercely intelligent and full of creative energy, Carmen was tiny and strikingly beautiful, with curly dark hair and flashing blue eyes. She called a spade a spade, usually to its face, and was known for her quick temper and her indefatigable loyalty to her friends. She recalled that during the lunch Angela announced that her boyfriend had thrown a typewriter at her: did Carmen think she should leave him? Carmen said that she certainly did. Remembering the occasion in 1982, Angela zoomed in on a different moment:

> somebody was indulging in a succession of the then newly fashionable Arab jokes. A slow freeze spread out from the person on my right but, unperturbed, the jester went on and on about white nightgowns and goats on Bayswater balconies until this woman . . . laid down her knife and fork and announced:
> 'An Arab would be most offended.'
> 'Surely,' said this insensitive man, undeterred, 'there are no Arabs here.'
> Petite as she is, Carmen was instantly the tallest person there. 'I am an Arab,' she said majestically. My first and abiding impression therefore . . . was of an extraordinary strength of character.

Carmen was in the process of setting up a publishing house for books by women, which she wanted to have a flavour of *Spare Rib*; it was going to be called Spare Rib Books, but the name was soon changed to Virago. Rosie Boycott and Marsha Rowe were already on board as directors. Shortly after the lunch for Jerzy Kosiński, when Virago was still very much at the drawing-board stage, Carmen and Rosie took Angela out for lunch at San Lorenzo, a fashionable Italian restaurant in the swanky central London district of Knightsbridge ('How we afforded such things, I don't know,' said Carmen, who was funding the project partially out of her own pocket), and asked if she'd write a book for them. Angela mentioned her ideas about Sade. Carmen thought that they were 'splendid', and asked her to develop a formal proposal.

Angela went away and typed up what she described as an 'advertisement' for *The Sadeian Woman*, which she said would be 'about de Sade and sexuality as a political phenomenon and the myth of gender'. It would be about 60,000 words long, she thought, and would be divided into seven chapters, 'because I like the number seven'. She wanted illustrations, and intended to spend time in France looking at Sade's manuscripts as part of her research. 'Hopefully, it will turn out both erudite and also elegant, somewhat French eighteenth century. Which is only apt. But I'm not sure, yet, what it <u>will</u> turn out like.'

Carmen wasn't fazed by this admission – 'I'm more enthusiastic about your "advertisement" than anything else that's come our way,' she wrote – and after Virago's first commissioning meeting in September she offered an advance of £1,000; Tony Godwin of Harcourt Brace Jovanovich paid a further $1,500 to publish the book in the United States. 'I won't be able to start work on it until the end of the year,' Angela warned, 'say, Jan 1, 1974, to be on the safe side; and I am a bugger about deadlines, I mean, I evade them, so it would be best to allow me <u>as long as a year to complete it</u>.' As it turned out, even this supposedly generous time frame was wildly optimistic. The project occupied her throughout the mid-1970s, and she was still fiddling with the manuscript as late as February 1978.

Her friendship with Carmen wasn't hindered by the delay, and she was soon placed on Virago's editorial committee. Over the next few years Angela brought several new authors (including Pat Barker and Lorna Tracy) to Carmen's attention and nursed them into print, wrote reports on various manuscripts, and from 1978 made recommendations for the Virago Modern Classics range, including some books by men – Sade's *Justine*, Richardson's *Clarissa* – that she felt were expressive of female 'pathology'.

Virago had its roots in the women's movement, but it didn't position itself at the radical end of the spectrum – it was sometimes derided as 'the accept-able face of feminism' – and Angela was sympathetic to its mass-market designs. She wanted the company to make proper money out of women's writing, to rescue it from the margins by rescuing it from the registers of passivity and victimhood. 'I suppose I am moved towards it', she wrote a couple of years later, 'by the desire that no daughter of mine should ever be in a position to be able to write: BY GRAND CENTRAL STATION I SAT DOWN AND WEPT [the title of Elizabeth Smart's vehemently poetic novel about a woman's affair with a married man, which Angela elsewhere described as 'a masochistic season in hell'], exquisite prose though it might contain. (BY GRAND CENTRAL STATION I TORE OFF HIS BALLS would be more like it, I should hope)'.

On a slightly less virtuous level, her relationship with Virago provided her with something she had never had before: a corner of the British literary world where her position as a great and totemic writer was assured. Of all the editors she worked with over the course of her career, Carmen was by some distance the one she became closest to, and probably the one who held her work in the highest esteem (Marsha Rowe remembers Carmen coming into the *Spare Rib* offices shortly after the lunch for Kosiński, and announcing: 'Angela Carter is a *real* writer'). Once Virago had established itself as a going concern – moving its headquarters from Carmen's house in bohemian Chelsea to private offices on Soho's Wardour Street, and publishing its first book in 1975 – Angela's status within it became that of a revered and beloved godmother. 'She was a very central author,' said Ursula Owen, who joined the company as a director in 1974. 'She was very supportive of Virago from the beginning . . . I loved everything about her, I loved her and I loved *The Sadeian Woman*.' Lennie Goodings, who joined the company in 1978 and went on to become its publisher (that is, chief editorial spirit), was equally effusive: 'She was so charming and caring. Angela had a tremendous curiosity and a generosity of spirit. She was very loyal to Carmen and very loyal to the Virago enterprise.'

In its earliest months, Virago was run under the auspices of Quartet Books, the new publishing house of John Boothe and William Miller, who had left Panther the year before. They intended to bring out both hardbacks and paperbacks under the same imprint – a revolutionary idea at the time. To help them get off the ground, Angela agreed to give them the short stories she had been writing since moving to Japan in 1970. They paid £1,000 for the collection that became *Fireworks*. 'She was very generous in allowing us to publish it,' remembered Boothe, who was conscious that the advance was less than she might have received from Hart-Davis.

Quartet operated out of rented offices above a fishmonger's at 29 Goodge Street, in the mournful central London district of Bloomsbury, a perennial haunt of writers, publishers and academics. The literary agent Deborah Rogers – whose clients included Anthony Burgess and Eva Figes – had her offices on the floor above. She was beginning to acquire a reputation as one of the most formidable of a new generation of agents, thanks to her powerful (and entirely justified) confidence in her literary tastes, her unflagging loyalty to her authors, and her simultaneously gentle and tenacious approach to deal-making. A couple of years older than Angela, blonde, mildly eccentric and rather posh, she had angular features, a kindly smile, and a perpetual twinkle to her pale blue eyes. She exuded warmth and curiosity, and took enormous pleasure in her work.

Angela drifted upstairs from the Quartet offices one day in May 1973, and asked Deborah if she might be happy to represent her. She had become frustrated with Irene Josephy's insouciant attitude (weeks would pass when it was impossible to get hold of her), and specifically with her failure to sell either *Love* or *The Infernal Desire Machines of Dr Hoffman* in any foreign territories.

Deborah wasn't familiar with Angela's work, and although they got on well, she said she'd have to read a few of the novels before knowing if she could take them on. A few weeks later, she wrote to Angela that 'DR HOFFMAN is the most extraordinary and exciting English novel that I have read for ages, and if nothing else I am grateful for your visit which prompted me to read it . . . after reading this I am absolutely certain that I would love to handle your work if you were to decide that the time was right for you to make a move, and if you wanted to entrust it to me.'

Now that she had set things in motion, Angela became anxious about sacking Irene ('due to having been with Irene for such a long time and not knowing precisely quite how to break it'), and it took her until 12 August, an interval of some four weeks, to write a rather formal notice of dismissal ('many, many thanks for your work with me over the past seven years . . . I guess there is an etiquette in these affairs, and I'm sure we'll both abide by it'). Its businesslike tone is an indication of how sensible she was to make the move to Deborah, who – in a manner strikingly similar to Carmen – not only provided a boost to her career, but became one of her closest friends. Angela and Deborah were both telephone junkies, and they made long calls to one another, sometimes on a daily basis, taking in business matters, but also dealing in politics and gossip. Deborah was on the left politically, but admitted that 'as far as being one of the Sisters was concerned, I was never very good . . . the fact was that, shamelessly, I used the fact of being a woman to promote stuff . . . I think in a way my, what I would like to think perhaps was an independence of spirit – which meant that I didn't sign up for [feminism], as I didn't sign up for anything else – was something Angela felt happy with.'

Angela tended to present the end of her relationship with Andrew Travers as a sudden rupture, followed by complete estrangement: 'I lived with a psychopath,' she told a friend from Japan the following year. 'I nearly got murdered & if he ever comes within 20 miles of me again I shall call the police.' In reality, things were less straightforward – and initially, less acrimonious – than that implies. At the start of April 1973, having apparently decided that living with Andrew wasn't conducive to writing novels, she went to stay with her old friend Edward Horesh in Bath. But she hadn't cut off contact with Andrew, and over the ensuing weeks she wrote him dozens of letters full of endearments ('at night, when I am about to go to sleep, I embrace you and kiss you goodnight'), tender practicalities ('I have been thinking about what you should eat, seeing how food prices are rising again, & we must arrange for me to teach you how to cook, because woman's liberation = man's liberation & it is very inconvenient not knowing how to cook'), and meditations on a shared future ('I should think we will have quite a good deal of time together, one way & another; but never grow stale, or bored, or angry, or destroying, neither of us, we mustn't'). Far from turning her back on the relationship, she appears to have been searching for a position from which she could maintain it:

> I forced you to commit yourself to me out of vanity & possessiveness & insecurity & other horrid things & so I deserved what I got, which was your confusion, I suppose, & its fruits. You are a funny one, no denying it, & so am I, & I can't live with you (probably not with anyone) & you can't live with me; but we can visit, & when I say I love you, it means I wish you well, I mean, wish you well for yourself, & that is all I want to say, now, because there are your beautiful eyes, also.

Her decision to decamp to Edward's house – rather than going to her father, or her brother, or any of her female friends – was mainly down to her sense that Bath was 'the ideal place to retrench for a while, to relax in provincial somnolence'. A self-consciously attractive city – with its sedate Georgian crescents, towering Gothic abbey, and colonnaded Roman bathhouse, all made from the same honey-coloured stone – it lies in a depression of the Somerset hills, over the natural hot springs to which it owes its living. Angela had loved the city since she first went there, on a day trip from Bristol, in the winter of 1962. On that occasion she had written: 'Everywhere you look in Bath you see something new & odd & beautiful . . . They knew where to decorate, where to lavish whimsies & gilding, plaster wreaths, wright iron; & they knew where to leave severely alone.' Such thoroughgoing elegance can make Bath feel like a sort of toy town, which as far as Angela was concerned was all to the good:

> The uselessness of the city contributes both to its charm and to its poignancy, which is part of its charm. It was not built to assert the pre-eminence of a particular family or the power of a certain region. It had no major industry in the eighteenth century, except tourism. The gentleman whose tastes this city was built (speculatively) to satisfy

had no interest in labour as such, only in his profits from a labour he hoped would take place as far away from his pleasures as possible; Bath was built to be happy in, which accounts for its innocence and its ineradicable melancholy.

Edward lived on Sydney Buildings, a long, narrow street off the stately thoroughfare of Bathwick Hill, which afforded spectacular views over the city, but was 'a bit off the beaten track, for Bath'. His house was 'v. much an academic's pad . . . a one-man house, you can draw the walls round you like a coat'. There was a small garden with a fig tree, which snapdragons and blackbirds frequented. Angela sat outside in the spring sunshine, working (prompted by a crotchety letter from Marion Boyars: the deadline had been and gone) on her translation of *Surréalisme et sexualité*. She wrote to Andrew: 'I am in the extensile & tensile mood that drives you mad.'

Staying with Edward wasn't a long-term solution to the problem of where to live: her father agreed to lend her the money to buy a house of her own in Bath. She soon found a place on Hay Hill, a narrow pedestrianised alley of eclectic architectural style. We don't know exactly how much she paid (the house wasn't listed with the Land Registry until 1982), but another property that she looked at was on the market for £2,500.

No. 5 Hay Hill was tallish but very thin, with three small rooms stacked one on top of the other. On the ground floor was a kitchen/dining room; on the first floor, a small bathroom and a small bedroom (which Angela used mainly as a study); and on the top floor the master bedroom. It was a bit of a wreck, and had to be done up – but in an effort to attract gentrifiers, the council was offering grants for renovations. By 17 May 1973, Angela had bought it. She wrote to Andrew:

> I've just been to look at my house and though it's by no means a palazzo, it really does seem to me very pretty indeed. Somehow, this strikes me as terribly unfair. Please forgive use of possessive 'my'. It's kind of a toy notion. It seems peculiarly amazing, to actually own this carapace of bricks and mortar. I don't really understand the notion of 'owning'. I <u>feel</u> it, all right; but I'm not sure what it is I feel.

Whatever it was she felt, it appears to have loosened her psychological connection to Andrew. In that same letter, she informed him that she'd be back in London the following week, looking after Andrea Newman's house and cats in the west London district of World's End: she suggested that

Andrew come over, 'and we can watch colour television and so forth only
not sleep in Andrea's bed – or, if we do, to leave no perceptible traces'.
But then Andrea cancelled her holiday, and Angela didn't go to London
after all. The delay in seeing Andrew seems to have allowed her emotions
to converge with her physical distance from the relationship. On 2 June
she wrote in her journal:

> Yesterday evening, I stopped loving Andrew. It arrived like a thunder-
> clap; falling out of love with the astonishing suddenness of falling
> in love, or even more so. I've been very naïve & foolish, he's been
> waiting for me like a big, fat spider in a web baited with libido. How
> childish it is.

On 6 June, she rang Fleur to ask for a tip-off when Andrew was out so that
she could come and collect her belongings from Lincoln Road. 'I sensed
that she was keeping something back,' Fleur recalled. Even so, she didn't
feel any personal loyalty to Andrew, and when she came home from work
to find a note saying that he'd be away for a few days, she called Angela.
Was the front room locked? Angela asked. Fleur said that it was. 'He's not
in there, is he?' She now claimed that Andrew had threatened suicide if she
ever left him. Andrew denies having done any such thing, and in light of
the calm and affectionate tone of their correspondence up to this point it
does seem like a melodramatic move on Angela's part.

Fleur, who wasn't to know this, felt suddenly afraid: she called Tony
Gould, who came over to offer moral support, and then called the police.
The young constable who attended said that it wouldn't be easy to break
down the door, a hypothesis he proceeded to test by ramming it several
times with his shoulder. Having cracked the frame but failed to shift the
door itself, he went outside and simply shone a torch through the window.
The room was empty.

When Andrew returned a day or two later, there was no way of disguising the damage to the entrance of his room: 'he said he had locked it
because there was a valuable typewriter inside', Fleur wrote in her diary.
The typewriter, Angela told Fleur, was hers. On 12 June Andrew moved
out, taking it with him, and went to stay with relatives in Minehead.

He was furious – seemingly less at being left by Angela than at the manner of his eviction from Lincoln Road. On 23 June he wrote a 1,500-word
letter (closely typed over three and a half A4 pages) to Andrea Newman,
consisting entirely of invective directed against Fleur and (mainly) Angela,

whom he accused of being a plagiarist, of having poor standards of personal hygiene, of being 'terribly immature and, worse than that, terribly resistant to any possibility in her of maturing', and of possessing a 'basic shiftiness and lack of confidence coupled to a prodigious vanity (that told her that what she did was always right) coupled to an abject failure to understand another person'. Though written in anger, the letter is worth considering: it represents a way of inventing Angela – by someone who, whatever his blind spots and biases, was unusually close to her – that differs markedly from the perceptions of most of her friends. But Angela's response to it was untroubled. She was staying at Andrea's flat when it arrived, and recognising the handwriting on the envelope, she opened and read it before passing it on. Her main complaint was that 'he's used <u>my</u> typewriter!'

CHAPTER FOURTEEN

Isn't the identity fragile?

Weary of romantic turmoil, and anxious to get back to work, Angela set about turning 5 Hay Hill into a one-woman sanctum. She painted the walls white, except for the bathroom, which she painted black and decorated with 'rather erotic pictures', according to her cousin Nicola Farthing. She had the doorbell removed 'for reasons of misanthropy', and fixed the telephone in a spot 'where it's virtually inaudible'. On 5 July, two months after her thirty-third birthday, she wrote to Fleur Adcock: 'It's paint pots, paint pots everywhere here – but I'm beginning to see an end to it, the house in which I'm going to live is peering through the surface of the house I bought.'

All of this took precedence over finishing her translation of *Surréalisme et sexualité*. On 7 July she wrote to Marion Boyars:

> The main body of the text was translated some weeks ago & now I'm working on the notes & bibliography which, hopefully, will only take a short while. I've been delayed by moving house . . . which move was occasioned by a crisis in my private life, it's been a rather difficult spring. But the work is done – & I should be able to get the manuscript off very soon. I feel very bad about the delay but things got hopelessly out of hand . . . anyway, it'll be with you within, I hope, a week or so.

In fact, she didn't deliver a completed typescript until 31 August – eight weeks after writing that letter, and five months after her original deadline – with notes, but still without a bibliography. The latter task was proving much harder than she'd anticipated. 'Could you not employ a researcher to do the bibliography?' she wrote in her covering letter. 'I simply can't afford the time as I have a novel that must be written.' Her brusque tone may have been a response to Boyars' nagging, but even nagging was preferable to the silence that ensued. On 17 September Angela wrote:

> I posted the translation of Xavière Gauthier's SURREALISM AND SEXUALITY to you a couple of weeks ago, with a letter explaining why I can't undertake to compile a bibliography, plus apologies – and was a little surprised to receive only a formal acceptance of ms. postcard in reply, since the work <u>was</u> commissioned and undertaken under contract.

But Boyars still didn't respond, and Angela soon became distracted by other work. As the months passed, and she didn't hear anything more about the translation, she must have assumed that Calder & Boyars had decided not to publish.

The pressure of the novel that 'must be written' had been building up for some time. Angela had begun making detailed notes for it in January 1972. Over the next eighteen months, the title had changed from *The Great Hermaphrodite* to *The Passion of New Eve*, and the setting had migrated from ancient Rome to an apocalyptic USA. What had remained constant was the idea of a vulgar, violent satire, debunking the cultural archetypes of masculinity and femininity. Like *The Sadeian Woman*, which it took shape alongside, *The Passion of New Eve* is concerned with deconstructing 'the myth of gender'.

Angela was always at pains to distinguish myth from folklore, and became irritated when people spoke about the 'mythic quality' of her work. 'I'm in the demythologising business,' she wrote in 1983. She saw myths as 'extraordinary lies designed to make people unfree', and felt that her duty as an artist was to do pretty much the opposite. The first stirrings of *The Passion of New Eve* came when she encountered the Greek myth of Tiresias, the prophet who was punished by the goddess Hera by being turned into a woman – quite as if, Angela thought, womanhood was synonymous with suffering. It struck her as pernicious propaganda. She began to work out a plot that would satirically entwine Tiresias with other ancient myths of gender identity (such as the story of the Fall) as well as taking in modern archetypes of femininity (such as the images produced by Hollywood), so as to lay bare some of the cultural forces acting on women's ideas about themselves, and on men's ideas about women. She thought of it as 'a piece of black comedy', but also as 'a deeply, deeply serious piece of fiction about gender identity, about our relation to the dream factory, our relation to imagery'. 'I intended it as a feminist novel,' she told an interviewer in 1979. 'I wanted to show the absurdity of making generalisations about male and female. I don't see much difference between men and women. The variations between people of the same sex are usually far greater.'

The incredibly baroque storyline combines elements of science fiction, parody and picaresque. It is narrated by Evelyn, a womanising English academic, who flees a chaotic, disintegrating New York for the California desert, only to be captured by gun-toting radical feminists and taken to their subterranean lair. The group is presided over by the Holy Mother, an enormous many-breasted matriarch, also known as the Great Parricide and the Grand Emasculator (Angela had no time for the essentialist sort of feminism that was the target of this caricature: 'Mother goddesses are just as silly a notion as father gods,' she wrote in *The Sadeian Woman*). By way of punishing Evelyn's misogynistic tendencies, the women intend to turn him into a 'perfect specimen of womanhood', and then impregnate him with his own sperm. So he is trimmed from Evelyn to Eve, and bombarded with cultural images of femininity: Hollywood actresses, the Madonna and child, and 'a video-tape intended, I think, to subliminally instil the maternal instinct itself; it showed cats with kittens, vixens with cubs, the mother whale with her offspring, ocelots, elephants, wallabies, all tumbling and suckling and watchfully tending'.

The 'passion' of the novel's title refers in part to the process of suffering and degradation that Eve undergoes during her crash course in gender studies. After escaping the matriarchal clutches of the Holy Mother and her followers, she is captured by their patriarchal equivalent, a sex-and-death cult led by a one-eyed, one-legged guru named Zero (plunging back into her memories of America in 1969, Angela had come up with the figure of Charles Manson; Zero was based partly on him). When Zero rapes her, Eve finally stops seeing herself as a man trapped in a woman's body: 'The mediation of Zero turned me into a woman.' At the same time, Zero's assault 'brought with it a shock of introspection, forced me to know myself as a former violator at the moment of my own violation'. The patent absurdity of this dualism isn't, as some readers have assumed, a comment on the respective natures of men and women, but a send-up of archetypal versions of masculinity and femininity. 'It is difficult not to laugh,' the critic

James Wood has written dismissively of the scene, before adding, as if the thought has suddenly occurred to him: 'perhaps this is the intention'.

In her former life as a man, Eve was an aficionado of the films of Tristessa de St Ange, a Marlene Dietrich / Greta Garbo style grande dame of the silent cinema – a mime artiste of 'emblematic despair' – who's described at the start of the novel as 'the most beautiful woman in the world.' Her films, demonstrating 'every kitsch excess of the mode of femininity', feature heavily in the bombardment of images Eve is subjected to after her sex-change operation. But when Zero leads his harem in a raid on Tristessa's mansion, it turns out she's been a transvestite all along. Angela liked the contrast between a man who (like Tiresias) has been forcibly turned into a woman, and another who's merely impersonating a woman:

> The story of Tristessa is, of course, that somebody who is as perfect as that couldn't possibly be anything but an invention. And it turns out that she is, in fact, a chap really, underneath it all. There was always the story that Garbo was a man really, because she was too perfect. Her manner, everything. She was too much like a woman. And the novel is about . . . the construction of sexual identity and how, for some particular reason, the cinema was the kind of medium for this. The cinema became one of the great mediums for the construction of certain kinds of sexual identity, both for women and for men.

The novel's conception of sexual identity is certainly more fluid than those typically offered by Hollywood: it ends with Eve setting sail from the California coast, pregnant with Tristessa's child.

Angela gave a great deal of thought to the uses and methods of political art while she was writing *The Passion of New Eve*. She wasn't under any illusions about whom it could reach. 'I make an elite product,' she told an interviewer shortly before the novel was published. 'If you've got these bourgeois elitist tools, you can only get at a very limited number of people.' But on the whole, she wasn't concerned about preaching to the masses: 'It's the tastes of the intelligentsia in this country that distresses me.'

One way of shaking up the intelligentsia was to go against received notions of aesthetics. Looking back at her early novels, Angela felt that she 'wasn't grappling with text at all' in them ('the surface . . . is absolutely bland'). In *The Passion of New Eve* she sought 'to beautify [the prose] to such an extent that it becomes like uglifying'. From its very first line ('The last night I spent in London, I took some girl or other to the movies and, through her mediation, I paid you a little tribute of spermatozoa, Tristessa' – which the novelist and critic Adam Mars-Jones has described as 'an opening that is actually easier to remember than forget'), the mood is sultry, sexy, violent – balefully stylish.

Not much of this came through in the first draft, which Angela began on 14 July 1973. She wrote it longhand, over 110 lined A4 sheets. The plot was more or less in place, but the prose didn't have much tang. Evelyn introduced himself in a blandly direct way, like the narrator of a conventional *Bildungsroman* ('I was a younger son & we were, as they say, comfortably off; my academic success, crowned by the post in New York, had gratified my parents & the contract, only for a year's duration, ensured I would not be too long away'). In her second draft Angela began hacking away at the expository padding, to reveal the glinting core.

It was a laborious process. 'I've been w[orkin]g,' she wrote to Fleur Adcock on 10 August. 'Superstitious fears make me nervous about talking about it. W[orkin]g (especially on a novel) is, for me, something like an extended version of "the pit & the pendulum" – the one thing worse than going on is giving up. This is going to be a very difficult one, & I've been forced to take up yoga to keep me in trim for it.' This was true: she was trying to teach herself yoga from a book, but she soon came to the conclusion that it 'improves one's posture but not one's tranquillity' – either that, or 'I bought the wrong book'.

Angela's social circles remained small throughout her time in Bath: the two most important friendships she made while living there were both with colleagues of Edward at the university. Christopher Frayling (who lived in a village outside the city) was appointed a junior lecturer in October 1973, when he was twenty-six. His interests overlapped at several points with Angela's: having just completed his PhD on Rousseau (with reference to Laclos and Sade), he taught courses on 'Film and Propaganda', and 'European Socialist Thought'. Angela went to a few of his lectures and sat at the back, smoking. He was also an aficionado of the western, and was writing a book about vampires in nineteenth-century literature. Angela became fascinated by this project. He lent her his copy of the script for the 1922 film *Nosferatu*, as well as various books about vampires and folklore. When he told her that he was planning a research trip to the Carpathian Mountains in Romania – following in the footsteps of Jonathan Harker in

Dracula – Angela was tickled. The character of Hero in her 1975 radio play *Vampirella* – a somewhat naïve, over-educated, gung-ho young Englishman, who sets out on a bicycle tour of the Carpathians, all unprepared for the darkness he'll encounter – is based on Frayling. She presented him with the typescript as a gift.

They tended to meet at Edward's house on Sydney Buildings, where Christine Downton – who, like Edward, was a left-wing lecturer in economics – sometimes joined them. Feminism, Downton remembered, was a foregone conclusion between her and Angela: 'to the extent that we had conversations about it, it would probably be to just relate new experiences of anti-feminism or gender bias, or if we'd read something or experienced something'. But their conversations tended to be light-hearted:

> Angela was a very gleeful person. She was a raconteur of glee, maybe that's the best way of putting it . . . a gleam would come into her eyes, and her whole face would sort of brighten up, when she was going to say something she thought was a bit on the naughty side, or on the provocative side.

Frayling agreed, but felt that Angela set out to provoke herself as much as anyone else:

> She was incredibly idiosyncratic when she talked, she'd say all sort of things for affect, a sort of hit-and-run approach. She loved 'swearing in church'. I mean, if she felt that at a dinner party or at an event, like a talk, everyone was being a bit too well mannered, she'd suddenly say something, usually an expletive . . . I think that like a lot of shy people, she'd explode occasionally, and these things would come out as her way of relating.

Angela had encouraged Edward to buy a colour television, and after supper at his house the four of them would gather around it with a drink. Christine remembers watching the Watergate hearings, which began on 17 May 1973 ('we were totally gripped by it . . . I think [Angela] found it an extraordinary spectacle'). The Bathwick Ward division of the Labour Party met once a month in Edward's sitting room, and although she lived on the other side of the city, Angela became its secretary ('since nobody else wanted to'). There were about eight active members, including Angela, Edward and Christopher Frayling. Angela's role was to take the minutes and report back to party headquarters.

Angela became increasingly keen on the opera during this period, and sometimes Edward would drive her and Frayling to Bristol to see Glyndebourne touring or the Welsh National Opera. The productions they saw included Mozart's *The Magic Flute* and *The Marriage of Figaro*, Verdi's *Falstaff*, and Weber's *Der Freischütz*, which Frayling remembers Angela talking about redoing as a 'kind of Satanic western' – this was the inspiration for *Gun for the Devil*, a television script that she wrote in 1975 about gunslingers dabbling in the occult (it hasn't ever been produced, but the script and a separate prose treatment were both published posthumously).

They also went to the cinema quite frequently, though never to the theatre. 'Angie had a thing about the theatre,' Frayling remembered. It's true that her attitude to a certain sort of English thespianism was often derisive. In a *New Society* piece about television drama in 1979, she wrote: '"Live" theatre – though it might be better to call it "undead" theatre – used to embarrass me so much I could hardly bear it, that dreadful spectacle of painted loons in the middle distance making fools of themselves.' But she had a deep affection for what she saw as a less pompous dramatic tradition – music hall, pantomime, the rambunctious Elizabethan stage. It's the contrast she sought to draw in *Wise Children* between the Hazards (who primly tread the boards) and the Chances (who go gleefully on the halls).

Money remained tight throughout this period, and Angela took whatever journalistic commissions she was offered (she continued to write for *Club International* until December 1974). In November 1973 she began contributing regularly to the *Radio Times*, the BBC listings magazine, by profiling six writers who had adapted individual short stories by Thomas Hardy for 'a major new television series': among them were the dramatist Dennis Potter and the novelist and short-story writer William Trevor (Angela enjoyed meeting the latter: 'he says he likes my work and is a lovely man besides', she told Carmen). Her subsequent contributions included an article about Gothic horror to tie in with a televised double bill of *Dracula* and *Frankenstein*, as well as profiles of Graham Miles (winner of the BBC snooker series *Pot Black*), and the composer Carl Orff (whose *Carmina Burana* was being broadcast live from Munich to mark his eightieth birthday in 1975). Christopher Frayling remembers her coming back from interviewing Iris Murdoch for the magazine, and being dismayed that Murdoch hadn't known who she was: 'she was really, really hurt. She was very thin-skinned actually, in some respects.'

The interview with Murdoch doesn't seem to have been published (at least, it wasn't published under the name Angela Carter: a short, anonymously authored profile to mark the televisation of *An Unofficial Rose* did appear in the issue dated 21 December 1974). But there's no doubt that it took place. Ann McFerran – a young researcher for the magazine – was sent to meet the two authors off their respective trains at Paddington station and introduce them to one another. She was a bit embarrassed by the task: 'I don't know what on earth possessed the *Radio Times* to think that two perfectly competent women like Iris Murdoch and Angela Carter couldn't actually say "hello" and "shall we go to the nearest coffee bar?"' Her discomfort only increased as the afternoon progressed: Murdoch assumed that McFerran was the person who had been sent to interview her, in the first of several knocks to Angela's pride (according to the account she gave Frayling, Murdoch turned to her at one point to ask: 'And what do you do?').

Angela got on well with McFerran, though, and that night she stayed with her and her partner, the playwright Snoo Wilson, in their house on The Chase, a long, wide, sloping south London street, whose broad semi-detached villas huddle closer and closer together the further they stray from Clapham Common, until by the time they meet the Wandsworth Road they've formed themselves into an Edwardian terrace. It was the start of a long friendship. 'The following morning she wrote up this interview in what seemed to me, enviously, like about an hour,' McFerran says: 'and [I remember] thinking, "Gosh, I wish I could write as brilliantly and as quickly as that."'

The speed with which Angela produced her article can probably be put down to insouciance. She wasn't proud of her contributions to the *Radio Times*, and felt 'furtive' whenever anybody noticed them. She told Fleur Adcock that she could only settle down to them by telling herself that they were paying her central-heating bill – 'every page is £75 towards a warmer home!'

In spite of these boosts to her household budget, Angela was living well beyond her means (the 'warmer home' never materialised: Christopher Frayling remembers that it was always uncomfortably cold at 5 Hay Hill). The anxious financial calculations scrawled in the back of her journal reveal the extent of her troubles: in November 1973 she received £8.96 in royalties, and made a further £250 through journalism. In December, her total income fell to just £44.20, all of it from journalism; that month she spent

£105.83, although excepting books and cigarettes the only luxuries she bought were a pair of boots (£11.99), some sweets (£1.42) and Christmas presents for her family (£9.94). Things were made even more difficult by her attempts to save money for builders to fix the roof, something that the council, in 'a piece of bureaucratic double-bind', required her to do before it would give her a grant for further renovations.

There were other demands on her time, most of which weren't adequately paid. She finished revising *Fireworks* late in the evening of 5 November (as she worked, the pyrotechnics of her title must have filled the air outside). Although Irene had sold most of the rights to Quartet, Angela sent the manuscript to Deborah with an accompanying note: 'I'm aware of my own natural prejudice, but I do think it's quite nice and has a certain internal consistency, like dreams dreamed on the same night.'

On 22 November she received proofs of the Japanese edition of *Love* (translated as *Rakuen*, meaning 'Paradise', in an echo of Angela's original working title), which Kodansha intended to publish in February. Angela decided to fly to Tokyo for the launch – it isn't clear who paid for the trip, although given the parlous state of her finances, it probably wasn't her. With this deadline looming, she redoubled her efforts to finish *The Passion of New Eve*. In December she wrote to Martin Hoyle, who was still living in Bristol, to apologise for her silence since moving back to the west of England:

> I've been working so hard this winter that I haven't emerged much from my little cocoon in Bath. I only come into Bristol when I can catch a lift, which isn't often, but I've looked for you at the opera . . . I plan to split next year for a while and learn the French they speak in France. I can read it, even translate it, but not speak it. This rather depends on whether I have any money left after getting the builders in to do my house up. Squatters have moved into the house next door, they play the drums a lot and sometimes scream late into the night. My own house has been occupied by mice who shit a lot in the kitchen and thunder about in the walls in the way mice do, making noise in inverse ratio to their size. Otherwise, Bath is quiet but beautiful, though I wish the Jesus freaks would stop doing whatever it is they're doing and do something useful. Forgive me for not writing before, I can't believe I have been here six months, it's gone in a flash. Jesus, six more months down the pan. Please come and see me.

As Christmas approached, the pressures of work were met with domestic adversity. Kitty Farthing – Angela's 'dotty' maternal aunt – died suddenly on 20 December, from a pulmonary embolism. The funeral was held on Christmas Eve. Angela wrote in her journal: 'My family has such a facility for dying in emblematic circumstances. Now, Kit; to be rejected by us & go mad to draw attention to her sorrow, her loneliness . . . And then to induce, by what magic means, the same death as my mother. At the same time of year.' It's unclear what she meant by saying that her aunt was 'rejected by us' – it wasn't true, as Angela later claimed, that Kitty died in Springfield Mental Hospital – but it suggests that guilt may have been one of the emotions feeding her portrayal in *Wise Children*.

All of this meant that with her trip to Japan almost upon her, Angela still hadn't finished *The Passion of New Eve*. On 25 January she sent Deborah a few sections of the novel, along with a detailed synopsis. 'Though it's possible I may change certain things in the story,' she wrote, 'I won't change the overall plan. It should work out at about 60,000 words, I think, or rather less . . . Do you think it will find a friendly home?' On the basis of the sections Angela had shown her, Deborah sold US rights to Tony Godwin at Harcourt Brace Jovanovich for $2,000, but it seems she couldn't persuade Hart-Davis – or any other British publisher – to come on board at such an early stage.

On 10 February 1974, Angela went to London for Fleur Adcock's birthday party, and slept on the floor. The following day she rose early to catch her flight to Tokyo. It wasn't the joyous return she had been anticipating. Shinjuku, she felt, had become 'bright & dark & soulless', the traditional wood-and-paper buildings (including the house she had lived in during her last eight months in the city) replaced by high-rise office blocks and new love hotels, which displayed their hourly rates in garish neon. The number of cars on the streets had dramatically increased; so had the number of skyscrapers. Angela thought it was 'the most ridiculous place in the world . . . like Balzac on speed'. There's no doubting the strength of her reaction, which she expressed in letters and articles as well as in her journal; but perhaps it says more about how she'd changed than about how Tokyo had (she'd been dazzled by the relentless traffic and pervasive neon when she first arrived there in 1969 – and had found it thrilling).

She was faced with a heavy schedule of publicity events, and quickly discerned a wider than usual gap between the amount her publishers hoped to make from the novel and the amount she had been paid. 'They are crooks, crooks, crooks! I have been ripped off to a point where the imagination fails,' she wrote to Deborah. 'Can you, in future, <u>always</u> make a special clause for Japanese rights 'cos it's an enormous and mysterious market and people more efficient than me ought to be able to do something with it.' As well as a laborious round of book signings and events, she was expected to write a series of articles under the rubric 'Confessions of a Free Woman' for 'a magazine of no significance' called *Young Lady*. 'This series (of which I chose neither the title nor the place of publication) ended up as undiluted women's lib propaganda,' she told Deborah. 'I suspect I have sold them world rights. (I didn't <u>intend</u> to do any such thing, God help me! I didn't even intend to write it!)' Her deadlines for the series are noted in her diary, but there's no trace of the articles themselves, either in the weekly magazine *Young Lady* or in the monthly magazine *Wakai-Josei* ('Young Lady' in Japanese). But the monthly magazine *Bungeishunju* does contain an article under Angela's byline from May 1974. Titled 'My Shinjuku', it vents her distress at the changes she perceived in her old neighbourhood: 'what has become of Tokyo since two years ago? Why do the willows look so ill and sad? What are those blue skyscrapers dominating the city?' (She presumably filed her copy in English, to be translated into Japanese by someone on the magazine's staff – these lines have been translated back again.)

It may be that some of her negative feelings about Tokyo were redirected from elsewhere. Among the old friends she caught up with was Kō, who – having travelled as far afield as France, India, and the southern states of the USA – had at last returned to Japan the previous year. Angela barely recognised him. He wore sharp suits, and had developed a fascination with knives. 'He talks in a new voice,' Angela wrote in her journal. 'He is trying to bark, butch, like a Japanese, & he mimics mirthless laughter a lot & makes animal noises, grunts, mews, barks.' She felt that he was consciously seeking to disguise the innocence that still endured beneath his newly assumed toughness: 'He no longer trusts people, I think . . . He who was Ariel is now Caliban & was always both.' His transformation pained and fascinated her in equal measure. She analysed it over and over again in her journal, sometimes addressing her thoughts to him:

Your ugliness is the same kind of thing as your beauty. It is a device, a disguise; a mask . . . Each condition, innocence, corruption, excludes the other; excludes, not negates. Behind this mask, you grow, in secret; you are changing, behind the mask, but the mask modifies the change. You must choose your masks carefully.

Ted Holst (Naine's former boyfriend, who was now in a relationship with Kō's sister Mina) recalled that the changes in Kō's personality had begun when Angela returned to England in 1972: 'what upset him was that Angela wanted to pursue her career rather than stay with him'. She seems to have intuited this, and to have been astonished by her own power. 'I know why I come bothering you, dear Kō,' she wrote in her journal. 'It is because I feel I can still cause you pain. So I come & stick the pins in & watch you twitch.' The more she saw of him, the more such self-consciously cruel impulses eclipsed her softer ones:

I should love to hold him in my arms, again, & feel his skin; I should like to force or persuade him to trust me, again, to put all his trust in me . . . I want to make him, again, utterly dependent on me & then I would leave him again, of course, & his last state would be worse than his first.

It appears that she succeeded in seducing him, although it's also possible that the following lines – written in her journal for 1974, but perhaps at a later date – refer to their initial parting in the spring of 1972. 'We made love,' she wrote, '& in my sentimentality, I had planned, in my fantasy, that he should weep. But, instead, he turned on me with eyes that had become all jagged, cold . . . a devil.' This image of Kō's poisoned beauty – and the question of how much responsibility for it she bore – returned to haunt her during the last weeks of her life.

In a mood of 'heroic stupidity', Angela decided to return to Britain via the USSR, taking in Samarkand, Kiev and Leningrad over the course of two weeks. On Saturday 20 April she boarded a Russian ferry – the MS *Baikal* – at Yokohama. She shared her cabin with a young Japanese couple whose final destination was Kabul. 'They are very fragile and delicate-looking and I fear for them, by God, I do,' she wrote in an abortive article about the trip. She might have saved some fear for herself. As had happened in

the summer of 1971 – when she had taken the ferry in the other direction
to find Sozo not waiting at Yokohama – she spent most of the journey con-
fined to her berth, retching into the paper bags provided. But she remained
sanguine: 'this ordeal by seasickness is all part of the magic, you don't go
to Russia to <u>enjoy</u> yourself. You go to see how you make out.'

A bus met foreigners off the ferry at Nakhodka and took them straight
to a waiting train. Angela shared her compartment with a nervous Japanese
boy ('the Russians have a grand disregard for gender'), who planned on
walking from Helsinki to Madrid. There were a few other Westerners on the
train – 'an Irish depressive', 'a middle-aged Antipodean hippy', and 'an
Australian who thinks he's got pneumonia'. They had plenty of time to get
to know one another in the restaurant car; the train chugged along, at an
unvarying speed of around fifty miles per hour, through nearly 600 miles
of wilderness between Nakhodka and Khabarovsk. Outside, an almost fea-
tureless white landscape trundled by: huge expanses of snow, broken only
by leafless black trees, black frozen lakes, and every hundred miles or so a
few brightly painted wooden buildings, huddled together as if for warmth.
In every direction, these desolate views extended to the horizon.

After a night in Khabarovsk, Angela flew to Samarkand. Swallows
swooped over the runway as the plane descended; desert was visible beyond.
She waited for an hour in the airport café – where the only refreshment
made available to her was a plastic cup of mineral water – before a driver
came and took her to a 'splendidly vulgar' hotel, 'all shiny, all new', among
clay houses that seemed to sink down into the soil.

Intourist (the Soviet agency responsible for looking after foreigners)
provided her with a guide named Akbar, who arrived the following day to
show her around the city. He took her to an archaeological site ('a herd
of sheep wandered over it; two sullen boys on a donkey passed. A small
wind blew; impossible to describe the loneliness') and to the observatory of
Ulugh-bed (which contained 'a photograph of the skull of Tamburlaine, &
fragments of his silk grave-clothes'). They went to the bazaar (where Angela
wanted to buy dried apricots, but Akbar suggested something better: 'he
showed me piles of dusty stones and invited me to taste them. They were
smoked, salted apricot pits; more delicious than pistachio nuts, even')
and to Tamburlaine's mausoleum ('where the scourge of Asia lies in a jade
tomb under a pepper-pot dome of intense blue'). But the highlight of the
trip came when they visited the ruins of the Bibi-Khanym mosque, with
its magnificent entranceway of fretted gold and lapis lazuli. As they sat on

a bench in the courtyard, with turtle doves darting between the branches of a flowering tree overhead, Akbar told Angela the legend of the mosque: how Tamburlaine's beautiful wife had overseen its construction while the great emperor was away on a campaign, and how she had been inveigled, by means of a clever argument about the properties of love, into granting the architect a single kiss – when Tamburlaine returned, he beat his wife and sent his executioners for the architect, who sprouted wings and flew away to Persia. 'It is impossible to describe the charm with which [Akbar] relates the story,' Angela wrote in her journal. 'Scheherazade has nothing on it.' She used the legend as the basis of her story 'The Kiss', which appeared in her 1985 collection Black Venus.

It isn't clear whether she continued, as she had originally planned, through Kiev and Leningrad – she didn't write anything about either city – but she did see enough of Russia to make a few generalisations about its people. In her journal she described them as having 'a fabulous rhetoric of the heart. Sentimentality so rich it transcends itself.' She was back in Bath in time for her thirty-fourth birthday, which she celebrated by dyeing her hair 'a flaming, Soviet red'.

The period between the summer of 1973 and the autumn of 1974 was the longest in Angela's adult life that passed without a significant romantic attachment. She was, on the whole, perfectly happy being single – after the theatrics of her most recent relationship, she was glad of a rest, and the casual encounters she'd had since moving to Bath were causing her to 'loathe Englishmen, as men, that is, with an almost insane passion' – but she was increasingly frustrated by the lack of opportunities for sex. By the time she returned from the USSR, her libido was tormenting her:

> I feel I am perched on top of this huge, gaping orifice that is brimming over with liquid, just the touch of a finger & it will spill over, spill out & drown everybody. I feel I am only an appendage of my cunt, which is ravenous & wants to cram cock into itself in immense quantities. I just want to fuck & fuck & fuck & fuck & I can't think of anything else, it's terrible.

One of her neighbours on Hay Hill was a twenty-two-year-old Welshman, to whom she had taken a liking: 'the furry Welsh animal', she called him in her journal. Shortly after returning from her trip, she went to bed with him. It was, she wrote, 'by far the best fuck I've ever had in GB'. She watched his house 'like a hawk, or a lovesick woman' over the ensuing weeks, daydreaming about 'his cock & his cunning fingers in my groin'. But she knew that a second liaison would encumber the simplicity of the first, and she had no interest in starting a relationship with him. 'Oh, Jesus,' she wrote in her journal, 'female sexuality is a cruel cross to bear!'

It was about to reveal how much crueller it could be. Over the next few weeks, her sexual craving gave way to a new and more disquieting set of sensations. She found herself inhabiting a state of 'dreamy slowness . . . like walking under water'. There was a constant 'sensuous pain' in her nipples, which were unusually hard. In all the times she had imagined herself to be pregnant, she had never experienced symptoms like these.

The first test she took came back negative; by the time she took a second, she was 'feeling like hell'. Even so, the positive result came as a shock. She became 'very ill, & extremely depressed'. At the mercy of her biology, the confidence and sense of autonomy she had accumulated over the past few years began to waver. 'I felt I was not my self, or myself,' she wrote:

> Against my will, I was slowed down. I felt . . . an intense lethargy, & the focus of this lethargy was the thing in my belly, the thing – or being – so undeniably, even implacably there, that had lodged there so casually, like a blown seed. Hazard. Fecundated at hazard, I had become the instrument of nature, of processes now entirely beyond my control, that changed me into this passive container, my belly into a waiting room, things were happening inside me, under this thick, warm snowfall of calm – which I did not want, I was involuntarily tranquilized – immense amounts of secret activity were taking place. And I felt most strange, I felt possessed.

Considering how often Angela had fantasised about having a baby, her dismay at finding herself pregnant at the age of thirty-four suggests an extreme ambivalence. Part of it may have been a deep-seated aversion to identifying with her own mother, a consequence of the effort it had cost her to put some psychological space between them during her teenage years (as the novelist and critic Nicole Ward Jouve has pointed out, Angela Carter's fiction never inhabits a maternal perspective). On a more conscious level, she had developed a profound hostility towards the cultural 'mystification' of motherhood. She disliked the ways it was portrayed as being the natural object of womanhood, and as the most important factor separating women from men. In *The Sadeian Woman*, she wrote that 'to deny the bankrupt enchantments of the womb is to pare a good deal of fraudulent magic from the idea of women . . . to force us to abandon, perhaps regretfully, perhaps with relief, the deluded priestesshood of a holy reproductive function'. But she understood the seductive power of these myths, and feared – as her comment about feeling 'not my self, or myself' suggests – that becoming a mother would overwhelm the identity she was still trying to fasten down. 'I really don't know how I would have managed if I'd had children when I was young, before I'd established a body of work,' she told an interviewer in 1985. 'I don't know what kind of person I would have been.'

The Abortion Act of 1967 had effectively legalised terminations up until the twenty-fourth week of pregnancy, shutting down an ugly and unsanitary backstreet trade – but the early stages of obtaining one were still complicated. Two separate doctors had to certify that the child's or the mother's mental or physical health was at risk. How this was interpreted was basically up to the individual practitioner – and since the vast majority of them were male, the Act was rather a qualified victory for the women's movement. Many doctors refused on religious grounds to approve any abortions at all, while others subjected their patients to invasive physical examinations before consenting. Even when consent was swiftly granted, there were often further hurdles to clear, owing to the patchy supply of abortion services at hospitals. The west of England was not generously served.

Writing from a later vantage point about the permissive society of the early 1970s, Angela recalled: 'many of us scarcely noticed we were women, such was the unisex confusion of our roles, until we entered the straight world in search of employment, or got pregnant . . . and found, to our astonishment, we had been second-class citizens all the time. Especially if you then decided, with a clear mind, in possession of all your faculties, that you wanted an NHS abortion.'

The whole topic was, by contemporary British standards, incredibly fraught. Feminist campaigners pressed hard for further reform, but they were met with ferocious opposition. The arguments against abortion tended to veer from the fondly patriarchal to the sternly religious – men telling women what they really want, and men telling women what God wants of them – a pair of strategies neatly combined by the journalist and moralist Malcolm Muggeridge, who wrote that 'the Magnificat continues to express the indestructible creativity of our mortal flesh, and few mothers, when they actually set eyes on the fruit of their womb, are inclined to reject it'. Women who confessed to having had abortions tended to be lionised by one side, and vilified by the other. Though Angela spoke quite openly about hers in later years, the only person she seems to have confided in at the time was Carmen Callil, who was probably the most vocal and committed feminist among her friends. 'There is nothing like this experience for radicalising a woman,' Angela wrote to her. 'And I thought I was radical already.'

What she doesn't seem to have admitted to Carmen was that, even if her response was generally one of discomfort and gloom, there were times when she 'adored' being pregnant: 'I felt estranged from myself but also enhanced,' she wrote in her journal afterwards: 'I loved my own slowness & the changes I could see in my body, my breasts enriching.' This ambivalence seemed to her a product of 'the magic of ambiguous states . . . it is always difficult to explore areas where so much mystification conceals a true mystery.'

On Thursday 11 July she checked into a charity clinic in London (a private abortion being well beyond her means, and an NHS one being impossible to arrange). When the nurse was explaining the procedure to her, she began to cry. Speaking about this a few years later, she denied that her tears hinted at any regret over the course of action she was pursuing. Rather, they sprang from a sense of how fortunate she was to be able to pursue it in the first place: 'I was remembering women I've known who had abortions before the law was changed, and I was seized with a deeply anguished guilt that it was so easy for me, when it had been so difficult for them.' There's no doubt that she did feel acute sympathy for such women: in *The Passion of New Eve*, Leilah – an exotic dancer – is forced into having a backstreet abortion 'at the price of her womb'. But that isn't to say that Angela's attitude to her own abortion was straightforwardly positive. 'Considering it was done in the best possible circumstances,' she wrote in her journal afterwards, 'God knows what scars it leaves when done in the worst possible circumstances.'

Early in the morning of Friday 12 July, she rang William Miller, who was going on holiday with Carmen, and asked him to take her a message:

'What's the message?' he says; 'Tell her I'm all right,' I said. 'What?' he said. 'What's that?' 'That I'm <u>all right</u>,' I repeated. It was 8.30 in the morning and it obviously seemed an extraordinary time to ring up and entrust him with this. So he says, perhaps suspiciously, 'Where are you . . .' and I got cold feet about telling him ('I'm at the abortionists,

William' – I mean, maybe he hasn't had breakfast yet) and never got around to asking him to buy me a restorative gin at lunchtime.

She went back to Bath still 'gently doped up from the anaesthetic'. In the weeks that followed, she tried to make sense of what had happened. 'The regression to timorousness, to a desire for protection, has left me with a certain confusion about my own nature,' she wrote in her journal. 'If all it takes is a fresh infusion of hormones in my metabolism to make me start inventing invisible companions, like a lonely child, then who am I? Isn't the identity fragile?'

Almost a year had passed since Angela had delivered her translation of *Surréalisme et sexualité* to Calder & Boyars, and she had heard nothing from the publishers in the intervening period. Then, on 15 July 1974 – three days after she returned from the clinic in London – she had a letter from Marion Boyars, informing her that there had been 'a great deal of criticism of the translation' from the editors at Basic Books, and that Calder & Boyars had after lengthy negotiations decided to go ahead without them – they intended to send the book to the printers in a week's time. 'I know this is giving you very short notice,' Boyars wrote, 'but if you want to see what has been done before it goes to the printer, you will have to come and visit Tim O'Grady in the office, since I am going off on holiday. But you will have to do this very quickly indeed.'

Angela rang the office that morning. She was understandably anxious about the idea that her work had been the subject of 'a great deal of criticism', and let Tim O'Grady know that she didn't want the book to come out if it was 'doomed to being ripped to pieces'. He wrote to Boyars:

she said she realised she took the project on leading everyone, including herself, to believe that she could handle all the technical language, but when she got into it she found that some portions of it were over her head (most notably the chapter on linguistics, which she isn't particularly up on – and which, by the way, she suggested you assign to a specialist to look at, if not rewrite). What she wants, basically, is details about what specifically is wrong with the translation and what she can do about it. She was very nice about it (though she did express some curiosity about why she hadn't heard from us in nearly a year) and above all worried that not only she, but we as well would suffer by a sloppy job . . . Finally, she asks that we please give her the facts and not try to soothe her.

The facts were that the editor at Basic Books had complained that 'what may be, in French, subtle and allusive discourse, becomes, in English, a hopeless garble of jargon and isms'. Calder & Boyars held off printing, and Angela took the manuscript away 'for two days' to see if she could do anything with it – but a letter from Boyars on 26 September (more than two months later) suggests she still hadn't returned it. That seems to be the last contact they had with one another, and the typescript was still among Angela's papers when she died, so it looks like she simply hung on to it and waited for the problem to go away. To date, no English translation of *Surréalisme et sexualité* has ever appeared in print.

Fireworks was published by Quartet on 15 August 1974, priced £2.50, and subtitled 'Nine Profane Pieces' at the suggestion of William Miller (when the book was reissued by Chatto & Windus in 1987, Angela asked for the subtitle to be removed). The reviews were mixed – across the various publications in which they appeared, and often in themselves as well. Auberon Waugh, writing in the *Evening Standard*, liked 'The Loves of Lady Purple', 'Master', 'Penetrating to the Heart of the Forest', and 'The Excecutioner's Beautiful Daughter', but liked the Japanese stories rather less, and complained that 'Miss Carter seems to have fallen heavily under Mr [Anthony] Burgess's influence – a useful enough influence for a young writer, I suppose, if not exactly what one would choose for one's daughters.' (That note of condescension is even more gratuitous than it might appear – Waugh was less than six months older than Angela.) But Norman Shrapnel, writing in the *Observer*, was most taken by 'A Souvenir of Japan', and wondered, 'if she can write as well as she does in that, why bother with the garish rest?' The collection received an equally ambivalent, though much more thoughtful and insightful review – perhaps the most insightful that Angela's work had yet been given – from Lorna Sage, who told readers of the *Guardian* that Angela Carter was 'one of the most rousing young writers around. At the same time, though, you have to reckon with the sheer vulgarity of her tastes; she substitutes the perverse delights of self-parody . . . for the discipline of self-awareness. All in all, *Fireworks* is a fair specimen of her talent – sometimes absorbing, often dreadful, always unrepentant.'

That frank assertion that Angela's writing was 'often dreadful' suggests that, if she and Lorna had encountered one another in person by August 1974, they weren't yet the close friends they soon became. They probably met at a *Guardian* party, or through mutual friends such as Ann McFerran and Snoo Wilson, or perhaps even off the back of that review, which in spite of its cavils demonstrated a sure enough sense of Angela's impulses and influences to suggest that she had found something like her ideal critic.

Lorna was exceptionally beautiful (with long blonde hair, mournful blue eyes and delicate features) and exceptionally glamorous (given to wearing fitted jackets and four-inch heels), but her most arresting qualities were her formidable intellect and her nervous energy. She chain-smoked, drank gin with trembling fingers, and stood with her shoulders hunched ('You always wanted to give her a back rub,' said her friend Peter Conradi). She talked constantly, in a breathless mix of black humour and literary and political argument, and had an eidetic memory. She and Angela formed an intimate, conspiratorial alliance. 'They liked being bad together,' remembered Lorna's daughter Sharon, who was in her early teens when they met. 'They used to cackle a lot, really laugh about things in a very wicked way that wasn't always understandable to me.' Their sensibilities were closely aligned – they were both dandyish in their style and tastes, were both committed to left-wing politics, and both of them wanted to increase the profile of women's writing – and their personalities had been forged in comparable psychological conditions. Lorna had overcome intense shyness and fought her way out of an oppressive, severely limited family environment (which provided the material for her bestselling memoir *Bad Blood* in 2001), via accidental motherhood and marriage at seventeen, to a first-class degree from Durham University, where she and her husband, Vic Sage, were the first ever married students (their admittance requiring a change in the rules). By 1974 the marriage had come apart, and Lorna was teaching at the University of East Anglia, while becoming increasingly well known to a non-academic audience as a reviewer, mainly for the *Guardian*, the *Observer*, the *New Statesman* and Ian Hamilton's *New Review* (the successor to the *Review*, which had ceased publication in 1972, the *New Review* had a broader remit, and a much better gender balance: Angela contributed two pieces to it later in the decade). Lorna soon began teaching such novels as *The Magic Toyshop* and *The Infernal Desire Machines of Dr Hoffman* at the University of East Anglia, and she had an important hand in the posthumous upsurge of Angela Carter's reputation. She was, Angela wrote to Pat Barker in 1983, 'a formidable ally'.

Lorna wasn't the only high-profile admirer Angela gained via *Fireworks*. She received fan letters from the authors Olivia Manning ('[the stories] are not only very well written but show an original imagination + visionary power that is extraordinary. I am sure you will do great things'), Ian McEwan, who at twenty-six was just about to publish his own first book ('how deeply I admire these stories . . . how beautifully they read out loud'), and Robert Coover ('you've got a really stunning talent . . . "Reflections" joins that small set of treasured moments . . . along with the best of Kafka, Beckett, Dostoevsky, Barth, Borges . . . I mean to say, I rarely praise anyone').

McEwan and Coover both suggested meeting, and though Angela put them off (she said she was lying low in Bath until she had finished *The Sadeian Woman*), she began corresponding with them both, and sent them copies of her other books in exchange for copies of theirs. After reading McEwan's collection of stories, *First Love, Last Rites*, she wrote to him: 'I liked especially SOLID GEOMETRY [in which a man disposes of his wife after she smashes the jar containing a pickled penis that he keeps on his desk], obviously – but all the stories are good . . . you have made an auspicious arrival, she said pompously, no – but you have.' That was written a month before the book was published to rather more extravagant praise ('a brilliant performance, showing an originality astonishing for a writer still in his mid-twenties', wrote Anthony Thwaite in the *Observer*), and Angela seems to have baulked when it was: in 1977 she remarked in a letter to Carmen that 'poor Ian has been dreadfully overrated'. She seems to have thought of him as existing in the same category as Angus Wilson: in other words, as having some flair for the grotesque, but not much facility for language or ideas, and as being too attached to the conventions of realism. But it's likely that what really upset her was a sense that his reception as the saviour of English fiction (a role he shared with the twenty-five-year-old Martin Amis, whose first novel, *The Rachel Papers*, had been published in 1973) meant that her own contribution had been sidelined. Even before *First Love, Last Rites* was published, she indicated a degree of wariness towards McEwan: 'I am shocked to see when you were born, in that I can feel my own joints stiffening,' she wrote to him. 'How much longer can I pass myself off as a "young writer" . . .'

As his list of 'treasured moments' suggested, Robert Coover was operating on a remarkably similar frequency to Angela's. American by nationality, but living since 1969 in the almost symbolically English county of Kent, he was, at forty-two, the author of two novels – *The Origin of the Brunists*, in which the sole survivor of a mining disaster becomes the focus of an apocalyptic religion, and *The Universal Baseball Association, Inc., J. Henry Waugh, Prop.*, in which an accountant retreats into the fantasy world of an invented sport league – as well as a collection of short stories, *Pricksongs & Descants*. He was beginning to acquire a reputation as one of the strangest and most significant American writers of his generation. When she sent him *The Infernal Desire Machines of Dr Hoffman*, he responded:

> I was utterly taken in by it and am still somewhat lost in nebulous time myself – in fact, you drew me into a hyper-attentiveness I haven't enjoyed in a book in a long time, so much so that I was intricately aware of your own rising and falling enthusiasms through the book, catching at the rare repetition or imprecision as though hearing the skipped heartbeat of a high-wire walker.

Coover was guest-editing the *Iowa Review* – a quarterly magazine put out by the University of Iowa, whose previous contributors had included William Burroughs and Samuel Beckett – and he offered to publish some of Angela's work. He wanted to kick-start her reputation in the United States, publishing several of her stories together with an interview and a critical essay. 'The <u>Iowa Review</u>, now into its sixth year, has never featured a writer like this before,' he told her. Angela, who was flattered by the proposal, began assembling a portfolio of her work.

Meanwhile, Deborah had sold US rights to *The Infernal Desire Machines of Dr Hoffman* to Tony Godwin at Harcourt Brace Jovanovich (who retitled it *The War of Dreams*). It was published in September 1974, and received a favourable notice from William Hjoortsberg in the *New York Times Book Review*, on the strength of which, Godwin wrote, 'we are printing an additional 2,500 copies and keeping our fingers crossed'.

None of this inflated Angela's sense of achievement much: 'I suffer rather badly from the alienation of the artist in our society,' she wrote to Neil Forsyth, a friend from Japan, in the short period between the publication of *Fireworks* and the publication of *The War of Dreams*. 'It is like shouting in an empty room.' Some of her despondency may have been down to concerns about her next book. *The Sadeian Woman* loomed over her ever more oppressively as the year pitched towards its conclusion. She had been reading the entire works of Sade, 'plus a bit of Freud to keep me sane', and had begun doubting her competence for the project. As long ago as March she had been apologising to Carmen and offering excuses for her slow progress ('I've had a dreadful "crise du nerfes" due to the buying of the house and the hiring of the builders . . . I feel so embarrassed . . . I feel I shouldn't visit until I've got something to show you'), but it's clear that by winter she still hadn't made much headway. 'When I think of the Sade book, I know I have bitten off more than I can chew & become hysterical,' she wrote to Neil Forsyth. A few months later she told Fleur Adcock that working on the book was making her 'agitated & depressed': 'I am beginning to think [*The Sadeian Woman*] was a Mistake, which will stamp me with the purplest kind of notoriety forever.'

CHAPTER FIFTEEN

The silences with which the English compose intimacies

In the autumn of 1974, Mark Pearce – a nineteen-year-old construction worker from Bristol – was building an extension onto a single-storey house on Hay Hill. It wasn't easy to concentrate: in the house opposite, directly on his level, he could see a woman sitting at her desk, absorbed in her work, her face framed by a shock of wiry red hair. When she had the window open, wafts of classical music drifted over to him. 'Every now and again I would look across and she'd have disappeared, obviously gone down to have a bit of lunch or put the kettle on or something, but [normally] she'd be up there working, and that's all she did.' He was 'completely intrigued by this person who was . . . in her own world'.

Mark hadn't been overburdened with opportunities before that summer. Raised in the shadow of a bullying, censorious father, he had left school without qualifications, and for almost a year he'd spent his dole money travelling back and forth across his native Bristol, and sometimes much further afield, looking for work. He'd eventually found it with a firm of builders based in Tetbury, a small town thirty miles outside the city. It was solid employment, but there was little to keep him from moving on. One day, the red-haired woman came rushing across the street to ask for help: one of her taps had burst, and there was water everywhere. Mark went over to fix it. 'He came in,' Angela told her friends, 'and never left.'

Some of those friends, when they met him a few months later, were a bit surprised. Deborah Rogers was typical in viewing the couple as 'the most improbable combination in so many ways'. Part of the improbability was to do with the fifteen-year age gap between them, although that becomes a lot less remarkable when viewed in the context of Angela's circle. Several of her friends – among them Lorna Sage, Corinna Sargood, and Deborah herself – ended up with considerably younger men. Perhaps these clever, ambitious, unconventional women were seeking to escape the chauvinistic attitudes of men of their own generation (to whom several of them had unsuccessful early marriages). A much more unusual difference between Angela and Mark was the gulf between their levels of education. It's clear that theirs wasn't the sort of literary 'marriage' that depends upon shared ambitions or intellectual adventures. Angela needed all of that much less than she needed a sense of domestic stability, and the space to be herself. A comparison might be drawn with the marriage of James and Nora Joyce, who also had a love that transcended differences of education and literary taste, a love that was sustained by the ways their personalities rhymed (Angela and Mark were both mild-mannered, both confident in their individuality, both given to esoteric enthusiasms), by deep mutual tenderness, and by sexual compatibility.

Mark cut a dramatic figure. He was tall, sinewy, long-haired and extravagantly bearded: Angela described him as looking 'like a werewolf', while others thought he looked 'like Christ'. Either way, he was phenomenally handsome, with brooding features and soulful, long-lashed green eyes (they were 'the colour of the inside of the ocean', Angela wrote). She described him as 'big and fierce', and 'so MALE'. He was given to boyish hobbies: he liked making things, was good with tools, and had what he describes as 'an affinity with fire'; at different times over the next twenty years he had fleeting passions for guns, archery and motorcycles. But his dominant quality, as far as most people were concerned, was his startling capacity for silence. He was quite capable of saying no more than five or six words (two of which would be 'hello' and 'goodbye') over the course of an entire evening. A few of Angela's friends found this hulking, mute presence at the dinner table a bit unnerving. Others understood that Mark was happiest observing: he didn't feel the need to interpose himself in a conversation. His silence was comfortable and self-contained, by contrast with Paul Carter's rebarbative, melancholy silence, and Angela clearly found it companionable. In September 1975, in a piece for *New Society*, she wrote: 'the haunting silences of Bath are those with which the English compose intimacies'.

For all that she liked to joke about Mark's fierceness, it was his mildness and apparent purity (as well as his 'Pre-Raphaelite' good looks) to which she was initially drawn. Shortly after meeting him, she wrote in her journal:

When I hold him in my arms, I hold all this country's sadness, its ineradicable poignancy, the rain, soft rain of early spring; the cold, pure weather, the fragility of the small flowers that hide themselves, the gentleness of the hills, their low lines of brown & grey, mists, mists coming down on a November afternoon, the magic silence of the wood. Your gentleness, your innocence, your sweetness, like the taste of rain & tears . . . I do not see you with my eyes but with my heart.

She found that she became calmer when she was with him, and although the relationship progressed in a fairly casual manner for its first few months, she was considering its long-term prospects from the beginning. In her journal, she wrote: 'I am remembering what John [Yoxall] said, how one has to work out how long a relationship will do, whether for a night, or a week, or a year, or a lifetime . . .'

The work that Mark had witnessed Angela absorbed in could have been any of several projects, but her major preoccupation throughout this period was *The Sadeian Woman*. She was reading assiduously – biographies of Sade and academic papers on his work, cultural critics from Roland Barthes to Michel Foucault, psychoanalytic theorists including Freud, Melanie Klein and Jacques Lacan – and filling up notebook after notebook with quotations and summaries. 'At least the bibliography is going to be enormously impressive,' she wrote to Deborah on 16 September 1975, enclosing draft versions of the first two chapters. 'I'd like to know what you think . . . although I am very, very nervous.'

There's no trace of these anxieties in the finished book. *The Sadeian Woman* is a work of brilliantly sustained cultural criticism, in a mode that English people rarely attempt: a fiercely felt, epigrammatic, unashamedly intellectual excursion into semiotics and group psychology. Almost every sentence provides a subtle provocation or dazzling insight. It owes something to Barthes, Foucault and Gauthier, but the intelligence and style that shape it are distinctively Angela Carter's own; it is the most explicit statement of her feminist and socialist beliefs that she ever made in print, and functions as a sort of guide to the other books that she wrote during this period – *The Passion of New Eve* and *The Bloody Chamber*.

The book opens with a 'Polemical Preface', the argument of which is incredibly dense and discursive ('the somewhat chaotic organisation is intentional', Angela told Deborah: 'Sade was a somewhat chaotic chap, and, dammit, so am I'). A very broad summary might go like this: sex always involves two (or more) particular individuals, with their respective histories, their intricate biographies. 'We do not go to bed in simple pairs; even if we choose not to refer to them, we still drag there with us the cultural impedimenta of our social class, our parents' lives, our bank balances, our sexual and emotional expectations . . . all the bits and pieces of our unique existences.' But pornography tends to ignore this fact. It 'departicularises' relations between men and women by reducing them to their mythic roles, that is, to the 'behavioural modes' of masculine and feminine (the book deals with gay pornography – in a slightly unconvincing manner – by arguing that femininity is 'a mode of experience that transcends gender'). Pornography thus reinforces a view of society as naturally riven between the sexes. This needn't, however, be the case. Pornographic writing that acquires the techniques of real literature, of real art, is capable of subverting rather than endorsing the status quo:

> A moral pornographer might use pornography as a critique of current relations between the sexes. His business would be the total demystification of the flesh and the subsequent revelation, through the infinite modulations of the sexual act, of the real relations of man and his kind. Such a pornographer would not be the enemy of women, perhaps because he might begin to penetrate to the heart of the contempt for women that distorts our culture even as he entered the realms of true obscenity as he describes it.

Angela viewed Sade as just such an artist, 'a terrorist of the imagination', who used pornography to transmit an unflinching and (for that reason) deeply uncomfortable vision of a society in which sexuality is at the mercy of political power. His work is 'more descriptive and diagnostic than proscriptive and prophetic':

> He creates, not an artificial paradise of gratified sexuality but a model of hell, in which the gratification of sexuality involves the infliction and the tolerance of extreme pain. He describes sexual relations in the

context of an unfree society as the expression of pure tyranny, usually by men upon women, sometimes by men upon men, sometimes by women upon men and other women; the one constant in all Sade's monstrous orgies is that the whip hand is always the hand with the real political power and the victim is a person who has little or no power at all.

In other words, Sade's concern is not really with the physical, but with the underlying structures of human relations: 'he is uncommon amongst pornographers in that he rarely, if ever, makes sexual activity seem attractive as such'. It was his vision of an oppressive, unjust world – a patriarchal one, certainly, but also a mercenary, conservative, class-bound one – that appealed to her. ('I did have problems keeping the book within a feminist perspective,' she told one interviewer.)

The main body of the text comprises extended readings of three of Sade's novels: *Justine*, *Juliette* and *Philosophy in the Boudoir* (an additional chapter, focussing on *The 120 Days of Sodom*, was cut after Carmen suggested that it was 'thinner than the others, and somehow the least convincing'). Sade recognised that the world wasn't fair to women – Justine is repeatedly raped, imprisoned and tortured, her only crime that of trying to live virtuously in the way society has ordained for members of her sex, by preserving her virginity; her sister Juliette plays by the same rules, but turns them to her advantage, exploiting her sexuality to gain wealth and power, and violently dominating others – but whether they wallow in their status as victims or greedily emulate their masters' habits, they are equally culpable, in Angela Carter's view, for failing to remake the world for themselves.

Along the way, *The Sadeian Woman* takes in the images of femininity produced by Hollywood (Marilyn Monroe's 'representative capacity for exquisite martyrdom' recalls Justine), the mystification of motherhood ('the biological iconography of women' is overturned in Sade's invention of Juliette), and the tensions between mothers and daughters (the extreme antipathy between Eugénie de Mistival and her mother in *Philosophy in the Boudoir* 'suggests that women, also, retain elements of the early erotic relation with the mother that has been more fully exposed and documented in men'). But at its heart, *The Sadeian Woman* is about how the world might be remade. It ends with a long quotation from the anarchist writer Emma Goldman:

The demand for equal rights in every vocation of life is just and fair; but, after all, the most vital right is the right to love and be loved. Indeed, if partial emancipation is to become a complete and true emancipation of woman, it will have to do away with the ridiculous notion that to be loved, to be sweetheart and mother, is synonymous with being slave or subordinate. It will have to do away with the absurd notion of the dualism of the sexes, or that man and woman represent two antagonistic worlds . . .

A true conception of the relation of the sexes will not admit of conqueror and conquered; it knows of but one great thing: to give of one's self boundlessly, in order to find one's self richer, deeper, better.

By the time Angela met Mark she had learned an inordinate amount about sexual power play over the course of her relationships with Paul, Sozo, Kō and Andrew. The sort of relationship described by Goldman – a sustaining and humanising partnership between equals – was what she now hoped to find.

The Sadeian Woman illuminates several of the ideas that underwrite Angela Carter's fiction, but as a book-length work of cultural history it stands alone in her *oeuvre*, and she frequently doubted its worth. When she had finished the first two chapters in the autumn of 1975, she sent them to John Berger. He returned them with notes in the margin and ticks of enthusiasm, along with an encouraging letter:

I believe in the book. Very much. At last somebody – and it could probably only be a woman – is intellectually <u>active</u> before Sade . . .

My only qualification is that at times your activity is so various and so fast, that it may confuse. Not that I think any lines of thought should be cut for this reason – rather I'd argue that sometimes they should be given more space – <u>so that they jostle a little less</u>.

I have no doubt at all that you should go on with the book – and that you should give it as much time as <u>it</u> needs. To hell with deadlines, publishers yelling, etc. It deserves to be constructed with all the space it demands.

Angela took most of Berger's suggestions on board. But if his encouragement dissuaded her from giving up, it didn't rally her much further than that. Almost a year later, when she sent the third and fourth chapters to Carmen, she was still struggling with 'the profound dread inspired by the idea that the book does not, maybe, work'.

* * *

Over the four years that it took her to research and write *The Sadeian Woman*, Angela found relief in a number of smaller projects. Early in 1975, she began writing her first radio play. It began with a sound:

> Sitting in my room, pencil in hand, staring vacantly into space instead of getting on with whatever it was I was meant to be doing, I ran the pencil idly along the top of the radiator. It made a metallic, almost musical rattle. It was just the noise that a long, pointed fingernail might make if it were run along the bars of a birdcage.
>
> Now, I thought, what kind of person might have such fingernails? Why, a vampire, famed for their long, sharp fingernails (all the better to eviscerate you with!)

The play tells the story of a lonely countess named Vampirella, who laments the dependence on human blood that keeps her at a distance from humanity: 'My name is exile. My name is anguish. My name is longing.' When Hero, an innocent young Englishman, arrives at her castle, he takes pity on her, and her status as a monster is exposed as nothing more than pathology. *Vampirella* is a voluptuous, slyly comic piece of work, full of knowing Gothic details and camp flourishes. The script was offered to the BBC, where it found its way onto the desk of the producer Glyn Dearman, a contemporary of Angela and a former child actor, known to her generation for his portrayal of Tiny Tim in the 1951 film *Scrooge* and of Jennings in the BBC *Children's Hour* serial *Jennings at School*. Angela loved working with him, and they went on to make several more radio programmes together. She wrote that his 'style, sensitivity and enthusiasm would irradiate dramatised readings of the London telephone directory'. The appreciation was mutual: 'Angela had an enormous sense of fun which bubbled through a natural shyness and irradiated everything she did,' Dearman wrote. 'Working with her was life-enhancing.'

Vampirella was broadcast on BBC Radio 3 on 20 July 1976. Angela used it as the 'raw material' for a short story, 'The Lady of the House of Love', which omits the stuff about literary vampires that had been sprinkled over the original play, turns Hero into a soldier on his way to the First World War, and exaggerates the elements of horror, in silky, supple, sumptuous prose. '"The Lady of the House of Love" is a Gothic tale about a reluctant vampire; the radio play, *Vampirella*, is about vampirism as a metaphor,' Angela commented in 1985. 'The one is neither better nor worse than the other. Only, each is quite different.'

She sent the story to Robert Coover, and on 10 August 1975 he told her that he had shipped it off to the *Iowa Review* along with two of the stories from *Fireworks* ('Master' and 'Reflections'), two of her poems ('The Named Thing' and 'Liede') and an essay, 'Notes on the Gothic Mode', in which she claimed that it had never occurred to her to apply the label to her own work before reviewers started doing so (this wasn't entirely true – she had described both *Shadow Dance* and *The Magic Toyshop* as Gothic in letters to Janice Robertson – but perhaps she'd forgotten that she had). The whole lot appeared in the summer/fall issue of the *Iowa Review*, along with an introduction by Coover, in which he described Angela Carter as a writer 'whose talent far exceeds her reputation'.

As autumn approached, Angela began work on a new short story. 'The Erl-King' is an evocation of the bearded, elfin woodland creature from German and Scandinavian folklore, best known in Britain through his malevolent incarnation in Goethe's poem 'Der Erlkönig'. Angela depicts him as 'gaunt . . . tall as a tree with birds in its branches', his eyes 'quite green, as if from too much looking at the wood'; in her journal she wrote: 'Mark is der erlkönig.' He seduces the narrator, who soon becomes alarmed by his hold over her. 'I am not afraid of him; only . . . of the vertigo with which he seizes me.' She doesn't blame him for this – 'in his innocence he never knew he might be the death of me' – but nonetheless imagines strangling him with the strands of his own long hair. The story is a beautifully tender and sensual nightmare; it suggests that Angela was becoming unnerved by how deeply she was falling for Mark. She considered putting it in a book with 'The Lady of the House of Love' and a novella about Lola Montez, the nineteenth-century dancer and mistress of both Franz Liszt and King Ludwig I of Bavaria (these relationships are the subject of Max Ophüls' film *Lola Montès*, which Angela had seen with Christopher Frayling), but she doesn't appear to have made much headway with this idea.

Bath provided Angela with plenty of ways to relax between her intensive bouts of work. Nicholas Saunders' influential guidebook *Alternative England and Wales*, published in 1975, describes the city (with perhaps a pinch of hyperbole) as becoming what London's Notting Hill had been in the 1960s: the geographical heart of the British counterculture. There were numerous craft shops, galleries and fringe theatres; what Angela described as '*proper cafés* where you can sit and read the papers and play dominoes and talk to strangers, just as if you were abroad'; and health shops, including Harvest, the finest 'natural foods' store outside London (it remains open today), which had a noticeboard where New Age Seekers advertised for like minds to 'get into organic smallholding', or sought 'good homes for vegetarian kittens'.

At around this time, Angela became involved with pioneering performance artists Shirley Cameron and Roland Miller through the Bath Arts Workshop. She participated in several of their performances, including one that she proposed and wrote herself. Titled *Ceremonies and Transformations of the Beasts*, it was centred around a man metamorphosing into a bird – a distant ancestor, perhaps, of Fevvers in *Nights at the Circus*, and a close cousin of the lycanthropes in *The Bloody Chamber*. 'It was very alternative,' remembered Christopher Frayling who went to see the piece at Walcot Village Hall. 'This deafening percussion, this performance artist, and the only words I remember in the whole thing were at the end, he suddenly put on these huge feathers . . . and he stood there in all his nakedness and said, "Big bird!"'

Angela stayed in touch with her friends in London via endless, meandering phone conversations, sometimes lasting an hour or two at a time. She would gossip, catch up, talk about politics and art, or go off on long comic tangents, often leaving monologues on friends' answering machines if they weren't around to speak to her. This was long before mobile phones, so her interlocutor would be anchored to the spot. 'When you talked to Angela on the phone, you had to make yourself comfortable,' remembered Mark. Ann McFerran agreed: 'Often she would call you in the middle of the morning and you would almost pack up your work for the day. But I wouldn't have missed those conversations for the world.'

Throughout this period, Angela's reputation as a critic was gathering momentum. She was still writing regular pieces for the *Radio Times*, but now her name also began to appear in the listings pages of the magazine – she started reviewing books for programmes such as *Now Read On* on BBC Radio 4 and *Read All About It* on BBC1. 'I am certainly not material for a public personality', she had written to Carole after her first TV appearance in 1969, and it's true that her eccentric manner of speaking could be testing for the broadcast mediums, but combined with her intellectual sharpness and her subversive sensibility it made for some magnificently unusual moments. Once, on a panel discussion about D. H. Lawrence, she said: 'I've always thought that Gudrun [from *Women in Love*] was, well' – there followed one of her drawn-out pauses – 'the vasectomy queen of the north.' Now it was her fellow panellists' turn to be silent.

She was also engaging regularly in a more considered form of cultural criticism. Since she first started writing for *New Society* in the mid-1960s, her contributions had developed from mildly idiosyncratic pieces of conventional reportage to lithe and witty semiotic analyses of contemporary culture. Much of this can be put down to the influence of the European critics she had been reading since 1968, and in particular that of Roland Barthes. It isn't clear exactly when she first encountered his work (John Hayes remembers talking to her about him while she was living in Japan, but Christopher Frayling has described introducing her to *Mythologies* in 1975, and the opening line of a letter that she sent him on 1 June 1976 is 'Ta for Barthes'). She went out of her way to throw commentators off the scent of his influence (in 1978 she told an interviewer that 'I've only just read Barthes. Last month'), but it remains pungent in spite of her efforts. His interests were uncannily similar to hers – Japan, cinema, fashion, Sade – and his approach, examining everyday phenomena for the myths they conceal, was one that she increasingly adopted for her own.

In 1976 she wrote a piece about wrestling for *New Society*. It is utterly unlike the chapter on wrestling in *A Bunch of Joys* (her unpublished nonfiction book about Bristol nightlife), and very like Barthes' take on the subject twenty years earlier in *Mythologies*. Both authors begin by analysing the effects of the light hitting the ring: a light 'without shadow [that] generates an emotion without reserve', writes Barthes; a 'theatrical' light that 'clothes the wrestlers' according to Carter. Barthes feels that wrestling 'presents man's suffering with all the amplification of tragic masks'; Carter sees it as 'a crude morality play'. Barthes talks of the 'moral mechanism' of the spectacle; Carter of its 'moral rhythm'. There are several other echoes between the two essays. They're much too soft to count as plagiarism – the most that they suggest is a level of conscious emulation – but neither can they be entirely coincidental.

John Yoxall returned to England once or twice a year to stay with his aging parents. At around the time that Angela was writing *Vampirella*, he visited her in Bath, bringing with him two friends from Japan, Sandy Brown and Takeshi Yasuda. They had met while learning to be potters in Mashiko, a small town about ninety miles north of Tokyo, and were now married and living on a farm in Devon. 'I remember liking [Angela] enormously,' Sandy says. 'She was a very good listener actually, as well as an interesting talker . . . I thought she was absolutely fascinating . . . very charismatic.' The affection was obviously mutual, and not long afterwards, Angela went to stay with Sandy and Takeshi in Devon.

Bourne Head Farm occupied twenty-five acres in the wild, rolling countryside near the village of Meshaw, not far from Exmoor. It belonged to Sandy's mother, who wanted it to be self-sufficient. They rose early each morning to milk the cows, made cream using old-fashioned equipment, fed the whey to the pigs, and turned the pigs into sausages and chops. They grew their own vegetables, baked their own bread, churned their own butter, and made their own cheese. There was a traditional stone-built farmhouse and various outbuildings, including a barn that Sandy and Takeshi had converted into a pottery, where they made the utensils with which they prepared the food, and the dishes from which they ate. 'Angela loved all of this, like it was some sort of amazing fantasy,' Sandy remembered:

> while we were eating we would be talking about the food that we were eating, and then after we had finished eating we would be talking about the next meal we were going to eat and then we would prepare that and then we would talk about that, and so there was this rolling conversation about food going on endlessly, and I just got the impression that Angela could have stayed there indefinitely.

Though her visits to the farm never lasted more than a week or two at a time, Angela returned most years until 1980. On that first occasion, John Yoxall stood in the kitchen while they sliced a pig in half, telling a rambling story about a man he'd met in the Philippines. In the evening, after the men had gone to bed, Sandy and Angela sat around the big inglenook fireplace and talked. Sandy remembers Angela telling her about 'this gorgeous young builder who had come in to do some work on her house . . . she was absolutely besotted with him'.

Angela began to entertain fantasies of living off the land. Hughie remembered her saying around this time (and remembered himself teasing her for saying) that she wanted to move to the Soviet Union and drive a tractor. She couldn't even drive a car. Back in Bath she asked Edward to teach her.

On the second or third lesson, she drove straight into a wall and knocked it over. They called Mark to come and fix it. Edward, when he saw them together, realised that the relationship was growing closer.

Angela hadn't touched *The Passion of New Eve* since February 1974; returning to it in the winter of 1975, she found herself drawn immediately back into its world, and the work consumed her for the rest of the year. 'I have never had such "baby blues" with any novel as I've had with this one,' she wrote to Deborah on 5 January 1976, enclosing the finished manuscript. 'Real gloom & anguish as I approached the finishing tape.' She feared that it was a bit of a mess, partly because of the long gap between writing the first and second drafts: 'I started off writing the novel thinking I was interested in myth with a capital M . . . and ending up realising that Myth bored me stiff,' she told the critic Elaine Jordan a few years later. 'I'm not sure that it hangs together,' she said on another occasion. 'I think the metaphysics gets in the way.' But it was among only three of her books – the others were *Nights at the Circus* and *Wise Children* – that she chose to be featured in the *Omnibus* programme in 1992, and in the mid-1980s she described it as 'my favourite of my novels because it is so ambitious, so serious and so helplessly flawed'.

Tony Godwin of Harcourt Brace Jovanovich agreed: 'It's nearly a masterpiece,' he wrote to her. 'Congratulations . . . it is a remarkable novel and I am full of admiration.' Her British publishers were less enthusiastic, but they came up with the goods. Mark Barty-King – who had taken over from Alan Brooke at Hart-Davis – offered £2,000, the same as the company had paid for each of Angela's last two novels. Deborah tried persuading him to go a little higher. He wrote to her on 26 February 1976:

> I am afraid I cannot report that we feel confident that this is a major step forward for Angela. The writing is certainly as beguiling as ever and many of the images in the book are extremely graphic and even lurid, but while, once again, to a certain extent I appreciate all the symbolic imagery in itself, I cannot see a truly original vision at work in the book . . . There have been, after all, a good many apocalyptic books signalling the devastation of the world as we know it. Possibly what I am saying is that I do not feel the book is as important as the author may think it is. Bearing all this in mind, I think we must stick

to our offer of £2,000 as previously formulated and perhaps you will let me know what you feel about it in due course.

The offer wasn't negligible, but Angela was put out by Barty-King's grudging tone, and by his obvious indifference to the novel itself. Deborah sent the manuscript to a number of other publishers, including Liz Calder, a young editor at the distinguished left-wing house of Victor Gollancz, who received a reader's report describing it as 'a startling mixture of apocalyptic Gothic, Sci Fi, soft porn and Women's Lib . . . a strange and fascinating book, not quite making the grade as a serious novel, but ranking high in Sci Fant.'

Calder was a former fashion model with a poised, serene manner that belied her taste for adventure both geographical (she had spent years living in Brazil) and literary. Even so, she remembers her initial lunch meeting with Angela as being a bit uncomfortable:

> I was fairly awestruck and tongue-tied, and terribly nervous . . . I think it was partly her manner, which was hard to figure when you didn't know her: there'd be a lot of hemming and hawing and laughter and so on, and at the beginning it was a bit hard to know how to take it. But that wasn't really what bothered me. It was just that I had great admiration for her, and I was anxious about how I was performing, in order to win her over. She gave the impression of being quite beady. She was obviously summing you up. And I remember that halfway through the lunch, which was going rather sporadically, really, she said to me: 'Who are your favourite authors?' And my mind just went blank. I came up with some really daft answers, and I thought, I've really blown it now . . . So nobody could have been more surprised than me when Deborah said, 'Well, she wants to come with you.'

On 28 April 1976, Calder offered £1,500 for British and Commonwealth rights to *The Passion of New Eve*. She wanted to publish it in a new 'Fantasy and Macabre' imprint, 'which would be likely to include writers such as Ursula Le Guin, in the future'. Deborah asked her to raise the offer to £2,250, so as to outbid Hart-Davis. Calder tried to find the extra money, noting in an internal Gollancz memo that 'Angela Carter is <u>exactly</u> the sort of writer we are looking for: young, already with her own following, something of a TV/radio pundit, committed, controversial, and enormously talented.' Her bosses were evidently unconvinced, and Angela eventually accepted the original offer of £1,500, signing a contract on 27 May.

Shortly afterwards, she was invited to a dinner in honour of the Chilean novelist José Donoso at Calder's home in London. One of the guests was the young British Indian writer Salman Rushdie, a 'great fan' of Angela's work, whose first novel *Grimus* had recently been published by Gollancz. 'Mr Donoso arrived looking like a Hispanic Buffalo Bill, complete with silver goatee, fringed jacket and cowboy boots, and proceeded, as I saw it, to patronize Angela terribly,' Rushdie remembered. 'I was completely unknown, but Angela had published a lot of books by that time, and the fact that he either didn't know or affected not to know who she was, that offended me on her behalf. So I guess I stood up for her . . . I made a speech at Donoso about how this was like the greatest writer in England. I think it endeared me to her.'

Over the next few years, Angela formed a close and mutually supportive friendship with Rushdie. 'In a literary sense she was one of my greatest allies,' he remembered. 'She was one of the people who really understood my work as I would have wished it to be understood, and was a great defender of it to anybody who would ask, and several who wouldn't ask.' In the neat, manicured landscape of contemporary British fiction, she had at last found a novelist whose wild, flamboyant sensibility corresponded with her own. They were both outsiders, with firmly held socialist principles; they were both interested in comedy and language and Joyce; both of them were drawn to fantasy, and both were blessed with spectacular powers of invention; and neither of them recognised the ways in which they were themselves invented in the media. When, in 1985, the young journalist Helen Simpson interviewed them together for *Vogue* (the headline was: 'Hackle Raisers'), she expressed surprise at how easy-going and witty they both were:

HS: I'm talking to you two because I was at a reading where you appeared together and seemed to be enjoying yourselves so much, seemed such good friends. I'm interested in books and writers, and I hadn't read anywhere else of your friendship. And I would have thought it a most unlikely friendship . . . Salman, your public image is not exactly one of approachable friendliness or bonhomie . . . And you, Angela, are often presented as a vatic, other-worldly fable-spinner.

AC: So you're a furious Third-Worlder, Salman, and I'm a stern-faced
    feminist.
SR: How strange. Am I?

*   *   *

Occasions like the dinner at which she met Rushdie were convincing
Angela that she needed to be closer to the literary action. Deborah Rogers
formed the impression that she was beginning to think in quite pragmatic
terms about her career: 'I think she was much more ambitious than she
let on.' Christopher Frayling agreed: 'It was odd . . . she quite wanted to
be famous.' That wouldn't be an easy thing to achieve in Bath, and by
the end of 1975, Angela had decided to move on. Fleur Adcock visited
her, and noted in her diary that Angela still found the city peaceful, 'but
after three years she's had almost enough of that particular kind of peace':

> Bath's full of retired people, she says: a lot of them retired at 17. The
> 'alternative society' is so evident that it's taken a large area of ground
> from what it offers to replace . . . the mixture has too few ingredients;
> Angela feels the need for London's multifarious mess again.

She began talking to Christine Downton – who for the past year had been
working as a contract economist at the Bank of England – about buying
a house together in the capital, and specifically in its lower hemisphere
('Angela was very firm that she wanted to be south of the river,' Downton
remembered). One Saturday afternoon, Rebecca Howard drove them both
around south London looking at different houses. 'We were dotting about,
with reasonable range, along the river,' she remembered. Her son Sam,
aged about three, was with them. When they got to 107 The Chase – a
derelict four-storey Victorian house with a large overgrown garden, on the
street in Clapham that Ann McFerran and Snoo Wilson lived on – Sam
peed on the doorstep. Angela said: 'Right, that's got to be it, he's scent-
marked the house.'

CHAPTER SIXTEEN
The tales of terror groove

In 1976, the historically working-class district of Clapham was changing fast. Around the Common there was a health-food shop, an antiques merchant, and an independent bookstore. There were plans to open an alternative-therapies centre on the High Street. The bankers and property speculators whose flashy loft conversions and double-parked Porsches saw the area become a byword for yuppiedom during the 1980s hadn't yet arrived in significant numbers, but there was already a solid constituency of literary and media types: as well as Snoo Wilson and Ann McFerran, Angela's new neighbours included the playwright David Hare and the cartoonist and television presenter Barry Fantoni, as well as Ian McEwan, whom she began seeing quite regularly for dinner.

Angela understood that she was implicated in the process of gentrification, but even so, she felt pained by the passing of the south London she had known as a girl. 'You can't walk home from the tube, these days, without seeing somebody moving their Swiss-cheese plants into a white-painted room, probably with a chrome and glass coffee table and maybe spotlight fittings,' she complained in an article for *New Society*. Dora Chance, a resident of nearby Brixton, has a similar gripe in *Wise Children*: 'There's been a diaspora of the affluent, they jumped into their diesel Saabs and dispersed throughout the city. You'd never believe the price of a house round here, these days.'

The price of 107 The Chase was £14,000, which Angela and Christine split between them, as they did the house itself, Angela taking the top two floors, Christine the bottom two and the garden. They stripped the wallpaper and did the plastering themselves, and painted the front of the house a shocking blood red (it faded over the years Angela lived there to a fleshy pink). Mark began the process of converting Angela's half into a self-contained maison-ette: on the first floor he constructed a spacious kitchen-cum-living-room, featuring 'a rather Beardslyesque black & yellow kitchen unit, which is like no other kitchen unit in Clapham, or indeed the world'. On the top floor was their bedroom and, facing the street, Angela's study.

Angela was happy with Mark's work but frustrated by its pace – she referred to it as 'Jurassic Productions' – and she spent the first few months of 1976 travelling back and forth between Bath and London, dealing with the sale of her old house, and overseeing the renovation of her new one. 'Everything is in chaos,' she wrote to Brenda Leys (who handled dramatic rights for the Deborah Rogers Agency) on 8 March. 'Am chewing Valium like they were sweeties.' On 1 June, when she officially moved into The Chase, it was still 'more building site than house'.

A few days later, burglars broke in through a downstairs window. Since Angela and Christine didn't own anything very valuable, they 'were reduced to taking odds and ends they thought the wife might fancy: a pretty teapot, all the forks and spoons but, oddly, no knives except the carving knife . . . Also a pair of black velvet trousers and a straw boater.' The incident cheered Angela up no end: south London hadn't changed too much.

The summer of 1976 was the hottest since records began. It didn't rain for forty-five consecutive days, from late June through to mid-August. Angela 'sweated [it] out' translating the *Histoires ou contes du temps passé avec des moralités* – Charles Perrault's pioneering seventeenth-century collection of fairy tales – 'on the pretext of improving my French'. It was a commission from Gollancz, who paid her an advance of £700. Angela found the experience revelatory: 'what an unexpected treat to find that in this great Ur-collection – whence sprang the Sleeping Beauty, Puss in Boots, Little Red Riding Hood, Cinderella, Tom Thumb, all the heroes of pantomime – all these nursery tales are purposely dressed up as fables of the politics of experience'.

That's a long way from the standard interpretation of the tales: the scholar Jack Zipes has described them as 'high literary recondite texts intended to provide examples of civility'. Perrault was a rather sycophantic poet at the court of Louis XIV. He cultivated a refined, ironic style. Angela more or less ignored these facts, describing him in the afterword to her translations as 'never artful. His tales retain the simplicity of form and the narrative directness of the country story-teller.' She was reinventing him in her grandmother's image – a project no less audacious than enlisting the Marquis de Sade as a proto-feminist. She tested the limits between translation and adaptation, converting Perrault's long, elegant sentences into short, blunt ones, adding colloquial phrases to them, and replacing his verse morals with prose homilies, many of which said the precise opposite of what he intended. The resulting text was 'almost word for word' the way her grandmother had told the stories to her, but Angela tended to present her deviations from the original as failures of comprehension: 'I'm told, quite kindly, that [my translation is] not extraordinarily accurate,' she demurred when complimented on the book. 'People have offered to correct my French.'

For all that she put her own stamp on Perrault's texts, Angela couldn't go too far without entirely neglecting her duties as translator. But her imagination had been piqued. As part of her research she read *The Uses of Enchantment*, Bruno Bettelheim's newly published psychoanalytic study of European folk-lore, in which he contended that fairy tales serve to console children about such terrifying mysteries as sex and death, by presenting them in symbolic form. Angela disagreed with some of the basic tenets of his argument – she knew a bit about the historical circumstances in which the tales were origi-nally told, and thought it was pretty obvious that in the densely wooded landscapes of medieval France, a story that warned children not to stray from the path had a more than therapeutic purpose – but from an artistic point of view, she was exhilarated by the vivid images of sex and violence, lurking in the familiar spaces of the nursery, that Bettelheim laid bare. She was particularly struck by his idea that the animals that populate fairy tales represent base desires. She copied the following lines into her journal:

> Fairy-tale animals come in two forms: dangerous & destructive animals, such as the wolf in 'Little Red Riding Hood', or the dragon [who] devastates an entire country unless each year a virgin is sacrificed to it . . . & wise & helpful animals which guide & rescue the hero . . .
>
> Both dangerous & helpful animals stand for our animal nature, our instinctual drives. The dangerous ones symbolize the untamed id – not yet subjected to ego & superego control, in all its dangerous energy. The helpful animals represent our natural energy – again the id – but now made to serve the best interests of the total personality.

'The animal is repressed sexuality – "the beast in man",' Angela wrote in her journal. She began dreaming up a collection of tales in which the latent sexual imagery would rise uncomfortably to the surface, a book that would expose as vainglorious lies the ways we try to distinguish ourselves from animals, in what she later described as 'a social realism of the unconscious' – its effect would be the very opposite of consoling. Her initial notes focus on 'Red Riding Hood', 'Cinderella', and 'Beauty and the Beast'. At the top of the page she wrote: '<u>Code name</u>: The New Mother Goose'.

This was the first flash of *The Bloody Chamber*. The finished book would also include versions of 'Bluebeard' (which Bettelheim groups together with 'Beauty and the Beast' as an 'animal groom' story), 'Snow White' and 'Puss-in-Boots', as well as 'The Erl-King' and 'The Lady of the House of Love', both of which Angela redrafted to echo more sharply the collection's themes. The 'Cinderella' material was eventually absorbed into 'Wolf-Alice', which also draws on 'Red Riding Hood' and 'Beauty and the Beast'. Most of the stories feature young girls discovering their sexuality, and there's no shortage of erotic and menstrual imagery, but Angela never thought of *The Bloody Chamber* as a crusading feminist book in the manner of *The Passion of New Eve* or *The Sadeian Woman*. When she was asked in 1985 if her intention had been to subvert and feminise a patriarchal form, she said: 'Not really. I was taking . . . the latent content of those traditional stories and using that; and the latent content is violently sexual. And because I am a woman, I read it that way.' She was being a little bit disingenuous – she knew perfectly well that to write frankly about female sexuality was to upset a cultural norm – but her remarks suggest that she was becoming irritated by the ways commentators were sealing the significance of the stories within the sphere of gender politics (their initial reception focussed much more intently on the theme of human versus animal nature).

As well as her work on Perrault and the persistent headache of *The Sadeian Woman*, Angela had been writing masses of journalism to pay for the house – in the year to October 1976 she wrote twelve long articles for *New Society*, two for the *Radio Times*, one for *Cosmopolitan*, one for *Vogue*, and one for the *New Review*, as well as various book reviews for publications including *Spare Rib* and the *Guardian* – and she was finding the constant cycle of deadlines and word-counts increasingly oppressive. She was thankful for Mark, who provided support and kept her from becoming too manic. 'At least this stress, ravaging though it is, isn't connected with affairs of the heart,' she wrote to Fleur Adcock. 'That would be <u>too much</u>.'

Teaching, it occurred to her, might be a less fraught way to earn a living. She came across an advertisement for an Arts Council of Great Britain fellowship at the University of Sheffield. The post was intended for a creative writer, who would make herself available to students, and perhaps take the odd class, but who would basically be free to get on with her own work. Angela was interviewed by a panel consisting of Brian Morris, the head of the university's English department; Neil Roberts, a lecturer in twentieth-century literature; and the Catholic novelist Piers Paul Read, as an external examiner. Read might not have been the most natural supporter of Angela Carter's work, but of the five or six candidates who were interviewed for the job, most had only published in magazines (Alexis Lykiard was the only one other than Angela who had published novels). Neil Roberts remembered that there wasn't much discussion about whom they should appoint:

> In the opinion of everyone on the panel, Angela was obviously the outstanding candidate . . . The most striking impression she made, given what I had read of her work, which was in a sort of fantasy mode, what really struck me and somewhat surprised me was quite how intellectual she was – a real sharpness of mind. And also, perhaps slightly paradoxically, in contrast to the extreme articulacy of her writing, that she talked in a sort of casual, hip manner. She didn't speak with the sort of fluency that you might expect from her writing. She spoke with a kind of false inarticulacy – I don't know whether it was deliberately false or not, but a sort of hesitancy. It may just have been that she didn't want to seem too forbidding. Also she was much more politically conscious and motivated than I had deduced from the stories.

At the start of October, then, Angela returned to the bleak industrial landscapes of South Yorkshire. Sheffield is just a short train journey from Wath-upon-Dearne, and lies under the same implacable skies (Angela told John Haffenden that she wrote most of *The Bloody Chamber* there, 'which is probably why they are all such cold, wintry stories'). It was a world away from the middle-class environments of London or Bath, and even Bradford struck Angela as having the edge in terms of sophistication. In 1976, Sheffield remained relatively untouched by immigration, and the older generation still spoke in the dialect Angela remembered from her grandmother, 'all "sithee" and "thyssen" and "'e were runnin' like buggery"'. People ate black pudding and tripe – it was more or less impossible to get hold of fancy foreign ingredients like garlic and olive oil – and brought jugs of beer home from the pub. Women aged over forty didn't leave the house without a hat or a scarf to cover their hair. 'Although I think I know more about the exquisite gradations & variations of provincial life in Britain than anyone else, either living or dead,' Angela wrote to Alan Ross of the *London Magazine*, 'Sheffield has opened up a whole new dimension of it.'

John Yoxall put her in touch with his friend Kaktus Leach (with whom he had hitch-hiked to India almost ten years earlier), who lived in a large Victorian house on Albert Road, not far from the city centre, with his wife, Naomi Brent. For £7 a week in rent they provided Angela with a narrow first-floor room, only just big enough for a single bed and a desk, looking out over the back garden towards a slope of terraced houses – a view that Angela thought was 'like a Lowry painting'.

Kaktus and Naomi were vigorously engaged in left-wing politics, and the house was a hotbed of radical activity. There was an offset lithograph in the basement and 'all sorts of nutty people used to come round to get posters or tickets or leaflets printed'. They also put up refugees from Augusto Pinochet's military dictatorship in Chile: a former political prisoner had been living there with his family before Angela arrived, and although he and his wife had since moved to permanent accommodation in Barnsley, their two oldest daughters were remaining at Albert Road until they finished school. They were 'naughty teenagers', and Angela, whose room was next to theirs, was 'rather amused by them'. A married couple called John and Joss LeCorney rented a room on the floor above (Joss was a feminist historian, who subsequently founded a woman's press), and when Angela first moved into the house, another woman and her baby were also living there. They all took turns to prepare meals (Naomi remembered Angela as 'a brilliant cook. She would do lovely puddings and then she wouldn't eat them'), and they all dined together most evenings. Angela described the house as a 'commune' in letters to her friends, but that was romanticising things a little: everybody paid rent to Kaktus and Naomi, except for the Chilean refugees, who were paid for by a government scheme.

In the evenings, when she wasn't working, Angela often came down to the living room, but she rarely took part in the rowdy discussions that went on between her housemates. 'She'd just quietly sit there,' Naomi remembered. On the whole, Naomi put this down to politeness rather than shyness: it seemed in keeping with other aspects of Angela's behaviour. It was clear that she had a ferocious tobacco habit (when she was writing, smoke would curl out from the keyhole of her room), but she never indulged it in the communal spaces of the house. Her thoughtfulness and discretion made her 'an extremely good lodger':

> she was away a lot, at weekends and holidays, and [when she was in the house] she was writing. She'd just lock herself in her room with her portable typewriter and I'd know to keep out of the way, and she'd get on with it . . . She was immensely unselfish, she was just so careful, about being here and about other people.

Kaktus agreed that Angela was 'very easy to live with':

> It was just her presence, in conversation, being polite to visitors, cooking, being considerate about what she did. It was just the way she was all the time . . . She had amazingly good manners. We knew her before she'd reached the zenith of her fame in literature, but she was totally un-big-headed about it.

Kaktus and Naomi had a two-year-old son, who was frightened of the illustrations in Judith Kerr's book *The Tiger Who Came to Tea*; Angela drew a picture of a friendlier-looking tiger, to comfort him. But something in her manner suggested that her gentleness and apparent tranquillity had been painfully acquired: 'I think she was one of these people who'd had a difficult time but [had] fought her way through it and had come to an equilibrium,' Kaktus says. 'It won't have been easy, but I had the impression she'd got there, and was content with herself.'

The University of Sheffield occupies a variegated sprawl of late Victorian and mid-twentieth-century buildings, beginning a mile away from the city centre, and about four miles from Albert Road. Angela had her own office – inherited from the Nigerian poet Wole Soyinka – in the Arts Tower, a functional skyscraper built in the 1960s, which on a rare clear day commanded unbroken views over the city. Since Soyinka had hardly ever been spotted on campus, the staff had become accustomed to using his office as a common room. Angela made it her own by plastering the walls with Dadaist posters and pictures cut out of *Vogue*.

Every weekday during the academic term she 'clocked on, like a worker'. As the phrase suggests, she didn't look on her new role with any great enthusiasm. She missed Mark, and it seemed increasingly mad to be so many miles away from the nest she'd only just begun to feather. The first day of term was Monday 4 October. That Wednesday she wrote to Christopher Frayling:

> the winds are wuthering round the arts tower, in which I sit in anomic revelry, contemplating a very aged typewriter & a 2-bus trip back to the commune, where my friends will be hard at work on the next edition of the 'Sheffield Free Press' . . . I keep thinking – that's 2 days done; only another three terms of 8 weeks each minus 2 days. I'm sure this is the wrong reaction.

In another letter to Frayling she wrote: 'I really don't want to do anything at all, except sit in my office & stare vacantly at the wall.' But depicting herself as indolent was never going to be convincing. She was busy research-ing the imagery of fairy tales, and admitted that she had borrowed from the 'excellent' university library a book called *Wolves and Were-Wolves* by John Pollard. 'I may try & cross were-wolves with "La Belle et la Bête",' she wrote.

In fact, she put the material to immediate use in a sequence of improvi-sations on 'Red Riding Hood'. She composed the first two stories between October 1976 and January 1977. 'The Werewolf' came first – a 'tiny little story' (it's about 1,000 words long) in which Red Riding Hood slices off the wolf's right forepaw when she meets him in the woods, only to find, when she reaches her grandmother's house, that the old woman has 'a bloody stump where her right hand should have been, festering already'. The idea of the old woman being the wolf – inherent in versions of the tale that feature him wearing her clothes to lure Red Riding Hood closer – is at once mesmeric and deeply disturbing, laying bare the Oedipal tensions that Bettelheim diagnosed in the tale.

Bettelheim observed that, although many versions of 'Red Riding Hood' exist, its basic elements are always 'a little girl with a red cap, [and] the company of wolves'. Angela knew that the last four words would be the title of the second story in the sequence, long before she had a clear sense of what she would do with it. Then the last line came to her: 'See! sweet and sound she sleeps in granny's bed, between the paws of the tender wolf.' The little girl would ignore her mother's warnings, embrace her animal nature, and find satisfaction in the company of wolves.

The story begins with a series of portentous statements about the evil nature of wolves ('They are grey as famine, they are as unkind as plague') and brief, cautionary accounts of lycanthropy, narrated in the voice of an ancient country storyteller. It conjures a primal, primary-coloured landscape (all virginal whites and carnal reds), steeped in danger. So when Red Riding Hood laughs in the wolf's face, rips off his shirt and '[flings] it into the fire, in the fiery wake of her own discarded clothing', it's an extraordinary moment, replacing Perrault's moralistic ending with an image of violent joy.

Angela knew that these stories were among the best things she had written. In the winter of her thirty-seventh year – with seven published books behind her, and another one about to come out – she had begun to produce the work on which her place in literary history rests.

During her first term in Sheffield, Angela became involved in a project with a group of four students, who co-authored a piece of fiction under her 'general, occasionally rather Stalinist' direction and editorship. In an introduction to the finished work, she offered some thoughts on the creative process:

> Writing fiction involves thinking laterally, that is, sideways – following through an idea by thinking in terms of connections, so as to create characters; it involves thinking structurally, that is, vertically, to make a coherent narrative with enough upward drive to go on until it stops; it also involves thinking in terms of images as well as words.

She helped the students to do all of this, making them compile dossiers on their characters and advising them on how to work through the plot. They began with 'one single, basic, archetypal theme – a quest', and went from there. Angela would set them a new task each week – they would have to go away and write a passage according to certain guidelines – then she would meet them to discuss the results and flesh out 'any emerging threads of imagery and symbolism'. One of the students, Steve Bownass, described the process as 'very enjoyable . . . a tangible form of discipline, leading, hopefully, to a tangible improvement'.

When it was finished, Angela tried to get the novella-length story published in the university magazine, but Gerard Langley, the student editor, wasn't keen. 'It just seemed really disconnected,' he remembered:

> It didn't have much thread. I tried to talk to her about it, and she got a bit huffy and said: 'Well, how would you do it then?' So for

about a year we worked on it, me and her and this guy called John Lake . . . [We] did quite a lot of this thing and then I left university and we never really finished it.

Even so, that year of working with Angela made a lasting impression on Langley. He subsequently became the lead singer of new-wave rock band the Blue Aeroplanes, whose 2011 album *Anti-Gravity* features a song named after her.

Angela got on well with her colleagues in the English department, and managed to insinuate herself onto a course titled 'The Gothic Imagination': 'The reading list comprises everything from "Melmoth the Wanderer" to Bram Stoker,' she wrote to Frayling, '& now also includes A. Carter, I'm happy to say.' But Neil Roberts recalled that she held herself apart to some extent: 'She was sociable – but I wouldn't describe her as uninhibited. There was a kind of reserve, although she mixed, she talked, she was friendly. There was a sense that she was holding something back.'

What she was holding back – or a large part of it – was her sense that life was happening elsewhere. She returned to London as frequently as she could, most weekends and throughout the academic holidays, 'since home (temporarily, at least) is where the heart is'. That 'temporarily' is just a talismanic bit of cynicism; her feelings for Mark showed no signs of abating. The following year she wrote in her journal:

> He still retains the look of how I first saw him, how I first saw him with the dazzled eye of love – a tree, with birds in it; a gaunt, tall, woodland being, with the shyness natural to those who live elsewhere . . . Grace & unsureness of a wild animal, a young horse, perhaps, or a deer, that comes to take bread from your hand & starts back when you speak to it. Nothing is changed.

They had soon established a harmonious domestic routine. Mark took care of most of the housework (in 1984 Angela told an interviewer that she'd gone off the idea of darkly passionate Heathcliff-type men: 'now I like people who know how to do the washing-up'), although she was usually responsible for the cooking. A couple of years later she told a friend that 'we (roughly) share the labour of looking after one another (we can't afford to employ one another, & besides, have other things to do). I say, "roughly", because it always seems to me that I do more, but he thinks he does more, too, so I suppose it is fair.'

'Mark made her very happy,' remembered Christine Downton. 'I think he sort of gave her a confidence in a domestic life, which she'd never really experienced before.' This wasn't lost on visitors to The Chase. 'He obviously adored her, and she him,' remembered Liz Calder. Salman Rushdie agreed: 'they were very at ease together.' 'They conspired to present their relationship as somehow *sui generis*,' wrote Lorna Sage: 'they had nothing much conventionally "in common", of course, except that they were both eccentrics, stubborn, intransigent, wordlessly intimate.'

In January, Angela sent 'The Company of Wolves' to the novelist Emma Tennant, who had been pestering her since 1975 to write something for her new magazine, *Bananas*. In her covering letter, Angela explained that ' "The Company of Wolves" is part of a work-in-progress called "New Mother Goose Tales", a collection of stories loosely derived from traditional fairy tales. This is part of the spin-off from a translation of the fairy tales of Charles Perrault . . . I seem to be stuck in the "tales of terror" groove for the time being.'

Tennant was a glamorous figure – an experimental novelist with an aristocratic background and strong feminist ideals – and *Bananas*, still only in its sixth issue, was making rapid incursions into the avant-gardish ground formerly occupied by *New Worlds*. J. G. Ballard was a contributing editor, and the magazine (or 'literary newspaper', as it was styled) had assembled a stable of distinctive writers, including William Burroughs, Philip Roth, Harold Pinter, Ian McEwan and Ted Hughes.

There have been rumours that Angela had a sexual relationship with Hughes. The only source for them appears to be Tennant, who in *Burnt Diaries* (her memoir of the 1970s, composed some years later in a spurious present tense) writes: 'Has Angela . . . I wonder . . . and it comes to me that she said a few months back when I spoke of Hughes's sudden nocturnal visit to my basement kitchen that there had been "something" between them . . . and her eyes gleamed from under her Red Riding Hood's Grandma coating of white hair.' This demonstrably false recollection (Angela's hair wasn't white at the time the conversation is supposed to have happened) is all that Hughes's biographer, Jonathan Bate, has in mind when he reports that 'Angela Carter, brilliant and beautiful magical realist, hinted that there had been "something" between her and Ted.' It seems vanishingly unlikely that such a relationship could have occurred without leaving any trace on the private or published writing of either participant. Quite apart from that, they only seem to have met on one occasion before Angela started writing for *Bananas* (by which time Hughes was having an affair with Tennant, and Angela's relationship with Mark was getting deeper) and, as far as these things can be determined, they weren't really one another's type. It's hard to treat the rumours as anything but invention of the most sensationalist kind.

The Passion of New Eve was published on 24 March 1977 in a striking black and gold jacket. The blurb, which Angela composed herself, described it as a 'dazzlingly imaginative novel . . . streaked with black humour'. 'Notice I curbed my natural reticence in the last paragraph,' she wrote to Liz Calder, 'but it is important to mention the black humour, since I've often noticed how easily people miss the irony and do not know when I am joking, often with embarrassing results.'

Most reviewers missed the irony even after she had flagged it up – as if funniness and feminism couldn't possibly coexist. There were a few positive responses (notably one by Lorna Sage in the *Observer*, which praised Angela for tackling 'the processes of myth-making and storytelling without puritan apologetics'), but most were irritated by what they saw as the novel's intractability. Jill Neville in the *Sunday Times* seemed to imagine that Angela thought of Evelyn's forced sex-change as just punishment for his past behaviour (primly remarking that he was 'not so terribly in the wrong it seems to me'), and felt that as the plot unravelled, 'any poor male reader would feel like a cat having its face rubbed in its own excrement'. The reflexively waspish journalist Julian Barnes – writing in the *New Statesman* under the pseudonym Paddy Beesley – echoed Ian Hamilton's review of *The Magic Toyshop* in painting Angela Carter as a cheap sensationalist, in poor control of her energies: 'If it all sounds jagged and cluttered in summary, then this is a good summary. Miss Carter leaves all plot on the escapes-and-captures level, shuns dialogue, and despite snatches of sharp phrasing, is prone to court silliness.' In the *Evening Standard*, the usually supportive Auberon Waugh, while affirming that 'her robust, unruly imagination has a matter-of-factness to it which I, at any rate, find attractive', felt that the novel was let down by 'self-indulgent passages in the middle' and a 'more or less incomprehensible' ending. 'It is all a little sad, because I am convinced that Miss Carter is one of the best writers of her generation,' he concluded, like a disappointed headmaster. 'One day she will reward my faith in her.'

'The Company of Wolves' appeared in the seventh issue of *Bananas* in April 1977, alongside work by J. G. Ballard, Tim Owens and John Sladek. To celebrate its launch, Angela was invited to a party at the *Bananas* offices in the semi-gentrified slum district of Notting Hill. It was a sunny day, and people spilled out of the small basement kitchen into the communal gardens at the back of the building. In her *Burnt Diaries*, Tennant evokes the scene:

> I wander outside, where the trees are newly in leaf and people are holding their *Bananas* No. 7 as if it had just floated down from above: Angela, I think secretly delighted with her 'Company of Wolves', comes over to kiss me and non-communicate her feelings. In fact, Angela's fascination is so great that it doesn't matter how long one has to wait for the tentatively begun sentence – this broken into by the chisel of high laughter, or the power-drill of an indrawn breath, for she is as amused as any by the kaleidoscope of thought processes which interrupt the consummation of her sentence. I imagine whole libraries and encyclopaedias of alternative meanings and parentheses lining up within Angela as she embarks bravely on speech. In the end, she has said only that she likes the way her story looks. But all the other possibilities, like bubbles blown high into the atmosphere, are there.

It was probably at the same party that Angela met Elizabeth Smart, the Canadian poet and author of *By Grand Central Station I Sat Down and Wept*, as she reported to Lorna Sage:

> 'It is hard for women,' [Smart] slurred. Actually, it was a very peculiar experience because she clearly wanted to talk in polished gnomic epigrams about anguish and death and boredom and I honestly couldn't think of anything to say. Except, I understand why men hate women and they are right, yes, right . . . And I began to plot a study of the Jean Rhys/ E. Smart/ E. O'Brien woman titled 'Self-inflicted Wounds'.

The personality that emerges from that letter – remorselessly observant, sharply funny – is hard to reconcile with the fey, other-worldly figure 'embarking bravely on speech' conjured by Emma Tennant. For all that the stories from *The Bloody Chamber* enhanced Angela's literary reputation, they also gave rise to a newly shallow way of inventing her – rather than as a sophisticated modern artist, she began to be portrayed as a primitive, quasi-mystical teller of tales – a tendency that only got worse after she stopped dyeing her hair in the 1980s, and the epithets 'white witch' and 'fairy godmother' began attaching themselves to her.

By the spring of 1977 Angela had begun writing the 'Beauty and the Beast' sequence for her New Mother Goose tales. 'Man & beast: benevolence & strangeness of the beasts,' she wrote in her journal. 'Beasts as other.' She looked at Madame Leprince de Beaumont's version of the tale, in which Beauty finds the Beast almost starved at the end, revives him, and agrees to marry him. His alarming animal associations thus tamed, he becomes a handsome man. Bettelheim viewed the tale as depicting the healthy transfer of affections from parent (Beauty's father) to sexual partner (the Beast); Angela thought that the way in which the Beast manipulates Beauty's feelings – 'Since you left me, I have been sick,' he whimpers – was anything but healthy, and that her sudden interest in him at this stage suggested deep reserves of masochism. 'The Courtship of Mr Lyon', the first of her versions of the tale, doesn't make these feelings explicit, though, ending as it does on a picture of apparent domestic bliss: 'Mr and Mrs Lyon walk in the garden; the old spaniel drowses on the grass, in a drift of fallen petals.' It is one of the richest and most oblique of the stories in *The Bloody Chamber*, and one of the most beautifully written.

She had the first sentence of 'The Tiger's Bride', the next story in the sequence, early on: 'My father lost me to The Beast at cards.' She later described this as 'one of my very favourite lines, if I may say this, in all my work . . . I was so thrilled with that line when I thought of it!' The narrator is initially terrified of her new husband, but eventually consents to sleep with him – he begins licking her, 'and each stroke of his tongue ripped off skin after successive skin, all the skins of a life in the world', to reveal the beautiful pelt beneath. During the Easter holidays Angela visited Italy with Edward Horesh, and decided to use Venice as the story's backdrop (there would be a scene with Beauty in 'a black gondola with a gondolier masked, all in black'), then changed her mind after visiting Mantua – the story is set there.

*   *   *

Gollancz published *The Fairy Tales of Charles Perrault* that summer, in a hardback edition featuring elegant, surreal etchings by Martin Ware (Angela loved them: 'His Mae West-like Lilac Fairy is particularly delicious,' she told Deborah). Barbara Hogan, writing in the *Daily Mail*, described the experience of reading Angela's translations as 'like coming suddenly upon a familiar building that has been cleaned'. 'Her plain prose is an admirable vehicle for Perrault's narratives,' agreed Philippa Pearce in the *Guardian*: 'The tartness of comment is most refreshing after so much sugaring-over of folk-tale for children.' In the *Times Literary Supplement*, the scholar A. J. Krailsheimer called the book 'stylish and lively', but noted that 'the version of Donkey-Skin translated by Angela Carter is not, as she claims, Perrault's own verse tale (in which the fairy is not called Lilac or anything else), but a much later, anonymous prose version (published 1781)'. Neither he nor any of the other reviewers commented on the liberties Angela had taken with Perrault's originals when she was working directly from them.

This may have freed her up to take further liberties. She spent the beginning of the summer working on a long story inspired by 'Bluebeard'. She felt that Perrault's original tale had a 'curious flavour':

> It was partly his blue beard that did it, he looked amazingly to me like Diaghilev. And then I realised that if it had been Diaghilev, I'd have . . . to do something very weird – and then I thought maybe I'd got the right type but the wrong character, and I realised I'd seen him before walking through the crowd in a short story by Colette – and as soon as I'd identified the situation, the corrupt old man and the young girl with enormous potential for corruption herself – as soon as I'd identified these characters as being characters in Colette, I knew that I'd got the setting, or got the period, at least.

'The Bloody Chamber', the story that resulted from these musings, is set in Mont Saint-Michel – the walled commune constructed, in pyramid formation, around an eighth-century monastery on a tiny island in Normandy. The narrator tells the story of her marriage, aged seventeen, to the marquis who lives there, a man who smells of 'leather and spices' and has a 'strange, heavy, almost waxen face . . . not lined by experience' (the resemblance to Sade is unmistakable), all of whose previous wives have disappeared under mysterious circumstances. After brusquely taking the narrator's virginity, the marquis is called out on business; he leaves her with keys to all the rooms in the castle, but forbids her to enter one of them: 'Every man must have one secret, if only one, from his wife,' he says. Inevitably, the narrator soon enters the forbidden room, only to discover that it's a torture chamber, strewn with the corpses of the marquis' previous wives. Just as he is about to add her to his collection, the narrator's mother rides in on horseback and dispatches him with a bullet to the brain ('the moment the story becomes an homage to Colette . . . it has to be the mother who [rescues] her rather than the brothers,' Angela explained). A brilliantly sustained pastiche of *fin de siècle* horror, 'The Bloody Chamber' is several times the length of most of the other tales Angela had been working on during this period. When she had finished writing it, in late July, she sent it to Deborah along with the other stories in the collection that would bear its name.

At the beginning of August, Angela went with the performance artists Shirley Cameron and Roland Miller, and their twin baby daughters Lois and Colette, to the international Meeting of Art festival – 'twelve days of exhibitions, debates, films, performances and God knows what else besides' – in Caldas da Rainha, 'a small town not too untypical of southern Portugal except the weather tends to be lousy'. For a week Cameron and Miller presented a different work each day; Angela watched and took notes, with a view to writing about the festival for *New Society*. After a while, she decided that she wanted to participate. In the park outside the museum were some permanent bronze statues; one was of a boy and a girl, like twins, larger than life-size. Shirley and Angela decided to concoct a performance: Angela washed the bronze twins while Shirley washed Lois and Colette.

It was perhaps not the most favourable setting for what Miller later described as 'an art-joke with the convention of sculpture'. The Portuguese democracy was still very young and vulnerable, and many of the inhabitants of Caldas da Rainha lived in dire poverty. The festival ended early when a group of right-wing thugs arrived at the fish market to smash up the decadent sculptures, cheered on by the locals. Then a group of Stalinists arrived. Shirley Cameron remembers how quickly the atmosphere turned menacing:

> there was this big demonstration and it became anti-foreigners, and suddenly, there was us with our pushchair, with our blonde twins – Roland, me and Angela, and a Portuguese friend – and we were going from café to café, we'd go into a café and be sitting there, and gradually

a crowd would form around us, just looking at us. We'd think, we'd better move on, so we moved on, and that happened about three times. So eventually we were [asking ourselves] 'Where are the organisers of this festival?' It looked like they'd got in their cars and cleared off. It was like serious trouble . . . There was a hostel there, a YMCA or something like that, so we and a lot of the foreign artists went to this hostel, [and] locked the doors. And our Portuguese friend went back to this house where we'd been staying, got our luggage, and in the morning we got the six o'clock train out.

Angela was as shocked by this turn of events as anybody else, but she was inclined to side with left-wing activists, and after returning to the safety of London she tried to see things from the demonstrators' point of view. In her account of the festival for *New Society* she wrote: 'desire, imagination and dream – the domains of art – these, too, should be distributed with care in a country where the very possibility of such things might seem to mock the reality of the inhabitants'.

Later that month she wrote a version of 'Puss-in-Boots' inflected with the themes and imagery of Pierre Beaumarchais' play *The Barber of Seville* – best known via Rossini's subsequent opera – which follows the adventures of a wily manservant called Figaro as he helps his master find love. Angela gave Figaro's personality to her Puss – he's 'a cat of the world, cosmopolitan, sophisticated' – in a story whose plot is much closer to that of Beaumarchais' play than that of Perrault's fairy tale, and which has the bawdy, buoyant mood of *opera buffa*. Puss's voice is garrulous and wry, although his air of refinement is sometimes let down by the inherent absurdity of his species ('I went about my ablutions,' he says at one point, 'tonguing my arsehole . . . one leg stuck in the air like a ham bone'). Ten years later, Angela told an interviewer that although she'd always thought of her work as being 'quite loaded with jokes', 'Puss-in-Boots' was 'the first story that I wrote that was supposed to be really funny, out-and-out funny'. She hurriedly sent it off to Deborah, with the instructions that it was

to go in between COURTSHIP OF MR LYON and THE ERL-KING. (The logic of this being, a lion-man, a superhuman cat and a non-human genius loci, juxtaposed in a collection that is about metarelations between humans and animals. No, honestly. The stories are planned as a whole & echo & reflect each other all the time.)

I'm sorry to make such a fuss about PUSS, but it really does seem to me to be a delicious little piece and I'd hate the fairy-tale-derived collection to go out without it in it! I guess you'll understand when you've had a look at it.

She needn't have worried: Deborah thought it would be a good idea for a few more of the stories to appear individually in magazines, to build up momentum, before she sent them out to publishers. 'The Courtship of Mr Lyon' appeared in *Vogue* in April 1978, and 'Wolf-Alice' appeared in *Stand* that winter.

In September Angela's contract at Sheffield was unexpectedly renewed ('I don't want to put any pressure on you,' Naomi remembers her saying, 'but I'm not coming back unless I can live with you again'). Mark was free to make plans of his own. He had become interested in ceramics after building a kiln for Naine Woodrow – who had left Japan shortly after Angela, and was now living near them in Clapham – and he decided to spend a few months at Bourne Head Farm with Sandy and Takeshi, helping out around the land, while learning what he could about working with clay.

Angela spent most of that term struggling with the 'endless, unfinishable' Sade project, which she had been working on, intermittently, for almost four years. She feared that it was turning out to be 'a very bad book indeed – half impossibly high-flown and highbrow, half helplessly sexploitative and god-awful'. She was bored of it and anxious about its reception, and she felt daunted by the amount of material involved – 'like doing finals'. She later said that she became very moody during this period, given to 'snapping and temper', and was difficult to be around. Mark doesn't remember it like that, but he was on the other side of the country a lot of the time. What's certain is that she obsessed over the book. Often, she would stay up late into the night, trying to make things work, but felt 'defeated and helpless'. She swore never to write non-fiction again.

But the initial responses to her efforts suggested that they hadn't been in vain. On 24 February she heard back about *The Sadeian Woman* from Marion Wheeler, her new editor at Harcourt Brace Jovanovich (Tony Godwin having died suddenly in 1976):

It is stunningly original, marvelously provocative and great fun to read. Nobody, but nobody, has applied that Carter sensibility to Sade and the modern social/sexual/political arena. Your intelligence and wicked wit illuminate the arena of sexual politics in a way that no one has come close to doing. As I go over it again – for the third time – I am still struck by the wonderful discoveries, felicities of interpretation and, always, your deft use of language. I congratulate you on what will probably be – here, anyway – a most controversial and enlightening book.

Meanwhile, Deborah had sent 'The Bloody Chamber' and 'The Courtship of Mr Lyon' to Liz Calder, who thought they were 'Peak Carter Country! Brilliant, imaginative, witty and very scary!' She received a reader's report from Catharine Carver, a former editor at Gollancz who had gone freelance. It read, in its entirety:

Yes yes yes. Marvellously funny and allusive and frightening, like a death-threat that spells itself out backwards on to your mirror while you're tweezing an eyebrow. If the stories all work as well as 'The Bloody Chamber' and 'Courtship of Mr Lyon' I don't see how a book of these can fail.

Angela signed a contract with Gollancz – her editor was now Joanna Goldsworthy, since Calder was leaving the company to join Jonathan Cape – for an advance of £1,000 for British and Commonwealth rights on 19 May 1978.

The summer of 1978 was punctuated by mini teaching jobs. In May Angela joined Fleur Adcock at a teachers' college in the Cumbrian town of Ambleside (a short drive – over roads commanding dramatic views of Lake Windermere – from Dove Cottage in Grasmere, where William and Dorothy Wordsworth had lived) for a writing course organised by Northern Arts. Fleur loaned her a copy of Dorothy Wordsworth's *Journals*, which Angela devoured, later turning her ideas about them into a piece for *New Society*. Shortly after returning to London she wrote to Fleur:

The trouble is, I am so badly versed in Wordsworth studies I can't even tell whether or not my observations are original. I <u>was</u> struck, though, by how ill they always were – 'I wandered lonely as – atishoo!'

And you can actually plot the way they left small ailments untreated so they grew into large ailments; one day, Dorothy cuts her thumb in the kitchen. Three days later, septic infection has set in. Does it stop her baking the bread? Does it not. Salmonella rules – next day, William is poorly. And Coleridge trotting around with exploded pupils. I think I've put my finger on something with the idea that behind every great man is a woman dedicated to his greatness whilst behind every great woman is a man dedicated to bringing her down. This is why Charlotte Brontë castrates Rochester and drowns Mr Emanuel, of course; spite. So there, you bastard. Also, had William been capable of changing a light bulb on his own, Dorothy wouldn't have felt superior to him in small things, and therefore might have felt less awed by his apparent superiority in great things.

The idea about every great woman having a man dedicated to bringing her down may have been prompted by encountering one of the students on the Ambleside course. Lorna Tracy was married to the poet Jon Silkin, whom she had met when she was a student and he a teacher at the Iowa Writers' Workshop: he had taken her back with him to Newcastle, from where they edited the literary magazine *Stand*. After reading a couple of Tracy's short stories, Angela had formed the opinion that she was a wonderful writer, and intuited that Silkin, feeling threatened by her superior talent, was hell-bent on wrecking her confidence. Tracy remembers being surprised by Angela's attentiveness to her that week in Ambleside: 'I expected to be entirely awed, because I knew something of what she'd written, but she didn't let you be awed. She was so forthcoming, so warm, and so encouraging.' As soon as she got back to London, Angela began campaigning to get Tracy into print with Virago. She wrote to Carmen: 'My first impression is that she is absolutely brilliant and <u>streets</u> ahead of Ian McEwan . . . The only snag is, the stories are mostly set in America and one or two are a bit unconventionally laid out, i.e. one is in the form of a script . . . But honestly – a FIND.' In 1981 Carmen published Tracy's stories in a collection titled *Amateur Passions*, which Angela reviewed for the *London Review of Books*: 'there is not one flabby sentence or second-hand image in the whole book . . . Tracy is a startling writer because her prose simply won't lie down on the page but keeps on getting up and drawing attention to itself, socking you in the eye, almost, changing direction and intention at the will of a formidably controlled intelligence.'

Two months after Ambleside, Angela taught a week-long residential course with the writer and artist Colin Spencer at Lumb Bank, the Arvon centre at Hebden Bridge, Yorkshire. It's situated in a valley, with a view over a brown and green river, surrounded by derelict mills ('The Ozymandias effect,' Angela wrote in her journal: 'in their decay, the dark, Satanic mills return quite gracefully to nature, moss grows over them, the worked stones tumble'). The course was a kind of structured retreat: there were no work-shops, only one-to-one tutorials, and the students were expected to spend most of the time by themselves, writing in an atmosphere of productive silence and seclusion. Every evening, a couple of them were invited to read an example of their work to the group. Tutors weren't exempt from this ritual. One of the students was the thirty-five-year-old Pat Barker, who remembered that Angela read 'The Company of Wolves'.

When her own turn came, Barker read a story about two elderly ladies in Tyneside – it became the final chapter of *Union Street*, her first published novel. By the late 1970s, the lives of working-class northerners had become deeply unfashionable as literary material – the feeling was that Alan Sillitoe had wrung them dry in the 1960s – but Angela thought that this was prob-ably in Barker's favour. 'You've acquired for yourself, and, it would seem, for your own exclusive use, an absolutely vast domain,' she wrote a couple of years later, after helping the novel to get published by Virago. 'You've actually inherited the real world.'

'[Angela] was very generous in her appreciation and encouragement of other writers,' Barker remembered. 'She was able to register merit in work that was very different to her own work, and that's very rare. She was very, very good in recognising and facilitating a voice that was unlike hers.' It was a sign that she was growing more comfortable with herself – she was no longer the woman who had rushed up to insult A. S. Byatt in 1968 – and it became increasingly pronounced over the next decade.

CHAPTER SEVENTEEN
No. 1 Lash Lady

Sequestered behind high trees on the western outskirts of Norwich, the campus of the University of East Anglia is emphatically modern, an austere, orthogonal landscape of concrete and glass, featuring a terraced central square and halls of residence shaped like ziggurats. It's a far cry from the Gothic splendours of Oxford and Cambridge, or even the Neo-Gothic ones of Bristol and Sheffield. Established in 1963, UEA was supposed to be a new kind of university: a hub of intellectual adventurousness, where energy was valued over solemnity, and innovation trumped tradition. Its founding motto was 'Do Different'.

One of the things it did differently was to offer an MA in creative writing. The first programme of its kind in Britain, it was founded in 1970 by the novelists Angus Wilson and Malcolm Bradbury, both of whom trailed considerable reputations – Wilson as one of Britain's leading novelists, a paragon of mordant humour and moral perspicuity; Bradbury as a dauntingly well-read critic and (following his 1975 novel *The History Man*) an ingenious postmodernist – and its first graduate was Ian McEwan, whose own reputation as the *enfant terrible* of English letters was, by the end of the decade, blossoming.

On the ground, things weren't quite so clear-cut. For all their impressive credentials, Wilson and Bradbury were both tweedy, mild-mannered, middle-aged men, with pronounced establishment tendencies (they were both members of London gentlemen's clubs, and both went on to accept knighthoods, in 1980 and 2000 respectively). Wilson was in his fifties and sixties when he taught at UEA, and did so partly as a way of reacquainting himself with youth, an encounter that rather shocked him. Bradbury was still in his forties at the end of the 1970s, but he cut a pipe-smoking, donnish, avuncular figure.

They both seemed extremely conservative in comparison to Lorna Sage, who delivered lectures on literary theory in a rush of nervous energy, her fingers visibly trembling as she took constant, deep pulls on her cigarette ('It was like she had come hotfoot from the barricades,' remembered one student), and who smuggled unanointed writers (such as Angela Carter) onto the reading lists. She disagreed with Bradbury about almost everything, and their colleagues in the School of English and American Studies were often forced to take sides. 'It was a hotbed of intrigue,' according to the novelist Paul Bailey, who occasionally taught creative writing there, and became friends with Angela around this time.

In 1978, Wilson retired his chair, and the School began looking for another novelist to teach with Bradbury on the creative writing MA. Such courses were still generally looked on with suspicion in Britain, and most established authors wouldn't have considered such a job. Angela was a bit suspicious herself:

> We were producing very, very much better writers in this country when people were leaving school between twelve and fourteen. I don't mean to be intemperate but I think this is very important. Reading and *living* are the real training for writing fiction. This may sound smug but it's true . . . People can put themselves through the most extraordinary privations to write a novel.

But unlike some of her peers, Angela needed to earn her living, and when Lorna asked how she'd feel about taking over Wilson's job at UEA, she jumped at the opportunity. She taught there from 1978, usually for one ten-week term each year (though with some years, such as 1980–1, off), until 1988. She would take the train to Norwich, do a day's teaching, stay overnight with Lorna and her daughter Sharon – in a house whose atmosphere she satirised as 'teabags, Tampax and the *TLS*' – and take the train back to London the following afternoon. Students remember her sitting with Lorna in the graduate bar, in a constant haze of laughter and smoke.

The course recruited between five and ten students a year. It comprised two terms of workshops, followed by a term of one-to-one tutorials. Bradbury tended to teach the workshops, and Angela the tutorials, although occasionally (as in the 1985–6 academic year) these roles were reversed. Angela found the course unexpectedly impressive. 'The students on it are very highly selected, are *extremely* highly motivated,' she told an interviewer in 1985. She saw her role as doing 'exactly as a copy editor in a publishing company does: to go through a piece of fiction and say, "look he's wearing odd socks here, what do you precisely mean, here, would so-and-so say such a thing?"' By that measure, she wasn't very good at the job: students don't remember her reading their work at all closely, or providing detailed feedback or annotations. Rather, she would form an impression of it, and talk in general terms. She sat in Malcolm Bradbury's office, which she seemed to occupy like a squatter, and the students would come to see her, one by one. 'She gave the impression of being wryly amused at finding herself in a teaching position, in an office,' remembered Lynne Bryan (class of 1985). 'There was a lot of silence. It was almost like you were going to the doctor and you had to say something first.' Anne Enright (class of 1987), who had applied to the course because of her admiration for Angela's work, recalled a typical tutorial:

> The student ahead of me came out of her office, made a big face and hurried away. I went in. Carter sat beside, rather than behind a desk. On the edge of it, facing me, were the pages I had submitted, with a handwritten note from her on the top sheet. She indicated the pages with a graceful hand. She said: 'Well this is all fine.'
> And then we talked of other things.

Not everyone found their encounters with Angela so easy. Perhaps the student ahead of Enright – the one who made 'a big face' – had a similar experience to Louise Doughty (also class of 1987):

> Sessions with Angela were fraught, but the fault was all mine – she was shrewd enough to spot a student in trouble and her advice often consisted of her gazing at me in a benign and enigmatic manner, while I tried – blatheringly – to justify my failures. It was a traumatic process. After one tutorial I emerged in tears and made my way over to the office of one of the administrative staff who had befriended me, a lovely warm lady who made me a coffee and handed me a box of tissues. She surmised, understandably but wrongly, that Angela had been mean to me.

'Everyone was terrified of Angela,' recalled Glenn Patterson (class of 1986), who had her for workshops rather than tutorials. Vic Sage – Lorna's ex-husband, who also taught at UEA and got to know Angela while she was teaching there – described her as 'radically unstable', and observed that 'she performed to [the students], which was disconcerting for some of them'. Lynne Bryan was one of those who was disconcerted:

On our first meeting she reached across to take a ruler from Malcolm's pen-pot. The ruler was expandable. She played with it a little. Smiled.

Lynne, she said; Do you think Malcolm measures his penis with this?

This remark was, Lynne later decided, Angela's way of putting her at her ease, but at the time it embarrassed her terribly. She wasn't put off, however, since Angela had 'a funny kind of fluid personality . . . I was intimidated by her but I also wanted to be her friend, because there was a kind of warmth there as well.' Andrew Cowan (class of 1985) agreed:

I liked her to such an extent that the fact that she didn't offer what I wanted in terms of feedback on my work didn't matter, because what she did was she kind of humanised the course, and unlike Malcolm, who seemed not terribly interested, she actually seemed interested in us as individuals, she made me feel it was worthwhile being there. She proceeded by indirection: she was sort of slyly encouraging. So one week, for instance, she gave me *Gulliver's Travels* . . .

Giving her students books as presents was one of Angela's characteristic pedagogical techniques. She also gave Cowan a copy of Raymond Carver's collection *What We Talk About When We Talk About Love* ('whereas it was clear that she thought *Gulliver's Travels* was a key book and an important book, she thought Raymond Carver wasn't worth her time,' Cowan recalls. 'But she thought I might get something out of it, and I did'); she gave Lynne Bryan a copy of Paul Bailey's novel *Old Soldiers*; she gave Glenn Patterson a novel by Peter Carey. Whether or not they enjoyed the books, the students were all delighted to be given something that seemed to have been selected specially for them. They often spent a long time trying to work out what kind of coded message the gift contained. 'I went away and I spent the week trying to understand why Angela had given me *Gulliver's Travels*,' Cowan remembered. 'I came back the following week and I said, "Why did you ask me to read that?" And she says, "Oh, I just thought you might enjoy it. That's all."'

Angela was particularly nurturing and generous towards those students who didn't come from traditional university-going backgrounds (Cowan,

Patterson and Bryan all fit this description). She gave the impression of being on their side. 'She was in a kind of equivalent relationship with the institution,' reflected Cowan. 'But a bit more self-confident, I think, about her tangential relationship to the university.'

Kazuo Ishiguro (class of 1980) was living in Cardiff during the summer term, so visited Angela at 107 The Chase rather than travelling all the way to Norwich for his tutorials. The domestic setting only increased the sense that she was unlike his other teachers: 'She talked very much out of her instincts, and she lived much more how a writer should live . . . She wasn't based around the university, her approach was not an academic one.' During their sessions at The Chase, they would sit at the kitchen table, discussing technical questions – a running debate was about the validity of manipulative suspense devices, what Angela called the 'slipping-noose method of narration', which Ishiguro liked using and which Angela didn't like him using – and Mark would sometimes sit silently on a sofa in the background. On one occasion, Angela left the room, and Ishiguro tried to make conversation, but Mark didn't really engage. Then one day Ishiguro asked about something he needed to know for his novel – 'After you drowned cats, would they bob to the surface, or would they sink?' – and Mark, who was sitting on the sofa reading a novel, answered. 'That was the first time I heard Mark speak.'

The narrator of Ishiguro's novel (which was published in 1982 as A Pale View of Hills) is pregnant for much of the story, and he was concerned about getting her psychology right. Angela was impressed: 'I thought that was very nice. Most male writers would have just plunged ahead. I thought it was a very good sign that he was so concerned about that, a good sign for his empathy.' He already had a publisher lined up, but no agent, so Angela introduced him to Deborah. She also introduced Glenn Patterson to Carmen, who published his first novel, Burning Your Own, in 1988, after she had moved from Virago to Chatto & Windus. When it came out, Angela interviewed Patterson at the Institute of Contemporary Arts in London, as part of the pioneering 'Writers in Conversation' series – 'It was fantastic,' he recalls, 'it was an extraordinary thing to do, actually, for a first-time novelist' – and invited him to dinner with Kazuo Ishiguro and Paul Bailey at The Chase.

There were many more students whom she didn't stay in touch with, but several of them – especially those who went on to become professional writers – remember being taught by Angela as a defining period in their lives. Andrew Cowan (who since 2004 has himself taught on the UEA writing programme) still feels grateful to her: 'You spend years carrying this impression with you, always carrying a flame, and yet when you examine it there's so little to go on, it's just this lifelong impression of a benign presence looking over you, at the time, and in a way subsequently, forever.'

During the time that Angela taught at UEA, her reputation underwent a series of small transformations. The first of these came with the publication of *The Sadeian Woman*, which was scheduled in both the UK and the USA for 28 March 1979. As the date approached, Angela recalled the doubts and anxieties that had dogged the writing of the book. 'I am now about to be incarnated by the media as No. 1 Lash Lady,' she wrote to Lorna Tracy. 'I feel very ambivalent about this, obviously, and rather ambivalent about the book, though a very nice lady from GAY NEWS, who interviewed me, assured me that anybody who bought it for a quick thrill would find it a long haul.' The lady from *Gay News* (whose name was Marsaili Cameron) may have been underestimating the stamina of thrill-seekers. For the rest of Angela's life, a proportion of her fan mail came from people whose primary interest in her doesn't appear to have been literary:

> Dear Ms Carter,
> I suppose all the boys say this to you. I am Tony and of course I would like to be your slave . . .

A few reviewers, mostly for the mainstream left-wing press, did see what *The Sadeian Woman* was getting at. Hermione Lee wrote in the *New Statesman* that while 'few women would feel inclined to treat the Marquis de Sade with affectionate familiarity . . . Angela Carter is neither ordinary nor timid. The tone is one of intellectual relish . . . rational, refined . . . witty.' Margaret Walters, writing in *New Society*, described the book as 'provocative, always readable . . . illuminating, witty, freewheeling', and Francis Huxley, reviewing it alongside Michel Foucault's newly translated *History of Sexuality* in the *Guardian*, declared himself 'grateful to Miss Carter' for showing how men 'might free themselves from some habitual tyrannies and become human'.

More frequently, though, the reviews were marked by peevish incomprehension. John Weightman, writing in the *Observer*, admitted that he was baffled by Angela Carter's project: 'I fail to see why she has tried to harness Sade to the cause of Women's Lib . . . The bewildered reader is kept going only by an occasional, surprising aside.' At least he was candid; others settled for reviewing the book they had been expecting, rather than the one they had read. Richard Gilman in the *New York Times*, while conceding that *The Sadeian Woman* contained 'a number of shrewd insights', presented it as a tirade against pornographers in general and against Sade in particular, describing its position as 'fierce, unaccommodating and aggressively stated', and its author as 'a rigid ideologue, fervidly feminist, furiously antireligious and against transcendence of any kind'.

The most vehement reaction, though, came from other feminists. The paperback edition was stickered by the Federation of Alternative Bookshops for having a cover that was offensive to women (a painting by the surrealist artist Clovis Trouille featuring several half-naked women, some of whom are being whipped). Carmen wrote to Eileen Fairweather, a representative of the federation: 'I don't know if you realise how upset Angela Carter has been about this . . . The cover was chosen by her with us. Without wishing to sound sanctimonious, she is someone who has been committed to feminism for many years, and obviously neither she – nor us – would have used the cover if we had thought it sexist.' Fairweather responded with a somewhat mollifying letter, but said that she wouldn't read a book like that on the Tube, 'for fear some man would think I was reading porn, and use that as an excuse to respond accordingly'.

The book's content was just as offensive to some sections of the women's movement, appearing at a time when the debate about pornography was growing increasingly heated, and writers such as the American radical feminist Andrea Dworkin were condemning Sade as the misogynist extraordinaire. Dworkin herself described *The Sadeian Woman* as 'a pseudofeminist literary essay'. Susanne Kappeler – another prominent anti-pornography feminist – conducted a masterclass in missing the point when she accused Angela of treating Sade as nothing but 'a Cultural Edifice . . . A literary artefact, removed by convention of the literary beyond the reach of political (or feminist) critique.' Angela was rather pleased with these denunciations: 'If I can get up Susanne Kappeler's nose, to say nothing of the Dworkin proboscis, then my living has not been in vain.'

Angela's next book was also a semi-calculated affront to Dworkin, who in 1974 had argued that the fairy-tale form entrenches gender stereotypes and so holds women back. But on this territory, Angela – who knew considerably more about folklore than Dworkin did – was at a definite advantage. *The Bloody Chamber* was published in May 1979 to glowing full-page reviews. Janice Elliott, writing in the *Sunday Telegraph*, called it 'a dazzling collection . . . Miss Carter leads us not so much into hallucination or illusion, as through the mirror into a parallel reality.' 'Ms Carter's stories are too rich and heady for casual consumption,' warned Patricia Craig in the *New Statesman*, 'but they do provide, at a very high level, romantic nourishment for the imagination.' Lorna Sage, reviewing the book for the *Observer*, explained that 'the main theme is the collusion between artificial and animal nature . . . But I mustn't make *The Bloody Chamber* sound too solemnly planned. It's a splendidly funny, erotic and adventurous book.' Lesley Garner, writing in *Cosmopolitan*, didn't seem to see the funny side, but she was impressed by the collection nonetheless: 'The stories . . . are presented to us like poisoned fruits, blooming, perfumed, delicious and rotten . . . They all make a horrid kind of sense, and they are painstakingly, exquisitely told.' Auberon Waugh, in a long review for the *Evening Standard*, felt that 'The best story in the book, "Puss-in-Boots", deserves to be included in every prose anthology of this century or any other . . . [it] had me gasping with admiration . . . If she can ease off a slight tendency to self-indulgence in nature descriptions, if she can hold back on the occasional lapse into coarseness – I don't think we really need biological case-histories of female puberty – and watch against the risk of repeating unusual effects in the same volume, nobody will be able to deny her the title of Great British Writer.' Guido Almansi, writing in the *Literary Review*, by contrast to Waugh, especially liked the 'moments of superb bad taste' and 'carnal humour', saying that the book was 'miles away from the drab of the Drabblian world of British female writers'. And Susan Kennedy, writing in the *Times Literary Supplement*, pronounced that with *The Bloody Chamber* 'Angela Carter extends her control over an area of the imagination on which she has already left her mark. Her re-telling of European folk and fairy tales has the power, not only to cause us to think again, and deeply, about the mythic sources of our common cultural touchstones, but to plunge us into hackle-raising speculation about aspects of our human/ animal nature.'

Angela's publicity schedule for *The Bloody Chamber* was considerably heavier than it had been for previous books: she made a number of television and radio appearances to promote it. On BBC2's *Word for Word* programme, she read 'The Snow Child', a story derived from an obscure variant of 'Snow White', in which a count and countess are riding through a wintry landscape, the count wishing for a girl, who soon appears, only to be murdered by the countess, and then have her corpse defiled by the count. When Angela had finished reading, the journalist and broadcaster Arthur Marshall bluntly told her that 'on the whole, I don't really like stories of fantasy . . . I like stories that begin: "Mrs Henderson walked slowly into Sainsbury's and purchased a pound of cod."' Angela cocked her head amusedly: 'I'd like to know the Sainsbury's where you can buy cod. You fantasist.'

Lorna Sage lived something of a double life. Her reputation as a self-made woman, a pioneering feminist academic, and a fearless journalist with passionately held socialist principles, wasn't in any danger. But as her friend James Fenton wrote a year after her death, 'there was a side to her that enjoyed and was amused by a certain brush with high life', a weakness that he put down to 'her sense perhaps of having conquered the castle, however absurd the results might sometimes seem'.

In the mid-1970s, when she was researching a book on Neoplatonism, Lorna had visited Florence for the first time. She had rented an apart-ment in the grounds of the sixteenth-century San Francesco di Paola, a dilapidated former monastery with beautiful, rambling gardens providing panoramic views over the city, which was used frequently as a location for period films. It was owned by Harry Brewster, who was one of the last surviving links to the cosmopolitan Florence described by Henry James: his grandfather was said to have been the model for Gilbert Osmond, the caddish American expatriate in *The Portrait of a Lady*. Brewster was in his late sixties when Lorna first arrived at San Francesco di Paola, but he gave the impression of being almost of an age with the crumbling stucco ('I used to think he was like a lizard,' remembered Lorna's daughter Sharon, 'he was just unimaginably old, crazily old . . . He had that papyrus skin of somebody who's always been in the sun'). His accent sounded faintly German to most ears, but his English had a fastidious clarity that conjured the ghosts of his Edwardian governesses. He wrote books with titles such as *The Cosmopolites* and *A Cosmopolite's Journey*. Half of literary and artistic Italy – from the writer Harold Acton to the film-maker Bernardo Bertolucci, who was married to his niece – used to visit him in his charmed garden overlooking the rooftops of Florence.

Lorna fell in love with the lifestyle she encountered at San Francesco di Paola, and specifically with one of the people who embodied it. Rupert Hodson was a rakish, foppish Englishman, thirteen years younger than her, and only a few years older than her daughter. He was an Old Etonian – a detail that Lorna, in spite of her politics, seems to have liked – who wore linen suits during the summer, tweed suits during the winter, and bright bow ties all year round. A brilliant cook and a gifted pianist, he was also a heavy drinker, who made the most of the long lunches that came with his job at the British Institute. 'Many thought him reminiscent of a character from Evelyn Waugh's *Decline and Fall*,' according to his obituary in the *Daily Telegraph*.

After she met Rupert, Lorna lived in Norwich only during the academic term, and went to Florence every holiday, writing endless articles and book reviews while she was there. Sharon remembered her constantly working – 'like a crazy person' – in order to pay for this lifestyle. She married Rupert in 1979, when she was thirty-six and he was twenty-three.

Angela and Mark visited San Francesco di Paola for the first time that summer, and returned almost every year until 1991, staying for at least a couple of weeks at a stretch, and sometimes for a month or more. Lorna would organise a separate apartment for them within the walls of the garden. During the day, Angela lounged around in the sun – eating nectarines, reading, drawing, and writing in her journal – or ventured into the city with Mark. In the evenings they all gathered for an al fresco dinner, and had 'very drink-fuelled, mad conversations', while semi-feral cats roamed around the table looking for scraps. It was a setting in which Angela felt blissfully relaxed, if also, sometimes, a tiny bit guilty. In her journal, she wrote: 'It is the earthly paradise, behind a wall, an iron gate . . . a magically enclosed place, privileged place.' She began plotting a story set in the garden. It was going to be a return to the theme of the Fall – the cosseted residents expelled from their sanctum – but it doesn't appear to have been written.

Towards the end of 1979, Susannah Clapp, an editor at the newly formed *London Review of Books*, got in touch through Liz Calder to ask if Angela would write something for the paper. Though still in her twenties, Clapp was a dynamic and well-connected figure in the London literary world (she had previously worked as an editor at Jonathan Cape, where her successes included Bruce Chatwin's cult travelogue *In Patagonia*). She remembered

Angela, 'swaddled in a big coat', coming into the paper's tiny office in the packing department of Dillons bookshop. Her first contribution to the *London Review of Books* was a review of Bertolucci's *La Luna*, published in March 1980, and she wrote another sixteen pieces for the paper over the next decade. She formed a constructive working relationship with Susannah, who also became one of her closest friends.

That winter Angela wrote 'Black Venus', a story about Jeanne Duval, the mixed-race mistress of Baudelaire. The genesis of the story was reading a biography of Baudelaire (whom Angela described a year later in a letter to the American writer Elizabeth Hardwick as 'the greatest poet of alienation . . . the architect of my sensibility') in conjunction with *The World the Slaves Made* by Eugene Genovese. She conceived of a story that would draw a connection between Duval and the Dark Lady of Shakespeare's sonnets, and through this juxtaposition say something about 'how awful it is to be a muse'. It is of a piece with the biographical fictions about Edgar Allan Poe and Lizzie Borden that she wrote the following year, but in its attempt to excavate the life of a forgotten, beleaguered woman, it goes one step further, anticipating some of the feminist biographies of writers' consorts (Brenda Maddox on Nora Joyce, Claire Tomalin on Dickens' mistress Nelly Ternan) that started to appear in the late 1980s. 'Black Venus' became the title story of Angela Carter's third collection, but it was initially published by itself, in a spiral-bound limited edition by Next Editions in association with Faber & Faber. With what she called 'the wincing, self-conscious narcissism peculiar to this profession', she sent a copy to the biographer Richard Holmes, who had chosen *The Bloody Chamber* as one of his 'books of the year' in *The Times*.

During the winter of 1979–80, she also wrote a radio version of 'The Company of Wolves', and the words for a children's book titled *Comic and Curious Cats*, an alphabet and vocabulary primer ('I love my cat with an A / Because he is Amiable/Amenable/His name is Abednigo', 'I love my cats with a B and a C / Because they are Beautiful and Capricious') with stylish, witty illustrations by the artist Martin Leman. It's worth noting that one thing she *didn't* do during this period was write a children's book called *The Music People*. Though widely attributed to her (for example in the *Oxford Encyclopaedia of British Literature*, and in the introduction to the Penguin Classics edition of *The Fairy Tales of Charles Perrault*), this fun-filled guide to learning the piano is, in fact, the work of a different Angela Carter.

* * *

Angela's love of opera had remained with her since her days in Bath. In 1971 her friend John Cox had been appointed director of production at Glyndebourne, and in the summer she often went to concerts there (Carmen remembers her wearing an inappropriate woolly jumper on one occasion, but she must have learned her lesson: in the only surviving photograph of her at Glyndebourne she's wearing a long and elegant summer dress). Towards the end of 1979, she was approached by Cox and the composer Michael Berkeley – who was married to Deborah Rogers – and asked to write the libretto for an adaptation of Virginia Woolf's novel *Orlando*, which details the 'biography' of a fictional poet who lives for several centuries, and whose sex fluctuates between male and female. Though the initial inspiration for the project was Cox's, he remembers that it was Berkeley who suggested involving Angela:

> I'd [already] directed a couple of things in which sexual ambiguity is fairly central, like the character of Cherubino [in *The Marriage of Figaro*], the character of Octavian [in *Der Rosenkavalier*]. And I happened to read *Orlando*, and immediately thought this would be a very interesting operatic project, if only because the sexual ambiguity of the leading character is embedded within the narrative . . . It would be a fascinating challenge for a singer and a director to have to change sex halfway through. So I proposed it to Michael Berkeley [who] seized on it as a project, as I hoped he would, for himself. It was entirely his idea to ask Angela, because he knew her pretty well through Deborah. And he was surprised and delighted to hear that I knew her as well. He said, 'Well, that makes it so much easier.' And so we talked to Angela and she took the bait, as it were.

It isn't surprising that she did. In many ways, Woolf was the canonical English writer whose sensibility was most closely aligned with hers – they both enjoyed fantasy, both were extraordinarily sensitive to and enamoured of the English language, and both expressed frustration and scepticism about conventional gender roles – but even so, Angela's feelings about Woolf were conflicted. It was the snobbery, the pervasive sense of Bloomsbury elitism, the cut-glass accent that got up her nose. Her scornful response, when she came across an anecdote in a book by Elizabeth David about Woolf 'kneading away like nobody's business' at a loaf of home-made bread, is typical:

Virginia Woolf? Yes. Although otherwise an indifferent cook, Virginia could certainly knock you up a lovely cottage loaf. You bet. This strikes me as just the sort of pretentiously frivolous and dilettantish thing a Bloomsbury *would* be good at – knowing how to do one, just one, fatuously complicated kitchen thing and doing that one thing well enough to put the cook's nose out of joint.

But she read *Orlando* with pleasure, interpreting it largely as a feminist document ('I am sure the poor showing the chaps make in this book is intentional on Woolf's part,' she wrote to Cox). Angela's adaptation takes a few structural liberties with the original text (such as having the heroine die at the end), but tries hard to be true to its spirit. She wanted to create an improvisational effect, to convey the impression that things were being made up as they happened, which was how the novel had seemed to her:

> as I was working . . . it began to seem a better and better idea to emphasise a certain quality as of country house charades, e.g. the idea of the servants <u>becoming</u> lords and ladies, and, especially, becoming the garden . . . They can quite easily become an Elizabethan formal garden by standing around with pot plants, or privet bushes cut into antic forms over their heads . . . It seemed to me that a fluidity of decor – one scene running into another – is part of the dreamlike quality of the whole; hence the use of gauzes, always a dreamlike effect.

She delivered a first draft in March 1980. Glyndebourne got back saying that although they thought there was a lot going for her version of *Orlando*, their programme was totally booked up until 1985. The project fizzled out, and Angela was never paid for the work she'd done.

By the end of the 1970s, the women's movement had broadened the scope of its operations from the struggle for equal rights to unmasking the patriarchal bias of the cultural order, including the very structures of the English language (the way the word *mankind* is allowed to stand for the whole of humankind, for example). Like all revolutions it had its excesses, and there were stories in the right-wing press about feminists insisting that semantically innocent words (*history, Manchester*) should be replaced with semantically self-conscious ones (*herstory, Personchester*). At around the same time, the phrase 'politically correct' was gaining some currency on the left, usually deployed with a bit of irony, in full cognisance of its Stalinist echoes. It was only later – towards the end of the next decade – that the phrase was co-opted by the right, as shorthand for the kind of puritan mentality that was supposed to have coined 'herstory' and 'Personchester'.

Since Angela Carter's death, hostile critics have sometimes attempted to tar her with this brush. The charge was put most directly by the Oxford don (and husband of Iris Murdoch) John Bayley, who in an essay for the *New York Review of Books* in 1992 accused her of 'political correctness: whatever spirited arabesques and feats of descriptive imagination Carter may perform she always comes to rest in the right ideological position'. She was, he continued, 'committed to the preoccupations and fashions of our moment', her work epitomising 'how a certain style of good writing has politicized itself today, constituting itself as the literary wing of militant orthodoxy'.

Bayley's failure to distinguish Angela's provocative, ironic and highly idiosyncratic sort of feminism (and thus, presumably, any sort of feminism) from 'the preoccupations and fashions of our moment' gets his argument off to a bad start. Her actual attitude to 'militant orthodoxy' is revealed in an essay of 1980 titled 'The Language of Sisterhood', in which she considered the feminist campaign 'to make English fit women as well as it fits men'. Though sympathetic to the impulse, and conscious that 'the language of my militant sisters reflects reality' (in a way that inherited linguistic structures often didn't), she cast a sceptical eye over the manifestations of 'Women's Lib newspeak'. On the idea that syntactical norms are patriarchal impositions – 'part of the conspiracy to stifle Woman's Voice in its unique-ness' – she pointed out that they are also 'part of a wider conspiracy to stifle everybody's voice in its uniqueness for the sake of our understanding one another more easily.'

Angela's individualism meant that she tended to take flak from both sides of the political divide (as the criticisms of *The Sadeian Woman* showed). The letters pages of the various magazines she wrote for – all of which were politically left of centre – contained plenty of vitriol directed at her. A response to her *New Society* piece about the porn star Linda Lovelace accused her of 'typical male chauvinist aggression towards [a] sexually out-spoken woman'; an interview with *City Limits* in which she talked about 'female masochism' was derided as 'heterosexist meanderings' by one cor-respondent and '60s pseudo-anarchy' by another, who particularly objected to the way 'she namedrops her way through a stew of sentimental male thinkers'. Others complained of her 'shrill rhetoric', 'moral superiority', 'glib, ill-informed comments' and 'terrible literal-mindedness'. For a writer who 'always comes to rest in the right ideological position', she inspired an extraordinary volume of dissent. Like many of her friends, Christopher Frayling was baffled by later portrayals of her as someone who toed the party line: 'If there was a kind of consensus in the room about anything, she'd immediately bowl a googly in order just to see what happened. She was the opposite, absolute opposite of political correctness.'

Since moving to London, Angela's housemate Christine Downton had been romantically involved with an American lawyer who, Angela wrote, 'seems to have an income roughly the equivalent of the GNP of a small Central American republic . . . on the rare occasions when he met Mark or myself he exhibited acute stress symptoms, as if he thought we'd nationalise him or something'. In the spring of 1980, Christine moved out of 107 The Chase to live with him (Angela's suspicion that she'd moved to the right politically seemed confirmed when it emerged that she'd left all her back issues of the *New Left Review* behind). Angela bought her out of her side of the house for £29,000 – a more than fourfold increase on what it had been worth four years previously – and hired an architect to plot a few structural changes: extending the ground-floor kitchen to incorporate a living area; installing a new bathroom with a shower. It was stretching her budget almost to breaking point (Mark had enrolled, with her encouragement, on a three-year course in ceramics at the Croydon College of Art and Design, so wasn't able to contribute much). They took in a lodger to help ease the financial burden.

Things were going to be tough for a while, but as she approached her fortieth birthday – 'one of those great meridians in a woman's life' – Angela looked around her and realised that she wasn't doing too badly. 'I had a nicer time in my thirties than I did in my twenties,' she reflected a few years later. 'I started doing things like foreign travel and having a house, and you know, watching television and things like that.' It struck her that her periods of intense melancholy and staggering self-consciousness had largely retreated into memory: 'I appear to be getting infinitely more light-hearted as I get older.'

That summer she wrote 'The Quilt Maker', a story that traces the outlines of her own biography, from the cloying, overindulged atmosphere of her early childhood, through the end of her marriage and her years in Japan, to her return to south London as a quietly confident middle-aged woman 'married to a house carpenter'. The narrator is clear that she sees herself as the only author of her own identity, and consequently of her own happiness:

> One theory is, we make our destinies like blind men chucking paint at a wall; we never understand nor even see the marks we leave behind us. But not too much of the grandly accidental abstract expressionist about *my* life, I trust; oh, no. I always try to live on the best possible terms with my unconscious and let my right hand know what my left is doing and, fresh every morning, scrutinise my dreams. Abandon, therefore, or rather, deconstruct the blind-action painter metaphor; take it apart, formalise it, put it back together again, strive for something a touch more hard-edged, intentional, altogether less arty, for I do believe we all have the right to choose.

CHAPTER EIGHTEEN

American ghosts

Angela's sense of fulfilment during the summer of 1980 was tempered by the strain of her financial worries. The purchase of Christine's side of the house had left her 'weak from an acute haemorrhage of the bank account', and the combination of journalism and teaching at the University of East Anglia couldn't provide an adequate transfusion of funds. Just as she was starting to fear that she'd over-reached, she had a letter from Robert Coover – who had returned to the USA the previous year to become professor of writing at Brown University, an Ivy League school in Providence, Rhode Island – asking whether she might be interested in teaching there for a year. The job came with a salary of $20,000 (about £9,000), and although Angela calculated that she would lose a quarter of that to American taxes – which she assumed she had to pay in addition to British taxes, not realising her mistake until after she received a rebate – it was an unexpected financial lifeline. She booked her flight out for 8 September, one week before the start of the semester.

It wasn't allowing much time to acclimatise, but she didn't want to be away from Mark – who would be staying in London to study for his diploma at the Croydon College of Art and Design – any longer than was necessary. She anticipated loneliness, and tried to think of her time in Providence as a period of constructive solitude. She considered learning Italian in her spare time, 'because that's where I want to go, eventually, if Europe isn't blasted off the face of the Earth within the next five years'.

She also decided to stop dyeing her hair, letting the natural grey emerge over the course of the year. At forty, she would allow herself to exhibit a symptom of aging which women twice as old took pains to conceal. It was perhaps the most outwardly dramatic touch in her lifelong project of self-invention: a visible rebuff to the prescriptions of a masculine society, and a sign that she was entirely comfortable with herself. She knew exactly what impact her altered appearance would have on people, and made some effort to prepare her friends. 'I have gone totally and startlingly grey,' she wrote to Carmen shortly before she returned to London, blaming her transformation on 'the ravages of a New England winter'.

Coover had found her an apartment on Arlington Avenue, a long, quiet, maple-lined street in the prosperous East Side of Providence, a short walk from his own home on University Avenue. A row of large clapboard houses with porches and swings out front – many of them sporting flagpoles from which stars and stripes fluttered patriotically in the breeze – faced a low wall that marked the boundary of the Brown University playing fields. Angela's apartment was on the second floor of number 41: it had two very spacious rooms, both with big windows and extensive wooden floors. One of them contained a 'very comfortable' four-poster bed. There was also a bathroom with an 'extraordinarily violent' shower, and a kitchen with a 'walk-in fridge'. The only downside was the rent: $300 a month, although that did at least include utilities.

She arrived towards the end of a brilliant summer. 'The light is wonderful,' she wrote to Mark, 'like English summer light but somehow richer & riper – huge skies, tiny frills of cloud.' But the temperature – which lingered in the mid-nineties for days on end – wasn't comparable to anything she had experienced in England. It was often too hot to sleep. On her first night, she tossed and turned for what felt like hours, then woke up jet-lagged at 5 a.m. and watched dawn break over the playing fields.

Later that day, Coover and his wife Pili – a tapestry artist of Spanish origin, to whom Angela became close while she was in Providence – drove her to a big warehouse off a freeway to buy sheets and furniture and cooking utensils. Angela was taken aback by how familiar it all seemed. 'All motorways & autoroutes & autostradas are imitations of these freeways,' she wrote. '<u>All the world</u> looks like America!' But she was relieved to discover that the real thing came somewhat cheaper than its foreign counterparts. 'Cigarettes are 60 cents – about 25p, at the current exchange rate,' she wrote excitedly to Mark. (In Britain they were more than twice that.) Her letters home were full of comments about money: she urged Mark not to buy any clothes until he came to visit her, and cautioned him against calling her too often or sending large packages. It's a sign of how necessary the job was: even with the salary it provided, they were desperate to make savings wherever they could.

Angela's distance from Mark tainted her whole experience of Providence. 'You know I am not good at writing it down or saying it in crowded kitchens full of interested & sympathetic people like on the [Coovers'] 'phone on Monday,' she wrote to him on Thursday 11 September, 'but I do love you and I do think, in a sense, I am always with you & you with me.' By the end of the week, the sense in which they were always with one another was proving less potent than the sense in which they weren't: 'I miss you in sharp, physical waves,' she wrote. She pinned a photograph of him (looking 'very stern') to the wall of her apartment. The letters she wrote him over the course of the year – which, though broken by his visits to Providence during the Christmas and Easter vacations, was by some stretch the long-est period they were ever apart – provide one of the best insights we have into the workings of their relationship. (There aren't any letters from him to her, but that reveals something in itself: 'my dear, I know words are not your language', she wrote.)

It's obvious from these letters that she had no doubts about his intel-ligence, and that his lack of formal education only troubled her in so far as it disadvantaged him. They evidently shared a sense of humour (she joked that her Indian hippy landlord had 'imported' the cockroaches she'd found in her apartment, 'to give the place local colour') as well as a set of values ('There is a conspicuous lack of cynicism round here that I find a bit unnerving'). It's also apparent that the power dynamic between them was, by comparison to some of her previous relationships, very elastic: she alternated between attitudes of maternal tenderness (encouraging him in his artistic endeavours, coaxing him to eat properly) and girlish playfulness (portraying herself as vulnerable and anxious without him to take care of her). But perhaps the most revealing thing of all is the bittersweet quality of her loneliness that year: it didn't cause her to do much soul-searching. Though she suffered a couple of minor relapses into insecurity and neurosis, her discontent was mainly turned outwards.

'I don't like America & never will,' she wrote to Carmen when she had been there for a few days. Her grievances centred on the symptoms of what she regarded as malignant capitalism. Even though she was a smoker, she thought that selling cigarettes in drugstores was 'a bit much'. Buying a phone for her apartment, she became irritated when the assistant tried to sell her a push-button one instead of a dial one, and to interest her in imitation antique ones, and ones shaped like Mickey Mouse or Snoopy. Even when she chose the most basic model she was given a choice of twelve colours, and invited to purchase kitchen, bathroom and bedroom extensions. She was surrounded by 'poor Americans being ripped off', and was shocked by the sight of a girl with vivid burn scars on her arms ('In Britain, the NHS would have patched her up'). 'I shall just keep my head down & try to ignore everything,' she wrote to Mark. 'It is a nice place to visit, I daresay. Maybe things will look up when I get into the swing. If there <u>is</u> a swing.'

Her opportunities for getting into the swing were limited by her inability to drive, or even ride a bicycle. She could walk to the university campus from her apartment, but she was largely reliant on the Coovers for travel further afield. She even needed them to take her grocery shopping once a week. 'She was incompetent in many ways,' Robert Coover remembered. 'Whenever she had a problem she would drop by and ask what to do about it. It was a sight to see her.'

To be fair, she had warned him about this: 'I am not the stuff of which empire builders were made,' she had written in June. 'Venturing out into the unknown fills me with terror and I was kind of hoping I'd be able to drop in on you and Pili a lot.' It's understandable, though, if he didn't take her at her word. He knew that she had upped sticks and gone to Japan by herself, and that far from seeking out familiar comforts while she was there, had found work as a bar hostess. The difference was that back then she had been fleeing a gloomy domestic life in England – she had felt she had nothing to lose – whereas now she was leaving behind a relationship that provided her with a sense of equilibrium.

Fortunately, a taste of home was soon at hand. When she had been in Providence for just over a week, Christopher Frayling and his girlfriend appeared, on their way to Boston. The three of them went on a pilgrimage to find the grave of the horror writer H. P. Lovecraft, who had spent most of his life in Providence (Angela was keen on his work, finding in it 'an odd stylistic resemblance' to Borges). But when they reached Swan Point Cemetery – which extends over sixty acres in the north-eastern corner of the city, with around 40,000 interments in beautifully manicured rows – they couldn't find Lovecraft's tomb. They walked around and around in circles, and Frayling remembers Angela becoming increasingly irritable: 'She didn't like walking.' But writing to Mark a couple of days later, she said that seeing Frayling and his girlfriend had rallied her: 'We all laughed hysterically about everything from the moment they arrived to the time they left, which has fairly set me up for the oncoming winter. And I shall be All Right.'

Brown University lies steeply uphill from the administrative and commercial centres of Providence, as if embodying a metaphor about the rarefied atmosphere of academe. The buildings are old and pretty, and though constructed in a mishmash of architectural styles, they tend to exhibit a certain genteel self-assurance. Angela thought that it was 'like a parody Cambridge'.

It was a 'progressive' school – meaning, basically, that the students didn't have to major in anything. Most of them came from fairly well-off families (tuition fees were $6,000 a year) and Angela soon became irritated by their apparently boundless sense of entitlement. They were 'eager to please, cocksure &, in the main, empty-headed', she told Mark. In one of her columns for New Society, she drew an unflattering picture of the 'prep' (i.e. private) school graduates whom she was teaching: 'The intellectual preppies are the hardest to handle, as they believe they have been trained to think for themselves.' What especially baffled and distressed her was how many of their public (i.e. state) school peers strove to emulate their prim outfits and patrician manners. 'I do think British education is better, actually,' she wrote to Lorna Tracy. 'It also seems much more egalitarian, somehow.'

But for all that Angela grumbled about the elements of social conservatism she encountered at Brown, she had arrived there at a time of intellectual upheaval. Strong currents of radical politics and avant-garde ideas were pulsing through the English department in the early 1980s. Jeffrey Eugenides – who graduated with a degree in English in 1983, but who was abroad during the 1980–1 academic year – recalled in his 2011 novel The Marriage Plot an environment in which students competed for places on a newly created Program in Semiotics Studies, where heated discussions about Derrida and Barthes followed them back to their residences, and where it was fashionable to read 'the Marquis de Sade . . . [whose] shocking sex scenes weren't really about sex but politics. They were therefore anti-imperialist, anti-bourgeois, anti-patriarchal, and anti-everything a smart young feminist should be against.' Perhaps the vogue for Sade reveals Angela's influence on the intellectual microclimate at Brown, but if so, she took away lots in exchange. She wrote to Susannah Clapp:

> I've fallen among semioticians & am trying to make head or tail of the deconstructionists. I haven't got a dictionary in my flat & keep forgetting to look 'hermeneutics' up in the library. It's been busy, busy, busy as far as thinking is concerned but I don't know how much use all this Derrida & stuff is going to be when I get home. I keep wondering just what Derrida is up to &, if he's so clever, why doesn't he write a novel of his own?

The writing programme at Brown was also inclined towards the avant-garde. It was headed by the African American poet Michael S. Harper, who was known for stirring jazz rhythms and syncopations into his work, and who wore a beret and tinted glasses even when he was indoors. Angela's job was covering for the postmodern novelist John Hawkes, who was on sabbatical. Also teaching at Brown (though not in the English department) was the historian and socialist campaigner E. P. Thompson, with whom Angela became 'quite chummy'. They discussed British politics with one another. Thompson suggested that if Michael Foot and Tony Benn formed a Labour government in the UK, then the US would step in to destabilise them, much as it had done in Chile and Jamaica. Angela objected that Foot and Benn were 'faintly risible' figures, and wouldn't be capable of posing the same threat to US foreign policy that Chile's Salvadore Allende or Jamaica's Michael Manley had.

Angela taught on Wednesdays and Thursdays, and had a mixture of graduate and undergraduate classes. She employed many of the techniques she had developed at the University of East Anglia. Rick Moody, one of her undergraduate students (and subsequently the author of such novels as *Garden State* and *The Ice Storm*), recalled that she announced early on in the semester that she didn't set much store by traditional workshops:

> Tutorial was a better way to instruct, she opined, so we were all to turn up a few times a semester and talk with her personally about what was going on with our work. I remember these conversations being rather impulsive. Only occasionally did we talk in depth about particular stories, but that didn't make the conversations any less thrilling. One time I turned up carrying a Vintage edition of *The Sound and the Fury*.

Angela pointed at the Faulkner, and then [at] the stack of student work on her desk and said, 'I wish I were reading *that* instead of these.'

Just as she tended to do with her students at UEA, she steered Moody towards writers she thought might be useful to him: William Burroughs and Jean Genet are the two he remembers her recommending. For all that this approach to teaching could come across as offhand, Angela took her responsibilities seriously. 'The last thing a teacher wants to know is that s/he is a <u>bad</u> teacher,' she wrote to Mark, 'because one always does know oneself, however unconsciously, when one isn't getting through, & it's actually a very painful experience. One feels hurt & rejected & everything, & then one takes it out on the students.' Although she didn't really believe in the efficacy of workshops, she devoted a lot of energy to them. In a letter to Fleur Adcock she complained that 'teaching creative writing as an ongoing thing in formal classes is very trying and I'm looking forward to the break'.

Meanwhile, the pedagogical instinct was extended to Mark, who was having to write essays for his course at the Croydon College of Art and Design. She gave him tips on how to construct them ('make a list of the major points you want to mention. Grade them 1, 2, 3 etc. in the order of importance. Use a paragraph per point') and offered a few general words of encouragement:

I <u>do</u> think it's quite important for everybody to acquire a reasonable facility in written English, to be able to express themselves clearly & logically on paper, and it probably won't hurt you to learn a bit of history of art, or whatever it is they want you to learn, because it never hurts anybody to learn anything, even if it doesn't seem particularly relevant to the task at hand. Don't be disheartened, though! You've managed to evade almost every form of education until now, so you <u>will</u> have to work hard to make up for lost time; but oh! how it will enrich you in the long term! Truly; I swear it.

*　　*　　*

However much Angela complained about being in America, the country had a bracing effect on her imagination. She became fascinated by historical accounts of oppression, alienation and violence in the quaint landscapes of New England. She read up on the Salem witch trials, which had occurred about seventy miles from Providence, and on the case of Lizzie Borden, who murdered her family with an axe in the town of Fall River, less than twenty miles away. She began contrasting these episodes with the founding myths of the republic, the emphasis placed on democracy, inclusiveness, and equality of opportunity. By the beginning of October she was regularly staying up all night to work, covering page after page in furious handwriting (she didn't have access to a typewriter).

The first fruit of this activity was 'The Cabinet of Edgar Allan Poe', a story about the American author whose work had most powerfully influenced her own. 'He came to Providence courting a local ether-addicted spiritualist who called herself the Seer of Providence & lived beside the graveyard,' she explained to Susannah Clapp. The finished story doesn't mention the Seer of Providence, but it mixes some of the other milestones of Poe's biography (the death of his mother, his adoption by Mr Allan of Virginia, his marriage to his thirteen-year-old cousin Virginia Clemm and her subsequent death from consumption) with astonishing scenes of barefaced fictionality (the infant Poe watches his father dematerialise: 'He unbecame . . . He said not one word to his boys but went on evaporating until he melted clean away, leaving behind him in the room as proof he had been there only a puddle of puke on the splintered floorboards'). It presents a complex psychological portrait of the author, paying special attention to the women in his life, and their influence on his character and compulsions. The story is (following on from 'Black Venus') another remarkable transmutation of biographical fact into the sprightly stuff of art.

After finishing her story about Poe, she turned her attention to Lizzie Borden, around whose biography she began constructing a novel. It was provisionally titled *In a Nameless Hour*, an allusion to the French symbolist writer Auguste Villiers de l'Isle-Adam, who wrote of the heroine of his unfinished novel *Isis*:

The character of her mind was self-determining and by obscure transitions it attained the immanent proportions where the self is affirmed for what it is. The nameless hour, the eternal hour when children cease to look vaguely at the sky and the earth rang for her in her ninth year. From this moment on, what was dreaming confusedly in the eyes of this little girl took on a more fixed glint: one would have said she was feeling the meaning of herself while awakening in our shadows.

As the passage from which she took her title suggests, Angela interpreted Lizzie's crime as a desperate break from engulfment to self-assertion. By the time of the murders, the Borden 'girls', Lizzie and Emma, were in their thirties and forties respectively, but 'they did not marry and so live[d] in their father's house, where they remain[ed] in a fictive, protracted childhood'. The claustrophobic atmosphere of the Borden home – 'a house of privacies sealed so close as if they had been sealed with wax on a legal document' – is chillingly done. But although Angela emphasised the patriarchal structure of the household ('the . . . old man owns all the women by either marriage, birth or contract'), the atmosphere of domestic tyranny was taken from her own more matriarchal upbringing. She gave Old Borden her mother's belief that submerging the body in water removes essential oils, and described Lizzie as 'a girl of Sargasso calm', just as she had once described her own adolescence as a 'Sargasso sea'.

Her work on Lizzie Borden occupied her for most of her year in Providence. The material was eventually boiled down into two short stories, one of which, 'The Fall Rivers Axe Murders' (covering the hours leading up to the killings in hallucinatory detail), appeared in *Black Venus*, while the other, 'Lizzie and the Tiger' (which follows the infant Lizzie on a momentous and disturbing trip to the circus), appeared in the posthumously published *American Ghosts and Old World Wonders* (the title of which was inspired by D. H. Lawrence: 'there are terrible spirits, ghosts in the air of America').

The setting of 'Lizzie and the Tiger' had migrated from the novel Angela intended to write next. During the period she was working on the Lizzie Borden material, she was also researching her next novel, about a woman born with wings in nineteenth-century London, which she was already referring to in her journal as *Nights at the Circus*. On 9 October she asked Mark to send her two histories of the Trans-Siberian Railway and a book about the folklore of Siberia, and shortly afterwards she read *Wild Tigers and Tame Fleas* by Bill Ballantine, who had toured America as a clown in the 1940s. 'There is something about circuses,' she wrote in her journal. 'Circuses & silences.'

By mid-October the summer was over: the temperature had settled down into the low sixties, the leaves were beginning to fall, and the first frosts were coming in at night. Angela had settled into a routine: dividing her days between writing, teaching, and researching in the university library, and seeing the Coovers or going to the cinema a couple of evenings a week. She avoided most social situations, but thought that it was ruder to turn down invitations from students than from colleagues, so went to the odd undergraduate party. 'I have some dishy students but feel not the slightest twinge of desire to offer them credits in advanced foreplay,' she wrote to Carmen. Her erotic attention was focussed on Mark. 'Please miss me,' she urged him.

At the end of October she took the train to New York to interview the novelist and critic Elizabeth Hardwick for *Vogue*. Her response to the city was a long way from the agitation and dislike she'd felt when she was last there in 1969. 'It is beautiful & monstrous & probably addictive,' she told Mark:

> It really does look like itself in the movies – just as it should do, I suppose; and there is indeed a great deal of public wealth & public squalor & ordinary people, in shops & stuff are, well, very nice indeed. I certainly wasn't expecting that. The woman I stayed with, a writer, lives in a sort of old-fashioned glamorous area, the sort of place that has seen better days fairly recently, & turned out to have heard of me & liked my work so it wasn't an interview thing so much as staying with a new friend. She is also an old American left-winger – rather to my surprise.

They got on well enough for Angela to confide in Hardwick about how much she was missing Mark, to which Hardwick wisely responded: 'It isn't being alone that's desolating, it is being without love.' The interview was 'a washout', Angela wrote to Carmen, 'because I decided I wanted her to adopt me and it was very difficult to ask incisive questions of somebody with whom one was discussing the American Old Left & menstruation – "all those young girls, <u>bleeding</u> all the time!" she said, with post-menopausal compassion'. They went to the Museum of Folk Art to see an exhibition on weathervanes, and Hardwick introduced her to the famous novelist and left-wing activist Mary McCarthy. 'I am not easily impressed,' Angela wrote to Carmen. 'I was impressed by them both.' Just how impressed is made clear in two breathless, coy letters she sent Hardwick, the first written shortly after she returned from New York to Providence ('Thank you for a <u>lovely</u> weekend. I can't tell you what a pleasure it was to meet you; and of course I took your front door key away with me! This was my unconscious stating in no uncertain terms that I'd like to come back'), the second written shortly after she returned from Providence to London ('I get tongue-tied, writing letters – I've been meaning to write & say just how much meeting you in New York meant to me . . . but I think you know that').

The intensity with which Angela embraced Hardwick – her desire for the older woman to 'adopt' her, even – isn't just an expression of her isolation that year in America. As she moved into her forties, she became increasingly drawn to mother figures. The writers who had meant the most to her during her formative years had almost all been male, but in the 1980s she became an extremely vocal champion not only of Hardwick, but also of Grace Paley (whom she described as a 'hero-mother' when she met her in New York in March 1981), Elizabeth Jolley (whom she described as '<u>wonderful!</u>' after meeting her in Australia in 1984, and to whom she subsequently sent pictures of her family) and Christina Stead (whom she never met, but described in an essay for the *London Review of Books* in 1982 as 'one of the greatest writers of our time' and 'one of the great articulators of family life'). These four writers – who were all aged between sixty and eighty when Angela became aware of them – don't have much in common except their linguistic vitality and a tough, indecorous attitude towards the experience of being a woman ('she writes *as* a woman, not *like* a woman', Angela wrote of Stead). Perhaps it was coincidence that Angela began proclaiming the genius of all four of them between 1980 and 1984, but the reverence she expressed for them and their work does suggest a new-found peace with the idea of female role models, and by extension – eleven years after her own mother's death – with the idea of motherhood.

The profile of Hardwick took a long time to write up; it never appeared, and it's possible that Angela never finished it. Her fiction, she felt, was also going badly. She wrote to Mark: 'you can imagine my mood & ought to be pleased you are so far away'. The initial rush of inspiration she'd felt at being in America had dissipated into the familiar daily grind. The idea of writing a novel about Lizzie Borden suddenly disgusted her. She wrote to Mark:

> I . . . found myself, quite quickly, utterly repelled by the subject matter, and seem to have dropped the idea of doing a quick shocker in order to make some bread for doing something very complicated about the nature of human relations in a mill town (which Fall River was). This

isn't coming out right, either, and, if the weather holds up, I'll take the bus over and have a look around. It <u>must</u> be an interesting place, because nobody ever, ever goes there and it is really quite a big city.

One readily available source of distraction was the presidential race between Jimmy Carter and Ronald Reagan, which was now entering its frenzied final stages. She followed it closely, hoping for a Carter victory. Reagan – who was 'probably senile' – alarmed her with his emphasis on military expenditure and his pronounced social conservatism. 'I tend to think of him as a figurehead for nameless, faceless forces of evil,' she wrote a few years later, 'but it is perfectly possible he <u>is</u> Lucifer in person himself. That would be a turn-up for the Moral Majority.' As the campaign progressed, though, it became increasingly obvious that he was going to win. 'Unfortunately, the mass of the population seems to put its trust in God & God is obviously a Reagan supporter,' she wrote to Mark.

On the evening of Tuesday 4 November, shortly after the polls closed, she went to watch the results come in with the Coovers and a few of their friends. When it became clear that Reagan had achieved a landslide victory, one of the guests stormed out, but Angela stayed until the early hours. The next day, in a small, impotent, yet – in the context of a private American college – not un-risky gesture of defiance, she took J. G. Ballard's story 'Why I Want to Fuck Ronald Reagan' (which discusses the former actor's psycho-sexual appeal, with reference to car crashes and Adolf Hitler) and read it to her undergraduate class. 'They laughed until they cried,' she wrote in a 1984 essay on Ballard, 'except those who vice versa'd.' Her account is backed up by Rick Moody, who recalled: 'it was a measure of Angela's persuasive talents that everyone enjoyed this bit of show and tell'.

The winter was as cold as the summer had been hot. Angela drank rum and hot orange juice, and used cocoa butter on her face against windburn. The radiators in her apartment didn't work, and although she bought an electric heater, it didn't provide much warmth. She bumped her head getting out of a car and sustained a bruise that swiftly blossomed into a black eye, making her look 'like a battered wife'. She tried not to count the days until Mark arrived for Christmas, fearing that it would bring bad luck in the form of them arguing. As the date approached, though, her neuroses snowballed. She became overwhelmingly anxious about his journey, fixating on the possibility of him dying in a plane crash. If he did make it to Providence in one piece, she was convinced that the house in Clapham would be burgled while he was there. 'My young man arrives in two days' time,' she wrote to Carmen on 11 December. 'Since the human heart is, actually, much simpler than one would have ever thought possible, I shall only say I am looking forward to seeing him very, very much indeed; & I am sure I would not have sustained a black eye had he been here to look after me.'

On 13 December, the Coovers drove her to Boston to meet Mark at Logan International Airport. 'When he came, she was transported,' Robert Coover remembered. 'She was just great.' Her father had sent her a cheque for $200 as a Christmas present, so she and Mark were able to eat out, and rent a car to go for day trips. They visited potteries in the seaside town of Newport, and went clothes shopping in Providence. Angela's newly grey hair accentuated the age difference between them. Buying army-surplus greatcoats together, the assistant asked if Mark was her son – 'How he chuckled,' Angela wrote.

Christmas Day was the coldest ever recorded in New England. 'We went for a walk,' Angela told an editor at Gollancz who had written to inform her that *The Passion of New Eve* was being remaindered, '& the mucus froze in our nostrils.' It snowed every day until 15 January, by which time Mark had returned to London. Angela missed him all the more after his visit. She swore never to take a foreign job again.

After five months in Providence, Angela had relaxed into the academic lifestyle, but her feelings about America remained frosty. 'It's a culture so utterly without sensuality that I find it very difficult to work here,' she wrote in her journal on 16 January. 'It's not something I can talk to Americans about, either; the sensuous apprehension of the world was written out of the script very, very early on.' On 31 January she wrote to Pat Barker:

> The snow has almost melted and the students are back. One of them keeps scratching swastikas, probably with the point of his fraternity pin, on the paint in the library. Another one has painted a swastika in red paint on the wall opposite my house; I don't think it's aimed specifically at me, it's just an expression of joie de vivre . . . I'm doing

perfectly well and have many nice friends but I do think the consensus in the US of A is utterly and irredeemably loony. Did you know they are stopping teaching evolution theory in some schools in the South? You can now take degrees in something called 'Creation Biology', which <u>proves</u> Darwin was wrong. It's quite startling.

In the second semester, Angela offered an undergraduate course titled Science Fiction and Fantasy Writing. It was another creative-writing module, but with a more substantial literature component than she'd been able to include the previous semester. She devised a reading list that included works by Borges, Italo Calvino and Bruno Schulz. One of the students, John Kwok, remembered the discussions in class as being largely of a theoretical nature: 'her seminar was devoted to challenging our pre-existing assumptions as to the relevance of fantasy – and in some respects, science fiction too – to mainstream literature, in the process "deconstructing", for example, such cherished works as the Brothers Grimm fairy tales'.

The second semester was made easier than the first by the proximity of one of her closest friends: Lorna Sage was spending a sabbatical term at Wellesley, a private all-women's college in a well-to-do suburb of Boston. She visited Angela towards the end of January; a month later Angela visited her, and they rang one another up regularly to gossip about the dysfunctionality of their respective faculties and to vent disbelief at the oddness of America ('she complained about having to buy milk by the gallon', Angela told Mark after the first such conversation. 'I discover I've got used to this').

'I'm having neither a nice nor a nasty time,' she wrote to Susannah Clapp on 1 March. 'Time passes, is all, & I have difficulty following some conversations, &, very often, feel like a hairy barbarian among all these gentle & polite & sensitive non-smokers.' But her homesickness hadn't been buried very deep, and it surfaced at odd times:

> One of my students gave me a story in which the narrator goes to London & takes a taxi in from Heathrow & the taxi driver says to him: 'That'll be fifteen bleedin' quid, you miserable wanker.' How did this upper-class Eastern seaboard American child capture the exact speech rhythms of the British working class? It made me weep with nostalgia for the sheer rudeness – the vile, obscene, funny <u>rudeness</u> – of everyday life at home. Certainly Europeans tolerate & probably actively enjoy a degree of verbal abuse amongst themselves that

would be unimaginable here. Here, <u>physical</u> violence is tolerated. The crime rates would go right down, I think, if Americans stopped saying: 'Have a nice day', to one another. At least it would stop me from contemplating violence; when people in shops & so on order me to have a nice day in this authoritative way, I want to kill, kill, kill. When I mutter 'sod off' under my breath, they think it is a Russian Orthodox benediction.

*   *   *

By the end of March, Angela was exhausted. Her teeth were giving her trouble and she was suffering shortness of breath climbing the hilly streets around the university. Her newly grey hair made her feel old. Mark came to visit her during his vacation, but she was still teaching, so they weren't able to spend as much time together as they had at Christmas. She was worried about how thin he was becoming. 'He is turning remorselessly into an art student,' she wrote to Carmen:

> We went to Salem, to look at this glorious colonial architecture, and he has the camera and is snapping away and what is he bloody photographing? Car parks! Car parks! 'It's the real America,' he said. At least he didn't say: 'It's the iconography of the real America.' Not yet, he doesn't.

The semester ended in May, but Angela was required to hang around for another month or so to supervise her graduate students as they completed their final portfolios, and to do publicity for the American edition of *Fireworks*, which was being published that month by Harper & Row with the subtitle 'Nine Stories in Various Disguises' (which Angela liked no better than 'Nine Profane Pieces', the subtitle Quartet had foisted on the collection). In addition to readings in New York, Chicago and Minneapolis, she had been invited to speak at a conference in Boston about the politics of women in publishing. 'What shall I say?' she asked Carmen. 'That all the women in publishing that I know think Michael Foot is the best we can do at the moment? Is that what they mean?'

Towards the end of the month she returned to New York. She saw Elizabeth Hardwick, who offered to be a godmother if she ever had a baby, and had lunch with Ted Solotaroff, her editor at Harper & Row. Solotaroff had risen to prominence in the 1960s at the helm of the now legendary

New American Review, and has been described by Ian McEwan as 'the most influential editor of his time' and by the writer Bobbie Ann Mason as 'one of the last of the great editors'. Angela wasn't fazed by his reputation. 'He informed me, with a perfectly straight face, that he's spent the last year heavily involved with Judaism,' she wrote to Carmen:

> [He] seems to have decided that I am too upmarket a commodity to benefit from the customary sales pitch so [*Fireworks*] hasn't had any reviews or anything. I do actually think he is a – a what? Hesitating exquisitely (shit? creep? jerk?) I realise none of these fit. He just doesn't seem to have much spark of life, poor sod. I feel I can say this to you because I know you've never got off on him like some of the other girls have and I don't get off on him at all, at all. I think this is going to make my US career very difficult indeed. Furthermore, the only magazine or enterprise or anything in the US that has exhibited any interest in me being here at all is PENTHOUSE . . . Anyway, I've been working on a piece about Lizzie Borden (capitalism, patriarchy and the textile industry in South Eastern New England) which is obviously not the thing to delight the heart of a born-again Talmudic scholar. On the other hand, <u>you</u> might like it, so we'll talk about it when I see you.

Carmen had more immediate plans for Angela, and raised the idea of putting together a collection of her journalism for Virago – a proposal which 'pleased & flattered' her. After toying with various titles – including *Yesterday's Papers* and *Sparking Off* – she agreed to Carmen's suggestion of *Nothing Sacred* (a nod to a line from her 'Notes for a Theory of Sixties Style': 'in the pursuit of magnificence, nothing is sacred'). She received an advance of £1,250, signing a contract when she was back in England on 1 July.

By the end of May, the hot weather had returned – 'sudden, real, steaming, humid American summer' – and Angela had lost the use of her right ear. She suggested that it was a psychosomatic response to the way her books had fallen on deaf ears in America, but her jokiness concealed genuine anxiety about the affliction. The doctor couldn't see her for a week, and in the meantime she mentioned her suffering to all her correspondents. 'Partial deafness has put me in a curious, dreamy, remote relation with the world,' she told Mark. 'It's tiring talking to people because I have to strain every nerve to hear them, whilst noises like this typewriter, or the water splashing in the sink, are positively thunderous.'

She even mentioned her hearing problems to the writer Rikki Ducornet, whom she had never actually met, but who'd been in touch praising her work and asking if she might include 'Puss-in-Boots' in an anthology titled *Shoes and Shit*. Ducornet's first collection of stories, *The Butcher's Tales*, had been published the previous year, and she had also written several volumes of poetry. She was friendly with Robert Coover (who had recommended Angela's work), shared several of her literary enthusiasms (Borges, Márquez, Sade) and lived in Le Puy-Notre-Dame, a village in the Loire Valley, with the painter and ceramicist Guy Ducornet. Angela was intrigued by her:

> Coover says you live with a potter. Is this right, or is he conflating us? Because I happen to live with a potter, a large, impressive, silent man, whose silence, no doubt, will prove compatible if I turn out to need my ear amputated. Anyway, if this is so, what a coincidence: and, if not, it means that Coover thinks we have a lot in common (if you follow me).

She suggested that she and Mark might visit the Ducornets in Le Puy on their way back from Florence that summer. Over the next few years their friendship blossomed – Angela returned to Le Puy several times, and recommended one of Rikki's novels to Carmen, who published it at Chatto & Windus – and for a while Angela and Mark toyed with the idea of buying themselves a house in the Loire Valley.

On 29 May Angela went to the doctor, who diagnosed her deafness as the result of a build-up of wax in her right ear. 'It was terribly humiliating,' she wrote to Carmen. 'The nurse syringed my ear & great chunks of impacted crap came out. You wouldn't have thought one ear could hold so much wax.'

As the time to leave drew closer, Angela started noticing things that she would miss about Providence: the architecture, the unfamiliar birdsong in the mornings, the light – and above all the Coovers. She also realised how much she liked living in a republic. It was a great relief to be able to ignore the wedding of Prince Charles and Lady Diana Spencer, which several of her correspondents complained about being saturated with in Britain.

She booked her flight home for 28 June, planning to go almost straight to Florence at the start of July, to stay in San Francesco di Paola, and then on to France to visit Rikki and Guy Ducornet in Le Puy-Notre-Dame at the end of August. When the time came for her to leave, the Coovers threw her a party. Most members of the English department were there, as well as a few students. By way of a parting gift they presented her – in a nod to her work on Lizzie Borden – with an axe.

CHAPTER NINETEEN

A psychedelic Dickens

In September 1981, the second novels of both Salman Rushdie and Ian McEwan – *Midnight's Children* and *The Comfort of Strangers* respectively – were shortlisted for that year's Booker Prize. Established in 1969 as Britain's answer to the Prix Goncourt, the Booker had been dominated for its first twelve years by a much older generation, with Iris Murdoch (b. 1919) and William Golding (b. 1911) among its star turns, and C. P. Snow (b. 1905) and Elizabeth Bowen (b. 1899) among its walk-on parts. It was respected, but not exactly sexy. There was a whiff of the senior common room about it.

When *Midnight's Children* was announced as the winner on 20 October – in a ceremony that was, for the first time ever, broadcast live on the BBC – it was widely seen as heralding a new, youthful, cosmopolitan era of British fiction. Although a few previous Booker winners (J. G. Farrell's *The Siege of Krishnapur*, Ruth Prawer Jhabvala's *Heat and Dust*, Paul Scott's *Staying On*) had been set in India, *Midnight's Children* was the first to be written by someone with Indian heritage, to achieve such lively comic prose, or to so gleefully defy the conventions of social realism. The thirty-four-year-old Rushdie became a superstar overnight. 'Our life just went haywire,' his first wife, Clarissa Luard, recalled.

Over the next few years, the idea that Britain was enjoying a literary renaissance – with the Rushdie-McEwan-Amis generation representing a clean break with a stuffy and unadventurous past – became orthodoxy. An explosion of popular interest in literary fiction ensued. Novelists (though rarely novels) became front-page news. Glossy publicity campaigns, such as the list of the twenty 'Best Young British Novelists' published by *Granta* magazine in April 1983, were set up to promote them. Advances soared.

It's important not to overstate the degree to which Angela missed out on all this. Her reputation was always that of a singular talent, and it became ever more robust during the last decade of her life. She made frequent television and radio appearances, was invited to speak at literary festivals and events, and had opportunities to go on foreign tours. Her books were reviewed widely and prominently, often enthusiastically, and sometimes reverently. She even received the odd tasteful little prize. But she was rarely spoken of in the same breath as Rushdie, McEwan and Amis. Her advances – though they increased dramatically during the silly season of the 1980s – were never in the same ballpark as some of theirs. She scarcely troubled the bestseller lists (unless you count the *City Limits* list of 'Alternative Bestsellers'), or the shortlists of the most prestigious prizes. She wasn't subjected to much media scrutiny outside the muffled cloisters of the review sections.

There are several possible explanations for this disparity. Angela Carter was arguably too much of an individualist, her writing too wilfully unique, to fit easily into the media narrative of a new trend in British fiction; and though she was born in the same decade as most members of the 'golden generation', she was usually seen as belonging to an earlier vintage. She was a couple of years too old to feature in *Granta*'s 'Best Young British Novelists' list – which cemented the reputations of Amis, McEwan and Rushdie, along with those of her former students Pat Barker and Kazuo Ishiguro – since the cut-off age was forty. No doubt these factors played their part in her neglect. But she also suspected that her gender might have something to do with it. When she was praised it was often as a trailblazing woman writer, rather than just as a trailblazing writer. Even Lorna Sage, one of her greatest supporters and most sensitive critics, was in the habit of framing her achievement in terms of her gender. When *Granta* ran a symposium on 'The End of the English Novel' in 1980, Sage was the only one of five contributors to mention Angela Carter, describing her as the 'most self-conscious, versatile and impressive' of the 'women writers . . . discovering monstrous cracks in English domestic architecture'.

A few years later, Angela told an interviewer:

I've never had any problem getting published. It would be whinge-ing to say that men who are no better than I are very much more famous and very much richer and also regarded as . . . the right stuff. It would ill become me. But it's amazing what the Old Boys' club does for itself. *They* list the 'important British contemporary writers', and they'll list Malcolm Bradbury and Kingsley Amis, and they'll leave out Doris Lessing, who's the only one with a really huge international reputation. And they'll leave out Beryl Bainbridge. And . . .

She trailed off before saying that they also left out Angela Carter.

Carmen understood her frustration: 'she didn't want to be the queen, but she knew she wasn't given the same attention that Ian and Martin and all those people were . . . It's really hard if you're a woman and you put up with these things in our generation. It's not a question of bitterness, just, fucking hell.' Liz Calder agreed that Angela was disappointed by the way her reputation stalled: 'She retained throughout her life a feeling that she hadn't really broken through, either to the literary world or to the world at large, in the way that she would have wanted . . . She was very funny about it – about how all the boys were getting the prizes, but she wasn't.'

The boys themselves were conscious of her feelings, but she never made them feel uncomfortable. 'One of the really lovely things about her is that she was not ever envious of other people's success,' remembered Rushdie, '[although] I think she did genuinely wish that people treated her work as more important.' Ishiguro agreed:

> I thought Angela was always very confident about her own writing. I never sensed in all the time I knew her that she was not confident about her own writing, about the worth of her own writing. But she seemed very resigned to the idea that she would never be well known. And I think she'd be very surprised now at the fact that she's taught in schools, [and] every bookshop has loads of her books. Angela was used to being neglected, used to publishers not taking her seriously. Even from the start I think she was kind of resigned to the idea, and very supportive of the idea, that I would probably be commercially more successful than she would be.

These impressions are illuminating in so far as they go, but they don't tell the whole story. If Angela valued a writer's work, as she valued both Rushdie's and Ishiguro's, then she was fiercely and selflessly supportive of them; but if she felt that they were being undeservedly celebrated, that they were getting an easy ride because of their youth or class or gender, then it was a different matter. That was what she felt about McEwan, and a note of bitterness did often sound when she talked about him. She referred to him as 'poor Ian' and 'little Ian', and once as 'a trendy kid on the crest of the wave'. He continued to visit The Chase quite frequently for dinner, which suggests that she didn't have anything against him on a personal level – but there's no doubt that she begrudged him his reputation.

The increased visibility of British literature during the 1980s went hand in hand with structural changes to the publishing industry, as medium-sized independent firms began forming themselves into corporate groups to retain influence in an ever more competitive market. The firms of Chatto & Windus, Jonathan Cape and the Bodley Head had banded together as early as 1973. In February 1982, it was announced that Virago was to join them. Carmen Callil would remain chair of the company she had founded, but she would withdraw from its day-to-day operations to take over in April as publishing director and joint managing director of Chatto & Windus, the publishers of Iris Murdoch and A. S. Byatt, with a backlist that included Mark Twain, William Faulkner and Marcel Proust. She would be replacing the pioneering editor Norah Smallwood, who had started her career as a secretary and worked her way up to the boardroom, but in spite of this precedent, it was still unusual for a woman – a foreign-born feminist, at that – to be in a position of power in mainstream publishing, and Carmen's appointment attracted coverage well beyond the literary pages. In a profile of her friend for Vogue, Angela provided a sense of her achievement: 'British publishing, in the elevated stratum of managing directors, chairpersons and those with access to the cupboard in which the vintage port is kept, is heavily male-dominated . . . the higher up you get, the thicker throng the three-piece suits.'

Angela used the Vogue piece as an opportunity to enumerate Carmen's virtues as an editor. 'I would never have finished [The Sadeian Woman] if Carmen hadn't nagged me,' she wrote. 'She loves to "do right" by a book, to make sure it has just the right typeface, just the right jacket. Just the right promotion, so the book will reach those very people for whom it was written.' These were qualities that Angela greatly appreciated, and – now that Carmen was in a position to compete with rivals such as Gollancz and Hart-Davis – they began talking about Chatto & Windus publishing Angela's next novel, which she envisaged as 'a huge, comic, phantasmagoric, epic extravaganza, with a cast of thousands!'

* * *

Nights at the Circus centres on the extraordinary figure of Fevvers, a woman born with wings, whose career as a famous *aerialiste* in nineteenth-century London is kept aloft by the skilfully maintained double bluff that she's only pretending to have them – a situation that Angela thought of as 'kind of emblematic'. Partly based on the actress Mae West, Fevvers is a raucous, indecorous, magnificently physical creation. Lustrously blonde-haired and radiantly blue-eyed, standing more than six feet tall, she is renowned throughout Europe for her beauty; at close quarters, though, she looks 'more like a dray mare than an angel', with a face as 'broad and oval as a meat dish' and 'a voice that clanged like dustbin lids'. A woman of massive appetites and meagre delicacy, she burps, farts, sweats, and eats 'with gargantuan enthusiasm'. Her dressing room has 'a highly personal aroma', and is littered with discarded undergarments: it is 'a misstresspiece of exquisitely feminine squalor'.

Fevvers is a much more centred, solid character than any of Angela Carter's previous heroines – by comparison to her, Melanie in *The Magic Toyshop* and Marianne in *Heroes and Villains* seem only half alive – and the theme of self-discovery that flavoured those novels has been replaced in *Nights at the Circus* by an interest in self-expression ('LOOK AT ME', Fevvers seems to cry). A couple of interviewers wondered if this was because Angela had become more settled in herself. 'I think you're probably right, actually,' she told one of them. 'I had all these questions to discuss [to do] with adolescent girls before. But Fevvers, oh, she's the sort of person who in British films was usually the second lead, she's often the barmaid . . . And I wanted to put her centre stage.' She had been thinking about the novel since she returned to England from Japan, and had begun making notes for it as early as 1977, but she told another interviewer that she'd had to wait 'until I was big enough, strong enough, to write about a winged woman'.

The novel is set in 1899, as the nineteenth century was just giving way to the twentieth ('it's very important, it's about cusps', Angela said). It was a moment when debates about women's suffrage were growing increasingly heated in Britain. The arguments centred on the question of whether women were fundamentally different to men – meeker and gentler, less able to cope with the knotty complexities of politics – or whether they had merely been forced to assume that role, to disguise their natural abilities and intelligence, just as Fevvers has to pretend she can't fly. The novel occasionally hammers home its leading lady's symbolic role – she's described at one point as 'the pure child of the century that just now is waiting in the wings, the New Age in which no woman will be bound down to the ground' – but the basic conceit of a winged woman 'enforces', as the critic Aidan Day has put it, 'a psychological point'. If we feel that Fevvers' abilities are implausible, our attitude is analogous to those of the nineteenth-century men who doubted that women had the ability to vote.

In the first part of the novel, the implausibilities are refracted through the sceptical perspective of Jack Walser, an American journalist (based on the young Jack London, who Angela thought had written 'some terrific journalism' in the 1900s) engaged on a series of articles titled 'Great Humbugs of the World'. Walser interviews Fevvers in her dressing room, where she tells him the story of her life: how she was abandoned as a baby on the doorstep of an east London brothel – where she had a comfortable enough upbringing, playing Cupid with a toy bow and arrow 'in the alcove of the drawing-room in which the ladies introduced themselves to the gentlemen' – before discovering that she had the power of flight. When she was seventeen the brothel closed, and she joined a sort of peep show – 'a museum of woman monsters', catering to 'those who were troubled in their . . . souls' – run by a sinister matriarch called Madame Schreck. One of the patrons, having identified Fevvers as an angel, kidnapped her with the intention of murdering her in a sadistic ritual and extracting her essence to gain eternal youth. She escaped – the first of several getaways that she makes from lecherous men – and decided to join the circus as a trapeze artist. Throughout this section of the novel, Fevvers' narrative is interrupted by her companion Lizzie – 'a tiny, wizened, gnome-like apparition who might have been any age between thirty and fifty . . . There was ex-whore written all over her' – who performs the function of a Greek chorus, making explicit the subtext of the story (a habit that Fevvers occasionally laments).

The story hurtles forth, vaulting and swooping, into Part Two, which finds Fevvers and Lizzie in St Petersburg with Colonel Kearney's circus, about to travel onwards via Siberia to Japan. What they don't know is that the journalist Walser has followed them, disguised as a clown. When he rescues Mignon, the Ape-Man's wife, from the jaws of a tigress – 'a questing sluice of brown and yellow, a hot and molten death' – and takes her to Fevvers' hotel room, the star *aerialiste* begins falling in love with him.

The third and final part of the novel begins when the train taking them through Siberia is blown up by a band of outlaws. Fevvers breaks a wing, and she and Lizzie are taken prisoner. Walser is dug out of the train's wreckage with amnesia, and runs off into the wilderness. Fevvers and Lizzie eventually escape when a whirlwind spirits off the outlaws. Setting off into the snow, they run into Walser, whose memory has returned. The novel ends with him and Fevvers in bed together. The final joke is a double revelation: not only are Fevvers' wings indeed real, but she isn't, as she has always maintained, a virgin. 'To think I really fooled you!' she hoots in the final sentence. 'It just goes to show there's nothing like confidence.'

The ebullient comedy and carnival atmosphere of *Nights at the Circus* are unlike anything in Angela Carter's earlier work. Even more than *Shadow Dance* and *The Passion of New Eve*, it unites high culture with low: allusions to Joyce, Milton, Shakespeare, Melville and Poe jostle for space with fart gags, comic-book tropes and music-hall motifs. But for all its postmodern richness and inclusiveness – for all its hospitality to the fantastic and the allegorical – the novel adopts a deeply traditional form. 'I wanted to have a real sense of nineteenth-century solidity about *Nights at the Circus*,' Angela told an interviewer. She parodied some of what she saw as the conventions of the realist novel: the characters in *Nights at the Circus* are always pouring cups of tea and lighting cigarettes, which she viewed as the kind of thing realist writers thought added verisimilitude. In a letter to Deborah Rogers, written when she had completed an early draft of Part One, she described it as being 'a bit like psychedelic Dickens . . . but this need be no bad thing!'

Angela's confidence in the material is demonstrated by her response (expressed in a letter to Carmen) when her American editor, Amanda Vaill at Viking Penguin, asked her to make a few changes to the manuscript:

> When I read that I felt a violent surge of hatred for the entire USA and especially its publishing profession. If I had meant <u>Nights at the Circus</u> to be different I would have written it differently. She can go fuck herself and if she 'insists' on changes . . . I shall instruct Deb to take the novel away from her . . . Am I overreacting? Yes, I am probably overreacting. But: <u>no changes</u>.

*   *   *

In the spring of 1982, as Angela's forty-second birthday approached, she and Mark began 'finally discussing whether or not to have a baby', since, she wrote, 'my fertility is now finite in terms of months rather than years'. They decided that they would try. She let some of her friends in on her plans, and presented herself as being entirely relaxed about them. 'It's easy to pretend this is a major decision but I don't think it is, really,' she wrote to Lorna Tracy on 1 April. 'I've always believed in giving in to sentimental impulses.'

She conceived fairly quickly, and recorded the symptoms in her journal: 'nausea; breasts no longer taut & always pointed, still painful to press but nipples now softening & spreading – slightly seasick feeling all the time but not unpleasantly so. Sometimes, excitement; sometimes, terror.' She gave up smoking, and couldn't tolerate even the smell of coffee or alcohol. But things didn't work out. Around the seventh or eighth week she wrote:

> to travel hopefully is better than to arrive; we did not arrive. Clots of black blood, as from an old-fashioned abortion; & one afternoon of atrocious grief & tears as from the bottom of the soul, although nobody to blame but me, but me.

Feelings of guilt are common enough after miscarriages, but Angela blamed herself with remarkable conviction. In subsequent journal entries she tended to speak as if the loss of the pregnancy had been premeditated. Reflecting on the 'unreality of the future', she wrote: 'but that was one reason why I didn't have it, want it'. She wrote that it was 'impossible to imagine nine more months of it, the nausea & bone weariness & sense of approaching doom'. Afterwards she suffered 'not [from] remorse, but regret, easy to regret now I feel well'.

It's evident that her old ambivalence towards motherhood hadn't entirely resolved itself. But trying to get a handle on her state of mind is complicated by the fact that she almost immediately recommenced trying to conceive. Perhaps what happened in the summer of 1982 was a transformative moment. Shortly afterwards she wrote: '[Mark] has never seemed more beautiful & beloved to me; I am breathless and as if shocked with love, appalled at the idea I might have lost him.'

In June Angela was one of a group of writers – also including Anthony Burgess, William Empson, Dennis Potter, Chinua Achebe, and (thrillingly) Jorge Luis Borges – invited to Dublin to celebrate James Joyce in his centenary year. They were put up at the five-star Shelbourne Hotel and lavishly entertained at the state's expense. Angela hadn't visited Ireland since the 1960s, and she was astonished by how much it had changed. It was no longer the beautiful eighteenth-century city of *Ulysses*, she felt, but a vast and ugly one defaced by tower blocks and takeaway outlets.

One evening that week, Angela had dinner with the writer and film director Neil Jordan in a Chinese restaurant on Dame Street. They had met on one previous occasion, in 1979, when Jordan had received the *Guardian* Fiction Prize for his first book, a collection of dreamlike short stories titled *Night in Tunisia*. His debut feature film, *Angel*, a story of murder and revenge on the Belfast jazz circuit, had opened earlier that month to what Angela called 'the kind of review that one writes for oneself', and his second novel, *The Dream of a Beast*, was due to be published by Chatto & Windus in 1983. His tastes were very similar to Angela's, and they got on well. 'I found her fascinating,' he says. 'Quite wicked. She was an extraordinary character [with] an imagination that was quite different to anything else that one would have encountered at that time in British fiction.' He had recently heard the radio version of 'The Company of Wolves', and after Angela returned to London, he contacted her to propose that they did a film version of the story together. Angela was delighted with the idea, and they arranged that Jordan would come to London in the summer of 1983 to work on the script.

They were joined that evening in Dublin by Colm Tóibín, the twenty-seven-year-old editor of the current affairs magazine *Magill* (and subsequently the author of such novels as *The Blackwater Lightship* and *Brooklyn*). '[Angela] asked about Ireland's relationship to England, and wanted to know how much of the old hatred remained, and what state it was in,' he remembered. 'She seemed genuinely curious about this.'

On 16 June – the anniversary of the twenty-four-hour period over which the action of *Ulysses* takes place – the whole of Dublin became an enormous stage, as episodes from Joyce's masterpiece were acted out. RTE broadcast a thirty-hour marathon reading of the novel, and speakers were set up around the city. Tóibín accompanied Angela as she wandered around. He remembers standing with her on Capel Street Bridge, watching people in Edwardian costume going in and out of the Ormond Hotel, where the 'Sirens' episode of *Ulysses* is set:

> She had a way of not saying much that was almost infectious. She looked around her a lot, taking in every detail. She had a way of

seeming bemused by things, puzzled, amused. Her gaze was soft, but still penetrating, but with much subtlety in her aura, much withheld. This made her very good company for a stroll in Dublin. I felt that she was noticing many small things, and might even, for all I knew, be thinking of something else as well.

That evening there was a reception in Dublin Castle ('the very kind of riotous party Joyce adored', Angela wrote). It began with a banquet, at which Borges gave a toast to Joyce and to Ireland ('because for me the two are inseparable'), and opined that one day, 'like all great books', *Ulysses* would be read to children. When she returned to London, Angela told Salman Rushdie – who had also been invited to the celebrations in Dublin, but who'd had to cancel due to illness – all about Borges, relaying what he had said and doing impressions of his accent. 'I think it was a very important moment for her, to be able to meet him,' Rushdie said. 'You can't imagine Angela Carter without Borges.'

Nothing Sacred – the volume of non-fiction writing that Carmen had proposed – was published on 31 October 1982 to reviews that tended to play spot the difference between Angela Carter's behaviour as an essayist and her behaviour as a novelist. In the *Guardian*, the novelist Frank Tuohy felt that the journalism had the advantage over the fiction of 'its involvement with the world we know, or think we know. Here is the first serious writer to describe working in a Tokyo girlie bar, but also one who ranges widely through autobiographical sketches, social criticism and literary demolition.' Angus Wilson, by contrast, began his review for the *Observer* with the announcement that 'few fiction writers in the last two decades have given me so much pleasure as Angela Carter' – praising *The Infernal Desire Machines of Dr Hoffman* and *Fireworks* in particular – before rebuking her journalism for 'the too intrusive force of her convictions' and summing up *Nothing Sacred* as 'a most enjoyable if occasionally infuriating book'.

In the *London Review of Books*, the poet and Oxford don Tom Paulin suggested that the 'easy fluency' of the fiction was 'won at the expense of form and mimesis', but described the journalism as 'remarkable for a style which arches brilliantly between sociological observation and self-delighting irony . . . Carter is the laureate of de-industrialised England and the hedonistic egalitarianism of her prose . . . makes her the most advanced stylist in the country.' He saw her as having 'the new post-imperial sensibility' and 'a splendidly Mediterranean sense of joy' in common with the school of 'Martian' poets (who sought to defamiliarise the everyday phenomena of late twentieth-century life), quoting a few lines from Christopher Reid's 'A Whole School of Bourgeois Primitives' to support his case. This indulgence drew fire from Angela's fans on the letters pages of subsequent issues. 'What excuse can there be for such gratuitous name-dropping in an article presumably about the excellent Ms Carter's writing?' demanded one correspondent: 'The comparisons are odious . . . That slab of Martian verse does not compare with Carter, and has no place here.' Another objected to the idea of comparing her with anyone at all: 'Isn't one of her great gifts the fact that the writer she's most like is herself, sharing her originality directly with her readers?'

CHAPTER TWENTY

Doomed to love

In February 1983, Angela was approached to be a judge for that year's Booker Prize. It would be hard work: she was expected to read a hundred novels (almost twice the number submitted in the years before Rushdie's triumph) for a fee of just £1,000, paid in two instalments. But she said yes within two days of receiving the invitation. Perhaps she thought that the role would invigorate her reputation. If so, her hopes were rapidly deflated: the press release sent out by Booker McConnell Ltd in April described her as a 'children's author'.

Her fellow judges were the novelist Fay Weldon (in the chair); the *Observer*'s literary editor Terence Kilmartin; the poet and cultural critic Peter Porter; and the BBC commentator and *Tatler* editor Libby Purves. There had never before been a female chair, nor had the women on the jury ever outnumbered the men, a pair of firsts seized on by journalists with little else to say so early in the proceedings. 'Do I detect a feminist slant among this years Booker Prize judges?' wondered the *Evening Standard*'s diarist. 'Weldon and Carter will be trying to make sure that women are better represented than usual,' *Time Out* confirmed. In *The Times*, E. J. Craddock predicted that the prize would 'probably go to a novel written by a woman, published by a small, under-capitalized, little-known imprint'. Carmen Callil was on the Booker Prize committee, and it was widely insinuated that her intervention was the only reason that Angela had been selected. At the first meeting, according to *The Times*, Libby Purves declared that the prize shouldn't go to a 'feminist tract': 'whether or not she said this to bait the [other] judges, Angela Carter was baited'.

Narrow-minded gossip from sections of the press wasn't all that Angela had to contend with during her Booker service. The vast majority of submissions struck her as staid, middle-class rubbish, 'novels of personal experience divorced from public context', all too frequently featuring a charlady among the minor characters, but never written from her point of view. This, she wrote, was 'the subtext underwriting the much-vaunted renaissance of British fiction and it is to do with as-you-were'. She found reading so many bad books in a row an arduous and dispiriting process. 'I'd confidently expected all manner of good things to happen,' she wrote ruefully in *New Society* when it was finally over:

> Fat lunches from publishers, perhaps; bottles of bubbly delivered in plain wrappers; flattery and sycophancy on all sides. Not on your life. This *is* Britain. The only unsolicited gift that arrived took the form of a package containing yet *more* books from a publisher who must remain nameless, lest that name become mud – books *in addition* to the ones this publisher had already submitted, sent, not for the competition, obviously, but to me, personally, as a freelance lover of literature . . . I leafed through the offerings it contained to check if there were any tenners slipped among the pages, but no such luck.

She liked to present her attitude to the judging process as one of detached amusement and vague impatience, and even told friends that she roped in Mark to read some of the submitted books for her. He dismisses the story as nonsense: 'she took those kinds of things very seriously. She would have read everything.' His account is supported by her own private reflections on her role. She asked herself what the purpose of a literary prize was: whether it was intended to reward the book or the author, and what kind of book or author it ought to reward. She decided that she was looking for novels that used language in new and interesting ways, and was particularly impressed in this respect by Rushdie's *Shame*, which she thought was an even better book than *Midnight's Children*. Rushdie remembered that she took pains to minimise her natural bias towards him: 'she was so scrupulous about not allowing her personal relationship with me to in any way give me an inside track that she just stopped talking to me for an entire summer'.

Just as the judging process was getting started, its importance in Angela's life was thrown into perspective: she learned that she was two months pregnant in April 1983. She was almost forty-three years old. In the early 1980s it was still extremely rare for a woman to have a baby in her forties, and Angela was advised not to tell anybody about it for another three months, while the doctors ran various tests. When she did eventually tell people, she tended to claim that the pregnancy hadn't been planned. 'They had to drag me, kicking and screaming, into the labour ward,' she told an interviewer a few years later. 'I kept insisting that it was too late, that I was too old for such things.'

It was difficult at first – she suffered from terrible morning sickness. (A couple of years later, when one of her creative-writing students needed help drawing a character who was pregnant, Angela's advice was to imagine what it was like to 'start off every day, except when you were lying down, seasick'.) But she doesn't appear to have suffered from the same ambivalence that had afflicted her the previous year. 'I think I was too old to redefine myself,' she told *Marxism Today* in January 1985. 'I couldn't redefine myself as a mother.' She offered the thought as a slice of self-criticism, but perhaps it was the certainty that she wouldn't start redefining herself – that she had the maturity and self-possession to withstand the cultural pressures put on mothers – that allowed her, at long last, to view the prospect more with pleasure than with apprehension.

Even if she was confident that motherhood wouldn't disrupt her identity, Angela knew that it would consume her time, and she worked like a woman possessed throughout the summer of 1983. In addition to her reading for the Booker, she had a number of writing projects to wrap up before the baby arrived, the most significant of which was *Nights at the Circus*. She sent a completed version of Part Two to Deborah on 5 May, with a promise that 'Part Three is in the typewriter at the moment.' Four months later – on 17 September – she was able to deliver a completed manuscript. It added up to a 'massive' 140,000 words, making it by some stretch her longest book. The slight rush in which she wrote the last third of the novel shows in a few loose ends in the published version – Lizzie loses her handbag at one point, only to produce a pack of cards from it two pages later (as Angela's former student Andrew Cowan cheekily wrote to inform her) – but overall it was a bravura performance, her most assured and accomplished novel to date.

She received an advance of £26,000 from Chatto & Windus (for hardback rights) and a further £25,000 from Pan/Picador (for paperback rights). Even allowing for inflation, the combined figure was roughly ten times what she had been paid for any of her previous books, and more than five times the average wage. She was delighted – the period of scraping around for money was over, at least for the time being – but her priority was to put her affairs in order, and she immediately wrote to the Arts Council withdrawing an application she'd made for a bursary a few months previously. Marghanita Laski, the chair of that year's literature panel, wrote her a slightly bewildered thank you: 'This kind of decency is enormously heart-warming . . . I hope I need hardly say that if you had still needed the money, your claim to some would have rated highly.' Charles Osborne, the Arts Council's literature director, reinforced the point in a separate letter: 'you would undoubtedly have been offered a bursary had you not informed us that your financial circumstances had improved . . . Your generosity was greatly appreciated and will be taken into account should you make another application to the Council at a later date.'

In spite of the jump in her income provided by *Nights at the Circus*, Angela continued to produce masses of journalism, and to take on other projects, throughout the summer of 1983. She couldn't review any new novels (at least none that were eligible for the Booker), but she reviewed non-fiction at an energetic rate for *New Society* and the *Guardian*. In May she recorded a programme about Jean-Luc Godard for *Visions* on Channel 4. In June she took part in a seminar on 'Women in Gothick Fiction' at the University of London, and wrote a long piece for the *New Statesman* about the general election and 'the Thatcher phenomenon' (in which she took an uncharacteristically patrician line, complaining, of all things, about the prime minister's 'artificial' voice, her 'lady magistrate's' dress sense, and her 'Aryan' face). She also contributed long essays to several books: a piece for a Virago collection of women writing against nuclear weapons; a piece about Hugh Stalker for another Virago collection on fathers ('She was terribly reluctant to do that,' remembered Ursula Owen, who edited the book, 'my God, it was like getting blood out of a stone'); a piece about her relationship to the women's movement for a collection titled *Gender and Writing* from Pandora Press; and a wonderful piece about Chaucer's women, for a collection titled *The Left and the Erotic* from Lawrence & Wishart.

In July she worked with Neil Jordan on their script for *The Company of Wolves*. Every morning for a period of three or four weeks they sat together at the kitchen table in 107 The Chase, drinking tea from a samovar, and mapping out scenes. In the afternoon they split up to write, dividing the

Mark Pearce, mid-1970s: Angela thought he looked 'like a werewolf'

Angela, around the time she met Mark

Carmen Callil, who became Angela's most
important publisher and one of her
closest friends

Fleur Adcock, whose spare room Angela rented
in the early 1970s, and whom she subsequently
became close to

Deborah Rogers, Angela's
literary agent from 1973

Ian McEwan, the *enfant terrible* of English
literature, in the 1970s

Angela and friends: (clockwise from top left) with Mark and Liz Calder, mid-1970s; with Carmen at Glyndebourne; with Salman Rushdie in 1985; teaching with Lorna Sage at the University of East Anglia; with Mark and Neil Jordan, mid-1980s

With Grace Paley in London, 1985. Angela described her as 'a hero-mother'

Robert Coover at home in
Providence, January 1987

Paul Bailey, Carmen Callil, Angela Carter,
Susannah Clapp, late 1980s

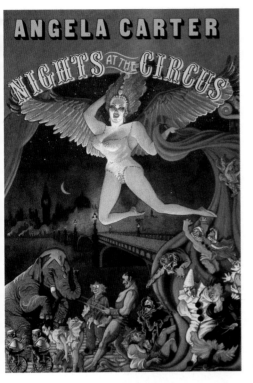
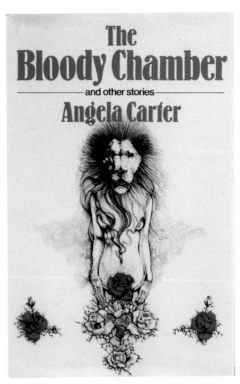

First editions of *Nights at the Circus* (1984) and *The Bloody Chamber* (1979)

A still from *The Company of Wolves* (1984). Angela was contemptuous when the London Underground refused to display posters featuring this image: 'they couldn't put their finger on it but they knew something was wrong'

Angela, Mark and Alex, 1984. 'You don't know anything about unrequited love until you've had children,' Angela told Lisa Appignanesi the following year

Far left: Alex, aged about three, fishing

Angela drew this portrait of Alex when they were living in Australia in 1984

Angela, Mark and Alex with Kazuo Ishiguro
and Lorna MacDougall on *Crowfoot*,
late 1980s

First edition of *Wise Children* (1991): the
cover shows the Dolly Sisters, whom
Angela's mother had admired as
a young woman

Angela, Mark and Alex with Susannah Clapp in the south of France, July 1991.
Angela had finished a course of radiotherapy just a few weeks earlier

Angela in her study at 107, The Chase, where she lived for the last
and the happiest sixteen years of her life

day's scenes between them, and reconvened the following morning to go over one another's work. It was the first time that Angela had collaborated on a piece of writing, and she found it an enormously enjoyable process. 'Occasionally we would squeak with pleasure over the perfection of the other's invention,' she remembered the following year. Jordan agreed: 'We were kind of trying to outdo each other, in a way, [over] what you could do with cinema, how you could make something that broke all the narrative rules.' Writing in the *Independent* several years later, he implied that it was she who drove this dynamic:

> I have never before or since felt the same sense of excitement, of the absolutely free play of an imagination at work as she translated the words, images and ironies of her fictional world into the blunt instrument that constitutes a screenplay. I received each page with a mixture of delight and terror – delight at the sheer originality of what was emerging, terror as I would wonder how on earth I was going to do justice to her conceptions on the screen.

They quickly realised that brief sentences in the original short story – 'A witch from up the valley once turned an entire wedding party into wolves because the groom had settled on another girl' – could be developed into whole narrative strands, and they decided to employ a framing device that would allow them to move freely between scenes that bore little or no direct relation to one another. Drawing on the structures of two films they both admired – *The Saragossa Manuscript* by Polish director Wojciech Has, and *Valerie and Her Week of Wonders* by Czechoslovakian director Jaromil Jireš – they constructed the script around the dream of an early-teenaged girl called Rosaleen, and the stories that her grandmother tells her within her dream. The film conjures the psychic atmosphere of Rosaleen's adolescence: we first encounter her in a room strewn with clothes and books, a room stuffy with 'a sense of oppressive heat, oppressive and unfocussed sensuality, adolescent turbulence'. She has been trying on her sister's make-up – a transgression into the forbidden world of adulthood. As in *The Magic Toyshop*, it is the heroine's attempts to slough off her childhood that make everything fall apart. Throughout the film runs the metaphor of adolescence as a dark, humid forest, filled with frights and enticements.

But while there's a thematic consistency to *The Company of Wolves*, the film makes no attempt to tell a coherent story. It is a work of high surrealism: the framing device of Rosaleen's dream is largely an excuse to bombard the viewer with strange and disturbing scenes and images. A lot of it wasn't intended to signify anything in particular. At one point, Rosaleen runs away from an 'amorous boy' and climbs a tree, towards a stork's nest in the crook of a bough. The bird flies away, and Rosaleen looks into the nest, which contains four eggs and a small mirror with a gilt handle. She begins applying her lipstick in the mirror. As she does so, the four eggs burst open to reveal four statuettes of babies (or actual babies in the original script). Rosaleen takes one home to show her grandmother; when she opens her cupped hands to reveal the statuette, it sheds a single tear. Angela, who was five months pregnant while they were working on the script, singled out this scene as a pure product of her unconscious. 'When we finished [the script] I realised there were a great many more eggs, babies, foetuses and pregnancies in that movie than there are in most movies,' she told an interviewer. 'I didn't do it intentionally, it just got in.'

The only constraints on the writing of the film were those of the medium of cinema itself. Angela wanted it to end with Rosaleen waking from her dream and diving into her bedroom floor, as into a pool of water. 'It was such a simple image, it would be so easy to do now,' Jordan reflected in 2014. 'But then it was impossible.' Instead, it ends with Rosaleen waking from her dream, and screaming in terror as a pack of wolves burst into her house. Angela was dismayed: 'When I went to the screening I sat with Neil and I was enjoying the film very much and thinking that it had turned out so well – just as I had hoped,' she told an interviewer a few years later. 'Until the ending, which I couldn't believe – I was so upset. I said, "You've ruined it." He was apologetic.'

By the middle of July, Angela's stamina was beginning to flag. 'It's been a tough spring and summer, so far,' she wrote to Rikki Ducornet:

> I've been working some eighteen or (as it seems) twenty hours a day on a movie project which may or may not come to anything – the project is arty as all hell, and happily it's not my job to persuade City bankers it will make them as much money as a fast-food concession. It's certainly useful work to have done, and I've learned a lot. But whether what I've learned will be put to any use is a different matter.

In fact, it was put to use almost immediately. Steve Woolley of Palace Pictures secured a budget of $2.5 million for The Company of Wolves via ITC Entertainment. 'I was surprised we got funding for it, I have to say,' Jordan later admitted. At the time, though, he didn't miss a beat. He quickly went to work with set designer Anton Furst (who went on to create the sets for Stanley Kubrick's *Full Metal Jacket* and Tim Burton's *Batman*) and prosthetics expert Christopher Tucker (who had turned John Hurt into John Merrick for David Lynch's *The Elephant Man*). Angela visited Shepperton Studios several times while the sets were being built. 'She was terribly excited by seeing this world that we had written together emerge in physical form,' remembered Jordan. 'I think it was a great experience for her.' The film was shot over nine weeks at Shepperton, from January to March 1984, with a cast that included Sarah Patterson as Rosaleen, Angela Lansbury as her grandmother, Terence Stamp as the Devil, and Stephen Rea as a young man who disappears on his wedding night, only to return, many years later, as a werewolf.

At the end of July – with a third draft of *The Company of Wolves* freshly completed – Angela and Mark returned to Florence, via Geneva on the outward journey. They had planned to visit Rikki and Guy Ducornet again on their way back to England, but heavily pregnant in the Italian heat, Angela found that she wasn't enjoying herself very much, and by the end of August she wanted to get home as quickly as possible. The symptoms of pregnancy were wearing her down: 'I sleep for approximately 12 hours a day, sometimes more, vast, deep, inexorable, irresistible sleep,' she wrote to Rikki Ducornet. 'My active life has dwindled to almost nothing, & I scarcely lift a pen.' She said that she and Mark were both 'nervous but cheerful'.

Back in London, she concentrated on the last of her reading for the Booker Prize. On 21 September she met with her fellow judges to hammer out a shortlist. They settled on *Rates of Exchange* by Malcolm Bradbury; *Life and Times of Michael K* by J. M. Coetzee; *Flying to Nowhere* by John Fuller; *The Illusionist* by Anita Mason; *Shame* by Salman Rushdie; and *Waterland* by Graham Swift. The media forecasts of a shortlist dominated by women had been hilariously wide of the mark, but the only journalist to comment on this turn-up was *Private Eye*'s 'Bookworm', who attributed it to infighting among the female judges ('there should have been three novels by women writers on the shortlist, but the three women judges couldn't agree on them, so there's only one').

The wider media response was less openly sexist, but it was just as full of sound and fury. In his *Sunday Telegraph* column, the reliably contrarian Auberon Waugh declared that the six shortlisted books were badly written and boring, and that by promoting them over the likes of William Trevor, Molly Keane and Francis King, 'Booker does a grave disservice to the novel.' There was a minor kerfuffle, a few days after the shortlist announcement, when 'similarities' were noticed between John Fuller's *Flying to Nowhere*, a whodunit set in a monastery in medieval Wales, and Umberto Eco's newly translated *The Name of the Rose*, a whodunit set in a monastery in medieval Italy. Fuller released a statement via his publishers, Salamander Press, to the effect that he had been working on the novel since 1977 – three years before *The Name of the Rose* appeared in Italy – and that he had the notebooks to prove it.

Over the next few weeks, Angela reread the six shortlisted titles, and tried to prepare for the arrival of her baby. In the second week of October, she went for her final scan, and learned that she was going to have a boy ('there was no way of ignoring it'). On 19 October – '3 weeks minus 3 days' before her due date – she wrote to Rikki Ducornet:

> There has been a lot of activity, internally, yesterday & the day before & I thought he was going to jump the gun, but it's all settled down, now. Thank goodness, since nothing is ready – my taxes not filed; the bedroom not painted; Mark's kiln not built; just a couple of sacks of second-hand babygros & a Moses basket leant by my oldest friend [Corinna Sargood] stacked up in the hallway. I am the size of a house & sleep approx. 18 hours a day. They tell me to make the most of sleeping, as it will be the last chance I have for some months, if not years. But all goes well, basically, & I'm sure <u>he</u> won't care if the bedroom isn't an interior decorator's masterpiece . . . Whether he'll care if the tax inspector takes his mother away to prison is another matter.

* * *

At 3.30 p.m. on Wednesday 26 October, the Booker judges met at Bucklersbury House – the monolithic building in the City of London where Booker McConnell Ltd had its headquarters – to decide on a winner. Angela was still supporting *Shame*, and so was Terence Kilmartin, but Peter Porter and Libby Purves were both behind *Life and Times of Michael K*. Fay Weldon was left to cast the deciding vote. She asked each of her fellow judges to read out a favourite sentence from the novel they thought should win, and to present a closing argument. Then they took a short break while she mulled it over. When they returned, she asked for another argument. After listening to them, she decided that the prize should go to Rushdie – no, Coetzee – no, Rushdie, definitely Rushdie. 'It was a to-and-fro thing,' she remembered. 'I've never known anything so knife-edge.' Finally, with only minutes to go until the start of an embargoed press conference for the literary editors of national newspapers – as Martyn Goff, the prize's administrator, had his hand on the door – Weldon decided that the winner was Coetzee. Angela was disappointed, but she bore it, by all accounts, with good grace.

The prize-giving ceremony at Stationers' Hall that evening was 'a nightmare & a strain'. It was a much more glamorous occasion than it had been in previous years, and it was clear that everything had been carefully arranged to facilitate the live television broadcast: the cameras were intrusive, and many of the guests became irritated when, before they started rolling, instructions were issued on when to applaud. The great and the good of the London literary world were there, including the novelists Margaret Drabble and Rosamond Lehmann; the biographer, critic and television presenter Hermione Lee; the editors of the *London Review of Books* and the *Times Literary Supplement*; the minister for the arts, Lord Gowrie; and all of the shortlisted authors except for J. M. Coetzee, who had asked if he could be 'excused the ordeal of travelling 8,000 miles' from South Africa. On Angela's table, as well as Mark, were the literary agent Peter Janson-Smith, the writer Derwent May, the translator and critic Malcolm Imrie, and a couple of people associated with Booker McConnell. They were subjected to a four-course meal accompanied by 'very good Italian wines', and followed by coffee and port. Eight and a half months pregnant, Angela found it all extremely trying.

Fay Weldon gave a speech in which she expressed pleasure at living in an age when novelists were 'highly thought of and eminently respectable,' before proceeding to berate the publishers in the room for not appreciating their 'raw material' properly. When she was finished, Clive Bradley, the president of the Publisher's Association, walked across the room and remonstrated with her agent, Giles Gordon – actually punching him according to some accounts.

But the occasion is remembered today less for Weldon's divisive speech than for breakfast television presenter Selina Scott's incompetent hosting for the BBC. She questioned 'how valid it is' for novelists to write about things that they haven't personally experienced, and on live television upset

Weldon, first of all, by asking if she'd actually read all the submitted books, and then Angela, by asking what she thought of the choice of winner. 'I'm one of the judges,' Angela said, visibly embarrassed. 'Does that exclude me from offering an opinion?' 'I'm sorry about that, what's your name?' Scott responded, before blundering on: Had Coetzee been her first choice? 'You shouldn't ask a question like that,' Angela demurred.

The following day, Angela was admitted to the South London Hospital for Women with high blood pressure and swollen feet. As she was being examined ('flat on my back, dress pulled up, knickers down, vulnerable, helpless, undignified'), the consultant obstetrician – a woman whom Angela described as looking like Margaret Thatcher 'minus the peroxide and the schlap' – asked her how she was feeling. Angela provided several versions of the exchange that followed this enquiry, the details of which vary in a few insignificant ways, but the basic gist of which remains the same. This one is from the brief account of her confinement that she wrote the following month for *New Society*:

> I try a little joke. It backfires. God, how it backfires. 'How do you feel?' 'A bit apprehensive,' I say. 'Not so much about the birth itself as about the next twenty or thirty years.' The consultant . . . turns on me a face costive with high moral seriousness. 'You have done the right thing in not having an abortion,' she says. 'But there is still time. If you have any doubts at all, I urge you to seriously discuss adoption with your husband – I know he's only a common-law husband, of course.'

If these remarks had been designed to upset Angela, they couldn't have succeeded much better than they did. Her indignation at the consultant's self-righteousness, intrusiveness and impregnable literal-mindedness is understandable, but perhaps she was also remembering her two previous pregnancies, and felt that she was being attacked at a point where she was vulnerable. That would certainly explain the violence of her reaction. 'Each time I think about it, the adrenalin surges through my veins. I want to kill this woman, I want the BMA [British Medical Association] to crucify her,' she wrote to Lorna Sage several days after the event. 'There would have been a round of *applause* if I'd kicked her in the crotch.'

She may also have felt that she was being persecuted because of her age. The consultant informed her that it was hospital policy to keep older women under observation for two weeks prior to delivery, and that she should go home to pack a bag, then return immediately; Angela suspected that she'd made this requirement up on the spot.

The ward in which she spent the next fortnight was 'perfectly okay . . . like a girls' dorm, & rather dreamy & soporific'. It was full of 'big, soft girls, all moving very slowly, as if under water'. Angela spent most of her time reading and watching television. She went into labour (or so she claimed in a letter to the writer and AIDS activist Simon Watney, whom she had met via an anti-censorship event at the Royal Festival Hall) watching Abel Gance's 1927 silent epic *Napoleon*.

Alexander Robert Pearce was born early in the morning of Monday 7 November 1983, when Angela was exactly forty-three and a half years old, and Mark was twenty-eight. Alexander was Hugh Stalker's middle name, and Robert was chosen in honour of Coover, whom Angela nominated as the baby's godfather ('in a secular way'), while Carmen Callil and Elizabeth Hardwick were his godmothers (or 'Marx-mother' and 'honorary aunt' respectively). An episiotomy had been required to deliver him, and Angela was doped with pethidine when the midwife gave him to her. 'I said something feeble to him,' she wrote in her journal. 'I forget what.'

Even at this heightened moment, she retained a no-nonsense attitude towards the requirements of motherhood. When the midwife instructed her to look deep into her son's eyes while breastfeeding ('It helps with the bonding'), she was severely unimpressed:

Good grief! Aren't we allowed any choice in the matter, he and I? Can't I learn to love him for himself, and vice versa, rather than trust to Mother Nature's psycho-physiological double bind? And what of his relationship with his father, who has no breasts? Besides, it's very difficult to look him in the eye. He fastens on the nipple with the furtive avidity of a secret tippler hitting the British sherry, glancing backwards to make sure nobody else gets there first. When he strikes oil, he instantly becomes comatose. Am I supposed to poke him into consciousness: 'Hey, baby, don't nod off, we're supposed to be bonding' . . . It's all part of the mystification in which the whole process of childbirth is so richly shrouded. For he is doomed to love us, at least for a significant period, because we are his parents. The same goes for us. That is life. That's the hell of it.

Angela tended, as in that passage, to frame the emotional consequences of having a baby in terms of parenthood rather than motherhood. The latter concept was too emphatically gendered, and loaded with too many difficult associations; the former allowed her to acknowledge her devotion to Alex in a way that didn't compromise her identity. With one small semantic switch she could talk freely about how happy he made her, and about how life-changing an event his birth had been. 'Possibly the only truth that I've established about being a parent', she told the writer Lisa Appignanesi just over a year later, 'is that you don't know anything about unrequited love until you've had children.'

CHAPTER TWENTY-ONE

A *lifestyle of paradoxical propriety*

Angela felt grotty for weeks after Alex's birth: she was constantly tired, and suffered from a fever, chills and stomach pains. On 23 November she was diagnosed as having a puerperal infection, which she recognised with some alarm as what had killed Mary Wollstonecraft in 1797. Fortunately, medical advances had reduced the affliction's mortality rate by 1983: Angela was given a ten-day course of antibiotics and advised to refrain from drinking and sex. But she retained a sense of having endured archaic hardships. 'The entire accouchement has been more like that of a 19th century literary lady than that of a twentieth century one,' she wrote to Simon Watney on 14 December.

They spent Christmas with Hughie and Joan, who had moved back to North Yorkshire, where Hughie had taught music at Giggleswick School in the 1960s. Angela's father came down from Scotland to exchange 'tooth-less grins' with the baby. Mark drove them the whole way from London on Christmas Eve. 'Being anxious parents, travelling that far with a baby, making sure he was comfortable and warm, we were tired,' he remembered. 'It took us so long to get up there . . . we stopped at practically every service station.'

Angela found it hard to relax even after they'd arrived. In her journal, on Christmas Day, she wrote: 'Anxiety – cot death; will he choke on the teat? get fat/thin? never shit again? cease to love me/never love me?' Christine Downton, who visited them in London around this time, immediately sensed Angela's unease around the baby: 'Having this tiny thing depend-ent on you physically when you don't feel physically self-confident, I think was something that she was sort of cautious about. I think she was afraid of almost breaking him.' A few years later, Angela told Susannah Clapp that having a child was 'the beginning of never not feeling anxious'.

Shortly before Alex's birth, Angela had been invited to spend the first academic term of 1984 as writer-in-residence at the University of Adelaide. The position lasted from 12 March until 11 May, and came with a fee of $4,000 (about £2,500) paid in two instalments, plus an additional weekly stipend of $155 (about £100) for food, rent and utilities. She was, according to her invitation, 'expected to provide a stimulus for the formal and informal study of literature, both within the Department and in the Adelaide community at large'. In practice this meant doing much what she had done at the University of Sheffield: making herself available to students, and giving the odd reading or lecture, but not teaching regular classes. After checking that she could bring Mark and Alex with her as dependants, she accepted. As the start of term approached, she looked forward to the trip: 'A friend of a friend . . . took his degree at Adelaide and makes the city sound paradisal. (Those flocks of cockatoos homing into the trees along the boulevards in the early evening light . . . Can it be true? I can't wait!)'

Returning to London after Christmas, she arranged everything – flights, visas, currency – in a rush. On 7 January she wrote to Michael Tolley, the chairman of the English department, letting him know her requirements vis-à-vis accommodation: 'Obviously, a pretty place, with a veranda or a balcony and slatted wooden blinds and so on would be nice . . . but not essential! But we do need somewhere fully, though not ~~necessarily~~ elaborately, furnished, with a minimum of cooking utensils, crockery, etc.' Finishing the letter, she worried that she'd been too delicate about the level of luxury she was after. As a PS, she added: 'a pretty place would be nice if it's possible; I admit it! (Perhaps more essential than we'd care to admit.)'

They set out on the morning of Sunday 26 February. At the airport in Singapore, where they had to transfer to another flight, Angela felt the 'wet heat of Asia' on her face, and was filled with nostalgia for her time in Japan. When they reached Adelaide, several hours later, it was the light, rather than the heat, that dazzled her: 'when I got out of the plane . . . I felt as if I'd just cleaned my glasses. It was the clearing of a haze.' Her enthusiasm only intensified as she saw more of the country. 'I like it more than anywhere I've ever been except Italy,' she told Carmen. In her journal, she wrote:

The drama of the birth of <u>this</u> nation is utterly different to that of the States; it is the story of how the poor, the outcast, the dispossessed of Britain came to inherit the most beautiful & most abundant country in the world . . . due to the negligence & stupidity & snobbism of the ruling class. It is a story with a moral too close to that of certain of the scriptures to be altogether comfortable, especially since, if Australia continues with its anti-nuclear policy, she may very well inherit the earth. But they're not in the least <u>meek</u>.

There were only a couple of drawbacks. 'The person at the Uni who invited me is <u>awful</u>,' she wrote to Carmen. 'He found us the most hideous apartment a ½ hour drive into the (hideous) suburbs; it's called a home unit, has a simulated leather 3 piece suite & a brick yard out back with a clothes drier in it.' It says something about Angela's outlook that – for all her expressions of solidarity with the working class – she was so distressed at the thought of staying there. After a week, they moved to a bungalow on Childers Street, a wide, tree-lined avenue in the sturdily bourgeois residential district of North Adelaide. It wasn't fancy – there was a simple sitting room at the front, a basic kitchen behind, and a small bedroom off to one side – but it was at least a free-standing house, a short walk from the city centre.

As it turned out, the lack of a pretty place didn't really matter when it was so pretty outside. 'It was like a miracle every day,' Mark remembered. Angela loved watching the sunsets – 'the most triumphantly vulgar sunsets in the world' – and being surrounded by so much exotic flora and wildlife. She wrote to Fleur Adcock, who had once given her a book about bird-watching, listing all the varieties of parrot that came to settle in the trees outside her window.

Above all, though, she liked the inhabitants of Australia: 'My! but they know how to have a good time,' she wrote in an abortive piece of journalism about the trip. 'It is one of those characteristics, like extraversion and being nice to children, that are so <u>unBritish</u> about Australians.' Peter Porter – her fellow Booker Prize judge and an expatriate Australian – had given her some advice on how to behave when she arrived: 'Don't praise anything,' he'd told her. 'They'll be suspicious of praise from a Pom. It'll make them think there may be something wrong.' In her article, Angela wrote: 'I now suspect this may have been my introduction to that . . . great Australian pastime, having people on.' She quickly came to admire this 'curiously selfless style of humour, planting a joke in an unsuspecting carrier and letting him take it away with him'. A British academic who'd recently returned from Australia had told her that koalas explode – she asked some Australians whether this was true. They 'slowly, richly, started to chuckle. It is a rare, a cherishable event when a tease such as this homes back to Australia. They were kind. They did not mock. They praised the anonymous perpetrator of the canard.'

In the week before the start of term, Angela participated in Writers' Week at the Adelaide Festival. Authors from across the English-speaking world, including André Brink (from South Africa), John McGahern (from Ireland), Bruce Chatwin, Salman Rushdie and David Harsent (from the UK), and Elizabeth Jolley and Thomas Keneally (from Australia), were there. On the evening of Saturday 3 March, a lavish dinner was put on for all of them. Among the guests was the Australian novelist and artist Barbara Hanrahan – a profoundly nervous forty-five-year-old woman, with long fair hair and broad, sculpted features – who revered Angela Carter's work. Meeting her hero in the flesh was an overwhelming experience for Hanrahan: 'I did like her so much,' she wrote in her diary. 'She is lovely with her crinkly grey hair and her pink face and her nose was running a little in the cold . . . She was so nice and unassuming and gentle.' The feeling was mutual: 'she's very, very nice', Angela wrote to Carmen. But Hanrahan was upset when she discovered that her idol had a baby: 'I felt disappointed, of course. I don't think of her and babies.' That was one downside of Angela's rapidly expanding reputation: the people she met from now on would often have a preconceived image of her in which they were passionately invested, and she wouldn't always correspond to the way they'd invented her for themselves.

Over the next week, Angela took part in panel discussions on 'Fantasy as Reality' and 'Living on the Edge', and gave several readings. The majority of events took place in a bright candy-striped marquee, with an adjoining bookshop and bar, on the lawns across from the Festival Centre. One day, over lunch, Rushdie introduced her to Bruce Chatwin – the famously charismatic author of In Patagonia – whose dusty blond hair, finely wrought features and brooding blue eyes tended to have a magnetic affect on men and women alike. 'Angela was initially quite reluctant, because I'm not sure that she was really that fond of his work,' Rushdie remembered. Chatwin picked up on her coolness at once, and made a determined effort to win her over – 'We must celebrate,' he announced as they shook hands, and immediately set off to find two bottles of expensive wine – and by the end of lunch they were laughing and gossiping like old friends. Angela had no patience for bullshit (especially if it involved mystification of any sort, a charge that might be levelled at some of Chatwin's work), but she wasn't immune to a bit of old-fashioned charm.

During that week she also met and became friends with the novelist Elizabeth Jolley. Born in England in 1923, Jolley had moved to Australia in her mid-thirties; she was almost sixty when she published her first novel, *Palomino*, in 1980, but she had soon established herself as 'the laureate of the dotty' (as her obituary in the *Guardian* put it), a witty chronicler of the eccentric and the grotesque. A physically slight, grey-haired woman – with birdlike features and intelligent blue eyes that gazed out sympathetically from behind wire-framed glasses – she cultivated a deceptively vague manner. She advised Angela on how to help Alex cope with the heat: 'You must do with him what we do with the chickens. Put him in the bath and pour lukewarm water over him from a watering can.' Angela was impressed: 'I decided I must at once read everything this woman had written.' Once she had done so, she was even more impressed. She wrote to Carmen, imploring her to publish some of Jolley's books in the UK: 'the only writer who is at all like her is Grace Paley . . . Surely you can do her! She ought to be a Virago Modern Classic; but anyway, ought to be published in the UK at all costs.'

Adelaide is a premeditated city, plotted with geometric precision: the streets are arranged in a grid, and the five major public squares are distributed in a quincunx. An enormous swathe of parkland enfolds the city centre. Angela walked into her office at the university every weekday morning, a mile and a half from Childers Street through the park. 'It was like walking into fairyland,' Mark remembered. He'd push Alex around the botanical gardens for a while each morning, before meeting Angela for lunch by the artificial river on campus. She sat in her office for most of the day, working on the stories that appeared in *Black Venus*, and Mark acted as a full-time father. (He always changed Alex's nappies, Barbara Hanrahan noted in her diary.)

Between February and May, Alex doubled in size, turned brown in the constant sunshine, and made frustrated attempts at crawling. Angela kitted him out in T-shirts emblazoned with such slogans as 'Little Aussie', 'Fair Dinkum Little Aussie', and 'All Australian Kid'. She regretted that he wouldn't remember anything about the trip: 'it would be nice to think that his first memories would be of parrots & kangaroos & frangipanis', she wrote to Elizabeth Hardwick.

At the end of term they rented a car and drove east, through almost 1,000 miles of grass and scrubland, to Sydney. Angela thought that it was 'ravishing . . . almost too beautiful a city, like a dress that is too good to wear'. After a week or so they headed south to Carmen Callil's home town of Melbourne, where Angela was giving a reading at Deakin University, before flying home on 27 May. ('No time to look around,' she wrote to Carmen, 'which makes me feel disloyal.') They were sad to be leaving: Angela thought she might return to write a travel book about South Australia, although she suspected that Chatwin and Rushdie, who had headed off into the interior after the Adelaide Festival, were planning to do just that. (In fact, their trip produced *The Songlines*, Chatwin's book about aboriginal culture, which Angela reviewed enthusiastically for the *Guardian* when it was published in 1987.) It's tantalising to imagine what Angela Carter could have made of this idea: the notes she made about Australia in her journal show just what a lively, fascinating book it might have been.

London seemed bleached and bitterly cold after three months in Australia. 'It was very depressing indeed returning home,' Angela wrote to Rikki Ducornet; neither she nor Mark could settle back down to work. They talked about returning to Australia for the long term: they would travel around for a while, deciding which part of the country they liked best – taking into consideration what was convenient for their work and Alex's schooling – and then put down roots. In the meantime, they dressed Alex in his 'Little Aussie' T-shirts, and bought a budgerigar that they named Adelaide. Their two cats – Cocker and Ponce – watched balefully as the bird swooped freely round the kitchen.

A few days after returning to London, Angela received a letter from the British–Pakistani novelist Zulfikar Ghose, who was professor of creative writing at the University of Texas. 'I'm in a position to recommend writers [for visiting professorships],' he told her. 'I admire your fiction and would like to recommend you.' Still pining for Australia, Angela jumped at the opportunity of living abroad for another few months (apparently forgetting the vow she had made never to return to the USA after her lonely year at Brown). It was agreed that she would spend January to May 1985 in Austin, Texas, receiving a salary of 'between $17,000 and $18,000'. She assured prospective landlords that 'me and my husband and, indeed, the baby are obsessively careful with other people's property, and engage in a lifestyle of such paradoxical propriety and primness it has been compared to that of Magritte'.

If describing Mark as her husband (even though 'we never got round to getting married') was true in spirit, then describing her lifestyle as one of 'paradoxical propriety and primness' was unimpeachably honest. The paradox arose because their domestic arrangements did have a fairly thick coating of bohemianism. Visitors to The Chase tended to emphasise the idiosyncratic decor and general disorganised clutter. 'Downstairs was carnival,' wrote Susannah Clapp: 'violet and marigold walls, and scarlet paintwork. A kite hung from the ceiling of the sitting room, the shelves supported menageries of wooden animals, books were piled on chairs.' Ian McEwan drew a similar picture: 'the comfortable junk-shop furniture is cat-violated, books cascade from the shelves above the television, an alp of dirty dishes dominates the sink.' The growing contingent of pets added to the anarchic atmosphere. Adelaide was soon joined by another budgerigar called Chubbeleigh, and the Persian rugs became scattered with feathers and birdseed. The kitchen surfaces were often invisible beneath assorted bric-a-brac: fairground art, Victorian mantel clocks, and the plates and bowls Mark made, which were 'beautiful, but also enormous', wrote Lorna Sage, 'so that they hardly fitted on the makeshift kitchen table, and you felt like a guest at a giants' feast.'

But in many other ways, Angela and Mark were by the mid-1980s paragons of middle-class respectability. They didn't take drugs or drink too much, or even smoke by the time Alex was born. They kept regular hours and observed orderly routines. They were increasingly well off – in the 1984–5 tax year, Angela anticipated an income of between £40,000 and £50,000 – and they had a few expensive tastes, such as foreign travel and (in Angela's case) opera. They read the *Guardian*, listened to BBC Radio 3, and watched the *Nine O'Clock News*. Friends came round for dinner at least a couple of times a month, and Angela cooked something inspired by Jane Grigson, Elizabeth David or Prosper Montagné: trout with flaked almonds, perhaps, or authentic cassoulet. They took care of their garden, which featured climbing roses and an apple tree, and enjoyed showing it off ('I particularly enjoy to see guests walking round the garden with glasses in their hands,' Angela wrote to Robert Coover. 'It fulfils some deep bourgeois fantasy of mine'). They even had a cleaning lady – the aptly named Sara Maclean – who came a couple of times a week until Alex was about two, when she began coming every day. 'Angela looked wild, but she was the gentlest of women,' Maclean remembered. 'The kind of woman you wanted your mum to be.'

The Company of Wolves was released in Britain on 21 September 1984, and received its premiere at the Odeon Leicester Square. It had been given an 18 certificate by the British Board of Film Classification, removing at a stroke a large share of its potential audience, and the London Underground had refused to display adverts that showed a wolf's snout protruding from a man's mouth. These setbacks annoyed Angela – she complained of 'Thatcherite censorship . . . [they] couldn't put their finger on it but they knew something was wrong' – but they didn't seem to slow the film's momentum much. The reviews were ecstatic. 'Regardless of whether the notion of a cinema renascence in this country is or is not a chimera,' wrote David Robinson in *The Times*, '*The Company of Wolves* is undeniably the most ambitious British film of the period.' In the *Observer*, Philip French agreed: 'Carter's feminist-gothic combines well with Jordan's mystical-cinematic tale-spinning, and they have come up with a magical picture that takes us back to the dream worlds of Cocteau and of Powell and Pressburger, and beyond that to German expressionist films of the 1920s like *Caligari* and Pabst's psychoanalytic *Secrets of the Soul*.' The film took $4 million worldwide at the box office and was nominated for four BAFTAS (Best Costume Design, Best Make-up, Best Production Design/Art Direction, and Best Visual Special Effects); the following year, Neil Jordan was named Director of the Year at the London Critics' Circle Film Awards.

That month, Angela was paid more attention by the British media than at any other point in her life. *Nights at the Circus* was published a week after *The Company of Wolves* was released, on 29 September 1984, and the publicity campaigns for the two works gained impetus from one another. The celebrated photographers Jerry Bauer and Eve Arnold both visited The Chase to take Angela's portrait. Long profiles appeared in the *Guardian* (where it was noted that 'having a baby at 44 [*sic*] has happened at the same time as her first great media success . . . her house in Clapham . . .

shows no mark of fame or fortune'), the *Sunday Times* (by Ian McEwan, who wrote that '*Nights at the Circus* will certainly confirm her as a stylist and fantasist, but will also force recognition of an impressive development in the writer's career') and *City Limits* (where she was described as 'the new hero of women's writing'). An interviewer for the *Face* was surprised to discover that 'Angela Carter . . . is not your typical tub-thumping feminist . . . Men per se are not high on her hit list. Her real contempt is reserved for those bastions of the Establishment that curtail freedom – the police and the church.' But she was certainly enough of a feminist to unnerve those men who were sensitive to criticism: a rave review of *The Company of Wolves* by the novelist, critic and biographer Peter Ackroyd in the *Spectator* ('one's pleasure in seeing it is more than a reaction against the ever-increasing restrictiveness of conventional social drama. This is, in fact, an alternative form of cinema') drew a furious letter from one reader:

> What we have in this hailed poetic and magical farrago is not only feminist hysteria and man-hatred but intellectual and artistic muddle purporting to be fantasy and imaginative subjectivity. The disgusting self-indulgence of Ms Carter in transforming wolves via their flayed carcasses into the hated phallus image is rendered worse by the occasional backtracking to suggest some men are tolerable. I protest against the adulation of this woman's interminable vapouring.

Angela enjoyed all the attention, both positive and negative. She went to the Toronto Film Festival, where *The Company of Wolves* was being screened, and wrote to Simon Watney: 'Fame has made me so unpleasant Mark packed me off to Canada for a week.'

The announcement of the Booker Prize shortlist on 19 September was a bit of a dampener on her spirits. It comprised *Empire of the Sun* by J. G. Ballard, *Flaubert's Parrot* by Julian Barnes, *Hotel du Lac* by Anita Brookner, *In Custody* by Anita Desai, *According to Mark* by Penelope Lively and *Small World* by David Lodge. *Nights at the Circus* – along with *The Only Problem* by Muriel Spark and *Money* by Martin Amis – was named by almost every commentator as a glaring omission. W. L. Webb, the literary editor of the *Guardian* and a close friend of Angela, hazarded that the novel 'may have been thought too overreaching by the rather conservative panel of judges'. In fact, two of them – the literary journalist Anthony Curtis and the novelist Polly Devlin – had included *Nights at the Circus* in their personal shortlists, but these weren't released to the public, and the remaining three judges (the Oxford don Richard Cobb, the poet and novelist John Fuller – whose *Flying to Nowhere* had been shortlisted when Angela was a judge the previous year – and the Labour MP Ted Rowlands) had dismissed it from the start. When the shortlist was announced, 'a deathly hush came through the Chatto offices', remembered Andrew Motion, who was the poetry editor there from 1983 to 1989. 'Carmen was devastated.' But she wasn't the type to stay quiet for long: 'I'm astounded,' she told the *Guardian* on 23 September. 'It's a great piece of writing, and she's a great writer . . . there should be some acknowledgement of great writing on the shortlist.' Polly Devlin broke the code of *omertà* that usually governs the Booker panel's deliberations to tell journalists that she was 'bewildered' by her fellow judges' indifference to *Nights at the Circus*: 'It's a tour de force, an amazing book.'

Most of the reviewers agreed, and several used their columns as clubs with which to bash the Booker. In the *Evening Standard*, Paul Bailey wrote that the omission of *Nights at the Circus* struck him as 'a calculated insult to one of the boldest and most brilliant novelists writing in English . . . Carter has been robbed of an important – temporarily important – recognition of her extraordinary powers, powers that have never before been so dazzlingly demonstrated as they are in this inventive and continuously entertaining novel.' Even Martyn Goff, the Booker Prize administrator, made it clear that he disagreed with the judges. In a review for the *Daily Telegraph* he called *Nights at the Circus* 'a most impressive tour de force . . . a work of an extraordinary imagination, projected in style and words with great, justified, self-confidence . . . I doubt whether its imaginative force will be matched by any other novel this year.'

Though all of the reviews were full of praise, there were some criticisms stirred in as well. In the *London Review of Books*, Michael Wood called *Nights at the Circus* 'a very disconcerting narrative . . . It all sounds like parody, but of what? We need to understand that we have climbed, not into an imitation of some aspect of the turn-of-the-century, but into a self-mocking myth which at first, unlike Fevvers, has a little trouble getting off the ground. Things are clearer once . . . the novel moves from London to St Petersburg and Siberia.' Adam Mars-Jones, by contrast, in a review for the *Times Literary Supplement*, heaped most of his praise on the first part of the novel: '*Nights at the Circus* doesn't so much start as break like a wave; the first third of Angela Carter's new novel is a glorious piece of work.' He was considerably less keen on the second and third parts: 'Without Fevvers's voice and Walser's point of view the narrative falters. There were just as many impossibilities in the London section as there are in St Petersburg, but now they are presented directly rather than mediated through a character who may only be a charlatan or a freak.'

The critical acclaim must have helped with the disappointment of being excluded from the Booker shortlist, and further consolation arrived the following year, when *Nights at the Circus* was recognised by a couple of the smaller literary prizes. It was shortlisted in the novel category of the Whitbread Book Awards (losing out to Christopher Hope's *Kruger's Alp*), and was named joint winner – with J. G. Ballard's Booker-shortlisted *Empire of the Sun* – of the James Tait Black Memorial Prize, worth £3,000. Neither of these accolades was paid more than cursory attention by the media (the Whitbread shortlist wasn't even made public: 'it is the most secret prize of the 20th century', Carmen wrote to Angela), but that isn't to say they were devoid of prestige. The James Tait Black was Britain's oldest surviving literary award, and was judged by academics and graduate students at the University of Edinburgh: it had a certain dusty gravitas. Angela was delighted to be named as a winner. She wrote to Alastair Fowler, the Regius Professor of Literature at the University of Edinburgh, to say that she was 'pleased and proud – indeed, honoured – to share the James Tait Black prize with J. G. Ballard's *Empire of the Sun*! . . . I prize my prize . . . thank you.' Her happiness at being put on an equal footing with Ballard is poignant in light of the later reputation of *Nights at the Circus*. In 2012, two decades after her death, it was voted the best novel to have won the James Tait Black Memorial Prize in its ninety-three-year history: a field that included not only *Empire of the Sun*, but also novels by D. H. Lawrence, Graham Greene, Evelyn Waugh, Muriel Spark, Iris Murdoch, William Golding, Salman Rushdie, Alan Hollinghurst and Zadie Smith.

By the time of his first birthday – 7 November 1984 – Alex had developed thick dark hair in glossy corkscrew curls, plump and rosy cheeks, and a beatific smile. 'He was an impossibly beautiful child,' remembered Paul Bailey. 'He looked like a cherub. He could have been painted by one of the Italian masters, he was that pretty.' He crawled around with gusto, and was beginning to haul himself into a standing position from which to fall over. He could say one word – 'nana' – to identify his favourite fruit. 'He often murmurs "banana" to himself in a pleased way when no bananas are about,' Angela wrote in her journal.

She was immensely proud of him, and she and Mark were fiercely devoted parents – 'They more or less hovered over the cot every night until he went to sleep,' remembered Rebecca Howard – but she was rather less proud of her efforts to absorb him into a varied and productive lifestyle. She had written nothing of any length since he had been born. '[Children] do take up a lot of time,' she told Lisa Appignanesi in a conversation at the Institute of Contemporary Arts. 'I mean, they demand it – and you don't mind giving it to them . . . Obviously, intellectual activity and small children are incompatible.' She tried to take courage from the example of J. G. Ballard – who had brought up three children single-handedly, while producing masses of first-rate writing – but found that she couldn't recover the mental freedom to even start a new novel. 'Organising your life is almost impossible,' she told another interviewer, 'especially when you're used to having a certain kind of rhythm of work which has to be completely changed':

> I was forced, after 43 years of evasion, to come to terms with my own incompetence. There are lots of things that you can brush under the carpet about yourself until you're faced with somebody whose needs won't be put off. You can't actually tell them to go away and come back in five minutes. I realised that I'm actually an extremely incompetent person and I idle a lot. I've got to learn to live with that.

Since writing a novel was out of the question for the time being, she took on projects that didn't need to be obsessive. She signed a contract with Virago to edit a collection of stories provisionally titled *Pirate Jenny's Book of Tales for Girls and Women* – it was eventually published as *Wayward Girls and Wicked Women* – for which she received £2,000 for hardback and paperback publication. She was struck by how few stories about women (whatever the sex of their authors) treated their protagonists as moral beings in the fullest sense – how morality tended to be associated entirely with sexual conduct, such that a wayward girl was one who lost her virginity before marriage, and a wicked woman was an adulteress – and she set out to construct her anthology around stories that allowed their heroines greater scope for moral responsibility. The result is a fantastically wide-ranging collection, featuring stories from around the world. Angela's original selection included 'O, if I could but shiver!' by Christina Stead (Australia), 'The Debutante' by Leonora Carrington (UK), 'Life' by Bessie Head (Botswana), 'Three Feminist Fables' by Suniti Namjoshi (India), 'The Plums' by Ama Ata Aidoo

(Ghana), 'A Woman Young and Old' by Grace Paley (USA), 'The Long Trial' by Andrée Chedid (France), 'Aunt Liu' by Luo Shu (China), 'The Monkey' by Isak Dinesen (Denmark), and 'Acceptance of their Ways' by Mavis Gallant (Canada). 'There are some others I could include,' Angela wrote to Sarah Baxter at Virago, 'if some of these e.g. the Isak Dinesen or the Mavis Gallant, prove too expensive':

> one of them, by the Edwardian writer of the supernatural, Vernon Lee, is a very nice ghost story but it is <u>amazingly</u> long – forty or fifty pages of closely printed prose. However, it is also blissfully out of copyright. I am tempted to slip in a Katherine Mansfield, as she, too, is blissfully out of copyright besides being very, very good, but I don't want to cross lines with Hermione Lee's *The Secret Self* [a two-volume anthology of stories by women, including one by Angela Carter, which was published that year by the Everyman's Library] . . . That's why I'm not including a story by myself. Actually, that's not so; I think it would be bad form, is why.

Virago didn't share Angela's concerns about overlapping with *The Secret Self*, nor her ideas about what constituted good form. In the published version of *Wayward Girls and Wicked Women*, Vernon Lee's 'Oke of Okehurst' and Katherine Mansfield's 'The Young Girl', as well as Angela Carter's own 'The Loves of Lady Purple', replaced the Gallant, the Dinesen and the Stead.

Angela arrived in Austin, with her family in tow, on 7 January 1985. Zulfikar Ghose met them at the airport. 'We make an immediately distinctive trio,' Angela had written to him. 'Mark has a beard & I have long grey hair & the baby (God help us) is teething . . . We will look lost until you speak.' Ghose drove them to the house they were renting at 1908 Stamford Lane. It was a smallish place (but with an extensive garden, where, on 10 February 1985, Alex took his first steps) in the old neighbourhood of Tarrytown, a couple of miles west of the university. In spite of its proximity to the city centre, Angela felt that the neighbourhood had pretentions to a pastoral atmosphere: 'Some of the properties have streams running through the front lot, with little rustic bridges over them,' she wrote in her journal. Many of them also had wind chimes: 'the sound of madness'.

There were no sidewalks. The gardens extended all the way to the curb. This didn't bother most of the locals, who tended to drive everywhere;

walking to the grocery store, Angela and Mark attracted funny looks. Mark thought that the dead dogs they often saw in the streets probably fell out of the backs of speeding pickup trucks, and Angela noted that the majority of Austinites knew their city only as a 'series of interiors.' She was dismayed by the narrowness of their horizons. She wrote to Simon Watney: 'No foreign news at all in the Austin paper . . . Actually, there is scarcely any news from Houston or Dallas, even. "Parochial" is the word.' The city is widely known as a liberal enclave in ferociously conservative Texas, but Angela was appalled by the small-minded attitudes she encountered. 'Everybody is loony, here,' she wrote to Susannah Clapp. In her journal, she made a few sweeping, scornful remarks about them: 'boiled faces – boiled, innocent, arrogant, indifferent'.

The rampant capitalism she had complained of in Providence five years earlier was even more pronounced in Austin. By the mid-1980s the city was at the heart of the booming tech and aerospace industries, with corporations including IBM, Lockheed and Motorola operating plants there. Dozens of new office blocks were transforming downtown Austin from a laid-back shuffle of bars and bookstores into a utilitarian business district; property developers were covering the attractive limestone hills to the west of the city with grandiose mansions. 'Jesus, there's a lot of money in this town!' Angela wrote to Simon Watney. 'I am trying to find the local chapter of the Spartacus League, so I can join.' Her visits to the USA often propelled her further to the left, but rarely with quite so much momentum.

Even her hopes of a pleasant climate were dashed. On 11 January – one week after they arrived – Texas was stunned by a record-breaking blizzard, shrouding the state in up to fourteen inches of snow. For several days, the freak weather led the television news; schools and businesses closed, and the life of the city effectively ground to a halt. It was the last straw, as far as Angela was concerned. 'Texans think Texas is like Australia,' she wrote to Elizabeth Jolley. 'They are so wrong . . . we couldn't resist the temptation of warm weather, and were suitably punished for not resisting temptation.'

The University of Texas is one of the largest in the USA. Its campus – located about a mile from the chambers of the Texas State Capitol – is made up of several vast, geometrically arranged pink and white buildings, constructed in the Beaux Arts style. 'The buildings are constantly being washed,' Angela wrote in her journal. 'Men in rubber suits, hosing them down – fine spray of water, looking like dust, so everything is pink & pristine as a baby's bum.'

The English department was located in the Main Building, conspicuous for its 300-foot central tower, from which, on 1 August 1966, a student had shot fourteen people dead. By the mid-1980s there were around a hundred members of staff in the department. 'When I first joined . . . all but three or four of the professors were white males,' remembered Zulfikar Ghose:

> Things began to change in the late 1970s as regards race and gender, and so when Angela came there were several females, including two or three committed feminists, in the department. What I found most curious was that for the first couple of months of her visit none of the female professors made any attempt to approach Angela who everyone knew to be an iconic feminist figure.

It meant that she was fairly isolated, and didn't enjoy her time at the university any more than she enjoyed her experience of the surrounding city. She taught two undergraduate modules: a beginners' creative-writing course, on which about twenty students were enrolled, and a more advanced one with only ten students. She met both classes twice a week, on Tuesdays and Thursdays, for an hour and a half at a time. She had told Ghose that she didn't want to teach the beginners' course in the form of a workshop:

> I'd like to start off with a handful of narrative models, i.e. folk tales, some Calvino, some Chekhov short stories, take them apart to show how they're done, and go on from there, having given some idea of the resources of fiction. If this seems somewhat ambitious, the general scheme can be scaled down so it does not seem formidable. But I occasionally find myself saying to writing students: 'You'd find it much easier to write fiction if you'd actually read some', and it seems [that this course] is an opportunity to begin at the beginning.

The format that Angela proposed may well be the most valuable method of teaching creative writing, but it's also a good deal more labour intensive than a traditional workshop. She didn't think much of her students in Texas – she barely mentioned them in her letters or journal, and didn't recommend any of them to Carmen or Deborah, or to her American editor, Amanda Vaill – but she devoted vast reserves of time and energy to them nonetheless. 'She was always there,' remembered Mark. Between preparing her classes and reading her students' work, she wasn't able to do much writing of her own. She revised some of the stories that appeared in *Black Venus*, but didn't begin any new projects, or even write any journalism during this period. 'I'm working very hard at the university, and at my share of childcare at home,' she wrote to Carmen. 'It is a bugger . . . I am stressed, bushed, depressed, and have NO TIME. It's no fun, being here.'

Angela and Mark made as many trips out of town as they could manage during their four months in Austin. They drove to the city of Taylor, through enormous flat landscapes strewn with 'wooden, crazy, ramshackle' homesteads, to watch a bout of 'rattlesnake sacking' that they had seen advertised in a local paper. The event took place at a sort of country fair. Men in snakeskin Stetsons and tight jeans went, one by one, into a ring with Perspex walls. The ring was full of rattlesnakes. Using a hooked stick, they scooped as many snakes as they could into a bag before the referee blew his whistle. 'Mucho macho,' Angela wrote in her journal. 'The erectile nature of the rattler – it rears up its head, it swells, it hisses, it rattles, before it spits its venom – makes the symbolism of the whole thing even more blatant.'

Shortly afterwards they went to New Mexico, to San Antonio and Santa Fe, and over the border into Chihuahua. 'So many Mexican things have the quality of being garish & sinister at the same time,' Angela wrote admiringly in her journal. On the way back to Austin they stopped at a Native American reservation. 'It was so depressed,' remembered Mark, 'all these people kind of lethargically sitting round not even taking you in, everybody's on drugs. We just couldn't bring ourselves to be tourists, gawping at them . . . so we just drove off.'

In March they flew east for a 'blissful' week in Providence with the Coovers. The highlight of the trip was meeting John Hawkes – the author of such lavishly experimental, hypnotically burnished novels as *The Blood Oranges* and *Second Skin* – whose job Angela had covered when she was at Brown a few years before. 'He is as near to a great writer as these puny times provide, and an enchanting man,' she wrote to Carmen:

> He has big, bulbous eyes that roll around, giving the impression of some sort of flighty winged bug – he's tiny – & a strange, cracked, high-pitched voice with the delivery, often, of W. C. Fields. One of a kind, I'd say. Mark said you'd always want to keep an eye on him,

in case he was up to something, & I know what he means. Anyway, he's really something, really irresistible.

Contrasting Austin with Providence, she realised what it was that she most disliked about the former city: 'it is the <u>racism</u> I can't stand in Texas. It is very rarely overt . . . but it deforms everything.' She did in fact witness overt racism while she was there – at the rattlesnake sacking, she and Mark had stumbled into a store run by the Ku Klux Klan – and Mark remembers Austin being visibly divided along racial lines, the white community living on one side of the railway tracks, the black and Hispanic communities on the other, with very little interaction between the two. His own deeply suntanned skin and voluminous frizzy hair – not unlike an afro in appearance – meant that they sometimes attracted hostile stares when they went out together in the evenings. They returned home on 10 May, a few days after Angela's forty-fifth birthday. Barbara Hanrahan, who was in London for the summer, visited them at The Chase and noted in her diary that 'they are both fatter [than they were in Adelaide], all the food in Austin – they just ate and drank because there was nothing to do'.

CHAPTER TWENTY-TWO

I refuse to play in tragedy

Not long after she returned from Texas, Angela began recording menopausal symptoms in her journal. She described the hot flushes that often woke her in the night, the erratic course of her periods, the recurrent stabbing pain in the base of her spine. She also noted the ways in which her appearance was changing:

> roll of suet round my belly; breasts bigger, heavier – strange, all of a sudden, to be for the first time in my life a big-breasted woman at the age of 45; I've put on a stone since Alex, & giving up smoking – but my face is thinner, almost gaunt-looking . . . more & more often, I catch myself in the mirror looking like my father.

The comparison suggests how unsexed she felt (her mother had lived to be sixty-five, and there were plenty of other female relatives to whom she could have likened herself). 'I'm taking the psychological aspects of all this much more badly than I would have thought,' she wrote: 'aging, losing looks, not being looked at in the street, not being <u>desired</u>. I feel that I will change into a crone overnight.' She became short-tempered with Mark ('he bores & irritates me about equally. I don't see why I should put up with it any more') and was given to sudden eruptions of unhappiness ('I am like a vase filled with tears, tip me up & they spill'). She suffered from a sense of 'intense miserable isolation, of unlovedness, of quite blinding self-pity, of being exploited, unappreciated etc.; very unattractive feelings, these, but <u>que faire</u>, I feel them, am tormented by them.'

The hot flushes subsided after a while, but she continued to wake at three or four o'clock in the morning. Too tired to work, she would potter aimlessly around the house until she heard Alex singing his 'sweet, raucous, tuneless songs' around eight. The doctor thought that she was depressed. In early August 1986, she wrote: 'fourth day of the anti-depressants. Perky-ish.' It isn't clear how long she remained on them, but a diary that she kept in 1990 to track the last of her periods is filled with references to 'suicidal' moods and 'despair', and in her journal she was still writing things like 'I can feel myself drying out' and 'I feel my ugly age.'

These entries would have surprised most of her friends. Going by the uncombed disarray of her long grey hair (she looked 'like someone who'd been left out in a hurricane', said Andrew Motion) and her increasing indifference to fashion (she had a 'madwoman-in-the-attic look', said Lennie Goodings, 'she never dressed in your classic female way'), they believed that she had boldly, brazenly embraced the aging process. Her appearance changed 'by her own choice,' stressed Paul Barker, 'from adolescent to grandmother, from smart sprite to sapient witch'. Susannah Clapp agreed: 'She abandoned fashion with caustic flair and childlike defiance.' That was evidently what she wanted people to think – like the Chance sisters in *Wise Children*, she refused to behave as if it was somehow shameful not to be a young woman any more – but it didn't come as naturally as some assumed. She was, in middle age, still inventing herself, still consciously performing the role of the person she wanted to be.

Angela had signed a contract for *Black Venus*, her third collection of stories, on 2 January 1985, receiving an advance of £6,000, and the book was published in October. It was only a year since *Nights at the Circus* and *The Company of Wolves* had announced Angela Carter to a wider audience, and the reviews of the new book tended to assume some knowledge of her earlier work, or at least of her reputation. Janice Elliot, the *Sunday Telegraph* reviewer who had applauded *The Bloody Chamber* six years earlier, wrote that 'Black Venus displays the superbly witchy Angela Carter at her best: less difficult than before but no less dazzling.' Lorna Sage, reviewing the collection in the *Times Literary Supplement* alongside *Come Unto These Yellow Sands* (a collection of Angela's radio plays which had been published that January by Bloodaxe Books) suggested that 'admirers who like to think of her as all artifice, transgressions and transformations will find this collection uncomfortable, because there's no escaping the fact that Carter . . . thinks that the stories we tell ourselves, however bizarrely archetypal, grow out of – and into – particular realities'.

Others felt that the acclaim was getting out of hand. The poet Douglas Dunn, writing in the *Glasgow Herald*, singled out 'The Kitchen Child' (a rambunctious comedy about below-stairs shenanigans in an English country house) for praise, but found the collection as a whole much too self-conscious for its own good: 'Excellent as the writing of the title story undoubtedly is, the same being true of "The Cabinet of Edgar Allan Poe", both stories strike me as extreme forms of imaginative literary history and criticism more than they impress me as stories . . . What I find irritating in her work is its literariness.' In the *New Statesman*, the novelist and poet Grace Ingoldby expressed similar reservations: 'Angela Carter's writing is . . . much easier to admire than to enjoy.' Criticisms of this sort had been levelled at her work from the very beginning ('Miss Carter is too clever by half,' wrote B. A. Young in a first-novel round-up for *Punch* on 24 August 1966), but it was only now, as her reputation gathered momentum, that they became a significant refrain. Angela regarded them as reactionary in the extreme. 'Anti-intellectualism is the traditional characteristic of the British intelligentsia,' she had noted wearily in her 1983 programme about Jean-Luc Godard.

All the same, she spent much of 1986 revisiting her early work with a severity that matched her harshest detractors. Following the success of *The Company of Wolves*, she had been approached by Granada Television to write a screenplay of *The Magic Toyshop*. As had happened in 1969 – when she had first tried to adapt the novel for the screen – she found it a dull and gruelling process. 'I'm actually finding it very hard going because I don't believe it's a very good novel,' she told an interviewer for the lesbian magazine *Square Peg*. 'I don't know why they picked that one. I hadn't looked at it for 15 or 20 years, and now I'm immensely embarrassed by it.' Even so, she constructed a script that remains largely faithful to the novel, but which makes use of the visual medium to add a few fresh touches (Jonathan's dreamy love of boats is illustrated by a close-up on his glasses: 'reflected within them, a three-masted barque riding huge waves'). David Wheatley, who directed *The Magic Toyshop*, remembered talking to Angela about *Valerie and Her Week of Wonders* (which had also influenced *The Company of Wolves*) and the Powell and Pressburger film *The Tales of Hoffmann* while she was working on the script. It was shot in Liverpool (because south London no longer resembled the area in which the story was set) in November 1986, and was broadcast on ITV on 5 November 1988.

Meanwhile, Chatto & Windus was planning to reissue *Fireworks* and *Love*. Rereading the latter book plunged Angela back into the psychic atmosphere of her twenties, the lonely, airless decade of her marriage to Paul Carter. 'It still haunts me,' she said when Lisa Appignanesi asked her about the novel at the Institute of Contemporary Arts. She told Carmen that she was finding the process of going back over it 'upsetting', and that she wanted to do 'some quite extensive things to it – not rewriting, if I started on that I'd have to rewrite it completely, but quite a lot of cutting out and emending . . . I <u>do</u> want to do a bit of an afterword for this one.'

The revised edition of *Love* appeared in February 1987. In the afterword, Angela mentioned the novel's 'almost sinister feat of male impersonation, its icy treatment of the mad girl and its penetrating aroma of unhappiness'. But rather than dwelling on these qualities, she suggested that 'perhaps the best way of discussing the novel would really be to write a bit more of it', and devoted herself to inventing afterlives for the characters. One result of this decision was that she didn't have to write much about Annabel – the character whose mental isolation was modelled on Paul Carter's – since her fate was sealed at the end of the book ('even the women's movement would have been no help to her'). Most of the others are treated with a mixture of affection and disapproval. The psychologist who was based on Carole Roffe becomes the director of three pharmaceutical companies, hosts a radio phone-in on neurosis, and writes a non-fiction bestseller titled *How To Succeed Even Though You Are A Woman*. She drives a Porsche, 'rather fast'. Buzz manages 'a few early punk bands' and perfects a lifestyle of 'terminal chic' and 'paranoid seclusion' in New York City. Lee becomes 'rather a good teacher', lives in a south London street 'that is the twin of the one in which he grew up', and is rewarded with a stable relationship and children about whom he thinks (as Angela had thought about Alex): 'Oh, the pain of it . . . the exquisite pain of unrequited love.'

'As for me,' Angela wrote in an early draft of the afterword, 'I discovered the Women's Movement and put on weight. To both these factors I attribute my present psychic good health' – a line which suggests either that her use of antidepressants had been short-lived, or that she was determined to present herself as happy under any circumstances. Even so, she couldn't resist ending on a plangent note: 'I retain a special relationship to this novel; it is a haunted house and I am the ghost inside, trapped in the exquisite misery of youth.'

* * *

On 20 September 1985, Angela had written to the folklore scholar Jack Zipes: 'Alexander now weighs 16 kilos, but he can still only say "banana".' By the following summer, he had mastered a few more words, and deployed them at great volume, but he still wasn't stringing them together into sentences. He had, however, 'taken a great shine to the alphabet, especially the letters Q & W, and spends a lot of time writing them on his blackboard . . . It is possible he will learn to write before he speaks properly.'

He was still only two and a half, but in spite of her breezy tone Angela was becoming concerned, and she made an appointment for him to see a speech therapist at Clapham Manor Clinic. She told Fleur Adcock about what happened when she took him there:

> The speech therapist said, 'Do you talk to him?' And she didn't talk to him! She said to me, 'What do you say to babies?' I said, 'You just do a running commentary . . . that's all you do, you just use the English language to babies.' She'd never thought of it. She'd sort of clean and cuddle him, and tuck him up, but she didn't say much, so he didn't get the idea. She probably thought it was a bit insulting to talk baby talk.

It was a mental block comparable to the problem she'd had speaking to foreigners when she lived in Japan. For Angela, speech was overwhelmingly a tool for self-expression – an attitude manifested in her willingness to leave people hanging while she searched for the right word, and also perhaps by the lack of dialogue in her novels, which tend to be dominated to an unusual extent by the narrator's voice. She didn't see the point in speaking when she had nothing to say, or when she couldn't say it in the best way possible. The idea of keeping the ball rolling – of speaking primarily for someone else's benefit – wasn't one she appears to have recognised. But she took note of the therapist's advice, and began talking to Alex more, as well as reading to him (Maurice Sendak, the author and illustrator of *Where the Wild Things Are*, became a particular favourite of theirs), and by the autumn of 1987 – perhaps even earlier – he was talking at an entirely respectable standard for his age.

Undeterred by her disagreeable stint in Texas, Angela had – only six months after returning to London – accepted an invitation from the biographer and memoirist John Leggett to spend the fall semester of 1986 at the University of Iowa Writers' Workshop. It's likely that the workshop's reputation, as much as the salary of $17,000 (about £12,000) that she was offered, was what tempted her back to the USA. The oldest creative-writing programme in the world, it had by the mid-1980s achieved an almost legendary status in American literary life. Over the past fifty years, many of the nation's outstanding authors (Flannery O'Connor, Raymond Carver, John Irving, Andre Dubus II) had emerged from the programme, and many more (Robert Lowell, John Berryman, Kurt Vonnegut, Philip Roth) had passed through as tutors. Iowa City had become, as the *Los Angeles Times* put it in May 1986 (three months before Angela arrived there) 'the Athens of America'. She told Leggett that she was 'delighted' to be approached.

Still, her negative feelings about the USA hadn't evaporated, and they displayed themselves in a neurotic outburst at the start of August, just over a fortnight before she was due to depart. The consular official at the American Embassy in London – 'a fat man with halitosis' – informed her that Mark wouldn't be permitted a spousal visa, since they weren't legally married. 'He was really quite offensive about it,' Angela wrote to Connie Brothers, the programme associate of the Iowa Writers' Workshop. '[He] jiggled his belly above his belt and said he wasn't being moralistic, it was the US law and that was that, and the previous visa [for their time in Texas] had been issued incorrectly.' She was advised to explain the situation to the immigration officials at Chicago, who would be able to grant Mark an extension on his tourist visa; she didn't find this reassuring. 'I am prone to anxiety at the best of times . . . I need him to ~~look after the baby~~ comfort and console us . . . I can't manage without him . . . Will they be capable of splitting up a family? . . . I am sure I am worrying well in excess of the problem; but that doesn't stop me.' She was indeed worrying in excess of the problem, and they were granted entry without any difficulties on 21 August.

Iowa came as a pleasant surprise: it wasn't remotely like Texas. A small, liberal state at the heart of the Corn Belt, in 1986 its economy was still largely based around farming. The landscapes were almost entirely unspoiled: rolling hills and golden cornfields predominated. There were butterflies everywhere. Even in the city, Angela felt that the atmosphere was bucolic. 'It's hard to remember . . . that Iowa City is part of an advanced, industrialised country,' she wrote to Jack Zipes. 'Even the computers seem to have straw in their hair.' That wasn't a problem as far as she was concerned – she still used a typewriter. On 15 September she wrote to Salman Rushdie:

You remember in [the Ray Bradbury book] *The Martian Chronicles*, the little clapboard town, with the church, that the Martians build as a decoy, to persuade the Earthlings they have come to their own, uncorrupted first beginnings, or, rather, to that dream home-town with the old folks swinging on the porch and etc.? Iowa City is like that . . . I haven't liked a part of the States so much since I first saw Washington Square . . . it all looks a bit like Ukraine – cornfields, and hedgerows full of sunflowers, and unpaved roads that send a plume of white dust into the air after the pickup truck.

The house they were renting was on the edge of the town – or 'right out in the countryside', as Angela wrote to her American editor Amanda Vaill – at 15 Woodland Heights. It was built on land that sloped away from the road, with views over the treetops behind, and was painted 'the colour of babyshit'. 'You never saw anything more tastefully vulgar,' she wrote to Carmen:

> but it is the most comfortable house I've ever lived in. Alex bounces on the plush carpets like they were trampolines. The showers – it is a 2 bathroom house – have little seats inside, in case you are too bushed to stand up. There is no end to it. The towels in the guest bathroom are the same colour – mint green – as the guest bedroom carpet . . . And the kitchen is almost too fully equipped. A fondue set. An artichoke cooker. A Cuisinart. Our landlords are gadget junkies, & they live in secluded bliss.

At the back of the house there was a small lake or large pond. Alex loved it. 'We watch him turn brown playing in the sun,' Angela told an interviewer. 'He has taken to catching crickets and keeping them in a cage.' Mark was also very happy in Iowa. 'It was just a gentle place,' he remembered. 'The food there was amazing . . . all the produce was so fresh.' Angela only mentioned one drawback to living there in letters to her friends, although she did mention it to several of them: 'It is very difficult to get a good loaf of <u>bread</u>. The best we've found so far is a pumpernickel trucked in twice a week from the Lithuanian bakery in Omaha.'

The Writers' Workshop was based in the English-Philosophy Building at 251 West Iowa Avenue, a mixture of modernist and classical forms facing the river. Angela found it an agreeable environment. 'The university here is scribbled all over with the right kind of graffiti,' she told Rushdie: '"Reagan

366

is a Terrorist", "Nicaragua – six years of indignity" ("six" crossed out and "seven" inserted in another colour spray can), "Sanctions now" and etc. These slogans go back a long way; one faded one on the air-conditioning plant says, "Dutch out of Indonesia" . . . suggesting a continuum of sanity and good sense.'

She taught two courses: a fiction workshop, and a literature seminar in which she traced 'the theme of alienation and moral disquiet' from Charlotte Brontë to J. G. Ballard; she titled it (quoting Thomas Wolfe) 'Life is strange and the world is bad'. Both courses had fifteen students, and both of them met only once a week – on Tuesday and Wednesday afternoons respectively – so Angela had every morning free, and her weekends lasted for longer than her weeks. David Michael Kaplan, who took the latter course, remembered it as being fairly intense:

> she was very rigorous, and very opinionated. I think she found the level of literary knowledge of the students was appalling, and she would often take them to task for it; I remember one day when she had us read a story by Kafka, not telling us who it was by, and then asking us the author, which I alone knew, and thus escaped her indignation . . . I'm not sure she was very popular with my fellow students, who I think found her too judgmental and too harsh . . . I did like her a lot though – her rigor, her depth of knowledge.

Kaplan's hunch about his fellow students seems to have been correct: a couple of them weren't willing to share their memories of her for this book. The aversion, if that's what it was, went both ways. Kaplan had lunch with Angela on one occasion and remembered her saying that she 'didn't much like the student writing she was critiquing, and was very disappointed by it'. She seems to have been mainly reacting against what she saw as their privilege. She wrote to her former student Rick Moody (who was now working at Simon & Schuster, and trying to bring his mentor's early work back into print in the USA): 'it is easy for kids from places like the Iowa Writing Programme . . . Oh, God! Basically, they don't know how much of it is sheer luck.'

In October, Angela travelled from Iowa to attend the International Festival of Authors in Toronto, which was at that time the biggest literary festival in the world. In 1986 it drew around fifty writers from a dozen countries, including Peter Ackroyd, Margaret Drabble and Timothy Mo (from the UK), Elizabeth Hardwick and Louise Erdrich (from the USA), Amos Oz (from Israel), Alice Munro (from Canada) and Josef Škvorecký (originally from Czechoslovakia, now based in Canada). They were all put up at the Toronto Hilton Harbour Castle Hotel, paid expenses on top of their fees, and generally given VIP treatment. In exchange they were required to give one twenty-minute reading each, and to take part in one panel discussion, for both of which they were guaranteed large audiences. Graham Swift – who was also there – has called the Harbourfront Centre 'the best venue I know . . . I believe no author appears there without feeling their work has been paid the immense respect of being offered a sense of occasion.'

During the day, the writers were subjected to various planned excursions and activities. On the morning of Tuesday 21 October, around twenty of them were bussed out to an aboriginal reserve outside the city. When they arrived, the inhabitants performed a 'war dance' for them. The twenty-eight-year-old novelist Caryl Phillips found it excruciating:

> We got to the ceremony and it became to me painfully, embarrassingly clear [that it was] heavily stage-managed nonsense that we were being offered as tourists. They were presenting their 'culture', and I remember thinking, I'm not sure if any of these people get it – and I turned around and I saw Angela with a big twinkle in her eye. She just raised her eyebrows at me and nodded and smiled, and I thought, she gets it . . . So we sort of became friends because of that gaze.

Phillips and Swift went out drinking together most evenings during the festival in a shabby bar called the Bamboo Club. They tended to appear visibly hungover at breakfast, and Angela would mockingly reprove them. 'She called us "the naughty boys",' remembered Phillips. 'She was wonderfully . . . maternal, as well as being wicked and witty during that week.'

Toronto aside, Angela didn't (by contrast with her time in Austin) do much travelling while she was in Iowa. 'Once we got settled in here, right in the middle of a Woody Guthrie song, we stuck,' she told Simon Watney. They enrolled Alex at the local Montessori school, where he went for a few hours every morning. Some of Angela's students – including Ann Patchett and Jane Satterfield – were enlisted to babysit in the afternoons, or if Angela and Mark went out in the evenings. Mark borrowed a studio from a local potter, and met a rancher who taught him how to ride ('which you can do in Iowa without having to speak with pebbles in your mouth',

Angela wrote). He took Alex fishing in the lake. 'It was almost as good as going to Australia,' he remembered. 'It was like being on holiday the whole time.' Angela agreed: 'I will return [to London] regretfully,' she told an interviewer for the *Cedar Rapids Gazette*. 'Alex . . . will kiss every cow in the cowshed at the bottom of our garden goodbye.'

By the time Angela was back in London in December 1986, Deborah Rogers had been her agent for almost fourteen years. During that period she had taken on a number of other young writers – including Bruce Chatwin, Salman Rushdie, Ian McEwan and Kazuo Ishiguro – whose reputations had become supercharged. In 1981, authors she represented had won the Somerset Maugham Award (Clive Sinclair), the Whitbread Awards for Best Novel and Best First Novel (Maurice Leitch and William Boyd), the Booker Prize (Rushdie) and the James Tait Black Memorial Prize (Rushdie again). A diary piece in the *Guardian* commended her for highlighting the importance of literary agents: 'a usually unsung part of the book-producing business'.

Six years later, though, the Deborah Rogers Agency was no longer so comfortably pre-eminent. She had recently adopted a baby and was by her own admission becoming distracted, and allowing her authors' interests to slide. 'The agency just wasn't functioning very efficiently, or even vaguely efficiently,' McEwan remembered:

> Angela and I had a lot of conversations at the time about how much we loved Deborah and how we couldn't leave, and then something would happen and Angela would say, 'That's it, I've had it, I'm leaving.' And then, 'I can't, because of Deborah.'

Not all of Deborah's clients shared Angela's sense of personal loyalty to her, and some of them were beginning to feel that a different agent might better serve their interests. The transformation of publishing from a genteel profession to a highly competitive industry had accelerated dramatically since the beginning of the 1980s. A cyclonic rush of mergers and takeovers had subsided with scarcely any independent publishing houses left standing – Pearson Longman had bought Penguin, which had in turn bought Viking and Hamish Hamilton; Random House had bought CVBC (the Chatto & Windus, Virago, Bodley Head and Jonathan Cape group); Collins had bought Granada and Harper & Row – and there had been a parallel upheaval in the world of bookselling, as a raft of new high-street chains (such as Waterstone's) emerged with the aim of turning literary fiction into a valuable commodity. While most of the money that resulted from these changes flowed upwards, towards the shareholders, a small number of authors were beginning to receive advances of unprecedented largesse. Among the most headline-grabbing were Graham Swift's £150,000 from Viking Penguin for his next two novels, Fay Weldon's £450,000 from Collins for her next three novels, and Michael Holroyd's £625,000 from Chatto & Windus for his three-volume biography of George Bernard Shaw. Not one · of those authors was represented by Deborah.

When her clients began considering their options, there was one that looked especially interesting. The New York-based agent Andrew Wylie was an arresting figure, with cool blue eyes that gazed unblinkingly out from behind fashionable glasses, a prominent brow, and a drawl that several commentators have compared to Jack Nicholson's. He had set himself up as a literary agent in 1980, and had swiftly acquired a reputation for doing whatever it took to secure large advances for his authors. 'He does not believe in the niceties which have hitherto governed the gentlemanly world of British publishing,' wrote Alan Rusbridger in a profile for the *Guardian* in 1988. One of these niceties was the convention that agents didn't poach authors from other agents; Wylie ominously said that if an author was being properly represented, then their agents had nothing to fear.

On 19 June 1987, Angela went to Salman Rushdie's fortieth birthday party at Homer End, Bruce Chatwin's house near the village of Ipsden in Oxfordshire, a verdant setting with impressive views over the Berkshire Downs. It was a beautiful, sunny day, and they spent a lot of time outside in the garden. The other guests included the novelists Nuruddin Farah and Pauline Melville (with both of whom Angela hit it off), Liz Calder, Deborah Rogers and Andrew Wylie.

'I just had an odd kind of feeling,' Deborah recalled twenty-five years later. 'Bruce and Salman were both slightly fulminating [about] how preposterous it was, how outrageous it was, that all the money went to the publishers rather than to the writers . . . and I felt terribly sort of uneasy, I knew that there was something [wrong].' Liz Calder remembers it being much more overt. 'It was absolutely unbelievable. You could see [Wylie] . . . sort of doing a number on them . . . It wasn't by stealth, it was just blatant wooing in front of all their friends and their current agent. It was horrible.'

On 16 September, Rushdie and Chatwin wrote simultaneous letters to Deborah informing her that they were moving to the agency Wylie shared with his two British partners, Gillon Aitken and Brian Stone. Rushdie had previously agreed to give his new novel, *The Satanic Verses*, to Liz Calder (who had published all his previous books, and had recently moved from Jonathan Cape to Bloomsbury, so could have done with the loyalty of her most successful author), but Wylie sold British and American rights to Viking Penguin in the US for $850,000 (about £525,000). It was a staggeringly high sum for a literary novel, eclipsing the previously record-breaking advances given to Weldon, Holroyd and Swift. The young novelists Caryl Phillips and Ben Okri – both of whom were friends of Rushdie – left the Deborah Rogers Agency for Wylie, Aitken & Stone shortly afterwards. It looked like the Deborah Rogers Agency was on the brink of collapse: there were several newspaper articles that hinted as much, in tones spiked with *Schadenfreude*. Deborah and Pat White (with whom she had been working since the 1970s) brought in fellow agent Gill Coleridge as a partner, and renamed the agency Rogers, Coleridge & White. Liz Calder wrote an angry letter to Rushdie that she came to regret (it was 'too angry' she told the *New Yorker* in 1995), and they didn't speak to one another for over a year.

Panic spread around the publishing industry. Carmen paused between trips to New York and Frankfurt to write Angela a heartfelt letter on 5 October:

> the situation with Salman has become so surrounded with monstrosity that I want to be particularly sure that you and I never get into the position that Liz has now arrived with Salman . . .
>
> I don't say this because I want you to ask anything less for any book you may write next. What I want to say in this letter . . . is that nothing will induce me to get into a position where you and I are no longer friends . . . I'm perfectly aware that I'm not the only publisher in the world capable of publishing Angela Carter . . . Suffice to say you can imagine when I think this may happen to you and me because of the way publishing is at the moment, I become anxious and write on paper my determination that this shall never be.

If Angela wrote a reply, it hasn't survived. But she clearly took note of the powerful position she found herself in. She had been planning a new novel – under the working title of *Chance and Hazard* – for over a year, but this was the moment she chose to mention it to Carmen. On 28 October, they had supper together and Angela pitched the book. The following morning,

Carmen sent a memo to her colleagues at Chatto & Windus: '[the novel] is based on Shakespeare's late comedies but it is quintessential Angela. A synopsis is coming. I <u>think</u> she will finish it in 1989 for publication in 1990.' But there was a catch:

> Angela wants money for this novel and a lot of it. She is both canny and realistic. She knows what Fay Weldon got . . . and knows it was for three novels. But she thinks she is a better writer than Fay Weldon, so my guess is she won't accept much less than Fay got per book. She knows she may not sell so much now, but is aware her books will last much longer than those of Fay Weldon . . .
>
> Basically I think she wants to know and get her market price . . . If we don't offer enough then my feeling is that she will offer herself on the open market. I asked Deborah if she could name a price for us, but she said no, Angela wants to know what <u>we</u> think she's worth . . .
>
> My guess is she'll want a minimum of £150,000 for UK rights to her book.

On 10 November, Angela sent Carmen a synopsis 'of the novel I've now decided to call *Wise Children*,' which she presented as 'a long, comic, pano-ramic novel that will parody whilst lovingly reduplicating the family saga genre and will use the theatre, both legit. and vaudeville, and the plays of Shakespeare, as a metaphor for British society over the last hundred years . . . Its subtext, evidently, is the general inefficacy of patriarchy.' Carmen was enthusiastic, but now that CVBC was owned by Random House, she had to run the acquisition past Simon Master, the newly installed chief executive of the group. He wouldn't allow her to offer more than £60,000 for Commonwealth rights. It was a bit more than Angela had received for *Nights at the Circus*, but considerably less than the sort of figures that Rushdie, Swift and Weldon were commanding (or the sort that Carmen had intuited she was holding out for). Perhaps she accepted that it was all she was worth – that a different publisher or a different agent couldn't have done any better for her – but it seems likely that she valued her friendships with Deborah and Carmen too highly to consider leaving either one of them. Wylie doesn't seem to have made any overtures towards her, which may have irritated her vanity and thickened her loyalties – but that's speculation. 'All I know is that I never doubted her,' said Deborah.

* * *

Angela sometimes told interviewers that she'd read 'most of Shakespeare' by the time she was ten. There are reasons for doubting that she had – a notebook that she kept while studying for her A levels contains what look like her earliest responses to several of the major plays – but it's entirely plausible (given her mother's partiality to him) that she had encountered at least some Shakespeare while her age was still in single digits. As an adult, she continued to frame her enjoyment of his work in terms a child would understand. She loved him for his language, his plots, his larger-than-life characters and his ribald sense of humour. 'I can curl up with a bag of apples and *Measure for Measure*, and it's like a racy novel,' she once said (although her favourite play of all was *A Midsummer Night's Dream*, which she liked 'almost beyond reason'). 'I do think there's something about Shakespeare that converts the most sophisticated person into the naïve observer,' she told Lorna Sage. He was, she said on another occasion, 'the great popular entertainer of all time'.

She knew that this wasn't the prevailing view of his significance. Since the late eighteenth century, Shakespeare had occupied an almost sanctified place in English culture. He was the national poet, but more than that, he was a symbol of 'national identity' – a concept that Angela tended to view as a means by which the culture of the ruling classes asserted itself over the rest. Shakespeare's plays were typically performed by plummy-voiced thespians (who were not infrequently rewarded for their exertions with knighthoods). He was regarded as a bastion of high culture. Angela was deeply suspicious of this tendency, feeling that England's greatest writer had been hitched to a particular (pompous, posh, patriarchal) version of Englishness. Her mother's family had revealed how much more inclusive his work could be: 'All of them knew . . . [that] to love Shakespeare was a kind of class revenge.'

Wise Children uses Shakespeare's plays, and especially his comedies, to celebrate the plurality of English culture, and to wryly interrogate distinctions between high and low, central and peripheral, legitimate and illegitimate. Angela wanted to allude to every one of the plays, and was frustrated that she couldn't find room for *Titus Andronicus* or *The Two Noble Kinsmen*. 'But I got a lot in!' she assured Paul Bailey, and so she did: the novel is crammed with identical twins, warring brothers, cuckolded husbands, substitute brides, errant fathers and triumphant returns from the dead. It's a splendidly busy, absurdly over-the-top burlesque of Shakespearian motifs.

The century-spanning, continent-crossing plot is framed by the events of a single day: 23 April, the feast day of St George (the patron saint of England), and the date usually taken to be Shakespeare's birthday. It's also the birthday of Dora Chance, the novel's rambunctious seventy-five-year-old narrator; of her twin sister Nora; of their natural father Sir Melchior Hazard; and of his twin brother, Dora's and Nora's legal father, Peregrine Hazard (presumed deceased). The story opens with Dora and Nora receiving a suspiciously last-minute invitation to Melchior's hundredth birthday celebrations. 'Something makes you think they don't want us to go?' Nora wonders. Not that feeling unwanted is a new experience for them: Melchior ('our greatest living Shakesperian') is 'a pillar of the legit. theatre', while the Chance girls are 'illegitimate in every way': they're bastards, they're from south London ('the wrong side of the tracks'), they went on the halls, and they're women. The tangled Hazard/Chance family tree – the solid central trunk indifferent to its rampant branches – is the novel's central metaphor for British society.

The day gets off with a bang when Tristram Hazard – a seedy game-show host, who believes himself to be Dora's and Nora's nephew, but is actually their half-brother – turns up on their doorstep to announce that their beloved mixed-race god-daughter Tiffany, with whom he's been having a relationship, is missing. He plays a videotape of the episode of his 'poxy show' that went out live the night before, in the course of which Tiffany had a very public breakdown (she's fallen pregnant with Tristram's child; he doesn't want to know). The first chapter ends with the news that a body, seemingly hers, has been found in the river.

For the next hundred pages or so the story circles back through Dora's memories, taking in her and Nora's childhoods under the indulgent eye of their guardian Grandma Chance; their occasional intersections with their father; the comings and goings of their uncle Perry; and various run-ins with their hated half-sisters (or cousins, as it turns out) Imogen and Saskia. It's full of gorgeous period detail ('the leatherette suite in the sitting room where the fumed-oak sideboard contained a single bottle of sweet sherry and a half a dozen dusty glasses stood on a tarnished silver tray inscribed "To a great little trouper from the Merry Martins, Frinton-on-Sea, 1919"') and amazing set-piece scenes (the Twelfth Night costume ball at Melchior's country pile that ends in a chaotic conflagration, or his centenary celebrations at the end of the novel, at which there's a giddy stampede of twists and revelations, not to mention a cheerful bout of incest between Perry and Dora).

Along the way, it presents a covert history of twentieth-century show business. Dora and Nora start their careers dancing in music halls in the 1920s. During their 1930s heyday they appear in a West End revue titled *What You Will* (or *What? You Will?* or *What! You Will!?!*) and go to Hollywood with Melchior – who wants 'to take North America back for England, Shakespeare and St George' – to make a film of *A Midsummer Night's Dream* (many of the details are based on Max Reinhardt's 1935 version). After the war, as their careers go into decline, they start appearing in shows called things like *Nudes of the World* and *Goldilocks and the Three Bares*.

All of Angela Carter's books are about performance and self-invention in one way or another, but *Wise Children* and *Nights at the Circus* are the only two that focus on professional entertainers. Angela talked about the reasons for this in the *Omnibus* documentary made a month before she died:

> They're useful people. I mean, it sounds beastly to talk about my characters in this way. But they're useful people, because, of course, their living, their whole livelihood, is based on the public presentation of certain kinds of aspects of sexuality, certain kinds of aspects of femininity, which they're quite conscious about. Show business, being a showgirl, is a very simple metaphor simply for being a woman, for being aware of your femininity, being aware of yourself as a woman and having to use it to negotiate with the world.

This becomes increasingly poignant as the characters grow older. When they were young, Dora and Nora were spoiled for work; as they entered middle age, they were forced into increasingly overt demonstrations of their femininity, even to the point of showing their breasts on stage. Now, in their dotage, they can't get any work at all. At its heart, *Wise Children* is about what happens to women's identities as they grow older and the culture ceases to treat them as sexual beings. Dora and Nora were consciously based on Angela's aunt Kitty ('She's recognisable in [Dora's] voice,' said Hughie), but they're also constructed from a lifetime's sympathetic observation of elderly women. In 1966, while working on her abortive non-fiction book *A Bunch of Joys*, Angela noted down two figures in a local pub:

> Two old ladies, one with a button nose, the other not, golden earrings in their ears, thick gold wedding rings on their hands, raise up their voices together. One has hair carefully combed under a net; the other has netted her hair down in strict rows, like corrugated iron. The veins

jut out like ropes on their arms. One had a gin and orange to drink, the other raised a golden goblet of light ale to her lips. They were sisters, or sisters-in-law, in best coats and a mass of jewellery. They sang in loud, shrill voices how love would live in their hearts. Their worn, aged femininity was still strong and sweet as tea.

Like these two, Dora and Nora have no intention of growing old gracefully. Towards the end of the novel, preparing for Melchior's party, they sit side by side in front of the mirror applying their make-up, just like they used to when they were young:

> It took an age but we did it; we painted the faces that we used to have on to the faces we have now. From a distance of thirty feet with the light behind us, we looked, at first glance, just like the girl who danced with the Prince of Wales when nightingales sang in Berkeley Square on a foggy day in London Town. The deceptions of memory. That girl was smooth as an egg and the lipstick never ran down little cracks and fissures round her mouth because, in those days, there were none.
>
> 'It's every woman's tragedy,' said Nora, as we contemplated our painted masterpieces, 'that, after a certain age, she looks like a female impersonator.'

That twinge of mournfulness is a rare note in *Wise Children*. 'I refuse point-blank to play in tragedy,' Dora says at one point, and the novel in which she stars is every inch a comedy – vulgar and bawdy, buoyant and optimistic. In the *Omnibus* documentary, Angela said: 'comedy stands for, you know, fertility, continuance, a sense of the protean nature of the world, of the inextinguishable, unappeasable nature of the world, the unappeasable nature of appetite and desire'. The prevailing tone is celebratory – almost every chapter is structured around a birthday – and Dora's and Nora's attitude to their fading looks tends to be one of defiant good cheer. When, at Melchior's party in the final chapter, they catch sight of themselves in the mirror and realise that they've overdone the slap, they don't feel abashed: 'we had to laugh at the spectacle we'd made of ourselves and, fortified by sisterly affection, strutted our stuff into the ballroom. We could still show them a thing or two, even if they couldn't stand the sight.'

Wise Children is by some distance Angela Carter's funniest and sunniest novel, her cleverest and most touching, but also her sprightliest. It is the product of a lifetime's thinking, looking, feeling and being. Even so, she didn't find the writing easy. She sent a very rough draft of the first chapter to Carmen on 20 March 1988: 'There is still quite a lot to do with it . . . the variations in tone and person of Dora's narrative will be made, finally, completely plausible. But this is the general way it's going and I'm not too dissatisfied with the general feel; and am extremely taken with the scene at the game show, in fact.'

During the period in which she wrote *Nights at the Circus* and *Wise Children* – her two novels about women involved in the dramatic arts – Angela was also working on several dramatic projects of her own. In September 1987, she was commissioned by Andrew Brown of Euston Films to write a screenplay based on the notorious murder by two New Zealand teenagers, Pauline Parker and Juliet Hulme, of Parker's mother in 1954. The two girls had constructed an obsessive fantasy world, in which they imagined themselves consorting with movie stars including James Mason, Ava Gardner and Orson Welles. When Parker's mother seemed ready to break up their friendship, they caved her head in with a brick. The case has inspired an extraordinary number of fictional interpretations over the past sixty years – ranging from Beryl Bainbridge's novel *Harriet Said...* to Peter Jackson's film *Heavenly Creatures* – and it offered several themes that Angela had visited in her previous work, including 1950s girlhood (*The Magic Toyshop*), parricide (her stories about Lizzie Borden) and the deceptions of Hollywood (*The Passion of New Eve*).

The commission arrived at an opportune moment. On 7 October Angela returned to Australia – taking Mark and Alex with her – for a three-week publicity tour. Before flying home to London they visited Christchurch, New Zealand, where the murder had occurred; Angela thought that the city was 'like being dead. Not unpleasant, exactly, but numb.' She spent time in the archives, poring over newspaper cuttings about the case, as well as the girls' police statements and a transcript of their trial. Back in London she worked on a first draft of the script, which she titled *The Christchurch Murder*. It relies on the apparatus of realism more heavily than anything she had written since the mid-1960s, and closely follows the details of the case, save a few name changes (Hulme becomes Nerissa Locke, Parker becomes Lena Ball) and other cosmetic alterations. Angela was surprisingly comfortable operating in this mode: the script has a powerfully baleful atmosphere, and presents an icily compelling vision of how tensions between mothers and daughters might bubble over into murder. She delivered a second draft in August 1988, but Euston Films couldn't find a production company to take it on – the Auckland-based South Pacific Pictures was briefly in the frame – and the project was eventually abandoned.

At around the same time, she was approached by Richard Eyre, director of the National Theatre, to write a modern version of Frank Wedekind's 'Lulu' plays – *Earth Spirit* and *Pandora's Box* – which follow their commandingly beautiful, sexually liberated, exuberantly mischievous heroine through an action-packed career as a femme fatale (involving murder, incest and lesbianism), to a bloody death at the hands of Jack the Ripper. Angela loved the idea. She had first encountered Lulu as a teenager, via G. W. Pabst's 1929 screen adaptation (starring Louise Brooks), which had remained one of her favourite films. In Iowa, she had shown it to her students: 'Nothing else but *Pandora's Box* would do . . . The role of Lulu . . . is one of the key representations of female sexuality in twentieth-century literature.'

She was considerably less keen on the original plays, however. While Pabst and Brooks had sought to discredit the 'peculiarly pernicious, if flattering' myth of the femme fatale, 'to both demonstrate [it] irresistibly in action while, at the same time, offering evidence of its manifest absurdity', Wedekind had remained in its thrall. Angela felt that his Lulu was a concatenation of hang-ups about sexually assertive women: a character 'who must die because she is free'. Her own version sets out to move the emphasis away from the mythical. She cut such unyielding elements as Wedekind's prologue – in which Lulu is brought onstage in Pierrot costume by an animal tamer, and described as the 'primal form of woman . . . created to incite sin,/to lure, seduce, corrupt, drop poison in' – and added stage directions emphasising that Lulu plays by the rules of a masculine society:

> she wears [her clothes] with a delightful wit, as if she saw the funny side of her own attractiveness . . . Like all those who make their living out of pleasing others, she is well aware of her precarious position in the world. She knows her role, the charming child (who, when she is naughty, can be punished 'for her own good'). She plays it, charmingly.

The tragedy of Angela Carter's Lulu is not her destructive sexuality, but her constructed femininity. It's a clever shift. But there was a tension between Angela's desire to refashion the material for herself, and the requirement of staying true to Wedekind's text. There was also the technical difficulty of squeezing two full-length tragedies into a single script. The resulting play is monstrously unwieldy (it takes around five hours to stage) and curiously stilted. Although Angela was becoming increasingly interested in the theatre during this period, she was never a regular theatregoer: it appealed to her more as a setting or metaphor for use in her fiction than as an artistic medium in its own right. This may explain why her only attempt at writing for it produced such disappointing results.

Angela admired Lulu's radiant lack of hypocrisy; it was a quality that she tried to cultivate in herself. But there was one area of her life in which she was happy enough to be a bit hypocritical. She had led her father to believe that she'd married Mark when Alex was born. Until then, Hugh had expected them to sleep in separate rooms, and the deception seemed a small thing if it made an old man happy. Angela's fondness for him had only increased as he'd grown more frail. 'The very words, "my father", always make me smile,' she had written in 1983. Because he'd built up a whole new existence for himself after her mother's death, she had 'never felt any of those succubus things people do about aged parents'. They went to stay with him a couple of times a year, and in recent months Angela had been talking about buying a house near him in Scotland, since she was beginning to worry about him, living all by himself above the Stalker shop.

She never managed to follow through on this plan. On Sunday 15 May 1988, a month short of his ninety-third birthday, Hugh was setting out for church when he slipped and 'cartwheeled' (according to his doctor, who witnessed the accident) down the stone steps that led up to his flat. He survived the fall, but contracted pneumonia while he was in hospital. Angela rushed up to Scotland, taking Alex with her; Hughie and Joan went too. They were all there when Hugh died on Monday 23 May.

His funeral took place the following week in Macduff, and he was cremated at Aberdeen, 600 miles away from Olive's final resting place in Wandsworth. Neither of them had ever attained much psychological distance from the worlds of their childhoods. Angela had forcefully rejected hers, but with her father's passing she felt bereft. 'I haven't felt like this since I lost my first great love,' she wrote in her journal. She wanted to keep as many of Hugh's possessions as she could, but Mark was resistant to clogging up their house with more junk. In August, Angela wrote in her journal:

Dad's things arrived on Sunday – the things Mark let me have, that is, i.e. what few heirloom things there were. The mahogany dining table & chairs they had made when they got married . . . Also the chest of drawers, likewise. The only concession to sentimentality Mark permitted me was a crate of photographs, which is maybe sufficient concession. All Sunday, which was beautifully sunny, & quiet, everybody in the street off out, I felt amazingly euphoric, & secure & easy in my mind, somehow, as though we'd got Dad home, at last . . .

I also began to feel reconciled to Mum, as if she'd breathed a sigh of relief, somewhere, to know this good furniture was finally going to be looked after. <u>She</u> really did like nice things, & wanted me to want nice things, too. She'd have appreciated Mark appreciating the chairs.

Shortly afterwards, they had a row over a glass-fronted cabinet. '<u>Furious</u> rage,' Angela wrote in her journal, '& a great deal came back to me during the rage – how hard it was, what a <u>struggle</u> it was, to become independent; how much I resent . . . being encroached on.'

CHAPTER TWENTY-THREE

Perhaps writing is a matter of life and death

By the summer of 1988, Britain barely resembled the country Angela had grown up in. The left-leaning consensus which had persisted more or less unchecked from 1945 until the mid-1970s – involving widespread support for the welfare state, a mixed economy, and the national ownership of key industries – had been roughly supplanted under the Conservative governments of Margaret Thatcher by an ideology of defiant individualism, underpinned by faith in the benefits of free markets, low taxes and a minimal state. The financial sector and the property markets had bloomed; the public sector and the trade unions had withered. Opponents of Thatcher felt that she was riding roughshod over civil liberties, and that a new, brash, acquisitive ethos was eroding the traditional British values of decency and decorum. The violence of the 1984–5 miners' strike had revealed the bitterness of that opposition among many working-class communities. But the wider electorate remained broadly supportive of her efforts to modernise Britain. On 11 June 1987, she had won her third successive general election with a slightly reduced (that is to say, still whopping) majority of 102 seats.

Angela made no secret of her antipathy towards Thatcher. In 1982 she had spoken at the Institute of Contemporary Arts – alongside Salman Rushdie and the writer and campaigner Anthony Barnett – about the British mission to recapture the Falkland Islands from Argentina, and had spent most of her time railing against the prime minister's jingoistic speeches. During the 1983 general election campaign, she had written her startlingly ad feminam attack on Thatcher for the *New Statesman*. 'Her hatred of Margaret Thatcher was operatic,' remembered Rushdie. 'She really, really loathed Margaret Thatcher.'

Even in the traditionally leftish worlds of the arts and the media, that wasn't a particularly popular attitude. Several of the most prominent stars in the literary firmament – among them Kingsley Amis, Philip Larkin, V. S. Naipaul, Iris Murdoch and Anthony Powell – were devoted cheerleaders for the government. The vast majority of national newspapers and magazines were also supportive of Thatcher's policies. Those who despaired of them often felt that they couldn't get their voices heard.

In June 1988, Angela received an invitation to the west London home of the playwright Harold Pinter and the biographer Lady Antonia Fraser, where a group of left-wing writers and intellectuals were meeting to discuss how to 're-establish the intellectual basis of the left'. Also present were the author and barrister John Mortimer, and his wife Penelope Gollop; the novelists Ian McEwan, Salman Rushdie, Emma Tennant and Margaret Drabble; the feminist writer and campaigner Germaine Greer; the playwright David Hare; the biographer Michael Holroyd; the former *New Statesman* editor Anthony Howard; the BBC journalist Margaret Jay; the Labour politicians Mark Fisher and Lord Williams; and the historian Ben Pimlott.

They sat cross-legged on the floor, and took it in turns to speak. John Mortimer acted as chairman, and began by describing 'a kind of intolerance and brutalism which to me seems quite new . . . something quite unusual in British public life'. Anthony Howard then spoke at length about how Thatcher had transformed the 'class appeal' of the Conservative Party, and what a dangerous opponent she was. Germaine Greer launched into a despairing analysis of the Labour Party ('We talk about the prospects for a future government. I would be a great deal happier if we had a bit of opposition'). Salman Rushdie objected that he hadn't thought he was coming to a meeting whose commitment was to a particular party. Ian McEwan raised the question of whether, as writers, they were bound to incorporate their politics into the structure of their work. After a while, the orderly arrangement of the meeting came apart, as people began accusing one another of 'accepting the basic tenets of Thatcherism' and of propping up the government by writing for the Murdoch press.

'I don't recall Angela saying a whole lot, actually, because I think she felt out of place somehow,' said Rushdie. The edited transcript of the meeting supports this interpretation: Angela's only contribution seems to have come out of nowhere, in the manner of someone who has been working up the courage to speak. Towards the end of the session, as they debated the direction their subsequent meetings should take – whether there should be an agenda, whether they should have guest speakers – she suddenly broke in to lament the closure of the hospital where she had given birth to Alex:

There is a small hospital near where I live – the South London Hospital for Women – that was the last general women's hospital. It was decided to close it down on the grounds that it cost two million a year to run. The health authority had in excess of two million signatures to keep the place open. People would come from as far as Glasgow and a great many women from ethnic minorities, because they like being treated by women. I think this sort of thing that has been done time and time again since 1979 actually fundamentally erodes people's convictions that they live in a democratic society. You want to keep the local hospital open. You do every conceivable thing you can to keep it open, and they close it. You think, I am not going to vote Tory, I am not going to vote Labour, I am going to sit at home in my own piss.

It was – conspicuously, after the grandstanding of some of her peers – a small, genuine howl of pain. After she had finished speaking, the conversation returned to logistics. It was decided that they would name themselves the 20 June Group (for the date of their first meeting, but also in allusion to the 20 July Plot of 1944, when a group of German aristocrats had tried to assassinate Hitler). This small act of pomposity swiftly returned to embarrass them.

Somehow or other – perhaps via an unsympathetic invitee – word of the gathering reached the press. A tsunami of derision was promptly unleashed. The *Independent* columnist Peter Jenkins led the charge: 'the news that Lady Antonia Fraser (-Pinter) and her friends were going to rethink the socialist future for us . . . presented a somewhat ridiculous spectacle. Who could suppose that these smart, talented, successful and rich London people – "champagne socialists", as John Mortimer pleases to call himself – were the ones who might turn the intellectual tide?' Writing in the *Evening Standard*, the novelist and critic D. J. Taylor was equally dismissive: 'It is not hard to sympathise with the people who find this sort of thing funny . . . The list of literary figures supposed to be joining this new alliance has a depressingly familiar ring. Margaret Drabble. Anthony Howard. John Mortimer. Harold Pinter. One does not wish to be ungallant, but they scarcely constitute a kaleidoscope of intellectual éclat.' Even Angela's friend Paul Bailey, a self-described 'old-fashioned Labour-voting writer', expressed the view that it was hypocritical and ridiculous of novelists who were doing very well under Thatcher to 'bite the hand that feeds them'.

Angela wasn't put off. She continued to attend meetings of the 20 June Group – which took place every couple of months for the next year or so – and became an increasingly vocal participant. Later that year, she was one of the founding signatories of Charter 88, which called for 'a new constitutional settlement' enshrining civil liberties. The following year, she signed an open letter protesting the poll tax, and predicted in an article for *City Limits* that after a few more years of Thatcherism, 'London will turn into a Third World city in the rain, with ceaseless traffic jams and people digging in the garbage while others drive by in their Porsches.'

In the years since her death – as her reputation has grown, and the facts of her life have been transmuted into the stuff of myth – her unwavering, yet hardly very effectual anti-Thatcherism has become the subject of extravagant claims. In an essay for the *London Review of Books* in 2013, the writer Iain Sinclair – whom Angela knew, and whose work she admired – went so far as to present her and Thatcher as the opposing spirits of the age:

> Where Thatcher was an absence, and more than an absence, a nega-
> tion, an assault on the notion of organic society, Carter was her
> contrary, a white witch, a perverse and libidinous celebrator of the
> stew of London . . . It struck me that these two women, strong, self-
> made, fierce in doctrine, gave a balance to whatever England was in
> the years between punk and John Major . . . In some weird way, we
> needed them both: dark and light.

It's a striking thought, but in its exaggerated contrast between 'dark and light' – exactly the sort of mythical bombast that Angela Carter was at pains to undermine – it rides roughshod over nuance. The reality was more complicated than Sinclair allows. 'England under Thatcher is boring, scary & dangerous,' Angela wrote to Rick Moody. 'We vaguely think of moving on . . . yet I'm earning more money under Thatcher than I have ever in my life before, and there is as yet only a general malaise abroad.' There's nothing intrinsically hypocritical – no matter what Paul Bailey thought – in believing that a government is bad for the country, while acknowledging that it hasn't been entirely bad for oneself. But it's an unusual consideration for a white witch.

*　　*　　*

Visiting positions at foreign universities had become an important part of Angela's life by the late 1980s: they were useful ways to keep some money coming in between novels, while at the same time seeing a bit of the world. In the fall semester of 1988, she took on yet another, at the Writers' Institute at New York State University in Albany. The city lies on the banks of the Hudson, 150 miles north of New York City, and is one of the oldest surviving British colonies. Angela liked it – although she found the number of supermarkets depressing – and she was enchanted by the surrounding countryside. She wrote to Lorna Sage: 'upstate New York is so beautiful. Rock, & water, & forest'. Elsewhere she described the Hudson as 'the most beautiful river in the world'.

She noted that the preponderance of 'fat girls' among her students was a sign of the university's social standing: 'if obesity is a sign of affluence in the Third World, in the First it is a sign of deprivation.' There was none of the sense of entitlement that had irritated her in both Providence and Iowa, and she worked hard to give her students as much help as she could. In addition to her regular classes she offered a pro bono 'community work-shop', for people who couldn't afford the fees. She enjoyed the work. The only downside to being there, she told Lorna Sage, was the 'truly terrifying' Women's Studies department, whose members were 'really hard-line radical feminists, who have virtually boycotted me'. Various well-known writers – including John Barth, T. C. Boyle and Marilynne Robinson – visited the institute to give readings and speak to the students over the course of the semester, but these regular injections of literary life probably didn't delight Angela, whose priority in Albany was 'isolating myself & working'. When she wasn't teaching she spent much of her time in the film sections of the university library, reading biographies 'with titles like *Too Late for Tears* or *Mascara in My Martini*' for the Hollywood section of *Wise Children*.

Towards the end of her time in Albany, Angela did a few events in dif-ferent parts of the country to promote *Saints and Strangers* – the American edition of *Black Venus* – which had just come out in paperback. She gave a reading in Gainsville, Florida on 3 November. She had been meant to give one in Providence later that week, but it was cancelled because she'd been double-booked with the poet Joseph Brodsky. The following week she gave two readings in New York City: one at the Lincoln Center on Monday 14 November, and one the following day at Endicott Books on Columbus Avenue. 'I'll be in the city with Mark & Alex, my man & my boy,' she wrote to Rick Moody. 'I may well be a disappointment after all these years, Rick, but it would be nice if you could get to either of these occasions.' That rather poignant note of apology suggests that Angela was becoming increasingly sensitive, as her fame increased, to the ways people built her up in their imaginations.

By the end of 1988, Angela's version of *Lulu* had gone through several drafts, incorporating editorial suggestions from Howard Davies – who had been lined up to direct it – and Richard Eyre. Privately, Eyre and Davies had begun to doubt that the project was viable ('maybe it was the wrong marriage', Eyre reflected in 1996), but they never put this to Angela in so many words. In December 1988, Davies wrote to inform her that *Lulu* would not be appearing 'in the current repertoire' at the National:

> I have always, as you will recall, found the 'style' of the play difficult – a sort of comic burlesque discursory narrative that seemed too wordy, and certainly difficult to act in any contemporary easy idiom. Whenever I edited – or brutalised – the text you shrugged in ironic resignation. I was never easy with it; and perhaps I am not in the end the right director for it.

Even so, he assured Angela that the play might well appear 'next year, or early in 1990'. Three months later another letter came, this time from Richard Eyre, telling her that the production had been delayed again:

> I think Howard made an initial mistake by thinking of it as an Olivier production . . . I think the more he imagined 'LULU' on the Olivier stage the more he felt that we would be in danger of having to turn it into the kind of play it isn't – that a difficult and elliptical text would be forced into a more accessible mode, in order to provide the kind of 'show' which the Olivier demands . . . I'm genuinely sorry that your fine and fluent version of the play is being kept waiting in the wings. (The introduction alone is superb dramaturgy.) I'm particularly sorry that your first venture in the theatre ended in a miasma of confusion and apparent bad faith, and I hope even more that it will be possible to stage your version of 'LULU' in the future.

By this point, Angela had learned to read between the lines. Susannah Clapp remembers running into her at a party in Tufnell Park shortly afterwards and finding her 'white-faced and narrow-eyed with fury: "The

National have just flushed my *Lulu* down the toilet.'" The work didn't entirely go to waste, though: Angela later suggested that the time she spent with Wedekind's work had informed *Wise Children*. 'I guess a lot of Lulu's personality, which I find very attractive, has gone into my twins,' she told Lorna Sage in 1991. But unlike Lulu, Dora and Nora refuse the fatality of the femme fatale – they refuse her tragic aspect – and gleefully, disgracefully grow old.

On Friday 10 February 1989, Alex's half-term began and the family went on holiday to Florence. It was there – four days later – that they heard about the fatwa issued by Iran's Ayatollah Khomeini against Salman Rushdie. Muslims across the world were encouraged to seek out and execute Rushdie and anyone who had been involved in the publication or distribution of his novel *The Satanic Verses*. The threat was considered serious, and Rushdie went into hiding the following day.

Angela was extremely agitated. She had reviewed the novel in glowing terms ('complicated, exhilarating . . . loquacious, sometimes hilarious, extraordinary') for the *Guardian* when it was published the previous September, but along with most Western commentators, she hadn't seemed to notice its potential for causing offence. That had become abundantly clear, however, in the months that followed. By the end of 1988, *The Satanic Verses* had been banned under blasphemy laws in India, Egypt and South Africa. In January 1989, it was burned on the streets of Bradford; on 13 February, one person had died and over a hundred had been injured during riots against it in Pakistan. With the announcement of the fatwa, the cycle of violence went into overdrive. By the end of March two moderate imams who'd defended the book had been shot dead in Brussels; several bookshops in Britain and the USA had been bombed; and twelve people had died during rioting in Mumbai.

The response in Britain was deeply equivocal. The government defended the principle of free speech and lightly reproached the Ayatollah for inciting murder against a British citizen, but they didn't break off diplomatic relations with Tehran (on 7 March, Tehran took the initiative and broke off relations with London), and both Margaret Thatcher and Geoffrey Howe, the foreign secretary, went out of their way to disparage *The Satanic Verses* and to express sympathy for those who wanted to murder its author. 'We have known in our own religion people doing things which are deeply offensive to some of us,' explained Thatcher, 'and we have felt it very much. And that is what has happened in Islam.'

This wretched hedging – yes, it's a nasty book and yes, he's a nasty piece of work, but no, he oughtn't really to be killed – was echoed by several well-known writers. The historian Hugh Trevor-Roper claimed to support Rushdie's right to police protection, but somewhat undermined that position by adding: 'he knew what he was doing and could foresee the consequences . . . I would not shed a tear if some British muslims, deploring his manners, should waylay him in a dark street and seek to improve them.' The thriller writer John le Carré likewise announced that the death sentence was 'outrageous', but went on to imply that some lesser form of punishment would have been quite suitable: 'I don't think it is given to any of us to be impertinent to great religions with impunity.' The children's author Roald Dahl wrote a mildly unhinged letter to *The Times* in which he called Rushdie 'a dangerous opportunist . . . he knew exactly what he was doing . . . This kind of sensationalism does indeed get an indifferent book to the top of the bestseller list . . . but to my mind it is a cheap way of doing it . . . In a civilized world we all have a moral obligation to apply a modicum of censorship to our own work in order to reinforce this principle of free speech.'

Angela's support for Rushdie was as unwavering as it was unqualified. 'She was somebody I could call up and kind of fulminate at,' he remembered. 'At that point there wasn't much she could do except be an ear.' Nonetheless, she made every effort to do more. On 1 March she put her name to a 'World Writers' Statement', declaring – along with thousands of literary figures from across the globe – that they were all involved in *The Satanic Verses* in so far as they supported its publication. The meeting of the 20 June Group that month was dominated by discussion of Rushdie's plight, and it was agreed that they would send a joint letter to Neil Kinnock, the leader of the Labour Party, urging him to make a statement on Rushdie's behalf. Shortly afterwards, Angela was part of a delegation of authors and intellectuals organised by Article 19 – the campaign group set up to defend freedom of expression – to speak to a gathering of moderate Muslim leaders about *The Satanic Verses*. On the day in question, only Angela and Kazuo Ishiguro turned up at the appointed time. Ishiguro remembered the atmosphere being uncomfortable:

Some of these guys were very, very angry about *The Satanic Verses*. And Angela of course was in her Angela mode. She was at her most eccentric and dreamy. Somebody would bark some sort of furious thing and she'd make some reference to ancient Greek something or other . . . and I just thought, what's happened to the other guys, all these actual professional campaigners from Article 19?

Angela stayed in touch with Rushdie throughout this period, and saw him as often as the cloak-and-dagger nature of his new existence would allow. He remembers that his protection officers liked visiting The Chase more than they liked visiting some of his other friends, because while most people tended to ignore them, 'she always made sure that they had a good meal, and were taken care of, and had a TV to watch'.

She retained a sense of outrage about what had happened to Rushdie until the very end of her life. One of the last things she ever wrote was the introduction to *Expletives Deleted*, a collection of her journalism that was published in 1992. It ends with these words:

> For more than three years, Salman Rushdie, Britain's most remarkable writer, has suffered the archaic and cruel penalty of a death sentence, passed on him for writing and publishing a book. All those who work in the same profession are affected by his dreadful predicament, whether they know it or not. Its reverberations upon the freedoms and responsibilities of writers are endless. Perhaps writing *is* a matter of life and death. All good fortune, Salman.

'That moved me to tears really, when I saw that,' Rushdie remembered. 'At that moment in my life I felt very weakened by what had happened . . . She was a friend in need.'

Although she still wasn't paid the sort of attention that Rushdie and McEwan were, Angela Carter had a robust, somewhat cultish reputation by the end of the 1980s. There were pockets of the London literary world – including those associated with Virago and the *London Review of Books* – that accorded her superstar status. 'She was always surrounded by people,' remembered Fleur Adcock, who often saw her at parties. 'Everybody was all over her.' 'More or less everybody around her sucked up to her,' agreed Andrew Motion. '"Oh Angela, you are wonderful." That was very much the mood in her close circle.' It was often the mood somewhat further afield, as well. By the time she was forty-eight she was receiving letters from students all over the world who were writing doctoral theses on her work, as well as regular invitations to give lectures and to speak at academic conferences.

In May 1989 she went to the University of Basel as guest of honour for a symposium 'On Strangeness' organised by the Swiss Association of University Teachers of English. Neil Forsyth, an old friend from Japan, was also there, giving a paper on Tom Stoppard, and Angela joined the audience. He remembered that it took him a while to recognise her because of her long grey hair, and that afterwards she teased him about 'how long it had taken me to see her beneath all the changes'. They talked about Stoppard rewriting Shakespeare in such plays as *Dogg's Hamlet, Cahoot's Macbeth* and *Rosencrantz and Guildenstern Are Dead*, a project that Angela felt 'overlapped' with *Wise Children*. For her own paper she read 'Alice in Prague' – a new story that mixed alchemical motifs with a version of *Alice in Wonderland* inspired by Jan Švankmajer's recent film – and made a few introductory remarks about its composition, saying that it was a privilege to read the story at the university where the alchemist and occultist Paracelsus had been a student.

The following month she travelled to Budapest. The Wheatland Foundation – a venture set up by the American heiress Ann Getty and the British publisher Lord Weidenfeld – had since 1987 been sponsoring an annual International Writers' Conference, at which authors from around the world made presentations (with the aid of simultaneous translations) about the state of literature in their respective countries. This was the first time that the conference had taken place in Eastern Europe – a development made possible by Soviet leader Mikhael Gorbachev's policy of glasnost, or openness to the West – and there was an excited atmosphere of being at the centre of world events. The talks took place in the Hilton hotel, in a grand hall where the Hungarian parliament had once met. Several of the great names in world literature were there: Alain Robbe-Grillet, Chinua Achebe, Nadine Gordimer, Nuruddin Farah, Susan Sontag and Richard Ford among them. Angela was joined on the British panel by Paul Bailey, Kazuo Ishiguro, Jeremy Treglown, David Hare, Christopher Hope and David Pryce-Jones.

Angela liked Budapest – 'a lovely, shabby city [with] that Middle Europe scent of summer, is it lime blossom?' – but most of the talks were impossibly dull. 'Authors suddenly thought they were at the United Nations representing their country', Kazuo Ishiguro remembered. Paul Bailey sat next to Angela for much of the proceedings, and recalled that they giggled like schoolchildren at the pomposity of it all:

> Susan Sontag graced us with a lecture one day . . . I can't remember exactly what she said but it was along these lines: 'I was reading Dickens at five . . . By the time I was ten I'd progressed to the real heavyweights, like Tolstoy and Dostoevsky.' And Angela leaned towards me and whispered, 'Wouldn't you fucking know.' She was no respecter of reputations at all. It didn't matter if they'd been praised to the skies, she took her own line on them.

The first ripple in the bland surface of the week came when the right-wing Russian writer and activist Eduard Limonov heckled the Polish Nobel laureate Czesław Miłosz during his keynote speech. Miłosz was talking about the Nazi–Soviet pact of 1939, when Limonov began shouting that Russia had done more than any other country to defeat Hitler: 'How many Soviet soldiers died in liberating Auschwitz?' he yelled. Miłosz ignored him.

But Limonov wasn't finished. On the evening of 24 June, the final night of the conference, the delegates were drinking champagne in the hotel bar. The British and Russian panels were sitting on nearby tables. Paul Bailey described what happened:

> Every country had to elect someone to say thank you to the Gettys and to the Hungarian Arts Council or whatever it was. So I thanked them, and I said, 'It's been a wonderful week, there's only been one drawback, there's one person whose behaviour has been shamelessly terrible.' But I didn't name him. And he . . . suddenly turned up at the table, he came straight to me and he said, 'Are you in favour of capital punishment?' I said, 'That's a strange question to ask at two o'clock in the morning.' And he said it again. 'Are you in favour of capital punishment?' I said, 'No, of course I'm not.' And he said, 'I thought so. You're one of those liberal cunts, aren't you.' And then I said, 'Is there something wrong with you? Are you a secret transvestite by any chance?' And he picked up the bottle of champagne and hit me over the head with it.

It was a startling moment. Paul collapsed to the floor and 'just sort of saw stars for a few minutes'. Angela was sitting close by and the swinging bottle only narrowly missed her. The other Russian delegates ran over and pulled Limonov off with the help of Leon Wieseltier, literary editor of the

New Republic ('people you don't expect to be involved in something like that', as Kazuo Ishiguro put it. 'The whole thing was quite surreal'). But Paul emerged with nothing worse than a bump on the head, and soon they were all regarding it as a funny story. The next day, Mark met them at the airport. As they were driving back into London, Angela told the story of Limonov as if it was a joke, but Mark was outraged. He wanted to find Limonov and do him over. 'He did always fiercely leap to Angela's defence,' Lorna MacDougall (who was married to Ishiguro, and had been with them in Budapest) remembered. 'I think partly she got a rise out of him sometimes so he could really leap to her defence because he was so good at that.' In this case, at least, Mark's defensive instincts were sound. Limonov surfaced again in 1992 at the side of Radovan Karadžić – the so-called 'Butcher of Bosnia', who in March 2016 was found guilty of genocide – and was filmed firing a sniper rifle at an apartment block in the besieged city of Sarajevo.

One of the reasons for the sudden improvement in Angela Carter's academic reputation during the 1980s was that the South American literary influences she had started to display in the previous decade – in *Fireworks* and *The Infernal Desire Machines of Dr Hoffman* – had suddenly become fashionable. She now began trying to distance herself from them, asserting her individuality in the face of attempts to identify her with a particular trend. In July 1989, during a conversation about magical realism at the Institute of Contemporary Arts, she vehemently denied that she was a representative of the genre, arguing that the phrase was meaningless when applied to any writing 'in which something out of the way happens', rather than being used in the specific context of Latin American literature.

Three months later, on 18 October, she gave the Jorge Luis Borges Memorial Lecture of the Anglo-Argentine Society at the Royal Society of Arts. Focussing mainly on *The Book of Imaginary Beings*, Borges's vivid and eccentric bestiary of fictional creatures, she said that 'the urge to categorise, to classify, to sort out, divide up, store away tidily – the taxonomic passion' was what she loved most about his work. It's a surprising claim. Her own passion was for disordering things, exploding categories, undermining divisions. Perhaps it was a way of acknowledging her weakness for the Argentinian – and for South American literature more generally – while drawing attention away from the true nature of her debt.

* * *

Angela had been contracted to deliver *Wise Children* in December 1988, but a year later she was still working frantically on the novel. 'I've never met anyone – apart maybe from Lucian [Freud] – who's quite so focussed on what they're doing,' Mark remembered. 'I would say it was obsessive, but not an obsessive regime. Everything was fluid . . . She always had room for something else, but she never got distracted by it. The main focus was always work.' Now that Alex was at school all day – he was six years old by the end of 1989 – she had largely returned to the working habits she had been used to before he was born. She took time off to prepare some food for him when he came home from school, and sat with him while he ate, but she often went back to work afterwards. Mark took him to school in the mornings, and was responsible for looking after him at weekends and during the holidays. Several of Angela's friends thought that Mark's style of parenting was excessively strict, but they noticed that Angela never interfered in that side of things.

Being a full-time parent meant that Mark was able to devote less and less of his time to pottery. He had given up the studio he rented in east London shortly after they returned from Austin in 1985, and had recently begun helping out around Alex's school. He enjoyed it, and decided to retrain as a teacher. 'Angela really encouraged me,' he remembered. He needed to get his English and maths GCSEs first, so he enrolled on an access course in Brixton, and went there every day after dropping Alex off at school.

Around this time, they bought a 'very second-hand' barge – named *Crowfoot* – which they moored on the canal near Regent's Park. Mark and Alex took it out quite regularly at the weekends; Angela sometimes joined them. It appealed to her sense of folksy romance. After one of her first excursions in the boat, she wrote to Lorna Sage:

> The canals are wonderful . . . You get this Ophelia-style view of the canal bank, huge juicy plants & flowers & grasses; and we saw herons, & a king-fisher, & it was that frail, chilly, early spring that is so English, & the East End – we went through Hackney – is now really one vast nature reserve, mile after mile of abandoned factories returning to the wild. I kept thinking: 'This dereliction produced the wealth that made London the richest city in the world.' All gone. It was like Ozymandias.

They went as far as Waltham Abbey on one occasion, and regularly went to the cemetery at Kensal Green. They sometimes took friends along with them. Liz Calder, who went with them to Little Venice one day, remembered that Mark 'took charge and ordered everyone around, including [Angela] . . . She loved it when people admired his pots, or in this case the barge – it was his toy.' Susannah Clapp remembers sitting in the cabin while Alex told her 'a long and intricate story about a mouse'. Fleur Adcock – who joined them on 11 February 1990, the day that Nelson Mandela was released from prison – remembered that they had a radio on board, and that Angela served olive bread and hearty soup. On a couple of occasions they spent the night on board: they were woken by the sound of ducks outside, and ate breakfast on deck with a view of the elephants at London Zoo. 'It was magic,' Mark remembered.

CHAPTER TWENTY-FOUR

Call it a happy ending

By the beginning of 1990, Angela's hair had started to turn from grey to white. She wore big glasses that covered half her face, and tended to dress in long, flowing skirts and baggy jumpers ('I've passed a point in the size barrier where what you like is quite different from what you can get,' she explained). Most of her friends felt that she was becoming happier and more self-assured as she got older, and people who met her for the first time during this period are inclined to describe her as grandmotherly: gentle, good-natured, and seemingly content. It was an image that she did nothing to discourage. When she went to Naples that summer on a British Council junket, a member of the audience asked: 'Who is Angela Carter?' To which she replied: 'A middle-aged woman who still has most of her teeth.'

There's little reason to doubt that she was as content as she appeared, although it isn't easy to measure the distance between her public and private selves during this period of her life. She had been keeping her journals less and less regularly since Alex's birth – the one that she began in 1983 had lasted her five years – and she stopped keeping them altogether after she was diagnosed with cancer in 1991. The menopause diary that she kept throughout 1990, with its frequent references to 'tears' and 'despair', does suggest that she wasn't always as happy and self-possessed as people tended to assume. But it's impossible to tell whether these brief (often single-word) entries are reports on her prevailing mental weather, or merely notes on fleeting moods. All we really know about her state of mind during the last two years of her life is what she allowed others to see – both on the page and in person – and that was someone who had successfully fashioned her own set of circumstances, someone who was entirely comfortable with her career, her family, her lifestyle and herself.

David Mitchell, then a twenty-one-year-old student at the University of Kent (and subsequently the author of the Booker-shortlisted novels *number9dream* and *Cloud Atlas*), remembers Angela visiting the campus in 1990 to give a reading. She looked 'like a benign witch', he wrote in 2010, 'with . . . an other-worldly serenity'. As she read from a work in progress (*Wise Children*), two elderly audience members sitting at opposite ends of the room fell asleep and began 'snoring in out-of-sync stereo'. Angela paused, glanced up at them, and said: 'My devotees follow me wherever I go.' 'The laughter woke the snorers, which was even funnier,' Mitchell remembered.

After the reading, he asked Angela to sign his second-hand copy of *The Bloody Chamber*:

> Happily, I was too nervous to tell Angela Carter how I, too, wanted to be a novelist some day . . . Less happily, I asked her a 60-second question about Jungian archetypes in her work, designed to impress her with how much Northrop Frye I had ingested. The sort of writer who enjoys hunting out fools to not suffer gladly would have atomised such a pretentious pest – who deserved no less – but Angela Carter's reply was a gentle, 'I didn't really mean that, no.' She didn't know she was teaching me anything, but she was, and it was this: be forgiving to the young idiot you too once were.

*   *   *

On 11 March, Angela flew to New Zealand for the Wellington International Festival, taking Mark and Alex with her (the festival organisers paid for them all to go first class). While she gave readings and participated in panel discussions, 'the boys' (as she called them) made excursions along the coast, where on one occasion, to their great delight, they saw an albatross. '[Angela] wanted them to experience the perks, if you like, the benefits of her career,' remembered Caryl Phillips, who was also present at the festival. The rest of the British contingent was made up of Ian McEwan, the poets James Fenton and Charles Causley, the composer Michael Tippett, and the members of the Lindsay String Quartet.

Phillips and McEwan played tennis every morning during the festival, and were quite competitive with one another. Angela was often sitting in the hotel lobby when they returned, and greeted them by saying: 'Hello boys, who won?' Phillips saw this as her way of 'basically taking the piss – in a gentle way, not a malicious way at all, but she was just a mischief maker . . . I was so happy to see her.' McEwan, who hadn't seen much of her since he moved from London to Oxford a few years earlier, was struck by how much she'd changed:

> By that time Angela had become quite a star, and was a very striking figure, with this hair that was turning white and spilling down her shoulders and back, and to my mind [she] had acquired this authority. She was always very tentative – she had a kind of stuttering speech, backtracking and having second thoughts halfway through a sentence, she would be interestingly tangled – and it struck me that now she'd settled into a new persona which was calmer and more certain . . . She just no longer spoke in that constant self-interrupting way.

After the festival, Angela, Mark and Alex drove to Lake Taupo and Auckland, then flew to the South Island on 29 March to visit Dunedin, Darfield and Christchurch. 'I've never been in a country – except maybe France – with such a variety of landscape, so various, mostly all beautiful,' Angela wrote in her journal. After a week they flew to Sydney, where they stayed with the painter Arthur Boyd. They returned to London on 13 April.

Three weeks later, Deborah Rogers threw Angela a lunch party to celebrate her fiftieth birthday. The guests included Kazuo Ishiguro and Lorna MacDougall, Carmen Callil, Susannah Clapp, Lorna Sage and Rupert Hodson, Robert and Pili Coover, Ursula Owen, Bill Webb, John Cox and John Hayes, Ann McFerran and Snoo Wilson, and Corinna Sargood. Alex played with Ann's and Snoo's children, while the adults stood around talking with plates of food and glasses of wine balanced precariously in their hands. Carmen took several photographs that day: in every one of them, Angela is beaming.

Towards the end of the summer, Angela sent an idea to Waldemar Januszczak, the head of arts at Channel 4 television. *The Holy Family Album* is a sort of pastiche documentary with a bold and provocative conceit: that representations of Christ in Western art – from Renaissance masterpieces to comic-book images – are photographs from God's own album. Januszczak loved the idea: 'I always saw it as rather like an Angela Carter short story, but done on television.' John Ellis of Large Door Productions was brought on board as the producer, and Jo Ann Kaplan as the director. Angela walked with Kaplan around the Victoria and Albert Museum in central London, pointing out some of the paintings and sculptures she had in mind for the film, and also took her to a shop called Padre Pio, which sold Catholic icons. 'She had lots of ideas for how to do certain things and what she intended,' Kaplan recalled. One of the things she had in mind was a grotto that Corinna Sargood – now living in east London, but spending a portion of each year in Mexico – had built in her garden. It appears in the film as the venue for an appearance of the Infant of Prague.

The script, which Angela delivered on 1 March 1991, went out of its way to be offensive to Christians. Footage of a cheap conjurer in a top hat and tails is juxtaposed with paintings of the feeding of the 5,000. A graphic shot of a woman's vagina during childbirth – a baby's head crowning bloodily out – segues into a scene of the nativity. '[God] did not forget to bring his camera to the birth, but he had to be circumspect about it, because he was the natural father, remember, not the legal father,' says the voiceover, which was done by Angela herself. When it comes to the crucifixion, she says:

> He was a cruel God. He was a cruel father. Remember, he'd planned all this. All the books say he'd planned it out, right from the very beginning . . . Perhaps we read Oedipal conflict the wrong way. Perhaps men don't want to kill their fathers – surely not, or how could Christianity have lasted all this time? – but deep down they want to kill their sons, just like God did, to get rid of the rival, the one she thought was dropped from heaven, the one, deep down, he knows she loves the best.

The other major project that Angela worked on during this period was an anthology of folk stories about girls and women – started under the working title *Feminist Fairy Tales*, it was eventually published as *The Virago Book of Fairy Tales* – for which she was paid £10,000 for world hardback and paperback rights. She had originally conceived of editing a series of anthologies (modelled on Andrew Lang's twelve 'coloured' Fairy Books – blue, red, green and so on) in the mid-1980s, and had signed a contract for the first one in November 1988. By that time Carmen was no longer involved with the day-to-day running of Virago, and the first volume was overseen by Ursula Owen, the second one by Lennie Goodings (Owen having left Virago by then to become cultural policy advisor to the Labour Party and director of the party's Paul Hamlyn Fund).

Angela's working definition of a fairy tale was simply a story derived from the oral tradition, one that had 'no particular author'. This tradition was, at least in European cultures, associated with the dismissive convention of Mother Goose, the old woman sitting by the fire and telling frivolous stories to the children. Angela chose her title somewhat in a spirit of defiance: 'Can you see Martin Amis allowing himself to be observed leafing through something called *The Virago Book of Fairy Tales*? He'd rather be seen reading *Guns and Ammunition*.' The majority of the tales that she selected are decidedly not children's stories, however: coarse wit and sexual wisdom abound. Nor are fairies prominent among the cast of characters, although supernatural beings of one kind or another do make appearances. The tales were selected from a wide variety of cultures – Chinese, Russian, Kashmiri, Inuit – but all of them feature a female protagonist. Angela chose to combine geographical range with sexual particularity not in order to show 'that we are all sisters under the skin . . . I don't believe that . . . Rather, I wanted to demonstrate the extraordinary richness and diversity of responses to the same common predicament – being alive – and the richness and diversity with which femininity, in practice, is represented in "unofficial" culture: its strategies, its plots, its hard work.' She appended incisive little footnotes to several of the tales, notes that were 'not so much scholarly as idiosyncratic', as she freely confessed. 'Swahili storytellers believe that women are incorrigibly wicked, diabolically cunning and sexually insatiable,' she observes in relation to one tale. 'I hope this is true, for the sake of the women.'

She derived 'a good deal of pleasure' from her research, much of which was conducted in the London Library on St James's Square, where she would go a couple of afternoons a week to wander round the stacks. After the stress of finishing *Wise Children* ('Being funny for 250 pages is <u>hell</u>,' she wrote to Fleur Adcock in December, 'it nearly killed me'), she was happy to concentrate on a project that gave her room to breathe, and allowed for a bit more time spent with Mark and Alex. A *Sunday Times* 'Life in the Day' feature, published in 1991, suggests that she achieved a perfect balance between work and family life during this period:

The radio alarm goes off at 7.30 a.m. so we wake up to the joyful sound of the news. Alex comes in with his *bon mot* for the day. 'When do ducks get up?' he'll say, to which the correct answer is: 'I don't know.' And he says: 'At the quack of dawn.'

There was a Fifties film called *Woman in a Dressing Gown*, and that's what I become for the next few hours. I put on this egg-stained dressing gown and become instantly squalid as I make breakfast. Once every three months Mark goes to Sainsbury's, and for six weeks after he eats muesli; Alex has toast and yoghurt, and I eat whatever is in the larder – cold leftovers from last night's takeaway curry if I can get away with it.

We drink proper coffee, and I read the *Guardian*; Alex reads the *Beano* or *Whizzer and Chips*, and Mark ostentatiously reads nothing. The mail has probably come by now. I seem to be on a lot of people's mailing lists. I get a lot of stuff asking me to subscribe to anti-pornography groups, and others asking me to subscribe to pro-pornography groups, but very little actual pornography.

I have radios throughout the house, tuned to Radio 3. After the 8.30 news bulletin we discover that Alex hasn't cleaned his teeth or washed his face, and Mark calls on me to do something maternal like comb his hair. Mark takes Alex to school before he goes off to be a mature student . . .

By about 10.30 I've slowly ascended to the top of the house where I work. Mark is always suggesting that I take up a flask or an electric kettle on the grounds that if I want coffee I come down to the kitchen where I find something to do or read. But I don't see why I should be secreted away like some sacred object. I think I should be more integrated into the house.

She quite often had lunch with either Carmen or Deborah. If she stayed at home then she tended to delay eating until about half-past two, so as to give herself a decent stretch of work beforehand. Eventually, when hunger got the better of her, she made a hasty meal of 'toasted cheese sandwiches, yoghurt, fruit, whatever's in the larder'. After lunch she did a bit more work before attending to domestic duties:

> I do a little shopping on the way to pick up Al, who is usually exhausted and keen to get home to take his shoes off and watch *Count Duckula* on TV. I might watch, too . . .
>
> On weekdays Al has tea at about six o'clock, and then we have our quality time together. We play ludo, or he reads to me and I read to him, or we just sit doing parallel play. I work on his scrapbook,

making collages out of postcards. Then his dad puts him to bed, while I cook supper.

'When I was 30, if I'd known what life would be like at 50, I'd have slit my wrists,' Angela told the *Sunday Times*. 'What I wanted then was a bit of flash.' But she had come to appreciate the less flashy things in life, and placed a high value on such quiet domestic intervals. 'Truthfully,' says Dora Chance, 'these glorious pauses do, sometimes, occur in the discordant but complementary narratives of our lives and if you choose to stop the story there, at such a pause, and refuse to take it any further, then you can call it a happy ending.'

CHAPTER TWENTY-FIVE

How sweet it was!

In September 1990 – as she was preparing for an event on the life and work of the film-maker Pier Paolo Pasolini – Angela began to experience chest pains. Not long afterwards, she developed a cough; it became so bad that she sometimes couldn't sleep. Her doctor prescribed antibiotics, which had no effect. By mid-January 1991 her chest was 'very, very painful', and she was presenting a number of other symptoms: she was constantly exhausted, and her stomach hurt when she sat down. By the end of February her breathing was becoming laborious. She went back to the doctor, who referred her to the Brompton Hospital for an X-ray on Thursday 21 March. It revealed a tumour on her right lung, which had spread to her lymph glands, making it inoperable.

'Things happened very quickly after that,' she wrote to Fleur Adcock. She was given various tests, and a course of radiotherapy was arranged. Wendy Burford, a nurse specialist in palliative care, spoke to her about managing her symptoms. Almost twenty-five years later, Burford still remembered the conversation:

> I can see her now walking across the outpatients [ward], with her very . . . sort of flyaway hair, and she had a very friendly, warm face, and the consultant had asked me to speak to her. And she kept talking about her boys, so I assumed she'd got more than one child . . . Most people, when they're newly diagnosed, are very anxious and very frightened about what's going to happen, then usually it settles down once treatment starts. She was going to fight it. She was anxious when I first met her, but she was going to fight it all the way. She had a very strong personality.

Mark quit his access course to look after her – ferrying her to and from appointments at the hospital, cooking and cleaning for her at home – and together they spoke to Alex about what was happening. 'We were very damning about the way the English culturally shield their children from that kind of thing,' remembered Mark. 'We decided that obviously we wouldn't be full-on, but Alex was introduced to the fact that Angela was ill, and then gradually, as we knew more, so he knew more.' The children in his class at school sent her 'Get Well Soon' cards.

The Brompton didn't have its own radiotherapy department, so Angela went at ten thirty every morning to the Royal Marsden, where she was 'blasted with gamma rays – ½ a minute on each side, like a minute steak – & sent home'. The treatment didn't cause her any pain or discomfort, but it did make her incredibly sleepy. She usually went to bed as soon as she got back from the hospital and stayed there until Alex came home from school, when she made an effort to appear a bit livelier than she felt. She told Salman Rushdie that the treatment was 'sufficiently enervating that you can't really think beyond it':

> I kept chanting to myself, 'Kill the mad, bad cells!' until I realised I was investing the horrid little things with a kind of Byronic glamour, like Lucifer in PARADISE LOST, all that anarchic, anti-authoritarian chaos . . . and <u>that</u> won't do at all, so now I chant 'Kill the psychotic cells!' and visualise them as teeny, tiny Rottweilers, vile, mindless, all teeth and no sensibility, and I am sure this is a much more positive attitude.

*   *   *

When she did think beyond the treatment, it was usually in a pragmatic frame of mind: she wanted to make sure that Mark and Alex were properly provided for in the event of her death. On 16 April she made her will. She bequeathed £20,000 to Hughie and Joan, left everything else to Mark, and appointed Susannah Clapp as her literary executor. 'Her requirements for her estate were relaxed, if not exactly straightforward,' Susannah remembered. 'I should do whatever was necessary to "make money for [her] boys".' Angela's other major concern was that, because they'd never married, Mark wouldn't have automatic custodial rights over Alex if she died. On 2 May, they made their union official at Lambeth Registry Office. Their next-door neighbours, Jeanne and Ian Maclean, acted as witnesses, and Alex was also there, wearing a blue velvet suit that they'd bought him specially for the occasion. They didn't invite anyone else. Afterwards they went for a meal in the local Indian restaurant.

At the same time as making these arrangements, Angela was planning to recover. On 1 June, as soon as her course of radiotherapy was over, she pitched a new novel to Carmen. *Adela* was to be a fantasia on the life of Jane Eyre's pupil Adèle Varens (sometimes known as Adela). It would pick up the story where Charlotte Brontë left off, with Jane's marriage to Adela's guardian Mr Rochester. Adela is packed off to boarding school, where she 'eventually learns, from a newly arrived French mistress, that her mother is not dead at all but alive and well in Paris'. After stopping by Thornton Hall to seduce Rochester, only to discover that he's (whoops) her father, Adela travels to Paris, and finds her mother 'singing incendiary revolutionary songs in a notorious cabaret. Old, raddled, haggard, her mother is an altogether unexpected discovery.' Then the Franco-Prussian War breaks out, followed by the Siege of Paris (the action of *Jane Eyre* takes place some fifty years earlier; *Adela* 'plays some tricks with history', Angela wrote). In the end, Jane rescues Adela from prison and reveals that Rochester has, at long last, acknowledged her as his child. 'Adela says she would rather be known as her mother's daughter.' These bare bones of the story are all we have, but it looks as though *Adela* was going to be a return to some of the themes – legitimacy and illegitimacy, remote fathers and plucky daughters, the general shortcomings of patriarchy – that went into *Wise Children*.

'I envisage it at around 50,000 words,' Angela told Carmen, 'very sulphurous and over-the-top, more in the style of "The Bloody Chamber" but with some laughs.' Carmen wanted to offer more money than she had for *Wise Children*, but Simon Master, her chief executive, was cautious: 'The last thing we want to do in the present circumstances is not be supportive of any writing that Angela is trying to do. However this is really only a novella based on a nice but rather "miniaturist" idea . . . It is clearly not a major work – which understandably Angela could hardly contemplate at the moment – and I wonder what you reckon you could do with it.' In the end, it was decided that Carmen would offer £100,000 for world hardback and paperback rights – but that the contract would include a new collection of journalism and a new collection of stories (both of which could be gathered from work that Angela had already completed) along with the novel. It was a canny move. *Adela* never made it past the proposal, but the journalism was published as *Expletives Deleted* in 1992, and the stories as *American Ghosts and Old World Wonders* in 1993.

On 12 June, *Wise Children* was published with great fanfare. There were posters all over the London Underground, elaborate displays in bookshop windows, and an ambitious publicity schedule lined up, though this had to be scaled back due to Angela's lack of energy. She did manage an appearance at the Birmingham Readers' and Writers' Festival on Saturday 11 May, as well as a few readings and bookshop signings in London. She was interviewed by Susannah Clapp for the *Independent on Sunday*, Peter Kemp for the *Sunday Times*, and Paul Bailey for BBC Radio 3.

Many of the reviews were written by other novelists, and the majority of them were extremely positive. In the *Scotsman*, Shena Mackay called *Wise Children* 'a bravura demonstration of [Carter's] gifts . . . a generous affirmation of life and love'. In the *Daily Telegraph*, Ruth Rendell agreed that it was 'wonderful . . . there is not much fiction around as good as this'. Reviewing the novel for the *Times Literary Supplement*, Edmund White pronounced it 'Angela Carter's best book. It deserves many prizes and, better than that, the affection of generations of readers.' Jonathan Coe, writing in the *Guardian*, thought that the interplay between high and low culture was 'an important subject for any novel. Importance need not entail solemnity, however, when we're dealing with a writer as quick-witted, as intelligent and as deeply in love with life as Angela Carter clearly is.' And Salman Rushdie, writing in the *Independent on Sunday*, called *Wise Children* 'a funny, funny, funny book . . . even better than *Nights at the Circus*. It deserves all the bouquets, diamonds, stage-door Johnnies and hollow crowns it can get.'

Negative responses tended to focus on the manic pitch and tendency towards excess. In a thoughtful, nuanced piece for *The Times*, the biographer Victoria Glendinning acknowledged the 'exuberant virtuosity' on display, but felt that 'the great comic set-pieces of pandemonium and bally-hoo go on rather too long, and numb the reader's response. The arch nudges and winks become tiresome.' The novelist and critic Harriet Waugh, writing in the *Evening Standard*, agreed that the hilarity came at the expense of emotional depth: 'It is all a jolly exercise in bringing to cartoon-life sepia photographs of those eras, and by the time the characters take their bow . . . just a little bit tedious.'

These dissenting voices were lost in the thunder of applause. *Wise Children* was named the *Sunday Express* Book of the Year, and became the greatest commercial success of Angela Carter's writing life, spending a fortnight in the lower reaches of the bestseller lists.

On Wednesday 12 June there was a launch party at Carmen's house in Chelsea. Jonathan Burnham from Chatto & Windus played the piano, while the writer Francis Wyndham sang songs from the shows. Angela sat down throughout, with Mark at her side, but otherwise she seemed more or less herself. Not all of the guests realised she was ill. It was only later that Pauline Melville could make sense of the 'flicker of . . . dislike or disapproval' that she caught when she asked whether Angela minded her smoking. Marina Warner, on the other hand, noticed a difference in Angela's voice: 'It sounded short of breath.' But when Susannah Clapp asked if she was enjoying herself, Angela replied: 'Yes . . . I feel loved.'

On 30 June, Angela went with Mark and Alex to Liz Calder's house near Carcassonne in the south of France. Liz wasn't there, but Carmen and Susannah both flew over to join them. A photograph taken by Carmen shows the others sitting outside one evening, glasses of red wine and mineral water on the table between them, smiling at the camera – all except Mark, who looks tired and preoccupied. During the day, he practised archery (his latest enthusiasm) by the pool and Angela sat around drawing. She left behind a picture of a watermelon, done in bright pink and green crayon, by way of a thank you, and Alex wrote a message in the guest book: 'LOVELY HERE WISH YOU WERE HERE TWO. LOVE ALEX.'

They returned to London on 12 July. Initial signs were that the radio-therapy had been successful. On 13 August, Carmen wrote to the novelist Margaret Forster:

> News on Angela is excellent: the radiotherapy is over and they report it's done very well. However she has a chest infection and a persistent cough due to the fact, I think, that she's run-down and she also has a very bad shoulder because she fell over in a taxi on the way to the hospital and sprained it. All these things seem much more important when you're low which, after radiotherapy, obviously she is. But the doctors are very pleased with her and we're all much more hopeful: it's been a grim time.

The chest infection turned into pneumonia, and Angela was admitted to the Brompton for a few days towards the end of the month. From her bed she worked on *Expletives Deleted*, the first of the three books she had promised Carmen. She had already started going through her journalism from the past three decades with the help of Mark Bell, an editorial assistant at Chatto & Windus (and previously an assistant at the Deborah Rogers Agency), whom she self-mockingly referred to as her amanuensis. He would visit her at The Chase – and on one occasion at the Brompton – and she would send him away again with piles of articles to photocopy and details of others to track down. 'I had no idea I'd done so much,' she wrote to him on 3 September. The selection process was guided as much by a desire to represent the full range of her interests as to showcase her best work. 'She was very much choosing the pieces to tie in with themes she thought were important in her life,' Bell remembered. On 26 September, she asked him to remove from the selection a negative review she'd written in 1974 of Borges's *Introduction to English Literature* ('an idiosyncratically bland little book . . . It appears to have been composed in the cosiest of panelled libraries at some eternal teatime') because 'I don't think it's fair to the grand old man to whom I owe so much.'

The results of new tests at the end of August showed that the disease was getting worse. For a brief period, Angela was given chemotherapy – Michael Moorcock provided her with cannabis, which she baked into cakes, to offset the side effects – and on 1 October she wrote to Connie Brothers, programme associate of the Iowa Writers' Workshop, to ask whether she might return there 'if I go into remission', since 'all 3 of us remember it with so much affection. And I think it would be good for my health.' But it soon became clear that remission wasn't on the cards. 'She coped very well,' Wendy Burford remembered. 'But she had moments when she was sad, and like most people she didn't want to die. She didn't want to leave her family behind.'

In spite of her sadness at leaving Mark and Alex, Angela refused to see death as a 'distinguished thing' (in Henry James's well-known phrase). As long ago as 1967, in *Several Perceptions*, she had written: 'Death was certainly not proud, nor even dignified; he was just a practical joker or fool with bells and [a] bladder.' She stuck to this view throughout her final illness. 'She was so brave about the whole thing,' remembered Rebecca Howard.

'I think she was furious that her life was being taken away from her. I'm sure she was scared, who wouldn't be, but she put a brave face on it, had great gallows humour.' Several examples of this have been preserved. 'Don't worry,' she said to Michael Moorcock when she went into a coughing fit while he was visiting her, 'I'm not bringing up bits of lung.' She told one correspondent that she was 'hanging on like grim death for the chance to vote this bloody government out. It's what the hospital calls "an excellent short-term goal".' Speaking to Corinna Sargood on the phone one day, she noted that a man was coming to the door. 'It's all right,' she said. 'I'll let him in. He hasn't got a scythe.'

Even in private, she never broke down. 'She was very stoical, didn't complain,' remembered Mark. The vibrant, defiantly humorous personality that she had begun crafting more than thirty years before – and that she had struggled so hard to assert – remained with her to the very end.

In September, there was a bizarre incident when a marketing consultant called David Carter was profiled by *World of Interiors*. The piece described his lushly decorated apartment, and also mentioned his fondness for lengthy monologues and fabulous tales. 'Only a newcomer or a fool would question the validity of his stories,' the journalist remarked. Several readers did, however, question his claim that he was 'raised in Ireland by Angela Carter: novelist, author of *The Company of Wolves*, and his mother'. Mark remembers Angela being 'absolutely fucking livid' about the article. The magazine's editor wrote her a jokey letter asking whether she might consider adopting David Carter. 'Not the greatest apology I've ever received,' she huffed. Even at this late stage in her life – with her identity and her originality so clearly established – people trying to 'take her over' could still cause her sense of humour to short-circuit.

The Booker Prize shortlist was another source of exasperation when it was announced later that month. *Wise Children* had been supported by two of the judges, the former *Times Literary Supplement* editor Jeremy Treglown and the writer and teacher Jonathan Keates. But this was in the days before the longlist was made public, and opposition from the remaining judges (the novelists Penelope Fitzgerald, Nicholas Mosley and Ann Schlee) kept the Chance sisters from advancing any further. 'I certainly don't seem to get the sympathy vote,' Angela reflected, when the news reached her. Others noticed that no women at all had made the shortlist that year – it consisted of *Time's Arrow* by Martin Amis, *The Van* by Roddy Doyle, *Such a Long Journey* by Rohinton Mistry, *The Redundancy of Courage* by Timothy Mo, *The Famished Road* by Ben Okri and *Reading Turgenev* by William Trevor – and plans were set in motion, by a group including Lennie Goodings of Virago, to found a prize specifically for women's fiction. This became the Orange Prize and subsequently the Baileys Prize – but it was originally going to be called the Angela Carter Prize.

In what looked to many commentators like a shameless attempt to stir up controversy, *The Holy Family Album* was shown to a group of Christian journalists and clergymen a week before the national broadcast. Within hours, Channel 4 was being bombarded with demands for the programme to be scrapped. Even liberal churchmen joined in the uproar. Canon Paul Bates of Westminster Abbey denounced the film as 'second-rate, confused and intellectually lightweight . . . I can't see the point in showing it. It's not an arts programme, it's not witty, it's not clever or profound.' In a highly unusual move, the Independent Television Commission vetted *The Holy Family Album* in advance of the broadcast. Waldemar Januszczak made the case for the defence in terms that sought to out-outrage the film's accusers: 'People are trying to fetter free speech. I see it as the same kind of repression Salman Rushdie experienced . . . We cannot allow religious fundamentalists to gag people when they are offering their own religious views.' Angela more gently fanned the flames: 'It was not my intention to blaspheme,' she told the *Observer*, 'because I do not believe that you can blaspheme against something which does not exist.' She did, however, ring up Wendy Burford – a practising Christian – to check that she was happy to continue treating her.

On 3 December 1991 – the day the film was broadcast – *The Times* criticised it in an editorial: 'That practising Christians are no longer in a majority is neither here nor there. Do Ms Carter and Channel 4 use this as an excuse to criticise blacks, Muslims or the disabled?' Four days later, *Right to Reply* – a programme that allowed viewers to air their concerns about Channel 4's output – staged a debate between the Roman Catholic theologian James Conroy and Waldemar Januszczak, who seemed to have abruptly lost his stomach for the fight. When Conroy complained about the 'crude' way the images were put together, and the 'sneering' in Angela's voiceover, Januszczak said – with an apologetic quaver – that it wasn't meant to be sneering. Rory McGrath, the host, chipped in to say: 'it clearly was sneering'. Januszczak replied: 'the fragility of her voice might have been open to some misinterpretation.' Conroy had the last word, describing the programme as 'intellectually weak', and saying that it trivialised not just religion, but also the viewer.

The reviews were no more sympathetic to the film's intentions. Alan Stanbrook, writing in the *Daily Telegraph*, was typical in calling *The Holy Family Album* 'undeniably offensive, not to say blasphemous . . . the sort of self-congratulatory twaddle that real artists leave behind in their school magazines . . . The sad thing about Angela Carter's script is that it is dishonest with itself. Glaringly absent from her neo-Freudian reading of the Gospels is any mention of the Resurrection or the Redemption. These, after all, are the central tenets of the faith . . . by ignoring them, because they don't fit conveniently into her theory, Angela Carter has not merely weakened her case but scuppered it.' Angela's friends and fellow novelists, however, were full of praise. J. G. Ballard wrote to her: 'Breton + Ernst would have been <u>proud</u> of you – your demolition job on Our Saviour was brilliant – so gentle, elegant + deadpan – congratulations.' Salman Rushdie also offered his support, to which Angela replied: 'I don't think I need any help from *you*.'

Wendy Burford and another specialist nurse, Stephen Barton, began visiting Angela at The Chase as she became more symptomatic. There was a Trinity Hospice on Clapham Common, but she was adamant that she didn't want to go there; she needed to feel that she was still essentially herself. She became fairly close to Burford during this period, discussing everything from her feelings about the friends who visited her – 'she'd comment if people had said something which she thought was particularly unhelpful, tactless' – to her anxieties about Mark and Alex. 'She was a lovely lady,' Burford remembered. 'I was very fond of her.'

Throughout this period, offers of work continued to arrive. She was asked to judge the Mind Book of the Year/Allen Lane Award, to give lectures at the universities of Stockholm and Cambridge, to write an essay for a book about William Burroughs and to contribute a short story to a *New Worlds* anthology. Neil Jordan got in touch to propose two new films that he hoped they could work on together: the first was an adaptation of her story 'The Cabinet of Edgar Allan Poe', the other was provisionally titled *Erotic Tales*, and would comprise 'tales of sexual intrigue and depravity, each with an ironic moral twist to it'. Angela declined all of these offers. She also had to cancel a trip to stay with Corinna Sargood in Mexico, and an ongoing visiting professorship at Washington University in St Louis, Missouri.

On 11 December she received a letter from the Royal Society of Literature, informing her that she had been elected a fellow. She wasn't able to make it to the ceremony. The only invitations that she appears to have accepted during this period were two requests for interviews with the BBC: the one from *Omnibus*, and another from the flagship Radio 4 programme *Desert Island Discs*. The latter was especially exciting – 'I've fantasised about being on <u>Desert Island Discs</u> for years,' she had written to Carmen in 1985 – but the production team wouldn't visit her at home, and she was too ill to make it to the studio. 'Fuck them, then', was her response. She did, however, get as far as selecting the records she would take with her to her desert island: 'The Girl with the Flaxen Hair' by Debussy (because she remembered Hughie playing it on the piano in the 1940s); 'Mannish Boy' by Muddy Waters (because she loved it and it reminded her of the late 1950s); 'Ich Liebe Dich' from Schumann's *Dichterliebe* (the first LP she ever bought); 'Willow Weep' by Billie Holliday (which reminded her of childhood visits to Streatham Ice Rink); 'Driving in my Car-Car' by Woodie Guthrie (which Alex was learning on his guitar); 'No Woman, No Cry' by Bob Marley (because it evoked south London for her); and 'Im Abendrot' by Richard Strauss (the song that was used in the David Lynch film *Wild at Heart*). Her book was *Larousse Gastronomique*, and her luxury item was a zebra.

She spent a lot of her time watching films and reading ('All those books, you understand, that one always meant to read . . .'), or just enjoying the company of Mark and Alex. 'I am still here,' she wrote to Caryl Phillips on 11 December:

> cursing & swearing vigorously, & able to hiss gleefully: 'I told you so!' about Ben Okri [the recipient of that year's Booker Prize], whose modest assumption of the role of genius has been, I am told, one of the delights of the autumn literary season, a season I am sitting out. There is an upside to everything. I haven't been to a literary party for 9 months & feel spiritually improved thereby.
>
> Mark is bearing up; we're all bearing up, in fact. Fuck it. We watch a lot of videos. Actually, it's rather a hedonistic time, in a funny way. Bed-rest & rich food.

She was wringing life for every bit of pleasure it could afford. She presented Wendy Burford with a handwritten story, an improvisation on a well-known Buddhist parable:

for Wendy

A Zen monk was walking across the mountains. He came to a narrow pass. On one side of the pass, a sheer precipice fell away into the void. On the other side, a sheer wall of rock ran up to the heavens.

As he crossed the pass, the monk saw a mountain lion approaching him from in front. Turning hastily, the monk saw another mountain lion approaching him from behind. A creeper hung over the lip of the precipice; hurriedly the monk seized hold of the creeper & swung down.

He dangled at the end of the creeper above the void. The sun shone, a refreshing breeze blew. A wild strawberry was growing just beside the creeper; the fruit was ripe and red. Above, on the pass, the two mountain lions stood roaring at one another, each refusing to permit the other to pass.

A mouse emerged from a crevice in the rock & began to nibble at the creeper. Soon it would nibble its way right through.

The monk stretched out & picked the strawberry. He ate it.

How sweet it was!

*   *   *

She was conscientious about putting her affairs in order. She took care of her finances, making provision for Mark and Alex, and gave precise instructions for her funeral. She finished editing *Expletives Deleted* and the second volume of *The Virago Book of Fairy Tales* (although she didn't get as far as writing the footnotes), and catalogued her remaining papers. While she was still relatively vigorous, she tried to see all the friends that she could, inviting them, one by one, to visit her at The Chase. It was clear to most of them that she was saying goodbye, but she resisted any note of solemnity or self-pity. Salman Rushdie remembered that on his last visit, she made the effort to dress for tea:

She was obviously in real pain. You could see it on her face that she was in considerable pain . . . [but she was] wearing a high-collared dress, with a frill . . . and sitting in an upright chair, very straight, pouring tea.

A real act of will, you know, to be herself for forty minutes or whatever it was. She managed it absolutely, and she was telling funny stories.

One of these stories – about a life insurance policy she had taken out just before her diagnosis – 'inspired a great gloating black comedy aria at which it was impossible not to laugh'. She also spoke about practical matters, instructing Rushdie that he was to read Andrew Marvell's 'On a Drop of Dew' at her funeral. The choice of such a frankly metaphysical poem surprised him: 'the Angela Carter I knew had always been the most scatologically irreligious, merrily godless of women'. This wasn't in fact indicative of a last-minute conversion to the faith: she had always loved Marvell. But before she could explain this, her energy began to flag. Mark stepped in to draw the conversation to a close: 'I think we're going to have to stop now.'

Lorna Sage had been one of her closest and most supportive friends since the mid-1970s, but a few people have suggested that the relationship faltered towards the end of Angela's life. Mark doesn't remember this – 'there was no argument or falling out that I know of, and I was there all the time' – but Carmen says that Lorna's drinking had started to upset Angela, and Sharon Sage recalls her mother being 'very hurt because someone, and I'm not quite sure who, didn't want her to come to [Angela's] funeral'. There is one contemporary bit of evidence for a cooling on Angela's side towards the friendship, although it's hardly conclusive. Lorna appeared in the *Omnibus* documentary as a talking head, but she wasn't on the list of names that Angela drew up for the producer on 20 January 1992, which contained the request: 'please do not accept anybody who is not on this list'. It's a pretty striking absence: the list included people who were extremely close to Angela (such as Hughie and Carmen) but also people to whom she was a lot less close than she had been to Lorna (such as her neighbours Jeanne and Ian Maclean, and the novelist Nuruddin Farah).

Rebecca Howard visited The Chase frequently during this period: 'Towards the end of her life Angie wanted to relive things . . . having been at Bristol and things like that. She wanted to talk, and she wanted gossip. She said: "Oh, we're not talking about serious things, I want gossip."' Even so, it's clear that Angela's journeys into the past towards the end of her life included reflecting on what kind of person she had been. In the introduction to *Expletives Deleted*, she wrote: 'I haven't changed much, over the years. I use less adjectives, now, and have a kinder heart, perhaps.' The question of her kindness was one that she returned to frequently during these weeks. 'There was a warmth about Angela which was very nice,' Wendy Burford remembered. 'But she used to say, "I haven't always been nice." I didn't know what she meant by that.'

One of the things she must have been thinking of was her treatment of Mansu Kō, the Korean boy whose heart she had broken in 1972, and then attempted to break again in 1974. His subsequent life hadn't been pretty: he had drifted in Tokyo, often sleeping in the coffee houses, and had become increasingly involved with drugs and knives. Eventually, in July 1991, he walked off the eighth floor of a building in Osaka; he didn't leave a note. On 14 January 1992, Angela wrote to Ted Holst, who had informed her of Kō's death: 'Don't think I'm immune to guilt . . . Oh, dear, oh, dear. Things turned out really badly.'

But however much pain Angela had caused Kō, she had enriched many other lives. As word that she was dying spread around the London literary world, she started to receive letters from people who wanted her to know what she had meant to them. The one that Lennie Goodings sent her on 11 February 1992 stands out for the grace and sincerity of its tone:

> I want to write & say thank you to you – for many things. For giv-ing me such delight as a reader; for all the support & encouragement you've given me & Virago; for the wonderful books you've published with us. I was talking to a friend this weekend & I mentioned your name & she said she didn't go in much for hero worship but you were her heroine – & I guess that's another way of saying what I feel too. Except that heroes are usually distant & cool, until you get close to them & then they have lead feet (or whatever that expression is!) and that's not you. You've been such fun; & such a tonic and such an interesting, good, generous human being. I feel very privileged to have had the chance to work with such a rich, rewarding writer – who also understands about being a mother . . .
>
> I send you & Mark & Alex love. From all accounts the three of you are dealing with this horribly sad & difficult time with great spirit and dignity & that is a tribute to you & Mark. You are a wonderful woman Angela.

*   *   *

As Angela's life contracted during the period of her illness – as she became progressively more housebound, and then bedbound – she came to rely on Mark for almost everything. He cooked, cleaned, took Alex back and forth from school, and dealt with the hospital; he increasingly had to help Angela move around, wash, and get dressed. 'He was devoted, he was very, very good,' remembered Rebecca Howard. On Sundays, Wendy Burford would arrive to look after Angela for a few hours, and Mark would go to the Crystal Palace National Sports Centre to practise archery: 'That was my meditation, that was my time off every week, and it kept me sane.'

By the end of January, Angela was rapidly losing weight around her face, and her energy levels were extremely low. She was set up in bed with a syringe-driver giving her morphine. A few close friends and family members – Deborah Rogers and Michael Berkeley; Rebecca Howard; Carmen Callil; Hughie and Joan Stalker; Susannah Clapp – visited her during this final phase of her life, but she didn't like people seeing her in such a depleted state. Her breathlessness meant that speech was becoming increasingly difficult, and she could often communicate only with a nod or a smile. She couldn't concentrate on books or films, but she liked listening to music on BBC Radio 3, finding it soothing.

On the morning of Sunday 16 February she was in terrible pain. It was clear that the end was close at hand. Wendy called the doctor for permission to increase the morphine dosage: 'We tried to make sure that she was comfortable, and that her breathing was as well-regulated as it could possibly be at that point in time.' Over the next few hours, Angela's awareness gradually faded. Mark stayed with her until she died, at twenty-five past two that afternoon.

Epilogue

Angela Carter's elevation to great-author status began the morning after she died. Her obituaries extolled her as a forerunner of the vibrant Rushdie generation, a unique interpreter of our common dreams, 'the Salvador Dalí of English letters'. Five weeks later, a memorial service at the Ritzy cinema in Brixton – featuring the music she had selected for *Desert Island Discs* and clips from her favourite films – was reported in the national press. 'I was just amazed,' remembered Ian McEwan. 'Usually when a writer dies their reputation collapses, and then ten years later it picks up.'

In the two and a half decades since, Angela Carter's place in the contemporary canon has never been in doubt. All of her novels and short stories are still in print. *Wise Children* and *The Bloody Chamber* are both among Vintage Classics' top ten bestsellers of all time, and *Nights at the Circus* is also among the top twenty-five. Occasions relating to her and her work – the twentieth anniversary of her death in 2012, the publication of a new edition of her poetry in 2015 – are marked by prime-time broadcasts and sell-out events. Her influence has been acknowledged by many of the outstanding writers in the generations following hers, including Jeanette Winterson, Ali Smith, Anne Enright, David Mitchell, Sarah Waters, China Miéville and Nicola Barker. Through the work of these authors, the spirit of Angela Carter – her stylistic brio and her intellectual sharpness, her indifference to realism and her fondness for pulp genres – lives on into the twenty-first century.

Dozens of books have now been written about her, but the vast majority of them have been aimed squarely at an academic audience. Anyone interested in her life hasn't had much to go on. For many years, the only substantial resource was a long essay that Lorna Sage published in *Granta* in November 1992, and subsequently adapted into a short book (titled

Angela Carter). It delivers the genuine, zesty flavour of Angela's personality, but its scope is intentionally limited to situating the work in a biographical framework, rather than providing a detailed account of the life. Since 2011, there have been a few other portraits by friends and students – a book-length memoir by Susannah Clapp, essays by Christopher Frayling, Rick Moody and Anne Enright – but in the absence of a full biography, the myth-making has largely gone unchecked.

I don't remember when or where I first became aware of her. By the time I reached university, in October 2001, I had an impression of her as a vibrant, vital force in English literature, but there was also something slightly off-putting about her reputation (a sense, perhaps, that she was just for girls – the academic literature has tended to stress her feminist consciousness at the expense of everything else), and I didn't get around to reading her at that stage. After graduating I moved to Berlin, where I spent a year giving walking tours of the city centre, writing for travel guides, and working on an unfinishable novel. One day I came across a second-hand copy of *The Magic Toyshop* in an English-language bookshop. I had recently heard Ali Smith, whose work I've always loved, speaking about her own love of Angela Carter's work – I think that was what convinced me to part with my euros. Back in my tiny room above a bakery I tore through the novel in a few intoxicated hours, stunned by the fearless quality of the imagination on display and by the luminous beauty of the prose. Over the course of that year I read as many of her books as I could get my hands on, and found out what little I could about the ebullient genius who had written them, so unlike any English writer I had previously encountered.

Five years ago I met Susannah Clapp, who since 1997 has been the theatre critic of the *Observer*. We fell to talking about Angela Carter, and I expressed my bafflement that there hadn't yet been a biography. She explained that although there was a flurry of interest immediately after Angela's death, it had been thought that the appointment of an official biographer should wait until Alex could be involved in the decision – but since he'd been old enough to have a say, there hadn't been many candidates. It hadn't previously occurred to me to propose myself, but somehow or other it came up over the course of our conversation (Susannah had read some of my journalism in the *London Review of Books* and the *Times Literary Supplement*, but I can't remember which of us first raised the idea), and a couple of days later I wrote to confirm that I'd be interested.

I'm aware that a number of my fellow Angela Carter fans have been disappointed to hear that the first biography was being written by a man. Like them, I've often worried about my ability to do her justice – but my gender hasn't been the greatest of my concerns. When it's been put to me that a man could never fully understand her, I've tended to point out that there have been many distinguished biographies of women written by men (and for that matter of men written by women); that almost all writing involves an act of identification with people who are in crucial respects unlike the author; and that Angela never thought of gender as the most important division between human beings. The last few hundred pages will have revealed the strengths or shortfalls of these arguments, and there doesn't seem much point in expanding on them here. But I'll admit that writing the life of a woman – a staunchly feminist, deeply sensual, sometimes irascible woman at that – has been more of an enlightening experience than I'd initially anticipated.

It's probably impossible to immerse yourself in another person's existence – reading their letters, retracing their journeys, spending time with their family and friends – without your own identity starting to merge with theirs in some way. By the time I was approaching the end of this book I knew on what day of 1976 Angela had finished writing *The Passion of New Eve* and exactly how long she'd spent at the University of Iowa, but I sometimes struggled to remember such basic facts about my own life as how old I was when I met my wife, or what year I graduated from university. It's been a strange and somewhat eerie process: a haunting, but there were times when I didn't know if the ghost was Angela, or me.

This feeling was at its strongest in the spring of 2013, when I retraced the fateful journey she'd made through Russia to Japan forty-two years earlier. Whatever lingering traces of tsarist luxury the Trans-Siberian Railway had retained in 1971, by the time I went they had entirely evaporated. The champagne-serving waiters in black tie had been replaced by thickly made-up *provodnitsa* who added smoke from their cigarettes to the reek of frying fat. From the inscrutable menu, I chose at random, and was presented with a stomach-turning array of knotty meats and fatty stews, garnished with bitter herbs and, often, a human hair or two. But I was constantly aware of Angela's experience – like the text on a palimpsest – beneath the surface of my own, and I drew on her courage and the power of her romanticism as I lay on my narrow berth, moving through the same desolate landscapes she'd described, towards the same unreliable man.

I had first come across the name Sozo Araki in Angela's letters to her friend Carole Roffe, and had managed to track him down with the help of a research student at Kanagawa University. It didn't take long. Although he never made it as a novelist, Sozo had by then published more than a dozen books with titles such as *Strategies for Love* and *Romance Outside Marriage*. On a cool, bright morning in early April, he walked me around Shinjuku, pointing out the sites of bars and coffee houses where he and Angela had spent time together, many of which (including the Fugetsudo) have long since vanished, replaced by faceless skyscrapers. At sixty-eight Sozo still cut a dapper, somewhat raffish figure in a sports jacket and trainers, his hair only just beginning to turn grey around the temples. He invited me back to his apartment to continue the interview. At one point I went to the bathroom: it was covered from floor to ceiling in photographs of Elvis Presley. For a moment I felt as though I'd stepped back forty years into the past, as if the aging man behind me at the sitting-room table was once again that restless, dreamy twenty-four-year-old whom Angela had loved.

At other times, the distance between Angela's life and mine has been much harder to bridge. While I've tried to be as diligent as possible, this book is not – that most chimerical of biographical aims – exhaustive. The world that Angela Carter inhabited (and to some extent shaped) is fast disappearing, and some of the people who played leading roles in the story of her life had followed her into history before I had a chance to speak to them. Lorna Sage died from emphysema in 2001, a week after *Bad Blood* received the Whitbread Prize for Biography. Her voice echoes throughout this book – her writing on Angela Carter has been among my primary sources – but the portrait of their friendship isn't what it might have been had she survived. A much more profound silence is that of Paul Carter. I had hoped that he would think twice about his refusal to speak to me, but he died a few months after I first contacted him in 2011, taking his memories of Angela, and his perspective on their marriage, with him to the grave.

Several others who did help to shape this book, and who were exceptionally generous to me during its early stages, didn't live to see it finished. Among those I'm most indebted to is Carole Roffe. When I first contacted her, in January 2012, Carole (who had by then reverted to her maiden name of Howells) said that she'd been waiting for a biographer to find her: she had kept hundreds of letters from Angela, and didn't know what to do with them. I visited her the following week at her home in Newcastle, where she allowed me to copy all the letters, and over countless cigarettes and cups of tea (displaced by glasses of wine as the evening wore on), she regaled me with her memories of Angela. Eighteen months later – while I was in Providence with Robert and Pili Coover – I received an email from Carole to say that she'd been diagnosed with cancer. I helped her transfer her letters to the British Library, where the majority of Angela Carter's papers are stored, and visited her on two further occasions over the next few months. As her condition worsened, Carole asked to read the parts of the book that I'd already finished; I'm glad that I was able to show her the chapters concerning her friendship with Angela before she died. It's a source of deep regret that I wasn't able to extend the same courtesy to Deborah Rogers, who suffered a fatal heart attack outside her home in London on 30 April 2014. Her memorial service, six months later, brought together many of the central figures of Angela's world, including Mark Pearce, Susannah Clapp, Kazuo Ishiguro, Paul Bailey and Carmen Callil. In January 2016, I received news that Angela's brother Hughie had also died – at almost the same age as his father did, and in eerily similar circumstances – after falling down the steps outside his house in Yorkshire. Each of these losses has affected me much more deeply than my own fleeting relationships with the deceased can explain.

There have been other, less poignant obstacles to exhaustiveness. A couple of people who expressed negative feelings about Angela weren't willing to go on record with them. A few others simply ignored my (increasingly insistent) requests for an interview. One person who did speak to me – someone who cared very deeply about Angela – got cold feet about showing me her letters. Many others had lost or discarded the letters that she sent them over the years. All of these gaps have produced distortions of one kind or another, and I'm especially sorry that, owing to a shortage of documentation, I haven't always done justice to the importance in Angela's life of her brother Hughie, or of her friendship with Corinna Sargood.

Ultimately, this biography is intended as a first step towards demythologising Angela Carter. I've tried to complicate the one-dimensional image of a 'white witch' or 'fairy godmother' by illuminating a few aspects – not all of them attractive – of the self she worked so hard to establish and protect. But of course, another biographer would have come at the material differently. It's taken twenty-five years for this first full account of Angela Carter's life to appear, but we won't be able to start seeing her in the round until a second one gets written, approaching her from a completely different perspective. She's much too big for any single book to contain.

Edmund Gordon, 28 February 2016

Acknowledgements

Of the many debts of gratitude I've incurred while writing this book, the most significant are to Mark and Alex Pearce, who gave me their time and eased my way, but never sought to interfere with what I wrote. Few biographers can ever have been so fortunate in their dealings with a literary estate. Susannah Clapp, as Angela Carter's literary executor, took a huge risk in appointing me, and has been answering my questions and fielding my anxieties ever since. I hope she knows how grateful I am.

For sharing their memories of Angela with me (and in many cases for allowing me to see letters, diaries and photographs), I'm indebted to Fleur Adcock, Jacqueline Anthony, Lisa Appignanesi, Sozo Araki, Paul Bailey, Pat Barker, Paul Barker, Mark Bell, Roger Bing, John Boothe, Naomi Brent and Kaktus Leach, John Brodie, Alan Brooke, Sandy Brown, A. S. Byatt, Lynne Bryan, Wendy Burford, Liz Calder, Carmen Callil, Shirley Cameron, Peter Carver, Peter Conradi, Robert and Pili Coover, Andrew Cowan, Christine Cox, John Cox and John Hayes, Tony Crofts, Neil Curry, Christine Downton, Rikki Ducornet, Anne Enright, Nicola Farthing, Neil Forsyth, Christopher Frayling, Elizabeth Graver, Zulfikar Ghose, Lennie Goodings, Tony Gould, Reg Hall, John Henty, Gary Hicks, Richard Holmes, Ted Holst, A. M. Homes, Edward Horesh, William Hossack, Rebecca Howard, the late Carole Howells, Martin Hoyle, Kazuo Ishiguro and Lorna MacDougall, Neil Jordan, Jay Jeff Jones, David Michael Kaplan, Jo Ann Kaplan, Hanif Kureishi, Hermione Lee, John Lockwood, Ray Lowry, Ian Maclean, the late Sara Maclean, Ian McEwan, Ann McFerran, Adam Mars-Jones, Pauline Melville, David Miller, Rick Moody, Andrew Motion, Michael and Linda Moorcock, Andrea Newman, Jenny Orsborn, Ursula Owen, Glenn Patterson, Caryl Phillips, Erica Rex, Neil Roberts, Janice Robertson, Jill Quantrill Robin, the late Deborah Rogers, Marsha Rowe,

Acknowledgements

Salman Rushdie, Corinna Sargood and Richard Wallace, Henry Scott Stokes, Helen Simpson, Oscar Smazlen, Philip Spencer, Harriet Spicer, Joan Stalker and the late Hugh Stalker, Joe Steeples, Peter and Janet Swan, Sharon Tolaini-Sage, Colm Tóibín, Lorna Tracy, Andrew Travers, Marina Warner, Simon Watney, Kate Webb, Fay Weldon, Naine Woodrow and Jack Zipes.

I've relied on the expertise of countless archivists and librarians while researching this book. I'd like to thank the staff of the BBC Written Archives, the British Library, the Bodleian Library at the University of Oxford, the Brotherton Library at the University of Leeds, the Colindale Newspaper Archive, the Dobkin Collection, the Emory University Manuscripts Library, the Harry Ransom Center at the University of Texas, the International Anthony Burgess Foundation, the Lilly Library at the University of Indiana, the London Library, the London Metropolitan Archives, the Maugham Library at King's College London, the Museum of London, the National Archives of the UK, the National Archives of Australia, the National Library of Australia, the National Library of Scotland, the Newcastle University Special Collections, the Ohio State University Rare Books and Manuscripts Library, the State Library of New South Wales, the State Library of South Australia, the University of Adelaide Archive, the University of Bristol Library, the University College London Library and Archive, the University of East Anglia Library and Archive, the University of Edinburgh Library, the University of Reading Library, the Oxford Brookes University Special Collections, the Random House Archive and Library, the Rogers, Coleridge & White Archive, the V&A Library, and the Women's Library at the London School of Economics.

For help with research, I'm grateful to Joseph Benavides, Naoko Choja and Simon Hammond. Francesca Wade deserves special mention: almost every chapter has benefited from her prodigious energy, resourcefulness and attention to detail.

My agent, Peter Straus, was in my corner before I ever dreamed of writing a biography of Angela Carter, and has been a source of advice and encouragement at every stage of the process. Thanks also to David Miller, Matthew Turner, and everybody else at Rogers, Coleridge & White. At Chatto & Windus, Clara Farmer (who commissioned the book) and Parisa Ebrahimi (who edited it) have been wonderful throughout. David Milner's copyediting, John Garrett's proofreading, and the index provided by Chris Bell, have all been amazingly thorough. Thanks to

Acknowledgements

Norman Hirschy and Brendan O'Neill at Oxford University Press for supervising the American edition.

I'm enormously grateful to Lisa Appignanesi, Ned Beauman, Jon Day, Lara Feigel, Adam Mars-Jones, Leo Robson and Francesca Wade for reading various sections of the manuscript and suggesting improvements; to Lindsay Duguid and John Murray-Browne for donating the beautiful desk at which most of the writing took place; to Colm Tóibín and Catarina and James Leigh-Pemberton for providing rural hideaways (on the Wexford coast and in the Aberdeenshire hills respectively) in which I was able to concentrate on my work; to Mayako Murai for looking after me in Tokyo and translating Angela Carter's Japanese articles for me; to Christian Lorentzen, Thomas Meaney and Davey Volner for looking after me in New York; to Robert and Pili Coover for showing me around Providence; and to Andrew Biswell, Rowan Boyson, Rick Gekoski, Natsumi Ikoma, Laura Kaye, Karen Shimwell, Danielle Shaw, Ivo Stourton and Andrew Wilson for sharing material and providing new leads. Thanks also to the Royal Society of Literature and the judges of the 2012 Jerwood Awards – Richard Davenport-Hines, Caroline Moorehead and Gaby Wood – whose provision of £5,000 allowed me, in the early spring of 2013, to visit Japan, and to recreate Angela's first trans-Siberian journey.

Throughout the time I've been working on this book, I've been blessed with more than my fair share of generous and inspiring friends. In addition to several of those already mentioned, I'd like to thank Alex Mavor, Amelie Hegardt, Adam O'Riordan, Andrew O'Hagan, Ed King, Tamara Atkin, William Brett, Claire Mookerjee, Tom Fleming and Jonathan Beckman. My colleagues in the English department at King's College London, and my students on the MA in Life-Writing and the MA in English: 1850–the present, have all helped sharpen my ideas. My parents, Jane and Richard Gordon, instilled me with a love of reading at an early age; for that, and for many other things, I can't thank them enough.

My wife, Sophie, has tolerated my absences and obsessive behaviour over the past five years with extraordinary good grace. This book is dedicated to her because without her generosity, optimism and strength – without her love – it could never have been written.

List of Illustrations

All photos, unless otherwise stated, are used by kind permission of the Angela Carter Estate.

Plate section I

List of Illustrations

Plate section II

Every effort has been made by the publishers to trace the holders of copyright. Any inadvertent omissions of acknowledgement or permission can be rectified in future editions.

Notes

Angela Carter's spelling was idiosyncratic. When her departures from standard English have been obviously unintentional, I've taken the liberty of correcting them. I haven't generally done the same for lapses in grammar, which apart from being much rarer, are more deeply woven into the fabric of her prose.

Some documents that were privately owned when I began my research – such as Angela's letters to Carole Roffe – have since been acquired by various archives. Many of these are still being catalogued, and a few of them have been placed under restricted access, but the references below correspond as far as possible to the current location of the material.

I've used the following abbreviations to identify major sources:

WORKS BY ANGELA CARTER:

BYB: *Burning Your Boats: Collected Stories* (London: Vintage, 1996)
CR: *The Curious Room: Collected Dramatic Works* (London: Vintage, 1997)
DH: *The Infernal Desire Machines of Dr Hoffman* (London: Penguin, 1982)
FTCP: *The Fairy Tales of Charles Perrault* (London: Penguin, 2008)
HV: *Heroes and Villains* (London: Penguin, 1981)
L: *Love* (London: Vintage, 2006)
MT: *The Magic Toyshop* (London: Virago, 1981)
NC: *Nights at the Circus* (London: Vintage, 1985)
NE: *The Passion of New Eve* (London: Virago, 1982)
NS: *Nothing Sacred* (London: Virago, 1982)
SD: *Shadow Dance* (London: Virago, 1995)
SL: *Shaking a Leg: Collected Journalism* (London: Vintage, 1998)
SP: *Several Perceptions* (London: Virago, 1995)
SW: *The Sadeian Woman* (London: Virago, 1979)

VBFT: *The Virago Book of Fairy Tales* (London: Virago, 1990)
WC: *Wise Children* (London: Vintage, 1992)

OTHER SOURCES:

Add. MS.: Additional Manuscripts collection of the British Library
AI: Author's interview with –
BLSA: The British Library Sound Archive
HRC: The Harry Ransom Center at the University of Texas
PC: Private collection of –
OS: Ohio State University Rare Books and Manuscripts Library
RCW: Rogers, Coleridge & White Archive
RH: The Random House Archive and Library

INTRODUCTION

xi 'tiny Rottweilers': Angela Carter to Salman Rushdie, 1 June 1991, Emory University Manuscripts Library, collection No. 1000/Series 4

xi 'I should stress . . .': Kim Evans to Angela Carter, 26 November 1991, Add. MS.88899/2/28

xi 'might we be able to matte . . .': Angela Carter to Kim Evans, undated, Add. MS. 88899/2/28

xii 'A funeral is no longer . . .': *SL*, p. 135

xii 'I always thought she knew who she was . . .': AI Salman Rushdie, 7 February 2014

xii 'Angela Carter . . . was one of the most important . . .': *Daily Telegraph*, 17 February 1992

xii 'She interpreted the times . . .': *Guardian*, 17 February 1992

xii 'Her imagination was one of the most dazzling . . .': *Independent*, 18 February 1992

xiii 'I never believe that I'm writing about the search for self . . .': *Omnibus: Angela Carter's Curious Room*, BBC1, 15 September 1992

xiii 'Why should anyone be interested . . .': *Vogue*, July 1982

xiii 'the nature of alienation': BLSA C1365/12

xiii 'integration means . . .': Angela Carter to Carole Roffe, undated, Add. MS. 89102

xiii 'social fiction': *SL*, p. 38

xiii She wasn't the first person to make this observation . . .: for some of the key influences on Angela Carter's thinking about gender identity, see Simone de Beauvoir, *The Second Sex*, trans. H. M. Parshley (New York: Knopf, 1953) and Theodor Adorno, *Minima Moralia*, trans. E. F. N. Jephcott

(London: Verso, 1974). For a comparison with Judith Butler's theory of gender performativity, see Joanne Trevenna, 'Gender as performance: questioning the "Butlerification" of Angela Carter's fiction', *Journal of Gender Studies*, Vol. 11, No. 3 (2002)

xii 'By the end her life fitted her . . .': Lorna Sage, *Angela Carter* (Plymouth: Northcote House, 1994), p. 4

xiv 'It was almost as if she was presenting . . .' AI Kazuo Ishiguro and Lorna MacDougall, 7 March 2014

xiv 'She had a sort of granny persona . . .': AI Sharon Tolaini-Sage, 16 April 2014

xiv 'watching her was sometimes like . . .': Susannah Clapp, *A Card from Angela Carter* (London: Bloomsbury, 2012), pp. 16–17

xiv 'I feel like Archimedes . . .': Angela Carter to Carole Roffe, undated, Add. MS. 89102

xv 'as a New Age role model . . .': *Observer*, 9 July 1995

xv 'he became his admirers': W. H. Auden, *Collected Poems*, ed. Edward Mendelson (London: Faber, 1976), p. 197

xv 'She had something of the Faerie Queene . . .': *Independent*, 18 February 1992

xv 'English literature has lost its high sorceress . . .': *New York Times*, 8 March 1992

xv 'the oracle we all consulted . . .': *Sunday Times*, 23 February 1992

xv 'The amazing thing about her . . .': *Observer*, 23 February 1992

xv 'She caught me smiling . . .': *Guardian*, 18 February 1992

xvi 'not seem in character . . .': *Guardian*, 19 February 1992

xvi 'I do exaggerate . . .': Angela Carter to Carole Roffe, undated, Add. MS. 89102

xvi 'Autobiography is closer to fiction . . .': *SL*, p. 358

xvii 'the *really* important thing . . .': ibid., p. 605

CHAPTER 1: A MATRIARCHAL CLAN

3 'Once upon a time . . .': Angela Carter frequently described this childhood ritual, including in *FTCP*, p. 13, *VBFT*, pp. 240–1, and John Haffenden, *Novelists in Interview* (London: Methuen, 1985), p. 83. The version of the story used here is Carter's own translation (*FTCP*, pp. 20–2), which she said was 'almost word for word' the way her grandmother told it to her.

4 'bloody awful': *SL*, p. 6

4 'Every word and gesture . . .': ibid.

4 'It's a wise child . . .': Angela Carter, 'The Language of Sisterhood' in *The State of Language*, ed. Leonard Michaels and Christopher Ricks (Berkeley: University of California Press, 1980), p. 227

4 'second sight . . .': *Vogue*, July 1982

4   'functionally illiterate': *Sunday Times*, 24 January 1981

5   'a national calamity': *Times*, 18 November 1893

5   one of the few things that can be ascertained . . .: The National Archives, WO 372/7/26904

5   she destroyed his letters, but kept the stamps: *SL*, p. 7

6   'one of the first acts of modern jihad': Helen James, 'The Assassination of Lord Mayo', *International Journal of Asia–Pacific Studies*, Vol. 5, No. 2 (July 2009)

6   all commerce had to be undertaken using rum or top hats . . .: Guthrie Moir, *The Suffolk Regiment (The 12th Regiment of Foot)* (London: Leo Cooper, 1969), p. 68

6   'we [began] to think seriously of discarding our clothes': cited in Edward Arthur Howard Webb, *History of the 12th (the Suffolk) Regiment, 1685–1913* (London: Spottiswoode, 1914), p. 337

6   There were also sinister medical experiments . . .: *Guardian*, 22 June 2001

6   that he 'became radicalised' . . .: *SL*, p. 7

6   'very much an ex-military . . .': AI Hugh and Joan Stalker, 7 February 2012

6   he impressed his superiors . . .: The National Archives, WO 372/7/26904

7   'He is <u>much depressed</u> . . .': ibid.

7   'an ebony elephant . . .': *SL*, p. 8

7   'of all the dead in my family . . .': ibid., p. 7

7   According to family legend . . .: AI Hugh and Joan Stalker, 17 April 2012

7   'stink industries': Peter Ackroyd, *London: The Biography* (London: Chatto & Windus, 2001), pp. 676–7

8   'the *bastard* side . . .': *WC*, p. 1

8   'the tendency of English fiction . . .': *In Conversation: Angela Carter with Lisa Appignanesi*, ICA video, 1985

8   'old men in flat caps . . .': *London Magazine*, March 1971

8   'a typical . . . headline from the local press . . .' *SL*, p. 178

8   'sounds of marital violence . . .': *WC*, p. 1

8   'My maternal grandparents . . .': BLSA C1365/12

8   'so out of tune it sounded like a harpsichord': *London Magazine*, March 1971

9   'Love is not too strong a term . . .': *Times*, 2 October 2001

9   'a matriarchal clan': *SL*, p. 6

10 When Olive was in her forties . . .: AI Hugh and Joan Stalker, 7 February 2012

10 'How are things in Glocca Morra?': ibid.

11 'clothes are the visible woman . . .': *Sunday Times Magazine*, 1 October 1978

11 'sometimes sorry for herself' . . .: *SL*, p. 10

11 'I wish God had thought of a better way . . .': AI Hugh and Joan Stalker, 17 April 2012

11 after he died, Angela found his membership . . .: Lorna Sage, *Angela Carter* (Plymouth: Northcote House, 1994), p. 7

12 'If he had pretensions . . .': *SL*, p. 12
12 A recording of Hugh . . .: 1987, PC William Hossack
12 The funerals of the drowned . . .: ibid.
12 Along with his loquacity . . .: *SL*, p. 20
12 'weird beyond belief': ibid.
12 'If you opened a drawer . . .': AI Hugh and Joan Stalker, 17 April 2012
13 he had already read *Don Quixote* . . .: BLSA C1365/12
13 On the morning of 15 August 1922 . . .: details of the case are taken from various reports in the *Manchester Guardian* and the *Dundee Courier*
14 'happy tourists, whose whole thought . . .': *Dundee Courier*, 18 August 1922
14 'the Scheherazade of Fleet Street': *Guardian*, 25 May 1988
15 'Evacuation was really rather like abduction . . .': AI Hugh and Joan Stalker, 7 February 2012
15 It had been an agitated pregnancy . . .: *SL*, p. 71
16 'the feeling of panic': AI Hugh and Joan Stalker, 7 February 2012
16 German planes passed over . . .: Richard Benson, *The Valley: A Hundred Years in the Life of a Family* (London: 4th Estate, 2014), p. 94
17 'swaggering' and 'mucky pastoral': *SL*, p. 5
17 'I think I became the child she had been . . .': ibid., p. 3
17 'seemed to my infant self . . .': ibid., p. 6
17 If she ever had a daughter . . .: *NS*, p. 130
17 'With the insight of hindsight . . .': *SL*, p. 9

CHAPTER 2: STATES OF GRACE ARE ALWAYS EVIL
18 light seeped . . .: *London Magazine*, March 1971
18 On one occasion she recalled . . .: ibid.
18 Their own house . . .: details from AI Hugh and Joan Stalker, 17 April 2012, *SL*, pp. 10–14, and *London Magazine*, March 1971
20 'She was always terribly serious . . .': AI Nicola Farthing, 27 January 2012
20 'My childhood had . . .': Add. MS. 88899/1/87
20 'one of the most potent memories . . .' *CR*, pp. 498–9
21 'to amuse myself . . .': Add. MS. 88899/2/28
21 'full of social realism . . .': *Sunday Times*, 24 January 1982
21 'an ill-spelt epic': Add. MS. 88899/1/100
21 'I get on well with cats . . .': *Bungeishunju*, May 1974, translated for the author by Mayako Murai
21 'just the age to be knocked sideways . . .': *SL*, p. 19
21 'I would say my father did not prepare me well . . .': ibid.
21 a 'dream cathedral' and an 'apotheosis of the fake': *Omnibus: Angela Carter's Curious Room*, BBC1, 15 September 1992
22 'anything might materialise . . .': ibid.
22 'at an age when there is no reason for anything to be real': *BYB*, p. 319

22   'it was like the unconscious itself': *Omnibus: Angela Carter's Curious Room*, BBC1, 15 September 1992

22   On winter evenings . . .: *London Magazine*, March 1971

23   'For us kids . . .': email to the author from Philip Spencer, 19 January 2012

23   Around a quarter of the 492 Jamaicans . . .: David Kynaston, *Austerity Britain, 1945–1951* (London: Bloomsbury, 2007), pp. 274–6

23   'Little Harlem': David Kynaston, *Family Britain, 1951–1957* (London: Bloomsbury, 2009), p. 100

24   'full of extrovert brown children . . .': *London Magazine*, March 1971

24   Angela's best friend . . .: ibid.

24   'a desire to make herself invisible': *Guardian*, 10 August 1972

24   'like many fat girls . . .': *London Magazine*, March 1971

24   'Canned fruit was a very big deal in my social class . . .': BYB, pp. 445–6

25   'I thought her mother was crazy . . .': AI Hugh and Joan Stalker, 7 January 2012

25   In her school report for 1949 . . .: Add. MS. 88899/6/7

26   'a bit of a failure': AI Jacqueline Anthony, 22 January 2012

26   'unencumbered of the need . . .': AI Jill Quantrill Robin, 25 January 2012

26   'in the last twenty years . . .': Janet Sondheimer and P. R. Bodington, *The Girls' Public Day School Trust, 1872–1972: Centenary Review* (London, 1972), p. 96

27   She channelled some of her enthusiasm . . .: *Streatham Hill & Clapham High School Magazine*, July 1952

28   'lots of people's second-best friend': *Independent on Sunday*, 9 June 1991

28   'off by heart': BLSA C1365/12

28   'a one-person "mixed ability" class': *Times Educational Supplement*, 7 December 1979

29   'I hated school . . .': ibid.

29   'I felt I had no right to *be* in the world': ibid.

29   'a sort of doll': AI Hugh and Joan Stalker, 17 April 2012

30   'blindingly unhappy': *Vogue*, July 1982

30   'bleak, blank stretch': Add. MS. 88899/1/87

30   'obsessed and indeed terrified': SL, p. 32

30   As late as her thirteenth or fourteenth year . . .: *Observer*, 10 April 1977

30   'I can remember . . .': Add. MS. 88899/1/96

30   'most elementary assertion of the self': SW, p. 12

30   She once told a friend . . .: AI Andrea Newman, 24 August 2012

31   'around the time I was 13 or 14': *Observer*, 9 November 1986

31   'nobody would ever love her . . .': MT, p. 3

31   'The summer she was fifteen . . .': ibid., p. 1

31   'in limbo . . .': ibid., p. 82

31   'terrifying maleness' and 'ferocious, unwashed, animal reek': ibid., pp. 45, 36

31 'with the intense sense . . .': *Observer*, 9 November 1986
32 'the fortunate expulsion . . .': Add. MS. 88899/2/28
32 'Eden is always evil . . .': ibid.
32 'A good deal of the joy evaporated . . .': SL, p. 13
32 'curious way of walking . . .': AI Jacqueline Anthony, 22 January 2012
32 'I longed to be like her . . .': ibid.
33 at the start of 1958 . . .: SL, p. 58
33 'a positive sign of depravity': ibid., p. 12
33 a typical outfit . . .: ibid., p. 8
33 'I remember going back to Balham . . .': AI Hugh and Joan Stalker, 7 February 2012
33 'I went back to my parents' flat one day . . .': AI Nicola Farthing, 27 January 2012
33 'to stay fat and dependent on her': AI Hugh and Joan Stalker, 17 April 2012
33 it would turn the inside of her belly black: Add. MS. 88899/1/90
33 'our later discords, our acrimonious squabblings': SL, p. 15
34 'My mother . . . always selected the susceptible point . . .': Angela Carter to Carole Roffe, undated, Add. MS. 89102
34 'a form of punishment uniquely fitted . . .': SW, p. 136
34 'I never properly thanked you . . .': Angela Carter to Cecil Farthing, undated, PC Nicola Farthing
35 'for lectures, music, social functions and so on': Janet Sondheimer and P. R. Bodington, *The Girls' Public Day School Trust, 1872–1972: Centenary Review* (London, 1972), p. 96
35 'My adolescent rebellion was considerably hampered . . .': SL, p. 22
35 'I loved these faces . . .': *Omnibus: Angela Carter's Curious Room*, BBC1, 15 September 1992
36 her 'very unusual' French teacher: *Times Educational Supplement*, 7 December 1979
36 'wore that record out' . . .: ibid.

CHAPTER 3: FLIGHT FROM A CLOSED ROOM
37 'some nitwit': SL, p. 23
37 'kicking and screaming . . .': BLSA C1365/12
37 'I never thanked him . . .': *Vogue*, July 1982
37 By the end of the 1950s . . .: 1961 census data
37 'the token woman': AI John Henty, Peter Carver and Roger Bing, 1 May 2012
37 The newsroom was smoke-filled and cacophonous . . .: ibid.
38 'It was obviously a better bet . . .': BLSA C1365/12
38 she gave her occupation as 'journalist' . . .: SL, p. 29

38 'one of the lads': AI John Henty, Peter Carver and Roger Bing, 1 May 2012

38 'I'd never heard a woman use the F-word . . .': ibid.; 'she was one of the most devout smokers on the staff . . .': AI Joe Steeples, 22 March 2013; 'back in those days, if you said to a girl . . .': AI John Henty, Peter Carver and Roger Bing, 1 May 2012

38 'a great, lumpy, butch cow . . .': Angela Carter to Carole Roffe, 21 March 1971, Add. MS. 89102

38 'Britannia on the old penny coins': Angela Carter to Carole Roffe, undated, Add. MS. 89102

38 'a Russian female all-in wrestler': Angela Carter to Janice Robertson, 14 November 1965, RH

39 'And I was <u>pleased</u> . . .': Angela Carter to Carole Roffe, 21 March 1971, Add. MS. 89102

39 'adolescent, clever, neurotic to a twinkling pitch': ibid.

39 'Attempted suicide by narcissism . . .': SL, p. 57

39 'between five and a half and six stone': ibid., p. 58

39 'At this point' . . .: ibid.

39 'Some analysts . . .': Lisa Appignanesi, *Mad, Bad and Sad: A History of Women and the Mind Doctors from 1800 to the Present* (London: Virago, 2007), pp. 448–9

39 The Italian psychotherapist Mara Selvini Palazolli . . .: cited in *SL*, pp. 56–60

39 'confessions of an ex-anorexic': SL, p. 58

40 'the talk of anorexia . . .': AI Hugh and Joan Stalker, 7 February 2012

40 'it was certainly on the edge of anorexia': ibid.

40 writing to a friend in 1969 . . .: Angela Carter to Carole Roffe, undated, Add. MS. 89102

40 an 'automatic . . . not-eating reaction': Add. MS. 88899/1/87

40 'her mum kept trying to get her to eat cream buns . . .': AI Hugh and Joan Stalker, 7 February 2012

40 when Olive discovered . . .: ibid.

40 'I didn't know what they wanted of me . . .': SL, p. 22

40 'functioned as a kind of benign day-clinic . . .': ibid., p. 58

40 'like a cross between . . .': 'Notes on Angela (Stalker) Carter', prepared for the author by Joe Steeples, March 2013

41 'One passes oneself off as another . . .': SL, p. 106

41 'What the fucking hell is that?': AI John Henty, Peter Carver and Roger Bing, 1 May 2012

41 'a demonic inaccuracy': *Independent on Sunday*, 9 June 1991

41 'they hadn't heard her knocking': AI Joe Steeples, 22 March 2013

41 'There was nothing stuffy and formal . . .': Croydon *Advertiser*, 7 October 1960

42 'a free course . . .': Croydon *Advertiser*, 30 September 1960

42   'so, indeed, in another 40 years' time . . .': Croydon *Advertiser*, 11 August 1961
42   'I think women admire Marlene Dietrich . . .': Croydon *Advertiser*, 31 March 1961
42   'I can date to . . . the summer of 1968 . . .': *SL*, p. 38
43   'the high, wild uplands of modern jazz': Croydon *Advertiser*, 20 February 1959
43   'the fancy-name brigade': Croydon *Advertiser*, 2 January 1959
43   'Prolonged study of best-selling-record charts . . .': Croydon *Advertiser*, 28 August 1959
43   'like a taxi office': AI Reg Hall, 6 February 2013
43   'Jazz fans and folk-music fanciers . . .': Croydon *Advertiser*, 18 December 1959
43   'a simple, artsy Soho fifties beatnik': Angela Carter to Carole Roffe, undated, Add. MS. 89102
43   'an amiable teddy bear': unpublished memoir by Carole Howells
43   Later, when she saw him eating bananas in bed . . .: Add. MS. 88899/1/88
43   'I finally bumped into somebody . . .': *SL*, p. 22
44   'gentleness' and 'moral virtue': Angela Carter to Carole Roffe, undated, Add. MS. 89102
44   'If you know some good songs . . .': Croydon *Advertiser*, 31 March 1961
44   'nice, witty, a little abrasive . . .': AI Reg Hall, 6 February 2013
44   Paul, she said, taught her everything she knew . . .: *Storyteller*, July 1962
44   'The study of the traditional song of these islands . . .': *SL*, p. 314
45   'creative urge of the anonymous masses': ibid., p. 323
45   J. B. Priestley's call . . .: cited in Dominic Sandbrook, *Never Had It So Good* (London: Little, Brown, 2005), p. 260
45   'From 1958 the Aldermaston march . . .': *Singing from the Floor*, ed. J. P. Bean (London: Faber, 2014), p. 100
45   'some people say the world's a horrible place . . .': *Songs from Aldermaston*, Collector, 1960
45   'a tremendous stimulation of . . . love affairs': *Spectator*, 15 January 1960
45   'We were always being picked up . . .': *SL*, p. 113
45   'a CND novel' . . .: Add. MS. 88899/1/87
46   'moving and beautiful memories' . . .: *SL*, p. 48
46   'wet behind the ears': AI Hugh and Joan Stalker, 17 April 2012
46   'the smell of omelette & fried potatoes . . .': Add. MS. 88899/1/87
46   'a desperate quality . . .': ibid.
47   The night before the wedding . . .: AI Hugh and Joan Stalker, 17 April 2012
47   Afterwards there was lunch . . .: ibid.
47   'in a wild surmise': *MT*, p. 200
47   'she loved nobody in this place . . .': *HV*, p. 19
47   'she had lived for only as long as the silence . . .': *Bananas*, January/ February 1979

47   'I admit it' . . .: Add. MS. 88899/1/100
48   'sense of perfect order . . .': Add. MS. 88899/1/86
48   Of her earliest sexual experiences . . .: *Observer*, 10 April 1977
48   On Friday nights . . .: 'Notes on Angela (Stalker) Carter', prepared for the author by Joe Steeples, March 2013
48   'My whole experience of the next decade . . .': Angela Carter, 'Truly, It Felt Like Year One' in *Very Heaven: Looking Back at the 1960s*, ed. Sara Maitland (London: Virago, 1988), p. 211
49   'It must have given me a certain degree . . .': BLSA C1365/12
49   'the period . . . 1903–23 . . .': *SL*, p. 506
49   'very much the first novel we all wanted to write . . .': ibid., p. 531
49   She believed that she 'would have given up reading altogether . . .': *Observer*, 10 April 1977
49   'D. H. Lawrence embarrasses me': Add. MS. 88899/1/89
49   'the uncomfortable fact remains . . .': *SL*, p. 532
50   'simple, minimal, stranger's response': Add. MS. 88899/1/86
50   'Angela depressed' . . .: John Henty's diary, PC John Henty
51   'I suppose you'll have to go with him' . . .: *SL*, p. 23
51   On 4 August she announced to her former colleagues . . .: John Henty's diary, PC John Henty
51   'She was happy' . . .: AI John Henty, Peter Carver and Roger Bing, 1 May 2012

CHAPTER 4: JUST A WIFE
52   'Many of the shops . . .': *SP*, pp. 9–10
52   'possibly the greatest work of art . . .': *Storyteller*, July 1962
53   'Everyone was terribly conscious . . .': AI Martin Hoyle, 7 April 2012
53   *Western Scene*, Bristol's very own beat paper . . .: cited in Add. MS. 88899/1/41
53   'across a crowded room': *New Review*, July 1977
53   She later said that her early years in the city . . .: unpublished memoir by Carole Howells
54   'sick, mindless wanders': Add. MS. 88899/1/86
54   'wilfully eccentric . . .': *Independent on Sunday*, 9 June 1991
54   'I must strive . . .': Add. MS. 88899/1/86
54   'I'm intelligent, I know . . .': Add. MS. 88899/1/87
55   Among the best of her early short fiction to have survived . . .: Add. MS. 88899/1/43
55   'depressed' . . .: Add. MS. 88899/1/86 and Add. MS. 88899/1/87
55   'It never ends . . .': Add. MS. 88899/1/87

55   It has been estimated . . .: David Kynaston, *Modernity Britain: A Shake of the Dice, 1959–62* (London: Bloomsbury, 2014), p. 204

56   'they simply bred in the corridor': AI Neil Curry, 28 September 2012

56   'vile, dirty habits': Add. MS. 88899/1/86

56   'another day wasted': Add. MS. 88899/1/88

56   'angry . . . & indrawn . . .': Add. MS. 88899/1/86

56   'My God,' she wrote in her journal . . .: ibid.

56   '[muddled] along . . .': Angela Carter to Carole Roffe, undated, Add. MS. 89102

57   'just a wife': *New Review*, July 1977

57   'I don't really want him to have a personality . . .': Add. MS. 88899/1/87

57   'I go all to pieces . . .': Add. MS. 88899/1/86

57   'accept expressions of love . . .': Add. MS. 88899/1/87

57   'I want to cry with love . . .': ibid.

57   'There's a flaw to this logic . . .': Angela Carter to Mark Pearce, 19 March 1981, Add. MS. 88899/3/3

58   'Too bad that so many writers have mucked around . . .': Add. MS. 88899/1/86

58   She woke the next morning . . .: ibid.

58   Years later, she told a friend . . .: Angela Carter to Neil Forsyth, 26 August 1974, PC Neil Forsyth

58   'I'm unhappy enough to die . . .': Add. MS. 88899/1/86

58   'My family is unique . . .': Add. MS. 88899/1/87

58   'wallowing pinkly . . .': ibid.

58   'Oh good, here comes the fucking turkey': AI Hugh and Joan Stalker, 17 April 2012

58   'Angela would do things . . .': ibid.

59   'mooning silently about' . . .: Add. MS. 88899/1/87

59   'full of fat, happy, giggling babies' . . .: ibid.

59   'wacky' . . .: AI Peter and Janet Swan, 9 September 2014

59   'there was a dramatic style about her . . .': ibid.

59   'twenty-one going on sixty-one' . . .: ibid.

60   'She played the sort of elderly aunt . . .': ibid.

60   'I always have to interpret my physical symptoms . . .': Angela Carter to Carole Roffe, undated, Add. MS. 89102

60   'a nice, old-fashioned feminist . . .': ibid.

61   'She had a nice sense of humour . . .': AI Jenny Orsborn, 12 July 2014

61   'awful teeth' . . . : AI Peter and Janet Swan, 9 September 2014

61   'shitbag' . . .: Add. MS. 88899/1/86

61   'nights in a garden of never-never Spain': *SD*, p. 1

61   Angela joked about making a film about Clifton society . . .: AI Corinna Sargood, 10 January 2012

61 'very innocent and pastoral . . .': *New Yorkshire Writing*, Winter 1978

62 'the genius loci of this strange area . . .': Add. MS. 88899/1/86

62 'as conventionally as possible' . . .: AI Corinna Sargood, 10 January 2012

62 'not of this world' . . .: Angela Carter to Carole Roffe, 2 November 1971, Add. MS. 89102

62 'being rather bored by them': AI Corinna Sargood, 10 January 2012

62 '[Angela] was a very visual person . . .': ibid.

63 'What I want is a voice . . .': Add. MS. 88899/1/88

63 'I like using a proper pen . . .': Add. MS. 88899/1/86

63 'great psychological blow . . .': Add. MS. 88899/1/87

63 The stories she was working on . . .: Add. MS. 88899/1/43

63 'The Events of a Night': ibid.

64 'souped-up version . . .': BYB, p. 4

64 'quite magnificent': Add. MS. 88899/1/87

64 'would not even have had . . .': SL, p. 539

65 'Few nations have spent quite as long as England . . .': *Western Daily Press*, 19 March 1962

65 'Love's Impossibility': Add. MS. 88899/1/87

65 'Through marriage & love one learns . . .': ibid.

66 'I married for privacy . . .': ibid.

66 'very hard line . . .': *Singing from the Floor*, ed. J. P. Bean (London: Faber, 2014), p. 141

66 'all these middle-class people singing Durham miners' songs': AI Corinna Sargood, 10 January 2012

66 'it was all very odd . . .': Angela Carter to Carole Roffe, undated, Add. MS. 89102

66 'Peggy Seeger sleeping on my floor': Add. MS. 88899/1/87

66 she has no memory of meeting Angela . . .: email to the author from Peggy Seeger, 23 July 2014

66 'empty and forlorn . . .': Add. MS. 88899/1/87

67 'If you've got a degree . . .': cited in Susannah Clapp, *A Card from Angela Carter* (London: Bloomsbury, 2012), p. 61

67 fewer than ten per cent of eighteen- to twenty-one-year-olds . . .: cited in Robert Anderson, *British Universities: Past and Present* (London: Bloomsbury, 2006), p. 47

CHAPTER 5: A SLAPSTICK NIGHTMARE

68 'not too many of them and not all compulsory': *Critical Survey*, Autumn 1963

69 'astonishingly brilliant': AI Neil Curry, 28 September 2012

69 'Professor Knights is a delicate . . .': Add. MS. 88899/1/100

69 'not just a journal . . .': Terry Eagleton, *Literary Theory: An Introduction* (Oxford: Blackwell, 1983), p. 33

69 'as a head of department . . .' cited in Edward Hilliard, *English as a Vocation: The Scrutiny Movement* (Oxford University Press, 2012), p. 93

69 'educational project associated with *Scrutiny*': ibid., p. 2

69 'eat up your broccoli': *Independent on Sunday*, 9 June 1991

70 'arrogant provincialism': Angela Carter to Carole Roffe, undated, Add. MS. 89102

70 whose teaching methods . . .: AI Neil Curry, 28 September 2012

70 'remarkable for their lack of plot or incident': *Independent*, 19 May 1994

70 'Tales are best divided . . .': Basil Cottle's lecture notes, University of Bristol Special Collections DM1582/56

70 'made the study . . .': Angela Carter to Basil Cottle, dated 'Wednesday', University of Bristol Special Collections, DM1582/4

70 'how can anyone take him seriously . . .': Add. MS. 88899/1/88

70 'I am shattered by Hume . . .': ibid.

71 'most of the female students . . .': AI Gary Hicks, 10 April 2012

71 'I wish they'd at least speak to me . . .': Add. MS. 88899/1/100

72 'It was obvious that Angela was writing . . .': AI Neil Curry, 28 September 2012

72 'She always struck me as someone . . .': AI Rebecca Howard, 26 April 2012

72 a dark stain on the floor . . .: AI Martin Hoyle, 7 April 2012

73 Angela spoke of having met situationists and anarchists . . .: *Independent on Sunday*, 9 June 1991

73 'to vindicate Mrs Pankhurst's gallant fight . . .': Angela Carter to Janice Robertson, 31 March 1966, RH

73 Asked in a late interview . . .: *Independent on Sunday*, 9 June 1991

73 'you would talk about feminism . . .': AI Rebecca Howard, 26 April 2012

73 'She'd sit there staring at people': AI Martin Hoyle, 7 April 2012

73 'holding court': AI Edward Horesh, 6 January 2012

73 'It is only recently . . .': Add. MS. 88899/1/89

73 'I talk about myself . . .': Add. MS. 88899/1/100

74 'Martin bored him to sleep': AI Martin Hoyle, 7 April 2012

74 'she could be cruel . . .': AI Neil Curry, 28 September 2012

74 'if you said something silly . . .' AI Rebecca Howard, 26 April 2012

74 'Presumably that was because Paul was at home . . .': ibid.

74 'I don't remember her ever saying anything against Paul . . .': AI Neil Curry, 28 September 2012

74 'Paul is sad' and 'eighteen months of purgatory': Add. MS. 88899/1/89

74 'Perhaps it's Paul . . .': ibid.

74 'It's clear that his depression . . .': Angela Carter to Carole Roffe, 14 February 1968, Add. MS. 89102

75 'I thought maybe . . .': AI Hugh and Joan Stalker, 7 February 2012
75 'the utterly crazy way we lived . . .': Angela Carter to Carole Roffe, 3 July 1968
75 'you can't waste love . . .': *SD*, pp. 43–4
75 from the notes she kept in her journal . . .: Add. MS. 88899/1/88 and Add. MS. 88899/1/100
76 'a brilliantly executed . . .': Add. MS. 88899/1/100
76 Angela said she couldn't countenance . . .: AI Neil Curry, 28 September 2012
77 'for the reasons most women who write . . .': Angela Carter to Cavan McCarthy, 20 October 1965, UCL Special Collections, MS. Add. 209
77 'My anatomy is only part . . .': *SW*, p. 4
77 'Men are different to women . . .': Angela Carter to Carole Roffe, undated, Add. MS. 89102
78 'soon leaps into her lap . . .': cited in *Vision* (undated), PC Neil Curry; Angela Carter's early poetry has recently been collected in *Unicorn: The Poetry of Angela Carter, with an essay by Rosemary Hill* (London: Profile, 2015)
78 'I have sharp teeth . . .' ibid.
78 'This sounds very pretentious . . .': Angela Carter to Jon Silkin, 15 January [1966?], the Brotherton Library, University of Leeds, BC MS 20c Stand
78 'of its period . . .': Angela Carter to Neil Astley, 14 December 1978, Newcastle University Special Collections, BXB-1-4-Car-1-4
79 'lavender ears' . . .: Add. MS. 88899/1/89
79 'I am twenty-four years old . . .': ibid.
79 'the semi-criminal, semi-beatnik . . .': Angela Carter to 'Fiction Editor, William Heinemann', 13 January 1965, RH
79 'Honeydripper crouched . . .': Add. MS. 88899/1/88
80 'a very hip short story' titled 'Fucking': Add. MS. 88899/1/89
80 'very thinly disguised': AI Jenny Orsborn, 12 July 2014
80 'based on an acquaintance of mine . . .': Angela Carter's inscription in John Hayes's copy of *Shadow Dance*, PC John Hayes
80 'from eyebrow to navel': *SD*, p. 17
80 the critic Marc O'Day has suggested . . .: Marc O'Day, '"Mutability is Having a Field Day": The Sixties Aura of Angela Carter's Bristol Trilogy' in *Flesh and the Mirror: Essays on the Art of Angela Carter*, ed. Lorna Sage (London: Virago, 1994)
81 'to weep and glitter with public tears . . .': *SD*, p. 8
81 'disordered attics': ibid., pp. 175–6
81 'I love him, I love him . . .': ibid., p. 105
81 'dregs of brown liquor . . .': ibid., p. 11
81 'browned at the edges . . .': ibid., p. 38
81 'as if butter wouldn't melt . . .': ibid., p. 41

81   'Morris felt like his own shadow . . .': ibid., p. 174
81   'a panting, wet-lipped nymphet . . .': ibid., p. 22
82   'used to look like the sort of young girl . . .': ibid., p. 2
82   'of her metallic deodorant sweat . . .': ibid., p. 5
82   'sweet, white, innocent and childish . . .': ibid., p. 16
82   'chasm': ibid., p. 39
82   'she would sigh . . .': ibid., p. 120
82   'she would have found some satisfaction . . .': ibid., p. 46
83   'What is the name of your cat? . . .': ibid., p. 70
83   she opted to write a dissertation . . .: Add. MS. 88899/1/116
83   'For relaxation' . . .: Angela Carter to Cavan McCarthy, undated, UCL Special Collections, MS. Add. 209
83   She changed a reference . . .: ibid.
84   she said that she decided on the firm . . .: AI Janice Robertson, 23 November 2014
84   'I think it is very funny . . .': Angela Carter to 'Fiction Editor, William Heinemann', 13 January 1965, RH
84   'I thought, "Here's a writer of exceptional talent" . . .': AI Janice Robertson, 23 November 2014
84   'several readings' . . .: Janice Robertson to Angela Carter, 7 April 1965, RH
84   'very nice, incredibly cheap': AI Janice Robertson, 23 November 2014
84   'was eccentric and delightful . . .': ibid.
85   'my mate says . . .': Angela Carter to Janice Robertson, undated, RH
85   But Jenny Orsborn remembered . . .: AI Jenny Orsborn, 12 July 2014
85   'I haven't changed the main structure . . .': Angela Carter to Janice Robertson, 27 June 1965, RH
85   'I don't think I can do any more . . .': Angela Carter to Janice Robertson, 16 August 1965, RH
85   'just like Joyce says it looks' . . .: Angela Carter to Lorna Tracy, undated, PC Lorna Tracy
85   'hair the colour of bitter beer': Add. MS. 88899/1/90
85   'the eyes round here . . .': ibid.
86   She decided to learn . . .: Angela Carter to Janice Robertson, 1 September 1965, RH
86   'I am extremely pleased . . .': ibid.
86   'I know it's awful . . .': BLSA C1365/12

CHAPTER 6: GIVING THE FLASH MORE SUBSTANCE
87   'My first husband . . .': Angela Carter to Lorna Tracy, 30 August 1980, PC Lorna Tracy
87   'I just don't want to work' . . .: Add. MS. 88899/1/87

88   'the beautiful is put at the service of liberty': *SL*, p. 510
88   'the old juices . . .': ibid. p. 512
88   'the marvellous alone . . .': Add. MS. 88899/1/90
89   'does "the marvellous alone is beautiful" mean . . .': Add. MS. 88899/1/87
89   'clockwork cat catching clockwork mouse . . .': ibid.
89   'I think writing . . .': Angela Carter to Carole Roffe, undated, Add. MS. 89102
89   'our external symbols . . .': *NE*, p. 7
89   'The bourgeois virgin' . . .: *Vogue*, July 1982
90   'She went into her bedroom . . .': *MT*, p. 24
90   'frail as a pressed flower': ibid., p. 73
90   'he wanted me to fuck you' . . .: ibid., pp. 151–2
90   'Nothing is left but us': ibid., p. 200
90   'but he was a depressed chemist . . .': BLSA C1365/12
90   'in & out of the house': Angela Carter's inscription in John Hayes's copy of *The Magic Toyshop*, PC John Hayes
90   'I thought, tentatively . . .': Angela Carter to Janice Robertson, 8 May 1966, RH
90   'a great deal about the methodology of fantasy': *New Yorkshire Writing*, Winter 1978
91   'quite consciously borrowed . . .': BLSA C1365/12
91   'not because of any religious thing . . .': Angela Carter to Carole Roffe, 3 September 1968, Add. MS. 89102
91   'a Gothic melodrama . . .': Angela Carter to Janice Robertson, 25 January 1966, RH
91   'a precursor to Angela Carter': *Observer*, 28 July 2013
91   'she's put her finger . . .': Angela Carter to Janice Robertson, 8 May 1966, RH
91   'a measure of confidence': Peter Schwed to Angela Carter, 4 June 1966, Add. MS. 88899/3/3
91   'neurotic compulsion': Angela Carter to Carole Roffe, 6 April 1972, Add. MS. 89102
92   'I feel nauseated . . .': Add. MS. 88899/1/89
92   'it is only very rarely . . .': Angela Carter to Carole Roffe, 17 February 1969, Add. MS. 89102
92   'I most wanted Paul's children . . .': Angela Carter to Carole Roffe, undated, Add. MS. 89102
92   'if only he would let me have babies . . .': Add. MS. 88899/1/89
92   'almost desperate': ibid.
92   'the drug seems to be working . . .': ibid.
92   'I don't really know the difference . . .': ibid.

93 'You will know by now . . .': Angela Carter to Basil Cottle, dated 'Wednesday', University of Bristol Special Collections, DM1582/4

93 'I need to be extraordinary': Add. MS. 88899/1/89

94 She admired such songs as 'Like a Rolling Stone' . . .: SL, p. 323

94 'shock of noise' . . .: *London Magazine*, October 1966 and Add. MS. 88899/1/91

94 'this orgy of destruction . . .': ibid.

94 'couple of birds . . .': Add. MS. 88899/1/91

94 'slightly spotted': ibid.

94 The café sold ham or pork pie . . .: *Guardian*, 17 September 1966

95 'the most awful, purplish colour . . .': Add. MS. 88899/1/91

95 'They are all old and most are fat . . .': *Guardian*, 17 September 1966

95 'huge as fate . . .': ibid.

95 'I am beginning to understand about femininity' . . .: Add. MS. 88899/1/91

95 'wouldn't have recognised Simone de Beauvoir . . .': *Vogue*, June 1991

96 Angela had last seen her in April . . .: Add. MS. 88899/1/90

96 The Stalkers went by car . . .: AI Hugh and Joan Stalker, 17 April 2012

96 'plastic' . . .: Add. MS. 88899/1/91

96 'People are always falling into graves . . .': ibid.

96 'I was surprised how . . .': ibid.

96 'knocked out . . .': Angela Carter to Janice Robertson, dated 'Thursday', RH

96 'enormously pleased and flattered': Angela Carter to Janice Robertson, dated 'Sunday', RH

97 'for all its strangeness' . . .: *Sunday Times*, 7 August 1966

97 'poetic vision of Heaven and Hell' . . .: *Times Literary Supplement*, 4 August 1966

97 'Victoriana, Pop Art . . .': *New Statesman*, 8 July 1966

97 'very promising indeed . . .': BBC Home Service, 5 July 1966

97 The worst notice . . .: *Manchester Evening News*, 26 July 1966

98 'in my experience . . .': Angela Carter to Pat Barker, 1 June 1982, PC Pat Barker

98 'I'm not giving autographs . . .': Angela Carter to Cavan McCarthy, undated, UCL Special Collections, MS. Add. 209

98 'Everything was kind of opening up . . .': AI Rebecca Howard, 26 April 2012

98 'Paul began to resent . . .': AI Hugh and Joan Stalker, 7 January 2012

98 Angela later told a friend . . .: Angela Carter to Lorna Tracy, 30 May 1981, PC Lorna Tracy

98 'lewd and outrageous': *Guardian*, 10 August 1972; 'What do you want to write about . . .': Angela Carter to Janice Robertson, dated 'Sunday', RH

99 'Is indecent exposure . . .': Angela Carter to Janice Robertson, 16 January 1967, RH

99   'self-questioning, anti-metropolitan . . .': Paul Barker's notes for his
     talk at 'Fireworks: Angela Carter and the Futures of Writing' (confer-
     ence at the University of York, 30 September to 2 October 1994), PC
     Paul Barker
99   'It pioneered . . .': *Vogue*, November 1982
99   'She was dressed all in black . . .': *Independent on Sunday*, 8 January 1995
99   'a bit too Hogarthian' . . .: Paul Barker to Mark Bell, 23 September 1994,
     PC Susannah Clapp
100 'She became central . . .': AI Paul Barker, 19 April 2012
100 'of the fifties . . .': Add. MS. 88899/1/41
101 'an unwise freedom of movement . . .': ibid.
101 'When young men are rude . . .': Angela Carter to Janice Robertson, dated
     'Sunday', RH
101 'with perhaps high hopes . . .': Add. MS. 88899/1/41
101 'more difficult and maybe less true . . .': Angela Carter to Janice Robertson,
     11 January 1967, RH
101 'dancing is ceasing . . .': Add. MS. 88899/1/41
102 'this one died . . .': Add. MS. 88899/1/90
102 'in a somewhat incestuous relationship' . . .: *Education & Training*, Vol.
     10, No. 1 (1968)
102 'His ability for abstract thought . . .': Add. MS. 88899/1/100
103 'a reasonably suave . . .': *Sunday Times*, 19 May 1968
103 'the only time I have genuinely wished . . .': Angela Carter to Carole
     Roffe, 3 July 1968, Add. MS. 89102
103 'took away the suspicion . . .': L, p. 12
103 'I think she went out of her way . . .': AI Edward Horesh, 6 January 2012
103 'the witch': ibid.
103 she played the students folk and pop records . . .: unpublished memoir by
     Carole Howells
103 she appears to have made around £60 . . .: Add. MS. 88899/1/91
103 'severe depressions': unpublished memoir by Carole Howells
104 'a young woman . . .': L, p. 54
104 'an ugly, gawky girl . . .': unpublished memoir by Carole Howells
104 'a fact hardly likely . . .': ibid.
104 'a nice bird . . .': Add. MS. 88899/1/91
104 'strength & peculiar integrity': Angela Carter to Carole Roffe,
     27 October 1971, Add. MS. 89102; 'in many ways much more . . .':
     Angela Carter to Carole Roffe, 21 December 1972, Add. MS. 89102
104 'our lives, our loves, our families . . .': unpublished memoir by Carole
     Howells
105 'They would talk to each other in virtual shorthand': AI John Lockwood,
     7 June 2013

105   'It was like a love affair': AI Carole Howells, 20 February 2012
105   'prodding & pushing . . .': Angela Carter to Carole Roffe, undated, Add. MS. 89102
105   'her background was such . . .': unpublished memoir by Carole Howells

CHAPTER 7: HAPPINESS IS EGO-SHAPED
106   Angela called them the *papillons dorées*: AI Martin Hoyle, 7 April 2012
106   'There was a yeastiness in the air . . .': Angela Carter, 'Truly, It Felt Like Year One' in *Very Heaven: Looking Back at the 1960s*, ed. Sara Maitland (London: Virago, 1988), pp. 211–12
106   'the startling dandyism . . .': *SL*, p. 106
106   'a haze of colour': *SP*, p. 17
107   'Wars are great catalysts . . .': Angela Carter, 'Truly, It Felt Like Year One' in *Very Heaven: Looking Back at the 1960s*, ed. Sara Maitland (London: Virago, 1988), p. 212
107   'a certain illegitimate intellectual status' . . .: *SP*, p. 4
107   'sad, hopeless . . .': ibid., p. 5
107   'the sweet evening air': ibid., p. 20
107   'Somehow, he thought . . .': ibid., p. 21
107   Angela was disappointed . . .: Angela Carter to Carole Roffe, 10 March 1969, Add. MS. 89102
107   'friends with time again': *SP*, p. 146
108   'Speaking very loosely . . .': BLSA C1365/12
108   'it made madness, alienation . . .': Angela Carter, 'Truly, It Felt Like Year One' in *Very Heaven: Looking Back at the 1960s*, ed. Sara Maitland (London: Virago, 1988), p. 215
108   'centrally firm sense . . .': R. D. Laing, *The Divided Self* (London: Tavistock, 1960), p. 39
108   'my own very strongly held self-image . . .': Angela Carter to Carole Roffe, undated, Add. MS. 89102
109   'I wasn't mothered I was smothered': R. D. Laing, *The Divided Self* (London: Tavistock, 1960), p. 200
109   'His father was a newsagent . . .': *SP*, pp. 6–7
109   'love is her business': ibid., p. 88
109   'terrifying naked eyes' . . .: ibid., p. 48
109   'expressionless voice . . .': ibid., p. 49
109   'retaining a ghostly female perfume': ibid., p. 30
109   'he wanted to reach the uncreated country . . .': ibid., p. 114
109   'gone for good . . .': ibid., p. 76
109   an 'engulfment image' . . .: Angela Carter to Carole Roffe, undated, Add. MS. 89102

110 'borrowed from Godard': Angela Carter to Janice Robertson, 16 December 1967, RH
110 'both bemused and excited . . .': ibid.
110 'I am less shuffling and furtive . . .': Angela Carter to Carole Roffe, 21 April 1968, Add. MS. 89102
110 'It is very short . . .': Angela Carter to Janice Robertson, 16 December 1967, RH
110 'I think it is the best . . .': Janice Robertson to Angela Carter, undated, RH
110 'a tiny desk . . .': Gyles Brandreth, *Something Sensational to Read in the Train: The Diary of a Lifetime* (London: John Murray, 2009), p. 230
110 'a bit like Angela, really': AI Janice Robertson, 23 November 2014
111 'Now I am permitted . . .': *SL*, p. 54
111 'I have nothing but praise . . .': Angela Carter to Carole Roffe, undated, Add. MS. 89102
111 'She started going out more . . .': AI Peter and Janet Swan, 9 September 2014
111 'Not because of Paul . . .': ibid.
111 One man . . .: email to the author from Andrew Travers, 20 March 2014
111 'reacted like . . .': Angela Carter to Carole Roffe, undated, Add. MS. 89102
112 'Women tend to be raised . . .': Angela Carter, 'Truly, It Felt Like Year One' in *Very Heaven: Looking Back at the 1960s*, ed. Sara Maitland (London: Virago, 1988), p. 214
112 'aborted' and 'one-sided': Add. MS. 88899/1/91; John gave friends to understand . . .: email to the author from Oscar Smazlen, 14 August 2014
112 'it didn't affect how I felt . . .': AI Jenny Orsborn, 12 July 2014
112 'this is the first thing that has happened . . .': Add. MS. 88899/1/91
112 'the classic climax . . .': ibid.
112 'Granny wasn't a witch for nothing': Angela Carter to Carole Roffe, 14 January 1971, Add. MS. 89102
113 'Since I do not fully understand . . .': Add. MS. 88899/1/91
113 'we are so happy together . . .': ibid.
113 'Paul is all new and shiny . . .': Angela Carter to Carole Roffe, undated, Add. MS. 89102
113 'Angela Carter has done that unusual thing . . .': *Daily Telegraph*, 6 July 1967
114 'Angela Carter has a bizarre . . .': *Times Literary Supplement*, 6 July 1967
114 'a cruel and lyrical little fantasy' . . .: *Guardian*, 23 June 1967
114 'suffering' and 'control': cited in Alan Jenkins' introduction to Ian Hamilton's *Collected Poems* (London: Faber, 2013), p. vi
114 'indulgent' . . .: *Listener*, 13 July 1967
114 'Angela Carter writes like a very up-to-date . . .': *Observer*, 25 June 1967
114 'Hans Andersen mixed with the Brothers Grimm': *Sunday Times*, 11 June 1967

114 'more like Grimm than Hans Andersen . . .': Angela Carter to Mary Whitehead, 27 July 1967, RH

114 'a simple narrative framework' . . .: Angela Carter to Mary Whitehead, dated 'Wednesday', RH

115 'a fairy tale is a story . . .': cited by Marina Warner, Introduction to *The Second Virago Book of Fairy Tales* (London: Virago, 1992), p. xi

115 'her magic dress and a paper bag . . .': Angela Carter, *Miss Z, the Dark Young Lady* (London: Heinemann, 1970) p. 9

115 'I fear you acted rashly': ibid., p. 7

115 'only to speak to them sensibly': ibid., p. 20

115 'A working girl knows how to use her wits': Angela Carter, *The Donkey Prince* (New York: Simon & Schuster, 1970), p. 28

115 'a book of 25,000 to 30,000 words': Mary Whitehead to Angela Carter, 29 August 1967, RH

115 'I fear my particular forte . . .': Angela Carter to Mary Whitehead, undated, RH

115 'exactly – even uncannily . . .': Angela Carter to Janet Chenery, undated, RH

116 'the worst art school in the country': Angela Carter to Carole Roffe, 14 February 1968, Add. MS. 89102

116 'doing therapy . . .': Add. MS. 88899/1/91

116 'And they wouldn't let me into art school . . .': Angela Carter's inscription in John Hayes' copy of *Shadow Dance*, PC John Hayes

116 'as I try & grow . . .': Add. MS. 88899/9/91

116 'Nobody is responsible . . .': ibid.

117 'It seems to me . . .': ibid.

117 'spontaneous remission period' . . .: Angela Carter to Carole Roffe, 14 February 1968, Add. MS. 89102

117 'I'd rather like . . .': ibid.

117 'I don't think I could stand . . .': ibid.

117 'I am dependent . . .': Angela Carter to Carole Roffe, undated, Add. MS. 89102

CHAPTER 8: THE EDGE OF THE UNIMAGINABLE

118 'the only truly alien planet . . .': J. G. Ballard, *A User's Guide to the Millennium: Essays and Reviews* (London: HarperCollins, 1996), p. 197

118 'immaculately glazed savagery': *Vogue*, July 1982

118 'When I read those mid-sixties issues . . .': *SL*, pp. 33–4

119 'twelve hours a day more or less': Angela Carter to Carole Roffe, undated, Add. MS. 89102

119 'a love story . . .': Angela Carter to Carole Roffe, 30 June 1969, Add. MS. 89102

119   'an autonomous power of their own': *HV*, p. 12

119   'What I was envisaging . . .': *In Conversation: Angela Carter with Lisa Appignanesi*, ICA video, 1985

119   'an attempt to cross-fertilise . . .': Angela Carter's inscription in John Hayes' copy of *Heroes and Villains*, PC John Hayes

119   'would make some kind of change': *HV*, p. 4

119   'made out of steel and concrete': ibid., p. 3

119   'tremendous confusion': ibid., p. 19

120   'a chronic gift for unhappiness': ibid., p. 84

120   Angela researched the novel carefully . . .: Add. MS. 88899/9/91

120   'It started to feel like living on a demolition site' . . .: Angela Carter, 'Truly, It Felt Like Year One' in *Very Heaven: Looking Back at the 1960s*, ed. Sara Maitland (London: Virago, 1988), p. 211

120   'the feminine character . . .': cited in *SL*, p. 110

120   'heightened awareness . . .': *SL*, p. 38

121   'I suppose I started getting interested . . .': BLSA C1365/12

121   'I have a jackdaw kind of a mind . . .': National Archives of Australia, C100/1164504

121   Writing to an academic . . .: Angela Carter to Elaine Jordan, cited in Elaine Jordan, 'The Dangerous Edge' in *Flesh and the Mirror: Essays on the Art of Angela Carter*, ed. Lorna Sage (London: Virago, 1994), pp. 197–8

121   'I'm not too sure . . .': Angela Carter to Carole Roffe, 30 June 1969, Add. MS. 89102

121   'it looks like pretentious gibberish . . .': Angela Carter to Janice Robertson, 20 December 1968, RH

121   'I am really quite pleased . . .': Angela Carter to Carole Roffe, 30 June 1969, Add. MS. 89102

121   'very good': Janice Robertson, internal Heinemann memo, undated, RH

122   'terribly pleased . . .': Angela Carter to Janice Robertson, 25 September 1970, PC Janice Robertson

122   'a look of [Jean-Paul] Belmondo': Angela Carter to Carole Roffe, 21 April 1968, Add. MS. 89102

122   'the idea was that . . .': AI Martin Hoyle, 7 April 2012

122   'a bizarre circus': Angela Carter to Carole Roffe, undated, Add. MS. 89102

122   'like a bullring . . .': *Paris Review*, Fall 2001

123   'self-conscious realism': cited in James Wood, 'England' in *The Oxford Guide to Contemporary Writing*, ed. John Sturrock (Oxford University Press, 1996), p. 125

123   'the sort of thing you and your sister . . .': AI A. S. Byatt, 26 May 2015

123   'I knew she was shy . . .': ibid.

123   'Byatt is a very intelligent literary lady . . .': Angela Carter to Carole Roffe, undated, Add. MS. 89102

123 'They fail to realise . . .': ibid.

123 'Things are happening . . .': *Sunday Times*, 19 May 1968

124 'muted and blurred': *Sunday Telegraph*, 28 July 1968

124 'what is so intriguing . . .': *Listener*, 1 August 1968

124 'compelling in its own obscure way': *Evening News*, 3 August 1968

124 'Miss [*sic*] Carter presents us . . .': *Observer*, 28 July 1968

124 'many small sunbursts': *Guardian*, 2 August 1968

124 'a pop record you liked . . .': *New Society*, 1 August 1968

124 'astonishingly brilliant . . .': *Country Life*, 22 August 1968

124 'a complete failure . . .': Angela Carter to Carole Roffe, undated, Add. MS. 89102

124 'a monster of sentimentality': ibid.

124 'more or less a confession . . .': ibid.

124 'I am becoming reconciled . . .': ibid.

125 'It does embarrass me . . .': BLSA C1365/12

125 'I've been haunted . . .': Angela Carter to Carole Roffe, 14 February 1948, Add. MS. 89102

125 'knocked [her] out': Angela Carter to Carole Roffe, undated, Add. MS. 89102

125 'sacrificing innumerable nuances . . .': Angela Carter to Carole Roffe, 3 July 1968

126 'sick' and 'disturbed': L, p. 15; 'very tender heart' . . .: ibid., p. 14; 'malign' . . .: ibid., p. 11

126 'quite incomprehensible': ibid., p. 29

126 'the palpable evidence of her own secrets': ibid., p. 7

126 'totally engulfing': ibid., p. 35

126 'she could not incorporate . . .': ibid., p. 44

126 'There is a condition . . .': ibid., p. 58

126 'think of it this way' . . .: ibid., p. 60

126 'by the conviction . . .': ibid., p. 36

126 'nothing but death . . .': ibid., p. 110

126 'anti-Laing novel' . . .: BLSA C1365/12

127 'in my terms . . .': ibid.

127 '"LOVE" is autobiographical' . . .: Angela Carter to Carole Roffe, 25 September 1970, Add. MS. 89102

127 'if some biographer . . .': Angela Carter to Carole Roffe, 16 December 1970, Add. MS. 89102

127 'since she felt . . .': L, p. 32

127 'to reduce him to not-being': ibid., p. 35

127 'only to be expected' . . .: ibid., p. 8

127 'precarious autonomy': ibid., p. 11

127 'he's come out of the pages . . .': Add. MS. 88899/1/98

127 'A lot of [Love] is an exercise in style' . . .: BLSA C1365/12

128 'for precision' . . .: Add. MS. 88899/1/92

128 'An unhappy adolescent . . .': L, pp. 70–1

128 'This novel, as promised . . .': Angela Carter to Carole Roffe, 19 May 1969, Add. MS. 89102

129 'the plump cheerfulness . . .': Add. MS. 88899/1/65

129 'The heroine's refusal to grow up . . .': Lorna Sage, 'Angela Carter: The Fairy Tale' in Angela Carter and the Fairy Tale, ed. Danielle Marie Roemer and Christina Bacchilega (Detroit: Wayne State University Press, 2000), p. 72

129 'although [Carter] feels sorry . . .': New York Review of Books, 23 April 1992

129 'to provide Annabel with an empowering femininity': Katie Garner, 'Blending the Pre-Raphaelite with the Surreal in Angela Carter's Shadow Dance (1966) and Love (1971)' in Angela Carter: New Critical Readings (London: Bloomsbury, 2014), p. 155

129 'she has no femininity . . .': Sue Roe, 'The Disorder of Love: Angela Carter's Surrealist Collage' in Flesh and the Mirror: Essays on the Art of Angela Carter, ed. Lorna Sage (London: Virago, 1994), pp. 81–94

129 'dreamed a gaggle of Eng Lit students . . .': Angela Carter to Carole Roffe, 19 May 1969, Add. MS. 89102

130 'I had no intention . . .': Angela Carter to Elaine [Jordan?], undated, Add. MS. 88899/1/84

130 'I once met someone . . .': Vector, Easter 1982

130 'straightforwardly intellectual arguments': John Haffenden, Novelists in Interview (London: Methuen, 1985), p. 79

130 'always got a tendency . . .': Omnibus: Angela Carter's Curious Room, BBC1, 15 September 1992

130 'I never know what a novel is about . . .': BLSA C1365/12

130 'I write to ask questions . . .': Angela Carter to Carole Roffe, undated, Add. MS. 89102

130 'it does Angela Carter no favours . . .': Independent, 29 July 1995

131 'I would regard myself . . .': SL, p. 37

131 a 'low-budget film . . .': Arnold Goodman to Janice Robertson, 20 February 1969, RH

131 'background is in motion pictures . . .': ibid.

131 'a not-very-successful theatre producer': Blake Bailey, Cheever: A Life (New York: Picador, 2009), p. 131

131 'getting along splendidly': Janice Robertson to Clarence Padgett, 9 May 1969, RH

131 'One Big Drag . . .': Angela Carter to Carole Roffe, undated, Add. MS. 89102

132 'This does not mean . . .': Clarence Padgett to Angela Carter, undated, RH

132   'the film thing appears to be falling apart': Angela Carter to Carole Roffe, undated, Add. MS. 89102

132   'I have been very handsomely paid . . .': Angela Carter to Janice Robertson, 20 December 1969, RH

132   'it is hard now to appreciate . . .': *Independent on Sunday*, 8 January 1995

132   'one of the world's great novelists': Ronald Bell, *The Japan Experience* (Tokyo: Weatherhill, 1973), p. 148

133   Corinna's husband . . .: AI Corinna Sargood, 10 January 2012

133   'a typical Clifton move': AI Martin Hoyle, 7 April 2012

133   'I think they particularly objected . . .': Angela Carter to Carole Roffe, 16 July 1969, Add. MS. 89102

133   'all these wretched men . . .': AI Martin Hoyle, 7 April 2012

134   'kept finding little bits . . .': Angela Carter to Carole Roffe, 16 July 1969, Add. MS. 89102

134   'in human terms . . .': *In Conversation: Angela Carter with Lisa Appignanesi*, ICA video, 1985

134   'couldn't hold on . . .': ibid.

134   'a very, very strange and disturbing . . .': *Vector*, Easter 1982

134   'only a very slightly exaggerated picture . . .': ibid.

134   'Riding the buses . . .': Angela Carter to Carole Roffe, undated, Add. MS. 89102

135   'brewed Typhoo . . .': ibid.

135   'the most beautiful . . .': *SL*, p. 275

135   'saffron-robed figures . . .': ibid., p. 203

135   'like a Godard movie . . .': Angela Carter to Carole Roffe, undated, Add. MS. 89102

135   'I think of the United States . . .': *SL*, p. 607

135   'somewhere along . . .': *BYB*, p. 445

CHAPTER 9: VERTIGO

137   'I arrived by air . . .': Add. MS. 88899/1/80

137   'hordes of purposeful human beings': *Vogue*, January 1970

137   'laugh and/or smile . . .': ibid.

137   'architecturally vile' . . .: ibid.

138   'garish, bedizened . . .': ibid.

138   'its history . . . before it . . .': Angela Carter to John Orsborn, 18 October 1969, PC Jenny Orsborn

138   'This is probably the most absolutely . . .': Angela Carter to Carole Roffe, undated, Add. MS. 89102

138   'spending most of [her] time . . .': *Vogue*, January 1970

138   'if you order a cup of coffee . . .': *Fujinkoron*, April 1972, translated for the author by Mayako Murai

138   'hashish-dream somnolence': Angela Carter to Neil Forsyth, undated, PC Neil Forsyth

138   'Japanese men pursue . . .': *Guardian*, 10 August 1972

138   'When they grow their hair long . . .': Ronald Bell, *The Japan Experience* (Tokyo: Weatherhill, 1973), p. 152

139   'nascent sense of independence . . .': Angela Carter to Carole Roffe, undated, Add. MS. 89102

139   'I didn't want to sleep with him . . .': ibid.

139   'a middle-aged Brooklyn Jew' . . .: Angela Carter to Carole Roffe, 25 September 1969, Add. MS. 89102

139   'in the Tokyo railroad station' . . .: Hal Burnell to Caryl Phillips, 21 January 2006, PC Caryl Phillips

139   'if he wants to come with me . . .': Angela Carter to Carole Roffe, 25 September 1969, Add. MS. 89102

139   'the colour of a brown paper parcel': Angela Carter to Carole Roffe, dated 'Friday', Add. MS. 89102

139   '"where are you from?" . . .': Add. MS. 88899/1/81

139   They talked about Dostoevsky . . .: AI Sozo Araki, 22 April 2013

140   'I thought she was like a Hollywood actress' . . .: ibid.

140   'incredibly beautiful': Angela Carter to Andrea Newman, 14 September 1970, PC Andrea Newman

140   'a mirror on the ceiling . . .': BYB, p. 69

140   'an authentic red light' . . .: Add. MS. 88899/1/93

140   'We were shown into a room like a paper box . . .': BYB, pp. 29–30

140   'The maid . . .': *Vogue*, January 1970

141   Sozo retained a memory . . .: AI Sozo Araki, 22 April 2013

141   'my First Real Affair': Angela Carter to Carmen Callil, undated, PC Carmen Callil

141   'a romantic of the most extreme kind . . .': Angela Carter to Carole Roffe, undated, Add. MS. 89102

141   'like a figure through the wrong end of a telescope': Angela Carter to Carole Roffe, 6 October 1969, Add. MS. 89102

141   'like a character in a cheap novel': *Guardian*, 10 August 1972

141   'very like Bristol' . . .: Angela Carter to Carole Roffe, undated, Add. MS. 89102

141   'His face did not . . .': Add. MS. 88899/1/80

141   'with a drunken . . .': Angela Carter to Carole Roffe, 6 October 1969, Add. MS. 89102

142   'I do feel a bit scared . . .': ibid.

142   in a final, private gesture . . .: Angela Carter to Carole Roffe, undated, Add. MS. 89102

142 'I fell in love . . .': ibid.

142 'I plan to go back to Japan . . .': Angela Carter to John Orsborn, 18 October 1969, PC Jenny Orsborn

143 'the British talent for seedy compromise . . .': ibid.

143 'everything the Americans touch . . .': Angela Carter to Carole Roffe, undated, Add. MS. 89102

143 'bowled over . . .': *Vogue*, July 1982

143 'an inventory of imaginary cities': Angela Carter to Carole Roffe, dated 'Wednesday/Thursday', Add. MS. 89102

143 'too hot to hold me': Angela Carter to Carole Roffe, 6 October 1969, Add. MS. 89102

144 'how much . . .': Add. MS. 88899/1/93

144 'a bad introduction to the permissive society': Angela Carter to Carole Roffe, undated, Add. MS. 89102

144 'irrational and . . .': Angela Carter to Carole Roffe, undated, Add. MS. 89102

144 'an interesting Freudian slip . . .': Angela Carter to Carole Roffe, dated 'Wednesday/Thursday', Add. MS. 89102

144 'he alternately blusters and cajoles . . .': ibid.

144 'the contemporary equivalent . . .': Angela Carter to Carole Roffe, undated, Add. MS. 89102

144 'it's no good saying . . .': Angela Carter to Carole Roffe, dated 'Wednesday/Thursday', Add. MS. 89102

145 'he's plainly in a bad way . . .': ibid.

145 'a free woman . . .': *SW*, p. 30

145 'I met him that morning . . .': AI Martin Hoyle, 7 April 2012

145 'I have no wish at all . . .': letter to the author from Paul Carter, 17 October 2011

145 'a remarkable step into the darkness . . .': *Times*, 15 November 1969

146 'richly imagined . . .': *Times Literary Supplement*, 20 November 1969

146 'I find I am not particularly interested in my reviews . . .': Angela Carter to Carole Roffe, undated, Add. MS. 89102

146 'as far as Heinemann . . .': Angela Carter to Carole Roffe, dated 'Wednesday', Add. MS. 89102

146 'vodka in the windows . . .': *SL*, p. 153

146 'installed happily . . .': Angela Carter to Janice Robertson, 28 November 1969, PC Janice Robertson

146 'She did not find writing novels easy' . . .: AI John Lockwood, 7 June 2013

147 'We'd be going to do something . . .': ibid.

147 'my maladroit handling . . .': Angela Carter to Carole Roffe, dated 'Thursday', Add. MS. 89102

147 'As soon as we started to have sex . . .': AI John Lockwood, 7 June 2013

148 'I suppose I feel . . .': Add. MS. 88899/1/93

148 'the significance of the femme fatale . . .': *SL*, p. 354

148   Olive took one look at her . . .: AI Hugh and Joan Stalker, 7 February 2012
148   'a sideboard . . .': Angela Carter to Carole Roffe, undated, Add. MS. 89102
149   'memorably ghastly': Angela Carter to Carole Roffe, 21 March 1971, Add. MS. 89102
149   'suddenly got old . . .': Angela Carter to Carole Roffe, 19 March 1970, Add. MS. 89102
149   asked in a late interview . . .: 'Angela Carter interviewed by Lorna Sage' in *New Writing*, ed. Malcolm Bradbury and Judith Cooke (London: Minerva, 1992), p. 190
149   'Afterwards, I really thought . . .': Angela Carter to Carole Roffe, dated 'Thursday', Add. MS. 89102
149   'a deplorable state': Angela Carter to Carole Roffe, 19 March 1970, Add. MS. 89102
149   'I feel so strange . . .': Add. MS. 88899/1/93

CHAPTER 10: THE DRESSING-UP BOX OF THE HEART
153   his legs shaking uncontrollably: unpublished memoir by Sozo Araki, trans. Natsumi Ikoma
153   'an awkward, forced smile': ibid.
153   'a living image . . .': Add. MS. 88899/1/80
153   Almost as soon . . .': Angela Carter to Carole Roffe, undated, Add. MS. 89102
153   'sustained by passion only . . .': Add. MS. 88899/1/93
154   'taken certain ideas . . .': Angela Carter to Carole Roffe, 5 March 1972, Add. MS. 89102
154   They went to a lettings agency . . .: unpublished memoir by Sozo Araki, trans. Natsumi Ikoma
154   'Sozo began to cry . . .': Angela Carter to Carole Roffe, undated, Add. MS. 89102
154   'I didn't want . . .': ibid.
155   'it always seems to be Sunday afternoon . . .': SL, p. 231
155   'I'm going to have to support him . . .': Angela Carter to Carole Roffe, undated, Add. MS. 89102
155   'They were playing 'catch' . . .': SL, p. 234
155   'the first coloured family . . .': ibid.
155   'a painful and enlightening experience . . .': ibid., p. 39
155   'When they put shit in it . . .': Add. MS. 88899/1/81
156   'very happy & very funny': Angela Carter to Carole Roffe, undated, Add. MS. 89102
156   'He shows no signs of dependence . . .': ibid.
156   'The most interesting and the most disturbing thing . . .': ibid.

156 'peculiar anguish' . . .: Angela Carter to Carole Roffe, dated 'Tuesday', Add. MS. 89102

156 'I knew him as intimately . . .': *BYB*, p. 32

156 'I am both absolutely in love . . .': Angela Carter to Carole Roffe, undated, Add. MS. 89102

157 'radiantly unreliable' . . .: Angela Carter to Carole Roffe, 31 July 1970, Add. MS. 89102

157 'because he's not published anything . . .': Angela Carter to Carole Roffe, 29 June 1970, Add. MS. 89102

157 'five or six lessons max': AI Sozo Araki, 22 April 2013

157 'apprenticeship in the language of signs': *NS*, p. 28

157 'I am a bit like a phoenix . . .': Angela Carter to Carole Roffe, dated 'Thursday', Add. MS. 89102

157 'English was necessary for her to enjoy life . . .': AI Sozo Araki, 22 April 2013

157 'she had a lot of small arguments . . .': ibid.

158 'On the other hand . . .': Angela Carter to Carole Roffe, undated, Add. MS. 89102

158 'I just wish I knew . . .': ibid.

158 'tinkering with another person's autonomy . . .': ibid.

158 'reading and chatting . . .': AI Sozo Araki, 22 April 2013

158 Shortly after she returned to England in 1972 . . .: *Guardian*, 30 March, 1973

159 'I can't work . . .': Angela Carter to Carole Roffe, 31 July, Add. MS. 89102

159 'I started to write short pieces . . .': *BYB*, p. 459

159 'a conversation I had . . .': BLSA C1365/12

159 'the first short piece I ever attempted to write': ibid.

159 'ongoing trauma': Angela Carter to Carole Roffe, 8 May 1970, Add. MS. 89102

159 'It Was Such a Nice Little Planet': Add. MS. 88899/1/61

160 'extraordinarily camp . . .': Angela Carter to Carole Roffe, undated, Add. MS. 89102

160 'What's a nice girl like you . . .': Add. MS. 88899/1/61

160 'I cut out the cunnilingus . . .': Angela Carter to Carole Roffe, undated, Add. MS. 89102

160 'fucking derisory': ibid.

160 'take its fivers . . .': ibid.

160 'Freud would no doubt say . . .': Angela Carter to Carole Roffe, dated 'Thursday', Add. MS. 89102

161 'I am far too many miles away . . .': Angela Carter to Andrea Newman, undated, PC Andrea Newman

161 'What the fuck am I going to do for a living?': Angela Carter to Carole Roffe, 1 September, Add. MS. 89102

161 'into some semblance . . .': Angela Carter to Andrea Newman, undated, PC Andrea Newman
161 'Because I was young and stupid . . .': AI Sozo Araki, 22 April 2013
161 'I suspect I <u>am</u> dominating him . . .': Angela Carter to Carole Roffe, dated 'Thursday', Add. MS. 89102
162 'the word for wife . . .': *BYB*, p. 28
162 'If he fancies being sucked off . . .': Angela Carter to Carole Roffe, dated 'Thursday', Add. MS. 89102
162 'I was young . . .': AI Sozo Araki, 22 April 2013
162 'to be <u>utterly</u> self-revealing . . .': Angela Carter to Carole Roffe, 10 March 1971, Add. MS. 89102
163 'It is rather like . . .': Angela Carter to Carole Roffe, undated, Add. MS. 89102
163 'extremely beautiful' . . .: Angela Carter to Carole Roffe, 27 September 1971, Add. MS. 89102
163 'he really likes, admires & respects . . .': Angela Carter to Carole Roffe, 11 January 1972, Add. MS. 89102
163 'He is, actually, someone I want to keep . . .': Angela Carter to Carole Roffe, 27 September 1971, Add. MS. 89102
163 'who made a . . .': Angela Carter to Carole Roffe, 5 March 1972, Add. MS. 89102
164 'at least [in Japan] they do not disguise the situation': *BYB*, p. 30
164 'intense polarity . . .': Angela Carter to Carole Roffe, 3 August 1971, Add. MS. 89102
164 'absolute femininity . . .': *Spare Rib*, May 1973
164 'Is she a good lay? . . .': Angela Carter to Carole Roffe, 3 August 1971, Add. MS. 89102
164 'This is a heartbreaking country for a feminist': Angela Carter to Andrea Newman, undated, PC Andrea Newman
164 'Mrs Pankhurst is right . . .': Angela Carter to Carole Roffe, 29 June 1970, Add. MS. 89102
164 'an ambulant penis': Angela Carter to Carole Roffe, 25 July 1971, Add. MS. 89102
164 'One has always wondered . . .': Angela Carter to Carole Roffe, dated 'Sunday', Add. MS. 89102
164 'My position in <u>any</u> revolution . . .': Angela Carter to Carole Roffe, 11 January 1972, Add. MS. 89102
165 'an American woman's lib. lady . . .': Angela Carter to Carole Roffe, 16 December 1970, Add. MS. 89102
165 'not yet fully radicalised': Angela Carter to Carole Roffe, undated, Add. MS. 89102
165 'curious elements of Uncle Tomism . . .': ibid.
165 'the woman I love best after you': ibid.

165   '[Naine] is all perception . . .': ibid.
165   'between practising romanticism and hard-headed realism': ibid.
165   'My own persistent discontent . . .': ibid.
166   'So much complexity . . .': *DH*, p. 4
166   'rummaging in the dressing-up box . . .': *BYB*, p. 69
166   'the real trouble . . .': Angela Carter to Carole Roffe, undated, Add. MS. 89102
166   'I am knocked out . . .': Angela Carter to Carole Roffe, dated 'Sunday', Add. MS. 89102
167   'what with working & S's alienation . . .': Angela Carter to Carole Roffe, 31 July 1970, Add. MS. 89102
167   'He was bored by the fireworks . . .': Angela Carter to Carole Roffe, 2/3 November 1970, Add. MS. 89102
167   '"Are you happy?" he asked . . .': *BYB*, p. 28
167   'not strictly true . . .': Angela Carter to Carole Roffe, 10 March 1971, Add. MS. 89102
167   'accurate': AI Sozo Araki, 22 April 2013
167   'we were surrounded by the most moving images . . .': *BYB*, p. 34
168   'THE GATES OF PARADISE . . .': Peter Schwed to Angela Carter, 7 August 1970, Add. MS. 88899/3/31
168   'it seems to me that Lee . . .': Angela Carter to Carole Roffe, 1 September 1970, Add. MS. 89102
168   'I am constantly meeting people . . .': Angela Carter to Janice Robertson, 25 September 1970, PC Janice Robertson
169   'e.g. Miss Z ought to be blonde . . .': ibid.
169   'probably the most boring man in the entire universe . . .': Angela Carter to Carole Roffe, 1 September 1970, Add. MS. 89102
169   'I am uneasy . . .': Angela Carter to Carole Roffe, dated 'Tuesday', Add. MS. 89102
169   'a vague promise of several thou . . .': Angela Carter to Carole Roffe, 11 October 1970, Add. MS. 89102
170   'I simply do not need to earn as much . . .': Angela Carter to Carole Roffe, 25 September 1970, Add. MS. 89102
170   'It's interesting for me . . .': Angela Carter to Carole Roffe, 6 October 1970, Add. MS. 89102
170   'either make the relationship absolute or shatter it': Angela Carter to Carole Roffe, dated 'Tuesday', Add. MS. 89102
170   'I really do both want & need . . .': Angela Carter to Carole Roffe, undated, Add. MS. 89102
171   'a buffoon': Ronald Bell, *The Japan Experience* (Tokyo: Weatherhill, 1973), p. 148
171   'was an orchestration . . .': *SL*, pp. 238–44

CHAPTER 11: BLUEPRINTS FOR NEW LIFESTYLES

172 'we have travelled further . . .': Add. MS. 88899/1/81

172 'similar weather-lacquered, inexpressive faces . . .': *Spare Rib*, May 1973

173 'like being inside a shell': Add. MS. 88899/1/81

173 'a most refined Japanese style': Angela Carter to Andrea Newman, 18 December 1970, PC Andrea Newman

173 'reminiscent of the Old West' . . .: Add. MS. 88899/1/81

173 'It was so boring' . . .: AI Sozo Araki, 22 April 2013

173 'I was so happy' . . .: ibid.

174 'God knows if I will write it': Angela Carter to Carole Roffe, 16 December 1970, Add. MS. 89102

174 'anxiety-ridden, frenetic, exhilarated . . .': ibid.

174 'solid, drab . . .': *DH*, p. 15

174 'a battle between an encyclopedist and a poet': ibid., p. 24

174 'as inconspicuously as possible': ibid., p. 40

175 'posterity's prostitute': ibid., p. 14

175 'the Doctor has liberated the streets . . .': ibid., p. 33; 'nothing in the city was what it seemed . . .': ibid., p. 11

175 'the time of actualised desire': ibid., p. 11

175 'his eyelids were vestigial . . .': ibid., p. 32

175 'Don't you think it would be very beautiful . . .': ibid., p. 57

175 'The speech of the river people . . .': ibid., p. 71

176 'Jesus, he could have written great science fiction': Angela Carter to Carole Roffe, 16 December 1970, Add. MS. 89102

176 'an allegorical novel . . .': V&A archive, ACGB/60/66

176 'a Dostoevskian novel . . .': Add. MS. 88899/1/95

176 '*The Infernal Desire Machines of Dr Hoffman*, that was when . . .': National Archives of Australia, C100/1148870

176 'theoretically matrilinear': *DH*, p. 80

177 'believed women were born . . .': ibid., p. 172, p. 174

177 'the English . . .': Angela Carter to Carole Roffe, 21 March 1971, Add. MS. 89102

177 'I experienced an almost instantaneous regret . . .': *DH*, p. 85

177 'I knew myself to be . . .': ibid., p. 97

177 'the death-defying double somersault . . .': ibid., p. 214

177 'fatal error . . .': ibid., p. 168

178 'I think I killed her to stop her killing me': ibid., p. 217

178 'I was peaking a bit . . .': BLSA C1365/12

178 'Doing <u>Dr H</u> . . .': Angela Carter to Carole Roffe, 29 March 1971, Add. MS. 89102

178 'HOFFMAN is probably . . .': Angela Carter to Carole Roffe, 5 August 1971, Add. MS. 89102

178 'very strange' . . .: email to the author from Alan Brooke, 21 June 2014

178 'We seem to get on very well . . .': Angela Carter to Carole Roffe, 16 December 1970, Add. MS. 89102

178 'when there is nobody else around . . .': Angela Carter to Carole Roffe, 1 January 1971, Add. MS. 89102

179 'He gave me a new me': Angela Carter to Carole Roffe, 27 September 1971, Add. MS. 89102

179 'I didn't get bored . . .': AI Sozo Araki, 22 April 2013

179 'a weird 2 days . . .': Angela Carter to Carole Roffe, 10 March 1971, Add. MS. 89102

179 Almost a year later . . .: Angela Carter to Carole Roffe, [illegible] September 1971, Add. MS. 89102

179 'That was one of the happiest times of my life . . .': AI Sozo Araki, 22 April 2013

179 't.b. of the skin . . .': Angela Carter to Carole Roffe, 31 March 1971, Add. MS. 89102

179 'she can't bear to leave the kids . . .': ibid.

180 'headaches, stiff arm . . .': Angela Carter to Carole Roffe, 21 April 1971, Add. MS. 89102

180 'I think I'd be rather a good . . .': Angela Carter to Carole Roffe, undated, Add. MS. 89102

180 'disgusting' . . .: Angela Carter to Carole Roffe, dated 'Friday', Add. MS. 89102

180 'a Japan bore': ibid.

180 'She was much more sociable . . .': AI Edward Horesh, 6 January 2012

180 'it was a huge thing . . .': AI Rebecca Howard, 26 April 2012

180 'a weekend with them . . .': Angela Carter to Carole Roffe, undated, Add. MS. 89102

181 'untraumatic': ibid.

181 'What I really feel . . .': ibid.

181 'that respectable working class area . . .': ibid.

181 'blueprints for new lifestyles': ibid.

181 'a Scot, a homosexual and a socialist': *Guardian*, 24 November 2009

182 'She was into it . . .': AI John Cox and John Hayes, 23 April 2012

182 'She always seemed to me . . .': ibid.

182 'a disappointing effort . . .': *Guardian*, 20 May 1971

182 'a trifle above the matter . . .': *Observer*, 16 May 1971

182 'what every Sicilian in New York . . .': SL, p. 20

182 'they haven't changed the sheets': Angela Carter to Carole Roffe, undated, Add. MS. 89102

182 'for the violence . . .': ibid.

183 'total atmosphere of hypocrisy . . .': ibid.

183 'My posthumous rapprochement . . .': ibid.

183   'an enormous parenthesis': *SL*, p. 20
183   'fantastically depressed' . . .: Angela Carter to Carole Roffe, undated, Add. MS. 89102
184   'both very excited & very trepidatious' . . .: ibid.
184   'like the girl . . .': ibid.
184   'I have suddenly realised . . .': ibid.
184   'a pretty place' . . .: ibid.
184   'there were not enough blankets . . .': Add. MS. 88899/1/94
184   'a desolate town . . .': ibid.
185   'a French woman and her awful child': Angela Carter to Carole Roffe, 18 July 1971, Add. MS. 89102
185   'It is possible . . .': *Vogue*, December 1973
185   '2 days of unremitting agony' . . .: Angela Carter to Carole Roffe, 18 July 1971, Add. MS. 89102
185   'as we rounded the coast . . .': *BYB*, p. 71
185   Angela was in such a hurry . . .: Angela Carter to Carole Roffe, 18 July 1971, Add. MS. 89102

CHAPTER 12: CONSTRUCTING A PERSONALITY
186   'making, I suppose . . .': Angela Carter to Carole Roffe, 18 July 1971, Add. MS. 89102
186   'from bar to bar, café to café': ibid.
186   'the poignancy of my own situation . . .': *BYB*, p. 68
186   'If you can't find him . . .': Angela Carter to Carole Roffe, 18 July 1971, Add. MS. 89102
186   'It was an absolutely delirious night . . .': ibid.
187   'I saw the flesh and the mirror . . .': *BYB*, p. 71
187   'I scrambled out of [his] arms . . .': ibid.
188   'busy': Unpublished memoir by Sozo Araki, trans. Natsumi Ikoma
188   'He is undergoing some sort of personality crisis . . .': Angela Carter to Carole Roffe, 18 July 1971, Add. MS. 89102
188   'Paul Carter activity': ibid.
188   'His passion for sex without contacts . . .': Angela Carter to Carole Roffe, 28 July 1971, Add. MS. 89102
188   'S. has perceived . . .': Angela Carter to Carole Roffe, undated, Add. MS. 89102
188   'a simpler & less competitive person . . .': Angela Carter to Carole Roffe, 5 August 1971, Add. MS. 89102
189   'Frankly . . .': AI Sozo Araki, 22 April 2013
189   '2 mat cupboard' . . .: Angela Carter to Carole Roffe, 20 July 1971, Add. MS. 89102

189 'The thrill has definitely gone . . .': Angela Carter to Andrea Newman, 22 July 1971, PC Andrea Newman

189 'the loss of face involved': Angela Carter to Carole Roffe, 18 July 1971, Add. MS. 89102

189 'Splittsville is definitely imminent': Angela Carter to Carole Roffe, 20 July 1971, Add. MS. 89102

189 'I am sure he thinks <u>he</u> has left me': Angela Carter to Carole Roffe, 25 July 1971, Add. MS. 89102

189 'the truth is that I left you': unpublished memoir by Sozo Araki, trans. Natsumi Ikoma

189 'I do not believe it is moral . . .': Add. MS. 88899/1/80

190 'my freedom appals me . . .': Angela Carter to Carole Roffe, 27/28 October 1971, Add. MS. 89102

190 'terrified of being alone': Angela Carter to Carole Roffe, undated, Add. MS. 89102

190 On one occasion, he failed to call . . .: Angela Carter to Carole Roffe, 25 July 1971, Add. MS. 89102

190 On another . . .: AI Sozo Araki, 22 April 2013

190 'to the extent that I am a romantic . . .': Angela Carter to Carole Roffe, 3 August 1971, Add. MS. 89102

190 'I can't eat . . .': ibid.

190 'used to keel over . . .': Angela Carter to Carmen Callil, undated, PC Carmen Callil

190 'just a leetle, leetle Valium . . .': ibid.

191 'You & I are far closer . . .': Angela Carter to Carole Roffe, 1 September 1971, Add. MS. 89102

191 'wee house' . . .: Angela Carter to Carole Roffe, undated, Add. MS. 89102

191 'in a coolish . . .': Add. MS. 88899/1/80

191 'more of a patchwork quilt . . .': Angela Carter to Carole Roffe, undated, Add. MS. 89102

191 The working title was *Fictions Written in a Certain City* . . .: Add. MS. 88899/1/80

192 'HOFFMAN rattled along . . .': Angela Carter to Carole Roffe, 8/9 February 1972, Add. MS. 89102

192 'this is a very, very hard patch of maturing . . .': Angela Carter to Carole Roffe, 27 October 1971, Add. MS. 89102

192 'I must perfect a new form . . .': Angela Carter to Carole Roffe, 8/9 February 1971, Add. MS. 89102

192 'I shall end up with . . .': ibid.

193 'Oh, Jesus, when will this torture end': Angela Carter to Carole Roffe, 27 October 1971, Add. MS. 89102

193 'though I want desperately . . .': ibid.

193 'a sufficiently well-established sense of self . . .': Angela Carter to Carole Roffe, 19–24 November 1971, Add. MS. 89102

193 'Kō. Yes, Kō . . .': Angela Carter to Carole Roffe, 17 November 1971, Add. MS. 89102

194 'I remember S. saying . . .': Angela Carter to Carole Roffe, undated, Add. MS. 89102

194 'he is already a complete person': Angela Carter to Carole Roffe, 21 December 1971, Add. MS. 89102

194 'God knows what's in his head . . .': Angela Carter to Carole Roffe, 19–24 November 1971, Add. MS. 89102

194 'more a mature 14 . . .': ibid.

194 'already contrived . . .': ibid.

194 'very strange': AI Ted Holst, 28 April 2013

194 'the relationship is so simple . . .': Angela Carter to Carole Roffe, 11 January 1972, Add. MS. 89102

195 'I suppose [Kō] is really a piece of sexual bric-a-brac . . .': Angela Carter to Carole Roffe, 17 November 1971, Add. MS. 89102

195 'about the size of a largish studio apartment . . .': SL, pp. 249–50

195 'creepy': AI Naine Woodrow, 21 May 2013

195 'regress to behaviour . . .': SL, pp. 251–2

196 'was never sure how close she got . . .': *Independent on Sunday*, 8 January 1995

196 'in the warm . . .': Angela Carter to Carole Roffe, 2 January 1972, Add. MS. 89102

196 'an old-fashioned Confucian type': AI Ted Holst, 28 April 2013

196 'faintly bewildered air': Angela Carter to Carole Roffe, 2 January 1972, Add. MS. 89102

196 'I have squared [their profession] . . .': Angela Carter to Carole Roffe, 2 January 1972, Add. MS. 89102

196 'Kō is lovely . . .': ibid.

196 'I went off the pill . . .': Angela Carter to Carole Roffe, 9 January 1972, Add. MS. 89102

196 'cessation of menstruation . . .': Angela Carter to Carole Roffe, 11 January 1972, Add. MS. 89102

197 'more or less convinced . . .': Angela Carter to Carole Roffe, 18 January 1972, Add. MS. 89102

197 'I know I will miss him . . .': Angela Carter to Carole Roffe, undated, Add. MS. 89102

197 'a good, English-speaking abortion . . .': Angela Carter to Carole Roffe, 2 February 1972, Add. MS. 89102

197 'I was just doing my thing . . .': Angela Carter to Carole Roffe, 8/9 February 1972, Add. MS. 89102

197 'doing all kinds of things . . .': Angela Carter to Carole Roffe, undated, Add. MS. 89102
197 'to comfort Kō' . . .: Add. MS. 88899/1/94
198 'It <u>was</u> – though blurred by my sickness . . .': ibid.
198 'I'm afraid I have nothing but bad news . . .': Peter Schwed to Angela Carter, 3 April 1972, Add. MS. 89102
198 'The letter from Simon & Schuster . . .': Angela Carter to Carole Roffe, 6 April 1972, Add. MS. 89102
198 'for God's sake get out of Japan . . .': Anthony Burgess to Angela Carter, 14 April 1972, Add. MS. 88899/3/1
199 'it really has been . . .': Angela Carter to Carole Roffe, undated, Add. MS. 89102
199 'what I do feel, really . . .': Angela Carter to Carole Roffe, 6 April 1972, Add. MS. 89102

CHAPTER 13: YET ANOTHER FOREIGN COUNTRY
203 'which, senses peeled . . .': Angela Carter to Carole Roffe, 16 June 1972, Add. MS. 89102
203 By way of decorating . . .: email to author from Andrew Travers, 20 March 2014
203 'The atavistic appeal . . .': Angela Carter to Carole Roffe, 16 June 1972, Add. MS. 89102
204 'I knew it was a man . . .': Add. MS. 88899/1/95
204 'I think he was exposing himself': ibid.
204 'dreadfully shocked . . .': Angela Carter to Carole Roffe, dated 'Monday', Add. MS. 89102
204 'it was like that F. Scott Fitzgerald story . . .': ibid.
204 'This feverish, hysterical feeling . . .': Angela Carter to Carole Roffe, undated, Add. MS. 89102
204 'it hardly seemed possible . . .': BYB, p. 97
204 'high up in an attic . . .': ibid., p. 96
204 'got on my tits like anything': Add. MS. 88899/1/94
205 'I was terribly impressed': ibid.
205 'the ache of loss . . .': ibid.
205 'I feel very bad about this . . .': Angela Carter to Carole Roffe, undated, Add. MS. 89102
205 'sensation of walking on thin ice' . . .: ibid.
205 'Carole, oh, Carole . . .': ibid.
205 'the trouble with travelling . . .': Angela Carter to Anthony Burgess, 29 July 1972, International Anthony Burgess Foundation
206 'I can't stand friction . . .': Angela Carter to Carole Roffe, 16 June 1972, Add. MS. 89102

206 'all I know is . . .': AI Rebecca Howard, 26 April 2012
206 'marked the beginning of my obscurity': cited in Susannah Clapp, *A Card from Angela Carter* (London: Bloomsbury, 2012), p. 32
206 'a real freak . . .': *Time Out*, 2 June 1972
206 'Angela Carter has the kind of electric talent . . .': *Financial Times*, 20 May 1972
207 'unique among her contemporaries . . .': *Daily Telegraph*, 18 May 1972
207 'peacock brilliance' . . .: *Sunday Times*, 14 May 1972
207 'I can only testify . . .': *Spectator*, 20 May 1972
207 'being a somewhat fey . . .': *Guardian*, 10 August 1972
207 'who [were] writing . . .': B. S. Johnson, *Aren't You Rather Young to be Writing Your Memoirs?* (London: Hutchinson, 1973), p. 29
207 'blood and brains everywhere': Angela Carter to Carole Roffe, undated, Add. MS. 89102
207 'I haven't yet actually dared . . .': ibid.
208 'I always find it easier . . .': BLSA C1365/8
208 'her first publishers . . .': Joe Scott-Clark to Charles Osborn, 25 September 1972, V&A archive, ACGB/60/66
208 'so God awful . . .': Angela Carter to Carole Roffe, undated, Add. MS. 89102
208 'I admire him very much . . .': Angela Carter to Neil Forsyth, 26 August 1974, PC Neil Forsyth
209 'When I really . . . ': ibid.
209 'ranging from the innocent child-woman . . .': Anna Watz, 'Angela Carter and Xavière Gauthier's *Surréalisme et sexualité*', *Contemporary Women's Writing*, July 2010
209 'a very good book indeed . . .': Angela Carter to Marion Boyars, undated, the Lilly Library, University of Indiana
209 'like to translate . . .': ibid.
209 'very freely . . .': ibid.
209 'On 18 October . . .: Marion Boyars to Angela Carter; 18 October 1972, the Lilly Library, University of Indiana
209 'not only insane . . .': Angela Carter to Carole Roffe, 25 September 1970, Add. MS. 89102
210 'We sat downstairs . . .': email to the author from Andrew Travers, 20 March 2014
210 'Time & ill fortune . . .': Angela Carter to Carole Roffe, undated, Add. MS. 89102
210 'one of the few people . . .': Angela Carter to Neil Forsyth, 26 August 1974, PC Neil Forsyth
210 'not [as] an emanation of myself . . .': Angela Carter to Andrew Travers, dated 'Saturday', PC Andrew Travers

210 'post-traumatic stress . . .': email to the author from Andrew Travers, 20 March 2014

210 'he brought his work home with him': AI Hugh and Joan Stalker, 17 April 2012

210 'I am not entirely innocent . . .': Angela Carter to Carole Roffe, dated 'Sunday/Monday', Add. MS. 89102

211 'In the interval before she actually moved in . . .': 'Angela Carter: some notes and a chronology', prepared for the author by Fleur Adcock

211 'my path has crossed with that of Andrew Travers . . .': Angela Carter to Carole Roffe, undated, Add. MS. 89102

211 'she said Angela's entire manner . . .': AI John Lockwood, 7 June 2013

211 'I am perceptive but not sensitive . . .': Angela Carter to Carole Roffe, undated, Add. MS. 89102

212 'godforsaken hole . . .': Angela Carter to Carole Roffe, undated, Add. MS. 89102

212 'I was always slightly in awe of her' . . .: AI Fleur Adcock, 5 February 2013

212 'she didn't start particularly early . . .': email to the author from Andrew Travers, 20 March 2014

212 'I think she found most social interactions . . .': AI Andrew Travers, 30 August 2014

212 'intensely sexual' . . . : email to the author from Andrew Travers, 17 February 2014

212 'midly tempestuous' . . .: AI Andrew Travers, 30 August 2014

213 'possessiveness' . . .: Angela Carter to Andrew Travers, undated, PC Andrew Travers

213 'Dear Andrew . . .': Add. MS. 88899/1/94

213 'He does not see me as a subject . . .': ibid.

213 'You knew you'd done something . . .': AI Andrew Travers, 30 August 2014

213 'He provokes violence . . .': Add. MS. 88899/1/94

213 'a spiritual/psychological crise . . .': Angela Carter to Anthony Burgess, 17 February 1973, International Anthony Burgess Foundation

214 'I think I threw a typewriter at something . . .': AI Andrew Travers, 30 August 2014

214 When she had left, there had only been four feminist groups . . .: Dominic Sandbrook, *State of Emergency: The Way We Were: Britain, 1970–1974* (London: Penguin, 2010), p. 376

215 at the end of that year . . .: ibid.

215 'actively involved . . .': *Face*, September 1984

215 'Imagine having to be macho . . .': *Gay News*, March 1979

215 'It's easily the most amusing thing . . .': *Observer*, 1 March 1970

215 'overriding impression' . . .: *Daily Telegraph*, 6 March 1971

215 At around the same time, Marsha Rowe . . .: Rosie Boycott, *A Nice Girl Like Me: A Story of the Seventies* (London: Chatto & Windus, 1984), pp. 59–60

216 'there was a huge gap . . .': ibid., p. 61

216 'with the onset of Women's Lib . . .': *Spare Rib*, July 1972

216 'a promise swathed in fantasy . . .': ibid.

216 'tall, slim, and scantily dressed, . . .: AI Marsha Rowe, 13 February 2014

216 'the loneliness of the child . . .': *Spare Rib*, March 1973

216 'the first thing you feel . . .': *Spare Rib*, May 1973

216 'the Turkish baths supply the needy . . .': *Men Only*, Vol. 38, No. 7, July 1973

217 '"You will get better lodging here," . . .': *Club International*, Vol. 3, No. 12, December 1974

217 'pornography is the theory . . .': Robin Morgan, *Going Too Far: The Personal Chronicle of a Feminist* (New York: Random House, 1977), p. 164

217 'I think some of the Sisters make too much of a fuss . . .': *Face*, November 1984

218 'We've almost forgotten . . .': *Observer*, 10 April 1977

218 'put pornography . . .': SW, p. 42

218 She recalled that during the lunch . . .: AI Carmen Callil, 5 January 2012

219 'somebody was indulging . . .': *Vogue*, July 1982

219 'How we afforded such things . . .': AI Carmen Callil, 5 January 2012

219 'advertisement' . . .: Angela Carter to Carmen Callil, 7 August 1973, Add. MS. 88904/1/60

219 'I'm more enthusiastic about your "advertisement" . . .': Carmen Callil to Angela Carter, 13 August 1973, Add. MS. 88904/1/60

220 'I won't be able to start work . . .': Angela Carter to Carmen Callil, 7 August 1973, Add. MS. 88904/1/60

220 'pathology': Lorna Sage, *Angela Carter* (Plymouth: Northcote House, 1994), p. 32

220 'the acceptable face of feminism': AI Lennie Goodings, 3 February 2015

220 'I suppose I am moved towards it . . .': Angela Carter to Lorna Sage, cited in Lorna Sage, *Angela Carter* (Plymouth: Northcote House, 1994), p. 32; 'a masochistic season in hell' is from Angela's review of the book, *Guardian*, 7 July 1977

220 'Angela Carter is a *real* writer': AI Marsha Rowe, 13 February 2014

221 'She was a very central author . . .': AI Ursula Owen, 25 February 2014

221 'She was so charming and caring . . .': AI Lennie Goodings, 3 February 2015

221 'She was very generous in allowing us . . .': AI John Boothe, 3 March 2014

222 'DR HOFFMAN is the most extraordinary . . .': Deborah Rogers to Angela Carter, 12 July 1973, RCW

222 'due to having been . . .': Angela Carter to Deborah Rogers, 12 August 1973, RCW

222 'as far as being one of the Sisters . . .': AI Deborah Rogers, 6 June 2012

222 'I lived with a psychopath . . .': Angela Carter to Neil Forsyth, 26 August 1974, PC Neil Forsyth

222 'at night . . .': various undated letters from Angela Carter to Andrew Travers, PC Andrew Travers

223 'I forced you to commit . . .': Angela Carter to Andrew Travers, undated, PC Andrew Travers

223 'the ideal place to retrench . . .': *Cosmopolitan*, July 1976

223 'Everywhere you look in Bath . . .': Add. MS. 88899/1/87

223 'The uselessness of the city . . .': *SL*, p. 163

224 'a bit off the beaten track . . .': Angela Carter to Deborah Rogers, undated, RCW

224 'I am in the extensile . . .': Angela Carter to Andrew Travers, undated, PC Andrew Travers

224 'I've just been to look at my house . . .': Angela Carter to Andrew Travers, 17 May 1973, PC Andrew Travers

225 'Yesterday evening . . .': Add. MS. 88899/1/94

225 'I sensed that she was keeping something back': 'Angela Carter: some notes and a chronology', prepared for the author by Fleur Adcock

225 'he said he had locked it . . .': Fleur Adcock's diary, PC Fleur Adcock

226 'terribly immature . . .': Andrew Travers to Andrea Newman, 23 June 1973, PC Andrea Newman

226 'he's used my typewriter!': Angela Carter's addendum to Andrew Travers' letter, op. cit.

CHAPTER 14: ISN'T THE IDENTITY FRAGILE?

227 'rather erotic pictures': AI Nicola Farthing, 27 January 2012

227 'for reasons of misanthropy' . . .: Angela Carter to Neil Forsyth, 26 August 1974

227 'It's paint pots, paint pots . . .': Angela Carter to Fleur Adcock, PC Fleur Adcock

227 'The main body of the text . . .': Angela Carter to Marion Boyars, 7 July 1973, the Lilly Library, University of Indiana

227 'Could you not . . .': Angela Carter to Marion Boyars, 31 August 1973, the Lilly Library, University of Indiana

228 'I posted . . .': Angela Carter to Marion Boyars, 17 September 1973, the Lilly Library, University of Indiana

228 'I'm in the demythologising business': *SL*, p. 38

228 'extraordinary lies . . .': ibid.

229 'a piece of black comedy': John Haffenden, *Novelists in Interview* (London: Methuen, 1985), p. 86

229 'a deeply, deeply serious piece . . .': *Omnibus: Angela Carter's Curious Room*, BBC1, 15 September 1992

229 'I intended it as a feminist novel . . .': *Gay News*, March 1979

229 'Mother goddesses . . .': *SW*, p. 11

229 a video-tape . . .': *NE*, p. 69

229 The 'passion' of the novel's title . . .: *SL*, p. 592

229 'The mediation of Zero . . .': *NE*, pp. 107–8

229 'brought with it . . .': ibid., p. 98

229 'It is difficult not to laugh' . . .: *London Review of Books*, 8 December 1994

230 the most beautiful woman in the world': *NE*, p. 4

230 'every kitsch excess . . .': ibid., p. 71

230 'The story of Tristessa . . .': *Omnibus: Angela Carter's Curious Room*, BBC1, 15 September 1992

230 'I make an elite product' . . .: BLSA C1365/12

230 'It's the tastes of the intelligentsia . . .': ibid.

230 'wasn't grappling . . .': ibid.

230 'to beautify . . .': ibid.

231 'an opening that is . . .': *London Review of Books*, 15 December 2005

231 'I was a younger son . . .': Add. MS. 88899/1/5

231 'I've been w[ork]ing' . . .: Angela Carter to Fleur Adcock, 10 August, PC Fleur Adcock

231 'improves one's posture . . .': ibid.

232 'to the extent that we had conversations . . .': AI Christine Downton, 19 March 2013

232 'She was incredibly idiosyncratic . . .': AI Christopher Frayling, 22 February 2013

232 'we were totally gripped by it . . .': AI Christine Downton, 19 March 2013

232 'since nobody else wanted to': Angela Carter to Deborah Rogers, undated, RCW

233 'Angie had a thing about the theatre': AI Christopher Frayling, 22 February 2013

233 '"Live" theatre . . .': *SL*, p. 405

233 'he says he likes my work . . .': Angela Carter to Carmen Callil, undated, Add. MS. 88904/1/60

233 'she was really, really hurt . . .': AI Christopher Frayling, 22 February 2013

234 'I don't know what on earth . . .': AI Ann McFerran, 5 June 2014

234 'And what do you do?': AI Christopher Frayling, 22 February 2013

234 'The following morning . . .': AI Ann McFerran, 5 June 2014

234 'furtive': Angela Carter to Fleur Adcock, undated, PC Fleur Adcock

234 'every page . . .': ibid.

234 The anxious financial calculations . . .: Add. MS. 88899/1/95

235 'a piece of bureaucratic double-bind': Angela Carter to Deborah Rogers, 17 July 1973, RCW

235 'I'm aware of my own natural prejudice . . .': Angela Carter to Deborah Rogers, 6 November 1973, RCW

235 'I've been working so hard this winter . . .': Angela Carter to Martin Hoyle, undated, PC Martin Hoyle

236 'My family has such a facility . . .': Add. MS. 88899/1/95

236 'Though it's possible I may change certain things . . .': Angela Carter to Deborah Rogers, 25 January 1974, RCW

236 'bright & dark & soulless': Add. MS. 88899/1/95

236 'the most ridiculous place in the world . . .': Angela Carter to Deborah Rogers, 25 March 1974

237 'They are crooks . . .': ibid.

237 'a magazine of no significance' . . .: ibid.

237 'what has become of Tokyo . . .': *Bungeishunju*, May 1974, translated for the author by Mayako Murai

237 'He talks in a new voice' . . .: Add. MS. 88899/1/95

237 'He no longer trusts people . . .': ibid.

238 'Your ugliness . . .': ibid.

238 'what upset him . . .': AI Ted Holst, 28 April 2013

238 'I know why I come bothering you . . .': Add. MS. 88899/1/95

238 'I should love to hold him in my arms . . .': ibid.

238 'We made love . . .': ibid.

238 'heroic stupidity': Angela Carter to Deborah Rogers, undated, RCW

238 On Saturday 20 April she boarded a Russian ferry . . .: details of the trip from Add. MS. 88899/1/84 and Add. MS. 88899/1/95

240 'a flaming, Soviet red': Angela Carter to Fleur Adcock, 7 May 1974, PC Fleur Adcock

240 'loathe Englishmen, as men . . .': Angela Carter to Neil Forsyth, 26 August 1974, PC Neil Forsyth

240 'I feel I am perched on top . . .': Add. MS. 88899/1/95

241 'by far the best fuck . . .': ibid.

241 'like a hawk . . .': ibid.

241 'Oh, Jesus . . .': ibid.

241 'dreamy slowness . . .': ibid.

241 'feeling like hell' . . .: Angela Carter to Carmen Callil, 14 July 1974, PC Carmen Callil

241 'very ill . . .': Add. MS. 88899/1/95

241 'I felt I was not my self, or myself . . .': Add. MS. 88899/1/95

241 as the novelist and critic Nicole Ward Jouve has pointed out . . .: Nicole Ward Jouve, 'Mother is a Figure of Speech' in *Flesh and the Mirror: Essays on the Art of Angela Carter* (London: Virago, 1994), pp. 136–71

242 'to deny the bankrupt enchantments of the womb . . .': SW, p. 109

242 'I really don't know how I would have managed . . .': *Marxism Today*, January 1985

242 Many doctors refused . . .: *Guardian*, 15 August 1975

242 'many of us scarcely noticed . . .': Add. MS. 88899/1/65

242 'the Magnificat . . .': *Guardian*, 3 April 1973

243 'There is nothing like this experience . . .': Angela Carter to Carmen Callil, 14 July 1974, PC Carmen Callil

243 'I felt estranged . . .': Add. MS. 88899/1/95

243 'I was remembering women I've known . . .': BLSA C1365/12

243 'at the price of her womb': *NE*, p. 34

243 'Considering it was done in the best possible circumstances . . .': Add. MS. 88899/1/95

243 '"What's the message?" he says . . .': Angela Carter to Carmen Callil, 14 July 1974, PC Carmen Callil

244 'The regression to timorousness . . .': Add. MS. 88899/1/95

244 'a great deal of criticism . . .': Marion Boyars to Angela Carter, 15 July 1974, the Lilly Library, University of Indiana

244 'she said she realised . . .': Tim O'Grady to Marion Boyars, 18 July 1974, the Lilly Library, University of Indiana

245 'what may be in French . . .': unsigned and undated letter to Marion Boyars, the Lilly Library, University of Indiana

245 'Miss [sic] Carter seems to have fallen heavily under . . .': *Evening Standard*, 10 September 1974

245 'if she can write as well as she does in that . . .': *Observer*, 29 August 1974

245 'one of the most rousing young writers around . . .': *Guardian*, 18 August 1974

246 'You always wanted to give her a back rub': AI Peter Conradi, 7 January 2014

246 'They liked being bad together . . .': AI Sharon Tolaini-Sage, 16 April 2014

247 'a formidable ally': Angela Carter to Pat Barker, 9 January 1983, PC Pat Barker

247 She received fan letters . . .: Add. MS. 88899/3/1

247 'I liked especially SOLID GEOMETRY . . .': Angela Carter to Ian McEwan, 26 April 1975, HRC, MS-4902

247 'a brilliant performance . . .': *Observer*, 4 May 1975

247 'poor Ian . . .': Angela Carter to Carmen Callil, 9 June 1977, PC Carmen Callil

247 'I am shocked . . .': Angela Carter to Ian McEwan, 26 April [1975], HRC, MS-4902

248 'I was utterly taken in by it . . .': Robert Coover to Angela Carter, 1 Feburary 1974, Add. MS. 88899/3/1

248 'The <u>Iowa Review</u>, now into its sixth year . . .': ibid.

248 'we are printing an additional . . .': Tony Godwin to Angela Carter, undated, Add. MS. 88899/3/1

248 'I suffer rather badly . . .': Angela Carter to Neil Forsyth, 26 August 1974, PC Neil Forsyth

249 'I've had a dreadful "crise du nerfes" . . .': Angela Carter to Carmen Callil, 16 March 1974, Add. MS. 88904/1/60

249 'When I think of the Sade book . . .': Angela Carter to Neil Forsyth, 26 August 1974, PC Neil Forsyth

249 'agitated & depressed' . . .: Angela Carter to Fleur Adcock, 30 January 1975, PC Fleur Adcock

CHAPTER 15: THE SILENCES WITH WHICH THE ENGLISH
COMPOSE INTIMACIES

250 It wasn't easy to concentrate . . .: AI Mark Pearce, 30 October 2014

250 'He came in . . .': *Granta* 41, Autumn 1992

250 'the most improbable combination . . .': AI Deborah Rogers, 6 June 2012

251 'the colour of the inside of the ocean': Add. MS. 88899/1/95

251 'big and fierce' . . .: cited in Susannah Clapp, *A Card from Angela Carter* (London: Bloomsbury, 2012), p. 76

251 'an affinity with fire': AI Mark Pearce, 30 October 2014

251 'the haunting silences of Bath . . .': *SL*, p. 161

252 'When I hold him in my arms . . .': Add. MS. 88899/1/95

252 'I am remembering what John . . .': ibid.

252 'At least the bibliography . . .': Angela Carter to Deborah Rogers, 16 September 1975, RCW

253 'the somewhat chaotic organisation . . .': ibid.

253 'We do not go to bed in simple pairs . . .': *SW*, p. 10

253 'A moral pornographer . . .': ibid., p. 22

253 'more descriptive . . .': ibid., pp. 27–8

254 'he is uncommon . . .': ibid., p. 28

254 'I did have problems . . .' *Gay News*, March 1979

254 'thinner than the others . . .': Carmen Callil to Angela Carter, undated, Add. MS. 88899/1/70

254 'representative capacity . . .': *SW*, p. 72

254 'the biological iconography . . .': ibid., p. 126

254 'suggests that women, also . . .': ibid., p. 143

254 'The demand for equal rights . . .': ibid., pp. 177–78

255 'I believe in the book . . .': John Berger to Angela Carter, 10 March 1976, Add. MS. 88899/1/70

255 'the profound dread . . .': Angela Carter to Carmen Callil, 11 December 1976, Add. MS. 88904/1/60

256 'Sitting in my room . . .': CR, p. 499

256 'My name is exile . . .': ibid., p. 9

256 his 'style, sensitivity . . .': ibid., p. 501

256 'Angela had an enormous sense of fun . . .': *Times*, 20 February 1992
256 '"The Lady of the House of Love" is a Gothic tale . . .': CR, p. 500
257 'gaunt . . .': BYB, p. 190
257 'quite green . . .': ibid., p. 187
257 'Mark is der erlkönig': Add. MS. 88899/1/95
257 'I am not afraid of him . . .': BYB, p. 189
257 'in his innocence . . .': pp. 191–92
257 She considered putting it . . .: Add. MS. 88899/1/95
257 '*proper* cafés . . .': *Cosmopolitan*, July 1976
258 'It was very alternative . . .': AI Christopher Frayling, 22 February 2013
258 'When you talked to Angela on the phone . . .': AI Mark Pearce, 30 October 2014
258 'she would call you in the middle of the morning . . .': AI Ann McFerran, 5 June 2014
258 'I am certainly not material . . .': Angela Carter to Carole Roffe, undated, Add. MS. 89102
258 'I've always thought . . .': cited in Susannah Clapp, *A Card From Angela Carter* (London: Bloomsbury, 2012), p. 19
259 'Ta for Barthes': Angela Carter to Christopher Frayling, 1 June 1976, PC Christopher Frayling
259 'I've only just read Barthes . . .': *New Yorkshire Writing*, Winter 1978
259 Both authors . . .: SL, pp. 332–6 and Roland Barthes, *Mythologies*, trans. Annette Lavers (London: Vintage, 2009), pp. 3–15
260 'I remember liking [Angela] enormously . . .': AI Sandy Brown, 4 April 2014
260 'Angela loved all of this . . .': ibid.
260 'this gorgeous young builder . . .': ibid.
260 Hughie remembered her saying . . .: AI Hugh and Joan Stalker, 7 February 2012
261 On the second or third lesson . . .: AI Edward Horesh, 6 January 2012
261 'I have never had such "baby blues" . . .': Angela Carter to Deborah Rogers, 5 January 1976, RCW
261 'I started off . . .': Angela Carter to Elaine Jordan, cited in Elaine Jordan, 'The Dangerous Edge' in *Flesh and the Mirror: Essays on the Art of Angela Carter*, ed. Lorna Sage (London: Virago, 1994), p. 213
261 'I'm not sure that it hangs together . . .': BLSA C1365/12
261 'my favourite of my novels . . .': *Omnibus: Angela Carter's Curious Room*, BBC1, 15 September 1992
261 'It's nearly a masterpiece . . .': Tony Godwin to Angela Carter, undated, Add. MS. 88899/3/1
261 'I am afraid I cannot report . . .': Mark Barty-King to Deborah Rogers, 26 February 1976, RCW
262 'a startling mixture . . .': Dobkin Collection

262 'I was fairly awestruck . . .': AI Liz Calder, 22 November 2011
262 'which would be likely . . .': Liz Calder to Deborah Rogers, 28 April 1976, Dobkin Collection
262 'Angela Carter is exactly the sort of writer . . .': Dobkin Collection
263 'Mr. Donoso arrived . . .': *New York Times*, 8 March 1992
263 'I was completely unknown . . .': AI Salman Rushdie, 7 February 2014
263 'In a literary sense . . .': ibid.
263 'I'm talking to you two . . .': *Vogue*, August 1985
264 'I think she was much more ambitious . . .': AI Deborah Rogers, 6 June 2012
264 'It was odd . . .': AI Christopher Frayling, 22 February 2013
264 'but after three years . . .': Fleur Adcock's diary, PC Fleur Adcock
264 'Angela was very firm . . .': AI Christine Downton, 19 March 2013
264 'We were dotting about . . .': AI Rebecca Howard, 26 April 2012
264 'Right, that's got to be it . . .': ibid.

CHAPTER 16: THE TALES OF TERROR GROOVE
265 'You can't walk home from the tube . . .': SL, p. 181
265 'There's been a diaspora of the affluent . . .': WC, p. 1
266 'a rather Beardslyesque . . .': Angela Carter to Lorna Tracy, 17 June 1979, PC Lorna Tracy
266 'Jurassic Productions': AI Christine Downton, 19 March 2013
266 'Everything is in chaos . . .': Angela Carter to Brenda Leys, 8 March 1976, RCW
266 'more building site than house': Angela Carter to Fleur Adcock, undated, PC Fleur Adcock
266 'were reduced to taking odds and ends . . .': SL, p. 180
266 'sweated [it] out' . . .: ibid., p. 452
266 'what an unexpected treat . . .': ibid.
266 'high literary recondite . . .': Jack Zipes, introduction to FTCP, p. xx
266 'never artful . . .': FTCP, p. 75
267 'I'm told, quite kindly . . .': Add. MS. 88899/2/28
267 'Fairy-tale animals . . .': Add. MS. 88899/1/96
268 'a social realism of the unconscious': National Archives of Australia, C100/1148870
268 'Code Name: The New Mother Goose': Add. MS. 88899/1/96
268 'Not really . . .': *Meanjin*, March 1985
268 'At least this stress . . .': Angela Carter to Fleur Adcock, undated, PC Fleur Adcock
269 'In the opinion of everyone on the panel . . .': AI Neil Roberts, 9 April 2014
269 'which is probably why . . .': John Haffenden, *Novelists in Interview* (London: Methuen, 1985), p. 86

269   'all "sithee" and "thyssen" . . .': *SL*, p. 5

269   People ate black pudding and tripe . . .: AI Naomi Brent and Kaktus Leach, 31 March 2015

270   'Although I think I know more . . .': Angela Carter to Alan Ross, undated, the Brotherton Library, University of Leeds, BC MS 20c London Magazine

270   'like a Lowry painting': AI Naomi Brent and Kaktus Leach, 31 March 2015

270   'all sorts of nutty people . . .': ibid.

270   'naughty teenagers' . . .: ibid.

270   'a brilliant cook . . .': ibid.

270   'She'd just quietly sit there': ibid.

271   'an extremely good lodger' . . .: ibid.

271   'very easy to live with' . . .: ibid.

271   'I think she was one of these people . . .': ibid.

271   Angela made it her own . . .: *New Yorkshire Writing*, Winter 1978

271   'clocked on, like a worker': *Harper's & Queen*, February 1979

272   'the winds are wuthering . . .': Angela Carter to Christopher Frayling, 6 October 1976, PC Christopher Frayling

272   'I really don't want to do anything . . .': Angela Carter to Christopher Frayling, undated, PC Christopher Frayling

272   'I may try & cross . . .': ibid.

272   a 'tiny little story': Angela Carter to Emma Tennant, 25 January 1977, HRC, *Bananas* archive, Box 4, Folder 1

272   'a bloody stump . . .': *BYB*, p. 211

272   'a little girl with a red cap . . .': Bruno Bettelheim, *The Uses of Enchantment* (London: Vintage, 1978), p. 168

272   'See! sweet and sound she sleeps . . .': *BYB*, p. 220

272   'They are grey as famine . . .': ibid., p. 212

273   '[flings] it into the fire . . .': ibid., p. 219

273   During her first term in Sheffield, Angela became involved in a project . . .: Add. MS. 88899/1/77

273   'It just seemed really disconnected' . . .: *Penny Black Music*, 23 April 2011

274   'The reading list comprises . . .': Angela Carter to Christopher Frayling, undated, PC Christopher Frayling

274   'She was sociable . . .': AI Neil Roberts, 9 April 2014

274   'since home (temporarily, at least) . . .': Angela Carter to Fleur Adcock, 25 January 1977, PC Fleur Adcock

274   'He still retains . . .': Add. MS. 88899/1/96

274   'now I like people . . .': *Globe and Mail*, 20 October 1984

274   'we (roughly) share the labour . . .': Angela Carter to Lorna Tracy, undated, PC Lorna Tracy

275   'Mark made her very happy . . .': AI Christine Downton, 19 March 2013

275   'He obviously adored her . . .': AI Liz Calder, 22 November 2011

275 'they were very at ease together': AI Salman Rushdie, 7 February 2014

275 'They conspired to present their relationship . . .': Lorna Sage, *Angela Carter* (Plymouth: Northcote House, 1994), p. 51

275 '"The Company of Wolves" is part of a work-in-progress . . .': Angela Carter to Emma Tennant, 25 January 1977, HRC, *Bananas* archive, Box 4, Folder 1

275 'Has Angela . . . I wonder . . .': Emma Tennant, *Burnt Diaries* (Edinburgh: Canongate, 2000), p. 96

275 'Angela Carter, brilliant and beautiful magical realist . . .': Jonathan Bate, *Ted Hughes: The Unauthorised Life* (London: Collins, 2015), p. 374

276 'Notice I curbed my natural reticence . . .': Angela Carter to Liz Calder, undated, Dobkin Collection

276 'the processes of myth-making . . .': *Observer*, 27 March 1977

276 'not so terribly . . .': *Sunday Times*, 2 March 1977

276 'If it all sounds jagged . . .': *New Statesman*, 25 March 1977

276 'her robust . . .': *Evening Standard*, 1 April 1977

277 'I wander outside . . .': Emma Tennant, *Burnt Diaries* (Edinburgh: Canongate, 2000), p. 88

277 '"It is hard for women," . . .': cited in Lorna Sage, *Angela Carter* (Plymouth: Northcote House, 1994), p. 32

278 'Man & beast . . .': Add. MS. 88899/1/96

278 'Since you left me . . .': BYB, p. 153

278 'Mr and Mrs Lyon . . .': ibid.

278 'My father lost me to The Beast at cards': ibid., p. 154

278 'one of my very favourite lines . . .': *The Coming Out Show*, 4 October 1987, ABC radio

278 'and each stroke of his tongue . . .': BYB, p. 169

278 'a black gondola . . .': Add. MS. 88899/1/96

279 'His Mae-West like Lilac Fairy . . .': Angela Carter to Deborah Rogers, 9 January 1977, RCW

279 'like coming suddenly upon a familiar building . . .': *Daily Mail*, 15 December 1977

279 'Her plain prose is an admirable vehicle . . .': *Guardian*, 29 September 1977

279 'stylish and lively . . .': *Times Literary Supplement*, 28 October 1977

279 'It was partly his blue beard . . .': *In Conversation: Angela Carter with Lisa Appignanesi*, ICA video, 1985

279 'leather and spices' . . .: BYB, p. 112

279 'Every man must have one secret . . .': ibid., p. 124

280 'the moment the story becomes an homage to Colette . . .': *In Conversation: Angela Carter with Lisa Appignanesi*, ICA video, 1985

280 'twelve days . . .': SL, pp. 219–23

280 'there was this big demonstration . . .': AI Shirley Cameron, 7 March 2012

281 'desire, imagination and dream . . .': *SL*, p. 222
281 'a cat of the world . . .': *BYB*, p. 170
281 'I went about my ablutions . . .': ibid., p. 172
281 Ten years later, Angela told an interviewer . . .: *The Review of Contemporary Fiction*, Fall 1994
281 'to go in between COURTSHIP OF MR LYON . . .': Angela Carter to Deborah Rogers, 24 August 1977, RCW
282 'I don't want to put any pressure on you . . .': AI Naomi Brent and Kaktus Leach, 31 March 2015
282 'endless, unfinishable' . . .: Angela Carter to Fleur Adcock, 17 October 1977, PC Fleur Adcock
282 'like doing finals': ibid.
282 'snapping and temper': Add. MS. 88899/3/1
283 'It is stunningly original . . .': Marion Wheeler to Angela Carter, 24 February 1978, RCW archive
283 'Peak Carter Country . . .': Liz Calder, internal Gollancz memorandum, 31 January 1978, Dobkin Collection
283 'Yes yes yes . . .': Dobkin Collection
283 'The trouble is, I am so badly versed . . .': Angela Carter to Fleur Adcock, 11 May 1978
284 'I expected to be entirely awed . . .': AI Lorna Tracy, 31 October 2014
284 'My first impression . . .': Angela Carter to Carmen Callil, 9 June 1977, Add. MS. 88904/1/60
284 'there is not one flabby sentence . . .': *London Review of Books*, 2 July 1981
285 'The Ozymandias effect . . .': Add. MS. 88899/1/96
285 One of the students . . .: AI Pat Barker, 5 May 2014
285 'You've acquired for yourself . . .': Angela Carter to Pat Barker, 9 January 1983, PC Pat Barker
285 '[Angela] was very generous . . .': AI Pat Barker, 5 May 2014

CHAPTER 17: NO. 1 LASH LADY
287 'It was like she had come hotfoot from the barricades': AI Lynne Bryan and Andrew Cowan, 24 January 2014
287 'It was a hotbed of intrigue': AI Paul Bailey, 6 March 2013
287 'We were producing very, very much better writers . . .': *Marxism Today*, January 1985
287 'teabags, Tampax and the *TLS*' . . .: 'Angela Carter interviewed by Lorna Sage' in *New Writing*, ed. Malcolm Bradbury and Judith Cooke (London: Minerva, 1992), p. 187
287 'The students on it are very highly selected . . .': *Marxism Today*, January 1985

288 'She gave the impression of being wryly amused . . .': AI Lynne Bryan and Andrew Cowan, 24 January 2014

288 'The student ahead of me came out . . .': *London Review of Books*, 17 February 2011

288 'Sessions with Angela were fraught . . .': Louise Doughty, 'A Traumatic Process' in *Body of Work: 40 Years of Creative Writing at UEA*, ed. Giles Foden (Ipswich: Full Circle Editions, 2011), p 70

288 'Everyone was terrified of Angela': *Books Ireland*, May 2003

289 'radically unstable' . . .: cited in 'Angela Carter: A Selective Biography', unpublished 2012 MA thesis by Danielle Shaw at the University of East Anglia

289 'On our first meeting . . .': Lynne Bryan, 'Questions I Never Asked My Creative Writing Tutors' in *Body of Work: 40 Years of Creative Writing at UEA*, ed. Giles Foden (Ipswich: Full Circle Editions, 2011), p. 140

289 'a funny kind of fluid personality . . .': AI Lynne Bryan and Andrew Cowan, 24 January 2014

289 'I liked her to such an extent . . .'and 'whereas it was clear . . .': ibid.

289 'I went away and I spent the week . . .': ibid.

290 'She was in a kind of equivalent relationship with the institution . . .': ibid.

290 'She talked very much out of her instincts . . .': AI Kazuo Ishiguro and Lorna MacDougall, 7 March 2014

290 'After you drowned . . .': ibid.

290 'I thought that was very nice . . .': *Guardian*, 28 February 1983

290 'It was fantastic . . .': AI Glenn Patterson, 15 February 2014

291 'You spend years carrying this impression with you . . .': AI Lynne Bryan and Andrew Cowan, 24 January 2014

291 'I am now about to be incarnated . . .': Angela Carter to Lorna Tracy, 20 March 1979, PC Lorna Tracy

291 'Dear Ms Carter . . .': Tony Willis ('age 42, 6ft, blonde') to Angela Carter, undated, Add. MS. 88899/3/2

291 'few women would feel inclined . . .': *New Statesman*, 4 April 1979

291 'provocative, always readable . . .': *New Society*, 7 April 1979

291 'grateful to Miss Carter . . .': *Guardian*, 29 March 1979

291 'I fail to see . . .': *Observer*, 8 April 1979

292 'a number of shrewd . . .': *New York Times*, 29 July 1979

292 'I don't know if you realise how upset Angela Carter has been . . .': Carmen Callil to Eileen Fairweather, undated, Add. MS. 88904/1/60

292 'for fear some man . . .': Eileen Fairweather to Angela Carter, 19 November 1979, Add. MS. 88904/1/60

292 'a pseudofeminist literary essay': Andrea Dworkin, *Pornography: Men Possessing Women* (New York: Putnam's, 1981), p. 85

292   'a Cultural Edifice . . .': Susanne Kappeler, *The Pornography of Representation* (Cambridge: Polity Press, 1986), pp. 2–3

292   'If I can get up Susanne Kappeler's nose . . .': Angela Carter to Elaine Jordan, cited in Elaine Jordan, 'The Dangerous Edge' in *Flesh and the Mirror: Essays on the Art of Angela Carter*, ed. Lorna Sage (London: Virago, 1994), p. 332, n. 5

293   'a dazzling collection . . .': *Sunday Telegraph*, 27 May 1979

293   'Ms Carter's stories are too rich and heady . . .': *New Statesman*, 24 May 1979

293   'the main theme . . .': *Observer*, 3 June 1979

293   'The stories . . . are presented to us like poisoned fruits . . .': *Cosmopolitan*, May 1979

293   'The best story in the book . . .': *Evening Standard*, 5 June 1979

293   'moments of superb bad taste . . .': *Literary Review*, 14 December 1979

293   'Angela Carter extends her control . . .': *Times Literary Supplement*, 8 February 1980

294   'on the whole . . .': *Word for Word*, 26 May 1979, BBC2

294   'there was a side to her . . .': *New York Review of Books*, 13 June 2002

294   'I used to think he was like a lizard . . .': AI Sharon Tolaini-Sage, 16 April 2014

294   His accent sounded faintly German . . .: *Independent*, 12 July 1999

295   'Many thought him reminiscent . . .': *Daily Telegraph*, 12 August 2006

295   'like a crazy person': AI Sharon Tolaini-Sage, 16 April 2014

295   'very drink-fuelled, mad conversations': ibid.

295   'It is the earthly paradise . . .': Add. MS. 88899/1/97

296   'swaddled in a big coat': Susannah Clapp, *A Card From Angela Carter* (London: Bloomsbury, 2012), p. 4

296   'the greatest poet of alienation . . .': Angela Carter to Elizabeth Hardwick, 6 November 1980, HRC, TXRC93-A46/5.1

296   'how awful it is to be a muse': ibid.

296   'the wincing, self-conscious narcissism . . .': Angela Carter to Richard Holmes, 18 June 1980, PC Richard Holmes

296   'I love my cat with an A . . .': Angela Carter and Martin Leman, *Comic and Curious Cats* (London: Orion, 1990), pp. 1–2

297   'I'd [already] directed . . .': AI John Cox and John Hayes, 23 April 2012

297   'kneading away like nobody's business . . .': *SL*, p. 95

298   'I am sure the poor showing the chaps make . . .': Angela Carter to John Cox, 8 January 1980, PC John Cox

298   'as I was working . . .': ibid.

299   'political correctness . . .': *New York Review of Books*, 23 April 1992

299   'to make English . . .': Angela Carter, 'The Language of Sisterhood' in *The State of Language*, ed. Leonard Michaels and Christopher Ricks (Berkeley: University of California Press, 1980), pp. 226–34

299 'typical male chauvinist aggression . . .': *New Society*, 25 July 1975

299 'heterosexist meanderings': *City Limits*, 5–11 October 1984

299 '60s pseudo-anarchy' . . .: *City Limits*, 28 September–4 October 1984

300 'If there was a kind of consensus . . .': AI Christopher Frayling, 22 February 2013

300 'seems to have an income . . .': Angela Carter to Robert Coover, 10 June 1980, PC Robert Coover

300 'one of those great meridians . . . ': *Vector*, Easter 1982

300 'I had a nicer time in my thirties . . .': BLSA C1365/8

300 'I appear to be getting infinitely more light-hearted . . .': *Vector*, Easter 1982

301 'One theory is . . .': BYB, p. 444

CHAPTER 18: AMERICAN GHOSTS

302 'weak from an acute haemorrhage . . .': Angela Carter to Robert Coover, 10 June 1980, PC Robert Coover

302 'because that's where I want to go . . .': ibid.

303 'I have gone totally and startlingly grey . . .': Angela Carter to Carmen Callil, 30 March 1981, PC Carmen Callil

303 Angela's apartment . . .: Angela Carter to Mark Pearce, 11 September 1980, Add. MS. 88899/3/3

303 'The light is wonderful . . .': ibid.

303 'All motorways . . .': ibid.

303 'Cigarettes are 60 cents . . .': ibid.

304 'You know I am not good . . .': ibid.

304 'I miss you in sharp, physical waves': Angela Carter to Mark Pearce, 17 September 1980, Add. MS. 88899/3/3

304 'my dear, I know words are not your language': Angela Carter to Mark Pearce, undated, Add. MS. 88899/3/3

304 'imported' . . .: Angela Carter to Mark Pearce, 22 September 1980, Add. MS. 88899/3/3

304 'There is a conspicuous lack . . .': Angela Carter to Mark Pearce, 17 September 1980, Add. MS. 88899/3/3

304 'I don't like America . . .': Angela Carter to Carmen Callil, 15 September 1980, PC Carmen Callil

305 'a bit much': Angela Carter to Carmen Callil, 26 October 1980, PC Carmen Callil

305 'poor Americans being ripped off' . . .: Angela Carter to Mark Pearce, 23 September 1980, Add. MS. 88899/3/3

305 'I shall just keep my head down . . .': Angela Carter to Mark Pearce, 17 September 1980, Add. Ms. 88899/3/3

305 'She was incompetent in many ways' . . .: AI Robert and Pili Coover, 18 September 2012

305 'I am not the stuff . . .': Angela Carter to Robert Coover, 10 June 1980, PC Robert Coover

305 'an odd stylistic resemblance': *SL*, p. 45

306 'She didn't like walking': AI Christopher Frayling, 22 February 2013

306 'We all laughed hysterically . . .': Angela Carter to Mark Pearce, 22 September 1980, Add. MS. 88899/3/3

306 'like a parody Cambridge': Angela Carter to Mark Pearce, 17 September 1980, Add. MS. 88899/3/3

306 'eager to please, cocksure . . .': Angela Carter to Mark Pearce, 25 September 1980, Add. MS. 88899/3/3

306 'The intellectual preppies are the hardest . . .': *SL*, p. 284

306 'I do think British education is better . . .': Angela Carter to Lorna Tracy, undated, PC Lorna Tracy

306 'the Marquis de Sade . . .': Jeffrey Eugenides, *The Marriage Plot* (London: 4th Estate, 2012), p. 24

307 'I've fallen among semioticians . . .': Angela Carter to Susannah Clapp, undated, PC Susannah Clapp

307 'quite chummy': Angela Carter to Lorna Tracy, undated, PC Lorna Tracy

307 'faintly risible': ibid.

307 'Tutorial was a better way to instruct . . .': *Tin House: Fantastic Women*, 28 September 2007

308 'The last thing a teacher wants . . .': Angela Carter to Mark Pearce, 26 February 1981, Add. MS. 88899/3/3

308 'teaching creative writing . . .': Angela Carter to Fleur Adcock, undated, PC Fleur Adcock

308 'make a list . . .': Angela Carter to Mark Pearce, 31 October 1980, Add. MS. 88899/3/3

309 'He came to Providence . . .': Angela Carter to Susannah Clapp, undated, PC Susannah Clapp

309 'He unbecame . . .': *BYB*, p. 264

309 'The character of her mind . . .': cited in Add. MS. 88899/1/97

310 'they did not marry . . .': *BYB*, p. 304

310 'a house of privacies . . .': ibid.

310 'the . . . old man . . .': ibid, p. 301

310 'a girl of Sargasso calm': ibid., p. 315

310 'There is something about circuses' . . .: Add. MS. 88899/1/97

311 'I have some dishy students . . .': Angela Carter to Carmen Callil, 26 October 1980, PC Carmen Callil

311 'Please miss me': Angela Carter to Mark Pearce, 9 October 1980, Add. MS. 88899/3/3

311 'It is beautiful & monstrous & probably addictive' . . .: Angela Carter to Mark Pearce, 22/23 October, Add. MS. 88899/3/3

311 'It isn't being alone that's desolating . . .': Angela Carter to Mark Pearce, 31 October 1980, Add. MS. 88899/3/3

311 'a washout' . . .: Angela Carter to Carmen Callil, 26 October 1980, PC Carmen Callil

311 'I am not easily impressed . . .': ibid.

311 'Thank you for a lovely weekend . . .': Angela Carter to Elizabeth Hardwick, 6 November 1980, HRC, TXRC93-A46/5.1

312 'I get tongue-tied . . .': Angela Carter to Elizabeth Hardwick, 3 October 1981, HRC, TXRC93-A46/5.1

312 'hero-mother': Angela Carter to Carmen Callil, 30 March 1981, PC Carmen Callil

312 'wonderful!': Angela Carter to Carmen Callil, 5 May 1984, RH

312 'one of the greatest writers of our time' . . .: SL, pp. 568–78

312 'you can imagine my mood . . .': Angela Carter to Mark Pearce, 2 November 1980, Add. MS. 88899/3/3

312 'I . . . found myself, quite quickly . . .': ibid.

313 'probably senile': Angela Carter to Mark Pearce, 22/23 October 1980, Add. MS. 88899/3/3

313 'I tend to think of him as a figurehead . . .': Angela Carter to Simon Watney, 23 November 1986, Add. MS. 83682

313 'Unfortunately, the mass of the population . . .': Angela Carter to Mark Pearce, 22/23 October 1980, Add. MS. 88899/3/3

313 one of the guests stormed out . . .: AI Robert and Pili Coover, 18 September 2012

313 'They laughed until they cried . . .': SL, p. 558

313 'it was a measure of Angela's persuasive talents . . .': Tin House: Fantastic Women, 28 September 2007

313 'like a battered wife': Angela Carter to Carmen Callil, 11 December 1980, PC Carmen Callil

314 'My young man arrives . . .': ibid.

314 'How he chuckled': Angela Carter to Carmen Callil, 15 January 1981, PC Carmen Callil

314 'We went for a walk . . .': Angela Carter to 'Victoria' at Gollancz, 1 January 1981, Dobkin Collection

314 'It's a culture so utterly without sensuality . . .': Add. Ms. 88899/1/97

314 'The snow has almost melted . . .': Angela Carter to Pat Barker, 31 January 1981, PC Pat Barker

315 'her seminar . . .': Tin House: Fantastic Women, 28 September 2007

315 'she complained . . .': Angela Carter to Mark Pearce, 26 January 1981, Add. MS. 88899/3/3

315 'I'm having neither a nice nor a nasty time' . . .: Angela Carter to Susannah Clapp, 1 March 1981, PC Susannah Clapp

315 'One of my students . . .': ibid.

316 'He is turning remorselessly into an art student' . . .: Angela Carter to Carmen Callil, undated, PC Carmen Callil

316 'What shall I say?' . . .: ibid.

317 'the most influential editor of his time' . . .: *New York Times*, 12 August 2008

317 'He informed me, with a perfectly straight face . . .': Angela Carter to Carmen Callil, undated, PC Carmen Callil

317 'pleased & flattered': Angela Carter to Carmen Callil, 5 August 1981, PC Carmen Callil

317 'sudden, real . . .': Angela Carter to Carmen Callil, undated, PC Carmen Callil

317 'Partial deafness . . .': Angela Carter to Mark Pearce, undated, Add. MS. 88899/3/3

318 'Coover says you live with a potter . . .': Angela Carter to Rikki Ducornet, 27 May 1981, OS

318 'It was terribly humiliating . . .': Angela Carter to Carmen Callil, 29 May, PC Carmen Callil

319 By way of a parting gift . . .: AI Erica Rex, 23 September 2013

CHAPTER 19: A PSYCHEDELIC DICKENS

320 'Our life just went haywire': *New Yorker*, 25 December 1995

321 'most self-conscious . . .': *Granta* 3, Autumn 1980

321 'I've never had any problem getting published . . .': *Guardian*, 25 September 1984

322 'she didn't want to be the queen . . .': AI Carmen Callil, 5 January 2012

322 'She retained throughout her life . . .': AI Liz Calder, 22 November 2011

322 'One of the really lovely things about her . . .': AI Salman Rushdie, 7 February 2014

322 'I thought Angela was always very confident . . .': AI Kazuo Ishiguro and Lorna MacDougall, 7 March 2014

323 'a trendy kid . . .': Angela Carter to Carmen Callil, 15 January 1981, PC Carmen Callil

323 'British publishing, in the elevated stratum . . .': *Vogue*, July 1982

323 'a huge, comic . . .': Angela Carter to Deborah Rogers, 16 August 1982, RCW

324 'kind of emblematic': *Face*, November 1984

324 'more like a dray . . .': NC, p. 9

324 'a voice that clanged . . .': ibid., p. 3

324 'with gargantuan enthusiasm': ibid., p. 6

324   'a mistresspiece of exquisitely feminine squalor': ibid., p. 9

324   'I think you're probably right . . .': *The Coming Out Show*, 4 October 1987, ABC radio

324   'until I was big enough . . .': cited in Sarah Gamble, *Angela Carter: Writing from the Front Line* (Edinburgh University Press, 1997), p. 157

324   'it's very important, it's about cusps': *Omnibus: Angela Carter's Curious Room*, BBC1, 15 September 1992

325   'pure child of the century . . .': *NC*, p. 25

325   'enforces' . . .: Aidan Day, *Angela Carter: The Rational Glass* (Manchester University Press, 1998), p. 175

325   'some terrific journalism': Add. MS. 88899/2/28

325   'in the alcove . . .': *NC*, p. 22

325   'a tiny, wizened . . .': ibid., p. 10

325   'a questing sluice . . .': ibid., p. 129

326   'To think I really fooled you!': ibid., p. 350

326   'I wanted to have . . .': Add. MS. 88899/2/28

326   'a bit like psychedelic Dickens . . .': Angela Carter to Deborah Rogers, 5 May 1982, RCW

326   'When I read that . . .': Angela Carter to Carmen Callil, 8 May 1984, RH

326   'finally discussing . . .': Angela Carter to Lorna Tracy, 1 April 1982, PC Lorna Tracy

326   'It's easy to pretend . . .': ibid.

327   'nausea . . .': Add. MS. 88899/1/97

327   'to travel hopefully . . .': ibid.

327   'unreality of the future' . . .: ibid.

327   '[Mark] has never seemed . . .': ibid.

328   'the kind of review that one writes for oneself': BLSA C95/67

328   'I found her fascinating . . .': AI Neil Jordan, 15 May 2014

328   '[Angela] asked about Ireland's relationship to England . . .': email to the author from Colm Tóibín, 8 January 2015

328   'She had a way of not saying much . . .': ibid.

329   'the very kind of riotous party Joyce adored': *SL*, p. 537

329   'I think it was a very important moment for her . . .': AI Salman Rushdie, 7 February 2014

329   'its involvement with the world . . .': *Guardian*, 25 November 1982

329   'few fiction writers . . .': *Observer*, 31 October 1982

329   'easy fluency' . . .: *London Review of Books*, 3 March 1983

330   'What excuse can there be . . .': *London Review of Books*, 1 April 1983

330   'Isn't one of her great gifts . . .': *London Review of Books*, 5 May 1983

CHAPTER 20: DOOMED TO LOVE

331 'children's author': Oxford Brookes University Special Collections, BP/1/15/1/1

331 'Do I detect . . .': *Evening Standard*, 20 April 1983

331 'Weldon and Carter . . .': *Time Out*, 22 April 1983

331 'probably go to a novel written by a woman . . .': *Times*, 7 August 1983

331 'feminist tract' . . .: ibid.

332 'novels of personal experience . . .': SL, p. 555

332 'the subtext . . .': ibid., p. 556

332 'I'd confidently expected . . .': ibid., p. 555

332 'she took those kinds of things very seriously . . .': AI Mark Pearce, 30 October 2014

332 'she was so scrupulous . . .': AI Salman Rushdie, 7 February 2014

333 'They had to drag me . . .': BOMB, Fall 1986

333 'start off every day . . .': Add. MS. 88899/2/28

333 'I think I was too old to redefine myself . . .': *Marxism Today*, January 1985

333 'Part Three is in the typewriter . . .': Angela Carter to Deborah Rogers, 5 May 1983, RCW

334 'This kind of decency . . .': Marghanita Laski to Angela Carter, 23 November 1983, Add. MS. 88899/3/1

334 'you would undoubtedly have been offered a bursary . . .': Charles Osborne to Angela Carter, 28 November 1983, RCW

334 'the Thatcher phenomenon' . . .: SL, pp. 189–95

334 'She was terribly reluctant . . .': AI Ursula Owen, 25 February 2014

335 'Occasionally we would squeak with pleasure . . .': BLSA C95/67

335 'We were kind of trying to outdo each other . . .': AI Neil Jordan, 15 May 2014

335 'I have never before or since . . .': *Independent*, 18 February 1992

335 'A witch from up the valley . . .': BYB, p. 213

335 'a sense of oppressive heat . . .': CR, p. 186

336 'When we finished . . .': *Face*, November 1984

336 'It was such a simple image . . .': AI Neil Jordan, 15 May 2014

336 'When I went to the screening . . .': BOMB, Fall 1986

336 'It's been a tough spring and summer . . .': Angela Carter to Rikki Ducornet, 17 July 1983, OS

336 'I was surprised we got funding for it . . .': AI Neil Jordan, 15 May 2014

337 'She was terribly excited . . .': ibid.

337 'I sleep for approximately 12 hours a day . . .': Angela Carter to Rikki Ducornet, 17 September 1983, OS

337 'there should have been three novels by women . . .': *Private Eye*, 10 October 1983

338 'Booker does a grave disservice to the novel': *Sunday Telegraph*, 25 September 1983

338 'There has been a lot of activity . . .': Angela Carter to Rikki Ducornet, 19 October 1983, OS
339 'It was a to-and-fro thing . . .': AI Fay Weldon, 26 February 2014
339 'a nightmare & a strain': Angela Carter to Susannah Clapp, 1 November 1983, PC Susannah Clapp
339 'excused the ordeal . . .': Oxford Brookes University Special Collections, BP/1/15/1/1
339 'very good Italian wines': ibid.
339 'highly thought of . . .': ibid.
339 Selina Scott's incompetent hosting . . .: *Bookmark: The 1983 Booker Prize*, BBC2, 26 October 1983
340 'flat on my back . . .': *SL*, p. 29
340 'I try a little joke . . .': ibid.
340 'Each time I think about it . . .': Angela Carter to Lorna Sage, cited in Lorna Sage, *Angela Carter* (Plymouth: Northcote House, 1994), p. 50
341 'perfectly okay . . .': Angela Carter to Susannah Clapp, 1 November 1983, PC Susannah Clapp
341 'big, soft girls . . .': Add. MS. 88899/1/98
341 She went into labour . . .: Angela Carter to Simon Watney, 14 November 1983, Add. MS. 83682
341 'I said something feeble . . .': Add. MS. 88899/1/98
341 'Good grief! Aren't we allowed any choice . . .': *SL*, pp. 30–1
342 'Possibly the only truth . . .': *In Conversation: Angela Carter with Lisa Appignanesi*, ICA video, 1985

CHAPTER 21: A LIFESTYLE OF PARADOXICAL PROPRIETY
343 'The entire accouchement . . .': Angela Carter to Simon Watney, 14 December 1984, Add. MS. 83682
343 'toothless grins': Add. MS. 88899/1/98
343 'Being anxious parents . . .': AI Mark Pearce, 30 October 2014
343 'Anxiety – cot death . . .': Add. MS. 88899/1/98
343 'Having this tiny thing . . .': AI Christine Downton, 19 March 2013
344 'the beginning of never not feeling anxious': AI Mark Pearce, 30 October 2014
344 'expected to provide a stimulus . . .': F. J. O'Neill to Angela Carter, 2 February 1984, University of Adelaide Archive, Series 200 1984/24
344 'A friend of a friend . . .': Angela Carter to Michael Tolley, 7 January 1984, University of Adelaide Archive, Series 200 1984/24
344 'Obviously, a pretty place . . .': ibid.
344 'wet heat of Asia': Add. MS. 88899/1/98
344 'when I got out of the plane . . .': Add. MS. 88899/1/65
344 'I like it more than anywhere . . .': Angela Carter to Carmen Callil, undated, RH

345 'The drama of the birth of <u>this</u> nation . . .': Add. MS. 88899/1/98

345 'The person at the Uni . . .': Angela Carter to Carmen Callil, undated, RH

345 'It was like a miracle . . .': AI Mark Pearce, 30 October 2014

345 'the most triumphantly vulgar sunsets . . .': Add. MS. 88899/1/65

345 'My! but they know how to have a good time' . . .: ibid.

346 'I did like her so much . . .': *The Diaries of Barbara Hanrahan*, ed. Elaine Lindsay (Brisbane: University of Queensland Press, 1998), p. 204

346 'she's very, very nice': Angela Carter to Carmen Callil, undated, RH

346 'I felt disappointed . . .': *The Diaries of Barbara Hanrahan*, ed. Elaine Lindsay (Brisbane: University of Queensland Press, 1998), p. 200

346 'Angela was initially quite reluctant . . .': AI Salman Rushdie, 7 February 2014

347 'We must celebrate': Susannah Clapp, *With Chatwin: Portrait of a Writer* (London: Vintage, 1998), p. 203

347 'the laureate of the dotty': *Guardian*, 6 March 2007

347 'You must do with him . . .': BLSA C95/397

347 'I decided I must at once . . .': ibid.

347 'the only writer who is at all like her . . .': Angela Carter to Carmen Callil, 5 May 1984, RH

347 'It was like walking into fairyland': AI Mark Pearce, 30 October 2014

348 'it would be nice to think . . .': Angela Carter to Elizabeth Hardwick, 9 April 1984, HRC, TXRC93-A46/5.1

348 'ravishing . . .': Add. MS. 88899/1/65

348 'No time to look around . . .': Angela Carter to Carmen Callil, 5 May 1984, RH

348 'It was very depressing . . .': Angela Carter to Rikki Ducornet, undated, OS

348 'I'm in a position . . .': Zulfikar Ghose to Angela Carter, 30 May 1984, HRC, TXRC03-A14

349 'me and my husband . . .': Angela Carter to Zulfikar Ghose, 28 October 1984, HRC, TXRC03-A14

349 'we never got round to getting married': Angela Carter to Zulfikar Ghose, 26 September 1984, HRC, TXRC03-A14

349 'Downstairs was carnival . . .': Susannah Clapp, *A Card from Angela Carter* (London: Bloomsbury, 2012), p. 1

349 'the comfortable junk-shop furniture . . .': *Sunday Times*, 9 September 1984

349 'beautiful, but also enormous . . .': Lorna Sage, *Angela Carter* (Plymouth: Northcote House, 1994), p. 50

349 in the 1984–5 tax year . . .: E. J. C. Wormald to Deborah Rogers, 25 November 1984, RCW

350 'I particularly enjoy . . .': Angela Carter to Robert Coover, 10 June 1980, PC Robert Coover

350 'Angela looked wild . . .': email to the author from Sara Maclean, 19 July 2014

350 'Thatcherite censorship . . .': *Marxism Today*, January 1985

350 'Regardless of whether . . .': *Times*, 15 August 1984

350 'Carter's feminist-gothic . . .': *Observer*, 26 August 1984

350 'having a baby at 44 . . .': *Guardian*, 25 September 1984

351 '*Nights at the Circus* will certainly confirm her as a stylist . . .': *Sunday Times*, 9 September 1984

351 'the new hero of women's writing': *City Limits*, 29 September–4 October 1984

351 'Angela Carter . . . is not your typical tub-thumping feminist . . .': *Face*, November 1984

351 'one's pleasure in seeing it . . .': *Spectator*, 29 September 1984

351 'What we have in this hailed poetic and magical farrago . . .': cited in *Vogue*, August 1985

351 'Fame has made me so unpleasant . . .': Angela Carter to Simon Watney, undated, Add. MS. 83682

351 'may have been thought too overreaching . . .': *Guardian*, 19 September 1984

351 In fact, two of them . . .: Oxford Brookes University Special Collections, BP 1/16/1/2

352 'a deathly hush . . .': AI Andrew Motion, 24 February 2014

352 'It's a tour de force . . .': *Guardian*, 23 September 1984

352 'a calculated insult . . .': *Evening Standard*, 26 September 1984

352 'a most impressive tour de force . . .': *Daily Telegraph*, 28 September 1984

352 'a very disconcerting narrative . . .': *London Review of Books*, 4 October 1984

352 '*Nights at the Circus* doesn't so much start . . .': *Times Literary Supplement*, 28 September 1984

353 'it is the most secret prize . . .': Carmen Callil to Angela Carter, 31 January 1985, RH

353 'pleased and proud . . .': Angela Carter to Alastair Fowler, 20 September 1985, National Library of Scotland, In Acc. 10093/43

353 'He was an impossibly beautiful child' . . .: AI Paul Bailey, 6 March 2013

353 'He often murmurs "banana" to himself . . .': Add. MS. 88899/1/98

354 'They more or less hovered . . .': AI Rebecca Howard, 26 April 2012

354 '[Children] do take up a lot of time . . .': *In Conversation: Angela Carter with Lisa Appignanesi*, ICA video, 1985

354 'Organising your life is almost impossible . . .': *Marxism Today*, January 1985

355 'There are some others I could include . . .': Angela Carter to Sarah Baxter, undated, Add. MS. 88899/1/77

355 'We make an immediately distinctive trio . . .': Angela Carter to Zulfikar Ghose, undated, HRC, TXRC03-A14

355 'Some of the properties . . .': Add. MS. 88899/1/98

356 'series of interiors': ibid.

356 'No foreign news at all . . .': Angela Carter to Simon Watney, 2 February 1985, Add. MS. 83682

356 'Everybody is loony, here': Angela Carter to Susannah Clapp, undated, PC Susannah Clapp

356 'boiled faces . . .': Add. MS. 88899/1/98

356 'Jesus, there's a lot of money . . .': Angela Carter to Simon Watney, 2 February 1985, Add. MS. 83682

356 'Texans think Texas . . .': Angela Carter to Elizabeth Jolley, 18 September 1985, State Library of New South Wales, MLMSS 4880

356 'The buildings are constantly being washed . . .': Add. MS. 88899/1/98

357 'When I first joined . . .': email to the author from Zulfikar Ghose, 16 July 2015

357 'I'd like to start off . . .': Angela Carter to Zulfikar Ghose, 28 October 1984, HRC, TXRC03-A14

358 'I'm working very hard . . .': Angela Carter to Carmen Callil, 31 January 1985, RH

358 'Mucho macho' . . .: Add. MS. 88899/1/98

358 'So many Mexican things . . .': ibid.

358 'It was so depressed . . .': AI Mark Pearce, 30 October 2014

358 'blissful': Angela Carter to Carmen Callil, 19 March 1985, RH

358 'He is as near to a great writer . . .': ibid.

359 'it is the racism . . .': ibid.

359 'they are both fatter . . .': *The Diaries of Barbara Hanrahan*, ed. Elaine Lindsay (Brisbane: University of Queensland Press, 1998), p. 229

CHAPTER 22: I REFUSE TO PLAY IN TRAGEDY

360 'roll of suet round my belly . . .': Add. MS. 88899/1/98

360 'I'm taking the psychological aspects . . .': ibid.

361 'fourth day of the anti-depressants . . .': ibid.

361 'suicidal' . . .: Add. MS. 88899/4/11

361 'like someone who'd been left out in a hurricane': AI Andrew Motion, 24 February 2014

361 'madwoman-in-the-attic look' . . .: AI Lennie Goodings, 3 February 2015

361 'by her own choice' . . .: *Independent on Sunday*, 7 January 1995

361 'She abandoned fashion . . .': Susannah Clapp, *A Card From Angela Carter* (London: Bloomsbury, 2012), p. 15

361 'Black Venus displays the superbly witchy . . .': *Sunday Telegraph*, 27 October 1985

361 'admirers who like to think of her . . .': *Times Literary Supplement*, 18 October 1985

362 'Excellent as the writing . . .': *Glasgow Herald*, 12 October 1985

362 'Angela Carter's writing . . .': *New Statesman*, 18 October 1985

362 'Anti-intellectualism . . .': SL, p. 381

362 'I'm actually finding it . . .': Add. MS. 88899/2/28

362 'reflected within them . . .': CR, p. 248

363 'It still haunts me': *In Conversation: Angela Carter with Lisa Appignanesi*, ICA video, 1985

363 'upsetting' . . .: Angela Carter to Carmen Callil, 25 July 1987, RH

363 'almost sinister feat . . .': L, p. 111

363 'even the women's movement . . .': ibid.

363 'rather fast': ibid., p. 113

363 'a few early punk bands' . . .: ibid., pp. 115–18

363 'As for me . . .': Add. MS. 88899/1/65

364 'Alexander now weighs 16 kilos . . .': Angela Carter to Jack Zipes, 20 September 1985, PC Jack Zipes

364 'taken a great shine to the alphabet . . .': Angela Carter to Jack Zipes, 1 June 1986, PC Jack Zipes

364 'The speech therapist said . . .': AI Fleur Adcock, 5 February 2013

365 'the Athens of America': *Los Angeles Times*, 28 May 1986

365 'a fat man with halitosis . . .': Angela Carter to Connie Brothers, 1 August 1986, administrative files of the University of Iowa

365 'It's hard to remember . . .': Angela Carter to Jack Zipes, undated, PC Jack Zipes

366 'You remember in [the Ray Bradbury book] . . .': Angela Carter to Salman Rushdie, 15 September 1986, Emory University Manuscripts Library, collection No. 1000/Series 4

366 'right out in the countryside' . . .: Angela Carter to Amanda Vaill, 28 August 1986, Dobkin Collection

366 'You never saw anything more tastefully vulgar . . .': Angela Carter to Carmen Callil, 26 August 1986, RH

366 'We watch him turn brown . . .': BOMB, Fall 1986

366 'It was just a gentle place . . .': AI Mark Pearce, 30 October 2014

366 'It is very difficult . . .': Angela Carter to Jack Zipes, undated, PC Jack Zipes

366 'The university here . . .': Angela Carter to Salman Rushdie, 15 September 1986, Emory University Manuscripts Library, collection No. 1000/Series 4

367 'the theme of alienation and moral disquiet': Angela Carter to John Leggett, undated, administrative files of the University of Iowa

367 'she was very rigorous . . .': email to the author from David Michael Kaplan, 9 February 2016

367 'didn't much like . . .': ibid.

367 'it is easy . . .': Angela Carter to Rick Moody, 19 January 1987, OS

368 'the best venue I know . . .': Graham Swift, *Making an Elephant: Writing from Within* (London: Picador, 2010), p. 279

368 'We got to the ceremony . . .': AI Caryl Phillips, 20 April 2012

368   'She called us "the naughty boys" . . .': ibid.
368   'Once we got settled . . .': Angela Carter to Simon Watney, 23 November 1986, Add. MS. 83682
368   'which you can do in Iowa . . .': ibid.
369   'It was almost as good . . .': AI Mark Pearce, 30 October 2014
369   'I will return . . .': *Cedar Rapids Gazette*, 30 November 1986
369   'a usually unsung part . . .': *Guardian*, 28 October 1981
369   'The agency just wasn't functioning . . .': AI Ian McEwan, 16 June 2013
370   'He does not believe in the niceties . . .': *Guardian*, 29 October 1988
370   'I just had an odd kind of feeling' . . .: AI Deborah Rogers, 6 June 2012
370   'It was absolutely unbelievable . . .': AI Liz Calder, 22 November 2011
371   'too angry': *New Yorker*, 25 December 1995
371   'the situation with Salman . . .': Carmen Callil to Angela Carter, 5 October 1987, PC Carmen Callil
372   '[the novel] is based . . .': Carmen Callil, memo, 28 October 1987, RH
372   'of the novel I've now decided to call *Wise Children*' . . .: Angela Carter to Carmen Callil, 10 November 1987, RH
372   'All I know is that I never doubted her': AI Deborah Rogers, 6 June 2012
373   'most of Shakespeare': BLSA C3165/8
373   'I can curl up with a bag of apples . . .': *Third Ear: Angela Carter*, BBC Radio 3, 25 June 1991
373   'I do think there's something about Shakespeare . . .': 'Angela Carter interviewed by Lorna Sage' in *New Writing*, ed. Malcolm Bradbury and Judith Cooke (London: Minerva, 1992), p. 192
373   'the great popular entertainer . . .': *Omnibus: Angela Carter's Curious Room*, BBC1, 15 September 1992
373   'All of them knew . . .': SL, p. 28
373   'But I got a lot in!': *Third Ear: Angela Carter*, BBC Radio 3, 25 June 1991
374   'Something makes you think . . .': WC, p. 5
374   'our greatest living . . .': ibid., p. 11
374   'the leatherette suite . . .': ibid., p. 59
375   'to take North America back . . .': ibid., p. 133
375   'They're useful people . . .': *Omnibus: Angela Carter's Curious Room*, BBC1, 15 September 1992
375   'She's recognisable in [Dora's] voice': AI Hugh and Joan Stalker, 17 April 2012
375   'Two old ladies . . .': Add. MS. 88899/1/41
376   'It took an age . . .': WC, p. 192
376   'I refuse point-blank . . .': ibid., p. 154
376   'comedy stands for . . .': *Omnibus: Angela Carter's Curious Room*, BBC1, 15 September 1992
376   'we had to laugh . . .': WC, p. 198

377 'There is still quite a lot to do . . .': Angela Carter to Carmen Callil, 20 March 1988, RH
377 'like being dead . . .': Add. MS. 88899/1/98
378 'Nothing else but *Pandora's Box* . . .': *SL*, p. 387
378 'peculiarly pernicious, if flattering' . . .: ibid., pp. 350–1
378 'primal form of woman . . .': Frank Wedekind, *Tragedies of Sex*, trans. Samuel Atkins Eliot Jr (New York: Boni & Liveright, 1923), p. 118
378 '*she wears [her clothes]* . . .': *CR*, p. 393
379 'The very words . . .': *SL*, p. 23
379 'never felt any . . .': Angela Carter to Rick Moody, 10 July [1988], OS
379 'I haven't felt like this . . .': Add. MS. 88899/1/98
380 'Dad's things . . .': ibid.

CHAPTER 23: PERHAPS WRITING IS A MATTER OF LIFE AND DEATH
381 'Her hatred of Margaret Thatcher . . .': AI Salman Rushdie, 7 February 2014
382 're-establish the intellectual . . .': Add. MS. 88899/6/8
382 'I don't recall Angela saying a whole lot . . .': AI Salman Rushdie, 7 February 2014
383 'There is a small hospital near where I live . . .': Add. MS. 88899/6/8
383 'the news that Lady Antonia Fraser (-Pinter) . . .': *Independent*, 12 July 1988
383 'It is not hard to sympathise . . .': *Evening Standard*, 5 July 1988
384 'bite the hand that feeds them': cited in Andrew Graham-Yooll, *Point of Arrival* (London: Pluto Press, 1992), pp. 170–1
384 'London will turn into a Third World city . . .': *City Limits*, 20–27 April 1989
384 'Where Thatcher was an absence . . .': *London Review of Books*, 9 May 2013
384 'England under Thatcher . . .': Angela Carter to Rick Moody, 19 February 1988, OS
385 'upstate New York is so beautiful . . .': Angela Carter to Lorna Sage, cited in Lorna Sage, *Angela Carter* (Plymouth: Northcote House, 1994), p. 41
385 'the most beautiful river in the world': *SL*, p. 439
385 'fat girls' . . .: Add. MS. 88899/1/98
385 'truly terrifying' . . .: Angela Carter to Lorna Sage, cited in Lorna Sage, *Angela Carter* (Plymouth: Northcote House, 1994), p. 41
385 'isolating myself & working': Angela Carter to Rick Moody, 7 November 1988, OS
385 'with titles like *Too Late for Tears* . . .': *Independent on Sunday*, 9 June 1991
385 'I'll be in the city . . .': Angela Carter to Rick Moody, 7 November 1988, OS
386 'maybe it was the wrong marriage': cited in *CR*, p. 510
386 'I have always . . .': Howard Davies to Angela Carter, undated, Add. MS. 88899/3/2

386 'I think Howard made an initial mistake . . .': Richard Eyre to Angela Carter, 11 March 1989, Add. MS. 88899/3/2

386 'white-faced and narrow-eyed . . .': Susannah Clapp, *A Card From Angela Carter* (London: Bloomsbury, 2012), p. 6

387 'I guess a lot of Lulu's personality . . .': 'Angela Carter interviewed by Lorna Sage' in *New Writing*, ed. Malcolm Bradbury and Judith Cooke (London: Minerva, 1992), p. 196

387 'complicated, exhilarating . . .': SL, pp. 586–8

387 'We have known in our own religion . . .': cited in *The Rushdie File*, ed. Lisa Appignanesi and Sara Maitland (London: 4th Estate, 1989), p. 141.

388 'he knew what he was doing . . .': cited in Paul Weller, *A Mirror for Our Times: The 'Rushdie Affair' and the Future of Multiculturalism* (London: Bloomsbury, 2009), p. 21

388 'I don't think it is given to any of us . . .': *International Herald Tribune*, 23 May 1989

388 'a dangerous opportunist . . .': *Times*, 28 February 1989

388 'She was somebody I could call up . . .': AI Salman Rushdie, 7 February 2014

388 'Some of these guys were very, very angry . . .': AI Kazuo Ishiguro and Lorna MacDougall, 7 March 2014

389 'she always made sure that they had a good meal . . .': AI Salman Rushdie, 7 February 2014

389 'For more than three years . . .': SL, p. 608

389 'That moved me to tears . . .': AI Salman Rushdie, 7 February 2014

389 'She was always surrounded . . .': AI Fleur Adcock, 5 February 2013

389 'More or less everybody . . .': AI Andrew Motion, 24 February 2014

390 'how long it had taken me . . .': email to the author from Neil Forsyth, 11 February 2014

390 'a lovely, shabby city . . .': Add. MS. 88899/1/99

391 'Susan Sontag graced us . . .': AI Paul Bailey, 6 March 2013

391 'How many Soviet soldiers died . . .': *New York Times*, 22 June 1989

391 'Every country had to elect someone . . .': AI Paul Bailey, 6 March 2013

392 'people you don't expect . . .': AI Kazuo Ishiguro and Lorna MacDougall, 7 March 2014

392 'He did always fiercely leap . . .': ibid.

392 'in which something out of the way happens': BLSA C95/490

392 'the urge to categorize . . .': Add. MS. 88899/1/65

393 'I've never met anyone . . .': AI Mark Pearce, 30 October 2014

393 'Angela really encouraged me . . .': ibid.

393 'The canals are wonderful . . .': Angela Carter to Lorna Sage, cited in Lorna Sage, *Angela Carter* (Plymouth: Northcote House, 1994), p. 57

394 'took charge . . .': AI Liz Calder, 22 November 2011

394 'a long and intricate story about a mouse': Susannah Clapp, *A Card from Angela Carter* (London: Bloomsbury, 2012), p. 77

394 Fleur Adcock . . .: AI Fleur Adcock, 5 February 2013

394 'It was magic': AI Mark Pearce, 30 October 2014

CHAPTER 24: CALL IT A HAPPY ENDING

395 'I've passed a point in the size barrier . . .': *Telegraph Weekend Magazine*, 13 May 1989

395 'Who is Angela Carter?' . . .: press cutting about Angela Carter in conversation with Lidia Curti, British Council Naples, 23 October 1990, PC Susannah Clapp

395 The menopause diary . . .: Add. MS. 88899/4/11

396 'like a benign witch' . . .: *Observer*, 9 May 2010

396 '[Angela] wanted them to experience . . .': AI Caryl Phillips, 20 April 2012

397 'basically taking the piss . . .': ibid.

397 'By that time Angela had become . . .': AI Ian McEwan, 16 June 2013

397 'I've never been in a country . . .': Add. MS. 88899/1/99

397 'I always saw it as rather like . . .': *Right to Reply*, Channel 4, 7 December 1991

398 'She had lots of ideas . . .': AI Jo Ann Kaplan, 12 March 2014

398 '[God] did not forget . . .': *Without Walls: The Holy Family Album*, Channel 4, 3 December 1991

398 'He was a cruel God . . .': ibid.

399 'Can you see Martin Amis . . .': 'Angela Carter interviewed by Lorna Sage' in *New Writing*, ed. Malcolm Bradbury and Judith Cooke (London: Minerva, 1992), p. 190

399 'that we are all sisters under the skin . . .': VBFT, p. xiv

399 'not so much scholarly . . .': ibid., p. 230

399 'Swahili storytellers . . .': ibid., p. 234

399 'a good deal of pleasure': ibid., p. xiii

399 'Being funny for 250 pages . . .': Angela Carter to Fleur Adcock, 'Christmas 1990', PC Fleur Adcock

399 'The radio alarm goes off . . .': *Sunday Times Magazine*, 25 August 1991

401 'Truthfully . . .': WC, p. 227

CHAPTER 25: HOW SWEET IT WAS!

402 Angela began to experience chest pains . . .: Add. MS. 88899/4/11

402 'very, very painful': ibid.

402 'Thinks happened very quickly . . .': Angela Carter to Fleur Adcock, 20 May 1991, PC Fleur Adcock

402 'I can see her now . . .': AI Wendy Burford, 8 September 2014

403 'We were very damning . . .': AI Mark Pearce, 30 October 2014

403 The children in his class . . .: Add. MS. 88899/3/2

403 'blasted with gamma rays . . .': Angela Carter to Fleur Adcock, 20 May 1991, PC Fleur Adcock

403 'sufficiently enervating . . .': Angela Carter to Salman Rushdie, 1 June 1991, Emory University Manuscripts Library, collection No. 1000/Series 4

403 'Her requirements for her estate . . .': Susannah Clapp, *A Card for Angela Carter* (London: Bloomsbury, 2012), p. 4

404 *Adela* was to be a fantasia . . .: Angela Carter to Carmen Callil, 1 June 1991, RH

404 'I envisage it . . .': ibid.

404 'The last thing we want to do . . .': Simon Master to Carmen Callil, 4 June 1991, RH

405 'a bravura demonstration . . .': *Scotsman*, 22 June 1991

405 'wonderful . . .': *Daily Telegraph*, 8 June 1991

405 'Angela Carter's best book . . .': *Times Literary Supplement*, 7 June 1991

405 'an important subject . . .': *Guardian*, 6 June 1991

405 'a funny, funny, funny book . . .': *Independent on Sunday*, 9 June 1991

405 'exuberant virtuosity' . . .: *Times*, 13 June 1991

405 'It is all a jolly exercise . . .': *Evening Standard*, 13 June 1991

406 'flicker of . . . dislike . . .': AI Pauline Melville, 20 February 2014

406 'It sounded short of breath': AI Marina Warner, 24 April 2014

406 'Yes . . . I feel loved': Susannah Clapp, *A Card for Angela Carter* (London: Bloomsbury, 2012), p. 95

406 'News on Angela . . .': Carmen Callil to Margaret Forster, 13 August 1991, Add. MS. 88899/3/3

407 'I had no idea . . .': Angela Carter to Mark Bell, 3 September 1991, RH

407 'She was very much choosing . . .': AI Mark Bell, 11 June 2014

407 'an idiosyncratically bland little book . . .': *SL*, p. 440

407 'I don't think it's fair . . .': Angela Carter to Mark Bell, 26 September 1991, RH

407 'if I go into remission' . . .: Angela Carter to Connie Brothers, 1 October 1991, administrative files of the University of Iowa

407 'She coped very well . . .': AI Wendy Burford, 6 September 2014

407 'Death was certainly not proud . . .': *SP*, p. 26

407 'She was so brave . . .': AI Rebecca Howard, 26 April 2012

407 'Don't worry . . .': Michael Moorcock, Introduction to Angela Carter, *Expletives Deleted* (London: Vintage, 1993), p. iv

408 'hanging on like grim death . . .': Angela Carter to Ted Holst, 14 January 1992, PC Ted Holst

408 'It's all right . . .': Susannah Clapp, *A Card for Angela Carter* (London: Bloomsbury, 2012), p. 94

408 'She was very stoical . . .': AI Mark Pearce, 30 October 2014

408 'Only a newcomer . . .': *World of Interiors*, September 1991

408 'absolutely fucking livid': AI Mark Pearce, 30 October 2014

408 'Not the greatest apology . . .': Angela Carter to Carmen Callil; undated, RH

408 *Wise Children* had been supported . . .: Oxford Brookes University Special Collections, BP/1/23/1/2

408 'I certainly don't seem . . .': *Granta* 41, Autumn 1992

409 it was originally going to be called . . .: AI Lennie Goodings, 3 February 2015

409 'second-rate, confused . . .': *Observer*, 1 December 1991

409 'People are trying to fetter . . .': ibid.

409 'It was not my intention . . .': ibid.

409 'That practising Christians . . .': *Times*, 3 December 1991

409 When Conroy complained . . .: *Right to Reply*, Channel 4, 7 December 1991

410 'undeniably offensive . . .': *Daily Telegraph*, 4 December 1991

410 'Breton + Ernst . . .': J. G. Ballard to Angela Carter, 4 December 1991, Add. MS. 88899/3/4

410 'I don't think I need . . .': cited in Susannah Clapp, *A Card for Angela Carter* (London: Bloomsbury, 2012), p. 98

410 'she'd comment . . .': AI Wendy Burford, 8 September 2014

411 'tales of sexual intrigue and depravity . . .': Neil Jordan to Angela Carter, 11 January 1992, Add. MS. 88899/3/2

411 On 11 December . . .: Add. MS. 88899/3/2

411 'I've fantasised . . .': Angela Carter to Carmen Callil, 31 January 1985, RH

411 'Fuck them, then': AI Wendy Burford

411 'All those books . . .': Angela Carter to Michael Moorcock, 'August Bank Holiday' [1991], PC Michael Moorcock

411 'I am still here . . .': Angela Carter to Caryl Phillips, 11 December 1991, Add. MS. 88899/1/99

412 'for Wendy . . .': PC Wendy Burford

412 'She was obviously in real pain . . .': AI Salman Rushdie, 7 February 2014

413 'I think we're going to have to stop now': ibid.

413 'there was no argument . . .': AI Mark Pearce, 30 October 2014

413 'very hurt because someone . . .': AI Sharon Tolaini-Sage, 16 April 2014

413 'please do not accept anybody who is not on this list': Angela Carter to Kim Evans, 20 January 1991, Add. MS. 88899/2/28

413 'Towards the end of her life . . .': AI Rebecca Howard, 26 April 2012

413 'I haven't changed much . . .': *SL*, p. 608

414 'There was a warmth . . .': AI Wendy Burford, 8 September 2014

414 'Don't think I'm immune to guilt . . .': Angela Carter to Ted Holst, 14 January 1992, PC Ted Holst

414 'I want to write & say thank you . . .': Lennie Goodings to Angela Carter, 11 February 1992, Add. MS. 88899/3/2
415 'He was devoted . . .': AI Rebecca Howard, 26 April 2012
415 'That was my meditation . . .': AI Mark Pearce, 30 October 2014
415 'We tried to make sure that she was comfortable . . .': AI Wendy Burford, 8 September 2014

EPILOGUE
416 'the Salvador Dalí of English letters': *Daily Telegraph*, 17 February 1992
416 'I was just amazed . . .': AI Ian McEwan, 16 June 2013

Index

Index

Index

Index

socialism 73, 215, 246, 252, 307, 311, 316, 334, 341, 381–4

solitariness, 20, 24–5, 28–9

smoking habit, xv–xvi, 33, 38, 231, 270–1, 303, 305, 315, 349, 360

teeth *see* dental problems

theatre, interest in 8–9, 68–9, 107, 233, 296, 326, 372–4, 390

warmth, friendliness xiv, 57, 59, 74, 284, 289, 402, 414

weight, 24–5, 28, 33, 38–40, 47, 179, 359, 360, 363

homes:

Albert Road, Sheffield 270–1, 282

Arlington Avenue, Providence 303

Arundel Place, Islington 203–4, 208, 210

Birdhurst Rise, Croydon 48–51

Chase, The, Clapham 264, 265–6, 274–5, 282, 290, 300, 302, 314, 323, 334, 348–50, 359, 389, 407, 410, 412, 413

Childers Street, Adelaide 345, 347

Hay Hill, Bath 224–6, 227, 234, 240, 247, 250–2

Kujukuri, Chiba 171, 172–4, 176, 178–9

Lincoln Road, East Finchley 211–14, 225

Meguro, Tokyo 154–8, 161, 170–1, 179

Ravenslea Road, Balham 16, 18–22, 23–5, 30, 33, 40, 46, 58, 75, 149, 160

Royal York Crescent, Bristol 52–61, 66, 68, 73, 74, 86, 90, 102, 107, 111, 133–4, 146, 156

Shinjuku, Tokyo 191, 194

Stamford Lane, Austin 355–6

Wath-upon-Dearne, Yorkshire 16–17, 96

Woodland Heights, Iowa City 366

influences:

cinema 21–2, 35, 48, 110, 128, 230, 231, 257, 324, 334, 335, 378

Continental theorists 181, 192, 259

fairy tales, folklore xii, 3, 4, 17, 20, 24, 28, 47, 70, 81, 83, 89, 114–15, 119, 228, 231, 257, 266, 267, 268, 272–3, 278–80, 292–4, 310, 364, 398–9

French literature 36, 89, 119, 128, 296

Gothic literature 63, 91, 121, 128, 145, 233, 256–7, 262, 274, 334

Latin American literature, magical realism 20, 143, 175-76, 178, 318, 329, 392, 407

medieval literature 70–1, 83, 85, 87

modernist literature 36, 49–50, 64, 68, 76

music-hall 8, 83, 233, 326

philosophy 70, 108, 181, 192, 259

psychoanalysis 70–1, 108, 121, 350, 363, 396, 410

science fiction xii, 30, 118, 130, 169, 176, 229, 262, 315

Shakespeare 8–9, 68–9, 107, 296, 326, 372–4, 390

surrealism 88–9, 118, 209, 271, 335, 410

relations with family:

Carter, Paul 43–51, 52–61, 65–6, 74–5, 79, 85–6, 87, 92, 94, 98, 102–5, 111–13, 116–17, 125–7, 133–6, 139, 141–9, 156, 158, 162, 178, 181, 183, 191, 194, 207, 213, 251, 255, 363, 419

Farthing, Ann 34

Farthing, Cecil 9, 34, 67

Farthing, Cynthia ('Kitty') 10, 236, 375

Farthing, Jane 3, 4, 16–17, 47, 96

Farthing, Nicola, 20, 33, 227

Farthing, Walter 6

Pearce, Alexander Robert 341–4, 347–8, 349–50, 353–5, 360–1, 363–4, 366, 369, 377, 379, 383, 385, 387, 393–4, 395, 397, 399–401, 403–4, 406–7, 410–15

Pearce, Mark 250–2, 255, 257–8, 261, 266, 268, 271–2, 274–6, 290, 295, 302–6, 308, 310–17, 326–7, 332–3, 339, 341, 344, 347, 348, 349, 351, 354, 355, 357–9, 360, 365, 377, 379–80, 385, 387, 392, 393–4, 397, 399–401, 403, 406, 407, 408, 410–15, 420

Stalker, Hugh 19, 21, 30, 34–5, 36, 37, 40, 149, 182–3, 334, 341, 360, 379–80

Stalker, Joan 25, 33, 40, 98, 148, 180, 210, 343, 379, 403, 415

Stalker, Olive 17, 19, 21, 24–5, 29, 30, 32–6, 38–40, 43, 46–7, 51, 57–8, 66, 98, 109, 148–9, 162, 183, 236, 360, 379–80

Stalker, William Hugh ('Hughie'), 29, 32, 33, 40, 46–7, 50, 58, 98, 148, 180, 210, 260, 343, 375, 379, 403, 411, 413, 415, 420

relations with friends and colleagues:

Adcock, Fleur 211, 212, 225, 231, 234, 236, 249, 264, 268, 283–4, 308, 345, 364, 389, 394, 399, 402

Anthony, Jacqueline 32–3

Appignanesi, Lisa 39, 342, 354, 363

Araki, Violet 179–80

Bailey, Paul 287, 290, 352, 353, 373, 383, 384, 390–2, 405, 420

Berkeley, Michael 297, 315

Boyd, Arthur 397

Bradbury, Malcolm 287–9

Brent, Naomi 270–1, 282

Brothers, Connie 365, 407

Burgess, Anthony 96, 198, 205, 207, 208, 213, 245

Cameron, Shirley 258, 280

Carver, Peter 48

Chatwin, Bruce 346–7, 348, 370–1

Coover, Pili 303–5, 311, 313, 318, 358, 397, 420

Index

Index

Index

Index

Index

Index

Index

Index

Index

Index

Index

Index

Index

Index

Index